THE POLITICAL ECONOMY OF NAMIBIA

An annotated, critical bibliography

Tore Linné Eriksen
with *Richard Moorsom*

The Scandinavian Institute of African Studies
in cooperation with
United Nations Institute for Namibia
Norwegian Institute of International Affairs

This book is published as

Norwegian Foreign Policy Studies, No. 50
(Norwegian Institute of International Affairs, Oslo)

FINAGLES LAW OF INFORMATION

The information you have
is not what you want
The information you want
is not what you need
The information you need
is not available

Of making many books there is no end.
                              - The Preacher.

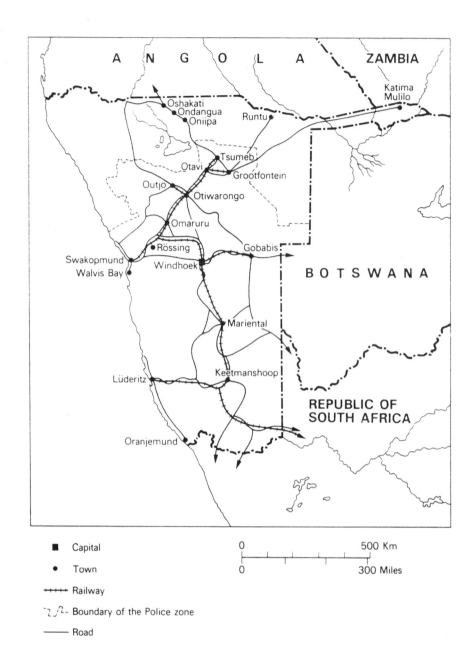

ANGOLA   ZAMBIA

Katima
Mulilo

Oshakati
Ondangua
Oniipa   Runtu

Tsumeb
Otavi
Grootfontein
Outjo
Otiwarongo

Omaruru

Rössing   Gobabis
Swakopmund
Walvis Bay   Windhoek   BOTSWANA

Mariental

Lüderitz   Keetmanshoop

REPUBLIC OF
SOUTH AFRICA

Oranjemund

■ Capital   0   500 Km
• Town   0   300 Miles
+++++ Railway
⌐⌐⌐ Boundary of the Police zone
——— Road

Map from: <u>Namibia - The Last Colony</u>. Edited by Reginald H. Green,
          Kimmo Kiljunen, Marja-Liisa Kiljunen. Longman 1981.

CONTENTS

ACKNOWLEDGEMENTS

It is hardly necessary to stress that preparing an annotated bibliography of this size and scope is not a one-person task, and that I owe a great deal to many friends and colleagues who have helped me with documentation, encouragement and criticism.

The work has been made possible by a generous research grant from the Norwegian Agency for International Development (NORAD). I have been employed by the Norwegian Institute of International Affairs since January 1982, and special thanks go to Liv Høivik and Tore Gustavsson for all their practical assistance to my project. Since June 1983 I have had the great pleasure of working closely with the United Nations Institute for Namibia. I should like to thank the staff of UNIN's Information and Documentation Division, and Christine Kisiedu in particular, for their encouragement and advice. I also wish to record my gratitude to the Scandinavian Institute of African Studies for taking on the daunting task of turning so bulky a manuscript into a book, and to Tore Gustavsson for preparing the index.

Richard Moorsom (Oxford) has been a great stimulus and a friend, and has written the drafts of a proportion of the manuscript, especially relating to agriculture and fisheries. Neither he nor the Institutes I have been privileged to work with, however, are in any sense responsible for the selection of entries and the views expressed in the annotations.

I am also very grateful to Werner Hillebrecht (Bremen) and Henning Melber (Kassel) for guiding me through the vast array of literature and sources in the German language. I have enjoyed the warm hospitality of Carl Schlettwein during two visits to his outstanding collection of Namibiana (Basler Afrika Bibliographien). I have also greatly benefitted from information and criticism of parts of the bibliography by Brigitte Lau (Windhoek) and Reginald H. Green (Sussex). Peter H. Katjavivi (Oxford), Susanne Linderos (Uppsala), Paul Spray (London), Peter Manning (London), Bettina Gebhardt (Frankfurt), Margaret Ling (London), Barbara König (London), David Simon (Leeds), Robert Gordon (Burlington), André du Pisani (Pretoria), Wolfgang Werner (London/ Windhoek), Justin Ellis (London), Eckard Strohmeyer (Karben), Sholto Cross (University of East Anglia), Kirsten Alnæs (London), Neville Alexander (Cape Town), amongst many, many others have supplied me with valuable information.

I have made use of the services of many libraries, research institutes, archives and organisations, especially in Great Britain and the Federal Republic of Germany. A brief presentation of some of the major resource centres will be found in the introduction, but I should like to express my special appreciation to the Catholic Institute for International Relations (London) and the research department of the International Defence and Aid Fund for Southern Africa (London) for their moral as well as practical support. Apart from the libraries and institutions already mentioned, the following libraries deserve a special thanks for their generous assistance: Institut für Weltwirtschaft (Kiel), Institut für Afrika-Kunde (Hamburg), Stadt- und Universitätbibliothek (Frankfurt), Royal Commonwealth Society (London), Overseas Development Group (University of East Anglia) and the School of Oriental and African Studies (University of London).

Finally, I must attribute my major source of inspiration to Agnete Eriksen and to friends in SWAPO of Namibia who are struggling for an independent Namibia.

Lusaka, July 1984

Tore Linné Eriksen

INTRODUCTION

A. AIMS, SCOPE AND STRUCTURE OF THE BIBLIOGRAPHY

When I was preparing a Namibia survey for the Norwegian Institute of
International Affairs/Swedish International Development Authority
(SIDA) back in 1981-82, I soon came to appreciate from my own direct
experience the need for an up-to-date bibliography on Namibia. Although several substantial bibliographies were indeed available at
the time (see chapter 14), they were, in my view, either too narrowly
focused or too outdated to serve as reliable guides. I must also admit that more often than not I found the annotations too brief, superficial and uncritical to be really useful.[1] Upon later discussing
this situation with friends and colleagues I was encouraged to
undertake a systematic collection of material, and to use this as a
basis for a select and more analytically annotated bibliography.
During a visit to Lusaka in June 1982 I was also informed that a
bibliography of this kind would fit well into the research and documentation programme of the United Nations Institute for Namibia. The
final decision to go ahead with the project was taken after several
meetings with the UNIN Information and Documentation Division and the
UNIN Management Committee.

At the time when I agreed to embark upon such a project, and a
research grant for this purpose was secured, I had a much more modest
and limited work in mind. The original idea was to spend about a
year on the bibliography as a first step towards a comprehensive
research project on Namibian economic history (1945-1955). As soon
as the bibliography started to live its own life, it proved to be a
far more time-consuming and demanding task. Its scope was broadened,
and much more effort was put into the laborious process of identifying, locating and tracing the relevant material. The main reasons
for this were that the volume of extant material was far greater than
had been anticipated, that a large number of new publications had
appeared in recent years and that I wanted the bibliography to be a
useful tool both for the academic community and for a more general
audience. When revising the original outline, the immediate needs of
people involved in planning and preparing for an independent Namibia
also came to figure more prominently in my mind. Thanks to the interest which many friends and colleagues have taken in the project, I
have also been urged to expand the bibliography to include academic
theses and conference papers, as well as a list of periodicals and
current bibliographies.

Since my aim has been to read, assess and review the literature
more critically than usually is the case with bibliographies, the
bibliography necessarily had to be a <u>select</u> one. Selection is always

---

1) It is, for example, not particularly instructive when all that is
said about a major book on Namibian history is that it "examines
the development of the territory", or that one of the most blatant
pro-apartheid propaganda pamphlets "gives background information
on the territory". Both examples are taken from Elna Schoeman:
<u>The Namibian issue, 1920-1980</u> (no 906), which is one of the better
bibliographies.

subjective - and sometimes arbitrary.[2] It could not be otherwise when the decision was made to restrict the number of entries to some 900, exclusive of theses, conference papers and periodicals. There is no overall consensus of agreement on the criteria for what is "useful" or "important", and not even the standard of what is considered to be a "scholarly" work gives any clear-cut set of guidelines.

I was also faced with the difficult task of defining more specifically the subjects to be included within the broad framework of "political economy". Some had necessarily to be excluded, others more briefly covered than the principal sections. I have, for instance, deliberately been very restrictive where Namibia as an "international issue" is concerned. A large research effort has gone into international law, diplomacy, international relations and related disciplines, while history (especially economic and social history), basic economic structures and social formations have remained neglected or under-researched. In addition, voluminous literature on the international status of Namibia has already been covered in Elna Schoeman's recent bibliography: The Namibian Issue, 1920-1980. A Select and Annotated Bibliography (no. 906).

With the exception of a few standard reference works and studies closely related to ecology and economic geography (especially water and energy), geography and natural sciences have generally been defined as being outside the scope of the present work. For recent publications in these fields, as well as in a wide range of other subjects, the reader will find valuable information in Eckhard Strohmeyer: Namibische National Bibliographie/Namibian National Bibliography, of which the three volumes published so far cover the period 1971-1979. The same author has also compiled a basic reference bibliography mainly concerned with anthropology and linguistics: Umfassende Bibliographie der Völker Namibiens und Südwestangolas (no. 912-13). On German colonialism and Namibia under German rule, German Africa. A select annotated bibliography (no. 871) is still a useful guide to literature published before 1963.

Although none of the bibliographies mentioned above are without major flaws, their existence nevertheless justifies my cursory treatment of certain disciplines and subjects. The decision to put less emphasis on literature already covered reasonably well also makes it possible to focus more attention on areas which have for a variety of reasons been neglected or not given due attention. Furthermore, I have purposely given fuller coverage to publications from the liberation movement (SWAPO of Namibia) or written more or less from the same

---

2) To give a few examples. The reader interested in ecology will find Hartmut Leser: Landschaftsökologische Studien im Kalahari-sandgebiet (no. 94), but not the many studies which have been published on the South African ostrich, Struthio camelus australis, in the arid veld. (See, inter alia, E.G.F. Sauer: "Aberrent sexual behaviour in the South African ostrich", The Auk, 89, no. 4, (October) 1972: 717-37). Likewise, the reader hunting for information on German colonialism in Namibia will find Helmut Bley: South West Africa under German rule (no. 179), but not Arthur von Creytz: Der Hund im Dienste des Farmers, der Schutz- und Polizeitruppe in Deutsch-Süd-West Afrika (Berlin: Schoetz, 1913, 80 p.).

perspective. Some of the existing bibliographies are based mainly
on material available in South Africa and Namibia itself, and thus
reflect a manifest lack of familiarity with literature arising from
liberation movements, solidarity groups and the more progressive
sections of the international academic community. Some of them are
also heavily biased against the struggle for Namibian independence,
a notable example being Richard F. Logan: <u>Bibliography of South</u>
<u>West Africa. Geography and related fields</u> (no. 893).[3] The decision
to try to redress this imbalance also, of course, stems from my own
position, which is politically identified with the liberation struggle and academically inspired by materialist historiography and radical political economy.

In order to provide a supplement - as well as an alternative -
to existing bibliographies, I have also tried to be as up-to-date as
possible, even at the risk of including items which may well be of no
more than passing interest. About two in every five items have been
published in the period 1980-1984. This fact is in itself a clear
indication of a growing research effort into Namibian history and
society, as well as of increasing international awareness of the
sufferings of the Namibian people under South African occupation and
of the issue of Namibia as one of the world's last remaining colonies.
Since some of the more recent publications and studies are not well
known, and since they often provide new insight and fresh interpretations, I have in general written lengthier annotations in order to
present and discuss the new - and often more radical - perspectives
of the 1980s. In this respect my hope has been to provide a modest
contribution to a historiographical discussion.

Despite this desire to be as up-to-date as possible, small items
published in current affairs periodicals are, with a few rare exceptions, not included. Most of these publications are readily available in libraries, and a systematic inclusion of news items of this
kind, however valuable for an understanding of current developments
they might be, would certainly have overwhelmed the bibliography.
<u>The Namibia Abstracts</u> compiled by the UNIN Information and Documenta-
tion Division has as one of its tasks to provide information of current literature of this kind (see no. 931). As a compensation,
chapter 15 contains an annotated list of relevant magazines, journals,
bulletins, newspapers, press digests, yearbooks and annual reports.

Adhering faithfully to the principle of "autopsy", I have strugg-
led my way through all the items included in the bibliography. It
goes without saying that in a number of cases I have had to rely on
the advice and comments of colleagues with expert knowledge in certain fields or languages (especially Afrikaans and Finnish). It is
also unavoidable that the quality of the annotations should vary
according to my own (restricted) familiarity with the different subjects, disciplines and specific works.

Despite these obvious limitations, my hope is that the annotations in all cases give the reader a fair introduction to the items
they present. What I have tried to do is, firstly, to provide a
straightforward <u>summary</u> of the content and ideas of a publication.

---

3) The writings by Heinrich Vedder are described as "excellent" and
    "thorough", while a book by Ruth First is depicted as "emotional
    anti-South African prejudice" and "distortions of the truth".

This can been done at varying length, depending on the character of
the work in question - in other words, the length of an annotation
cannot in itself be taken as an indication of how significant the
item is considered to be.

Secondly, I have wanted to say a few words about what I have
perceived to be the purpose of the publication. For instance: is it
a scholarly study prepared for a university degree, a polemical piece
distributed as a public relations effort on behalf of the occupying
regime, an official SWAPO document, a serious discussion of alternative development strategies for an independent Namibia, or personal
settler reminiscences written with the purpose of attracting immigrants?

Thirdly, wherever appropriate, I have tried to assess what use
researchers can make of the publication, irrespective of the purpose
of the author. This applies above all to the quantity, quality and
presentation of hard data, both statistical and descriptive, which it
contains and to the sources on which it relies and the way in which it
uses them.

Fourthly, in many cases I have given biographical information on
the author, including references to other published or unpublished
works. A principal reason for doing so is the opportunity it will
give the reader to approach the author directly.

Fifthly, I have also included in the bibliographical references
which head each annotation details on the number of tables and illustrations, as well as on internal bibliographies and guides to further
reading. Hopefully, this information will assist the reader in assessing the character and usefulness of a work. From my own experience,
it is often a help to know if a work contains statistical information
and a substantial bibliography before embarking upon the arduous task
of trying to acquire it through a library or through direct enquiries
to a university or an organisation. This is also one of the reasons
for including a certain amount of unpublished theses, the value of
which often lies more in the bibliography and references to archives
than in the amount of original insight.

B. THE ARRANGEMENT

The entries have been listed under broad subject categories, beginning with items which either serve as a general introduction to Namibia or which address themselves to issues which are not easily cate-
gorised. The subject divisions are followed by an annotated list of
bibliographies exclusively or mainly concerned with Namibia. For a
list of more general, current bibliographies, see chapter 14 B.

As is always the case with bibliographies of this kind, a considerable number of entries could fit different sections. Readers
are, therefore, strongly recommended to hunt for material in the text
as a whole. I have also made a number of cross-references at the end
of each chapter. To give an example: a book on Walvis Bay (no. 420)
is listed under chapter 6 C ("The Namibian economy under military
occupation, 1966-1984"), but cross-references are given at the end
of chapters concerned with international law, the colonial economy,
fisheries and international relations.

Bibliographies (ch. 14) and periodical publications (ch. 15) are
also included in the cross-reference system when they are found to be

particularly relevant to a specific subject, but theses (ch. 16) and
conference papers (ch. 17) are not included since these two chapters
contain unannotated lists of items which have not necessarily been
examined. This means that the reader has to consult these sections
of the bibliography in addition to making use of the broad subject
division into chapters and the cross-reference system.

One of the most awkward problems has been to decide where to place
literature whose principal purpose is to discuss development strategies or to provide sectoral reviews of importance to planners and
decision-makers in a future, independent Namibia. I have tried to
solve this dilemma by filing the items under the appropriate subject
where clearly defined chapters already exist, as in the cases of
mining, agriculture, fisheries, education and health. More general
surveys on the economic future of Namibia are put in a separate chapter 6 D ("Planning for an independent Namibia"), and the readers will
find that more specific sectoral studies are also referred to at the
end of this chapter. It should also be mentioned that as a rule
entries on Ovamboland before 1915 are listed under chapter 3 ("Pre-
colonial Namibia").

I would also like to admit that some sections reflect the conventional academic and politico-administrative departmentalisation, but
I do hope for an understanding of one of the basic dilemmas of a bib-
liographer: simultaneously to reflect and to try to transcend the
given literature, the commonly used concepts and the established subject divisions. In one particular case, chapter 9 on women in Namibia,
I have chosen to make a separate section although the number of items
is extremely limited. This is deliberately done in order to demonstrate the lack of both popular and scholarly work in this field, and to
make it possible to give cross-references to literature which has some
information on the position of women in Namibian society and in the
struggle for national liberation.

Although a fair number of academic theses have been incorporated
in the main text, chapter 16 presents a more extensive list of theses
relating to the study of the political economy of Namibia, including
some registered theses in progress. This is, of course, a select list,
and those readers interested in a wider range of subjects are referred
to Werner Hillebrecht: Hochschulschriften zu Namibia unter Einbezieh-
ung von Arbeiten zur deutschen Kolonialpolitik, Kolonialrecht und
Kolonialwirtschaft sowie zum Völkerbundsmandatsrecht (no. 882).

Since the mid-sixties there has been a succession of international
conferences concerned with Namibia. Chapter 17 lists the papers submitted to some of these conferences, presenting valuable material
which to a large extent still remains unpublished. Many of these
conference papers are also annotated where they merit separate inclusion. The same is the case for theses.

The main entries (chapters 1-15), as well as the lists of theses
and conference papers, are organised alphabetically according to the
general Anglo-American cataloguing rules. South African names are
listed under their prefix: DE VRIES, DU PISANI, VAN DER WAAL etc.
When filing, the German Umlaute (ä, ö, ü) are treated as 'ae', 'oe',
'ue'. Governmental publications are listed under South Africa (Union
or Republic), and under South West Africa (Admin.) if the colonial
administration in Windhoek or the local representative of the South
African occupying regime is the author or publisher.

In the case of a publication written by two or more authors, it
is listed under the name of the author who appears first on the title

page of the given item, but with cross-references to the other authors
where appropriate. If two or more works by separate authors are annotated together, the entry is under the author of the first of the
publications, with cross-references to the other(s). An institution
like, for instance, The Chamber of Mines is listed under Chamber,
which is the first substantive word. Wherever there is reasonable
doubt on classification, I have tried to make cross-references. As
mentioned above, I also hope that the author index at the end will
be a useful tool.

C. THE SOURCES

It is outside the scope of the present work to provide a comprehensive
guide to archives, libraries, documentation centres and organisations
which hold material relating to a study of Namibia. One of the reasons for this is that I have - for various reasons - not been in a
position to visit South Africa and Namibia itself. What I intend to
do in the following is mainly to indicate some of the sources I have
used in compiling the bibliography, in the hope that this will provide readers with some ideas on how to go about acquiring material.
    It is a striking consequence of the general indifference towards
Namibia in the Western academic community that few collections of any
substance exist outside the major colonial reference libraries and
that the latter are usually weak in coverage of the past two decades
and on material from within Namibia itself. In this regard the gaps
have been partially filled by specific projects (Basler Afrika Bibliographien), private institutions (International Defence and Aid Fund
for Southern Africa, Catholic Institute for International Relations)
and campaigning organisations (Namibia Support Committee, Informationsstelle Südliches Afrika). Also of significance are the private
resources of scholars engaged in serious research on Namibia, not all
University-based, who are generally willing to assist and advise on
research resources. In many cases it is necessary to approach an
aouthor, an organisation or a publisher directly. For this purpose,
a list of addresses is given in chapter 18. Addresses to most academic institutions can be found in The World of Learning. The SCOLMA
Directory of Libraries and Special Collections on Africa in the United
Kingdom and Western Europe and The African Book World & Press. A
Directory are also two indispensable reference works which provide a
wealth of information on libraries and archives, including addresses.[4]

---

4) The World of Learning. 33rd edition (London: Europa Publica-
   tions, 1982, 2 vols.); Harry Hannam (ed.): The SCOLMA Direc-
   tory of Libraries and Special Collections on Africa in the United
   Kingdom and Western Europe. Fourth revised and expanded edition,
   (Oxford: Zell/München, New York, London, Paris: Saur, 1983);
   Hans M. Zell & Carol Bundy (eds.): The African Book World &
   Press. A Directory. Third ed. (Oxford: Zell/München, New York,
   London, Paris: Saur, 1983).

Western Europe

To start with England, I have made extensive use of several major resource centres in London.[5] The library of the London School of Economics and Political Science (LSE) specialises both in official publications and on the countries of Southern Africa. It has complete runs
of parliamentary printed papers (commissions, select committees, departmental annual reports) for South Africa and the pre-Union states
stretching back well into the 19th century, as well as a range of
official economic and statistical publications, including censuses.
On the publications of the South African administration in Namibia it
is less complete, although more so than most other UK libraries. It
has a continuous run of the SWA Administration's annual Estimates of
Revenue and Expenditure from 1945 and incomplete series of the annual
reports of state bodies such as the Grain Board and the Promotion of
Farming Interests Board. Although under the SCOLMA Area Specialisa-
tion Scheme the LSE is responsible for South Africa in the fields of
economics and politics, its stock of books and documents on Namibia
is rather weak.[6]
     The second major London library, still privately run, is that of
the Royal Commonwealth Society. In terms of books, periodicals and
official publications, it is undoubtedly the best for the German period, and is generally strong on South Africa and Namibia, though
rather less so after the Second World War. It has an extensive collection of the 19th century travel accounts and a rare complete run
of the SWA Official Gazette. The holdings are made readily accessible by a uniquely detailed card index, in which entries are organised by country, sub-divided by subject and arranged in date order
of publication. The index includes articles from a wide range of 19th
and early 20th century periodicals and is thus a major bibliographic
reference in its own right.
     Amongst other institutional libraries, the School of Oriental and
African Studies, University of London, has a broad range of Africanist
journals, a substantial collection of political and historical literature on South Africa and Namibia, primarily post 1945, and one of the
best sets of bibliographic resources on Southern Africa in the UK,
although few official publications are stocked. Namibia is more
sparsely represented in the holdings of the Institute of Commonwealth

5) For an excellent introduction to the major archives and libraries
    in the UK as well as in other Western European countries, see
    Harry Hannam, note 4. See also T.L. Eriksen: Resources for
    Namibian studies: report from a visit to United Kingdom, May 1982
    (Oslo: Norwegian Institute of International Affairs, 1982, 13 p.)

6) The Standing Conference on Library Materials on Africa (SCOLMA)
    and its Area Specialisation Scheme is presented in Harry Hannam
    (ed.), see note 4. SCOLMA has also published UK library resour-
    ces for Southern African studies (London: SCOLMA, 1984, 35 p.).
    The papers in this publication represent a statement on the cur-
    rent status and collection policies for Southern African materials
    in several British libraries. See also the SCOLMA Bulletin:
    Africa Research and Documentation.

Studies, but SWAPO and SWANU appear in the special collection of documents from Commonwealth political parties.[7] The Institute's card
index of thesis titles registered at UK Universities provides an up-
to-date checklist of research in progress. The central Senate House
Library of the University of London is most valuable for its extensive international range of journals. The British Library is not so
accessible a research environment for work on Namibia, but together
with the Public Records Office stocks official documents, including
a number from the SWA Administration. Important for current economic
research is the City Business Library, which stocks key business literature and journals, specialised data sources on trades and businesses, trade directories and company reports, including those of a
large number of British and South African companies operating in
Namibia.

For effective research on contemporary Namibia, two private resource centres are indispensable. The first is the research, information and publications department of the International Defence and
Aid Fund for Southern Africa (IDAF), which collects a wide range of
books, pamphlets, official reports, UN documents and conference papers
on Namibia, many of them difficult or impossible to obtain through the
research libraries. Above all, for the last 15 years IDAF has maintained extensive subject files of cuttings from the South African,
Namibian and UK press, building a current affairs data bank unique in
its depth of coverage. In the past five years its scope has been
considerably broadened to embrace economic as well as political affairs. The cuttings files are the chief foundation for IDAF's extensive range of publications of Namibia. More recent in origin, the
Namibia collection of the Catholic Institute for International Relations (CIIR), built in part to support its publications series A Future for Namibia, is at least as comprehensive as IDAF's in books,
reports and journals, especially from inside Namibia itself, but much
less so in UN documentation and press cuttings.[8] It is also the
principal UK source of documents produced under the auspices of the
Southern African Development Coordination Conference (SADCC). In
addition to these, both the Namibia Support Committee and SWAPO's
Western European Office are significant sources of current documentation and information.

Outside London, the principal library for research on Namibia is
Rhodes House, Oxford. Part of Oxford University's decentralised Bodleian Library, it specialises on the British Empire/Commonwealth and
has extensive holdings of official publications, periodicals, books,
theses and manuscripts on and from South Africa and Namibia, especially up to c 1950. Included are a substantial unpublished review by
Lord Hailey of the South African mandate administration and a major
private archive, the papers of the late Rev. Michael Scott. The
library is well organised and possesses a card index arranged by
country and sub-divided by subject. Additional material, notably

7) ICS has recently decided to pay more attention to Namibia, and
for this purpose a symposium on research priorities in Namibian
studies took place in London 23-25 July 1984.

8) Five volumes have been published in the outstanding A Future for
Namibia series, see nos. 9, 532, 562, 580, 695).

periodicals, specialised literature and departmental annual reports, is scattered through other libraries in the Bodleian network.

The Centre for Southern African Studies of the University of York is responsible under the SCOLMA scheme for gathering material on Namibia, but to date has progressed little further than a collection of political documents from the 1970s and a few microfilms, including a run of the Windhoek Advertiser (1919-45) and the SWA Administrator's Annual Report to the League of Nations (1918-46).[9] A more specific and quite substantial Namibia collection is housed in the School of Development Studies of the University of East Anglia. It was assembled to support the FAO study on food security in post-independence Namibia (see no. 514), which was produced by the School's Overseas Development Group, and contains a wide range of books, articles, reports and theses - mainly but not exclusively on agriculture - some of them not available elsewhere outside Namibia itself. Unfortunately the collection is not integrated with the University library and is accessible only by privately arranged visits. Most of the items are, however, indexed in a bibliography produced by the ODG (see nos. 888-89).

Reflecting Namibia's history as a German colony, as well as the high standard of libraries in general, there are rich Namibia collections to be consulted in the Federal Republic of Germany.[10] The main university library for literature on Africa south of the Sahara is the Stadt- und Universitätbibliothek, Frankfurt, which also holds the extensive library of the former Deutsche Kolonialgesellschaft (1890-1940).[11] This collection consists of more than 20 000 books, theses, pamphlets, official reports and works of fiction. The main catalogue of the Frankfurt university library contains ca 1 500 entries on Namibia, general literature on German colonialism not included. The library also has a complete run of a large number of colonial journals and magazines (Deutsche Kolonialzeitung, Koloniale Rundschau, Deutsches Kolonialblatt etc.), Namibian newspapers and the records of the Legislative Assembly up to 1939. The Deutsche Bibliothek, which also is situated in Frankfurt, has a fine collection of more recent lite-

---

9) See Jane Henley: "Library provision for Southern African studies at the University of York, p. 26-29 in UK library resources for Southern African studies (see note 6).

10) The SCOLMA Directory (see note 4) presents the major West German libraries and archives, p. 137-49. Although partly out-of-date, valuable information can still be found in Dokumentationsdienst Afrika. Vol. 1: Institutionen der Afrika-Arbeit in der Bundesrepublik und Berlin (West); Vol 2: Afrika-bezogene Literatursammlungen in der Bundesrepublik und Berlin (West). (Hamburg: Deutsches Institut für Afrika-Forschung, 1971). For an inventory of archives, see also Quellen zur Geschichte Afrikas südlich der Sahara in den Archiven der Bundesrepublik Deutschland. Guide to the Sources of the History of Africa, vol. 1. (Zug/London: International Council on Archives, 1970).

11) The extensive catalogues of the Frankfurt university library are in the process of being published. So far, the Fachkatalog Afrika/ Subject Catalogue Africa, vols. 1-7 (München: Saur, 1976-82) has appeared, and regional catalogues will follow.

rature on Namibia, including academic theses from both German states.
Several libraries other than Frankfurt can also be recommended, especially Göttingen (Niedersächsische Staats- und Universitätsbibliothek), Berlin (Staatsbibliothek Preussischer Kulturbesitz), Hamburg
(Staats- und Universitätsbibliothek), München (Bayerische Staatsbibliothek), Bremen (Universitätsbibliothek Bremen, Übersee-Museum Bre-
men/Bremer Afrika Archiv) and Stuttgart (Landesbibliothek including
Bibliothek für Zeitgeschichte, Institut für Auslandsbeziehungen).[12]
     In the Federal Republic of Germany there are also several research
institutes and libraries specialising on literature related to economic development. The library at the Institut für Weltwirtschaft (Institute for World Economy), Kiel, is a case in point. The main focus
of this library is on economics, statistics, official publications
and the annual reports of companies, and the holdings on South Africa
and Namibia are rich in respect of both historical material and current literature. The library is well organised and easy to use. The
Namibia catalogue contains ca. 1 200 entries, which includes articles
in periodicals and chapters in books.[13] The Institut für Wirtschafts-
forschung/Hamburgisches Weltwirtschaft-Archiv (HWWA) is another research institute specialising in documentation. As its origins lie
in the old colonial institute before World War I, there is a particularly large collection of literature on Namibia, including theses
and articles from colonial journals. HWWA is also famous for its
vast collection of ca. 15 million newspaper clippings on raw materials, corporations and the economics of all countries of the world
sub-divided by sectors. The collection has been microfilmed up to
1960.
     There are also several research institutes devoted to the study
of Africa and developing countries, such as the Institut für Afrika-
Kunde (Hamburg) and the Deutsches Institut für Entwicklungspolitik/
German Development Institute (Berlin).[14] The Institute für Afrika-
Kunde has a special documentation division attached to it (Dokumenta-
tions-Leitstelle Afrika), where books, research publications and articles concerned with Africa are registered in a subject and country
catalogue which is open for consultation. In 1979 the German Development Institute completed a number of sectoral studies on the Namibian
economy (see no. 464), and the library is said to be well stocked in
literature and documents, including material collected during study
trips to Namibia. There is also a substantial collection at the University of Bremen, where a research project, "Politische Landeskunde

---

12) For the Staatsarchiv Bremen there exists a comprehensive guide:
     Führer durch die Quellen zur Geschichte Afrikas im Staatsarchiv
     Bremen. Bearbeitet von Sabine Birkenstock und Hartmut Müller.
     Mit einem Register von Horst Vogel. (Bremen, 1982, 245 p.).

13) See Institut für Weltwirtschaft: Regionenkatalog, Band 41
     (no. 883).

14) The Institut für Afrika-Kunde is also the publisher of a quarter-
     ly bibliographical bulletin: Ausgewählte neuere Literatur, as
     well as a bi-weekly compilation of clippings from African news-
     papers: Aktueller Informationsdienst Africa (no. 997).

Namibias" has been undertaken in cooperation with UNIN and SWAPO. One
of the aims of the project has been to prepare social science textbooks on Namibia for West German as well as for Namibian schools and
refugee settlements (see nos. 53, 64).[15] Deutsches Institut für Tropische und Subtropische Landwirtschaft, Witzenhausen, has a lot of
agricultural literature not available elsewhere in Europe.

Source material from the German colonial period is to be found in
several archives in both the Federal Republic of Germany and the German Democratic Republic. Unfortunately, I have not had the opportunity to consult the Deutsches Zentralarchiv Potsdam, which holds the
record of the Reichskolonialamt (Ministry of Colonial Affairs).[16]
This collection contains a vast quantity of official reports and correspondence, and is invaluable for a study of Namibia under colonial
rule. The documents of the Imperial Governor's Office in Windhoek
have now been made available on microfilm in the Bundesarchiv in
Koblenz, while the originals are kept in the State Archives in Windhoek. The Bundesarchiv also contains important collections of former
colonial officials as well as a collection of photographs. Material
relating to "German South West Africa" is also to be found in Archiv
des Auswärtigen Amts in Bonn, in the Bundesarchiv/Militärarchiv in
Freiburg and in the Staatsarchiv Bremen. The archives of the Vereinigte Evangelische Mission (United Evangelical Mission, formerly the
Rhenish Missionary Society) in Wuppertal contain a wide range of general literature on Namibia as well as a comprehensive collection of
source material relating to the activities of the mission since the
early 1840s.[17] There is also a set of documents microfilmed from the
missionary archives in Windhoek.

In the Federal Republic of Germany I have also benefitted very
much from consulting two unique private bibliographical projects.
Eckhard Strohmeyer (Karben) is, as mentioned above, the long-standing
compiler of Namibia National Bibliography (nos. 914-16). His remarkable collection of Namibiana, partly based on acquisition of material
in Namibia itself, is particularly valuable with regard to anthropology, linguistics and various Namibian publications in the vernacular.
Werner Hillebrecht (Bremen) has for some years been working on a large-
scale project, Namibian Bibliographic Data Project, whose ambitious
purpose is to register all items related to Namibia to be found in
West German libraries. The register, which is approaching completion,
now contains some 9000 entries on index cards, of which 6000 have
been verified to date, with full bibliographical details and locations.

15) The project is presented in Diskurs, no. 6 (August) 1982, Thema:
Namibia Die Aktualität des kolonialen Verhältnisses (no. 16). So
far two textbooks have been published, see nos. 52, 64 .

16) See Übersicht über die Bestände des Deutschen Zentralarchivs
Potsdam (Berlin: Rütten & Loenig, 1957, 232 p.). See also the
guide to the Namibia files given in the dissertations of, among
others, Drechsler (no. 188), Loth (no. 140) and Wege (no. 346).

17) Two major studies by Lothar Engel (nos. 192, 233) contain a guide
to the Namibia holdings.

The Basler Afrika Bibliographien/Basel Africa Bibliography (BAB), run by Carl Schlettwein, is also a unique institution which offers a wide range of services for research on Namibia.[18] On Namibia it contains more than 1 000 monographs in addition to xerox-copied material and numerous off-prints. Of special value is a complete run of periodicals, such as SWA Annual, Namib und Meer and Afrikanischer Heimatkalender, as well as publications from the SWA Scientific Society, The State Museum, and several of the bantustan "legislative assemblies". The collection of material published in Namibia since the early 1950s is probably more extensive than in any other libraries outside Southern Africa. BAB is also the publisher of the Namibia National Bibliography as well as other books relating to Namibia. It distributes an informative newsletter (Nachrichten/Newsletter) and is associated with a small antiquarian bookshop specialising on Namibia as well as other African countries.[19]

Archival sources in Finland are of particular interest for a study of the northern part of Namibia, as the Finnish Missionary Society has worked in Ovamboland since 1870.[20] The sources are in the Archives of the Finnish Missionary Society as well as in the possession of several individuals. An inventory of the Finnish material has been made in Martti Eirola et al.: The cultural and social change in Ovamboland 1870-1915 (no. 126), which also contains a discussion of sources and literature on the same topic in the Federal Republic of Germany and the German Democratic Republic. The missionary archives have now been microfilmed up to 1938, and copies are available at the Finnish Missionary Society, the UN Institute for Namibia and the Department of History at the University of Joensuu. The latter institute has obtained on microfilm from the Potsdam archives the documents of the German Colonial Office (Reichskolonialamt) dealing with Ovamboland, the Ovambo collections of the Archiv der Vereinigten Mission in Wuppertal and from Koblenz the source material of the Bundesarchiv concerning the northern part of Namibia up to 1915.

Before leaving the Nordic countries, it should be mentioned that in recent years the Scandinavian Institute of African Studies (Upp-

---

18) For a brief presentation of BAB, see K. Peter Johanson: "An African reference centre in Switzerland: the Basler Afrika Bibliographien", Mitteilungen der Basler Afrika Bibliographien, no. 16, 1976.

19) Antiquariat am Klosterberg, Klosterberg 21, CH-4051 Basel, Switzerland.

20) I have not yet had the opportunity to visit the University of Joensuu. The information in this section is taken from Martti Eirola et al.: The cultural and social change in Ovamboland 1870-1915 (no. 126). I have, however, consulted the material which has been microfilmed for the UN Institute for Namibia. See also Martti Eirola: "Archives and other sources on Namibian history in Finland", Nytt från Nordiska Afrikainstitutet (Uppsala), no. 11, 1983, and Susanne Linderos: Scandinavian studies on Namibia, paper presented to the International Conference on Namibia, London, 10-13 September 1984.

sala) has taken a keen interest in collecting material on Namibia.[21]
The library of the Development Research and Action Programme (DERAP)
at the Christian Michelsen Institute (Bergen) has a substantial collection on the economy and development strategy.[22] Both institutes
also have a wide range of literature on the Southern African region
in general. For litterature on Namibia, the Norwegian Institute
of International Affairs (Oslo) should also be consulted.

The United States

In the United States, I have benefitted from information on current
research and available resources supplied by the Africa Studies Association (ASA). At the annual ASA Conference in 1983 there was for
the first time a special session devoted to Namibian history and
anthropology, chaired by Ben Fuller (Boston University). Current
information may be found in ASA News, African Studies Review and
Issue, all published by ASA. The principal reference works which
have both been compiled by ASA and are scheduled for publication in
1984/85, are Handbook of American Resources for African Studies
and Guide to Non-Federal Archives and Manuscripts related to Africa.
There are valuable Southern Africa and Namibia collections at
several US libraries, notably the university libraries of Yale,
Northwestern, Boston and California, the Library of Congress, and
the Hoover Institution on War, Revolution, and Peace (Stanford University). The Joint Acquisition List of Africana (no. 930) is a
bi-monthly publication listing books, journals and microfilm acquisitions from 20 leading African studies libraries.
Namibian publications have been assigned to Yale University Library as a special collecting responsibility under the Association of
Research Libraries Foreign Acquisitions Plan and also under an agreement among members of the Research Libraries Group.[23] The Yale
libraries' holdings on Southern Africa are among the most extensive
in the world outside South Africa, and include most English language
publications on Namibia and a high proportion of German language items.
They also have broken runs of official publications of the SWA Administration and most South African official publications on Namibia,
as well as German Colonial and Foreign Office reports on the area.

---

21) The Institute convened a seminar on Namibia and the Nordic coun-
    tries in Helsinki, March 1981, and the bulletin Nytt från Nordiska
    Afrikainstitutet has carried several articles on Namibia and
    Namibian studies in Scandinavian languages as well as in English.

22) The collection was put together in 1984 as part of a project under
    the UN Nationhood Programme (no. 489), and a bibliography prepared
    by Richard Moorsom is due to appear in 1985 as a DERAP Working
    Paper (no. 896).

23) See the Guide to library resources for the study of Southern
    Africa, compiled by Beverly Grier for the Yale Southern Africa
    Research Program, edited by J.M.D. Crossey. (New Haven: African
    Collection, Yale University Library, 1977). The Yale Southern
    African Research Program also issues a newsletter.

For research on the German colonial period, there is an extensive collection of literature and microfilmed primary sources at the Hoover Institution. A select annotated bibliography based on this collection has been published, see Jon Bridgman and David E. Clarke: German Africa (no. 871). Mention should also be made of the unique collection of conference papers at the Melville J. Herskovits Library of African Studies, Northwestern University, indexed in The Africana Conference Paper index (no. 894).

The Cooperative Africana Microform Project (CAMP) was created in 1963 to bring together in microform a collection of research materials related to Africa.[24] Acquisitions are made both through filming rarely held materials (e.g. newspapers, official documents and archival and primary sources) and by purchasing positive copies of material which has already been filmed by some other organisations. The CAMP collection includes a wide range of Southern African materials, including a complete run of Windhoek Advertiser from 1919.

As one of the main protagonists in the struggle for Namibian independence since 1945, the United Nations (New York) is itself a major repository of documents and information on Namibia, though it is usually more easily found through the national UN deposit libraries. The Office of the Commissioner for Namibia has a rather patchy collection, which does however include most of the many consultancy reports prepared under the UN Nationhood Programme.

The Southern African region

Not unexpectedly, several major libraries, research centres and archives in South Africa hold extensive collections on Namibia.[25]

The State Library (Pretoria) is one of the two principal national libraries and a clearing house for interlibrary loans. There is a fully computerised national bibliographic system, including periodicals and theses, to which all university libraries are linked. The State Library is the compiler of the ongoing South African National Bibliography (SANB) (see no. 932). Being the national deposit library, by law it is supposed to receive all material published in Namibia, but in practice its collection is far from complete and this is reflected in the SANB. The library contains a number of important documents, such as annual South African administrative reports on the reserves in Namibia. It is also coordinating the systematic microfilming of a complete run of Namibian newspapers. So far the filming of the Allgemeine Zeitung and the Windhoek Advertiser has been comple-

---

24) See CAMP catalog: 1977 cumulative edition (Chicago: The Cooperative Africana Microform Project and the Center for Research Libraries, 1977, 203 p.) and CAMP catalog: 1981 cumulative supplement (Chicago: The Cooperative Africana Microform Project and the Center for Research Libraries, 1982, 151 p.).

25) The African Book World & Press. A Directory (see note 4) comprises a useful list, including addresses, of South African university and public libraries as well as special libraries and institutional publishers (p. 155-81).

ted, and the idea is to include the other Namibian journals and newspapers.[26] These films will also be available in the Windhoek State
Archives.

The other national library, the South African Library (Cape Town),
has a large Namibia collection which comprises the major part of the
published literature and periodicals, as well as historical manuscripts
in the substantial Grey Collection. It also holds complete runs of
Cape newspapers. The South African Library is also the centre for
retrospective bibliography, which so far has been indexed up to 1925.[27]

Of the municipal libraries, the South African Public Library (Johannesburg) has a valuable collection. It is noteworthy for its extensive coverage of newspapers and journals from the Cape, which are
especially relevant for a study of the links to Nama- and Damaraland
from mid-19th century onwards. This library compiles an index to
periodical literature, which also indexes some Namibian periodicals
(see no. 928).

There is no South African research institute or university which
specialises on Namibia, but an increasing number of scholars have
recently been involved in research on various aspects of Namibian
history, economy and current affairs.[28] Information on ongoing research in South Africa is provided by the Human Sciences Reserach
Council (HSRC), which issues a register of research in the human
sciences as well as a list of newly registered doctoral theses in its
quarterly journal, Humanities. The annual supplement to the catalogue
of theses and dissertations accepted for degrees by South African universities is compiled at the Ferdinand Postma Library, University of
Potchefstroom.[29]

Of the universities, Cape Town has served as a base for several
scholars working on Namibia. At intervals it has organised symposia
and summer schools on Namibia, the most recent being a series of lectures in 1982, which together with supplementary contributions were

---

26) The microfilming is partly coordinated with CAMP, see note 24.

27) This retrospective bibliography has so far been brought up to
1925. See A South Africa bibliography to the year 1925. Being
a revision of Sidney Mendelssohn's South African Bibliography
(1910). Edited at the South African Library, Cape Town. vols.
1-4 (London: Mansell, 1979).

28) For stimulating historiographical reviews, see Christopher Saunders (no. 69) and Brigitte Lau (no. 136).

29) South African theses are recorded in A.M.L. Robinson: Catalogue
of theses and dissertations accepted for degrees by the South
African Universities, 1918-1941 (Cape Town, 1950), and S.I.
Malan: Union catalogue of theses and dissertations of South
African Universities, 1942-1958 (Potchefstroom, 1959). Since
1957 annual supplements have been published by the Potchefstroom
University Library. The catalogues and the supplements have been
out of print for some time, but in 1978 a cumulative edition,
covering the years 1918-1977, was published on microfiche. This
catalogue consists of an author catalogue and a subject catalogue.
Annual supplements for the years after 1978 are also available on
microfiche from the Ferdinand Postma Library, University of Potchefstroom.

published in <u>Perspectives on Namibia: past and present</u> (no. 68).
<u>The J.W. Jagger Library at the University of Cape Town</u> has a sub-
stantial collection of literature on Namibia, partly indexed in a
series of subject bibliographies prepared by students at the School
of Librarianship. The Library is amply provided with finding aids.
Its Special Collection Department is particularly strong on periodicals and theses, and also holds official publications from Namibia.
It is complemented by the <u>Parliament Library</u> of Cape Town, which is
strong on official publications and serials from Namibia.

Attention should also be drawn to the <u>Institute for Contemporary
History</u> at the University of the Orange Free State (Bloemfontein),
which has published a three-volume bibliography and register of private document collections on the political history of South Africa,
which partly includes Namibia. The Institute itself has a remarkably
comprehensive press clipping archive covering the post-1945 period.
The collection has been thoroughly indexed and computerised. The
separate index of its holdings on Namibia is also available on microfiche in the Windhoek State Archives. The Institute also holds a
rich collection of primary source material on contemporary history,
including the archives of the Namibia branch of the National Party
(1939-1966) as well as the papers of South Africans prominent in Namibian administration and politics.[30]

Of the other universities, the <u>Cory Library for Historical Re-
search</u> at Rhodes University (Grahamstown) holds the archives of the
Wesleyan Missionary Society on micro-film. The <u>University of Stellen-
bosch</u>'s library contains a wide range of theses and some important
items, including a duplicate copy of the 30-volume collection of Heind-
rich Vedder's papers and source extracts, which are otherwise only
available at the State Archives, Windhoek. In view of their active
role in government commissioned consultancy work on Namibia, one may
also expect that a considerable quantity of material has been collected by the University's Institute for Planning Research, Transport
Research Centre and the Institute for Cartographic Analysis. The
archives section of the <u>University of Witwatersrand's library</u> (Johannesburg) holds several relevant collections, including the archives
of the South African Institute of Race Relations and most importantly
of the Anglican Church's Diocese of Damaraland. Mention should also
be made of the Documentation Centre for African Studies at the <u>Uni-
versity of South Africa</u> (Pretoria), which has a collection of documents and source material mainly concerned with political developments
in Namibia in the 1970s (see no. 918).

Of the South African Archives Depots, the <u>Central Archives</u> (Pretoria) stands out as the most important source for the study of Namibian
history. For the period up to 1910, there is also a valuable collection in the <u>Cape Archives</u>, of which a preliminary synopsis is given in
Brigitte Lau: "Sources for the study of Namibian history in the Cape
Archives".[31] A consolidated list of finding aids in the Archives De-

---

30) The IFHC collection includes the papers of, among others, J.D.
     du Basson, J. von S. von Moltke, D.T. du P. Viljoen, W.C. du
     Plessis and J.P.S. Bruwer.

31) The review will be published in a forthcoming issue of the <u>South
     African Archives Journal</u>.

pots was published in 1969, and supplements to this list have since
been issued. See also the Bibliography of South African Government
Publications (BISAGOB), published by the Department of National Education.[32]

Among private institutions, the South African Institute of Race
Relations prepares the annual Survey of Race Relations (see no. 979),
which also includes a separate section on Namibia. The Jan Hofmeyr
Library at the Institute is generally strong on legislation, labour,
education, health and social conditions.[33]

The Jan Smuts House Library at the South Africa Institute of International Affairs (Braamfontein) specialises in international relations
in Southern Africa, and has an extensive collection of press clippings
in additions to books and documents. The Institute is the publisher of
several journals and bibliographies, including Elna Schoeman: The
Namibian Issue, 1920-1980 (no. 906).

The reference library of the Africa Institute of South Africa
(Pretoria) has one of the most comprehensive and specialised collections of books, periodicals, newspaper clippings and microfiches on
Southern Africa. The Institute has been involved in Namibian studies,
and has, inter alia, compiled a semi-official survey of the Namibian
economy (no. 415).

The State Archives, Windhoek, is well organised, easily accessible
(for researchers who are allowed to enter South Africa/Namibia) and
largely untapped.[34] It holds the substantial records of the German
colonial administration as well as of the South West African Administration after 1915.[35] Its List of Archivalia gives a broad indica-

---

32) 10 volumes have so far been published, covering, inter alia,
     Department of Statistics, 1910-1977; Department of Agriculture,
     1910-1978; Sea Fisheries Branch, 1920-1980, with volumes on Mines
     and Commerce scheduled for publication in 1984. For a detailed
     list of these volumes, see Africa Research and Documentation,
     no. 33, 1983, p. 6.

33) See Records of the South African Institute of Race Relations.
     Part I. Compiled by A.M. Cunningham. (Johannesburg: University
     of the Witswatersrand Library, 1981, 227 p.). This first volume
     spans the years 1930-1950.

34) For a general survey of libraries and archives in Namibia, see
     Carl Schlettwein and Lisa Gebhardt: "Libraries and archives in
     South West Africa", Mitteilungen der Basler Afrika Bibliographien,
     no. 13, 1975: 3-20. There are also brief sections concerned with
     Namibian libraries, including addresses in Directory of Southern
     African Libraries. 1975 (Pretoria: The State Library, 1976) and
     in The African Book World & Press. A Directory (see note 4   ).
     Namibian libraries and the critical bibliographical situation in
     the 1970s are discussed in the introduction to Eckhard Strohmeyer:
     Namibische National Bibliographie/Namibian National Bibliography
     (nos. 914-16).

35) The Archives are open up to 1950, and in 1985 this period will be
    extended to 1955. There are, however, certain parts which either
    have been moved to South Africa or are restricted.

tion of the range of the records, and there are also numerous, very
detailed finding aids.[36] More than two-thirds of the collection have
so far been computerised and indexed by key words. The Archives also
embraces the C.J. Lemmer collection of more than 1000 books, many of
them rare, as well as c 8000 indexed photos and ca 7000 maps and plans.
Of particular value is the collection of all the background documents
to the Administrator's reports to the League of Nation (see no. 258),
which contain departmental and district reports on an annual basis.
In recent years the Archives has received reports, gazettes and other
documents from the second-tier "Representative Authorities", set up
by South Africa on a tribal basis in 1980, complementing the material
previously acquired on the bantustans and the reserves. The Archives
has also been provided with material relevant to Namibia from the Cape
Archives Depot, and is in the process of strengthening its holdings
by cooperation and exchange agreements with other archives and libraries in South Africa as well as in Western Europe. The first volume
in a series of source editions appeared in 1984 (no. 135). The compilation of a Central Register of Theses on Namibia has also been
completed in conjunction with the Library Services Division.

One of the most urgent tasks in terms of documentation, bibliographical work and the collection of primary source material in an
independent Namibia will undoubtedly be to incorporate the holdings
of the Administrative Library in Windhoek into a national library and
documentation system. Established in 1926 as the library of the Legislative Assembly, its collection of books, pamphlets and periodicals is reputed to be outstanding. In the 1960s a serious effort was
made to reorganise the Africana Section, to update the library to a
national library and to compile a national bibliography. For various
reasons these efforts were not followed up in the 1970s, and after the
administrative reorganisation in 1978 the Library was strictly controlled by the White second-tier administration and was later stored
away and made inaccessible. According to press reports the library
will reopen in late 1984.

The South West Africa Scientific Society, which published an
annual Journal as well as several newsletters and other publications,
also runs a substantial library. It is especially strong on botany,
zoology and ecology, but also has a certain amount of more general
literature. Of special historical interest is the Fritz Jaeger Collection, which includes c 2000 photos, manuscripts and material gathered during his research visits and travels in Namibia in the early
part of this century.

There is also a most valuable library (the Sam Cohen Library)
attached to the Society for Scientific Development and Museum, Swakopmund, which was established in the early 1950s. The content of
the Ferdinand Stich Africana Collection, which forms part of this

36) List of Archivalia in South West African Archives Depots.
(Windhoek: State Archives, rev. ed., 1983, 43 p. See also
Guide to accessions in the South West Africa Archives Depot.
(Windhoek: Archives Service, 1983, 136 p.) and the Annual
Report of the Director of Archives.

library, is given in a special issue of Bibliotheka (no. 879). The
library is also worth consulting for its collection of newspapers,
which is said to be largely complete from the late 1890s, as well as
for its local periodicals which are now being indexed.

The State Museum, Windhoek, has a library dating from the German
colonial period. Apart from science, it has a significant collection
on history, ethnology and archaeology.

The Windhoek Public Library is presently the major lending library
in Namibia. In addition to the general literature it has a separate
Africana collection of books and pamphlets mainly related to Namibian
history. The library also files current clippings from local newspapers by subject. The special Africana section contains a few items
which are not found elsewhere in Namibia.[37]

The archives of the former Rhenish Missionary Society in Windhoek
is only partly organised and catalogued, but researchers working on
the archives have found it very rewarding.[38] It comprises missionary
reports, conference papers and minutes, as well as correspondence between missionaries and African leaders. There are also a number of unpublished manuscripts by Heinrich Vedder and parts of his library.

Not so well-known is a private museum and a rich archive in Tsumeb,
which contains the records of the Otavi Minen- und Eisenbahngesellschaft (OMEG). The collection offers a wide range of documents, photos and other material relating to early land sales, railway construction, migrant labour and pre-colonial and colonial copper mining. A
more substantial research project on Namibian history has also to take
into account numerous other libraries, archives and collections, such
as company records, farm records, town libraries, churches, newspapers,
economic interest groups, private and official boards and municipal
archives.

In the Southern African region, attention should also be focused
on the United Nations Institute for Namibia. UNIN was set up in Lusaka in 1976, under the aegis of the UN Council for Namibia, to enable
Namibians to develop the necessary skills required for manning the
public service of an independent Namibia, to carry out research and
prepare studies on future policy options, and to serve as an information and documentation centre on Namibia. The Information and Documentation Division of UNIN provides services for the Institute's
teaching and research programmes and has a small but growing collection with emphasis on the social sciences, Namibiana and UN material.
The special collection on Namibia comprises a number of rare manuscripts, political documents and consultancy reports. The Information and Documentation Division also provides various bibliographic
services including Namibia Abstracts. Guide to selected literature
on Namibia and other Southern African countries (no. 931).

---

37) An example is the background material to Fragebogen... (no. 638).

38) See, among others, Engel (nos. 192, 233) and Diehl (no. 1096).

SAMPLE ENTRIES

22. FIRST, RUTH. South West Africa. Harmondsworth: Penguin, 1963, 269 p. Bibl.: 255-61. (Penguin African Library AP 10).

Author or editor:	Ruth First
Title of the book:	South West Africa
Place of publication:	Harmondsworth
Publisher:	Penguin
Date of publication:	1963
Number of pages:	269
Page numbers of the bibliography:	255-261
Additional information:	Penguin Africa Library AP 10

503. BRANDT, HELMUT. "Perspektiven der Agrarentwicklung eines unabhängigen Namibia". Afrika Spectrum, 14, no. 2, 1979:

Author:	Hartmut Brandt
Title of article:	Perspektiven der Agrarentwicklung eines unabhängigen Namibia
Title of periodical:	Afrika Spectrum
Volume number:	14
Part of volume:	No. 2
Date of publication:	1979
Page numbers of article:	203-17

248. PEARSON, PATRICK. "The Rehoboth rebellion". In Working papers in Southern African studies, vol. 2, edited by P. Bonner, p. 31-51. Johannesburg: Ravan Press, 1981.

Author:	Patrick Pearson
Title of article:	The Rehoboth rebellion
Title of the book/anthology in which the article is published:	Working papers in Southern Africa studies, vol. 2
Editor of the book/anthology:	P. Bonner
Page numbers of article:	31-51
Place of publication:	Johannesburg
Publisher:	Ravan Press
Date of publication:	1981

662. LOFFLER, JOHN. Labour and politics in Namibia in the 1970s. York: Centre for Southern African Studies, 1979, 68 p. Bibl.: 66-8 (MA thesis).

Author:	John Loffler
Title of the thesis:	Labour and politics in Namibia in the 1970s
Place of publication:	York
University/institution:	Centre for Southern African Studies
Degree date:	1979
Number of pages:	68
Page numbers of the bibliography:	66-68
Degree:	MA thesis

1. GENERAL AND INTRODUCTORY

1. ABRAHAMS, KENNETH (ed.). <u>Seminar on Namibian history</u>. Windhoek:
Namibian Review Publications, 1983, 119 p. (Namibian Review Publications,
no. 2).

This important contribution to the study of Namibian history consists
of six essays and talks presented to a seminar on Namibian history in
Windhoek 10-12 December 1982. The seminar was sponsored by the <u>Namibian</u>
<u>Review</u> (no. 955), and provided scholars with an opportunity to present
their works to a wider audience and to undertake a critical evaluation
of recent research. Most of the contributions reflect the efforts of
the small group of committed researchers based in Namibia and South
Africa to assist in laying the foundations for a radical reinterpretation
of Namibian history. For separate annotations, see Lau (no. 134),
Alexander (no. 177), Gottschalk (no. 237), Ngavirue (no. 246), and
Werner (no. 550).

<u>Africa Contemporary Record</u>, see no. 985.

2. ANTI-APARTHEID MOVEMENT/UNESCO. <u>Racism and apartheid in southern Africa.</u>
<u>South Africa and Namibia</u>. Paris: UNESCO, 1974, 156 p. 11 maps, 13
photos, 16 tables, bibl.: 153-56.

Based on material prepared by the British Anti-Apartheid Movement, this
well illustrated popular account of the apartheid system is mainly
concerned with South Africa. Although only 25 pages long, the section
on Namibia summarises a wide range of information on the economic and
political situation up to the beginning of the 1970s.

3. AUSTRALIA (THE PARLIAMENT OF THE COMMONWEALTH OF AUSTRALIA/JOINT COMMITTEE
ON FOREIGN AFFAIRS AND DEFENCE). <u>Report on Namibia</u>. Canberra: Australian
Government Publishing Service, 1982, 170 p. 19 tables, 4 figures.

Prepared by an Australian parliamentary committee, this report is a
factual and balanced introduction to the Namibian issue. It is evidently
based on a wide range of books and documents, and deals with the history
of the legal dispute, the struggle for independence and current socio-
economic conditions. There is a particularly detailed chapter on the
1977-82 period, as well as a separate chapter concerned with Walvis Bay
and the Penguin Islands. The report is supported by documentary appendices
and a large number of tables. The Committee concludes that the linking
of a withdrawal of Cuban troops from Angola with a Namibian settlement
only serves further to delay Namibian independence, that South Africa's
preferred - but unlikely - solution is "the establishment of a stable,
ethnically-based and friendly government which would allow Namibia to
remain a buffer against external attack by nationalist forces and which
would permit continuing South African domination of the Namibian economy",

and that there is an overwhelming case for Walvis Bay and the Penguin Islands to become part of an independent Namibia.

4. BABING, ALFRED and HANS-DIETER BRÄUER. Namibia. From the Waterberg to Ongurumbashe. Persian lamb and diamonds. Hendrik Witbooi's heirs. Dresden: Verlag Zeit im Bild, 1981, 372 p. 102 photos. (German original: Namibia. Vom Waterberg nach Ongurumbashe - Kampf um Diamanten und Persianer - Die Erben Hendrik Witboois. Berlin (GDR): Verlag der Nation, 1979, 368 p. Also published as Namibia. Kolonialzeit, Widerstand, Befreiungskampf heute. Ein Report. Köln: Pahl-Rugenstein Verlag, 1980, 221 p.).

Written by two East Germans involved in the solidarity campaign for the liberation movements in Southern Africa, the purpose of this rather polemical book is to provide a popular introduction to Namibia's history and the present struggle for independence. The first part, which is somewhat fragmented and anecdotal, is mainly concerned with the German colonial period and the Nazi colonial revanchism in the 1930s. The role played by the German-speaking community and the West German corporations in the 1970s is then described very schematically in the second part. An interview with the SWAPO president, Sam Nujoma, concludes the book.

5. BANNISTER, ANTHONY and PETER JOHNSON. Africa's harsh paradise. Namibia. London: Country Life Books/Hamlyn, 1979, 224 p. 264 photos. (Original edition: Cape Town: Struik, 1978. German edition: Afrikas herbes Paradies. Namibia. Hannover: Landbuchverlag, 1979, 224 p.).

This lavishly illustrated book - there are more than 250 colour photographs - is an impressive visual introduction to "the natural splendour" of Namibia. The text consists of contributions by different authors on ecology, wildlife, the Namib Desert, Etosha Pan and anthropology. The book is mainly concerned with wildlife and breathtaking landscapes, but it also gives a certain amount of information on the history, culture and living conditions of the Namibian people. By no means an account of suffering and struggle, the book nevertheless avoids the paternalistic and esoteric excesses commonly found in books of this kind. The two photographers have received international acclaim for other books, such as Okavango, Sea of land. Land of water. (Cape Town: Struik, 1978, 202 p.).

6. BEYERS, C.J. (ed.) Dictionary of South African biography. Cape Town: Tafelberg. Vol. 1. 1968 (sec. print 1978), 895 p. Vol. 2, 1972, 870 p. Vol. 3, 1977, 861 p. Vol. 4, 1982, 803 p. + index.

Initiated by the Human Sciences Research Council, this is the standard South African historical dictionary of biographies. It does not, however, include anybody who has died after 1970. Among the more than 3500 entries there are also a number of biographies of relevance to the study of Namibian history. The dictionary is strongest on European travellers, German and South African military officers and colonial administrators, and leading missionaries. Some of these biographical accounts are rather uncritical, even hagiographic, praising the "civilising role" of prominent colonisers. There are also biographies of a few African leaders, among them Jonker Afrikaner, Samuel Maharero,

Jakob Morenga (Marengo), Abraham Morris, Hendrik Witbooi and Amraal
Lamberts. All biographies include sources and suggestions for further
reading, and vol. 4 has a very useful cumulative name index.

BRÄUER, HANS-DIETER, see no. 45.

THE BRITISH COUNCIL OF CHURCHES, see no. 9.

7. BRITTAN, MICHAEL. Discover Namibia. Cape Town/Johannesburg: Struik,
   1979, 304 p. 84 photos, bibl.: 285-94.

   Written by a South African chemical engineer and businessman with an
   obvious fascination for Namibian geology, wildlife, botany and history,
   this is a collection of well-informed accounts on a wide range of subjects such as rock paintings of the Stone Age, the Namib Desert, the
   wildlife of Etosha Pan, the petrified forests and the Hoba meteorite.
   There are also two chapters of interest for the study of the economic
   history of mining and minerals: on diamonds (p. 163-201) and on Tsumeb
   (p. 232-61). The book is beautifully illustrated and has an extensive
   bibliography.

8. BRUWER, JOHANNES PETRUS VAN SCHALKWYK. South West Africa: the disputed
   land. Cape Town: Nasionale Boekhandel, 1966, 147 p. Bibl.: 133-36.

   Based on the author's experience as an ethnologist and "Commissioner-
   General for the Bantu Population of South West Africa", this book takes
   the South African standpoint on Namibia for granted. Professor
   Bruwer was a prominent member of the Commission of Enquiry into South
   West African Affairs (Odendaal Commission) during 1962-63, the author
   of an anthropological study of the Kwanyama in Ovamboland (no. 617),
   and an influential Afrikaner academic until his early death in the
   mid-1960s. His analysis is the best informed and most sophisticated
   of the crop of pro-apartheid publications on Namibia which appeared
   during the 1960s. The major part of the book deals with the history
   and peoples of Namibia before the colonisation. Although it is admitted
   that South Africa is not above criticism, it is maintained that the
   period under South African rule is characterised by the "civilised
   rule of law" and by remarkable economic progress. The book ends with
   a chapter arguing the South African case against the United Nations
   and the International Court of Justice.

9. CATHOLIC INSTITUTE FOR INTERNATIONAL RELATIONS and THE BRITISH COUNCIL
   OF CHURCHES. Namibia in the 1980s. London: CIIR/BCC, 1981, 84 p.
   (In German: Namibia in den achtziger Jahren. Hamburg: Evangelisches
   Missionswerk im Bereich der Bundesrepublik Deutschland und Berlin
   West e.v., 1982, 82 p. The text is also translated into French by
   Comité Catholique contre la Faim et pour le Développement, and pub-
   lished in Demain la Namibie. L'Afrique du Sud dans l'impasse? Paris:
   Editions Karthala, 1983, 163 p.).

   Although not representing official church policy, this is an important
   statement of progressive Christian opinion. The authors have consulted
   widely amongst Namibians at home and in exile, Christian and non-Christian,

as well as other experts on the country. The prime mover, CIIR, has been actively involved with contemporary economic and political issues in Southern Africa for some years, and published in the late 1970s an influential series of booklets on the problems of transition from colonialism to independence in Zimbabwe. The booklet is the first of a similar series on Namibia, see nos. 532, 580, 562, 695. It develops a concise and closely argued critique of economic exploitation and political and military repression under South African rule, concentrating on recent years, on which the benefits of its contact with grass-root Namibian sources are strongly evident. Particularly valuable is its penetrating analysis of the political motives and strategic manoeuvres of South Africa and the Western Contact Group and of the problem and priorities in the transition to independence. In its final section the booklet assumes and implicitly endorses the leading role and commit-ment to social justice of the liberation movement, SWAPO. Documentary appendices include several important statements by the churches in Namibia and Britain.

10. CENTRE D ´INFORMATION ET DE DOCUMENTATION SUR LE MOZAMBIQUE ET L ´AFRIQUE AUSTRALE (C.I.D.M.A.A.). Towards Namibian independence: prospects for development and assistance. Montréal, Québéc: 1984, 72 p. 4 maps, 11 photos. (Also published in French).

Prepared by a Namibia Study Team of C.I.D.M.A.A. for the Canadian Council for International Cooperation, this general introduction to Namibia is based on a visit to the territory in 1983 as well as on extensive consultations with SWAPO leaders, UN agencies and non-govern-mental organizations (NGO's) in Europe and Canada. Written in a popular style, the major part of the booklet describes the basic features of Namibian colonial society, the main sectors of the economy, the critical problems facing an independent Namibia, and SWAPO's position on a wide range of issues. It also reviews the Namibia solidarity activities of the Canadian NGO's since the 1970s, including projects situated inside Namibia and in the refugee settlements in Angola and Zambia, and recom-mends the creation of a Namibia Coordinating Committee to set sectoral priorities, to choose the projects, to plan information and educational campaigns among the Canadian public, and to present NGO requests to the Canadian government.

11. THE CENTRE FOR EXTRA-MURAL STUDIES, UNIVERSITY OF CAPE TOWN. South West Africa: problems and alternatives. Cape Town, 1975, 210 p.

A compendium of very uneven quality, based on the lectures and back-ground papers prepared for a course on Namibia at the Summer School, University of Cape Town in February 1975. The papers reflect the con-cern with Namibia as an international issue, but there are also contributions on the economy (W.H. Thomas, Francis Wilson) and labour (John Kane-Berman). Apart from South African scholars, a number of Namibians of different political persuasions are represented in state-ments on the churches, the liberation struggle, the black theology of liberation, and the political future of Namibia.

12. CROCKER, CHESTER A. and PENELOPE HARTLAND-THUNBERG. Namibia at the crossroads: economic and political prospects. Washington DC: Georgetown University, 1978, 55 p. 7 tables. (Center for Strategic

and International Studies Monograph).

Based on the assumption that Namibia would achieve independence in
1978, the purpose of this booklet was to stimulate discussion on
the economic and political future of the territory. The fact that
one of the authors later was appointed Assistant State Secretary for
African Affairs in the Reagan Administration lends added significance,
especially in view of its naive optimism over South African intentions.
The assessment of the political forces at work in Namibia is more
well-balanced, and both the strength of SWAPO and the ethnic parti-
cularity which serves as the principal focus of political loyalty
of nearly all the anti-SWAPO forces are duly recognized. The section
on the Namibian economy is mainly based on the official South West
Africa Survey 1974 (no. 306), and apart from an attempt to compare
Namibia to Botswana it adds nothing to the existing literature.

13. CROS, GÉRARD. La Namibie. Paris: Presses Universitaires de France,
    1983, 127 p. Bibl.: 126-7. (Que sais-je?).

This is one of the very few publications on Namibia in French, written
for a general audience and published in the prestigeous "Que sais-je?"
series. The book opens with two brief and straightforward chapters
on the geography and economy of the country, followed by a historical
introduction. The legal conflict, the constitutional development, the
liberation struggle and the international negotiations are also covered
by separate chapters, and important UN documents and resolutions are
reproduced. Although the author attempts an unbiased approach, the
bibliography reflects the lack of familiarity with progressive literature.

14. CULLINAN, SUE. "The Namibian dispute". Work in Progress, no. 24,
    (October) 1982: 28-39.

15. ------- "Military policy and the Namibian dispute". In South African
    Review I, p. 33-41. Johannesburg: Ravan Press, 1983.

The first of these two perceptive articles provides a brief overview
of the diplomatic, political, military and economic situation between
the Geneva conference in early 1981 and mid-1982, written from a
progressive standpoint. It describes and analyses South African and
Western attempts to sabotage the UN peace plan and introduce "constitutional guarantees", South African efforts to "namibianise" the
army of occupation, military aggression against Angola, the dissension
amongst pro-South African political parties and the deteriorating
capitalist economy. The contribution to South African Review I discusses the military aspects in more detail. The author is a South
African scholar and journalist who is preparing a PhD thesis on SWAPO
and political developments in Namibia since 1960. (University of
Cape Town).

16. DISKURS. Thema: Namibia: Die Aktualität des kolonialen Verhältnisses.
    Beitrage aus dem Projekt "Politische Landeskunde Namibias". Univer-
    sität Bremen, 1982, 276 p. (Diskurs, Bremer Beiträge zu Wissenschaft
    und Gesellschaft, no. 6, August 1982.).

This special issue of DISKURS is devoted to the project "Politische Landeskunde Namibias", which is a joint initiative of the University of Bremen and the UN Institute for Namibia to prepare textbooks and teaching materials for Namibian as well as West German schools. The background and the aims of the project are explained by Manfred O. Hinz, Helgard Patemann presents a critical analysis of German textbooks concerned with Namibia, colonisation and decolonisation, and Hartmut Müller gives an account of the colonial movement in Bremen with special emphasis on the role of the colonial pioneer F.A. Lüderitz. The major contribution to the issue is an extended and stimulating essay on Namibia under German rule, by Henning Melber (no. 202).

17. ERIKSEN, TORE LINNÉ. Namibia. Kolonialisme, apartheid og frigjørings-kamp i det sørlige Afrika. Oslo: Universitetsforlaget/Uppsala: Nordiska Afrikainstitutet, 1982, 251 p. 5 maps, 13 tables, bibl.: 222-34.

18. -------Namibia. Landanalys. Stockholm: SIDA, 1982, 97 p. 5 maps, 7 tables, bibl.: 72-9. (Revised edition to be published in 1985).

19. -------Namibia - hindringer og muligheter for utvikling. Oslo: Norsk Utenrikspolitisk Institutt, 1981, 72 p. (Forum for Utviklingsstudier, nos. 1-3, 1981).

20. -------"Råvarer, gruveselskaper og politikk: Namibia som eksempel". Internasjonal Politikk, no. 2, 1981: 237-66.

Written in Norwegian and intended for a Scandinavian audience, Namibia is a comprehensive and factual introduction to the history of colo-nialism, the apartheid economy and the struggle for liberation. There is a separate chapter dealing with Namibia in the context of SADCC and South African regional destabilisation, and the book ends with a dis-cussion of the political and economic prospects for an independent Namibia. Several documents, a chronology, a list of foreign companies, tables, and an extensive bibliography are included as appendices. Namibia. Landanalys is a translation into Swedish of a shortened ver-sion of the book, published in the SIDA series of "country reports". Namibia - hindringer og muligheter for utvikling provides a brief out-line of the economic structure, followed by a more detailed discussion of the possibilities for, and constraints on, economic development and socialist transformation in an independent Namibia. Råvarer, grueselskaper og politikk. is a case study of the role played by the international mining corporations in the exploitation of Namibia and the protracted diplomatic manoeuvers of recent years. Written from a standpoint of solidarity with the struggle for Namibian independence, these works provide one of the most comprehensive general introductions to the situation and key issues in contemporary Namibia.

21. ERMACORA, FELIX. Namibia/Südwestafrika. München: Bayerische Landes-zentrale für Politische Bildungsarbeit, 1981, 187 p. Tables, maps.

This general introduction to Namibia, one of many of its kind, focuses on Namibia mainly as an international political and legal issue. It also outlines the main features of the apartheid system. The first half is written by a leading Austrian expert on international law, while the second part contains a large number of UN and other documents, maps and tables.

22. FIRST, RUTH. <u>South West Africa</u>. Harmondsworth: Penguin, 1963, 269 p. Bibl.: 255-61. (Penguin Africa Library AP 10).

Ruth First, political journalist, leading member of the South African liberation movement and inspiration to generations of activists, was a major figure in postwar radical African scholarship until her assass- ination by a parcel bomb in Maputo in 1982. She was the first to attempt a book-length account of Namibian history and politics from a progressive point of view. Researched in depth from local sources and interviews and written for a popular readership with admirable analytical clarity, the resulting study remains one of the best and most readable introductory presentations of its kind, and differs from most in giving prominence to the views of Namibians themselves. It surveys more than a hundred years of Namibian history, with special em- phasis on the repressive methods of German and South African rule and their impact on the Namibian people. A central section discusses eco- nomic and social conditions, focusing on the every-day life of migrant workers, the crowding of Africans into small reserves, the oppressive lab- our regulations and the exploitative role played by the mining corpora- tions. There is also a chapter concerned with the liberation movements and their origins, which to a great extent is based on information given by the SWANU leader at that time, J.F. Kozonguizi. The book ends with an informative survey of reference and sources.

FIRST, RUTH, see no. 71.

23. FRAENKEL, PETER. <u>The Namibians of South West Africa</u>. London: Minority Rights Group, sec. ed. 1978, 44 p. Maps, 10 photos. (MRG Report no. 10).

Prepared on the basis of a trip to Namibia, this is a short and well- written introduction. The sections on the bantustans and on labour are still relevant, deploying information on wages and living con- ditions, put together from press cuttings and the author's own observations. The booklet is strong on maps and photos, reflecting the author's experience as a free-lance journalist and photographer. He has travelled extensively in Asia and Africa, and is currently associated with the Intermediate Technology Development Group. The first (1974) edition has been translated into French: <u>Les Namibiens</u> (Paris: Editions Entente, 1976, 147 p.).

24. GOLDBLATT, ISRAEL. <u>History of South West Africa from the beginning of the nineteenth century</u>. Cape Town: Juta, 1971, 273 p. 8 tables, bibl.: xi-xiii.

This narrative history is one of the few in English to cover the whole of the period for which documentary sources are available. Written by a liberal lawyer, recently deceased after a lifetime's residence in Namibia, it is sharply critical of the most extreme aspects of colonial repression. The main focus is on political events, but there are also several chapters on economic history, notably the mining and land companies, land settlement and diamond mining (chs. 22, 28, 34, 41, 44), and an appendix contains tables of post-1920 economic and demographic data. The author's principal interest is in the pre- colonial and German colonial period and coverage becomes very sketchy after 1920. His approach is, however, antiquarian, the text consisting of a series of factual statements unified by little more than chronological sequence and cut up into a large number of short chapters. This feature, together with the lack of an index, makes it difficult to make full use of the extensive range of archival and published sources which the author has consulted and frequently quotes in the text. Goldblatt also published an early assessment of the dispute between South Africa and the UN over Namibia's international legal status (The Mandated Territory of South West Africa in relation to the United Nations. Cape Town: Struik, 1961, 67 p.).

25. GREEN, LAWRENCE G. The coast of treasure. London/New York: Putnam, 1933, 269 p. (Reprinted, Cape Town: Timmins, 1983).

26. -------Where men still dream. Cape Town: Timmins, 1945, 280 p.

27. -------Lords of the last frontier. The story of South West Africa and its people of all races. Cape Town: Timmins, 1952, 369 p. (Also published: London/New York: Stanley Paul, 1953, 237 p.).

28. -------Like diamond blazing. The story of the diamonds of South Africa and the men who sought and found and stole diamonds in strange places. London: Robert Hale, 1967, 206 p.

Written by an adventurer, journalist and prolific popular author who travelled extensively in and around Namibia, these four well illustrated books make fascinating reading. L.H. Green was one of the very few to write books on Namibia in English before 1960, and his accounts are based on wide reading, but above all on personal observation and historical anecdotes picked up from sailors, farmers, miners, and colonial administrators. The paradigm is very much that of colonial rule, but his descriptive accounts show him to be a perceptive observer and carry a certain conviction. His first book, The coast of treasure, describes a voyage mostly by sea down the coast from Walvis Bay to Cape Town, covering fishing, guano collection and diamond mining. Where men still dream deals in part with a trek from Cape Town to Ovamboland; Lords of the last frontier is a more ambitious - and less successful - general introduction to the history and people of Namibia; and Like diamond blazing describes diamond mining in Namibia (p. 75-192). Material on Namibia appears in several other books by the same author, amongst others Old Africa untamed (London: Paul, 1940, 260 p., reprint Cape Town: Timmins, 1974); Panter Head: the full story of the Bird Islands of the southern coast of Africa, the men of the islands and the birds in their millions (London: Paul, 1955, 256 p.); So few are free (Cape Town: Timmons, 1946, 250 p.); Strange Africa (London: Paul, 1938. 288 p.); To the river's end (Cape Town: Timmins, 1945, 280 p., reprinted 1981); and On wings of fire (Cape Town: Timmins, 1967, reprinted 1982, 249 p.).

29. GREEN, REGINALD H., MARJA-LIISA KILJUNEN and KIMMO KILJUNEN (eds.). Namibia. The last colony. London: Longman, 1981, 310 p. 56 tables, 11 maps, bibl.: 293-303.

Together with SWAPO: To be born a nation (no. 74), this is still the best English-language introduction to the history, politics, economy and liberation struggle of Namibia. A wide-ranging introduction is followed by essays covering the colonial economy, the role of South African capital, living conditions under apartheid, the role of the

churches, contract work through Ovambo eyes, national resistance
and the ideology of the liberation struggle, agrarian changes and
transnational corporations. Important aspects, such as class
relations, Namibia in the Southern Africa/SADCC context and the
devastating effects of the war are, however, not covered. Apart
from the editors, who have themselves written two-thirds of the
text, there are contributions by Duncan Innes (no. 366), Justin
Ellis (no. 857), Sam Nujoma (no. 826), Constantine Vaitsos, Rauha
Voipio (no. 679) and Robert Chambers (no. 516). The book also
contains a very valuable and extensive statistical appendix, based
on the work of Reginald H. Green, as well as a comprehensive bibliography. The English version is a revised edition of Kimmo Kuljunen
and Marja-Liisa Kiljunen(eds.): Namibia viimeinen siirtomaa.
Helsinki: Tammi, 1980, 322 p.

30. GREEN, REGINALD H. and JEAN DE LA PAIX. "A nation in agony: the
Namibian people's struggle for solidarity, freedom and justice".
Development Dialogue, nos. 1-2, 1982: 141-64.

Essentially an extended review essay of four major publications on
Namibia (nos. 9, 29, 74, 470), this article serves also as a lucid
introduction to the history of "the economy of theft" and the
course of the struggle for liberation in Namibia. The authors
assess South Africa's strategy for control and the diplomatic
manoeuvres during 1982, and update the description and analysis
of current economic developments given by R.H. Green in other
articles and books (see, inter alia, no. 470).

31. GROTPETER, JOHN J. Historical dictionary of Namibia. Metuchen,
N.J./ London: The Scarecrow Press. (African Historical Diction-
aries). In preparation.

HARTLAND-THUNBERG, PENELOPE, see. no. 12.

32. HAYTHORNTHWAITE, FRANK. All the way to Abenab. London: Faber &
Faber, 1956, 288 p. 31 photos, 2 maps.

Based on the author's experience as an Anglican priest in Namibia
in the 1950s, this is an interesting source on a wide range of
subjects in a period which is poorly covered in the literature. The
author was an informed and acute observer, and writes in a popular
style. Apart from the activities of the churches, the book covers
geography, social history and economic conditions (mining, fisheries,
industry and transport). Although the main focus is on Walvis Bay
and Swakopmund, there are also descriptions of areas such as Tsumeb,
Grootfontein, Otjiwarongo and Outjo. There is a detailed index.

33. HELBIG, HELGA and LUDWIG HELBIG. Mythos Deutsch-Südwest. Namibia
und die Deutschen. Weinheim/Basel: Beltz, 1983, 284 p. 11 maps,
50 photos, bibl.: 276-84.

This book provides a lucid, perceptive and well illustrated introduction to Namibian history and the present political situation,
written in a popular style for a general German readership. The

authors were teachers in the German school in Lüderitz in the early
1960s, and have paid several later visits to the country. The book
is at the same time a travel account, a historical survey and an
analysis of the current situation. There are also separate chapters
on SWAPO and on the South African strategy for control through an
"internal solution". Special emphasis is put on the German missionaries and traders, German colonialism and the role played by the
German community both in the interwar period and today. There is
also a fascinating chapter on the past and present of Lüderitz,
based on the authors' visit during the celebration of its 100th
anniversary in 1983. The book is weaker on the economic structure
of Namibia and the living conditions of the black majority, but
remains on a whole a significant contribution to the literature on
Namibia in German. It serves also as a most welcome corrective to
the wide range of right-wing books set in a cold-war perspective
(see no. 786).

34. HILLEBRECHT, WERNER, HENNING MELBER and MARY MELBER (eds.). IM
TREUE FEST, SÜDWEST ! - Ein kolonialpolitisches Lesebuch von der
Eroberung Namibias über die deutsche Fremdherrschaft bis zur
Kolonialapologie der Gegenwart. Bonn: Informationsstelle Südliches
Afrika (ISSA), 1985, c. 176 p. (edition südliches Afrika). In
preparation.

35. HODGSON, BRYAN. "Namibia. Nearly a nation?". National Geographic,
161, (June) 1982: 755-97. 33 photos by Jim Brandenburg.

Published in a magazine with a very wide circulation, this is a
journalistic account of Namibia, lavishly illustrated in the typical
"one day in the human zoo" fashion of the magazine. Apart from a
brief geographical background and some glimpses of Etosha Pan and
everyday life, the article is mainly concerned with explaining
the virtues of the South African-controlled economy and the policies
of the pro-South African "Democratic Turnhalle Alliance". The
author, a senior National Geographic staffer, seems to believe that
all apartheid laws have been abolished.

35. HUBRICH, HEINRICH-GEORG and HENNING MELBER. Namibia-Geschichte und
Gegenwart zur Frage der Dekolonisation einer Siedlerkolonie. Bonn:
Informationsstelle Südliches Afrika, 1977, 274 p. Bibl.: 265-74.

This excellent introduction to Namibia, which is still one of the
best general works in any language, originated from a joint thesis
presented at the Free University, Berlin. It has been revised and
updated for publication, but there remains unfortunately too much
of what the authors themselves describe as the "academic-elitist
jargon of left-wing intellectuals". The main sections of the book
deal with the history of Namibia, the socio-economic structure,
the Turnhalle-strategy for "decolonisation" and the international
negotiations in 1977. The study is analytically strong and deploys
a wealth of detailed information, drawn partly from the authors'
careful reading of the Namibian press. There is also an extensive
bibliography.

37. HUNKE, HEINZ. Namibia: the strength of the powerless. Rome: IDOC
International, 1980, 161 p.

Describing itself as a "dossier", this book is in effect a set of
seven essays complemented by a detailed chronology. They cover in
turn the policies of the US, West Germany, the UK, Scandinavian
and Communist governments towards Namibia; military and nuclear
collaboration with South Africa; arguments for and against the
economic boycott and disinvestment; the liberation movement and
the main political parties in Namibia; the struggle over Namibian
independence; the role of the churches; and South Africa's moves
towards an "internal settlement". The analysis of the Namibian
churches' attitude and response to colonialism and the liberation
struggle is particularly authoritative. The book is richly documented with a mass of illuminating detail, but is often poorly
organised. The author, a radical catholic who is now employed by
the IDOC documentation centre, was expelled from Namibia in 1979
because of his courageous exposure of South African repression and
torture.

38. HURLICH, SUSAN and RICHARD L. LEE. "Colonialism, apartheid and
liberation. A Namibian example". In Challenging anthropology,
edited by David H. Turner and Gavin A. Smith, p. 353-69. Toronto:
McGraw-Hill Ryerson, 1979.

Taking Namibia as a case, the authors of this study argue that just
as no student could hope to understand African societies of yes-
terday without a firm grasp of kinship theory, today the student
must understand the wider system of political economy and class
struggles. After a brief introduction to the colonial history
of Namibia and the development of apartheid, it is demonstrated
how the ! Kung San in a space of twenty-five years have been transformed from an independent hunting and gathering people into an
appendage of the apartheid system. The final section is concerned
with the dynamics of African resistance to colonialism and apartheid, both in the early stage and in the more recent liberation
struggle led by SWAPO.

39. IDOC. Namibia now! Rome: IDOC, 1973, 116 p. Bibl.: 113-6.
(IDOC International documentation participation project on "The
Future of the Missionary Enterprise", no. 3).

A collection of documents on political and economic issues as well
as on the role of the churches. Areas of coverage include appeals
to the UN, the contract labour system, the general strike in 1971-72
and multinational corporations. Two of the most interesting documents are the full text of the influential letter sent by the Lutheran church to the South African prime minister, J.B. Vorster, in
1971, followed by excerpts and part of the transcript - nowhere
else published - of the subsequent meeting between Vorster and the
church leaders.

40. IDS BULLETIN. Southern Africa: the political economy of inequality.
Sussex: Institute of Development Studies, 1980, 80 p. (IDS Bulletin,
11, no. 4, (September) 1980).

Several of the contributions in this special issue of the IDS Bulletin
are of interest for an understanding of Namibia in its regional
context, and two articles address themselves directly to Namibia,
Kimmo Kiljunen: "Namibia: The ideology of national liberation",
p. 65-71, and Reginald H. Green: "The unforgiving land - basis for
a post-liberation programme in Namibia", p. 72-76.

41. INFORMATIONSDIENST SÜDLICHES AFRIKA. Schwerpunkt :Namibia 1983.
Bonn: ISSA, 1983, 32 p. (Informationsdienst südliches Afrika,
no. 7-8, (July-August) 1983).

A special issue of the journal of the West German anti-apartheid
movement, concerned with the recent development of the struggle
for Namibian independence. The articles cover such important
topical themes as the diplomatic manoeuvres of the Western powers,
the deteriorating social and economic conditions in Namibia, the
present crisis in agriculture, the activities of the multinational
corporations, the role of the churches and the South African military
escalation. There are also penetrating reviews of several books
on Namibia in German.

42. INTERNATIONAL DEFENCE AND AID FUND FOR SOUTHERN AFRICA. Namibia.
The facts. London: IDAF, 1980, 100 p. Bibl.: 98-9.

Bringing together a wide range of information, this is a well
organised compilation of facts and figures on Namibian history,
international status, economy, labour force, the apartheid system,
the war and the liberation struggle. It contains also a selected
bibliography and suggestions for further reading. For a brief
updating of information on poverty, living conditions and racial
segregation, see Apartheid in Namibia Today (IDAF, Briefing Paper
No. 4, March 1982). The recent development of the armed struggle
is covered by Fighting for Namibia. Documentation on the guerilla
war (IDAF, Briefing Paper, No. 8, July 1983) and the international
negotiations are discussed in Namibia: settlement negotiations
(IDAF, Briefing Paper, No. 12, July 1984).

43. INTERNATIONAL UNIVERSITY EXCHANGE FUND. Namibia Dossier. Geneva:
IEUF, 1978/79, 127 p.

During 1978 the National Union of South African Students (NUSAS)
published Focus on Namibia which brought together material on
Namibia normally not accessible to the South African public. The
publication was banned by the authorities, but was later reproduced by IUEF under another name for distribution inside South
Africa. The major part of the collection consists of UN publications, church statements, reports documenting the atrocities
of the South African troops and comments on the Turnhalle conference. Also included are several SWAPO documents and interviews with
SWAPO leaders.

44. JENNY, HANS. South West Africa. Land of extremes. Windhoek:
SWA Scientific Society, 1976, 299 p. Bibl.: 280-84. (German
original: Südwestafrika - Land zwischen den Extremen. Stuttgart:
Kohlhammer, 1966, 298 p.).

Written by a Swiss journalist specialising in African affairs, this
is - unfortunately - one of the very few general introductions to
Namibia available both in German and English. The report is based
on six journeys to Namibia as well as extensive reading, and offers
a well-written account from a colonialist/paternalistic perspective.
Apartheid and occupation is generally regarded as "an experiment in
black-white co-existence", "egalitarian conformity" is seen as the
most immediate danger to the "poor but happy tribesmen" and the
author's main concern is how to "keep SWA free" from "the revolution
of black Pan-Africanism and the red dictatorship of the proletariat".
There is, however, a certain amount of information on agriculture,
fisheries, mining and water supply (p. 141-83), and on European
politics and administration.

JOHNSON, PETER, see no. 5.

45. KATJAVIVI, PETER H. Some aspects of Namibia's political sociology.
University of Warwick, 1980, 164 p. Bibl.: 157-64. (MA thesis).

Written by a Namibian scholar who served as SWAPO Representative to
Western Europe and subsequently as Secretary of Information, this
dissertation deserves wider attention. The first part examines the
nature of colonialism in Namibia, summarising recent writings on the
economy and social and working conditions. The second part is concerned with the development of anti-colonial forces from the turn
of the century, with special emphasis on SWAPO and the role of the
churches in the liberation struggle. The research is based on a
wide range of Namibian sources, not widely accessible, including
material from private collections. The author is extending his
research on the origins and rise of nationalism in Namibia for
submission as a PhD thesis to St. Antony's College, Oxford.

46. KERINA, MBURUMBA. Namibia. The making of a nation. New York:
Books in Focus, 1981, 314 p. Bibl.: 301-06.

Written by a controversial Namibian political figure who has over
the years belonged to numerous different groupings, this is a fragmented and disappointing book which adds little to the literature
on Namibia. It is essentially a collection of old notes and documents which have been written over the last 20 years, mainly concerned
with history and diplomacy. The list of foreign companies operating
in the early 1960s (p. 214-37) contains some interesting information
on the fishing companies, which was included to show "the economic
potential of the country under the sort of stable black coalition
government which will emerge at the end of 1978". It is remarkable
that the account of the struggle for independence fails to give a
single reference to SWAPO.

KILJUNEN, KIMMO, see no. 29.

KILJUNEN, MARJA-LIISA, see no.29.

LA PAIX, JEAN DE, see no.30.

47. LAZAR, LEONARD. Namibia. London: The Africa Bureau, 1972, 107 p.

The purpose of this book is to give a first introduction to Namibia.

Apart from a historical survey from the German colonial conquest
to 1972, which contains no original material, the chief merit of
the publication is the reproduction of important documents, excerpts
from treaties and laws, UN resolutions and petitions. Prepared by
Roger Murray, there is also a well researched section on the history
and current operations of the mining sector.

LEE, RICHARD L., see no. 38.

48. LEUMER, WOLFGANG. Namibia – auf dem Weg zur Unabhängigkeit. Bonn:
Forschungsinstitut der Friedrich-Ebert-Stiftung, 1976, 53 p.
(Arbeiten aus der Abteilung Entwicklungsländerforschung, no. 60).

Published by the Ebert Foundation, which is connected to the West
German Social Democratic Party, this paper gives a brief description
of history, economic structure and the struggle for national
liberation. Some of the problems and possibilities facing Namibia
at independence are discussed, with some critical comments on the
works of W. Schneider-Barthold (no. 430) and W.H. Thomas (no. 75).
The report also includes a German translation of the SWAPO political
programme, two important UN resolutions, and comments on the role
of the German-speaking community in Namibia and the activities of
the churches.

49. LEVINSON, OLGA. Story of Namibia. Cape Town: Tafelberg, 1978,
155 p. 104 photos, bibl.: 141-42.

Originally published as The ageless land. The story of SWA (1961),
this is a revised and updated version of an impressionistic introduction to Namibian history. The writer is well-informed about
politics, parties and personalities, and also provides some glimpses
of pre-colonial and colonial history. There are several brief
chapters on the "black diamonds" (karakul), fisheries, mineral
riches, diamonds, tourism and conservation, which although not
scholarly economic history, offer a variety of detailed information.
Due attention is also paid to the growth of African nationalism,
although the author is clearly hostile to the liberation movement
(SWAPO). The book as a whole is badly organised and lacks references,
but has a good index.

50. LOTH, HEINRICH. From insurrection to an organised liberation
struggle. Namibia's struggle against racism, colonialism and
imperialism. Berlin (GDR): Solidarity Committee of the German
Democratic Republic, 1979, 56 p.

A brief, popularised account of Namibian history over the last
hundred years, written with the aim of making the struggle for
independence, led by SWAPO, more widely known in the GDR as well
as internationally. The author is a prominent East German historian and a prolific writer on Southern African affairs (see no.
140).

51. MBUENDE, KAIRE. Namibia – the broken shield: anatomy of imperialism
and revolution. Lund (Sweden): University of Lund, Department of
Sociology (PhD thesis). In preparation.

52. MELBER, HENNING (ed.). Namibia. Kolonialismus und Widerstand. Bonn:
    Informationsstelle Südliches Afrika (ISSA), 1981, 320 p. Bibl.: 311-
    20. (edition südliches afrika 8).

    This is a comprehensive collection of background articles and source
    material on Namibia, which serves as an introduction to Namibian
    history and the struggle for liberation. The book is especially
    valuable for schools and includes an annotated list of other publica-
    tions on Namibia available in German. The first part is devoted
    to the period of German colonialism, in which racism and ruthless
    exploitation are revealed through contemporary sources such as
    official reports and memoirs written by colonial administrators
    and settlers. There is also a section on labour and working con-
    ditions, mainly based on interviews with Namibians, as well as a
    collection of documents related to SWAPO and the struggle for
    independence.

53. MELBER, HENNING (compiler). Our Namibia. A social studies textbook.
    Osnabrück: terre des hommes (F.R.G.), 1984, 167 p. Illus.,
    bibl.: 166-67.

    This is a stimulating textbook for teaching social studies to Namibian
    pupils in upper primary and lower secondary classes, written within
    the framework of a new educational system that is helping in the
    making of an independent Namibia. Together with Lernbuch Namibia
    (no. 64), it originates from an extensive project of cooperation
    between the University of Bremen and the UN Institute for Namibia
    (Lusaka), in consultation with the Department of Education and
    Culture of SWAPO. The book covers the basic features of Namibian
    geography and economy, Namibian history and the main characteristics
    of contemporary society and the struggle for liberation. It is
    well illustrated with photos, maps and drawings, and a substantial
    part of the book consists of poems and excerpts from documents,
    books, and letters written by young Namibians in Health and Education
    Centres in Angola and Zambia. It also provides some inspiring ex-
    amples of the use of oral history.

    MELBER, HENNING, see no. 36.

    MELBER, HENNING, see no. 34.

    MELBER, MARY, see no. 34.

54. MOLEAH, ALFRED T. Namibia. The struggle for liberation. Wilmington,
    DE: Disa Press/Moleah Publishers, 1983, 341 p. 18 photos, bibl.:
    325-29.

    Written by a South African scholar based in the United States, the
    aim of this committed and somewhat rhetorical work is to provide US
    readers with a comprehensive introduction to Namibian history and
    the struggle for liberation. The author makes use of a wide range
    of secondary sources in presenting the major features of the
    settler-colonial system, African resistance and the evolution of
    South African strategy from incorporation to "internal settlement".

The chapter on "The African condition" (p. 42-88) offers a valuable summary of the literature on African workers and the migrant labour system, but the book is otherwise disappointingly weak in description and analysis of the economic and social structure of Namibia. The final chapters concentrate on the recent development of the conflict up to early 1983. The author argues strongly that South Africa's efforts to create an alternative to SWAPO are doomed to failure, and that the effects of the Reagan Administration's policy of "constructive engagement" have been to prolong the misery and agony of the Namibian people rather than to move South Africa towards a settlement.

55. MOORSOM, RICHARD. Colonisation and proletarianisation: an exploratory investigation of the formation of the working class in Namibia under German and South African colonial rule to 1945. University of Sussex, 1973, 257 p. 26 maps, 12 tables, bibl.: 229-57. (MA thesis).

This is a pioneering study in Namibian history, the main value of which lies in the construction of an analytical framework inspired by underdevelopment theory and historical materialism, in particular the writings by Martin Legassick and Harold Wolpe on the role of the reserve system in the evolution of the capitalist economy of South Africa. The dissertation progresses from an outline of the precolonial "subsistence" modes of production and social formations to an analysis of incipient class formation and the destructive impact of the "informal colonisers" (traders, miners, missionaries). The chapters devoted to the German and South African period concentrate on capital formation and labour demand, on the evolution of reserves and labour repression in southern and central Namibia, and of the imposition of the contract labour system in the north. The discussion of the complex process of proletarianisation ends with a brief account of the composition, consciousness and organisation of the working class. There are also 80 pages of informative references, several maps and tables and an extensive bibliography. The thesis served as a basis for further and more refined research by the same author, paying more attention to class formation and class struggle (see nos. 123, 664, 667).

56. MOORSOM, RICHARD. "Namibia in the frontline: the political economy of decolonisation in South Africa's colony". Review of African Political Economy, no. 17, (January-April) 1980: 71-82.

A brief but concentrated analysis of the political and economic interests at stake in the struggle for and against Namibian independence. The first section gives a general description of the economic structure, concluding that "the perfect harmony of exploiters" has begun to break up in dissension. The critical divide is seen to be between those who are strong enough to hope to salvage and perhaps enhance their long-term stake by accomodating themselves to a reformed or neo-colonial regime (the mining multinationals), and those who cannot afford even minimal concessions (the local settlers/ranchers). It is also argued that the systematic and extreme nature of colonial exploitation has left little space for the rise of a class of potential black collaborators in a neo-colonial solution. The conclusion is that both the South Africans and the Western powers find themselves confronted with contradictions they are not yet willing to resolve, and that SWAPO, therefore, has good reason to downgrade any expectation that diplomatic pressure on South Africa will be either seriously applied or yield results.

57. NACHTWEI, WINFRIED. Namibia. Von der antikolonialen Revolte zum nationalen Befreiungskampf. Geschichte der ehemaligen deutschen Kolonie Südwestafrika. Mannheim: Verlag Jürgen Sendler, 1976, 187 p. Bibl.: 182-87.

Written from a progressive standpoint, the purpose of this book is to provide the general reader with a popular account of colonialism and the liberation struggle in Namibia. The historical section gives a summary of the German literature, while the treatment of the contemporary scene is at times too polemical and simplified to be particularly useful.

58. NAMIBIA SUPPORT COMMITTEE. Turnhalle: South Africa's neo-colonial solution for Namibia. London, 1977, 12 p.

59. ------- Namibia... a nation held hostage. London, 1979, 8 p. (Occasional paper, no. 1).

60. ------- Foreign companies in Namibia. A shortlist of Western firms. London, 1980, 8 p. (Occasional paper, no. 2).

61. ------- Postponed indefinitely. Free elections in Namibia. A briefing on the failure of Western diplomacy. London, 1980, 22 p. (Occasional paper, no. 3).

62. ------- Namibia. A Guide to action. London, 1983, 34 p. (Action on Namibia, nos. 3-4, 1983).

Together these five pamphlets, produced by the foremost solidarity group on Namibia in Western Europe, provide a basic briefing on the general situation in Namibia, with special emphasis on Western diplomacy, South African repression, the role of international capital, the South African neo-colonial strategy and the need for solidarity compaigning in Western Europe.

63. PALMBERG, MAI (ed.). The struggle for Africa. London: Zed Press, 1983, 286 p. (Swedish original: Befrielsekampen i Afrika. Stockholm: AGIS, 1980).

A revised English edition of a popular Swedish introduction to colonialism and the struggle for independence in Africa. The book is primarily intended for schools, study circles and organisations, but as a readable and well illustrated account it can also be recommended to individual readers. It opens with three general background chapters on the colonisation of Africa, decolonisation and the nationalist movements, and neo-colonialism, followed by separate chapters devoted to Guinea-Bissau, Mozambique, Angola, Zimbabwe, Namibia and South Africa. The chapter of Namibia (p. 206-36) is a concise presentation of the economics of exploitation and the history of the struggle for liberation.

THE PARLIAMENT OF THE COMMONWEALTH OF AUSTRALIA, see no. 3.

64. PATEMANN, HELGARD. Lernbuch Namibia. Deutsche Kolonie 1884-1915.
Ein Lese- und Arbeitsbuch. Wuppertal: Hammer, 1984, 264 p. Illus.,
bibl.: 263-64. (First edition: Osnabrück: terre des hommes
Deutschland e.v./Bremen: Projekt "Politische Landeskunde Namibias").

Together with Our Namibia (no. 53), this textbook for West German
schools is one of the results of a joint project between the UN
Institute for Namibia (Lusaka) and the Namibia Project Group at the
University of Bremen. Its main focus in on the German colonial
period, the German-speaking community today and the relations between
the Federal Republic of Germany and Namibia. But there are also
chapters on pre-colonial Namibia, the basic features of the present
apartheid society (bantustans, migrant labour, economic exploitation)
and the struggle for liberation. A separate chapter relates the
colonisation process to German history in the second part of the
19th century. The book is well illustrated with pictures, drawings,
maps and excerpts from contemporary sources, and is intended for
use at various levels and in various disciplines (e.g., history,
geography, social science and religion).

65. PENDLETON, WADE and WOLFGANG H. THOMAS. The people of Namibia. Cape
Town: David Philip. (In the series "The People of Southern Africa").
In preparation.

66. RHOODIE, ESCHEL. South West: the last frontier in Africa.
Johannesburg: Voortrekkerpers, 1967, 284 p. 31 photos, 5 maps,
8 tables, bibl.: 273-75.

Written by a leading protagonist in South Africa's clandestine propaganda efforts in the 1960s and 1970s - the so-called "Muldergate"
scandal - this book is an interesting reflection of the official
view on Namibia prevailing in South Africa in the mid-1960s. The
major part is concerned with arguing the case for South Africa
against the UN "onslaught" in the aftermath of the revocation of
the mandate in 1966, but there are also sections which offer a
semi-official interpretation of the history, the contemporary
socio-economic structure and the strategic importance of Namibia
in the cold war. The final chapter summarises the proposals of
the Odendaal Commission, supporting the idea of a regional
"Community of South African States" and opposing democratic self-
determination, going so far as to assert that "anyone who talks
about an independent South West Africa under a system of one-man-
one-vote... reveals abysmal ignorance of the history of South
West Africa".

67. ROTBERG, ROBERT I. (ed.). Namibia: political and economic prospects.
Lexington: Lexington Books, D.C. Heath/Cape Town: David Philip,
1983, 133 p. Bibl.: 115-22.

This uneven collection of papers flows in part from a conference
organised in 1981 by the World Peace Foundation of Boston and the
Ditchley Foundation of Britain, which drew diplomatic, economic
and academic participants from Southern Africa, Western Europe and

the United States. The only substantial - although controversial -
contribution to the discussion of the prospects for an independent
Namibia is made by Wolfgang H. Thomas, whose economic analysis
occupies nearly half the book. (For a separate annotation, see no.
480.) Two brief background papers by N.H.Z. Watts and R.I. Rotberg
add little to the established liberal perspective. Kate Jowell's
paper is mainly a summary of the consensus of the conference concerning the economic priorities for an independent Namibia, and
strongly argues the need for maintaining the confidence of the
white commercial farmers, the mining multinationals, the colonial
civil servants, the South African state-run transport corporation
and potential Western donors. A brief final chapter, by veteran
South African liberal journalist Stanley Uys, adopts a perspective
more sympathetic to the liberation movement. The South African
economic grip on Namibia is essentially regarded as a stranglehold,
which, according to the author, one cannot expect SWAPO to maintain
or stabilise. It is also pointed out that SWAPO would be more concerned with establishing genuine independence than with subordin-
ating itself to either South Africa or to the Soviet Union. The
editor of this book, who is professor of political science and
history at the Massachusetts Institute of Technology, has previously
published a general introduction to Namibia, see p. 171-227 in
his Suffer the Future. Policy Choices in Southern Africa (Cambridge,
Mass./London: Harvard Unversity Press, 1980).

68. SAUNDERS, CHRISTOPHER (ed.). Perspectives on Namibia: past and
    present. Cape Town: Centre for African Studies, University of
    Cape Town, 1983, 162 p. Bibl.: 156-61. (Occasional Papers, no.
    4/1983).

    This very stimulating, although somewhat uneven, collection of
    recent essays on Namibia stems from a series of lectures delivered
    at the University of Cape Town during 1982. The original contribu-
    tions are strengthened with two additional papers, an informative
    introduction by the editor and a select bibliography. The section
    on history comprises three substantial contributions by Brigitte Lau
    (no. 134), Neville Alexander (no. 177) and Keith Gottschalk (no.
    237), reflecting the emergence of a new generation of South African-
    based historians committed to a radical reinterpretation of Namibian
    pre-colonial and colonial history. There is also a chapter on
    the historical evolution of Windhoek, written by David Simon
    (no. 104), followed by two comments on current political affairs:
    "Strategic Options on the Independence Dispute" (Ottilié Abrahams)
    and "Prospects for an International Settlement" (André du Pisani).
    The book ends with a discussion of the economic prospects by Wolfgang
    H. Thomas.

69. SAUNDERS, CHRISTOPHER. "Towards the decolonisation of Namibian
    history: notes on some recent work in English". The Namibian
    Review, no. 25, (January-March) 1983: 29-36. Also presented to
    the African Studies Association, 26th Annual Conference, Boston,
    December 7-10, 1983, 18 p.

    This is one of the few serious attempts to discuss Namibian histor-
    iography, and is exceptionally well informed on current research.
    The author, a senior lecturer at the University of Cape Town, makes

the point that although Namibian history is under-researched, a
new momentum was gained in the 1970s. He draws attention to some
recent works in English, by, inter alia, Kienetz, Lau, Werner,
Moorsom, Alexander, Bley and Drechsler, and argues on this basis
that the colonialist perspective has been profoundly challenged
by new scholarly interpretations. He considers that the focus has
shifted from Eurocentricity and "ethnic" explanations to an explicitly Namibian focus and a growing awareness of social differentiation, social relations and modes of production. The survey
contains a large number of references to papers, theses and books.

70. SEELEMANN, MARTIN. Ich liebe Südwest. Aus Südwestafrikas Geschichte,
von seinen Menschen und Tieren, vom Land und seiner Verwaltung, seiner
Wirtschaft und Industrie sowie seiner Stellung in der Weltpolitik.
Erlebnisse auf mehreren Studienreisen. Goslar: H. Hübener Verlag,
1971, 278 p.

The aim of this propagandist book is to serve as a general introduction
to Namibia for West German readers. It covers history from the
German colonisation onwards, as well as the economic structure
and the international dispute over the territory. The book is
written from the perspective of the conservative elements of the
German-speaking community in Namibia, and reflects the official
South African position in the chapters on the United Nations, the
liberation struggle ("Die Terroristen") and the bantustan policy.
The sections on agriculture contain information on farm labour and
karakul breeding.

71. SEGAL, RONALD and RUTH FIRST (eds.). South West Africa: A travesty
of trust. London: Deutsch, 1967, 352 p.

This valuable collection of expert papers was produced for the first
ever international conference on Namibia, held in Oxford in March,
1966, and is clearly based on a formidable research effort. Together
with First (no. 22) it is by far the best early introduction to
Namibia and was an important contribution to the international campaign
against South African colonialism at a time when a number of simplistic, popularised propaganda accounts were produced by the apartheid
regime. The papers cover a wide range of subjects, including the
history of the German period, the origins of the Mandate, South
African techniques of domination, the Namibian economy and the
economic relationship with South Africa, the legal apparatus,
education, social conditions of the black population, the Odendaal
Report, and the labour force. For separate annotations, see Bley
(no. 181), Louis (no. 244), Bradford (no. 225), Simons (no. 254),
Gervasi (no. 358), Sutcliffe (no. 390), Rogaly (no. 383), McGill
(no. 701), Ngavirue (no. 331) and Vilakazi (no. 276). The other
contributors are J.F. Kozonguizi, A. O'Dowd, E. Mondlane, R. Gott,
G.H. Geingob and I. McGibbon.

72. SIMON, DAVID. Contemporary Namibia: the political geography of
decolonisation. Oxford: School of Geography, 1983, 36 p. (Research Paper 31).

The aim of this research paper, which is based on a recent D.Phil. thesis mainly concerned with urbanisation (no. 102), is to provide a general introduction to the political geography of Namibia. It describes the economic system as inherently inefficient, financially unviable, unacceptable to a large proportion of the population as well as being an instrument for exacerbating socio-economic inequalities. It depicts the purpose of South African political strategy since 1975 as being to retain as much as possible of the status quo while giving the appearance of meaningful change away from white and South African control. The paper also discusses Namibia in a wider regional context, especially in the light of cooperation among SADCC-states. The geo-political analysis is thus more sophisticated than the crude cold-war framework employed by Brohman/Knight (no. 770), although the author seems to believe that it is still possible to reach a compromise "which meets the major demands of the contending interest groups".

SOUTH AFRICAN INSTITUTE OF RACE RELATIONS. A survey of race relations in South Africa, see no. 979.

73. STUDENTS AFRICAN MOVEMENT. Namibia review. Johannesburg: 1979 (?), 87 p.

Prepared by the Namibia Study Group of the Students African Movement from a progressive standpoint, this well-informed introduction to Namibia is directed to a South African readership. Separate chapters are devoted to history, labour, SWAPO and the liberation struggle, a critical analysis of other parties and groups, foreign interest, the Kassinga massacre, the "elections" in 1978 and the role of the churches. A wide range of documents and press reports are reproduced partly or at full length.

74. SWAPO OF NAMIBIA (SOUTH WEST AFRICA PEOPLE'S ORGANISATION). To be born a nation. The liberation struggle for Namibia. London: Zed Press, 1981, 357 p. 6 maps, 27 figures, 31 tables, bibl.: 349-55.

Originating from a research and publicity drive by SWAPO in the late 1970s, this is a popular history and a general introduction to Namibia and the liberation struggle from a radical nationalist point of view. The sections on the economy and on the living conditions for blacks under apartheid are both informative and clearly structured, offering a sharply anti-imperialist and class-based analysis. The major part of the book is devoted to a detailed political history of the liberation struggle over the last 20 years with a retrospective overview covering the different forms and stages of popular resistance before 1960. The statistical appendix incorporates and partly reworks some of the original calculations by R.H. Green, as well as other sources, and the extensive bibliography serves as a guide to further reading. Several SWAPO documents and statements are reproduced as appendices, enhancing the value of the book as a historical source. Important information is also concentrated in a large number of box inserts and graphs. Ch. 6 ("Traditions of Popular Resistance") has appeared in a slightly different form under the same title in Race & Class, 22, no. 1,

1980: 23-46. For a brief account of the history of SWAPO and the
liberation struggle, see: 20th Anniversary of the Founding of SWAPO,
1960-1980. Two Decades of Heroic Struggle (Luanda: SWAPO, 1980,
16 p.). See also nos. 828-34.

75. THOMAS, WOLFGANG H. Economic development in Namibia. Towards
acceptable development strategies for independent Namibia. München:
Chr. Kaiser Verlag/Mainz: Matthias-Grünewald-Verlag, 1978, 368 p.
6 diagrams, 52 tables, bibl.: 316-50.

This is one of the most widely used and quoted accounts of the
economic potential of Namibia, written by a West German economist
now back at the University of Western Cape after his expulsion from
South Africa in 1977. The author was a member of a committee of
financial experts responsible to the Turnhalle conference, and his
theoretical framework is largely the "free-market" perspective of
that conference. The book contains a great deal of detailed and
occasionally original economic data, partly reflecting the author's
access to confidential sources, and is undoubtedly the most effective
statement of a neo-colonial economic strategy. Despite his official
role, the author's analysis impels him to dispute the South African
contention that the Namibian economy is not independently viable
and has no economic development potential, although he also stresses
the need for close future cooperation between the two countries.
The major part of the book is devoted to a political discussion of
development strategies regarded by the author as "acceptable" - to
whom is never clearly defined. His highly questionable assumption
is that common ground for pro- and anti-colonial forces can be found,
and that flexibility, cooperation with South Africa and foreign aid
can lead to "socio-economic development and structural change".
There is also a large number of tables and a full bibliography.
For more recent works, see nos. 480-2.

THOMAS, WOLFGANG H., see no. 65.

76. UNITED NATIONS. Decolonization. Issue on Namiba. New York, 1977,
72 p. (A publication of the UN Department of Political Affairs,
Trusteeship and Decolonization. No. 9/Revised edition, December
1977).

This special issue on Namibia gives a useful background to the
situation prevailing in the territory in the mid-1970s, covering
economic conditions, legislation and the growth of the national
liberation struggle as well as the Turnhalle conference and the
diplomatic undertakings by the Western powers. The second part
deals with the history of the relations between the UN and South
Africa concerning Namibia, and includes the texts of the relevant
General Assembly and Security Council resolutions from the termination of the mandate (1966) up to 1977. The SWAPO Central Committee
Declaration of September 1977 is reproduced as an appendix.

77. UNITED NATIONS. Namibia. Working paper prepared by the Secretariat.
New York, 1983, 21 p. (Special Committee on the Situation with
regard to the Implementation of the Declaration of Independence to
Colonial Countries and Peoples. A/AC. 109/748, 22 August 1983).

Updated annually, this is a UN report which provides a general
introduction to Namibia. Special attention is paid to the illegal
occupation by South Africa, the oppression of the Nambian people,
the struggle for national independence and the efforts to achieve
a peaceful settlement. There is also a brief review of recent
economic developments.

78. UNITED NATIONS INSTITUTE FOR NAMIBIA. Handbook on Namibia. (Tentative title). Lusaka: UNIN, 1985. In preparation.

UNIVERSITÄT BREMEN, see no. 16.

79. VAN ROOYEN, INA (ed.). SWA/Namibia Today = SWA/Namibië Vandag =
SWA/Namibia Heute. Windhoek: SWA/Namibia Information Service,
1979, 120 p.

Published as three separate booklets in English, Afrikaans and
German, this is an introduction to Namibia whose purpose is to
paint a rosy picture of economic, social and cultural conditions.
The text is supported by numerous colour photos and basic official
facts and figures.

80. VIGNE, RANDOLPH. A dwelling place of our own. The story of the
Namibian nation. London: International Defence and Aid Fund for
Southern Africa, rev. ed. 1975, 52 p.

First published as early as 1973, A dwelling place... remains one
of the clearest and best-written short introductions to Namibian
history. It highlights the essential features of colonial repression
and exploitation, and makes graphic use of hitherto untouched
original material. The sections concerned with international
negotiations and the prospects for independence are updated in
"The Namibia file", Third World Quarterly, 5, no. 2, (April) 1983:
345-60. A South African in exile, the author has been actively
involved with the solidarity movement over the years, and is honorary
secretary of the Namibia Support Committee.

81. WELLINGTON, JOHN H. South West Africa and its human issues. London:
Oxford University Press, 1967, 461 p. 7 tables, 18 figures, 25
photos.

Written by a leading South African geographer, this book is one of
the weightiest contributions to Namibian geography and history.
The treatment of Namibia's geography, especially its physical and
ecological aspects, is wide-ranging and authoritative. The background chapter on the economy, although analytically rather weak,
provides a useful factual survey of the main features in the 1960s.
The historical sections on the 19th and early 20th centuries reflect
extensive and committed research and present a classic liberal
indictment of German and early South African colonialism, which is
neither so dry as Goldblatt (no. 24) nor so blantantly racist as
Vedder (no. 157). On the interwar period the author's account is
enhanced by a thorough examination of the annual reports of the
SWA Administrator (no. 258), as well as some key unpublished sources.

Beyond 1945 the text is thinner and more selectively preoccupied with the international dispute. Although the general framework is far from anti-colonialist, there is some trenchant criticism of the apartheid system and the inequitable distribution of land and resources.

SEE ALSO:

95, 111, 304, 312, 407, 740, 756, 765, 903, 906, 914-916, 964, 977, 979, 985, 987, 991, 992, 1013, 1017.

2. GEOGRAPHY, WATER AND ENERGY

82. BÄHR, JÜRGEN."Windhoek - eine stadtgeographische Skizze". Erdkunde, 24, no. 1, 1970: 39-59. 8 maps, 5 photos, 8 tables.

Written by a West German geographer at the University of Kiel, this brief descriptive account sets Windhoek in its historical and geographical perspective. The article outlines the history of Windhoek from the pre-colonial period up to the late 1960s, stressing the town's rapid expansion and diversification after the Second World War. It also covers the implementation of the policy of apartheid, in particular in the form of segregated townships for Africans and Coloureds outside the city centre. There are also several informative maps and tables.

83. BARNARD, W.S. Die Streekpatrone van Suidwes-Afrika. University of Stellenbosch, 1964, 393 p. 79 figures, 79 tables, bibl.: 384-93. (PhD thesis).

The primary concern of this geographical study is to determine the regional divisions for each of a range of categories: physical landforms, climate, natural resources, population, agriculture, mining, industry and transport. Each is discussed in consecutive chapters organised under three main headings: physical background, natural and social resources, and economic geography. In pursuing his analysis the author presents a wide range of data, much of it covering the 1950s and early 1960s but sometimes also earlier periods. The sources from which the tables are derived are unfortunately in most cases not attributed, but there is a full bibliography which is of particular value for the range of the South African publications listed. There is a copy of the thesis in the University of Frankfurt Library.

84. BRANDMAYR, JOSEF. Eine Landeskunde von Südwestafrika mit besonderer Berücksichtigung der ethnisch und historisch-politisch bedingten Raumprobleme. Univ. Salzburg, 1977, 553 p. 68 figures (maps, diagrams), bibl.: 540-53 (Dissertation).

This long thesis aims to provide a general introduction to the history, geography and geo-politics of Namibia as a background to a discussion of the development of the "homelands". These sections contain a fair amount of data, partly based on field research, but have been largely superseded by more recent works, see, for example, Leser (no. 95). Accepting the colonial framework, the major part of the thesis outlines the main structures of each of the "homelands", with emphasis on geography, administration, economy and infrastructure. The author seems to accept the Turnhalle rhetoric, believes that the apartheid system was dissolved in 1977 and maintains that the crea-

tion of "homelands" provided adequately for the economic and social security of the African "peoples".

85. BRETSCHER, J.B. Energy survey. New York: UN Department of Technical Cooperation, 1982, 46 p. 25 tables, 2 maps. (UN Nationhood Programme for Namibia, NAM/79/011, draft).

This general overview of the present uses and future requirements for energy in the national economy was intended to do no more than provide a preliminary assessment, but in a field almost untouched in the planning literature it is probably the most competent study to date. Starved of hard data both by South African secrecy and lack of opportunity for extensive research, the author relies extensively on comparative analogy, especially to Zambia in respect of mining and to Zimbabwe in respect of manufacturing and construction. The method at least yields rough estimates of energy demand, which the author's expertise in the fields helps to set in their Namibian context. Discussion of sources of energy supply, infrastructure and transport is concluded with brief remarks on high-grade personnel requirements for an Energy Department in an independent Namibia.

86. CHRISTIE, RENFREW. The political economy of the Kunene hydro-electric schemes. University of Cape Town, 1975, 242 p. Tables, maps, diagrams. Bibl.: 220-42. (MA thesis).

87. ------- "Who benefits by the Kunene hydroelectric schemes?". Social Dynamics, 2, no. 1, 1976: 31-43.

One of the few studies of the material infrastructure in Namibia, this is an important contribution to the analysis of the political economy of South African - and to a lesser extent Portuguese - colonial rule. The author, now serving a long prison sentence in South Africa for his commitment to the political and economic liberation of his country, researched extensively in the published literature, both historical and recent, and interviewed several of the South African officials directly involved. The first part of the thesis, an expansion of a BA (Hons) dissertation the previous year, presents the economic and political setting in a historical perspective. The second part gives a detailed analysis of the evolution, scope and purposes of the Kunene scheme itself, concluding with an assessment of the distribution of benefits from its completion. This analysis, in particular the final chapter, is summarised in the subsequently published article in Social Dynamics.

88. COMMITTEE FOR FREEDOM IN MOZAMBIQUE, ANGOLA & GUINÉ. White power. The Cunene river scheme. London, 1975, 24 p. 3 maps, illus.

Although some of the information is outdated, this pamphlet still serves as a brief introduction to the Cunene River Scheme and in particular the Calueque barrage and the power station at the Ruacana Falls. The information given supports the contention that Portugal and South Africa embarked upon this large project in order to intensity their exploitation of the region's agricultural and mineral resources, to reinforce their political control over the population and to attract international capital (and military support) to the area. The long-term aims of the Cunene River Scheme are also seen in the context of South Africa's expansionist policy in Southern Africa as a whole.

89. CUBITT, GERALD and GARTH OWEN-SMITH. Namibia - the untamed land. Cape Town: Dan Nelson, 1981, 208 p. 171 photos.

This is a lavishly illustrated "coffee-table" book on Namibia, concentrating on its ecosystems and the exceptional variety of wildlife. The photos (Cubitt) are complemented by six brief essays (Owen-Smith), which are mainly concerned with ecology and the need for conservation. To judge from the photos, there seem to be no human beings in Namibia. Gerald Cubitt has previously published another book with equally splendid illustrations, see Gerald Cubitt and Johann Richter: South West (Cape Town: Struik, 1976).

90. DINTER, KURT. Die vegetabilische Veldkost Deutsch - Südwest-Afrikas. Okahandja: Selbstverlag, 1912, 47 p. + 13 photos. (Also published by Kommissionsverlag E. Rühls, Bautzen).

Written by a prominent botanist in the German colonial service, this booklet describes the vegetable "veldkost" which formed a considerable part of the diet before colonial times, then slowly decreasing in importance. The register covers tuberous plants, fruits, mushrooms, onions, and leafgreens. See also by the same author: Deutsch-Südwest-Afrika. Flora. Forst- und landwirtschaftliche Fragmente. Leipzig: Weigel, 1909, 191 p.) and W. Geiss: "Veldkost in S.W.A.", Journal - SWA Wissenschaftliche Gesellschaft, 20, 1965-66: 59-68.

91. FAO. Assessment of potential land suitability, Namibia. Satellite imagery analysis for reconnaissance survey of natural resources. Rome: FAO, 1981, 40 p. 4 figures, 13 maps, bibl.: 38-40. (AG: DP/NAM/78/004, Technical report 1, based on the work of C. Travaglia and J. Schade, Remote Sensing Centre, Land and Water Development Division).

Based on frames taken by the Landsat satellite during the dry seasons of 1972 and 1973, this survey covers the northwestern quarter of Namibia. Following an explanation of the remote sensing technique and its uses, the study describes in some detail, with supplementary maps, the geology, surface drainage, climate, soil, vegetation, types of farming, mines and transport network. The analysis demonstrates the potential of this new form of geographical research for enhancing and even supplementing ground data, indicating, for example, zones of land use and areas of severe overgrazing. It also breaks new ground in demonstrating that much of the groundwater that underlies the Ovambo floodplain derives from large-scale seepage from the middle Kunene. The lack of correlation with published ground data leads to occasional errors of fact or judgement, but the utility of this new research method is convincingly demonstrated.

92. FERREIRA, EDUARDO DE SOUSA. "Namibia and the Cunene project in Angola". In Portuguese colonialism from South Africa to Europe, p. 91-121. Freiburg: Aktion Dritte Welt, 1972. (German original: "Namibia und das Cunene-Project in Angola", p. 81-114 in E. de Sousa Ferreira: Portugiesischer Kolonialismus zwischen Südafrika und Europa. Freiburg:

Aktion Dritte Welt, 1972).

This chapter forms part of a revised edition of articles, originally
published in German in 1970 and 1971. The author, who at the time
was living in West Germany and was actively involved in solidarity
campaigns for the liberation movements in the Portuguese colonies,
presents a brief general analysis of the political economy of Namibia. The argument, although informed by anti-imperialist theory, is
rather simplistic and thinly researched, and there are also factual
errors. There is, however, substantive information on the Cunene
hydro-electric scheme and on the background to West German economic
interests in Namibian uranium.

93. FINKELDEY, HELMUT. "Kostenlose Energie von der Sonne. Anwendung der
photovoltaischen Solarenergie in SWA". SWA Annual 1983: 33-42.

This short review (probably intended as a public relations drive by
SWE Power & Pumps (Pty) Ltd, Windhoek), is the first survey of the
already widespread utilisation of solar energy in Namibia. The
article is also published as an annex to Newsletter of the SWA Scientific Society, vol. XXXIV, no. 7.

FOOD AND AGRICULTURAL ORGANISATION, see no. 91.

INSTITUTE FOR CARTOGRAPHIC ANALYSIS, see no. 111.

94. LESER, HARTMUT. Landschaftsökologische Studien im Kalaharisandgebiet
um Auob und Nossob (östliches Südwestafrika). Wiesbaden: Franz Steiner
Verlag, 1971, 243 p. 96 illus., 9 maps, bibl.: 229-35.

Although the bulk of this monograph comprises a technical study of
vegetation and landscape, its final section gives a detailed, perceptive and partly historical analysis of the relationships between
ecology and farm economy in its study area, a section of the eastern
sandveld south of Gobabis. The author links the clear degradation of
the natural vegetation with a number of economic, managerial and administrative factors, including the clearance of bush cover for gra-
zing and dryland cropping, the inappropriate and incomplete introduction of fenced pasture rotation, the inadequate capital resources of
many of the smaller settler farmers, inadequate transport, and the
area's peripheral position in the South African marketing system.
Even by the yardstick of successful commercial farming and land-use
planning, both settler farming practices and official colonial policy
come in for serious criticism. Aspects of this critique are developed
in a comparative framework in a separate article ("Landschaftsökologische Grundlageforschung in Trockengebieten. Dargestellt an Beispiel-
en aus der Kalahari und ihren Randlandschaften", Erdkunde, 25, 1971:
209-33). A later article ("Weidewirtschaft und Regenfeldbau im Sandveld: westliche Kalahari um Schwarzen Nossob und Epukiro, östliches
SWA", Geographische Rundschau, 27, 1975: 108-22), based on a questionnaire survey of farmers in the same area during 1971, develops the
logical and economic analysis in greater depth. All three publications are well supported by original diagrams and maps; of particular
value are those specifying the structure of land ownership.

95. LESER, HARTMUT, Namibia. Stuttgart: Ernst Klett, 1982, 259 p. 36 tables, 42 illus., bibl.: 249-56. (Länderprofile-Geographische Strukturen, Daten, Entwicklungen).

96. ------- Südwestafrika. Eine geographische Landeskunde. Windhoek: SWA Wissenschaftliche Gesellschaft, 1976, 247 p. 40 maps and figures, 30 photos, tables.

   Written by a prominent physical geographer, who has published a wide range of scholarly studies, Namibia is a standard introduction to Namibian geography. The most valuable and authoritative part of the book is the third (p. 75-171), which is devoted to natural resources, ecosystems, climate, vegetation, agriculture, fisheries and mining. This section also contains a critical discussion of the exploitation of water resources, especially by the mines. The value is enhanced by numerous well-organised tables, often of some historical depth, as well as nearly 50 maps, diagrams etc. The cursory treatment of pre-colonial history is mainly based on the "missionary - colonialist" interpretation (Vedder et al.), and the development perspectives are largely discussed within a neo-colonial framework. The lack of familiarity with parts of the recent literature, especially by authors who are more critical of South African rule, is also evident in the sections on economic history, spatial structure and geo-political aspects. There are also several serious mistakes - for instance, identifying the "SWAPO-Democrats" as the internal wing of SWAPO - which cast doubts on the author's reliability when he moves beyond his professional fields. The 1976 edition is largely superseded by this new book, but the wide range of maps and statistics, which are mainly concerned with the first half of the 1970s, are still a useful source. This edition has also extensive bibliographies at the end of each chapter. For a detailed critique of past and present cartography in Namibia, see by the same author Namibia, Südwestafrika: Kartographische Probleme der neuen topographischen Karten 1:50 000 und 1:250 000 und ihre Perspektiven für die Landesentwicklung (Basel: Basler Afrika Bibliographien, 1982, 56 p.).

97. LOGAN, RICHARD F. The Central Namib desert, South West Africa. Washington: National Academy of Sciences, National Research Council, 1960, 162 p. 32 tables, 15 figures, 16 maps and charts.

   A district geography with arbitrarily defined boundaries, this study by a well-known US geographer concentrates on physical and environmental relationships, but has descriptive information on the economy of Walvis Bay and its hinterland. It also notes the ecologically damaging spread of settler stock-farming into the inner Namib shortly before it was halted by the implementation of the Odendaal Report. See also "The geography of the Central Namib desert" in Arid lands in perspective, edited by W.G. McGinnies and B. Goldman, p. 127-44 (Tucson: The University of Arizona Press, 1969), and "The utilization of the Namib desert, South West Africa" in Coastal deserts: their natural and human environments, edited by D.H.K. Amiran and A.K. Wilson, p. 177-86 (Tucson: The University of Arizona Press, 1973).

98. LOGAN, RICHARD F. "The geographical divisions of the deserts of South West Africa". In Impulse eines Landes extremer Bedingungen für die

Wissenschaft. Festschrift zum 80. Geburtstag von Fritz Gaerdes, Okahandja, Südwestafrika, p. 46-65. Basel: Basler Afrika Bibliographien,
1972.

A brief, readable and informative survey of the deserts of Namibia.
The author argues that despite their diversity the deserts are all
vulnerable to overexploitation. His conclusion is, consequently,
that protection of their surfaces, soils, vegetation and animals is
essential, and that drastic and thoroughly enforced conservation
planning is urgent.

99. LOGAN, RICHARD F. "Namibia". In African perspectives: an exchange of
essays on the economic geography of nine African states, edited by
Harm de Blij and Esmond Martin, p. 173-92. New York/London: Methuen,
1981.

Appearing in a collection of academic essays, this is an introduction
to the economic geography of Namibia which completely ignores the
bantustan policies, the inequitable land distribution, the effects of
the contract labour system, the ravages of the war and the extraction
of large profits by the transnational corporations. The purpose of
the article is quite clearly to tell the "success story" of Namibia
under colonial rule, concluding that an impressive improvement in the
social and economic conditions for "Non-Europeans" has taken place.
The author, who has published several studies on the Namib desert,
was one of the witness called to support the South African case before
the International Court of Justice in the 1960s.

100. MITCHELL, M.P. The politics of water. The significance of dams and
river valley development projects in the political and economic history of Southern Africa, with particular reference to the Cunene river
schemes. York: Centre for Southern African Studies, 1976, 101 p. 6
tables, 9 maps, bibl.: 97-101. (B. Phil thesis).

This dissertation is based on the premise that the great river schemes
in Southern Africa of the 1960s and early 1970s have broad political
ramifications, and that the massive Cunene River Schemes must be seen
in the context of the Odendaal plan for separate development, the
supremacy of the South Africa-controlled economy and the maintenance
of the existing social structures. It is more specifically argued
that the Cunene River Schemes were a necessary result of the claim
the mining sector makes on water resources in Namibia and that a huge
hydro-electric project will serve the expansion of the mining industry at the expense of the agricultural sector. The thesis does
not add much to the study conducted by Christie (nos. 86-7), but the
lack of literature on water and power supply makes it interesting
reading.

101. OLIVIER, H. "Angola/S.W. Africa" and "South West Africa". In Great
dams in southern Africa, p. 123-37 (ch. 8+9), 3 maps, 8 diagrams, 11
photos. Cape Town: Purnell, 1979.

A summary history of the construction of the Kunene River dams and
hydro-electric scheme in Namibia and Angola, and of the von Bach and
Naute dams inside Namibia, in a book devoted largely to South Africa.
There is much useful technical information, supplemented by maps of

the catchment areas, site diagrams and detailed technical drawings.

OWEN-SMITH, GARTH, see no. 89.

102. SIMON, DAVID. Aspects of urban change in Windhoek, Namibia, during the transition to independence. Oxford: Linacre College, 1983, 546 p. 88 tables, 34 figures, 10 photos, bibl.: 530-34 (D. Phil. thesis).

This thesis is one of the most impressive examples of recent post-graduate scholarship on Namibia, combining a wealth of empirical data with an analysis informed by a liberal political perspective. The author, a South African geographer who has undertaken extensive field research in Windhoek, supports his analysis with numerous tables and citations of primary sources. The study is broad in scope and metho-dology, succeeding chapters covering the historical geography of Wind-hoek, the city's position within the reorganisation of government since 1977, statutory desegregation and residential mobility, the political geography of housing, the urban economy, and social services and pub-lic amenities. An introductory chapter outlines the basic features of Namibian colonial history and economic dependency. The detailed examination of the period after the installation of the Administrator-General in September 1977 demonstrates clearly that the changes have been cosmetic rather than structural. The author's rather pessimistic conclusion that the new post-colonial order may not be as radically different as anticipated, reflects a wide reading of contemporary literature on urbanisation and social change in African and other Third World countries. Parts of this thesis have been published in journals and anthologies, see nos. 103, 104, 719.

103. SIMON, DAVID: "Recent trends in Namibian urbanization". Tijdschrift voor economische en sociale geografie, 73, no. 4, 1982:237-49.

Based on extensive research conducted for a D. Phil thesis (no. 102), this essay focuses on demographic aspects of urbanisation in Namibia since World War II. The author shows how urbanisation in this period has been closely related to the expansion of mining (Tsumeb, Swakop-mund) and the fishing industry (Walvis Bay), and that economic cent-res in the "white" areas have grown increasingly dominant at the ex-pense of the "homelands". A detailed examination of the racial com-position of the urban population reveals a steady urbanisation of blacks, despite the elaborate repressive influx and migrant labour controls. Several tables have been derived from the population cen-suses in 1951, 1960, 1970.

104. SIMON, DAVID. "The evolution of Windhoek". In Perspectives on Namibia: past and present, edited by Christopher Saunders, p. 83-108. Cape Town: Centre for African Studies, 1983.

Based on the author's D. Phil. thesis (no. 102) this is a narrative account of the development of Windhoek from pre-colonial occupation through German colonialism and South African rule. It points out that only since 1970 have whites been in the minority in the capital, reflecting the degree of control they exercise over the colonial pol-itical economy. It also clearly documents how the implementation of a rigid apartheid policy in the 1950s led to three racial settlements and "a city divided against itself", with the blacks getto of Katatura designed as a deprived, bleak urban dormitory for temporary residents staying in Windhoek only to provide labour.

SOUTH WEST AFRICA (ADM.) , DIRECTORATE OF DEVELOPMENT COOPERATION, see no. 111.

SOUTH WEST AFRICA (ADM.). Report of the Secretary for Water Affairs, see no. 1038.

105. SOUTH WEST AFRICA (ADM.), THE GEOLOGICAL SURVEY. The geology of South West Africa/Namibia. Windhoek, 1982, 7 p. 1 map.

A brief summary of the geology of Namibia, providing important technical information, especially on mineral occurrences and potential mineralisation. See also Geological map of South West Africa/Namibia (Pretoria: The Government Printer, 1980.)

106. SOUTH WEST AFRICA (ADM.), SWA/NAMIBIA, DIRECTORATE OF WATER AFFAIRS. 25 years of water supply to South West Africa, 1954-79. Windhoek, 1980, 28 p. 4 tables, 4 diagrams, 1 map, 28 photos. (Afrikaans edition: 25 Jaar van Watervoorsiening aan Suidwes-Afrika 1954-1979. Windhoek, 1980, 28 p.).

An unusually detailed and lucid historical review of state water policy, planning and infrastructural investment. The review covers all major aspects of the activities of the Water Affairs Branch, including dam and pipeline construction, the exploitation of groundwater, bulk water supply, maintenance and services, quality control, staff, finance, and legislation. The Branch also occasionally publishes booklets on specific topics, for instance, Water quality in SWA (1977) and Underground water in South West Africa (1978), and on projects, such as major dams.

107. STENGEL, HEINZ WALTER. "Die wasserwirtschaftliche Entwicklung einer Farm in Südwestafrika". Journal- SWA Wissenschaftliche Gesellschaft 17, 1962/63:37-102. Diagrams, maps, tables, photos.

A detailed case study of the development of water infrastructure on one of the oldest commercial farms in Namibia, presented largely in historical sequence. The author, the foremost state water engineer in Namibia for many years, is primarily concerned with technology and hydrology, but economic aspects are not ignored.

108. STENGEL, H.W. (ed.). Wasserwirtschaft - Waterwese-Water affairs in S.W.A. Windhoek: Afrika-Verlag der Kreis, 1963, 467 p. Tables, photos.

This book, part celebration and part exposition of the works of one of the most technically competent and informative branches of the colonial state, was published by a newly established local publisher in whose journal (Der Kreis) several of its chapters first appeared as articles. Being trilingual, the substantive text is shorter than might first appear (English p. 327-467); but the chapters are thoroughly researched, well written and packed with factual information. The topics covered include the water supply and infrastructure at

Walvis Bay, hydrography and water planning in Ovamboland, the uses of
perennial and seasonal rivers, evaporation and sedimentation in storage dams, and a general overview of water resources and planning in
Namibia. The book offers both a detailed insight into the planning
and programmes of the Branch – unique before or since in official publications – and scholarly contributions of considerable historical
depth. Of the two principal authors, Otto Wipplinger was then Director of the Branch and Heinz Stengel was to become its principal water
engineer and planner.

109. STENGEL, HEINZ WALTER. Der Schwarze Nossob. Eine wasserwirtschaftliche
      Studie über die Entwicklung eines Flussgebietes in Südwestafrika in
      Vergangenheit und Zukunft. Windhoek: SWA Wissenschaftliche Gesell-
      schaft, 1965, 60 p. Diagrams, maps, tables, photos. (English edition:
      The Black Nossob. Windhoek: SWA Scientific Society, 1966, 60 p.).

      This is a largely technical study of the development of the water
      infrastructure in the catchment area of the Black Nossob, which drains
      the plateau and sandveld west of Gobabis. It concentrates on the com-
      mercial farms, although the town of Gobabis is also featured. Brief
      sections on transport, stockfarming and land-ownership are followed
      by appendices on geology and vegetation and an extensive collection
      of plans and maps.

110. TURNER, TERISA. Energy and South African independence, Inter-
      national Oil Working Group Inc. , 1983. Document presented to
      the International conference in support of the struggle of the
      Namibian People (Paris, 25-29 April 1983). 89+19 p. 11 tables,
      4 figures, 7 maps.

      This consultancy study was presented to a major conference on
      Namibia, convened by the UN Council for Namibia, together with a
      shorter paper which represents a condensed version (Namibian in-
      dependence and oil embargo against South Africa).

It describes the Namibia energy system, showing that Namibia's energy
infrastructure has been engineered not only to render profitable the
exploitation of mineral resources but also to service the white farming sector and a massive military occupation. The study also reviews the ways in which existing energy relations are obstacles to
independence: by fuelling the South African military occupation, by
providing energy for lucrative and strategic mining operations, by
providing electricity from the Kunene hydroelectric scheme at Ruacana
for export to South Africa, and by constituting attractive prospects
for extraction of fuel minerals, especially uranium. The paper concludes that the territory, and above all the South African military
machine, is highly vulnerable to oil sanctions. The study remains however, rather thin in empirical detail and substantive analysis; and
only cursory attention is devoted to policy issues in general and to
non-industrial and renewable sources of energy in particular. These
aspects are being taken up more systematically in a report now in preparation for the – UN Office of Technical Cooperation and Development.

111. VAN DER MERWE , J.H. (ed.). National Atlas of South West Africa (Namibia) = Nasionale Atlas van Suidwes -Afrika (Namibië). Windhoek: Directorate of Development Cooperation/Stellenbosch: Institute for Cartographic Analysis, University of Stellenbosch, 1983, 202 p. 92 maps, 28 tables, 54 diagrams. (Distributed by Department of Civic Affairs and Manpower, Windhoek).

The publication of the National Atlas marks a partial but significant departure from the general stream of official political propaganda: it is primarily a textbook; and it contains a wealth of hard information, important parts of it from unpublished official sources. The project was initiated by the former SWA Administration, taken up by the new central government under the Administrator-General, and assigned to Stellenbosch whose Institute for Cartographic Analysis had done excellent map work for the three bantustan studies of the 1970s (see nos. 450-2). The result is a technically suberb general atlas whose cartographic quality stands international comparison. Each map is complemented by an explanatory or illustrative text, more often than not with references to sources and/or a diagram or table summarising some of the data it contains. The maps are divided under seven thematic heads: orientation (4), natural environment (24), settlement structure, in effect the history of land theft (12), population structure (11), economic structure (15), infrastructure (15) and urban structure (10). Of greatest value amongst the new data will be those on population (since even the preliminary results of the 1981 census remain unpublished), infrastructure, and several branches of economic activity, although because most of the base statistics are not given in the text the reader is reduced to measuring from the maps to derive actual quantities. For all its technical excellence, though, politics loom large through much of the atlas. Walvis Bay is religiously excluded even from historical maps of pre-colonial times; the text is blatantly although not always consistently supportive of the official view of Namibian history and constitutional evolution; and several of the maps are tendentious, notably "pre-colonial conflict" and the endless sub-divisions by "population groups". The political objective is clearly to show a sound capitalist economy under wise and generous colonial stewardship. But the obvious bias does not seriously detract from the atlas' empirical and cartographic value.

VOLK, OTTO HEINRICH, see no. 112.

112. WALTER, HEINRICH and OTTO HEINRICH VOLK. Grundlagen der Weidewirtschaft in Südwestafrika. Stuttgart: Eugen Ulmer, 1954, 281 p.

Based on several study trips and visits to more than 60 farms all over the country, this is a revised and modernised version of a four-volume work: Die Farmwirtschaft in Deutsch Südwest-Afrika (Berlin: Verlag von Paul Parey, 1940-41). A wide range of issues of relevance to karakul and cattle breeding are discussed, with the main emphasis on climatic conditions and the natural vegetation which serves as pasturage. The

first chapter contains valuable information on climate and rainfall,
followed by a close examination of the different forms of soil erosion
and prospects for the reclamation of the veld. The second part of the
book (p. 183-281) is a detailed classification of the forage plants of
Namibia, with more than 100 drawings of the various kinds of grasses,
herbs, shrubs, bushes and trees. See also a more recent publication
by O.H. Volk: Gräser des Farmgebietes von Südwestafrika (Windhoek:
SWA Wissenschaftliche Gesellschaft, 1974).

SEE ALSO:

5, 7, 35, 44, 68, 72, 81, 336, 341, 476, 489, 498, 515, 516, 532,
536, 562, 579, 594, 603, 609-10, 612, 623, 770, 815, 849, 870, 893,
908, 952, 1038.

3. PRE-COLONIAL NAMIBIA

113. ALEXANDER, JAMES E. <u>An expedition of discovery into the interior of</u>
<u>Africa, through the hitherto undescribed countries of the Great</u>
<u>Namaquas, Boschmans, and Hill Damaras</u>. London: Henry Colburn, 1838.
Vol. 1: 302 p. Vol. 2: 306 p. 15 illus., 1 map. (Facsimile reprint:
Cape Town: Struik, 1967. Vol. 1: 302 p. Vol. 2: 331 p. Africana
Collecteana Series vol. XXII & XXIII./New York: Johnson, 1967).

The first published account in English by a European visitor to Namibia.
Backed by the Royal Geographical Society and the British government,
Sir James Alexander, a well-to-do British army officer, undertook a
year-long overland expedition in 1836-7 from Cape Town to Walvis Bay
and Windhoek, the first European to reach central Namibia. The narrative is disappointingly thin on social observation and the author's
cultural chauvinism is at times obtrusive. It does nevertheless contain much social economic and political detail from what was a formative early phase in the integration of pre-colonial Namibia into the
world capitalist economy. It also has the first detailed map of the
Namibian interior.

114. AL-NAGAR, UMAR. <u>African initiative in the pre-colonial period</u>. Paper
presented to the <u>International Conference on Southern African History</u>,
Roma, Lesotho, 1977, 15 p.

This unpublished conference paper is essentially a critique of Heinrich
Vedder (no. 157), whose emphasis on tribal warfare and the destructive
role of Jonker Afrikaner is seen as providing the rationale for the
present-day divide-and-rule policy of the apartheid regime. The underlying assumptions of the "revision" are that state formations and concentrated power exercised by pre-colonial black rulers are good things
<u>per se</u> as examples of African pride and initiative. The role of pre-
colonial rulers and the question of state formation are bound to be
controversial areas in future writing of Namibian history, and there
is indeed room for other interpretations than the nationalist and
"etatist" thesis advanced in a raw form in this brief and not very
well researched paper. The author is a Sudanese historian, who was
at the time a lecturer at the UN Institute for Namibia.

115. ANDERSSON, CHARLES J. Lake Ngami; or, explorations and discoveries during four years' wanderings in the wilds of South Western Africa. London: Hurst and Blackett, 1856, 545 p. 1 map, 57 pictures. (Facsimile reprint, Cape Town: Struik, 1967).

116. ------- The Okavango river: a narrative of travel, exploration, and adventure. London: Hurst and Blackett, 1861, 364 p. 17 pictures. (Facsimile reprint, Cape Town: Struik, 1968).

117. ------- Notes of travel in South Africa. London: Hurst and Blackett, 1875, 338 p. (Facsimile reprint, Cape Town: Struik, 1969).

Charles Andersson was one of the foremost of the wave of European adventurers and traders to penetrate the Southern African interior in the mid-19th century, and unlike several of his contemporaries, concentrated his activities in central and northern Namibia. His travel narratives provide the most wide-ranging published account of the period from a European perspective, and although largely taken up with the conduct of his expeditions and his interest in natural history, contain much direct observation of interest as well as general commentary on the economic, social and political affairs of the peoples he encountered. Apart from reports and papers submitted to the Royal Geographical Society, London, for which its Journal may be consulted, Andersson published three major autobiographical books, containing narrative descriptions of his expeditions as hunter and explorer to Ovamboland in 1850-1 (with Francis Galton, see no. 128) and again in 1866-7, in the course of which he died; to Lake Ngami in 1852-3; and to the Okavango River in 1858-9. They also cover his trading activities and political interventions in central Namibia in the early 1860s. In the 1861 volume there is in addition a geographic and economic survey of the Namibian coast and a detailed account of the guano rush in the 1840s. These three volumes have been translated into German as well as several other languages.

ATMORE, ANTHONY, see no. 142.

118. BERGER, LOTHAR. Der Einfluss der Grenzziehung auf die Ovambo. Wiesbaden: Univ. Maiz, 1980, 148 p. 4 maps, bibl.: 134-44. (MA thesis).

This perceptive German dissertation develops a lucidly argued class analysis of the impact of European economic and military pressure on the Ovambo social formation up to the completion of the colonial conquest in 1917. The first section discusses the ecology of the Ovambo floodplain, the forces and relations of production, and social and political tendencies towards class formation and state-building. The second part provides a historical analysis of the colonisation process, identifying three distinct phases and concentrating on internal social and political change. Among the topics discussed is the impact of "Die Arbeiterfrage" (the need for migrant labour) on the northern part of Namibia, especially at a time when the societies were characterised by economic problems (rinderpest, the end of the ivory boom etc.) as well as growing internal contradictions. The study is based on a broad reading of contemporary German accounts and more recent secondary literature, and is informed by similar work by Clarence-Smith and Moorsom on Ovambo and southern Angolan society (see nos. 123, 124).

119. BORKOWSKY, CHRISTOPH. Zu einigen Aspekten des Ovambolebens. Berlin: Freie Universität, 1975, 122 p. 3 maps, bibl.: 119-20. (MA thesis).

This dissertation is one of two pioneering attempts - ironically each in complete ignorance of the other - to apply the methods and insights of historical materialist analysis to pre-colonial Ovambo society. It lacks the depth of source material, especially from the side of Portuguese colonialism in Angola, of Clarence-Smith and Moorsom (see nos. 123, 124), but covers a wide range of the German colonial literature and is strong on applied theory. Together with Berger (no. 118), it forms the most extended marxist analysis of the Ovambo social formation before formal conquest in 1915. The four principal sections discuss in turn the resources, means and methods of production; the forms of cooperation and differentiation in the labour process; the relations of production and appropriation of the product; and the form of the state, considering in particular the concepts of "despotism", "feudalism" and "divine kingship".

120. CAPE OF GOOD HOPE, DEPARTMENT OF NATIVE AFFAIRS. Report of W. Coates Palgrave, Esq., special commissioner to the tribes north of the Orange river, of his mission to Damaraland and Great Namaqualand in 1876. Cape Town, 1877, 117 p. + xli. (Pretoria: The State Library, 1969, Reprint no. 40).

121. DAVIES, JOAN H. "Palgrave and Damaraland". Archives Yearbook of South African History, 1942, part 2: 93-203. (MA thesis, Grahamstown University, 1939).

In 1875 the Parliament of the Colony of the Cape of Good Hope expressed its interest in acquiring Walvis Bay and the interior to safeguard the positions of the traders and missionaries and to avoid competition from other powers, and W. Coates Palgrave was subsequently appointed special commissioner to enquire into the resources of the country. His report is based on extensive travels in the central and southern part of what is today Namibia, and contains much first-hand information on political and economic conditions. There are also several historical documents, such as letters, petitions and minutes of meetings with local political leaders. Palgrave entered into an agreement with the Herero, later to be disregarded, but his efforts to persuade Nama leaders to ask for "protection" failed completely. The thesis by J.H. Davies provides a discussion of the Palgrave mission and his report, set in the context of Cape commerical expansion.

122. CHAPMAN, JAMES. Travels in the interior of South Africa. London: Bell and Daldy, 1868. 27 pictures. Vol. 1: 454 p. Vol. 2: 480 p. (New edition: E.C. Tabler (ed.). Travels in the interior of South Africa, 1849-63. Cape Town: Balkema, 1971, 48 pictures. Vol. 1: 258 p. Vol. 2: 244 p. South African biographical and historical studies no. 10).

James Chapman was amongst the most active of the mid-19th century traders and missionaries, reaching the area of the present Caprivi Strip several times and traversing central Namibia via Walvis Bay and Gobabis on three expeditions between 1855 and 1863. As a self-financed trader and hunter, Chapman was in constant contact with the people and political authorities of the areas through which he

passed. His extensive travel diaries provide a detailed account
of the conduct of his own and others' trading and hunting activities.
Commentary on local politics and social and economic conditions
is infrequently developed at any length. But although often coloured
by dogmatic cultural chauvinism, there is much sharply and familiarly
observed detail - in this respect the account of the final major
expedition from Walvis Bay to the Zambezi is superior in its Namibian
sections to that of the author's travelling companion, the artist
Thomas Baines (Explorations in South West Africa. London: 1864,
523 p.). Both the published versions have been edited from Chapman's
original manuscripts. The modern edition lacks the chapter summaries
of the original, but includes previously omitted manuscripts, a
selection of Baines' illustrations and Chapman's photographs,
probably the first to be taken in Namibia, a useful introduction,
notes, and an index.

123. CLARENCE-SMITH, W. GERVASE and RICHARD MOORSOM. "Underdevelopment
and class-formation in Ovamboland, 1844-1917". In The roots of
rural poverty in central and southern Africa, edited by Robin Palmer
and Neil Parsons, p. 96-112. London: Heinemann, 1977.

This slightly amended version of an earlier article (Journal of
African History, 16, no. 3, 1975) is a pioneering attempt to apply
the insights of class analysis to the history of pre-colonial
peasant society in northern Namibia. Its argument is rigorous,
concentrated and based on a wealth of source material, combining
Clarence-Smith's extensive archival research on southern Angola
with Moorsom's use of published Namibian sources. The authors argue
that pre-colonial contact with industrial capitalism through European
traders generated class divisions in the social structure of Ovambo
society which left it ultimately more vulnerable to incorporation
into the colonial system of labour migration. The use of class
analysis is perhaps more explicit in Moorsom's "Underdevelopment
and class-formation: the origins of migrant labour in Namibia,
1850-1915", in Perspectives on South Africa: a collection of working
papers, edited by T.Adler, Johannesburg: Witwatersrand University,
African Studies Institute, 1977, and in Clarence-Smith's published
study of southern Angola (no. 124). See also no. 667.

124. CLARENCE-SMITH, W. GERVASE. Slaves, peasants and capitalists in
southern Angola, 1840-1926. Cambridge University Press, 1979,
132 p. 4 diagrams, 7 maps, bibl.: 116-27.

This seminal book is based on the author's doctoral thesis on the
history of the colonisation of southern Angola (Mossamedes and its
hinterland, 1875-1915, PhD thesis, London: SOAS, 1975). Although
criticised by Clarence-Smith himself as doing "little more than
elaborate a general history of the area, with a much greater
stress on African societies than was the rule in colonialist historiography", the thesis deploys a wealth of archival and published
source material to characterise an area and a historical period
hitherto left largely to colonialist propaganda and ethnography.
The entirely rewritten published version may err in the opposite
direction in its selective use of source material. The text is
organised thematically and the main emphasis is laid on the economic and social structures of local social formations, both settler

and indigenous. The author's principal theoretical inspiration is
class analysis and marxist anthropology, and it is as a major case
study of the economic and social processes of colonial conquest
that the study is chiefly valuable. It is also, however, of considerable direct Namibian interest, since the area covered includes
Ovamboland and its northern neighbours.

125. CRAIG, ROBERT. "The African guano trade". Mariner's Mirror,
50, no. 7, 1964: 25-55.

A detailed and expert account of the tumultuous guano rush of
1843-4, when hundreds of vessels descended on Ichaboe Island and
removed more than 200,000 tons within two years. The author's
research embraced a wide range of published and private records
and he sets the episode in the context of the economics of
international merchant shipping in the 1840s.

DAVIES, JOAN H., see no. 121.

126. EIROLA, MARTTI et al. The cultural and social change in Ovamboland
1870-1915. University of Joensuu (Finland), 1983, 123 p. Bibl.:
66-122.

The pilot study described in this report was concerned with Ovamboland
in the period immediately before and during the German colonial
period. It was carried out by a team of Finnish researchers associated with the University of Joensuu, the University of Oulu and
the Scandinavian Institute of African Studies. Its aims were to
devise a detailed research programme for an inderdisciplinary project focusing on cultural, economic, social and political changes
in Ovamboland during the period 1870-1915, to make an inventory of
relevant source material and literature in Finland, the German
Democratic Republic and the Federal Republic of Germany, and to make
contact with Finnish and foreign research workers and institutes
interested in Namibian history. The main value of the report lies
in the overview of the unique material on Ovamboland which has
been collected in Finland as a result of the activities of the
Finnish Missionary Society. The report also contains useful information on some of the German archival sources, a brief bibliographical discussion of Northern Namibia and an outline of the
major themes of the research project which will follow as the next
step. The second half of the report consists of an extensive
listing of 750 publications of relevance to the project, covering
early travel, colonial and missionary literature and environmental
sciences as well as modern historical and social science literature.
See also no. 191.

127. FREY, C. "Jonker Afrikaner and his time". Journal - SWA Scientific
Society, 1, 1925/6: 17-35.

A general summary of the history of central Namibia during Jonker
Afrikaner's ascendancy (c. 1825-61). It is drawn largely from the
published accounts of European traders, explorers and missionaries
and concentrates as much on their activities as on the biography
of Jonker, who is depicted, as in Vedder's influential defence of

the missionaries' "civilising" role (see no. 157), as a barbarous despot bent on plunder and personal aggrandisement.

128. GALTON, FRANCIS. The narrative of an explorer in tropical South Africa. London: John Murray, 1853, 314 p. 10 pictures, 1 map. (New edition: London: Ward, Lock & Co., 1980, 314 p. 3 pictures, 1 map. Reprint: New York: Johnson Reprint Comp., 1971, 314 p.).

Francis Galton, an explorer and anthropologist from a wealthy Victorian background and soon to become a pillar of the Royal Geographical Society, was the first European traveller to visit Ovamboland from the south. His detailed narrative account of that 17-month expedition, which ranged widely over the central-northern plateau as well as to Ondonga in Ovamboland, mixes perceptive social, economic and political commentary with the usual travel anecdotes and exploits. The self-confidence of a well-connected adventurer from an expanding imperial power is in these circum- stances an advantage, for on the one hand his thoughts and motives are transparent at every stage, while on the other his account is sympathetic to the economic prosperity and the social and political order he encountered in the Ondonga kingdom. Of the two available editions, the 1980 reprint omits the travel itinerary and most of the colour prints, but adds an index and an appendix containing extracts from published descriptions of several subsequent exped- itions to Ovamboland, as well as the author's vigorous criticism of one of the more hostile of them. The German translation has recently been reprinted: Bericht eines Forschers in Tropischen Südafrika (Swakopmund: Gesellschaft für Wissenschaftliche Entwicklung und Museum, 1980, 180 p.).

129. IRLE, JAKOB. Die Herero. Ein Beitrag zur Landes-, Volks- und Missionskunde. Gütersloh: Bertelsmann, 1906, 352 p. 56 illus.

This is the leading missionary work and the standard account of Herero society in the late 19th century, based on the author's experience as a missionary since early 1870s. The book is re- garded as an equivalent to the work by Tönjes on Ovamboland (no. 156), and provides a unique insight into the life of the Herero in the period after 1870, seen through the eyes of an acute and not unsympathic observer. There is a great deal of information on geography, rainfall (tables for 1886-1903), droughts (from 1740 onwards) daily life, kinship, property rights, housing, work, social relations, trade (calculations of prices of consumer goods in Cape, Walvis Bay and Otjimbingwe), cattle routes, and modes of exchange. The last third of the book is devoted to the history and the future prospects of missionary activities. There are also numerous photos and drawings. The manuscript was comp- leted before the war of anti-colonial resistance, but published at a time when a paternalistic and balanced presentation of the Herero people was not what the authorities really wanted.

130. KIENETZ, ALVIN. "The key role of the Orlam migrations in the early Europeanization of South West Africa (Namibia)". The International Journal of African Historical Studies, 10, no. 4, 1977: 553-72.

This thought-provoking essay argues that the early 19th century
Orlam migrations have had a profound impact on the culture and
history of Namibia. While pro-colonialist historiography has emphasized
the role of European traders and missionaries as "pioneers", the
main concern of the author is to demonstrate the role played by
the Orlams through three basic components of their economy and culture: rifles, horses and ox-wagons. The basic conclusion is,
therefore, that a wave-like process of cultural diffusion took
place in the 19th century. The article is also a stimulating contribution to the historiographical discussion, and criticises the
colonialist historians as well as the "rather mechanistic" East
German school represented by Loth (no. 140) and Drechsler (no. 188).

131. LAU, BRIGITTE. A critique of the historical sources and historiography relating to the 'Damaras'in pre-colonial Namibia. University
of Cape Town, 1979, 105 p. Bibl.: 97-105. (BA, Honours).

This research essay breaks new ground in its critical assessment of
the historiography of pre-colonial Namibia, providing a penetrating
examination of the primary source material and the secondary
literature on the Damara in the 19th century. The author has
undertaken the important task of questioning the value and reliability of the source material, including the missionary information
often repeated uncritically by historians and anthropologists. The
essay contains also an illuminating discussion of some major historical
works, especially Heinrich Vedder (no. 157), Heinrich Loth (no. 140),
Richard Moorsom (nos. 55, 123) and Israel Goldblatt (no. 24). The
concluding chapter offers some tentative suggestions as to directions
for further research. While the subordination of Damara communities
to Nama/Orlam groups and the Herero has often been described as a
patron-client relationship between individuals, it is suggested that
a more useful approach is to understand this relationships of dependency and subservience in the light of the Orlam migrations and
the penetration of mercantile capital.

132. LAU, BRIGITTE. "'Thank God the Germans came': Vedder and Namibian
historiography". In Africa Seminar, Collected Papers, vol. 2,
edited by Keith Gottschalk and Christopher Saunders, p. 24-53.
Cape Town: Centre for African Studies, University of Cape Town,
1981.

Partly based on a BA thesis (no. 131), this essay offers a critical
examination of the writings of Heinrich Vedder, the influential
missionary and amateur historian. In a significant contribution
to Namibian historiography, the author points out that the ideas
and historical studies of Vedder have all centred on the role and
responsibility of the white race as the carrier of Christian White
Civilization, in which the German settlers of Namibia had a special
place. The essay demonstrates convincingly how colonial settler
myths were propagated through his South West Africa in early times
(no. 157), and that the overriding impulse behind his magnum opus
was to idealize the colonisation of Namibia by distorting the
history of the pre-colonial societies. These conclusions are
drawn from analysis of Vedder's writings on the Damara and his views
on pre-colonial violence and the concept of "tribe". The essay is

also published in three parts in The Namibia Review (no. 21, January-March 1981; no. 22, April-June 1981; and no. 26, September-December 1982).

133. LAU, BRIGITTE. The emergence of Kommando politics in Namaland, Southern Namibia 1800-1870. University of Cape Town, 1982, 388 p. Bibl.: 371-86. (MA thesis).

134. ------- "The Kommando and the 1860s traders' and missionaries' 'war of liberation'". In Seminar on Namibian history, p. 17-42. Windhoek, 1983. (Namibian Review Publications, no. 2).

This is a major historical study and a fresh and thoughtful reinterpretation of a critical period in Namibia's under-researched pre-colonial history, based on extensive archival work in Cape Town and Windhoek and inspired by materialist historiography and French anthropology. After a critical discussion of other historical interpretations (especially Vedder, Loth and Moorsom), the author describes the early Nama social formation (1800-1820) and the effects of the Orlam invasion. The main focus is on the rise and fall of the "kommando groups" as a particular pattern of social organisation, based on commodity exchange (the entrenchment of the dependency on the Cape nexus), cattle raiding, tributary relations with the Herero and the Damara, and more advanced military and transport technology, including the use of guns, horses and ox-wagons. It is argued that this system was fundamentally challenged in the middle of the century by the attempt of European traders and missionaries to usurp the political and economic power of the leading Orlam/Nama groups, this coming in a period of depletion of natural resources, the negative effects of the entrenchment of the dependency on the Cape nexus, a small-pox epidemic and lung-sickness amongst cattle. The wars in the 1860s, which have been portrayed by Vedder and others as a "Herero war of liberation" are seen in this perspective as a much more complex process in which European traders and missionaries extended their control of central Namibia by administering the final blow to the crumbling base of kommando power. This process is aptly summed up: "With kommando power broken, Europeans could now exploit the riches of the northern and eastern hunting velds without having to fear the payment of fees and duties. They could trade and settle where they planned... The country was freer than ever before - to be controlled by agents of merchant capital and colonialism". The essay in Seminar on Namibian history is a succinct introduction to the thesis. It is also published in Perspectives on Namibia (no. 68), but in this version the extensive footnotes and bibliographical references are unfortunately omitted.

135. LAU, BRIGITTE (ed.). Carl Hugo Hahn. Tagebücher, 1837-1860. Diaries. Windhoek: Archives Services Division of the Department of National Education, 1984. Part I: 1837 - 1845, 291p. ; Part II: 1846 - 1851, p. 291-579. (Archeia, Windhoek Archives Source Publications Series, No. 1-2). Avaliable in Western Europe from Basler Afrika Bibliographien.

This is a most welcome and carefully prepared source edition of the diaries of Carl Hugo Hahn, who was a missionary amongst the Herero and one of the key European political figures in central Namibia in the period 1842-1873. As pointed out by the editor in her

introduction, in the absence of extensive oral history research and
a well-established 19th century archeology, these documents are
among the earliest and most detailed sources on socio-political
conditions in Nama- and Hereroland. Their importance is further
enhanced by the fact that most of the early history of Herero communities is based on sources dating from the 1870s and 1880s, at
a time when major social and political changes had already occurred.
The diaries also throw a revealing light on the role of the missionaries and their own perceptions of the societies in which they worked.
The text is in German, but the introduction as well as the 240 informative notes are in English. There are also a bibliography and
a detailed index. The first two volumes cover the period 1837 -
1851 and the two other are expected to be published in the 1985.
The editor, herself a leading historian of 19th century Namibia
(see nos. 131-4), is Publications Officer at the State Archives,
Windhoek.

136. LAU, BRIGITTE. 'Pre-colonial' Namibian historiography: what is to
be done? Paper presented to the Conference on Research Priorities
in Namibia, ICS, University of London, 23-25 July 1984, 22 p.

This fully referenced paper draws on the author's previous studies
(see nos. 131-4) to make a most welcome contribution to the sparse
historiographical debate on pre-colonial Namibian societies. The
first part focuses on the colonial apologetic literature, and leads
into a critical assessment of the more recent Africanist and
historical materialist works, including a stimulating discussion
of authors such as Loth, Moorsom and Werner. The author points
to the vast blank spaces in existing literature, and stresses the
need for, inter alia, the study of ecological and demographic
changes in the 19th century, an oral history project and the preparation of a reader on pre-colonial Namibian history.

137. LEHMANN, F. RUDOLF. "Die politische und soziale Stellung der
Häuptlinge in Ovambo-Land während der deutschens Schutzherrschaft
in Südwest-Afrika". Tribus, N.F., 4-5, 1954/5: 265-328.

138. ------- "Die anthropogeographischen Verhältnisse des Ambolandes im
nördlichen Südwestafrika". Zeitschrift für Ethnologie, 79, 1954:
8-58. 7 photos.

The first of this pair of articles is concerned primarily with the
political status of the Ovambo kings and their relations with
the German authorities, on which a good deal of descriptive information from archival and literary sources is deployed. The concluding section tests the 'divine kingship' hypothesis in the
Ovambo context, discussing at length the pre-colonial forms of
social and political authority and the analyses of earlier authors.
The second article speculates on various aspects of the ecology
of Ovamboland, with lengthy descriptions and extensive historical
references on climate, water supply, natural environment, forms
of agriculture and trade, population, and social and political
history. Relatively little on-the-spot research appears to
have been undertaken, but the use of several unpublished offical
sources brings out new information. See also "Die verhouding van
die Duitse Beskermingsadministrasie in Suidwes-Afrika tot die

Ambovolke". Journal - SWA Scientific Society, 9, 1955-56.

139. LOEB, EDWIN M. In feudal Africa. Bloomington, 1962, 382 p. + xxii.
5 maps, 13 photos, bibl.: 378-83. (Publications 23, Indiana University, Research Center in Anthropology, Folklore and Linguistics.
Also part II of The International Journal of American Linguistics,
28, no. 3, 1962).

This is an original but controversial anthropological study of the
Kwanyama, the largest of the pre-colonial Ovambo population groups.
Through detailed fieldwork as a member of a large US expedition to
the area in 1947-48, the author has been able to provide new insight
into the late pre-colonial and early colonial period in the north.
The study represents a welcome departure from the timeless framework
of physical anthropology and ethnology in employing a historical
perspective on societal change. The sections on ecology, agriculture, trade, craftsmanship and other aspects of material culture
are strong, and differentiation by occupational and social rank
is discussed, prefiguring the class analyses of such authors as
Moorsom, Berger and Borkowsky. The author obviously wanted to
define societies as feudal, and he was consequently looking for
suitable characteristics. Despite its forced and at times speculative interpretations, the study is original in analysis and rich
as an empirical source.

140. LOTH, HEINRICH. Die christliche Mission in Südwestafrika. Zur
destruktiven Rolle der Rheinischen Missionsgesellschaft beim Prozess
der Staatsbildung in Südwestafrika (1842-1893). Berlin (GDR):
Akademie-Verlag, 1963, 180 p. Bibl.: 174-80. (Studien zur
Kolonialgeschichte und Geschichte der nationalen und kolonialen
Befreiungsbewegung, 8).

A major work of historical research and interpretation, offering
a forceful, original and controversial analysis of pre-colonial
central Namibian history. The author, a leading East German historian, made the first serious attempt to challenge the influential
and colonialist interpretation of the same period advanced by Heinrich
Vedder (no. 157). Where Vedder could see nothing but an endless
drama of bloody repression, internecine tribal warfare and the
individual despotism of African rulers, this study focuses attention
more on what is called "state formation" as one of the main themes
of 19th century Namibian history. The development of larger states
is regarded as a progressive and necessary step in social evolution , and the overriding aim of the book is to demonstrate the
destructiveness of missionary interventions in this process in the
1850s and 1860s. Typical of the 1960s, the author is more preoccupied with the actions of Europeans than with the internal
dynamism of the African societies. Some of the assumptions of the
study have been questioned by other historians, see for example
Kienetz (no. 130) and Lau (nos. 133, 136), who are more concerned
with external dependency and the influence of commodity production
on social and political relations than with the activities of the
missionaries. The book contains more than twenty historical documents in the appendix, as well as a guide to the relevant archival
files and to literature for further studies. Unfortunately, the

author himself was barred from the Rhenish missionary archives in
Wuppertal, West Germany. The same author has also published a
study of "Christian rebels" in Southern Africa and their fight against
colonialism and apartheid, which includes separate chapters on
Jonker Afrikaaner, Hendrik Witbooi and Markus Witbooi: Rebellen im
Priesterrock. Christen im Süden Afrikas und ihre Rolle im Widerstand gegen Kolonialismus und Apartheid. Eine historische Untersuchung. (Berlin: Union Verlag, 1977, 239 p.).

141. MCKIERNAN, GERALD. The narrative and journal of Gerald McKiernan
in South West Africa, 1874-1879. Cape Town: van Riebeeck Society,
1954, 193 p. 3 photos, 1 map. (Edited by P. Serton, van Riebeeck
Society Publications no. 35).

Gerald McKiernan was an American hunter and trader who travelled
widely through central and northern Namibia in the decade before
the German colonial annexation. The published text consists of
an uncompleted narrative (1874-6), written from memory after the
author's return to the US, and a travel journal (1877-9). It is
valuable for being the work not of a missionary, explorer or
well-to-do adventurer, each with a readership to play to or a
publicist aim to promote, but of one the ordinary traders who went
simply to make money. The author was not entirely free of the
pervasive racist ideology of the period, but frequent close contact
in the course of barter trading renders it less obtrusive than in
many similar accounts. His memory is accurate, his attitude re-
strained and unsentimentally pragmatic, and there is much carefully
observed detail on his and others' trading activities and, less
frequently, on the economy and society of the peasant farmers on
whom he depended for a living. This edition is enhanced by an
informative introduction and notes, and by appendices listing
the names of geographic locations and persons appearing in the text.

142. MARKS, SHULA and ANTHONY ATMORE. "Firearms in southern Africa: a
survey". Journal of African History, 12, no. 4, 1971: 517-30.

This article includes a brief but valuable early overview of the role
of firearms in the central and southern Namibian conflicts of the
19th century and the resistance to German conquest at the turn of
this century. The link between trade penetration, access to
European weapons technology, the raiding economy and internal class
and state formation is developed further in particularly Moorsom,
Clarence-Smith and Lau (see nos. 55, 123, 124, 133).

143. MEYER, FELIX. Wirtschaft und Recht der Herero. Berlin: Springer,
1905, 105 p.

An attempt to discuss the material culture and the customary law
of the Herero around the turn of the century, based on the extensive
writings of travellers, missionaries, anthropologists and colonial
administrators. The text is badly organised, lacking chapters and
sub-titles, and is not without racist overtones, but the compilation
of information on political organisation, "the cattle complex",
social differentiation and rules of inheritance, although frag-
mentary, has reference value. The text almost totally fails to note

the profound historical changes which the Herero were subject to in
the last part of the 19th century, and is set within the anthropological framework of a timeless "primitive society".

144. MÖLLER, PETER AUGUST. Journey in Africa through Angola, Ovampoland
and Damaraland. Cape Town: Struik, 1974, 216 p. 30 pictures, 3
maps, bibl.: 202-04. (Translated by Ione and Jalmar Rudner from
the Swedish original Resa i Afrika genom Angola, Ovampo och Damaraland. Stockholm: W. Billes Bokförlag, 1899).

At the time of his 1895-6 expedition through southern Angola,
Ovamboland and central Namibia to Walvis Bay, Peter Möller was
already a long-serving Swedish army officer and experienced in
African conditions, having been for several years a colonial administrator in the Congo. He was an accurate and observant reporter and
as well as the usual descriptions of hunting and wildlife, there
is much detailed information and perceptive general commentary
on the peoples amongst whom he travelled. His account gives a rare
and invaluable insight into social and economic conditions in
Ovamboland at a turning-point in its history, when the pressures of
unequal exchange and colonial conquest were setting in motion major
internal changes, confirming, for instance that the new class of
war-leaders (lenga) was well established before the devastating
rinderpest made cattle-raiding an economic necessity. This translation is complemented by extensive factual footnotes and by Möller's
portrait and landscape photographs.

MOORSOM, RICHARD, see no. 123.

145. MORITZ, EDUARD (ed.). "Aus den ältesten Reiseberichte über Deutsch-
Südwest-afrika". Mitteilungen aus den deutschen Schutzgebieten,
28, 1915: 161-268; 29, 1916: 135-253; 31, 1918: 17-44.

This is a unique collection of source material on Namibian pre-
colonial history, as seen through the eyes of voyagers, traders,
missionaries and travellers. The editor has brought together letters,
diaries and excerpts from published books, translated from Dutch,
Portuguese, French and English in addition to material originally
written in German, and provides brief biographical introductions.
The first part (1915) is concerned with the period 1760 up to
1842, when the Rhenish Missionary Society established itself in
Namibia, the second part (1916) mainly with diaries and letters
from missionaries (Knudsen, Hahn, Kleinschmidt, Scheppman) in the
period 1842-1852, while the third part (1918) opens with Portuguese reports from the 1480s and ends with an account of the
Namibian coast and the whaling activities in the 1830s.

146. NITSCHE, GEORG. Ovamboland. Versuch einer landeskundlichen Darstellung nach dem gegenwärtigen Stand unserer geographischen Kenntnis.
Univ. Kiel, 1913, 154 p. 4 maps, bibl.: 5-9.

The most comprehensive geographical and economic study of Ovamboland
to appear during the German colonial period, drawing on a wide range
of travel reports and secondary literature as well as the author's
academic training. More than two-thirds of the text is taken up

with physical geography and the natural environment. The concluding
chapters, although briefer, provide an ordered discussion on the
political and social structure of Ovambo society as well as
valuable data, not least on the earliest phase of labour migration.
The final chapter discusses the potential for colonial economic
exploitation. Writing at a time of growing German interest in
northwards expansion after the devastation of the Herero/Nama
war of resistance, the author, while urging military conquest,
rates large-scale labour migration as being of greater economic
value to the colonial regime than land seizure and plantation
agriculture.

147. PÉLISSIER, RÉNE. "Campagnes militaires au Sud-Angola (1885-1915)",
Cahiers d´Etudes Africaines, vol. 9, 1969: 54-111.

148. ------- "Mandume (c. 1890-1917) et la résistance Ovambo au colonial-
isme portugais en Angola". In Les Africains , vol. VIII, edited by
Charles-André Julien, p. 205-35. Paris: editions j.a., 1977.

Written by a prominent French historian specialising on Angola, the
first of these two essays provides a well researched survey on the
military dimensions of Portuguese attempts to colonise southern
Angola. It contains considerable factual detail on a period in
the history of northern Namibia and southern Angola which is poorly
covered in the modern literature (see no. 124). The second contribution offers a biographical sketch of the last Kwanyama king and one
of the most far-sighted leaders of the resistance to colonisation.
Mandume, who confronted the final South African/Portuguese assault
on Ovamboland in 1915 and was killed by the South Africans two
years later, is so far the only Namibian represented in a pres-
tigious series of volumes on "famous" African leaders.

149. PFOUTS, ANITA. "Social structure in precolonial Namibia: a linguistic analysis", UFAHAMU, 13, nos. 2-3, 1984: 283-302.

Originally presented as a paper to the African Studies Association
1983 Annual Conference, this preliminary and pioneering essay explores important aspects of pre-colonial history by using archeo-
logical and linguistic evidence to shed light on migration, settlement
and historical links between ethnic groups represented in Namibia
today. The author links Namibia to the stream of Central African
history, documents the strong historical ties between Ovambo and
Herero people, shows how class formation can be studied through
the existence of words for concepts of class formation, such as
"rich man", "pauper" and "slave", and argues that the collection
of words for iron and metal-working in several of the Southwest
Bantu languages indicates that the knowledge of the technology
already existed between 500-700 AD.

150. RIDSDALE, BENJAMIN. Scenes and adventures in Great Namaqualand.
London: T. Woolmer, 1883, 293 p.

Composed in diary form, this is the account of the experiences of

a Wesleyan missionary based in Warmbad in the late 1840s. The
major part of the book, which is badly organised and lacks a proper
contents list, consists of missionary reminiscences of limited
general value. There are, however, some original observations on
the political and social situation in the middle of the last century, notably the chapter "Great Namaqualand and its people" (p.
57-107).

151. SCHINZ, HANS. Deutsch- Südwest-Afrika. Forschungsreisen durch
die deutschen Schutzgebiete Gross-Nama- und Hereroland, nach dem
Kunene, dem Ngami-See und der Kalaxari, 1884-1887. Oldenburg/
Leipzig: Schultze, 1891, 568 p. 40 pictures.

This book, one of the first of a stream of autobiographical reminiscences from German travellers, missionaries and officials, was
the product of a two-year expedition in 1885-7 which ranged over
the whole of Namibia and northwestern Botswana. The travel narrative, which makes up the bulk of the text, is supplemented by
substantial general chapters on the Nama, the Herero, and the
Ovambo. The author's interest in botany and anthropology predom-
inates but economic and social themes regularly recur both in discussion
and in detailed observation, and there are brief excursions into
recent political and missionary history. Two concluding chapters
outline the potential for colonial exploitation, especially through
settler farming, and provide a certain amount of economic information on the first years of the German Protectorate. The
ethnographical collection based on Hans Schinz's visit to Namibia
forms a part of the Völkerkundemuseum der Universität Zürich. For
an informative presentation of the collection and its initiator,
see Miklós Szalay: Die ethnographische Südwestafrika-Sammlung
Hans Schinz, 1884-1886 (Zurich, Völkerkundemuseum der Universität
Zürich, 1979).

152. STENGEL, HEINZ WALTER. "Der Baiweg". Namib und Meer, 3, (October)
1972: 5-20.

This brief note describes the first road connection between the
coast and the interior of Namibia, which was built in the 1840s on
the initiative of the foremost African ruler in central Namibia
at the time, Jonker Afrikaner. The road, which greatly impressed
European travellers, was the first permanent trade link between
Namibia and the world market which was not dependent on the Cape
Colony. It served as the only link to Walvis Bay/Swakopmund until
a small-gauge railway line was built around the turn of the century.
The article sheds some light on pre-colonial and early colonial
economic history, but is marred by the use of tendentious terms
like "the warlike and rapacious native tribes". There is a summary
in English and Afrikaans.

153. STUCHLIK, MILAN. "Social stratification of the Herero". In Social
stratification in tribal Africa, edited by L. Holy and M. Stuchlik,
p. 151-66. Prague: Czech Academy of Sciences, 1963.

The author sets out to analyse in broad terms economic, social and
political differentiation in Herero society before it was sub-
stantially transformed by external pressures. His sources are

limited to the few available anthropological works, but within this framework he provides a perceptive synthesis.

154. TABLER, EDWARD C. Pioneers of South West Africa and Ngamiland, 1738-1880. Cape Town: Balkema, 1973, 142 p. Bibl.: 133-40. (South African Bibliographical and Historical Studies, 19).

Based on extensive research, this is a biographical dictionary and a reference work which provides information on European explorers, hunters, traders, settlers, agents, mine managers, tourists, missionaries, naturalists, photographers, concessionaires, military advisors, collectors, sportsmen, and cattle farmers, who travelled and settled in Namibia from 1738 to 1880. The book helps map the early penetration by Europeans in the area, and the index and the bibliography make it a practical reference source. It should be noted, however, that it also includes incorrect and superficial information, and that far from all relevant biographical sources have been exploited. For a critique of Tabler for not having taken into account the African "pioneers" (esp. the Orlams), see Kienitz (no. 130).

155. TINDALL, JOSEPH. The journal of Joseph Tindall. Missionary in South West Africa 1839-55. Cape Town: van Riebeeck Society, 1959, 198 p. Bibl.: 197-8. (Edited by B.A. Tindall).

Written in the form of a diary, with a chapter for each year, this book is mainly concerned with missionary activities, although there are also references to economic and social conditions and to conversations with local leaders. The published version, edited by the author's grandson, is suppled with foot-notes, a sketch-map, an introduction and a bibliography.

156. TÖNJES, HERMANN. Ovamboland: Land, Leute, Mission. Berlin: Martin Warneck, 1911, 317 p. 37 photos.

This book, one of the first to be specifically devoted to Ovamboland, gives a general account of economic, social, political and ideo-logical life in Ukwanyama, the largest of the Ovambo population settlement areas. The author based his book on his nine years' experience as a missionary. Organised broadly within an anthro-pological framework, it provides much descriptive information on the local economy and social order only a few years before the final colonial conquest. A final section describes the history and the work of the Lutheran Mission in Ovamboland.

157. VEDDER, HEINRICH. Das alte Südwestafrika. Südwestafrikas Geschichte bis zum Tode Mahareros 1890. Windhoek: SWA Wissenschaftliche Gesellschaft, 1981, 686 p. Bibl.: p. 664-66. (First edition: Berlin: Martin Warneck, 1934. English edition translated and edited by C.G. Hall: South West Africa in early times. Being the story of South West Africa up to the date of Maharero's death in 1890. Oxford University Press, 1938, 525 p. Reprint: London: Frank Cass & Co., 1966. Afrikaans edition: Die Voorgeskiedenis van van Suidwes-Afrika. Windhoek: Meinert, 1937, 751 p.).

Published in German, Afrikaans and English, this book has until very
recently been taken as the standard account of 19th century Namibian
history. The English edition is a shortened version of the original,
in that numerous letters and documents, as well as detailed accounts
of the development of individual missions, have been omitted. The
1981 German edition is the easiest to use, due to the inclusion of
an extensive subject and name index (p. 667-88), prepared by Vita
von Schwind. The legendary author, who lived in Namibia from 1902
until his death in 1972, was a leading missionary, an amateur
linguist, historian and anthropologist, as well as a prolific
writer. He was also an influential colonial propagandist and
played an important political role as a prominent member of the
German community and an appointed member of the South African
Senate after the apartheid victory in 1948. His magnum opus is
essentially a narrative account of European "discoveries", missionary
activities and "tribal warfare" up to 1890, mainly based on letters,
notes, diaries and reports by European missionaries, travellers and
colonial officials. There is, however, no discussion of the status
and reliability of missionary records, and without references very
little of the narrative is verifiable by academic standards. The
pre-colonial African societies are depicted as stereotyped "tribes"
engaged in endless wars and battles and ruled by blood-thirsty
despots, a description which has been echoed by others who have
written on the same period. The works of Vedder have recently come
under heavy attack from a new generation of historians, who have
maintained that his writings do not contain history "but at best a
chronicle of events and at worst a thinly-veiled political propaganda
from a settler point of view" (see Lau, nos. 131, 132). Hagiographic
accounts of his life and works have also been challenged by scholarly
examinations of his theology and close affinity to fascist ideology
(see Engel, no. 233). The background notes and documents for his
major historical study are available in 30 volumes at the State
Archives, Windhoek and at the Stellenbosch University. (Quellen
zur Geschichte von Südwestafrika; zusammengestellt im Auftrage der
Administration). For a celebration of Vedder and his ideas, see
Drascher, W./Rust, H.J. (eds.): Ein Leben für Südwestafrika.
Festschrift. Dr. h.c. Heinrich Vedder (Windhoek: SWA Wissen-
schaftliche Gesellschaft, 1961, 168 p.). See also the sketchy
biography written by Walter Moritz: Dr. Heinrich Vedder. Vom
Ravensberger Seidenweber zum berühmten Afrika-Missionar (Schwäbisch
Gmünd: Afrika-Verlag der Kreis bei Lempp Verlag, 1973, 33 p.) and
Julius Baumann: Mission und Ökumene in Südwestafrika. Dargestellt
am Lebenswerk von Hermann Heinrich Vedder (Leiden/Köln: E.J.
Brill, 1965, 168 p.). Vedder has also published his reminiscences:
Kurze Geschichten aus einem langen Leben (Wuppertal: Verlag der
Rheinischen Missionsgesellschaft, 1953, 246 p.), which is also avail-
able in a shortened Afrikaans version: Kort verhale uit 'n lang lewe
(Cape Town: Balkema, 1957, 138 p.).

158. WATSON, ARTHUR C. "The guano islands of southwestern Africa".
Geographical Review, 20, (October) 1930: 631-41.

An account of the guano rush of 1843-4, concentrating on its central
focus, Ichaboe Island, but also with descriptions of other islands
and of the sealing expeditions along the southern Namibian coast
which preceded it. The author uses mainly US sources and follows the

involvement of US vessels, in particular through the private journal
of a crew-member on board an American schooner, large extracts of
which are quoted.

159. WERNER, WOLFGANG. An exploratory investigation into the mode of
production of the Herero in pre-colonial Namibia to ca. 1870.
University of Cape Town, 1980, 112 p. Bibl.: 103-12.
(Dissertation, B. Sos. Sc., Honours).

A significant departure from the anthropological and missionary
literature in applying a marxist analytical framework to pre-colonial
Herero society, this dissertation poses some important questions
and issues for further research, although, as the author readily
acknowledges, the analysis is exploratory for lack of empirical
material on the production process, political organisation and the
dominated classes. His thesis is that a transition took place in
the first half of the 19th century from a lineage-based to a
tributary mode of production, based on an amalgamation of smaller
productive units defined by membership of a particular patrilineage
into large entities, and that social stratification based on control
over cattle and people began to take the shape of class relations.
Although the activities of missionaries and merchant capital led to
important changes, especially in the use of technology and imported
goods, it is argued that the relations of production did not change
significantly and that the missionaries and merchants were forced to
work through – and thus to strengthen – the dominant chiefs. This
continuity, in turn, explains why the conditions for an economic
and political unification of the Herero people did not exist before
the colonial annexation.

SEE ALSO:

1, 8, 24, 55, 68, 81, 182, 186, 191, 198, 202-03, 211, 553, 561,
619, 637, 641.

4. UNDER GERMAN RULE (1884-1915)

A. The German empire

60. ALBERTINI, RUDOLF VON with ALBERT WIRTZ. European colonial rule, 1880-1940. The impact of the West in India, Southeast Asia, and Africa. Westport, Connecticut: Greenwood Press/Oxford: Clio Press, 1982, 568 p. Bibl.: 541-64. (German edition: Europäische Kolonialherrschaft: die Expansion in Übersee von 1880-1940. München: Heyne, 1982, 656 p. Bibl.: 602-32.).

This is a revised edition of a standard German textbook on the history of European colonialism, originally published in 1976. It includes a lucid survey of German colonialism in Africa, written by Albert Wirtz, (p. 388-417 in the English edition, p. 444-80 in the German edition). This chapter places Namibia in the broader context of German economic interests and colonial policy. The book also has an extensive bibliography.

61. DÜLFFER, JOST. "Deutsche Kolonialherrschaft in Afrika". Neue Politische Literatur 26, no. 4, 1981: 458-73.

This is an informative and critical examination of recent scholarly studies concerned with German colonialism and the period of German colonial rule in Africa, discussing general works as well as case studies from Tanzania, Togo, Cameroon and Namibia. The author is a historian at the University of Köln.

DUIGNAN, PETER, see no. 162.

62. GANN, L.H. and PETER DUIGNAN. The rulers of German Africa 1884-1914. Stanford, California: Stanford University Press, 1977, 286 p. 26 tables + statistical appendix. (Hoover Institution Publications).

This is the first volume in a multi-volume work which defines its purpose as being "to elucidate the sociological and functional characteristics, the achievements as well as shortcomings, of the white empire builders, civilian and military during the age of the

New Imperialism in Africa". Written by two right-wing US scholars
(see no. 776), the study concentrates on the colonial elite and how
the Germans ran Namibia and the other parts of their empire. The
authors regard German colonialism as "an engine of modernization", and
argue against the Hannah Arendt's thesis linking colonialism to
the emergence of fascism. The work benefits from extensive archival
research, and is strong on the machinery of administration and
the role of the German administrators, armed forces and civilians
in Namibia. There are also two chapters discussing the social
and economic impact of conquest, covering the same ground as L.H.
Gann: "Economic development in Germany's African empire, 1984-1914",
published in The Economics of Colonialism, edited by L.H. Gann and
Peter Duignan (Cambridge University Press, 1975).

163. GIFFORD, PROSSER and WM. ROGER LOUIS (eds.). Britain and Germany in
Africa. Imperial rivalry and colonial rule. New Haven/London:
Yale U.P., 1967, 825 p.

This collection of essays on colonialism, focusing more on the European
powers than on the African side of history, contains several contributions of direct relevance for Namibian studies. The chapters by
Helmut Bley and Maynard W. Swanson are annotated separately (nos. 180,
272). Of relevance too are articles on British and German colonial
attitudes by W.W. Schmokel ("The hard death of imperialism: British
and German colonial attitudes, 1919-1939", p. 301-355) and a concluding chapter by John D. Fage ("British and German colonial rule:
a synthesis and summary", p. 691-706.). The book has a wide-ranging
historiographical essay by H. Pogge von Strandmann and Alison Smith
(no. 910).

164. GRAUDENZ, KARLHEINZ and HANNS MICHAEL SCHINDLER. Die deutschen
Kolonien. Geschichte der deutschen Schutzgebiete in Wort, Bild
und Karte. München: Südwest Verlag, 1982, 320 p. C 450 photos,
bibl.: 318-20.

The main value of this book lies in the wide array of photos, maps
and documents, which together throw light on German colonialism and
life in the colonies. In spite of the author's professed "objectiv-
ity", the chapter on Namibia (p. 31-95) is at times very close to
an apology for colonialism and shows little concern for the history
as experienced from an African point of view. The fascination
with missionaries, "pioneers", and military leaders gives a
one-sided perspective on Namibian history, and in general the
illustrations reveal more of the true character of German colonialism than does the written text. The final section on the contemporary situation in Namibia pays little attention to the national
struggle for independence, and is partly based on the South African
propaganda myth of Namibia as being torn apart by ethnic ("tribal")
rivalries. See also another pictorial review of German colonialism:
Uwe Timm: Deutsche Kolonien (München: Verlag Autoren Edition,
1981, 218 p.). The section on Namibia (p. 64-97) is very weak, and
does not contain many pictures which have not been used before.
Some of the most interesting - and revealing - photos are still to
be found in E. Schultz-Ewerth (ed.): Deutschlands Weg zur Kolonialmacht (Berlin: Verlag Scherl, 1934), which contains more than 230
illustrations.

65. HENDERSON, W.O. Studies in German colonial history. London:
F. Cass & Co., 1976, 142 p. (First edition: 1962).

This collection of essays by a well-known British historian is
mainly concerned with various aspects of the economic history
of the German colonies, in particular German trade and the colonies,
chartered companies and British economic activity in the German
colonies. The appendices contain statistics on Germany's commercial
relations with the colonies and the role of raw materials.

166. LEWIN, PERCY EVANS. The Germans and Africa. Their aims on the dark
continent and how they acquired their African colonies. London:
Cassell, 1939, 372 p. (First edition: 1915).

A revised and rewritten edition of a classic work on German colonialism in Africa, originally published during the First World War with the
propagandist purpose of showing that the Germans were not "worthy"
of keeping their colonies. Despite its bias, it contains some
useful information, including a chapter specifically dealing with
Namibia ("German administration in South-West Africa", p. 127-48).
The author was for many years librarian at the Royal Empire Society
(now Royal Commonwealth Society).

LOUIS, WM. ROGER, see no. 163.

167. MAMOZAI, MARTHA. Herrenmenschen. Frauen im deutschen Kolonialismus. Reinbek bei Hamburg: Rowohlt, 1982, 312 p. 44 photos.
(Frauen aktuell/rororo aktuell 4959).

Based on an academic study concerned with colonialism and the role
of women, this readable and thought-provoking book covers a wide
range of subjects: German colonialism in general, the predominance
of men (colonial "pioneers", missionaries, officers, etc.), the
position of women in pre-colonial societies and the impact of
colonialism on their status and working conditions, sexual abuse
and extreme violence directed against African women, and the role
played by German women in the colonies and in the colonial movements. The author draws heavily on contemporary sources, and
quotes extensively from books written by German women living in
Namibia before 1915 (Lydia Höpker, Margarethe von Eckenbrecher,
Ada Cramer, Clara Brockmann, Helene von Falkenhausen, Maria
Karow and others).

168. MEYER, HANS H.J. (ed.). Das deutsche Kolonialreich. Eine Länderkunde der deutschen Schutzgebiet. Leipzig/Wien: Bibliographisches
Institut. Vol. 1: Ostafrika und Kamerun. 1909, 650 p. Vol 2:
Togo, Südwestafrika, Schutzgebiete in der Südsee und Kiautchougebiete.
1910, 575 p. Maps, photos, graphs.

This is the standard contemporary work on the geography of the German
colonies, written by experts on the different territories. The
major part of the work is devoted to flora, fauna, physical geography and "colonial anthropology"; by contrast the treatment of
economic geography is surprisingly weak. This is also reflected
in the section dealing with Namibia, authored by Leonard Schultze
(vol. 2, p. 131-298).

169. MÜLLER, FRITZ FERDINAND (ed.). Kolonien unter der Peitsche. Eine Dokumentation. Berlin (GDR): Rütten & Loenig, 1962, 172 p.

This is a collection of 87 documents from the Deutsches Zentralarchiv, Potsdam, which together provide a graphic account of the methods of forced labour, violence and harsh punishment which were systematically used against the indigenous population of the former German colonies. The major part of the book is concerned with German East Africa (Tanganyika), but there are also several Namibian reports, documents and excerpts from the files of convicted persons. The editor has written an introduction to each of the nine chapters.

170. PIERARD, RICHARD VICTOR. The German Colonial Society. State University of Iowa, 1974, 407 p. (PhD thesis).

This is a detailed study of the Deutsche Kolonialgesellschaft, which played a prominent role in the scramble for colonies, the economic exploitation of the German territories, including Namibia, and colonial propaganda. The thesis, which is mainly based on the papers of the Society in the Deutsches Zentralarchiv in Potsdam, sheds light on the economic and political development of Namibia under colonial rule. The author argues that the primary motive behind the activities of the Society was nationalist, and that it did not draw its main support from big business. See also by the same author: "The Transportation of White Women to German Southwest Africa, 1898-1914"., Race, 12, no. 3, 1971: 317-22.

SCHINDLER, HANNS MICHAEL, see no. 164.

171. SCHMITT-EGNER, PETER. Kolonialismus und Faschismus. Eine Studie zur historischen und begrifflichen Genesis faschistischer Bewusstseinformen am deutschen Beispiel. Giessen/Lollar: Verlag Andreas Achenbach, 1975, 224 p. Bibl.: 199-224.

Submitted as a sociology dissertation in 1974 at the University of Frankfurt, this thesis uses many examples from Namibia to highlight issues of general importance to the theoretical discussion of colonial ideology. Starting from the works of Hannah Arendt, Fanon and Césaire, the author sets out to investigate the socio-economic basis of German colonial ideology, the origins of racist and expansionist ideology, and the subjective and objective functions of ideologies. The author advocates a strictly materialist approach to ideological phenomena, and argues that the radical racism of German settlers in Namibia also has to be understood in terms of their conflicts with land companies, monopoly capital and the colonial state bureaucracy. The final chapter contains a sketchy but suggestive outlook on the importance of colonial ideology in the genesis of fascism.

172. SCHNEE, HEINRICH (ed.). Deutsches Kolonial- Lexikon. Leipzig: Quelle & Meyer, 1920. Vol. 1: 776 p. Vol. 2: 698 p. Vol. 3: 778 p.

Edited by a former colonial governor (Tanganyika) and a leading colonial propagandist during the Nazi era, this encyclopedia is packed with information on a wide range of subjects. Apart from articles concerned with geography, the main value as a reference

work and source lies in the extensive treatment of colonial officials
and companies, such as the Siedelungsgesellschaft für Deutsch-
Südwestafrika and the Otavi Minen- und Eisenbahn- Gesellschaft (the
forerunner of the Tsumeb Corporation). The encyclopedia is, of
course, less reliable when it comes to the more controversial
issues of colonial policy. The manuscript was completed in 1914
and published after the World War I.

173. SMITH, WOODRUFF D. The German colonial empire. Chapel Hill: The
University of North Carolina Press, 1978, 274 p. Bibl.: 255-68.

The aim of this book is to serve as a summary history of the German
empire, and it is as such a useful indication of recent directions
in German colonial historiography. The main focus is on the interaction between Germany's colonial empire and domestic German politics
and socio-economic development. There are also brief chapters
devoted to each of the colonies ("South West Africa, 1885-1907:
white man's country and the roots of genocide", p. 51-65). The
principal argument is that the war of anti-colonial resistance in
Namibia contributed to a major crisis of the entire German colonial
empire, and that the methods of the German warfare presaged the
genocidal policies of a later era in German history. The author
is a US historian at the University of Texas.

174. STOECKER, HELMUTH (ed.). Drang nach Afrika. Die koloniale Expan-
sionpolitik und Herrschaft des deutschen Imperialismus in Afrika
von den Anfängen bis zum Ende des zweiten Weltkrieges. Berlin
(GDR): Akademie-Verlag, 1977, 370 p. 6 maps.

The objective of this collective work by East German historians is
to summarise the substantial body of recent research on the history
of Germany's relationship with Africa from the initial colonisation
up to the Second World War. Among the contributors are Helmuth
Stoecker, Heinrich Loth, Jolanda Ballhaus, Eberhard Czaya, and
Horst Drechsler, covering both the individual colonies and more
general themes such as the drive for colonies, colonial rule and
the relationship between the National Socialist Party and the
German Colonial Movement. Two chapters by Horst Drechsler, (p.
29-51 and p. 113- 23) do not add to his monograph (no. 188), but
review the history of "German South West Africa" in a comparative
perspective, with heavy emphasis on the brutality of the German
conquest and the ruthless exploitation of the Namibian people. There
is no bibliography, but the editor has contributed a brief note on
"Bürgerliche Literatur seit 1945 zur Geschichte der deutschen
Kolonialherrschaft in Afrika", p. 353-57.

WIRTZ, ALBERT, see no. 160.

175. WEHLER, HANS-ULRICH. Bismarck und der Imperialismus. München:
Deutscher Taschenbuch Verlag, 1976, 586 p. Bibl.: 507-70. (First
edition: Köln/Berlin: Kiepenheuer & Witsch, 1969, 582 p. Bibl.:
505-66.).

Written by a prominent West German historian, this is an important
landmark in the historical study of the German drive for colonies.

The meticulously researched book argues that German colonialism has
to be understood against the background of the Great Depression,
a structural crisis in the German economy and the struggle for
"ideological consensus" (nationalism, expansionism, colonialism)
in order to pacify sections of the working class. A separate section
(p. 263-92) is devoted to Namibia, Lüderitz and the Deutsche
Kolonialgesellschaft für Südwestafrika. The value of the study
is further enhanced by a massive bibliography and a critical
discussion of the main body of literature on German colonialism. The
principal ideas are summarised in English in "Bismarck's Imperialism",
Past & Present, no. 48, 1970: 119-58. The same article is published
in German as "Bismarck's Imperialismus", in Hans-Ulrich Wehler
(ed.): Imperialismus (Düsseldorf: Athenäum-Verlag, 1979). The
main thesis is supported by another scholarly work which also touches
on Namibia, see Klaus J. Bade: Friedrich Fabri und der Imperialismus
der Bismarckzeit: Revolution, Depression, Expansion (Freiburg:
Atlantis, 1975, 579 p.).

176. WORCH, HERBERT. Die Entwicklung der deutschen Kolonien in Afrika.
Ihre Bedeutung als Erzeuger und Verbraucher. Berlin, 1939, 144 p.
Bibl.: 129-43. (Dissertation, Friedrich- Wilhelms- Universität
zu Berlin).

The aim of this thesis was to show the extent to which the economic
conditions in the former German colonies had been deteriorating
under Mandate rule. The treatment of the subject bears evidence
of this propagandist purpose, but there are nevertheless some useful figures on trade, foreign debts, and production which are not
easily available from the interwar period. The bibliography will
also assist a comparative study of the former German colonies.

SEE ALSO:

16, 33, 34, 52, 64, chapter 4 b(177-219), chapter 6 a(317-49),
871, 872-4, 875, 877, 910-11, 934, 936, 937, 938.

. Colonisation and resistance

7. ALEXANDER, NEVILLE. Three essays on Namibian history. Windhoek: Namibian Review Publications, 1983, 34 p. (Namibian Review Publications, no. 1).

The first of a new series of Namibian studies, this collection of essays by a prominent South African activist and scholar forms a part of an investigation into Namibian history at the turn of the century. Although written in the preparatory stage of a long-term project on Namibian resistance and the origins of national consciousness, these three essays stand on their own as seminal contributions to a "revisionist" historiography. The opening essay on "Jakob Marengo and the Namibian history" (published under the same title in Social Dynamics, 7, no. 1, 1981: 1-7) is a brief and perceptive discussion of the role played by the Namibian guerilla leaders in the war of anti-colonial resistance (1903-1907). It is suggested that Marengo represents one of the main bridges between the so-called primary resistance against German colonial rule and the modern national liberation struggle led by SWAPO. The second essay - "Responses to German rule in Namibia or the engima of the Khowesin" - discusses the fate of the Khowesin (more generally known as the Witbooi people) during the period 1885-1905 in an attempt to come to grips with the notion of "collaboration" in the Namibian context. Drawing on the writings of Allan and Barbara Isaacman, Shula Marks, T.O. Ranger and Edward Steinhart, the point is made that most pre-colonial societies responded to colonial conquest by at times collaborating and at times resisting, and that the specific nature of the response has to be analysed in terms of the social structure and the objective historical situation. This essay is also published in Perspectives on Namibia: past and present, edited by C. Saunders, p. 45-68. (Cape Town: Centre for African Studies, 1983). The final contribution offers a stimulating historiographical review of "The Namibian war of anti-colonial resistance". It argues, inter alia, that the uprising was far more than a "Herero rebellion", that land was the central question and that the main thrust of the war therefore was anti-colonial without amounting to a "national war of liberation" in the modern sense. This essay, which is also reproduced in Seminar on Namibian History (no. 1), ends with a plea for an oral history project.

8. BAYER, MAXIMILIAN. The Rehoboth Baster Nation of Namibia. Basel: Basler Afrika Bibliographien, 1984, 54 p. 2 maps. Translated from the German and edited with an introduction by Peter Carstens. (German original: Die Nation der Bastards. Berlin: Süsserott,

1906, 24 p. "Die Nation der Bastards". Zeitschrift für Kolonial-politik, Kolonialrecht, und Kolonialwirtschaft, 8, no. 9, 1906: 625-48.).

Written by a German officer in praise of the Rehoboth Basters' "out-standing military service" in the period 1894-1904, this brief essay provides some information on social differentiation and on economic and social conditions in the Rehoboth Gebiet around the turn of the century. The text has been translated and edited by a professor of anthropology at the University of Toronto, who has written extensively on the "Baster" communities in Southern Africa (see no. 619). This edition also contains a succinct introduction, which sets the original text in its historical context, a bio-graphical note on Bayer, a bibliography and a number of informative references. The editor points out that Bayer wrote from a pers-pective sympathetic to the Baster cause, and that he did not share the extreme views on biological determinism and racial psychology put forward by Eugen Fischer (no. 622). The predominant attitude of the author is instead the wish to improve the conditions of the Rehoboth Basters, for instance in the field of education, in order to make them the loyal allies of the German colonial establishment. ("The more we promote education, the more the Basters will feel themselves like Germans, the more they will be strengthened, and the might of the German Empire will be more comprehensible to them"). Maximilian Bayer also published Mit dem Hauptquartier in Südwestafrika (Berlin: Weicher, 1909) as well as several popu-lar novels written for young people.

179. BLEY, HELMUTH. South-West Africa under German rule 1894-1914. London: Heinemann/Evanston: Northwestern University Press, 1971, 303 p. Bibl.: 286-89. Translated and edited by Hugh Ridley. (German original: Kolonialherrschaft und Sozialstruktur in Deutsch-Südwestafrika. Hamburg: Leibniz-Verlag, 1968, 390 p. Bibl.: 377-86).

180. ------- "Social discord in South-West Africa". In Britain and Germany in Africa, edited by P. Gifford and Wm. R. Louis, p. 607-30. New Haven/London: Yale U.P., 1967).

181. ------- "German South-West Africa after the conquest 1904-1914". In South-West Africa: A travesty of trust, edited by Ronald Segal and Ruth First, p. 35-53. London: Deutsch, 1967.

This major study by a leading West German scholar is a landmark in the historical study of German colonialism and Namibia. It is a complex, careful and solidly researched work, although not without its problems and inconsistencies, which attempts to pro-vide a multi-layered and integrated analysis where most other historians restrict themselves to narrative accounts of oppression and resistance. The author makes use of archival sources, as well as sociological and psychological theory, to support Hannah Arendt's thesis that the seeds of totalitarianism can be found in the period of colonial rule, and that racial, social and bureau-cratic predispositions to fascism manifested themselves in the specific conditions of a Namibian settler society based on brutal military methods. The study concentrates mainly on German policies

and conflicts within the settler society, while the treatment of
African societies and their reactions and initiatives is much weaker.
The central figure in the book is Major Theodor Leutwein, and it
is argued that the principal aim of the colonial governor was to
incorporate the Africans into the colonial system but that he was
opposed by die-hard settlers who favoured a "final solution". In
this respect, the author has been criticised for painting too
favourable a picture of Leutwein. The contributions to the books
edited by Gifford/Louis and Segal/First are valuable essays in their
own right, and in particular the latter provides a pioneering account
of African resistance after the war and partly redresses imbalance
in his book.

82. BOCHERT, CHRISTIAN. The Witboois and the Germans in South West
Africa. A study of their interaction between 1863 and 1905. Durban:
University of Natal, 1980, 207 p. 3 maps, 3 photos, bibl.:
199-207.

Although not the definitive treatment of the subject, this is one
of the few serious attempts to describe and analyse the interaction
between an African "tribe", the Khowesin, and the Germans as a
colonial power. The focal point is the relationships at the
socio-economic and political levels, covering the period from the
first settlement at Gibeon (1863) to the rebellion against colonial
rule (1904). Based on extensive archival research in Windhoek
and Cape Town, the author offers new insight into the penetration
of traders and missionaries, African reaction to colonial rule,
the aims of the Khowesin ("the Witboois") through the various stages
of opposition, collaboration and rebellion, and the impact of German
colonialism on the local, social structures. The introduction and
the bibliography also provide a comprehensive guide to primary
source material and the secondary literature. The thesis is, however, far stronger on assembling information than on methodology
and analysis, and there is still a need for more rigorous research
and a critical examination of the subject informed by the recent
historigraphical discussion of collaboration and resistance.

83. BRIDGMAN, JON M. The Revolt of the Hereros. Berkeley: University
of California Press, 1981, 184 p. 8 maps, bibl.: 175-77. (Perspectives on Southern Africa, 30).

Compared to some other scholarly work dealing with the war of anti-
colonial resistance, such as Bley (nos. 179-81) and Drechsler (no.
188), this study is disappointingly weak when it comes to setting
the social and economic context. The chief merit of the book is
its contribution to military history, with detailed accounts of
battles, campaigns and guerrilla techniques. This part of the study
draws on the official accounts by the Imperial German General Staff,
and primary documentary material has, unfortunately, not been consulted. Apart from documenting the German reign of terror, the
author puts more emphasis on the motives, plans and actions of the
Herero armies than is usually the case in conventional military
history. In this sense there is an attempt to describe the war
from an "African point of view", although that would require
another perspective and access to other sources, as well as insights

from oral traditions, to be successful. Despite the title, the
book contains a section on the war of the southern part of the
country, which the author insists on calling "The Hottentot Revolt".
There is also a survey of the source material, reports and books
covering this critical period on Namibian history. The author
is associate professor of history at the University of Washington,
Seattle, and has previously published a bibliography on German
Africa (no. 871). For a critical discussion of the book, which
also documents several inaccuracies, see the perceptive review
by Kirsten Alnaes in International Journal of Historical Studies,
16, no. 2, 1983: 290-3.

184. BÜLOW, FRANZ JOSEF VON. Deutsch - Südwestafrika. Drei Jahre im
Lande Hendrik Witboois. Schilderungen von Land und Leuten. Berlin:
Mittler, 1896, 365 p. 15 photos.

Written by one of the foremost German military leaders and colonial
officials, this account throws light on the early part of the
colonisation process, German military campaigns and African resistance.
The campaign against Hendrik Witbooi is described in particular
detail. The final part of the book presents a sketchy discussion
of the economic future of the colony.

185. THE CAMBRIDGE HISTORY OF THE BRITISH EMPIRE. Volume 8. Cambridge:
Cambridge University Press, 1936, 1005 p. (Second edition: 1963).

This standard account of this history of the British Empire includes
a brief chapter on Namibia ("The Germans in South West Africa", p.
694-709). The contribution is an uninspired piece of old-fashioned
colonial history, which was not revised for the second edition in
1963 (p. 723-38). The first section, written by Heinrich Vedder,
is mainly concerned with the German military occupation and the
1904-07 uprising. The second section focuses on administration
and economic conditions, based on the explicit assumptions that
"The economic history of South-West Africa is to a great extent the
history of the Deutsche Kolonialgesellschaft für Südwestafrika",
and that the mistakes made by the Germans were far outweighed
by "the achievements of constructive enterprise". The author of
the latter part was Veit Valentin.

CARSTENS, PETER, see no. 178.

186. CLAUSS, RAINER. Reaktionen auf Kolonialismus und Imperialismus.
Untersuchung der Völker Namibias. Berlin: Freie Universität,
1977, 104 p. Bibl.: 96-104. (Dissertation).

The chief merit of this thesis is to ask some urgent questions
on the connections between the structures of pre-colonial Namibian
societies and the different forms of resistance and colonial experience. There is, however, a stark contrast between the elaborate
theoretical objectives and the lack of empirical research to support
the discussion. The thesis also contains a useful summary of the
controversy over the roots of German imperialism. It is heavily
footnoted, and includes an extensive bibliography.

87. DEUTSCHLAND, REICHSKOLONMIALAMT. Die Behandlung der einheimischen
Bevölkerung in den kolonialen Besitzungen Deutschlands und
Englands. Eine Erwiderung auf das englische Blaubuch vom August
1918: Report on the natives of South West Africa and their treatment by Germany. Berlin: Verlag von Hans Robert Engelmann, 1919,
201 p. (English edition: The treatment of native and other populations in the colonial possessions of Germany and England. An
answers to the English Blue Book of August 1918: "Report on the
natives of South-West Africa and their treatment by Germany".
Berlin: German Colonial Office/Hans Robert Engelmann, 1919,
312 p.).

Written in a polemical style, this is the offical reply to the
British attacks on German colonial policies in Namibia (see no. 214).
The first part argues that during the years preceding the World
War many English colonial authorities paid tribute to the methods
of German colonisation. It also states that the treatment of
the local population was a necessary "corrective measure" against
"laziness, disobedience and insubordination". Apart from questioning
the population statistics of the British Blue Book and the credibility
of African witnesses, the book is mainly concerned with counter-
attacks on British colonialism in Egypt, South Africa, India and
Australia, with emphasis on forced labour, brutality, crimes, enslave-
ment and other atrocities.

88. DRECHSLER, HORST. Let us die fighting: the struggle of the Herero
and Nama against German imperialism (1884-1915). London: Zed
Press, 1980, 278 p. Bibl.: 256-75. (German original: Südwestafrika unter deutscher Kolonialherrschaft. Der Kampf der Herero
und Nama gegen den deutschen Imperialismus (1884-1915). Berlin
(GDR): Akademie-Verlag, 1966, 372 p. Bibl.: 291-321).

89. ------- "Jacob Morenga: a new kind of South-West African leader".
In Etudes Africaines/African Studies/Afrika Studien, edited by
Walter Markov, p. 95-105. Leipzig: VEB Verlag Enzyklopädie/
Karl Marx Universität, 1967.

90. ------- Aufstände in Südwestafrika. Der Kampf der Herero und Nama
1904 bis 1907 gegen die deutsche Kolonialherrschaft. Berlin(GDR):
Dietz, 1984, 180 p. 57 photos.

Based on a thesis submitted as early as 1963, this major study
is the foremost example of the flowering of East German historical
scholarship on 19th and early 20th century Namibian history which
followed the opening of the Imperial German State Archives in
Potsdam in 1956. Drawing extensively on the records of the colonial
office, as well as a wide range of books, periodicals and newpapers
from the colonial period, it presents a scholarly and lucid history of Namibian political and military resistance to the German
conquest and of the shifts in German strategy to overcome it.
The three central chapters examine the general uprising and
genocide of 1904-07 and the decade preceding it. Although primarily
a narrative history of resistance and the conquest, this account
is informed by historical materialism and in particular by the
Leninist theory of imperialism as applied in a number of East
German studies of pre-1914 German colonialism. Considerable

attention is given, particularly in the first and last chapters, to the economic motives and activities of both state and private interests, and also to the forced labour regime after 1907. A brief epilogue summarises the political history of Namibia up to 1978. The English edition is also provided with a preface by Sam Nujoma, the president of SWAPO. The article on Jacob Morenga (Marengo) brings together the then known facts about the extra-ordinary life of one of Namibia's guerrilla commanders in the war of anti-colonial resistance (1903-07), arguing that he was a new kind of leader in contrast to the traditional tribal chiefs who very often had been compromised through their previous collabora-tion with the Germans. Aufstände in Südwestafrika is based on the author's major historical study, and offers a popular and well ill-ustrated account of the struggle against German colonialism. Horst Drechsler, a professor at the University of Rostock, is working on a study of the land companies in Namibia under German rule.

191. EIROLA, MARTTI. Ambolaisten vastarinta Saksan siirtomaavaltaa vastaan 1885-1908. University of Oulu, 1980, 150 p. Bibl.: 145-50. (MA thesis). (The Ovambo people's resistance to German colonialism 1885-1908).

This unpublished MA thesis in Finnish concentrates on the Ovambo people's resistance to German colonialism. The study is based on Finnish archival sources as well as published Finnish, German and South African sources. It outlines pre-colonial social, economic and political structures in Ovamboland, and examines the German colonial strategy and the response of the Ovambo up to 1908. The author, a Finnish historian who grew up in Ovamboland, is partici-pating in a substantial research project on cultural and social change in Ovamboland 1870-1915 (see no. 126).

192. ENGEL, LOTHAR. Die Stellung der Rheinischen Missionsgesellschaft zu den politischen und gesellschaftlichen Verhältnissen Südwest-afrikas und ihr Beitrag zur dortigen kirchlichen Entwicklung bis zum Nama-Herero-Aufstand 1904-1907. Hamburg: Evang.- Theologischen Fakultät, Univ. Hamburg, 1972, 504 p. 4 maps, bibl.: 477-504.

Mainly drawing on the extensive archives of the missionary society, this meticulously researched thesis is concerned with the role of the Rheinische Missionsgesellschaft from the beginning in 1842 to the war of anti-colonial resistance in 1904. The author's interest lies primarily in the social and political functions of the church and the individual missionaries. The concept of mission-ary activities isolated from "worldly" conflicts and interests is completely rejected, and the close examination of the missionaries' attitudes to economic changes and policies towards the "natives" leads the author to conclude that they clearly were guided by values and ideas formed in imperial Germany and reinforced by other members of the European community in Namibia. The extensive bibliography also serves as an introduction to the relevant archives. For a follow-up study covering the period up to 1945, see no. 233.

193. ESTERHUYSE, J.H. South West Africa 1880-1894. The establishment
of German authority in South West Africa. Cape Town: Struik,
1968, 262 p. 21 photos, bibl.: 240-51.

Originally submitted in Afrikaans as a PhD thesis at the University
of Cape Town in 1964, this is a dry, narrative history of colonisation
and the first ten years of German administration. The main focus is
on the ways in which Germany established "law and order". It is a
detailed and thoroughly researched study, more concerned with compilation of facts than with discussion and analysis, reflecting the
author's work as an archivist in the Windhoek Archives, and there
are still valuable sources to which Esterhuyse draws attention that
have not at all or only marginally been used. Apart from a brief
chapter on the Deutsche Kolonialgesellschaft für Sudwestafrika
(p. 88-97), this book is very weak on economic and social history,
and the impact of German administration on the African population
is barely touched upon. The book concludes with a list of sources
and a bibliography.

194. FRANCOIS, CURT VON. Deutsch-Südwest-Afrika. Geschichte der Kolonisation bis zum Ausbruch des Krieges mit Witbooi, April 1893.
Berlin: Reimer, 1899, 223 p. 14 maps and plans.

The author was commander of the small German military force in Namibia
between 1889 and 1893. Written in at times embittered self-defence
against the greed of colonial enthusiasts and the criticism of
opponents, his account is primarily a detailed political and military
history of the first decade of German efforts to colonise central
and southern Namibia. There is also valuable economic information
from the early years of German settlement, in particular on the
concession companies, whose activities the author was in a good
position to assess.

195. FRANCOIS, HUGO VON. Nama und Damara in Deutsch-Südwest-Afrika.
Magdeburg: Baensch, 1895(1896?), 334 p, xxviii. Illus. (Reprint,
New York: Johnson, 1969).

Yet another massive account of the military campaigns and the establishment of a colonial administration, written by one of the leading
military commanders during the occupation of Namibia, and a brother
of the first German "Landeshauptmann" (see no. 194). The aim of the
book is to glorify the colonial system as well as to provide a
general introduction to Namibia. There are separate chapters
covering history, ethnology, geography, the fauna, and the indigenous
populations and their "backward cultures". A brief chapter is also
devoted to economic life in the 1890s, in particular farming, cattle-
breeding, trade and hunting. There are some 75 illustrations,
both pictures and drawings, some of them quite informative.

196. HINTRAGER, OSKAR. Südwestafrika in der deutschen Zeit. München:
Kommissionsverlag R. Oldenbourg, 1955, 261 p. 56 photos, bibl.:
240-55.

This is a conventional narrative within an apologetic framework,
published as late as 1955 by one of the leading German colonial
administrators in the period from 1906 to 1914. The book reflects

the author's closeness to the views of the local settlers on issues
of colonial policy and race. The chapters are organised according
to the ruling periods of the German governors. There are also a
few brief chapters on the economy, including some tables, but despite
occasional descriptive detail on particular aspects or events, the
chronicle is generally weak when it comes to economic and social
conditions. For a brief - and quite revealing - autobiographical
sketch, written just before he died in 1960, see: "Lebenslauf
des Geheimrats Dr. Oskar Hintrager", Afrikanischer Heimatkalender,
1982: 57-62.

197. ILIFFE, JOHN. "The Herero and Nama risings: South West Africa,
1904-1907". In Aspects of South African History, edited by G.
Kibodya, p. 95-111. Dar es Salaam: Institute of Education, University College, 1968.

The purpose of this paper, written by a prominent British historian,
is to summarise the accounts of the war of anti-colonial resistance
(1904-1907) given by Bley (no. 179) and Drechsler (no. 188), as well
as to compare the struggle for liberation from German rule in
Namibia to attempts made simultaneously by Tanzanian peoples in the
Maji-Maji rising. It argues that the long history of conflict between the Herero and the Nama for cattle, pasture and water was one
of the factors explaining why they failed to achieve the coordinated
action that the Ndebele and the Shona of Zimbabwe achieved in 1896
and the peoples of southern Tanzania achieved in 1905. It also notes
that the Herero and Nama were more formidable in terms of arms,
organisation, education and diplomacy than most other peoples of
tropical Africa, and that this might have been one of the reasons
why the Herero started the war before assuring themselves of the
support of the Nama.

198. KIENETZ, ALVIN. Nineteenth-century South West Africa as a German
settlement colony. University of Minnesota, 1975, 959 p. 12 tables,
35 figures, bibl.: 938-59. (PhD thesis).

This is an immensely detailed and heavily footnoted thesis, based on
a wide reading of contemporary sources dealing with settlement
policies in the first decade of German colonial rule (1884-1893).
Employing a historical-geographical approach, the thesis also explores in considerable depth the ecological basis for the settling of
agricultural communities in Namibia. An introductory chapter relates
the German colonialist arguments for overseas settlement to the
general phenomenon of nineteenth-century mass emigration from Europe.
It is followed by two chapters on the early "Europeanization" of
pre-colonial Namibia and its ecological effects. This part (p. 157-
331) is a contribution to Namibian historiography in its own right.
The rest of the thesis presents and analyses a wide range of contemporary statements about agricultural settlement possibilities, focusing
more on impressions, attitudes and plans than on activities. Among
the main issues to be discussed extensively are the two main strands
of agrarian settlement strategy, the small-holder communities and
large-scale stock farming. See also by the same author: "The demographic rationale for European settlement colonies in Africa: the
example of South-West Africa (Namibia) " Zambia Geographical Journal,
no. 33-34 1978-79: 17-29.

99. KÜLZ, WILHELM. Deutsch-Südafrika im 25.Jahre deutscher Schutzherrschaft. Skizzen und Beiträge und Geschichte Deutsch-Südafrikas.
Berlin: Süsserott, 1909, 375 p.

This is an attempt to write a serious contemporary history of German
colonial rule in Namibia, which should of course not be mistaken for
a general history of the territory or of its people. The first part
provides a detailed account of the establishment of German control
of various districts, reflecting the author's concern with local
administration. The section on economic history (p. 247-375)
describes the different sectors of the economy, mining corporations,
money and credit supply and communications. It is rather narrow
in scope, but can be used as a source for documenting the changes
which took place in settlement and economic strutures after the
German genocide. The author spent two years in Namibia advising the
colonial government on local administration, and was also involved
in setting up a society for the production of wool (see no. 349). He
was later to become a prominent member of the Weimar Cabinet 1926-
1927, and was the first chairman of the Liberal-Democratic Party
in East Germany after the Second World War. See also: Die Selbstverwaltung in Deutsch Südafrika (Berlin, 1909).

00. LENSSEN, H.E. Chronik von Deutsch-Südwestafrika. Eine kurz gefasste
Aufzählung geschichtlicher Ereignisse aus der Deutschen Kolonialzeit
von 1883 bis 1915. Windhoek: Verlag der SWA Wissenschaftlichen
Gesellschaft. 1966, 246 p.

A straightforward record of the main "events" in Namibia under German
rule, chronologically organised and seen through the eyes of a
German settler who also was involved in colonial administration. The
books contain bits and pieces of original information on German
administration, the establishment of companies, the arrival of settlers,
prices, the transport system, droughts, and the profitability of
farms. There are also some glimpses from the authors visit to
Ovamboland in 1905, commissioned by the German Governor. As there
is no index or systematic treatment of any subject, the book is
difficult to use as a source.

01. LEUTWEIN, THEODOR. Elf Jahre Gouverneur in Deutsch-Südwestafrika.
Berlin: Mittler, 1906, 589 p. Ca. 200 illus. (maps, photos,
sketches).

Written by the first German colonial Governor (1894-1904) shortly
after his replacement by the military commander von Trotha, this is
a vigorous defence of "the Leutwein system" and a classic text on
German Southwest-Africa. The author argues the case for cooperation
with the indigenous chiefs ("divide and rule"), and stresses that too
brutal repression is unprofitable for colonialism as a "business
venture". The colonial period is treated chronologically as well
as thematically, with the main emphasis on the military and administrative aspects of German rule. There are also two lengthy chapters
on the economy and biographical sketches of the leading African
personalities; and observations on a variety of related topics are
interspersed in the text. A large number of photos, maps and
drawings enhances the value of the book as a source. For a
critical discussion of the "Leutwein system", see, for example,

Helmut Bley (no. 179) and Horst Drechsler (no. 188).

LÜDERITZ, C.A., see no. 208.

202. MELBER, HENNING. "Das doppelte Vermächtnis der Geschichte. Nations-
werdung, Kolonisierungsprozess und deutsche Fremdherrschaft in
Namibia (ca. 1800-1914)". Diskurs, no. 6, 1982: 32-124. (Univ.
Bremen).

203. ------- Shadows of the past: the consequences of colonisation and
German colonial rule in Namibia. Paper presented to The International
Seminars on The Role of the Transnational Corporations in Namibia,
Washington, 1982. 28 p.

This seminal contribution by a prominent West German scholar is a
stimulating exposé of the main features of Namibian history from
c 1800 to the end of German colonial rule. The longer essay opens
with a perceptive discussion of pre-colonial societies and their
internal dynamics. This section is followed by a presentation of
pre-colonial European penetration, headed by missionaries, traders and
representatives of mining companies, arguing that their interventions
destroyed tendencies towards "state formation" and caused a stagnation of the social conditions. The sections on the establishment
of colonial rule and the development of the colonial economy after
the defeat of the Namibian resistance in 1907 offer an excellent
summary - as well as a critical discussion - of the scholarly works
covering this period. The author's main argument is that the German
colonial system prepared and created the structures of a racist
class society, which were afterwards perfected by the South African
regime and supplied with a specific ideology and doctrine of racial
rule. In this sense, the struggle for independence and liberation
is seen as a struggle against the colonial heritage of the German
past. The extensive list of references and the bibliography give a
good general introduction to the main body of literature. The paper
in English is essentially a shortened version of the essay. It
covers the same ground but is especially brief on the pre-colonial
period.

OTTO, ANTJE, see no. 206.

204. POOL, GERHARDUS. Die Herero-Opstand 1904-1907. Cape Town/Pretoria:
Hollandsch Afrikaansche Uitgevers Maatschappij, 1979, 311 p. 9 photos,
23 maps, bibl.: 290-99.

One of a small group of historical works on Namibia by Afrikaner
scholars, this is the published text of the author's MA thesis.
It is based on extensive research in the official and mission
archives in Windhoek, and provides a detailed narrative history
of the devastating German - Herero war of 1904-7, concentrating on
the main period of military conflict, January - October 1904. It
is principally a history of events, and as such stands in strong contrast to the more analytical history of Bley and the broad sweep
of Drechsler (see nos. 179, 188). The introductory chapter devotes
considerable attention to the economic background to the Herero

decision to rise against German rule. The author, a teacher in
Namibia (1962-74) before taking up a lectureship at the University
of Stellenbosch, is now researching a biography of Samuel Maharero.

205. RAUTENBERG, HULDA. Das alte Swakopmund, 1892-1919. Swakopmund zum
75. Geburtstag. Neumünster: Karl Wachholtz Verlag, 1967, 359 p.
5 maps, 30 photos, bibl.: 326-30. (Published by International
Lions Club, Swakopmund and Das Swakopmunder Museum).

This is a meticulously researched local history of Swakopmund under
German rule, based on archival material in Namibia as well as in
West Germany. It is by far the best local history produced in
Namibia to date, although the focus is mainly on the German traders,
German cultural institutions and the role of the port and railway
in supporting German economic interests. Within this framework,
the book offers a wealth of information and observations. Also
included are several appendices, such as a list of all registered
trade companies, rainfall statistics, population censuses and several
documents and primary sources. The text is supported by more than
500 references, a comprehensive bibliography and 30 photos.

REINHARD, WOLFGANG, see no. 219.

RUSCH, WALTER, see no. 206.

206. SCHOEDDER, EDDA, ANTJE OTTO and WALTER RUSCH. Lüderitzbucht - damals
und gestern. Windhoek: SWA Wissenschaftliche Gesellschaft, 1983,
186 p. 218 photos.

Published in conjunction with the 100th anniversary of the occupation
of Lüderitzbucht, this nostalgic pictorial review tells the story
of the town from the arrival of Lüdertiz, through the diamond rush
and into the 1930s. The fascinating pictures, selected by the
editors from the Lüderitz Museum, the National Archives and private
collections, are supplemented by articles and facsimile prints of
advertisements from local newspapers. There are special sections
concerned with the port, the fishing industry and local business,
but the main emphasis is on the social life of the German community.

207. SCHÜSSLER, WILHELM. Adolf Lüderitz: ein deutscher Kampf um Süd-
Afrika, 1883-1886: Geschichte des ersten Kolonialpioniers im
Zeitalter Bismarcks. Bremen: Schünemann, 1936. Maps, 15 illus.

208. LÜDERITZ, C.A. (ed.). Die Erschliessung von Deutsch-Südwest-Afrika:
Akten, Briefe und Denkschriften. Oldenburg: G. Stallings Verlag,
1945, 166 p.

Written in the context of Nazi attempts of reviving colonialism and
canonising "colonial pioneers", the book by Schüssler is a biography
of Adolf Lüderitz as well as a diplomatic history of the annexation of
Namibia. The diplomatic entanglements and German intrigues are
meticulously described, but as a nephew of Lüderitz, the author
carefully avoids mentioning facts such as the well-known "mile-fraud"
of Lüderitz in his treaty with the Nama at Bethanie. On the whole,
the negotiations with the Africans are poorly presented in comparison

with Anglo-German relations. The collection of documents is a most
welcome complement to the biography. It contains a wide range of
unabridged documents and letters, which include information on prices
and general economic conditions. There are also several other books
and essays concerned with Lüderitz, such as Meno Holst: Lüderitz
erkämpft Südwest (Berlin: Deutscher Verlag, 1941, 243 p.), but most
of them are merely hagiographic or purely fictional.

209. SCHWABE, KURD. Im deutschen Diamantenlande. Deutsch-Südwestafrika
von der Errichtung der deutschen Herrschaft bis zur Gegenwart (1884-
1910). Berlin: Mittler, 1910, 443 p. 100 photos.

This is a mixture of travel accounts, war memoirs and a general
description of the colonial economy, written by one of the best-known
German military leaders and settler spokesmen. The value of the
book as a source is strengthened by the large number of good quality
photos. There are separate chapters on the impact of the 1904-07
war on the commercial economy and the prospects for settlement, as
well as on trade and communications. The northern part of the country
is not given much attention, but the author notes that it constitutes
a major reservoir of "strong and intelligent labour" to be tapped.
For the personal reminiscences of Major Schwabe and accounts of the
wars, see also his Mit Schwert und Pflug in Deutsch - Südwestafrika.
Vier Kriegs- und Wanderjahre. (2. Aufl., Berlin: Mittler und Sohn,
1904, 514 p.), and Der Krieg in Deutsch Südwest-Afrika, 1904-1906
(Berlin: Weller, 1907, 440 p.).

210. SEITZ, THEODOR. Vom Aufstieg und Niederbruch deutscher Kolonialmacht,
Band 3: Die Gouverneursjahre in Südwestafrika. Karlsruhe: Müller,
1929, 144 p. 24 photos.

This is the third volume of the autobiography of one of the most prominent German colonial governors. He was the last German governor of
Namibia (1910-1915), after having served in a similar position in
the Cameroon, and was also president of the Deutsche Kolonialgesellschaft 1920-30. The first - and most interesting - part of the book
is mainly concerned with the military and civil administration of the
territory, but gives also some information on settler agriculture,
mining, communications and the credit system. There are also
superficial descriptions of the various population groups and a more
detailed chapter on the war with South Africa (1914/1915). The book
ends with a brief epilogue lamenting the loss of colonies following
"das Diktat von Versailles".

211. STALS, E.L.P. "Die aanraking tussen blankes en Ovambo's in
Suidwes-Afrika,1850-1915". Die Argiefjaarboek vir Suid-Afrikaanse
Geskiedenis 31, deel 2, 1968: 219-349. 4 photos, bibl.: 345-49.

This study, submitted as a PhD thesis to the University of Stellenbosch
in 1967, details European contact with Ovambo society from the
arrival of the first travellers from the south to the final conquest
of Ovamboland by the Portuguese and South African armies in 1915.
It is based mainly on German and South African colonial archives and
deals almost exclusively with contacts from the Namibian side.
It is thus complemented by Clarence-Smith's study of southwestern
Angola over the same period from Portuguese archival sources (see

no.124). In contrast to Clarence-Smith, Stals provides a detailed
descriptive account rather than an analysis of the process of
colonisation, but there is much valuable information as well as
specific commentary on the motivation of the principal interests
involved: travellers, traders, missionaries and the German colonial
administration. The final chapter gives one of the few accounts of
the early years of labour migration to be based on archival sources
(p. 321-44). The study also contains an extensive bibliography and
a guide to the archival sources.

212. STREITWOLF, KURT. Der Caprivizipfel. Berlin: Süsserott, 1911, 234
p. 38 photos, 5 maps.

Written by a leading military officer and colonial administrator,
this is primarily an account of an expedition in 1909 to establish
a German administrative presence. The emphasis is, not surprisingly,
on political relationships , but there is also descriptive detail
on economic and social conditions, as well as on the local ecology.
Kurt Streitwolf's material is deposited in the Federal military
archives in Freiburg (Bundes-Archiv-Militärarchiv), and includes a
collection of 500 photos. See also the biography of the author by
a South African historian (E.L.P. Stals. Kurt Streitwolf . Sy werk
in Suidwes-Afrika, 1899-1914. Johannesburg: Perskor, 1978, 142 p.).

213. SUDHOLT, GERT. Die deutsche Eingeborenenpolitik in Südwestafrika.
Von den Anfängen bis 1904. Hildesheim/New York: Georg Olms Verlag,
1975, 241 p. Bibl.: 195-202. (Historische Texte und Studien,
Band 1).

The modern historiography of German rule has been characterised by a
series of academic works which develop a critical examination of
colonialism and of the bloody suppression of Namibian peoples during
the 1903-07 war. The purpose of this study, however, is to produce
a scholarly revision of the "negative" picture of German rule in
Namibia under the Leutwein system from the "pacification" up to
1904. Although there are several attempts to refute both factual
evidence and the interpretations presented by Helmut Bley (no. 179)
and Horst Drechsler (no. 188), the author does not advance any coherent, alternative thesis. The book amounts to little more than
a somewhat rhapsodic endorsement of different aspects of German
"native policy". It argues that the idea behind the reserves was
to safeguard the interests of the "natives" and make it possible
for peoples to co-exist in the same territory; that the real cause
of the uprising was Herero "hate" and loss of pride; that the number
of Africans killed has been grossly exaggerated and that there are
no reasons whatsoever to apply the term "genocide". The study is
based on extensive research in the Windhoek Archives and in West
Germany, and the bibliography offers a useful guide to some of
the principal sources. The author was employed by Allgemeine Zeitung,
Windhoek, as a journalist in the period 1964-66.

214. UNITED KINGDOM. Report on the natives of South-West Africa and
their treatment by Germany. Prepared in the Administrator's
Office, Windhuk. London: HMSO, 1918, 212 p. (Cd. 9146).

Prepared as a contribution to the campaign against German colonialism, this is the often quoted "Blue Book" on the German ill-treatment of the African population in Namibia. The report provides a brief history of the "liberated" territory, focusing on German acquisitions of land, massacres of the civilian population, cattle confiscation, the extermination of the Herero and the "natives and the Criminal Law". A medical report on German methods of punishment (with photos) is also included as an appendix. The main value of the report lies in the excerpts from sworn affidavits from Namibians and extensive quotations from books and reports by German colonial officials and officers (Leutwein, Rohrbach, Dove, etc.). For an official German reply, see no. 187. Some of the statements in the "Blue Book" are summarised in Correspondence relating to the wishes of the natives of the German colonies as to their future government (London: HMSO, 1918, 59 p., Cd. 9210). See also Papers relating to certain trials in German South West Africa (London: HMSO, 1916, 50 p., Cd. 8371).

215. WALLENKAMPF, ARNOLD VALENTIN. The Herero rebellion in South West Africa, 1904-1906; a study in German colonialism. Los Angeles: University of California, 1969, 394 p. Bibl.: 373-83. (PhD thesis).

This well researched thesis was at the time the first comprehensive study of the Herero uprising to have been written in English, and provides a far more informative - although somewhat uneven - account than several later works (see, for instance, Bridgman no. 183). One of its chief merits is to make available in English the main findings of the scholarly German literature on the subject. The author has also made full use of the debates in the "Reichstag", which often contained quite frank discussions and critical remarks by the Social Democratic Party opposition. In terms of primary source material, a major weakness is that the author relies almost exclusively on the accounts by the German General Staff, the reports of army officers and German newspapers. The study is, however, far more than a narrative of military campaigns, and due attention is paid to a discussion of the fundamental reasons for Herero discontent, in particular exploitation by traders, rinderpest, loss of cattle in exchange for manufactured goods at high prices, land alienation and the influx of German settlers. It also stresses that to the Herero the German hold in Namibia did not appear unbreakable, and that the Germans were certainly not prepared to cope with a general insurrection. A major section of the thesis deals with the postwar situation, arguing that the handling of the Hereros was even more merciless than during the war, and that this cruelty, in terms of land and cattle expropriation, social control, forced labour and outright violence, was not perpetrated by soldiers in the field, but derived primarily from a policy decision by the Imperial Government. The study reproduces several "friendship and protection" treaties as an appendix, and there is a full bibliography.

216. WEBER, OTTO VON. Geschichte des Schutzgebietes Deutsch-Südwest-Afrika. Windhoek: SWA Wissenschaftliche Gesellschaft, 1979, 308 p. 24 photos.

The primary objective of this colonial narrative is to provide the

Germans in Namibia with a history of the territory under German rule.
The presentation draws mainly on the contemporary writings of administrators, settlers and missionaries such as C. von Francois, O. Hintrager,
von Bülow, Th. Leutwein, P. Rohrbach, K. Schwabe, H. Vedder and W.
Külz, supplemented with a few scholarly accounts of a more recent
origin. Given this apologetic framework and lack of understanding
of the Namibians as historical subjects, the book nevertheless has
some value as a chronicle of events and as a source of information
on colonial policy, including bits and pieces of interest for the
study of economic history. This revision of the 1971 edition (which
had been published by the author himself) has a very full index
(p. 238-64) and a number of photos.

217. WEINBERGER, GERDA. An den Quellen der Apartheid. Studien über
koloniale Ausbeutungs- und Herrschaftsmethoden in Südafrika und die
Zusammenarbeit des deutschen Imperialismus mit dem englischen
Imperialismus und den burischen Nationalisten (1902-1914). Berlin
(GDR): Akademie-Verlag, 1975, 217 p. Bibl.: 205-17. (Forschungen
zur Wirtschaftsgeschichte, vol 7).

Another well researched contribution from the East German marxist
school to the study of Southern Africa in the context of German
colonial history. One of the chapters is concerned with the German
suppression of the war of resistance and the British reaction to
it (ch. II, p. 51-95). Also discussed is the conflict between
hard-liners and more "enlightened" colonial officials over the merits
of extreme violence as against more "economic" methods of colonial
exploitation (ch. III, p. 96-133). In this regard, the author shows
that spokemen of the former school came to play an important role
as ideologists of the fascist colonial movement after World War I.

218. WITBOOI, HENDRIK. Die Dagboek van Hendrik Witbooi. Kaptein van
die Witbooi-Hottentotte. Bewerk na die oorspronklike Dokumente in
die Regeringsargief, Windhoek. Cape Town: The van Riebeek Society,
1929, 244 p. Maps.

219. ------- Afrika den Afrikanern ! Aufzeichnungen eines Nama-Häuptlings
aus der Zeit der deutschen Eroberung Südwestafrikas 1884 bis 1894.
(Berlin/Bonn: Dietz, 212 p. 18 photos. Edited by Wolfgang Reinhard).

This diary (or rather, copy-book of letters) is one of the very few
primary sources on early anti-colonial resistance in Namibia to have
been published. The collection of more than 100 notes and letters
by and to Hendrik Witbooi covers the period 1884-1894, and fell into
the hands of the German colonial regime during a raid on Witbooi's
headquarters in 1895. The extensive correspondence with other African
leaders and German colonial officials covers the confrontation with
the colonial intruders, Witbooi's struggle to remain independent
and sovereign leader of his people, the attempts to form concerted
actions contrary to the colonial myth of incessant internecine tribal
warfare, as well as Witbooi's strong religious beliefs and sense of
"divine mission". The diary was published in 1929 in its original
Cape Dutch version, with the letters arranged in chronological
order and a forword giving useful background information on the
project. (There is also a racist introduction in English, written
by the trader-farmer Gustav Voigts). This edition has recently

been complemented by the publication of a German translation by a
settler farmer, originally presented to Hermann Göring in the
1930s. Edited by Wolfgang Reinhard, who has also added a few more
documents and an introduction, the book is certainly not without
its weaknesses. The opportunity to revise the original translation has
not been fully used, several other Witbooi texts have been neglected,
racist and discriminatory terms of the colonial period are handled
uncritically and there is no attempt to provide a biographical
sketch of Hendrik Witbooi or to discuss his relevance to the present
struggle for independence. There is, consequently, still a need for
a more complete and carefully edited source edition as well as a
serious biographical study, a project which now has been embarked
upon by two West German scholars (Henning Melber and Werner Hillebrecht)

SEE ALSO:

1, 4, 16, 22, 24, 33, 34, 36, 52, 64, 68, 74, 81, 118, 119, 126,
137-8, chapter 4 a(160-76), chapter 6 a(317-49), 553, 622, 637,
711, 818, 856, 933.

5. UNDER SOUTH AFRICAN RULE

A. A trust betrayed (1915-1966)

220. BALLINGER, RONALD B. South-West Africa. The case against the union. Johannesburg: South African Institute of Race Relations, 1961, 56 p.

Written at the time of the first International Court of Justice deliberations over Namibia, this pamphlet outlines the legal and historical background to the international dispute from a liberal perspective. It points out that the overriding goal of South Africa has always been the incorporation of the territory, but that this course is likely to lead to isolation and conflict in an international situation where condemnation of racial discrimination and concern for dependent peoples are realities which have to be taken into account. The author was a senior lecturer, Department of History, University of Witwatersrand.

BARRON SMYTHE, L., see SMYTHE BARRON, L., no. 255.

221. BERTELSMANN, WERNER. Die deutsche Sprachgruppe Südwestafrikas in Politik und Recht seit 1915. Windhoek: SWA Wissenschaftliche Gesellschaft, 1979, 172 p. Bibl.: v-xvi.

This is a narrow and legalistic survey of the history of the German minority in Namibia since 1915, which is valuable chiefly as a compilation of facts on constitutional affairs, political parties, and the development of schools and other cultural institutions, including some information on the economic role of the German population. The author was a senior researcher at the University of South Africa when this treatise was written, and had previously lived in Namibia in 1952-1962 working for the Allgemeine Zeitung and the SWA Adminstration. The study was originally submitted as a dissertation at the University of Göttingen in 1970.

222. BLUMHAGEN, HUGO. Südwestafrika: einst und jetzt. Berlin: Reimer, 1934, 145 p. 21 tables, 27 photos.

223. ------- Entscheidungsjahre in Deutsch-Südwestafrika. Berlin: Reimer, 1939, 110 p. 15 tables, 35 photos.

These two books are representative products of the propaganda drive in the 1930s for the return of Germany's former colonies, written by an ex-official with 14 years' experience in the German colonial administration. They present a general overview of political, cultural and economic conditions in the territory, concentrating on the position of white, especially German, settlers. The first book covers the period from the First World War up to 1933, while the second focuses on the "fatal years" from 1934 to 1938. Both volumes contain detailed economic statistics. The author has also published a survey of the legal and constitutional development in the interwar period: Die Rechtsentwicklung in Deutsch-Südwestafrika unter dem Mandat der Südafrikanischen Union (Berlin: Duncker & Humblot, 1939, 127 p.).

224. BRADFORD, ROBERT LAROY. The origin and concession of the League of Nation's class 'C' mandate for South West Africa and fulfilment of of the sacred trust, 1919-1939. Yale University, 1965, 493 p. 13 tables, bibl.: 467-493. (PhD thesis).

225. ------- "Blacks to the wall". In South West Africa. A travesty of trust, edited by Ronald Segal and Ruth First, p. 87-101. London: Deutsch, 1967).

This is a well-researched thesis on Namibia in the interwar period, based mainly on the rich source material originating from the League of Nations as well as South African official documents. The first part of the study consists of an account of the deliberations at the Paris Peace Conference, concluding that South Africa right from the beginning interpreted the 'C' mandate as tantamount to annexation. It is followed by a close examination of important aspects of South African "native administration": vagrancy laws, pass requirements, forced labour, education, health care, land reserves, etc. There is also a separate chapter on the Bondelswarts uprising in 1922. The reports and minutes of the Permanent Mandates Commission show quite clearly that the great majority of the Commission members were of the opinion that South Africa did not fulfil her mandate responsibilities, but were unable to bring about significant changes in South African policy. The appendices contain a series of tables on contract labour, expenditure on health care and education, mortality rates, and the number of workers on farms, mines and railways, and are supplemented by an extensive bibliography. The contribution to South West Africa gives a brief summary of the main findings of the thesis, with the main emphasis on the living conditions of the black population.

226. BRAUM, ROBERT L. (ed.). Southwest Africa under mandate. Documents on the administration of the former German protectorate of Southwest Africa by the Union of South Africa under mandate of the League of Nations, 1919-1929. Salisbury, North Carolina: Documentary Publications, 1976, 241 p.

39 original documents are collected in this volume, which is of great
importance for the study of Namibian economic and political history
in the 1920s. The collection includes several unpublished US consular reports, press reports (Cape Times, Cape Argus) as well as
documents such as the first Report of the SWA Administrator (1919),
the reports of the commission appointed to advise on the future form
of government (1921), a lengthy survey of mineral resources and the
mining industry (1922) and the South West Africa Constitutional Bill
(1925). This volume complements a similar collection of documents
(Native Uprisings in South West Africa), see no. 231.

227. BUNTING, BRIAN. Namibia between the two wars: South Africa, the
mandate and the League of Nations. Paper presented to the Namibia
International Conference, Brussels, 1972, 13 p.

This is a brief conference paper which sets out to survey the interwar period, demonstrating how Namibia was in most respects administered by South Africa as a province. The author, a South African
writer and a leading member of the South African Communist Party
in exile, gives a straightforward account of the major instruments
of suppression and exploitation: the land theft, the migratory
labour system, the colour bar and the pass laws. He also points
out - citing official estimates - that the gaps between the population groups in the fields of education, wages and health were even
more extreme than in South Africa itself.

228. CROWELL, WILLIAM U. The evolution of South African control over
South West Africa. St. Johns University, New York, 1975, 433 p.
Bibl.: 393-433. (PhD thesis).

A descriptive and very uneven account of Namibia under South African
rule, touching upon a wide range of topics without any serious attempt
to weave together the political, social, economic and diplomatic
factors to explain the historical evolution of South African control.
The chapters concerned with Namibia as an international issue (the
South African acquisition of the territory, the Mandate and the UN/
South African dispute) contain no new material. There is however,
quite a useful chapter on "native affairs" and land settlement in
the interwar period, as well as a final chapter on "indigenous
political participation" which offers some insight into the early
years of organised struggle for independence. There is also a
brief discussion of the shift in the official South African policy
in the mid-seventies, leading the author to conclude that "it seems
inconceivable that South Africa would allow the emergence of a
Namibia which is free of its control".

229. D´AMATO, ANTHONY A. "The bantustan proposals for South-West Africa".
The Journal of Modern African Studies, 4, no. 2, 1966: 177-92.

This article, written by a US political scientist, examines the claims
made by South Africa that the bantustan proposals for Namibia will
eliminate discrimination through a "separation of races". The author
doubts that the outside world will regard the proposals as reasonable
and fair, and supports this argument by pointing to the inequitable
distribution of land and the fact that the African majority is not

given any voice in the central government which vests in itself
ownership of all mineral rights and unallocated land.

230. DAVEY, ARTHUR M. The Bondelzwarts affair: a study in the reper-
cussions, 1922-1959. Pretoria: University of South Africa, 1961,
28 p. (Communications of the University of South Africa, C 31).

This pamphlet by a South African historian is an attempt to examine
the reactions to the "Bondelzwarts affair" in the South African
Parliament, in the press, in the League of Nations and in England
and the US. It does not, however, offer new information or insights on the revolt and the massacre. In the author's own opinion,
the South African Administrator was justified in resorting to force,
but it is argued in retrospect that the "affair" was a grave setback
to South Africa because of the unfavourable impression which was
created abroad.

231. DEWALDT, FRANZ (ed.). Native uprisings in Southwest Africa. Documents on the armed uprising of the Bondelswart tribe (1922) and the
bloodless revolt of the Rehoboth Bastards (1925) in ex-German South-
West Africa under mandate. Salisbury, North Carolina: Documentary
Publications, 1976, 243 p.

This collection of documents, which complements a similar collection
of source material on economic conditions in the interwar period
(no. 226), is mainly concerned with the Bondelswarts rebellion
of 1922. Among the documents reproduced are several contemporary
US consular reports, press clippings, newspaper editorials, official
statements, the Report of the SWA Administrator (1921, 1922) as well as
the Report of the Administrator on the Bondelswarts Rising (1922),
and the Report of the Commission appointed to Enquire into the
Rebellion of the Bondelzwarts (1923).

232. DUNDAS, CHARLES (SIR). South-West Africa: the factual background.
Johannesburg: The South African Institute of International Affairs,
1946, 53 p.

Written by a former Governor of Uganda, this pamphlet was at the time
one of the best available surveys of political, financial and
economic conditions in Namibia. It provides a summary of important
official documents, annual reports of the SWA Administrator and
South African official yearbooks, and discusses in particular the
future relationship between the Union and the mandated territory.
It argues that economically Namibia had been able to maintain itself only by the generosity of South Africa, but at the same time
it emphasizes that the Territory is strategically important for
South Africa and economically of considerable value "as affording
an outlet for enterprise and settlement, as also a market for Union
manufactures".

233. ENGEL, LOTHAR. Kolonialismus und Nationalismus im deutschen Pro-
testantismus in Namibia 1907-1945. Beiträge zur Geschichte der
deutschen evangelischen Mission und Kirche im ehemaligen Kolonial-
und Mandatsgebiet Südwestafrika. Bern: Herbert Lang/Frankfurt:

Peter Lang, 1976, 612 p. Bibl.: 567-609. (Studien zur inter-
kulturellen Geschichte des Christentums, band 7).

Based on extensive archival research in Namibia and West Germany, this
is an exceptionally rich study of the role of the German protestant
church in Namibia. The author, a West German theologian and church
historian, has also written a major study of the Rhenish Missionary
Society from 1842 to 1907 (no. 192). He examines critically the
legitimising functions of the church vis-à-vis German national
and colonial interests in the period after the war of anti-colonial
resistance, adopting the standpoint that there can be no apolitical
theology. There is also a wealth of material of interest for a
general historical study of the interwar period, not least with
regard to the political and cultural role of the German community.
Special attention is paid to the attitudes of the churches and
individual clergymen such as Heinrich Vedder, and the widespread
sympathy with fascism and the German Nazi party is well documented.
This study is much more than a narrow church history, and the extensive bibliography and archival guide are useful tools for all students of Namibian history in the 1907-1945 period. For a brief
discussion in English of some of the major themes of the book,
especially in the 1920s, see "The Mission and the Political Awakening
of the Namibians After the First World War", in Lutheran Churches -
Salt or Mirror of Society?, edited by V. Duchrow, p. 130-44. (Geneva:
Lutheran World Federation, 1977).

234. FREISLICH, RICHARD. The last tribal war. A history of the Bondelswart uprising which took place in South West Africa in 1922. Cape
Town: Struik, 1964, 117 p. 8 photos.

A narrative account of the military campaign during the suppression
of the Bondelswart uprising, based on official reports and the private
papers of Colonel H. Prinsloo. The appendix (p. 87-117) reproduces
the 1922 report by Colonel Prinsloo, the Chief of Police. For a more
scholarly work, set in a broader historical perspective, see Lewis
(no. 243).

235. FREYER, E.P.W. Chronik von Otavi und Umgebung, 1906-66. Windhoek:
SWA Wissenschaftliche Gesellschaft, 1966, 36 p. Photos.

A brief narrative town history, with scattered information on the
growth of local businesses and farms, including a list, in date
order, of the foundation of all "shops, workshops and factories in
Otavi".

236. GAERDES, FRITZ. Geschichte und Entwicklung der Stadt Okahandja.
Windhoek: SWA Wissenschaftliche Gesellschaft, 1970, 86 p. 26
photos, 1 map, 3 tables. (In Afrikaans: Geskiedenis en Ontwikkeling
van die Stad Okahandja. Windhoek, SWA Wetenskaplike Vereniging,
1971, 69 p.).

This unambitious town history of Okahandja is primarily a brief chronicle of events from 1800 to 1970. The focal points of the booklet
are the history of the European population, education and the role
of churches, but there are also bits and pieces of information

on economic development, rainfall, drought and foot-and-mouth disease,
establishment of new businesses, etc. For a brief biography of the
author, as well as a list of his prolific writings (mainly natural
sciences, zoology and education), see Impulse. Festschrift zum 80.
Geburtstag von Fritz Gaerdes, Okahandja, Südwestafrika (Basel: Basler
Afrika Bibliographien, 1972,195 p.).

237. GOTTSCHALK, KEITH. "South Africa in Namibia, 1915-1980". In Perspectives on Namibia: past and present, edited by Christopher
Saunders, p. 69-82. (Cape Town: University of Cape Town, Centre
for African Studies, 1983).

This is the text of one in a series of lectures on Namibia given
at the Centre for African Studies during August 1982. In fact it
provides a concise, scholarly synopsis of the author's major
research project on South African colonialism in Namibia, for which
he is registered for a doctoral thesis at the University of Cape
Town. Ranging over the whole period of South African rule and
drawing on a wide range of historical instances and sources, the
paper analyses the general strategy of the colonial state, its
political economy, land theft and labour repression, and finally
Namibian resistance and South African "counter-revolutionary"
strategy. The essay is also reprinted in Seminar on Namibian history,
p. 78-96 (Windhoek: Namibian Review Publications, 1983).

238. HAILEY, WILLIAM MALCOLM (LORD). "South West Africa". African Affairs,
no. 183, 1947: 77-86.

This is a brief account of Namibia in the immediate aftermath of
the Second World War, written in the classic tradition of British
colonialism by a well-informed author with long colonial administrative experience. The article is based on a visit in 1946 to study
"native policies". The author makes the point that the philosophy
of the Europeans has many affinities with that of Europeans in South
Africa itself, and that it is not contemplated that the Africans
shall have any direct share in the government of the country. He
considers that although limited economic growth has taken place,
educational and medical facilities are sadly deficient. "Paternal
rule" in Ovamboland receives some favourable comments, but the author
remarks that "a generation may arise which may ask for a type of
justice different from that administered by the tribal organisation,
..., for some system which could be a more definite preparation
for the management of their own affairs". The long original report,
of which this article is a summary, contains much more factual
detail on living conditions. It can be consulted as a manuscript in
Rhodes House, Oxford (A survey of Native Affairs in South West Africa,
MS., 1946, 133 p.). See also the author's An African Survey (Oxford
U.P., 1956, 1676 p.), which has several references to Namibia.

239. HILDEBRAND, KLAUS. Vom Reich zum Weltreich. Hitler, NSDAP und
Koloniale Frage. München: Wilhelm Fink Verlag, 1969, 955 p.
Bibl.: 777-843.

Although mainly concerned with the "colonial question" and the rise
of fascism in Germany, this massive and immensely detailed study is

also a fascinating account of the role played in the campaign for
"Lebensraum" by propagandists with their background in Namibia
(Rohrbach, Blumhagen, Lindequist, Seitz etc.). There are also
numerous references to publications on the colonies which appeared
in Germany in the interwar period, and the importance attached to
Namibia is also reflected in the comprehensive bibliography.

HIRSEKORN, HANS B.K., see no. 264.

JONES, J.D. RHEINALLT, see RHEINALLT JONES, no. 250-1.

40. KILJUNEN, MARJA-LIISA. South African colonialism in Namibia. From
segregation to "ethnic democracy". University of Sussex, 1977, 61 p.
(MA thesis).

This brief dissertation examines South African colonial rule in
Namibia, from the segregationist phase through the introduction of
apartheid to the system of ethnic fragmentation and bantustans
following the Odendaal Commission. It summarises the main features
of the land theft, labour repression and legal apparatus up to the
early 1970s, but it adds little to the general literature and lacks
a proper discussion of the forces behind the changes in colonial
strategy.

41. KÜHNE, HORST. Faschistische Kolonialideologie und zweiter Weltkrieg.
Berlin (GDR): Dietz Verlag, 1982, 227 p. Bibl.: 201-21. (Dissertation, Institut für Gesellschaftswissenschaften beim Zentralkomitee der Sozialistischen Einheitspartei Deutschlands).

A rather simplistic and dogmatic academic work, mainly concerned with
the relationship between colonial propaganda and Nazi ideology. It
does, however, contain a descriptive account of Nazi activities in
Namibia in the 1930s ("Die Organisierung der nazistischen Kolonial -
propaganda in den Kolonien- dargestellt am Beispiel Südwestafrikas",
p. 119-145). See also "Die fünfte Kolonne des faschistischen deutschen
Imperialismus in Südwestafrika, 1933-39", Zeitschrift für Geschichts-
wissenschaft, 8, no. 4, 1960: 765-90.

42. LAWRIE, GORDON. "New light on South West Africa. Some extracts from
and comments on the Odendaal report". African Studies, 23, nos.
1-2, 1963: 1-15.

This is in the main a straightforward summary of the voluminous
Odendaal Report, drawing the ordinary reader's attention to some of
the main findings and recommendations. There is also a supplementary section dealing with the South African government's decisions on
the report. The author has added some critical comments of his
own, noting, inter alia, that the most important recommendations -
"Native homelands" and the relations with South Africa - are controversial political matters of international concern, and that they
may exacerbate rather than modify criticism at the UN. The author
was at the time director of the South African Institute of International Affairs.

243. LEWIS, GAVIN L.M. <u>The Bondelswarts rebellion of 1922</u>. Grahamstown: Rhodes University, 1977, 248 p. Bibl.: 235-40. (MA thesis).

This is a thoroughly researched study of the Bondelswarts rebellion and "native policies" in the early years of South African rule. The theoretical perspective is less developed, but the thesis benefits from extensive and careful use of the primary source material, such as the minutes of evidence and the various drafts prepared by the commission of inquiry, documents in the Transvaal Archives, the Windhoek Archives and the Prime Minister's Office. The author was also in a position to do a certain amount of fieldwork, and among his informants are several Bondelswarts with excellent memories for detail and a deep sense of grievance at the losses suffered under German and South African rule. The first part of the thesis is essentially a descriptive account of the events leading up to the rebellion, the rebellion itself and its bloody suppression, including a detailed discussion of the conflict between liberal and die-hard conservative representatives serving on the Native Affairs Commission. The second part consists of an assessment of the evidence, concluding that the Bondelswarts originally had held great hopes for the redress of their loss of land and independence under German rule, but that disillusionment, poverty, harsh treatment at the hands of European settlers, heavy taxes and further erosion of their economic independence led to the decision to fight rather than to surrender to the claims of the South African Administration.

244. LOUIS, WM. ROGER. "The South West African origins of the 'sacred trust', 1914-1919". In <u>South West Africa: A travesty of trust</u>, edited by Ronald Segal and Ruth First, p. 54-86. London: Deutsch, 1967. (Also published in <u>African Affairs</u>, 66, no. 262, (January) 1967: 20-39).

Partly based on the opening of the British official records of the peace-making at Versailles, this essay sets out to re-examine the origins of the South West Africa mandate. The main conclusions are that up to the end of the war it was generally assumed - in Britain as well as in South Africa - that the future of the German colony lay in annexation to the Union and that, despite its classification as a Mandate, South Africa was from the outset determined not to accept any external interference of importance. See also by the same author <u>Great Britain and Germany's lost Colonies, 1914-1919</u> (Oxford U.P., 1967, 168 p.).

245. NGAVIRUE, ZEDEKIA. <u>Political parties and interest groups in South West Africa: a study of plural societies</u>. Oxford: St. Antony's College, 1972, 424 p. 21 photos, bibl.: 414-24. (PhD thesis).

The aim of this thesis is to investigate the historical origins and the socio-economic, cultural and ideological bases of political parties and interest groups in Namibia. The research is based on extensive archival work, especially in German archives, and the appendices contain several important political documents. There are also an extensive bibliography and a number of tables and photos. The thesis is broad in historical scope, and discusses the ways in which different groups of people have contested economic and political power for more than a century. The author argues that ethnicity was never the sole causal factor, but interacted with political and economic forces. In his historical exposition he nevertheless sets out to show that the main conflict was between the Nama and the Herero in the pre-colonial period, between the Germans and the Herero, and the Nama in the years up to 1907, between German and South African whites in the interwar period, and between blacks and whites after 1945. The resurgence of Namibian nationalism after 1945 is described in some detail, partly based on the author's personal experience as a SWANU leader. This part of the thesis is characterised by slander and personal rivalry rather than by analysis and critical distance to the material. The author, who was chairman of the SWANU External Council (1965-68), returned to Namibia in the late 1970s and is now Deputy Chairman of Rössing Uranium Ltd.

6. NGAVIRUE, ZEDEKIA. "Economic competition between the Germans and the South Africans in Namibia". In Seminar on Namibian history, edited by Kenneth Abrahams, p. 97-118. Windhoek: Namibian Review Publications, 1983.

Based on his PhD thesis (see no. 245), the author's contribution to the collection of essays on Namibian history is mainly concerned with the efforts of the German community to recover lost ground in the interwar period. He makes the point that the policies of the South African administration favoured the economic struggle of the Afrikaners, and that the mandate administration used its political power to modify the land, minerals and banking concessions which had been acquired during the German colonial period. The decline in German economic predominance is well documented, and the author describes the subsequent political attempts by the German community to counter the process of incorporation into the Union of South Africa.

7. OLIVIER, MATTHEUS J. Inboorlingsbeleid en administrasie in Suidwes-Afrika. University of Stellenbosch, 1961, 444 p. (PhD thesis).

This is one of a handful of South African theses, mainly in Afrikaans, which are invaluable to outside researchers for their factual detail and their access, sometimes privileged, to official and archival sources. The author, a Bantu Affairs administrator in northern Namibia for a period during the 1950s, presents an orthodox but exhaustively researched history of "native administration" in Namibia, taking his account up to near the date of writing. Unpublished official records are not only extensively used but quoted at length in the text, providing a rare primary resource on official policy-making and action. There is also much economic information on peasant agriculture and labour migration.

8. PEARSON, PATRICK. "The Rehoboth rebellion". In Working papers in Southern African studies, vol. 2, edited by P. Bonner, p. 31-51. Johannesburg: Ravan Press, 1981.

While the Rehoboth rebellion in 1925 has traditionally been described as a conflict between the Rehoboth rebels and the South African

authorities, this perceptive working paper, written by a South African
anthropologist,contends that there were strong elements of intra-
community conflict and class struggle apparent in the rebellion.
This claim is convincingly supported by an examination of the growing
poverty and increasingly uneven distribution of wealth on the one
hand, and a corrupt and cabalistic ruling Rehoboth Council, collaborating with the colonial power, on the other. The article is
based on research conducted for an MA thesis, at the University of
Witwatersrand.

249. PIRIO, GREGORY A. The role of Garveyism in the making of the Southern
African working classes and Namibian nationalism. University of
California, 1982, 43 p.

Drawing on the records of Marcus Garvey's Universal Negro Improvement
Association as well as local administrative archives, this paper
explores a little known episode in the early history of black
nationalism in Namibia. The author, who is Senior Editor, Marcus
Garvey Papers, documents how in the early 1920s U.N.I.A. activists
established local branches in Lüderitz as well as Windhoek and other
places in central Namibia. The ideology of the movement was built
on the notion of "Negro consciousness" and the slogan "Africa for
the Africans". As in Cape Town, the interconnectedness of U.N.I.A.
and the trade union Industrial and Commercial Workers Union (I.C.U.)
was complete in the Lüderitz division, which drew its members mainly
from the dockers. The U.N.I.A. parent body went so far as to request
the League of Nations to hand the territory over to the African
people, inspired by the experience of the black republic of Liberia.
The paper was originally presented to the Joint Committee on African
Studies Conference on South Africa in the Contemporary Study of Race,
Class and Nationalism in 1982.

PRITCHARD, S.M., see no. 256.

250. RHEINALLT JONES, J.D. The future of South-West Africa. Johannesburg:
South African Institute of Race Relations, 1946, 30 p.

251. ------- The administration of South West Africa. Welfare of the
indigenous population. Johannesburg: South African Institute of
Race Relations, 1952, 19 p. (Also published in Race Relations Journal,
19, no. 7, 1952: 3-21).

Based on official documents, the proceedings of the Permanent Mandates
Commission and reports from the International Labour Organisation,
the first of these two booklets gives some factual background to
the debate on the incorporation of the territory as a province of
South Africa. The author argues that there are no legal obstacles
to the incorporation, but that it might be desirable for the "non-
European" population to be protected by guarantees on matters such
as land allocation, political representation, freedom of movement
and equality of economic opportunity. The 1952 publication is an
important contemporary source highlighting the main features of the
social and economic conditions for the African population in Namibia
in the late 1940s and early 1950s. There is detailed information
on agriculture in the reserves, distribution of land, health conditions, education, employment and wages for farm labourers, industrial

workers and domestic servants. The pamphlet clearly benefits from
a close examination of the spate of official reports in the late
1940s, in particular reports on long-term agricultural policy (1945),
the minimum area of farms (1946), health (1946) and native labourers
(1945-48). J.D. Rheinallt Jones was director of the South African
Institute of Race Relations when the booklets were written.

52. SCOTT, MICHAEL. The orphans' heritage: the story of the South West
African mandate, London: The Africa Bureau, 1958, 24 p.

53. ------- A time to speak. London: Faber & Faber, 1958, 365 p.

Written by one of the first and most courageous champions of Namibian
self-determination, now recently deceased, this pamphlet presents a
lucid and eloquent short history of the colonisation and brutal repression of the people of Namibia under German and South African
rule. International responsibility for ending South African oppression is here the author's foremost concern. (See also no. 274.)
The autobiography describes the author's activities at the UN for
the rights of the Namibian people, starting with the campaign for the
Herero in 1946 (p. 219-68). It also contains several statements
and petitions and appendices. The collection of Michael Scott's
papers is deposited at Rhodes House, Oxford, and is currently being
organised.

54. SIMONS, H.J. "Techniques of domination: South Africa's colonialism".
In South West Africa: A travesty of trust, edited by Ronald Segal
and Ruth First, p. 103-17. London: Deutsch, 1967.

Written by a prominent South African socialist and scholar in exile,
this article examines the ways in which all South Africa's varieties
of discrimination are applied to its colony in an accentuated form.
It is argued that Namibia has been absorbed into South Africa's own
colonial structure, that the Africans have been subjected to increased
direct control from Pretoria since 1949 and that the attempt to
revive tribalism and underpin tribal leaders - while at the same
time suppressing the national liberation movement - is used as a
technique of domination.

55. SMYTHE BARRON, L. (ed.). The Nazis in Africa. Salisbury, North
Carolina: Documentary Publications, 1978, 207 p. (Lost Documents
on the Third Reich, vol. 3).

This collection of fifty documents from unpublished US diplomatic
files sheds light on the extensive efforts by the German Nazi party
to extend their influence into the former German empire in Africa.
The majority of the documents are concerned with Namibia, where
thousands of settlers retained close economic, social and cultural
ties with their "fatherland". Some of the diplomatic documents
deal with the general development in the territory in the 1930s,
and they are supplemented with contemporary reports from the South
African press (The Star, Cape Times). There is also a well organised
index.

256. SOUTH AFRICA (UNION). Report on tour to Ovamboland by Major S.M.
Pritchard. Pretoria: Government Printer, 1915, 22 p. (U.G. -1915).

One of the first official descriptions of Ovamboland in English, this
brief report was written by a senior South African "native affairs"
official shortly after the surrender of the German troops in 1915.
The visit was undertaken to ensure the subordination of the chiefs
to South African authority, and to explore how to organise the
supply of labour to the railways, mines and other industries. The
report describes the appalling living conditions during a period of
total famine with thousands dying of starvation, and hopes that
economic pressure and deprivation, together with encouragement from
chiefs and missionaries, would result in large numbers leaving
the area in search of employment. Major Pritchard also offers his
personal observations on the political situation in the north, praising
the activities of the missionaries and describing "Mandume and his
people (as) real savages". The conclusion is that famine, political
upheavals and the attacks of Portuguese forces gave South Africa
a unique opportunity for "establishing a political administration in
a country in which, in other circumstances, resistance to authority
might with reason have been anticipated".

257. SOUTH AFRICA (UNION). Official yearbook of the Union of South Africa
and of Basutoland, Bechuanaland Protectorate and Swaziland. Pretoria:
Government Printer, 1917 (vol. 1) - 1960 (vol. 30).

Usually in the range of 700-1200 pages long, this is an important
historial reference work with a wide range of official information.
Each volume contains a separate chapter on Namibia (40-60 pages),
providing a review of government activities and a wealth of statistical material on agriculture, mining, fisheries, industry, transport,
prices, labour, health, social conditions and other subjects.

258. SOUTH AFRICA (UNION). Report presented by the Government of the Union
of South Africa to the Council of the League of Nations concerning
the administration of South West Africa for the year 19--. Pretoria:
Government Printer, 1918-1939, 1946.

These annual reports are the closest one gets to traditional
colonial reports after the South African takeover, and like their
counterparts prepared by colonial governments they contain invaluable
factual material. They also serve as a source for analysing the
image which the South African government sought to present of its
administration to the outside world. The reports cover a wide range
of subjects: legislation, international relations, consitutional
affairs, judicial and administrative organisation, police and defence, demographic statistics, public finance and taxation, trade
statistics, agriculture, land settlement and land tenure, mining,
"native affairs" and "native labour", education, missions, public
health, railways and various departmental activities. The length
varies from 14 p. (1919) to 240 p. (1939), and the text is usually
supplemented with a considerable number of photos. The large amount
of detailed statistics on social and economic conditions make the
reports an indispensable tool for research into the interwar
period, but they have yet to be fully utilised by historians. The
reports are available in several libraries, as well as on microfilm

(New York, Andronicus Publ., 1972). Before 1928 they were published under slightly different titles: Report of the Administrator of South West Africa for the Year (up to 1924), Report of the Government of the Union of South Africa on South-West Africa for the Year (up to 1927). For a discussion of the reports in the League of Nations, see Permanent Mandates Commission. Minutes of the ... session, held at Geneva, ... to ... (Geneva: League of Nations, 1921-39).

59. SOUTH AFRICA (UNION). Interim and final reports of the commission appointed to enquire into the question of the future form of government in the South-West African protectorate. Cape Town: Cape Times/ Government Printer, 1921, 12 p. (U.G. 24-21).

This is the brief report of a commission appointed in 1920 to enquire into the form of Government for the newly acquired territory, recommending that Namibia should move towards representative government as the fifth province of South Africa. It concentrates mainly on the "German problem", and warns against full representation until more "British males of European descents" had moved into Namibia in order to balance the predominantly German white population. The report is reproduced in Braum (no. 226).

60. SOUTH AFRICA (UNION). Report of the Administrator on the Bondelzwarts rising. Cape Town: Cape Times/Government Printer, 1922, 21 p. (U.G. 30-22).

61. ------- Report of the commission appointed to enquire into the rebellion of the Bondelzwarts. Cape Town: Cape Times/Government Printer, 1923, 33 p. (U.G. 16-23).

These two documents are important sources for the study of the Bondelwarts rebellion and South African "native policies" in the early 1920s. The first report was hastily drawn up by the Administrator, G.H. Hofmeyr, and includes an official account of the military operation. The document presents the "facts" as seen by the Administrator himself, arguing that the grievances were unjustified, that the administration exercised great patience, that the revolt was only a part of a widespread plot among blacks in the territory and that it was necessary "to inflict a severe and lasting lesson" on the Bondelswarts. The report of the Native Affairs Commission is a more balanced document, which covers all the major grievances and offers some critical remarks on the policies of the administration. G.L.M. Lewis's thesis (no. 243) reveals that the drafts of the report contained harsher criticism, but that the two liberal members (A.W. Roberts and C.T. Loram) were opposed by the reactionary/racist Grenadier-General L.A.S. Lemmer. Both documents are reproduced in Dewaldt, Franz (ed.): Native Uprisings in Southwest Africa (no. 231). See also a brief comment by the Permanent Mandates Commission: Report on the Bondelzwarts Rebellion (Geneva: League of Nations, 1923, 7 p.).

62. SOUTH AFRICA (UNION). Report of the Rehoboth commission. Cape Town: Cape Times/Government Printer, 1927, 309 p. Bibl.: 108-11. (U.G. 41-26).

This is an enquiry into some of the issues - notably boundaries,
land alienation and legal rights - which caused unrest in the
Rehoboth Gebiet in the 1920s. Its chief value is as a compilation
of a large amount of documents, letters, proclamations, statements
and interviews, as well as a complete record of evidence from the
sittings of the commission. Among the historical documents are minutes
from the Captains Meeting in 1858, the Law Book of 1871 and 1874, the
"Treaty of Protection and Friendship" with the Germans, excerpts from
the Witbooi diary (nos. 218, 219), and the South African proclamation
of 1923. The sole commissioner, Jacob de Villiers (a Judge of Appeal
of South Africa Supreme Court) deals in his report mainly with the
legal issues involved, but offers also some details on land alienation,
trade licenses, taxation and other matters of importance to a study
of economic history. One of his main recommendations is a prohibition
on further land alienation to Europeans.

263. SOUTH AFRICA (UNION). Report of the South West Africa commission.
Pretoria: Government Printer, 1936, 104 p. (U.G. 26-1936).

264. HIRSEKORN, HANS B.K. (ed.). Comments on the report of the South West
Africa commission. Windhoek, 1937, 112 p.

The report of the 1936 Commission reflected the growing dissatisfaction,
mainly of the local settlers, with the existing form of government in
the mid-1930s. The Commission was set up to enquire into the reasons
for this state of affairs and to consider changes in the structure
of the government. The report acknowledged that the white ranchers
suffered economically from the protection afforded to their counterparts in South Africa itself, and recommended that more financial
support should be given to the Territory. It also proposed that more
active steps be taken "for the development of the Non-European races
from their present backward condition" in order to avoid unrest in
the central and southern parts of the country. The report dealt
extensively with the German community and the Nazi influence, and
concluded that as long as the Germans were "subject to external
dictation", settler unity and democratic participation would be impossible. It recommended that no further automatic naturalisation
of Germans take place in the future. As a general conclusion the
Commission supported the idea of further incorporation into South
Africa, and claimed that there was no legal obstacle to administering
the Territory as a province of South Africa. The Comments on the Report
is a collection of documents prepared for the Permanent Mandates
Commission of the League of Nations, and submitted by H.B.K. Hirsekorn
on behalf of the German population. The major part consists of a
lengthy statement by 6 members of the Legislative Assembly, arguing
against the pro-incorporation resolution passed by a majority of
the Assembly. The report is mainly concerned with legal issues,
naturalisation and the position of the German language, but it also
presents a critique of South African economic policy, especially
on taxation and the transfer of surplus to the Union.

265. SOUTH AFRICA (UNION). South West Africa and the Union of South Africa:
the history of a mandate. New York: South Africa Government Information Office, 1946, 108 p. Photos.

Presented as "a factual and objective introduction", this document was
published in the US in propagandist support of the South African
government's diplomatic offensive to hustle the newly created UN to
allow it to incorporate Namibia formally into its own territory.
Lavishly illustrated and with a substantial text, which draws heavily
on the works of Vedder (see no. 157), its principal themes – endemic
tribal warfare in pre-colonial Namibia, German brutality, South African
economic benevolence and political liberality, and support from
tribal leaders – set the pattern for a series of similar publications in
later years. It includes the official account, with selected statements by tribal officials on the South African payroll, of the
notorious "referendum" in 1946 which inspired Rev. Michael Scott's
devastating exposure of South African oppression and deception (see
nos. 252, 253, 274).

66. SOUTH AFRICA (REPUBLIC). Report of the commission of enquiry into
South West Africa affairs, 1962–1963/Verslag van die kommisie van
ondersoek na aangeleenthede van Suidwes-Afrika, 1962–1963. Pretoria/
Cape Town: Government Printer, 1964. 558 p. 148 tables, 64 maps
and figures, bibl.: 553–58. (R.P. No. 12/64).

67. ------- Memorandum. Decisions by the Government on the recommendations
of the Commission of enquiry into South West Africa affairs. Pretoria/
Cape Town: Government Printer, 15 p. (W.P.H- '64).

68. ------- South West Africa: a five year plan for the development of
the native areas. Pretoria: Department of Bantu Administration
and Development, 1965, 196 p.

69. ------- Memorandum. Decisions by the Government on the financial and
administrative relations between the Republic and South West Africa.
Pretoria/Cape Town: Government Printer, 1968(?), 28 p.

70. ------- Explanatory memorandum explaining the background and the objects
of the Development of Self-Government for Native Nations in South-West
Africa Bill, 1968. Pretoria, 1968.

Taken together, these five important documents give a coherent and
illuminating picture of the official aims of apartheid policy in
Namibia, as well as of the increased incorporation of Namibia into
South Africa in the 1960s. The Commission of Enquiry (known as the
Odendaal Commission after its chairman) was appointed in 1962 to
submit a report, within the context of "what has already been planned
and put into practice", on the development of the "native territories".
The report is essentially a studied attempt to prepare a rationale for
further extension of the system of apartheid in the territory, excluding
any other alternatives than "separate development" and the setting
up of bantustans (or "homelands"). This massive report serves also
as a basic reference work with its wealth of official and detailed
information on administration, the economy (African agriculture) and
social conditions. In its 1964 Memorandum, the Government accepts
the Report in   broad principle, and outlines some of the decisions
regarding projects (for instance water supply and electricity) to be
undertaken immediately. At the same time it was decided to postpone
the implementation of the system of "self-governing territories",
mainly because of the pending case before the International Court
at the Hague. The 1965 Five-Year Development Plan is, however, based

on the proposed "homelands", and provides basic data on each of them
together with some proposals for the development of agriculture.
The "non-decision" at the Hague in 1966 is followed by the 1968
Memorandum on financial and administrative rearrangements, transferring
the responsibility for "native affairs" to the relevant South African
ministries and leaving only the administration of the "White Area"
and a few other tasks to the Legislative Assembly and the Administration in Windhoek. The background to the 1968/69 legislation on
the new dispensation is outlined in the Explanatory Memorandum of 1968.

271. STEER, GEORG L. Judgment on German Africa. London: Hodder &
Stoughton, 1939, 351 p.

Written in a popular style by a British foreign correspondent based in
South Africa, this book opens with a discussion of the Nazi claims
for colonies. The author provides a journalistic description of
Tanganyika, Namibia and Cameroon, and argues that the administration
of these countries as mandated territories is a qualitative improvement on the German colonial system. A lengthy chapter on Namibia
(p. 37-136) contains a range of information on the role of the German
community in the 1930s and on political, administrative and economic
conditions in general. Although the analysis of Namibia under South
African rule is not entirely uncritical, the author accepts the
official position that "Southwest is theirs and they intend to keep
it".

272. SWANSON, MAYNARD W. "South West Africa in trust, 1915-1939". In
Britain and Germany in Africa, edited by P. Gifford and Wm. R. Louis,
p. 631-65. New Haven/London: Yale University Press, 1967.

The purpose of this well-documented essay is to examine the circumstances under which South Africa's rule was established and maintained
in Namibia. The occupation of the former German colony was at the
time seen "as a natural step toward fulfilment of a greater Union"
and the author argues that a total incorporation of the Territory -
both for geographic, political, economic, strategic and ethnic
reasons - was the underlying assumption that governed South Africa's
administration between the two world wars. The article also contains
a certain amount of information on the main administrative and
economic features in a period which witnessed great economic expansion and increased white settlement followed by depression, drought
and financial crises.

273. THEODOROPOULAS, CHRISTOS. "Racialism and international law. "Native
Law" or the regulation of capital-labour relations in Namibia". The
Indian Journal of International Law, nos. 3-4, (July-December) 1978:
299-321. (Also published in The Korean Journal of International
Studies, 10, no. 3, 1979: 251-74).

While there is a multitude of studies concerned with international law
and the legal aspects of the "Namibia question", this is one of the
very few attempts to discuss the racial institutional framework and
the socio-economic implications of "native law". The author, who was
a lecturer at the Faculty of Law, University of Ife, Nigeria, when
the article was written, outlines the main features of the legal
system in Namibia from the German colonisation onwards. This system is

seen to give legal expression to the dominant settler racialism and
super-exploitation of black workers by converting it into binding
rules of social control. Special attention is given to labour
regulations, the bantustan policy aimed at destroying national unity
and territorial integrity and the extension of a wide range of
apartheid laws to Namibia.

74. TROUP, FREDA. In face of fear: Michael Scott's challenge to South
Africa. London: Faber & Faber, 1950, 227 p. 5 photos, 3 maps.

This seminal work, edited by Freda Troup from the notes of Rev.
Michael Scott, was the first major critique of colonial repression
in Namibia to be published after the Second World War and remains
today one of the most eloquent of its kind. Its inspiration was
Scott's 1947 mission to the UN on behalf of the Herero to oppose the
South African attempt to incorporate Namibia into its own territory.
A full account of both attempt and mission makes up the second half
of the book. Earlier chapters describe with considerable analytical
clarity and historical detail the pre-colonial economy and society,
the brutal German colonisation and land robbery, and the poverty and
exploitation of black workers and peasants under the South African
regime. Perhaps the book's greatest value is the wealth of letters
and statements from Namibian leaders, most of them taken down by
Scott during 1947-8 and here reproduced at length, making it a
rare published repositary of Namibian oral history. Inevitably
the Herero occupy the centre stage, but other black Namibian
groups are far from excluded. See also Scott (nos. 252, 253).

275. VAN DER MERWE, PAUL. Otjiwarongo 1906-1981. Otjiwarongo: the
Municipality, 1981, 246 p. Illus. (Printed by Transvaal Drukkers,
Cape Town).

Published in cooperation with the municipality of Otjiwarongo,
this is an uncritical tribute to the white Afrikaans-speaking
community camouflaged as a town history. The author is an academic
and National Party leader with family roots in Otjiwarongo. There
is much factual detail, mostly on church, education, culture and
sports, but also to some extent on topics of interest for the study
of economic history, such as railway building, agriculture and rainfall. Unfortunately there are neither references nor bibliography,
but more than 300 pictures are reproduced, illustrating the social
history of the "dorslandtrekkers" and their descendants.

276. VILAKAZI, ABSALOM L. "The Odendaal Report: social and economic aspects".
in South West Africa: A travesty of trust, edited by Ronald Segal
and Ruth First, p. 222-41. London: Deutsch, 1967.

In this review of the Odendaal Commission, its report is treated as
a studied attempt to prepare a rationale for the further extension
of the system of apartheid. The author points out that the given
planning framework was the apartheid-oriented socio-political structure,
and the proposal to create "homelands" is, therefore, seen as a
logical development of what the colonial regime had already planned
and put into practice. By examining land distribution, systems of
government, health services and social development and welfare,

the author concludes that the economic gap between the white developed
areas and the homelands will be widened by the proposals of the
Commission. The author was at the time professor of African Studies,
American University, Washington. He later returned to South Africa
where he is Director, Centre for Research and Documentation,
University of Zululand, as well as serving on the Anglo American
Corporation's Board of Directors.

SEE ALSO:

1, 22, 24, 32, 36, 44, 45, 49, 51, 66, 74, 78, 81, 206, chapter 6
b(350-93), 553, 546, 592, 627, 637, 640, 675, 702, 705, 706,
709, 722, 728, 730, 754, 818, 838, 863, 884, 902.

. Illegal occupation (1966-1984)

77. AMNESTY INTERNATIONAL. Human rights violations in Namibia. New York:
Amnesty International, 1982, 20 p. (In German: Menschenrechtsverlet-
zungen in Namibia. Bonn, 1982, 34 p.).

This factually detailed Amnesty International briefing has been
translated into several languages as part of a campaign against the
severe violations of human rights in Namibia, such as detention
without trial, political trials, "disappearances" and executions.
It also includes a list of political prisoners.

78. THE COMMITTEE ON SOUTH AFRICAN WAR RESISTANCE. "Namibia - a nation
under siege". Resister, no. 27, (August-September) 1983: 12-18.

79. ------- "The occupation of Namibia - Special Forces". Resister,
no. 28, (October-November) 1983: 20-23.

80. ------- "The SWA Territory Force". Resister, no. 29, (December-
January) 1983/84: 4-9.

81. ------- "Battle for the hearts and minds". Resister, no. 30,
(February-March) 1984: 12-19.

This is a four-part series focusing on the South African war against
Namibia, published in the bi-monthly magazine of the Committee on
South African War Resistance (COSAWR). The articles provide a
detailed and authoritative overview of the history of the military
build-up in Namibia, the military commando structures, life (and
death) in the main operational zones (Caprivi, Kavango, Ovamboland),
the attacks against Angola, the special military forces (Koevoet,
32 Battalion etc.) and the unsuccessful South African campaign to
win the hearts and minds of the Namibian people. There are also
several references to Namibia in a recent booklet published by
COSAWR: State of War. Apartheid South Africa's decade of militarism
(London: COSAWR, 1984, 24 p.).

82. DU PISANI, ANDRÉ. "Namibia: from incorporation to controlled
change". Journal of Contemporary African Studies, 1, no. 2, (April)
1982: 281-305.

83. ------- Namibia: the politics of continuity and change.
Johannesburg: Jonathan Ball, 1985. In preparation.

The aim of the essay in Journal of Contemporary African Studies
is to explain South Africa's official policies towards Namibia
from 1915 to the early 1980s. The author argues that an analysis

of the relationship reveals a shift of emphasis away from a policy
of incorporation and towards a process of controlled change. The
major part of the article deals with policy formulation in the
post-1975 period, and the overriding objective of South Africa's
policy is described as an attempt to ensure a dependent Namibia
under neo-colonial control. These themes are elaborated in much
greater detail and historical depth in the same author's forthcoming book, which covers the period up to 1984. The author is a
Namibian-born political scientist based at the University of South
Africa (UNISA), Pretoria. For comments on more recent developments,
see nos. 777-80. p. 289.

284. ELLIS, JUSTIN and HEINZ HUNKE. Torture - a cancer in our society.
London: Catholic Institute for International Relations/British
Council of Churches, 1978, 67 p.

This exposure of the systematic use of torture in Namibia was banned
by the South African authorities prior to its publication. The
purpose of the booklet is to support the protests against torture
which have been made by the churches in Namibia on several occasions
since 1967, not least in the form of pastoral letter signed by the
most prominent church leaders in 1977. The major part of the booklet
consists of a number of sworn statements which were filed in a case
before the Windhoek Supreme Court.

285. ELLIS, JUSTIN. Elections in Namibia? London: British Council of
Churches/Catholic Institute for International Relations, 1979,
63 p. (In German: Wahlen in Namibia? Bonn: ISSA, 1979, 46 p.).

This is a clear and succinct overview of the international negotiations in the critical period 1976-78, as well as a well-documented
analysis of the "elections" held in Namibia in December 1978. The
latter part draws on the same author's report on the intimidation
employed by the South African administration in the registration
of voters before the election campaign, a report which was published
by the Cristian Centre and led to the expulsion of the author. (Report
on the registration and election campaign in Namibia, 1978, Christian
Centre, 28 November 1978, 14 p.). The second half of the booklet
consists of UN documents and some background data on the Namibian
economy.

286. FIRST, RUTH. The bantustans: the implementation of the Odendaal
Report. Paper presented to the Namibia International Conference,
Brussels, 1972, 11 p.

Prepared for an international conference on Namibia, this detailed
and well organised paper offers a critical examination of the
background and general policies of the Odendaal Report and an outline of the implementation of the bantustan policy up to 1972.
The objective of the paper is to explain the colonial subjugation
of the territory and the internal colonisation of the Namibian people
under apartheid. It also shows how economically the "homelands"
were intentionally designed to be unviable, and how politically
the South African sought to establish seemingly legitimate ethnic

institutions in order to deflect discontent from the regime and
internalise conflicts within the bantustans.

7. HORRELL, MURIEL. South-West Africa. Johannesburg: South African
Institute of Race Relations, 1967, 94 p. Tables.

This booklet provides a general introduction to Namibia in the mid-
1960s. It relies heavily for its factual information on official
data from the Odendaal Commission and the 1967 South-West Africa
Survey, but benefits also from independent observations informed by
a visit to the territory. The principal chapters give an overview
of government policies, legislation, demography, economic conditions
and local politics. The booklet concludes with comments on the increasing resentment against discriminatory laws, the poverty of
the Reserves, the pass laws, police repression and restrictions on
economic progress. It is suggested that the acquiescent and powerless chiefs are increasingly seen as tools of the Government and
that a more radical generation is emerging. The author was for
many years research officer of the liberal South African Institute
of Race Relations.

8. HORRELL, MURIEL (comp.). Race relations as regulated by law in South
Africa, 1948-1979. Johannesburg: South African Institute of Race
Relations, 1982, 349 p.

This comprehensive survey of the laws and the administrative/political
structures of apartheid includes a separate chapter on Namibia
(p. 285-318), outlining the major decisions and laws concerned with
constitutional development, education, pass laws, emergency regulations
etc. This edition supersedes Laws affecting race relations in South
Africa (1978), which also contained a chapter on Namibia (p. 480-507).

HUNKE, HEINZ, see no. 284.

HURLICH, SUSAN, see no. 295.

9. INTERNATIONAL DEFENCE AND AID FUND FOR SOUTHERN AFRICA. Remember
Kassinga and other papers on political prisoners and detainees in
Namibia. London: IDAF, 1981, 52 p. (Fact Paper on Southern Africa
No. 9).

This is a graphic description of the main features of the machinery of
repression built up by the South African occupying regime, including
first-hand accounts of detention and torture. An interview with one
of the survivors of the massacre at Kassinga in 1978 is also given
together with a list of convicted political prisoners.

0. INTERNATIONAL DEFENCE AND AID FUND FOR SOUTHERN AFRICA. Apartheid
army in Namibia. South Africa's illegal military occupation.
London: IDAF, 1982, 74 p. (Fact Paper on Southern Africa No. 10).

The purpose of this booklet is to document the military occupation
of Namibia, and at the same time to discuss the ways in which the

territory is used as a springboard for attacks against neighbouring
countries. The military build-up in the 1970s is described in detail
and special attention is given to the "namibianisation" of the
war through "tribal armies" and conscription. It demonstrates how
military operations overshadow the daily life of Namibians, and how
the South African military and police are in the forefront of the
state apparatus of control. For an updated examination of South
Africa's warfare, see nos. 278-81, 293.

291. INTERNATIONAL DEFENCE AND AID FUND FOR SOUTHERN AFRICA. Namibia
under apartheid. Documentation on the situation inside the
country. London: IDAF, 1984, 12 p.

Prepared by IDAF's research department for a hearing on South African
aggression against its neighbouring states (Oslo, 22-24 March 1984),
this is a succinct and up-to-date survey of the effects of the South
African occupation on the civilian population. The paper deals
with the militarisation of Namibia, the socio-economic effects of
military rule, the occupation of Angola, the repression of political
activity, torture, detentions, atrocities and political trials.

292. INTERNATIONAL DEFENCE AND AID FUND FOR SOUTHERN AFRICA. Children
of Namibia. Growing up under apartheid. London: IDAF, 1984,
4 p. (IDAF briefing paper, no. 10, March 1984).

Children and young people have received little attention even in
the radical literature, and the aim of this briefing paper is
to bring together information and to focus greater interest and
concern on living conditions, health risks, education, insecurity
and deprivation of black children in a militarised and occupied
Namibia.

293. KÖNIG, BARBARA. Namibia. The ravages of war. London: International Defence and Aid Fund for Southern Africa, 1983, 60 p. 33
photos.

This factually detailed account of the devastating consequences
of the South African war for the civilian population is compulsory
reading for an understanding of the present situation in Namibia.
While most other current publications on Namibia address themselves
to the international dispute and the prospects for an independent
Namibia, this booklet focuses on the conditions of life for black
Namibians under military occupation, forced removals, the machinery of repression and the destruction of social infrastructure.
It shows how the pervasive military presence serves to underpin
the exploitative economic structures and racial policies, and how
the military apparatus has increasingly become the dominant force
in Namibia. The author concludes that the South Africans have
not achieved their aim of subduing the population, and that support
for SWAPO has grown despite the sufferings inflicted on all sections
of the Namibian population. The evidence presented is drawn largely
from church reports and Namibian newspapers. The author works at
IDAF as a researcher and writer on Namibia.

. LANDIS, ELIZABETH S. "The Turnhalle constitution: an analysis". Africa Today, 24, no. 3, 1977: 12-23.

This is a brief but hard-hitting examination of the Turnhalle Constitution, a document which was drafted under the close super-vision of the South African occupying power. The author's analysis exposes its important failings as being, firstly, that it does not ensure the national unity and territorial integrity of Namibia, but rather preserves and extends its fragmentation into bantustans; secondly, that it preserves the de facto dominance of whites; thirdly, that it is unlikely to provide meaningful protection for fundamental human rights; and, fourthly, that it does not provide for any election or popular participation in the interim government.

. LEE, RICHARD B. and SUSAN HURLICH. "From foragers to fighters: South Africa's militarization of the Namibian San". In Politics and history in band societies, edited by Eleanor Leacock and Richard Lee, p. 327-46. Cambridge University Press, 1982.

Written by two Canadian scholars, this case study reveals how the South African occupying forces have pressured the Namibian San people to participate directly in the war against SWAPO. The authors argue that this move is part of a major assault on the social, economic and cultural life of the San, in order to create dependent allies for South Africa out of indigenous ethnic groups in the north and northeast. These sinister efforts notwithstanding, they point out that by no means all have been deceived and that some San have assisted or joined SWAPO.

. LISSNER, JÖRGEN (ed.). Namibia 1975. Hope, fear and ambiguity. Geneva: Lutheran World Federation, 1976, 153 p.

This wide-ranging collection of documents, statements, articles and excerpts from books is intended to shed some light on events in Namibia during the dramatic year of 1975. With few exceptions, only material produced during 1975 is included, and preference has been given to publications originating in Namibia or South Africa. The main focus is on political developments, such as the bantustan "elections" of Ovamboland, the Turnhalle Constitutional Conference and the role of the churches, but there is also some coverage of the economic situation. Of special interest is the text of a lecture given in Windhoek by the well-known South African economist Francis Wilson ("Present and Future Aspects of Namibia's economy", p. 84-93).

. LOUW, WALTER. Owambo. Sandton: Southern African Freedom Founda-tion, 1979, 91 p. Tables, 14 photos.

A polemical and highly tendentious presentation of South African apartheid policy in the "Owambo" bantustan by one of the govern-ment's leading publicists in Namibia. Published by an extreme right-wing South African propaganda institution, the first half of this booklet is taken up with a crude political attack on SWAPO,

and much of the remainder with promotion of South Africa's "Turnhalle"
political strategy and economic "development" activities in Ovamboland.
On this latter aspect there is useful economic data despite gross
political distortion and factual inaccuracy in the presentation. The
discussion of "development" policy fully reflects the South African
switch in emphasis from shoring up "traditional" land tenure to the
promotion of individual land tenure and profit-motivated black
businessmen as the motor of economic expansion.

298. LUBOWSKI, ANTON. Speech on security legislation applicable in Namibia.
Windhoek, 1983, 14 p. (Addressed to the Namibia Educational Forum,
31.8.1983. Typescript).

299. ------- Speech at the Council of Churches of Namibia's ecumenical theological consultation on security legislation in Namibia and suggested
action to be taken to present evidence to the recently appointed
commission of inquiry into security legislation. Windhoek, 1983,
21 p. (Held at Catholic Hall, Katutura, 21.9.1983. Typescript).

The aim of these two speeches was to review the "security" legislation
in operation in Namibia, concentrating on how the laws and regulations
came into being and how they are structured. They stress that the
major part of the legislation has been imposed by the local representative of the occupying power (the Administrator-General), that
the laws exclude the jurisdiction of the courts, that numerous
people are detained and banned in terms of these laws, and that they
allow terror to be exercised by the people that apply them. Anton
Lubowski is a Namibian lawyer who joined SWAPO in 1984.

300. MASON, PHILIP. "Separate development and South West Africa: some
aspects of the Odendaal report". Race, 5 no. 4, 1964: 83-97.

Considering the assumptions underlying the Odendaal Report, this
article concludes that the main recommendations aim at a closer link
between Namibia and South Africa and an even more vigorous and
thorough implementation of the policy of separate development. The
author was director of the Institute of Race Relations, London.

301. PENDLETON, WADE C. Katutura: a place where we do not stay. The
social structure and social relationships of people in an African
township in South West Africa. San Diego: San Diego State University
Press, 1974, 197 p. 34 tables, 3 maps, 3 figures, 9 photos, bibl.:
181-89.

The objective of this academic work, which is based on a somewhat
pedantic doctoral dissertation in anthropology, is to focus on
urban social structure, social relationships and ethnicity in Windhoek.
Its principal argument is that ethnic distinctions within the African
population in Katutura - where most Africans are required to live -
are still significant, and that low wages, unskilled work, lack of
trade unions and limited education explain why there are few cross-
cutting mechanisms in the form of economic and occupational stratification. It also claims that the importance of ethnicity and race
has been further strengthened by the implementation of apartheid
and residential segregation in Windhoek. The conclusion drawn from
a detailed examination of conjugal unions is that few opportunities

exist for men and women of different ethnic groups to establish personal
relations. The book was published in the aftermath of several
important events in Namibia, such as the general strike of 1971-72
and a more pronounced opposition to South African rule by the churches,
leading the author to conclude that "possibly the new era in African
life in Katutura will see a rise of black consciousness which will
override ethnic and other considerations to force a change in the
socioeconomic-political conditions of the people". See also by the
same author: "Social categorization and language usage in Windhoek,
South West Africa", in Urban man in Southern Africa, edited by C.
Kileff and W.C. Pendleton, p. 63-80 (Gwelo: Mambo Press, 1975) and
"Urban ethnicity in Windhoek", in Ethnicity in modern Africa, edited
by B.M. du Toit, p. 135-42 (Boulder, Colorado: Westview Press, 1979).

302. PICKERING, ARTHUR. Law, state and social control in contemporary
Namibia. University of Warwick, 1983, 150 p. Bibl.: 144-50.
(LL.M. thesis).

Submitted as a dissertation by a Namibian lawyer who was also a
National Union of Namibian Workers (NUNW) activist before he was
imprisoned and forced to leave the country, this is a perceptive
study of the various forms of social control in Namibia. Its
principal hypothesis is that the South African regime has attempted
to implement a new strategy, called the "New Society", based on the
creation of a black petty bourgeoisie wholly dependent on the colonial
state. The author's concern is to discuss the role played by law
and state in promoting this strategy, focusing on economic institutions, in particular the First National Development Corporation
(ENOK) and the National Building and Investment Corporation, as
well as on political structures, notably the apartheid "Representative
Authorities", the territorial fragmentation and disorganisation of
the peasantry. He concludes that this strategy has failed due to
the inherent contradiction between national capitalists and settlers
on the one hand, who oppose any concessions, and on the other, international capital which believes that black nationalism can be bought
off by promoting a privileged section within the ranks of the
dominated classes. These conflicting perceptions, it is argued, are
reflected in the contradictory functions of law in the 1977-82
period, with the removal of some legal barriers blocking the advance
of the black petty bourgeoisie while others have remained.

303. PRINSLOO, DANIEL S. SWA: the Turnhalle and independence. Pretoria:
Foreign Affairs Association, 1976, 36 p. 12 photos, bibl.: 34-5.
(FAA Study Report No. 4).

This is a representative defence of the new South African strategy which
was developed in the mid-1970s, centring on the Turnhalle Conference
and an "interim government" to exclude SWAPO. The Turnhalle Conference is seen by the author, a leading South African political scientist
and Senior Research Fellow at the F.A.A., as "representing the
majority of all the peoples of South West Africa". He also argues
that a process has been initiated whereby the deadlock over the
status of Namibia is being finally cleared up, and that the Turnhalle
Conference is a clear indication "that the true value of human self-
determination is still being recognised on a continent of which so

many of its peoples have recently lost their freedom". See also by
the same author: SWA/Namibia. Towards a negotiated settlement
(Pretoria: Foreign Affairs Association, 1977, 38 p.).

304. SERFONTEIN, J.H.P. Namibia? Randburg: Fokus Suid Publishers/London:
Rex Collings, 1976, 323 p.

Written by a leading South African journalist who has followed the
Namibian scene closely since the early 1960s, this descriptive
account of political events reflects a growing disillusionment
with the official policies of the South African regime. The author
is well-informed, and his book provides a factual survey of events,
parties, personalities, shifting strategies and international negotiations in the decade leading to the Turnhalle conference in 1975.
Its main strength lies in the author's intimate knowledge of the
machinations of "white politics" in South Africa and Namibia, but it
is disappointingly weak on explanation. The description of black
politics is to a large extent concerned with ethnic and personal
rivalries, and there are few attempts to analyse the economic and
class interests blocking the road to independence. Several important
political statements, representing a broad spectrum of opinions, are
reproduced in an annex.

305. SOUTH AFRICA (REPUBLIC), DEPARTMENT OF FOREIGN AFFAIRS. South West
Africa Survey 1967. Cape/Pretoria: Government Printer, 1967, 190
p. 29 tables, 175 photos.

306. ------- South West Africa Survey 1974. Cape Town/Pretoria: Government
Printer, 1974, 70 p. + photos.

Published by the South African government, the stated aim of these
two surveys is "to put South Africa's view-point to the world more
actively". The 1967 Survey was one of the major South African
publications on Namibia in the 1960s, complementing the Odendaal
report (no. 266). The first part gives an official interpretation
of Namibian history and political development, while the section on
the economy is an important source for economic and infrastructural
data, however partisan the presentation. In contrast, the 1974
Survey is less informative and more defensive and glossy.

307. SOUTH AFRICA, DEPARTMENT OF FOREIGN AFFAIRS. Owambo. Pretoria, 1971,
37 p. + photos. 4 tables, 6 maps, 112 photos.

Published when South Africa's attempt to promote "Owambo" as its showpiece Namibian "homeland" was in full swing, this glossy propaganda
tract, more than half of which consists of a lavishly produced
photographic appendix, had no sooner appeared than the illusion
of the "bantustan without tears" was shattered by the 1971-2 contract
workers' strike and the associated peasant rebellion in Ovamboland
itself. The book is nonetheless a serious attempt to bolster the
South African case. The photo collection is superbly executed and
wide-ranging, containing, for example, informative views of the terrain
of peasant farming, the physical infrastructure, and the few local
factories. In the text, unpublished official data, much of it economic,
is deployed in the effort to boost the image of South African "development". Subjected to proper critical review, such data may be used

to complement the earlier SWA Survey 1967 and the later and in some
respects less informative Stellenbosch study (nos. 450-2).

308. SOUTH WEST AFRICA (ADM.). Constitutional conference of South West
Africa. Lansdowne, Cape: Citadel Press, 1976, 128 p. (In Afrikaans:
Staatkundige Beraad van Suidwes-Afrika. Lansdowne, Cape: Citadel
Press, 1976, 128 p.).

This is a representative collection of reports and documents from the
various working committees of the Constitutional Conference which
ran from the late 1975 to early 1977. It is mainly concerned with
proposals for economic and social reforms and the abolishment of
"petty apartheid". There are a few original tables on wages and
the occupation structure, followed by an outline of a new salary
structure which later was blocked. By and large, the document is a
symbol of the early optimism of the Turnhalle era.

309. SOUTH WEST AFRICA (ADM.). South West Africa/Namibia survey. Windhoek:
The Press Relations Office of the Administrator-General, 1980, 51 p.

This survey concentrates on the proceedings of the "Ministers'
Council" and the main activities of the Windhoek administration in
1979-80. It gives the impression of an independent, democratically
answerable bureaucracy smoothly working to promote development and
abolish discrimination. Given this propagandist purpose, the survey
provides some interesting information on the new administrative set-up
and a chronology of government decision-making.

310. SOUTH WEST AFRICA (ADM.). Verslag van die kommissie insake munisipale
wetgeving. Windhoek, 1980, 270 p. Tweede verslag: Kommentaar een
aanbevelings oor wetgeving wat munisipaliteite raak. Windhoek,
n.d. 27 p. Derde verslag: finansieringskorporasie vir munisipaliteite. Windhoek, n.d. 31 p. Vierde verslag: die finansiering van
plaaslike owerhede. Windhoek, 1981, 56 p. + 31 p. (annexes).

The precise circumstances and sequence of the compilation of this
series of reports are by no means clear from the texts themselves.
Taken as a whole, however, they represent a concerted attempt to bring
the legal and financial status of local authorities in line with
the Turnhalle constitution in which they form the third tier. Of
the four reports of the Commission, commonly known as the Arnold
Commission after its chairman, the long-serving town clerk of
Windhoek, the most substantial in terms of economic data is the
fourth. It includes unpublished statistics on municipal finance
(annex A), especially Katatura (annex B), for which detailed data
are given on expenditure, income, social and housing policy, and
the average incomes of residents by occupation. The Commission
has also released a number of technical and legal reports of its
"Commission of experts", the most extensive of which deals with the
proposed municipal law.

311. SOUTH WEST AFRICA (ADM.). Commission of inquiry into alleged irregularities and misapplication of property in Representative Authorities
and the Central Authority of South West Africa. Interim Reports.
Windhoek, 1983, 1984.

Known as the Thirion Commission – named after its chairman who is a
judge in the Natal Supreme Court – this Commission started its work
at the same time as the South African authorities dissolved the
"internal" DTA institutions in early 1983. It followed public
criticism of the malpractices (or "corruption") of the second-tier
authorities set up under the ethnic constitution of 1980 (AG 8).
The strategy behind its work has been to give the South African
colonial administration authority to exert increased financial
control in the light of the economic crisis and to call for greater
centralisation of various administrative departments (e.g. health
and education). The seven interim reports which were released in
1984 documented serious irregularities by the Ovambo, Kavango,
Herero, Coloured, Tswana, Caprivi and Damara "Representative Authorities", but despite the massive evidence the Commission has so far
not led to any prosecution. A background study to the Commission
was reported in the Namibian press in June 1984 to have exposed
transfer pricing and non-payment of taxes by key multinational
corporations, especially in the diamond business.

312. TÖTEMEYER, GERHARD. South West Africa/Namibia. Facts, attitudes,
assessment. Randburg: Fokus Suid Publishers, 1977, 323 p.

Written by a leading Namibian/South African political scientist, who
was expelled from the National Party because of his divergent views
on the Namibian issue, this is essentially a guide to the various
political parties, churches, movements and groupings in Namibia.
The author's presentation is supported by excerpts from statements,
programmes and speeches , but there are few attempts to examine
critically the parties and the interests they represent. Although
it is stated in the introduction that the intention is "to present
the reader with a factual background against which subsequent events
in the territory may be judged", the text is heavily biased by the
author's concern with cultural heterogeneity, ethnic conflicts and
elites, while very little attention is paid to class conflict and
economic interests.

313. TÖTEMEYER, GERHARD. Namibia, old and new: traditional and modern
leaders in Ovamboland. London: Hurst, 1978, 257 p. 7 maps, tables,
bibl.: 236-49.

An expanded, updated (to 1976/7) but only lightly revised version of
the author's doctoral thesis in Afrikaans. After introductory,
largely historial chapters, the book presents, together with background data, an extended discussion of the attitudes of South African
politicians and administrators and of Ovambo traders, clergy, bantustan
officials and white-collar employees on a range of political and
economic issues. Combining the tabulated results of a questionnaire
survey with a wide range of documentary evidence and the author's
own assessments, it provides an at times exceptionally detailed
account of the failure of South Africa's attempt between 1967 and
1976 to make Ovamboland its showpiece Namibian bantustan. Its
analysis is, however, weakened by a rather naive political sociology
derived from modernisation theory, counterposing "traditional" and
"modern" elites. The statistical significance of the survey method
is also highly questionable. The study is nonetheless valuable not

only for its empirical detail but also for being the work of an insider:
at the time of his research in 1971-2 the author had privileged access
to Ovamboland and the bantustan administration, and despite his
subsequent estrangement from the National Party hierarchy, a reformist
concern with the ineffectiveness of repressive policies informs his
analysis. The extensive bibliography includes a list of government
publications and unpublished dissertations. UNITED NATIONS ECON-
OMIC AND SOCIAL COUNCIL. Violations of human rights in South Africa,
See No. 1028.

14. USHEWOKUNZE, C.M. Turnhalle constitutional proposals for an interim
government in Namibia: an endorsement of apartheid injustice.
Lusaka: UNIN, 1977, 26 p.

Written by a former senior lecturer at the UN Institute for Namibia,
this paper provides a critical discussion of the draft constitution
for an interim government produced by the Turnhalle Constitutional
Conference in 1977. The paper places the proposals in the context
of the development of constitutional structures from 1920 up to the
Turnhalle neo-colonial strategy in the 1970s, concluding that the proposed constitutional basis for the "interim government" of Namibia
exposes the determination of the South African government to continue
its illegal control of the territory under the pretext that this has
been agreed to by the Namibian people themselves.

15. VOSLOO, WILLEM B. "Local government in South West Africa". In
Local government in southern Africa, edited by W.B. Vosloo, D.A.
Kotzé and W.J.O. Jeppe, p. 100-19. Pretoria/Cape Town: Academia,
1974.

A short synopsis of the administrative functions and legal authority
of central and local government in Namibia in the period before the
Turnhalle dispensation. The author is wholly uncritical of official
policy and restricts his account to a description of the arrangements at the time. There are, however, few other studies which
throw light on this level of the administrative and legal structure.

16. WEAVER, TONY. "Caught in the crossfire: the war in Namibia".
Work in Progress, no. 29, 1983: 4-10.

Written by the Windhoek correspondent of the South African Morning
Group of Newspapers, this is an informed account of the present state
of war in the northern areas. In spite of strict censorship, the
article offers a detailed description of the role played by the
Special Police Counter Insurgency Unit known as Koevoet (Crowbar).
There is also a section dealing with the social costs of the war:
the breakdown in health services, the spread of bubonic plague,
forced removals and restrictions on transport. An edited version of
a letter addressed to the United Nations Secretary General on his
visit to Namibia in August 1983, written by the Council of Churches
on Namibia, is reproduced in an appendix. For a more up-to-date
survey on the Namibian situation, see the same author's "Namibian
Review, p.211-27 in South African Review Two. (Johannesburg:
Ravan Press, 1984).

SEE ALSO:

1, 2, 3, 8, 9, 10, 14, 15, 17, 18, 22, 29, 33, 36, 41, 42, 43, 45, 49, 51, 56, 73, 74, 75, 78, 79, 102, 111, 237, 240, 275, 282-3, chapter 6 b(394-56), 462, 476, 485, 542, 656, 662, 681, 705, 838, 853, 854, 862, 864, 1003, 1028, 1032, 1035.

6. THE NAMIBIAN ECONOMY

A. Conquest and land theft (1884-1915)

417. BEINART, WILLIAM. "Cape workers in German South-West Africa, 1904-1912. Patterns of migrancy and the closing of options on the Southern African labour market". In Collected Seminar Papers No. 27. The societies of Southern Africa in the 19th and 20th centuries, vol. 11, p. 48-65. London: Institute of Commonwealth Studies, 1981.

Although presented mainly as a contribution to the economic history of the Cape Colony, focusing on the patterns of migration during a period of recession and ongoing proletarianisation in rural areas, this research paper also illuminates important aspects of Namibian labour history under German rule. Based on research in the Cape Archives, the study demonstrates how a large number of Cape workers were recruited to work in Namibia at a time when Ovamboland had not been fully opened up for contract labour, and when there was a heavy demand for labour as a result of the war of genocide. The paper quotes extensively from the letters and complaints sent to the Cape Native Affairs Dept., documenting, inter alia, the harsh working conditions and the physical violence of labour repression in Namibia.

418. CALVERT, A.F. South-west Africa during German occupation, 1884-1914. London: T.W. Laurie, 1915, 105 p. + photos (230 plates).

This is one of the first books in English to deal with the German colony, written in a polemical anti-German style. The author argues that a South African annexation will solve the pressing local problem of providing South Africa with land for its "bywoners" (the poor white class), and indicates the lines along which Namibia may be most profitably developed. The second half of the book describes "the country and its resources", dealing mainly with the diamonds industry. The value of the book as a source is enhanced by the facts and figures derived from British consular reports, as well as its 230 photos. The chapters on geology and minerals are mainly based on the works of the leading geologist at the time, Percy Wagner (see nos. 609, 610).

319. DEMUTH, JEAN. Der Diamantenmarkt mit besonderer Berücksichtigung der deutsch-südwestafrikanischen Ausbeute. Karlsruhe: Braun, 1912, 132 p. (Dissertation).

This is a detailed account of the first three years of the Namibian diamond industry, with a wealth of material on resources, companies, production, marketing, mining legislation, taxation, prices and the impact on the colonial economy in general.

320. DOVE, KARL. Deutsch-Südwestafrika. Berlin: Süsserott, 1913, 227 p. 16 photos.

Originally published in 1909, this is the second and revised edition of a classic and often cited German "Landeskunde". The author was a leading geographer and colonial propagandist, and the book is clearly written with the purpose of attracting settlers. His approach to colonial policy is summed up in one of the widely quoted phrases: "Leniency toward the natives is cruelty to the whites". The chapters on the geographical regions, the climate (with rainfall statistics from the 1890s), the flora and wildlife are quite good, but the sections dealing with history, economic structure and ethnography are rather thin. See also by the same author: Deutsch-Südwestafrika. Ergebnisse einer wissenschaftlichen Reise im südlichen Damaralande (Gotha: J. Perthes, 1896).

321. EVELEIGH, WILLIAM. South West Africa. London: T. Fisher Unwin, 1915, 255 p.

The aim of this general description of Namibia was to set before British readers a comprehensive account of the country, its history, its people and its economic potential. When it was published at the end of the German period, it was the first book in the English language to provide such an overview of the territory. The presentation is blatantly anti-German, but the book is an interesting source because of its attempt to synthesise offical documents and a large number of contemporary books by German scholars, administrators and writers of more popular books. There are separate chapters on "The Development of the Country", "The Diamond Fields" and "The Economic Future", where one can find bits and pieces of valuable information on the economy (p. 173-249). The author supports the idea of incorporating Namibia as an integral part of the Union of South Africa, and emphasizes the value of the mineral wealth and stock-farming.

322. GAD, JOHANNES. Die Betriebsverhältnisse der Farmen des mittleren Hererolandes (Deutsch Südwest-Afrika). Hamburg: L. Friederichsen & Co., 1915, 147 p. 93 figures. (Abhandlungen des Hamburgischen Kolonialinstituts, 28).

This detailed case study of 54 settler farms, one of the very few undertaken during the German colonial occupation, is especially valuable for its thoroughness and breadth of scope. The investigation, undertaken in 1912, covered half of the allocated farms - in practice most of those actually operating - in an area located in the heartland of the cattle-raising country from which the Herero had been driven less than eight years previously. The micro-economics of commercial farming are analysed in great detail, with as many as 93 tables, covering natural environment, water infrastructure, transport and marketing, a critique of official settlement policy, methods and costs of production, capital and credit. Also, unusually in both German and South African literature, considerable attention is devoted to labour, especially wages. One of the author's conclusions was that in the great majority of cases farm rations were below the bare minimum standards of nutrition.

23. HERMANN, ERNST. Viehzucht und Bodenkultur in Südwestafrika. Zugleich Ratgeber für Auswanderer. Berlin: Deutscher Kolonial-Verlag, 1914, 160 p. (4th enlarged edition, revised by Walter Mittelstaedt and F. Hermann).

Originally published in 1900, this is an informative source on farming and living conditions of German settlers. The author was himself a prominent settler, and sets out in his book to give prospective German immigrants a realistic picture of what a farming life in Namibia is like. Apart from a technical description of different kinds of farming and ranching, the book contains fragments of information on the costs of production, wages, health care and "how to treat the natives".

24. HESSE, HERMAN. Die Landfrage und die Frage der Rechtsgültigkeit der Konzessionen in Südwestafrika. Ein Beitrag zur wirtschaftlichen und finanziellen Entwicklung des Schutzgebietes. Jena: Costenoble, 1906. Vol. 1: xvi, 373 p. Vol. 2: ix, 288 p. Bibl.: vol. 1, xiv-xvi.

A very detailed study of the land companies, their legal rights and their economic role. The first volume opens with a general survey of the economic development up to 1906, with emphasis on the war of anti-colonial resistance and its impact on the economy. The major part of the volume consists of an examination of each of the eight companies. The second volume brings together 100 documents (agreements, proclamations, regulations, concessions, licenses, etc.) for the period 1880-1906. For a general and uncritical presentation of the main features of colonial law, see the thesis by the same author: Die Schutzverträge in Südwestafrika. Ein Beitrag zur rechtsgeschichtlichen und politischen Entwicklung des Schutzgebietes (Berlin: Süsserott, 1905, 170 p.).

25. JÄCKEL, HERBERT. Die Landgesellschaften in den deutschen Schutzgebieten. Denkschrift zur Kolonialen Landfrage. Jena: Fischer, 1909, 315 p. 3 diagrams, bibl.: ix-xiv. (Mitteilungen der Gesellschaft für wirtschaftliche Ausbildung Neue Folge, Heft 5).

A thoroughly researched investigation of the concession and land companies in the German colonies, concentrating on legal issues. The main focus is on the major companies operating in Namibia, such as Deutsche Kolonialgesellschaft, Kaoko-Land und Minen-Gesellschaft, South West Africa Company and Otavi Minen- und Eisenbahngesellschaft. There is a detailed examination of the origins and legal rights, but the study is weak on economic development and statistical data.

Though repeating the usual patriotic phraseology, the author also questions the motives of the companies and provides the most complete description of this controversial issue in German colonial policy.

326. KAROW, MARIA. Wo sonst der Fuss des Kriegers trat: Farmleben in Südwest nach dem Kriege. Berlin: Mittler, 1909, 255 p. 30 photos.

A fairly representative example of about a dozen of books which describe the daily "farming life" from a settler's point of view, having its value mainly as a source and as a contribution to the writing of social history "from above". There is a rather detailed description of the farm (18,000 hectares), the household and the work by the domestic servants and the garden workers. The photos are documents in their own right, and so are the paternalistic language and the racial stereotypes employed by the author.

327. LEUTWEIN, PAUL. Die Leistungen der Regierung in der Südwest- afrikanischen Land- und Minenfrage. Berlin: Süsserott, 1911, 130 p. Bibl.: 5-7. (Dissertation, Friedrich- Wilhelms- Universität, Berlin. Koloniale Abhandlungen, Heft 42-46).

The chief merit of this thesis lies in the detailed examination of the concessions given by the German government to large agricultural and mining companies. The author is highly critical of the policies implemented to support the companies (land distribution, mining regulations, credit policy, financial support etc.). Apart from this academic study, the author published a collection of poems and reminiscences from the early period of German colonisation (Du weitest deine Brust, der Blick wird freier: Kriegs- und Wander- Fahrten in Südwest, Berlin: Deutscher Kolonialverlag, 1909), a hagiographic account of his father (Afrikanerschicksal: Gouverneur Leutwein und seine Zeit, Stuttgart: Union Deutsche Verlagsgesell- schaft, 1929) and several pieces of colonial propaganda during the Nazi era.

328. LITTER, DR. Die Arbeiterfrage in Deutsch- Südwestafrika. Hamburg, 1913, 133 p. (Typescript).

A discussion of ways in which the chronic labour shortage might be overcome, with data on employment, methods of labour control, Ovambo labour migration and the health of black workers. Available only as a manuscript in Hamburgisches Weltwirtschaft- Archiv (HWWA), it will nonetheless repay consultation for research into labour repression and working conditions in the German colonial period.

329. MACDONALD, WILLIAM. The destiny of Walvis Bay. Johannesburg: Transvaal Leader, 1915, 96 p. 23 photos. (Reprinted by the State Library, Pretoria, 1979).

One of the few detailed descriptions of the Walvis Bay enclave, written just before the South African conquest made it Namibia's main port. The text consists of a series of feature articles - part travel diary and anecdote, part social and economic description - which first appeared in a Johannesburg newspaper. The author, editor of the Agricultural Journal of South Africa, was interested in Walvis

Bay both as an outlet for the settler farmers of the central African
interior and for its agricultural potential, which he describes
in some detail. His commentary on the social, economic and political
state of affairs in the enclave is observant and sometimes sharply
critical. He also provides a rare early account of the unique mode
of subsistence of the Topnaar peasants of the Kuiseb River.

330. MOSSOLOW, NICOLAI. Windhoek damals= Die Windhoek van weleer= This
was old Windhoek. Windhoek, 1965, 173 p. 29 photos.

Published by the author himself, this is a narrative history of the
town and its vicinity, concentrating on the German period and ending
in 1918. There is some detail on economic and social conditions,
the formation of colonial businesses and the smallholder settlement
at Klein Windhoek. The text is not footnoted and the author, a
former archivist, states that he had "no intention of producing a
detailed reference book". Nevertheless, the narrative is packed with
detail and is clearly based on wide reading. See also by the same author:
Windhoek Today/Windhoek Heute (Windhoek, 1967, 132 p.), which is made
up mainly of photographs.

331. NGAVIRUE, ZEDEKIA. "The land theft". In South West Africa: A
travesty of trust, edited by Ronald Segal and Ruth First, p. 178-
88. London: Deutsch, 1967.

A short history of the creation of the reserves by a prominent Herero
politician and then chairperson of the SWANU External Council. The
most detailed coverage is of the Herero reserves and forced removals
in the German and early South African periods. For a more comprehensive treatment, see the author's PhD thesis (no. 245).

332. OELHAFEN VON SCHÖLLENBACH, HANS. Die Besiedelung Deutsch-Südwest-
afrikas bis zum Weltkriege. Berlin: Reimer, 1926, 132 p. 3 maps,
tables.

Despite its obvious German-colonial overtones, this is one of the
best contemporary studies of Namibia as a settlement colony in the
period before the First World War. The main focus is on the settling
of the territory up to 1903, the change in colonial policy resulting
from the war of anti-colonial resistance , the constructions of railways,
land ownership structure and water supply. The author, who was a
leading army officer, has also written one of the few published
accounts of the First World War in Namibia: Der Feldzug in Südwestafrika. 1914-1915 (Berlin: Safari-Verlag, 1923, 268 p.).

333. PHILLIPS, JOHN A.S. "The Pomona story based on the Dr. George
Wunderlich collection". Journal - SWA Scientific Society 36/37,
1981/82-1982/83: 11-44.

This is a detailed and fascinating story of a central episode in
the long history of struggle for control over Namibian mineral resources. The first diamonds were discovered in 1909 in an area which
was claimed by several companies and prospectors, and the article
describes the fight between different interest groups until the
question was finally "resolved" when the South African Consolidated

Diamond Mines gained the upper hand after the First World War. The
research draws mainly on the rich collection donated to the Windhoek
State Archives by George Wunderlich, who served as a legal advisor
to Pomona Diamanten-Gesellschaft and to Daniel de Pass. Several maps
and documents are reproduced at the end of the article.

334. POOL, GERHARDUS. Pionierspoorweë in Duits-Suidwes-Afrika, 1897-1915.
Durban/Pretoria: Butterworth, 1982, 301 p. 6 figures, 81 photos,
12 maps, 15 tables, bibl.: 269-92.

This is the published version of a dissertation which sets out a
detailed history of the financing, construction, running and economic
significance of the state railways during the German period. There
is also scattered information on social history, such as the conditions
of construction and railway workers. The study is based on extensive
archival research, and contains many photos and a full bibliography.
The author is one of the few South African historians specialising
on Namibian history in the 1884-1915 period. (See also no. 204).

335. QUIRING, ERICH. Die Eisenbahnen Deutsch-Südwestafrikas und ihre
Bedeutung für die wirtschaftliche Entwicklung der Kolonie. Borna-
Leipzig: R. Noske, 1911, 63 p. (Dissertation, Friedrich-Alexanders-
Universität, Erlangen).

This is a straightforward and factual description of the railways in
"German Southwest-Africa" up to 1910, with emphasis on their origins,
operations, profitability and importance for agriculture and mining.

336. REHBOCK, THEODOR. Deutsch-Südwest-Afrika. Seine wirtschaftliche
Erschliessung unter besonderer Berücksichtigung der Nutzbarmachung
des Wassers. Bericht über das Ergebnis einer im Auftrage des
"Syndikats für Bewässerungsanlagen in Deutsch-Südwest-Afrika" durch
das Herero-und Gross-Namaland unternommenen Reise. Berlin: Reimer,
1898, 237 p. Maps, photos, bibl.: xi-xv.

This is one of the first attempts to survey the water resources and
the prospects for agricultural development in the central and southern
part of Namibia, commissioned by a German syndicate considering large-
scale settlements. Although conducted rather hastily, the study
contains some interesting observations and a wealth of information
on climate, water and geology. The author is primarily concerned
with the utilisation of water resources through boreholes, reser-
voirs and dams, and seeks to identify areas suitable for German
settlements, such as the proposed "colony" at Hatsamas.

337. ROHRBACH, PAUL. Deutsche Kolonialwirtschaft. I. Band: Südwest-
Afrika. Berlin-Schöneberg: Buchverlag der "Hilfe", 1907, 510 p.
25 photos.

A classic - and often quoted - introduction to the geography and
economy of Namibia under German rule. The author served as an
economic adviser and "Ansiedlungskommissar" (Imperial Emigration

Commissioner) in 1903-1907, and the book was written in order to
justify the German colonial system, to attract more settlers and
to argue the case for more financial support to further their economic
interests. As a source, the book also has its value in describing
the economic impact of the war of anti-colonial resistance on the
colonial economy and the reconstruction and building of railways
after the war. Paul Rohrbach was later to become one of the chief
colonial propagandists in the 1920s and during the Nazi period.
Among his other writings should also be mentioned Dernburg und die
Südwestafrikaner. Diamantenfrage. Selbstverwaltung. Landeshilfe.
(Berlin: Deutscher Kolonialverlag, 1911, 323 p.) and Wie machen wir
unsere Kolonien rentabel? Grundzüge eines Wirtschaftsprogramms für
Deutschlands afrikanischen Kolonialbesitz (Halle : Gebauer-Schwetschke
Druckerei u. Verlag, 1907, 279 p.). For a stimulating biographical
study, see Walter Mogk: Paul Rohrbach und das "Grössere Deutschland"
(München: Wilhelm Goldmann Verlag, 1972, 307 p.).

38. SANDER, LUDWIG. Die Rinderpest und ihr Einfluss auf die wirtschaftlichen Verhältnisse in Deutsch-Südwestafrika. Berlin: Verlag Hermann
Paetel, 1897, 44 p.

A descriptive eye-witness account of the catastrophic rinderpest
epidemic and its economic impact on both the settlers and the Herero.
It was written just after the height of the epidemic by a doctor who
was also the chief representative of one of the main land settlement
companies.

39. SANDER, K. LUDWIG G. Geschichte der Deutschen Kolonial-Gesellschaft
für Südwest-Afrika von ihrer Gründung bis zum Jahre 1910. Nach den
Akten bearbeitet und dargestellt. Berlin: Reimer, 1912. Band I:
Geschichtliche Darstellung, 315 p. Band II: Grundlegende Urkunden
in wörtlicher Wiedergabe und Karten, 477 p. Maps, photos.

This is a traditional and extensive company history in two volumes,
which at the same time sheds light on the colonial economy in general.
The first volume is essentially a detailed chronicle of events year
by year, while the second volume comprises a large collection of
primary documents, including treaties, mining regulations and administrative proclamations relevant for private companies. There are also
several high quality maps and photos.

40. SCHLETTWEIN, CARL. Der Farmer in Deutsch-Südwest-Afrika. Eine
Darstellung sämtlicher für den afrikanischen Farmer in Betracht
kommenden Erwerbszweigen ind ein Leitfaden für Anfänger. Wisman:
Hinstorff'sche Verlagsbuchhandlung, 1914, 273 p. 74 photos.
(Second revised and enlarged edition).

Written by a prominent settler and a leading political figure in the
Landesrat, this is one of the most useful introductions to capitalist
agriculture in Namibia under German rule. The purpose of the book is
to encourage young Germans to settle in Namibia, in order to fulfil
the "civilising mission" of colonialism. The book provides a general
geographical and historical background to the country, as well as
a description of a wide range of technical and practical issues related
to farming. The wealth of factual detail on crop cultivation,

cattle-breeding, prices, production costs and marketing, together with 74 photos and a subject index, makes the book a valuable source. It is also of interest that the author focuses attention on projects specifically designed to make the farming community self-sufficient and independent from South Africa and Germany. The technology considered falls well into what is today referred to as "intermediate technology", but such projects were entirely "forgotten" under South African rule. For a brief biographical note on Schlettwein, see Fritz Gaerdes: "Carl Schlettwein", SWA Annual 1972, p. 41-2.

SCHÖLLENBACH, HANS OELHAFEN VON, see OELHAFEN VON SCHÖLLENBACH, no. 332.

341. SCHMIDT, CARL. Geographie der Europäersiedelungen im deutschen Südwestafrika. Jena: Fischer, 1922, 132 p. 9 maps, 8 diagrams, bibl.: 123-32.

A scholarly monograph on the history and geography of European settlement from early 19th century up to the First World War, focusing on changes between 1894 and 1903. The main value of the survey lies in the detailed information on settlements and population distribution, supplemented with excellent analytical maps. There is also a comprehensive bibliography, listing more than 250 items.

342. SCHUBERT, EMMERICH. Landwirtschaft und ihre Nebenbetriebe in Südwestafrika. Heidelberg: Winter, 1913, 127 p. Figures, bibl.: v-vii. (Dissertation, Heidelberg).

A detailed study of the economics of European agriculture and related activities in Namibia in the period 1900-1912, covering both large-scale commercial farming and smallholdings. There is considerable data on production costs, debts, various forms of ownership and leasehold, size of farms, wages, agricultural research, crops and livestock statistics, and foreign trade. The thesis reflects the official racist/colonial prejudices, especially when "native policy" and the attitudes of the various African "population groups" toward farm labour are discussed.

343. SOUTH AFRICA (UNION). Memorandum on the country known as German South-West Africa. Pretoria: Government Printer, 1915, 95 p.

Based on German official material and British consular reports, this is a well-informed survey of Namibia with emphasis on the structure and expansion of the economy in the years preceding the South African takeover of the colony. It is packed with data, especially tables, covering administration, local government, land companies, agriculture, public works, irrigation, education, commerce, banking, customs and excise, mining, railways, harbours and shipping.

344. STRÄHUBER, HERMANN. Die Entwicklung des landwirtschaftlichen Kreditwesens in Deutsch-Südwestafrika. Ein Beitrag zur Wirtschaftsgeschichte dieser Kolonie. Nürnberg: George Heydolph, 1915, 109 p. (Dissertation, Erlangen).

Although not adding very much to the general economic history of "German South-West Africa" this thesis has its merits in offering a detailed examination of the banking and credit system. The main focus is on the origins of the "Landwirtschaftsbank für Deutsch-Südwestafrika", which was established to further the interests of the European settler community. It also shows how the bank assumed the responsibilities of a "national bank" after the outbreak of the war.

345. UNITED KINGDOM, FOREIGN OFFICE. South-West Africa. London: H.M.S.O., 1920, 114 p. Tables, bibl.: 112-14. (Handbooks prepared under the direction of the Historial Section of the Foreign office - No. 112). Published in German African possessions (late). (Peace handbooks. Issued by the Historical Section of the Foreign office, vol. 18). Reprinted under the same title by Greenwood Press, New York, 1969.

This report was prepared in 1917 by a special section established by the Foreign Office to provide the British delegates to the Peace Conference with information on the German colonies, and was later published together with similar studies on Togoland, Cameroon, Tanganyika and a report on "German treatment of natives". It contains much invaluable data on economic and social conditions, focusing on the period 1907-14, including the volume of trade, industry, shipping, agriculture, land companies, minerals, domestic commerce, public finance, and banking. The section on transport is particularly detailed, reflecting the interest of the General Staff of the War Office in railways, roads and ports.

345b. VOELTZ, RICHARD ANDREW. The origins and early years of The South West Africa Company, Ltd. A study of a British concession company in German South West Africa. Los Angeles: University of California, 1980, 260 p. 3 figures, 3 maps, bibl.: 250-60.

Based on the archives of South West Africa Company Ltd. in London, this mainly descriptive thesis is a history of a British concession company in Namibia in the period 1892-1914. It is shown how SWACO influenced the early economic history of the colony, and how the company's activities were firmly tied to the German colonial effort and to the colonising power's desire to expand its empire in Ovamboland and southern Angola at the expense of Portugal. Considerable attention is given to the origins of the company and the manner in which the "Damara concession" was obtained. The thesis also sheds light on a number of critical questions, such as the struggle between German interests favouring a settlement colony and those favouring large-scale investments and concessionary companies.

346. WEGE, FRITZ. Zur Entstehung und Entwicklung der Arbeiterklasse in Südwestafrika während der deutschen Kolonialherrschaft. Halle: Martin Luther-Universität, 1966, 360 p. 2 vols. Bibl.: 333-55. (Dissertation).

347. ------- "Die Anfänge der Herausbildung einer Arbeiterklasse in Südwestafrika unter der deutschen Kolonialherrschaft". Jahrbuch für

Wirtschaftsgeschichte 1, 1969: 183-221.

348. ------- "Zur sozialen Lage der Arbeiter Namibias unter der deutschen Kolonialherrschaft in den Jahren vor dem ersten Weltkrieg". Jahrbuch für Wirtschaftsgeschichte 3, 1971: 201-18.

The author of this well documented thesis was - together with Drechsler and Loth (see nos. 188, 140) - among the first East German scholars to base his work on the Potsdam archives. The thesis is concerned with "Die Arbeiterfrage", that is, how Africans were mobilised as workers in the interest of the exploitative colonial system. There is a propagandistic introduction, but the study itself is a meticulously researched and highly informative work. The sections on the general colonial economy add little to the existing literature, but the main chapters on "the making of the working class" is a documentation of the various mechanisms used to get workers into the mines, the railways and the farms (forced labour, pass laws, recruitment of migrant labour from the north, etc.). Focusing on the period 1910-1914, there are several chapters describing the conditions of workers: forms of contract, wages, sanitary conditions, and other important aspects of social history. The last section deals with the various forms of protest and resistance of the workers against colonial suppression and economic exploitation, and includes a rudimentary discussion of the origins of class consciousness. There are a large number of references and footnotes (p. 268-332), as well as an extensive bibliography which also serves as a guide to the Potsdam archives. The articles in Jahrbuch summarise two important aspects of the thesis, dealing with the origins of the working class and the living conditions of Namibian workers before the First World War.

349. WIEDEN, HELGE BEI DER. "Wollschafzucht in Deutsch-Südwestafrika". Vierteljahreschrift für Social- und Wirtschaftsgeschichte 58, no. 7, 1971: 67-87.

An account of wool farming from its origins in the 1890s to the late 1930s. The author examines in particular the history of a German syndicate established in 1909 specifically to promote wool sheep farming, using the archives of the town of which its chief promoter, Wilhelm Külz (see no. 199), was mayor. The article covers an aspect of farming on which there is scanty information in other works.

SEE ALSO:

4, 16, 22, 24, 33, 34, 36, 52, 55, 64, 74, 81, 118, 146, 151, chapter 4 a(160-76), chapter 4 b(177-219), 235, 236, 501, 667, 933.

B. Under the mandate (1915-1966)

350. BARTH, PAUL. Südwestafrika: wirtschaftlicher Ratgeber und allgemeine Anleitung, besonders für Auswanderungslustige. Windhoek: Meinert, 1926, 304 p. Photos.

A lengthy prospectus for would-be settlers, compiled by a leading German farmer together with the publisher. It gives a full description of colonial institutions, conditions of settlement and the commercial economy, especially farming.

351. BEWERSDORF, RICHARD. Die Industrialisierung der Südafrikanischen Union und Deutsch-Südwestafrikas. Berlin: Mier & Glasemann, 1939, 100 p. Bibl.: 87-90. (Dissertation, Friedrich-Wilhelms-Universität zu Bonn).

This thesis is mainly concerned with South Africa, but there are also references to manufacturing industry in Namibia in the interwar period. The author is stronger on compilation than analysis, but the study is one of the few sources of information on the industrial section in Namibia in this period. There are also brief sections on labour policy and the role of the state in industry.

352. BRENNER, HARRO. Südwestafrika und sein Aussenhandel. Berlin, 1933, 87 p. Bibl.: 4-6. (Dissertation, Friedrich-Wilhelms-Universität zu Berlin).

Based on the assumption that it was a compelling necessity for Germany to reconquer its former colonies, this thesis was primarily a contribution to the colonial campaign for "Lebensraum" in the early 1930s. It contains, nevertheless, a wide range of economic data on Namibia's state finances, the size and composition of foreign trade, mineral production, price indexes and railway rates in the years from 1920 to 1932. The analysis of the economic relations with South Africa contrasts sharply with the story put out by South African propaganda during the same period, which emphasized the large financial contributions made by the Union government to the mandated territory.

53. COOPER, ALLAN D. U.S. economic power and political influence in Namibia, 1700-1982. Boulder, Colorado: Westview Press, 1982, 222 p. 18 tables, 9 charts, bibl.: 197-208. (A Westview Replica Edition).

This is a thoroughly researched and critical examination of US relations with Namibia from the first commercial contact in the 18th century to the present. While most other studies of US interests

tend to restrict themselves to more recent mining operations, the
author gives a much broader historical perspective and includes
an analysis of the fishing industry and karakul farming as well as
financial services, manufacturing, shipping and oil exploration.
More than 100 corporations with interests in Namibia are identified and
described in detail. He also demonstrates how legislation and
policies are shaped by formal and informal linkages among company directors and policy-makers. The study includes calculations of profits
of some of the major American business interests in Namibia, and
the author argues that US corporations have reaped enormous benefits
from South Africa's subjugation of Namibia. An extensive bibliography
adds to the value of the book. See also a brief conference paper
on the same subject: "American corporate investments in Namibia",
Africa Today, 30, nos. 1-2, 1983: 23-33. The author is assistant
professor of political science, St. Augustine's College, Raleigh,
North Carolina.

354. CZAYA, EBERHARD. Der deutsche Imperialismus in Süd- and Südwestafrika.
Ein Beispiel für Kontinuität und Elastizität deutscher kolonialer
Bestrebungen. Berlin (DDR): Humboldt- Universität, 1967, vii, 476 p.
21 tables, bibl:: 462-76. (Dissertation).

This meticulously researched thesis within a marxist framework is a
significant contribution to the history of international capital and
German imperialism in Africa between the two wars, mainly - but not
exclusively - focusing on Namibia. There is a detailed examination
of the role played by major companies (especially Otavi Minen- und
Eisenbahngesellschaft) and some prominent businessmen (Lübberts,
Stauch). The author also discusses the movements in Germany for
colonial restoration during the Weimar republic and the Nazi era, and
relates these colonial endeavours to the activities and the annexation
plans of German groups inside Namibia itself. There is a comprehensive
bibliography, which also serves as a guide to the archival material
and the relevant company reports.

355. DAY, JOHN R. Railways of Southern Africa. London: Arthur Baker,
1963, 143 p. 65 photos.

This popular account of railway building and railways in Southern
Africa includes a brief narrative of the history of railways in
Namibia: "Unification in South Africa: South West Africa (p. 47-60).

356. DEUTSCHLAND, RUTH. Die Lage der afrikanischen Bevölkerung Südwest-
afrikas und ihr Kampf um nationale Befreiung (1945-1959). Berlin
(GDR): Humboldt-Universität, 1967, 285 p. Bibl.: 266-84.
(Dissertation).

Written by an East German historian, this thesis deals with an under-
researched period in Namibian history: the years between 1945 and
the beginning of the liberation struggle under the leadership of SWAPO.
The study is in the main a descriptive account of the social and
economic conditions of the African population, mainly the workers,
followed by a rather sketchy outline of struggle for independence
before 1960. The research is primarily based on UN material,
especially the large number of petitions from Namibian individuals

and organisations and the annual reports of the Committee on South
West Africa. The study benefits also from a reading of a local
newspaper (<u>Allgemeine Zeitung</u>) as well as South African official
documents and the series of ethnological studies published by the
Department for Native Affairs. See also two brief articles by the
same author: "Zu einigen Besdonderheiten des nationalen Befreiung-
skampfes in Südwestafrika nach den 2. Weltkrieg" p. 173- 84, in
<u>Nationalismus und Sozialismus im Befreiungskampf der Völker Asiens und
Afrikas</u> (Berlin, 1970) and "Die Lage der südwestafrikanischen Bevölkerung und ihr Kampf gegen das südafrikanische Apartheid-Regime",
<u>Deutsche Aussenpolitik</u>, 13, No. 6, 1968: 710-19.

357. DOWD, HERBERT WALTER. <u>Non-white land and labour policies in South
West Africa from 1918 to 1948</u>. Tufts, Fletcher School of Law and
Diplomacy, 1954, 397 p. 19 tables, bibl.: 380-97. (PhD thesis).

Submitted as early as 1954, this US thesis still deserves attention
and a wide readership. The chief value of the study lies in the
wealth of information compiled by the author on land distribution,
agricultural policies, various forms of labour repression and
coercion, taxation, wages, working conditions, health and education.
The analysis is, however, less rigorous and more conventional than
one perhaps could have expected on the basis of the material
presented. For general readers, the thesis offers a succinct summary
of the annual reports to the League of Nations, the Minutes of the
Permanent Mandates Commission, the ILO debates on forced labour as
well as several important South African commissions of inquiry. The
study benefits especially from a careful reading of the <u>Report of the
South West Africa National Labourers Commission, 1945-48</u> (1948) and
<u>Report of the Long Term Agricultural Commission</u> (1945). There are
also a large number of informative tables, an extensive summary
(p. 342-79) and a bibliography.

358. GERVASI, SEAN. "The South West African economy". In <u>South West Africa:
A travesty of trust</u>, edited by Ronald Segal and Ruth First, p. 128-
50. London: Deutsch, 1967.

Prepared for the 1966 international conference on Namibia, this brief
survey by a noted US scholar describes and analyses the Namibian
economy in the 1950s and the early 1960s. The historical overview
documents the considerable expansion of the capitalist sector (mining,
ranching and fisheries) in the postwar period. The author argues,
however, that dependence on the growth of mineral exports entails
instability as well as the exploitation of wasting assets, and that
economic expansion under apartheid has brought little benefit to
the black population.

359. GREEN, REGINALD H. and KIMMO KILJUNEN. "The colonial economy:
structures of growth and exploitation". In <u>Namibia. The last
colony</u>, edited by Reginald H. Green, Marja-Liisa Kiljunen and
Kimmo Kiljunen, p. 30-58. London: Longman, 1981.

A concise and well organised survey of the main characteristics of
the colonial economy of Namibia, concentrating on the period 1945-
1975. It offers some insight into the historical evolution of

the present system, and provides basic information on the patterns
of exploitation as well as on the different sectors of the economy.
The article concludes by emphasizing the need for this foreign-
dominated, vulnerable and externally dependent economy to be struct-
urally changed after independence.

360. HALBACH, AXEL J. Die Wirtschaft Südwestafrikas. München: IFO-
Institut für Wirtschaftsforschung, Afrika-Studienstelle, 1967,
210 p. 39 tables, 19 maps, 15 diagrams, bibl.: appendix, I-XI.

361. ------- Namibia. Wirtschaftsstruktur. Ausgabe 1981. Köln:
Bundesstelle für Aussenhandelsinformation, 1981, 107 p. 22 tables.
(Marktinformation, Reihe MI-A).

362. ------- Entwicklungsprobleme im südlichen Afrika. München: Weltforum
Verlag, 1982, 99 p. (IFO Forschungsberichte 60).

The first of these three studies by a West German economist is a
thorough and detailed analysis of the Namibian economy. It is based
on several visits to the territory, and concentrates mainly on the
period 1958-65. Its value lies chiefly in the compilation of facts
and figures illustrating the structure of the economy in an important
period which has been sparsely documented. The author draws heavily
on official sources, such as the White Papers of the SWA Administration and annual reports from local boards of South African government
departments, as well as the Population Census of 1960, the Industrial
Census of 1961/62 and the Agricultural Census of 1964. The large
number of tables, maps and diagrams make it possible to "mine" the
study for important information, which can also be used for interpretations which differ from the author's framework of conventional
economic geography which does not question the South African occupation of the country. There is also an extensive bibliography.
Wirtschaftsstruktur is a much more condensed factual survey, mainly
based on the statistical data released by the Department of Finance
(Windhoek) in the early 1980s and the multi-sectoral study prepared
by the German Development Institute. It also contains some information of special relevance to potential German investors. Entwicklungsprobleme is a collection of three articles concerned with South
Africa, Zimbabwe and Namibia. The contribution on Namibia provides
a sectoral survey and a brief discussion of the economic prospects
("Namibias wirtschaftliche Entwicklungsperspektiven", p. 41-70).
For a short summary of this article, see "Namibia. Wirtschaftliche
Entwicklungsperspektiven", Internationales Afrikaforum, 18, no. 1,
1982: 51-64.

363. HERRIGEL, OTTO. Studien zur Bevölkerungs- und Wirtschaftsentwicklung
Südwestafrikas. Univ. Basel, 1971, 123 p. 13 tables, bibl.:
119-22. (PhD thesis).

The aim of this thesis is to outline the main features of the socio-
economic system of Namibia, drawing on official data in a descriptive
rather than an analytical way. The author devotes a special section
to demography, and offers a summary of the main findings of the
censuses from 1921 onwards. The chapters covering the various
sectors of the economy present statistical series which have been
compiled and estimated from a wide range of sources (White papers,

Commission reports, annual reports from the Meat Control Board, the
South African Department of Mines etc). The final section is devoted
to a brief and in places critical discussion of the Odendaal report,
and the author argues that higher priority should be given to
education and health services, industrialisation and the construction
of a railway to Botswana and Zimbabwe. Otto Herrigel, a Namibian
by birth, is a lawyer in Windhoek.

364. HEYER, ADOLF BERNHARD. Die wirtschaftliche und finanzielle Lage
Südwest-Afrikas. Marburg: "Deutscher Lebensraum", 1937, 112 p.
(Dissertation, Phillips-Universität zu Margburg).

Yet another thesis arguing the case for Namibia to be returned to
the "true motherland", written by an editor of the magazine "Deutscher
Lebensraum" and a member of a settler family which was repatriated from
Namibia in 1919. The thesis contains a selection of data, especially
on climate, agriculture and mining.

365. HOPPE, THEODOR. Wirtschaftsstruktur und Wirtschaftsentwicklung
von Deutsch- Südwestafrika. Borna-Leipzig: Noske, 1936, 109 p.
Bibl.: 103-06. (Dissertation der Handels-Hochschule Leipzig).

Although written with the explicit purpose of supporting Germany's
claims to its former colonies, this thesis offers an unconventional
analysis of the economy in the interwar period. The depression of
the 1930s, on which a range of data is adduced, is explained as a
result not merely of the world crisis and the disastrous drought,
but also of the measures taken to protect the interests of South
African mines and industries, the Boer settlers and the South African
transport network.

366. INNES, DUNCAN. "South African capital and Namibia". In Namibia.
The last colony, edited by Reginald H. Green, Marja-Liisa Kiljunen
and Kimmo Kiljunen, p. 59-86. London: Longman, 1981.

367. ------- "Imperialism and the national struggle in Namibia". Review
of African Political Economy, no. 9, (May-August) 1978: 44-59.

368. ------- Anglo American and the rise of modern South Africa.
Johannesburg: Ravan Press/London: Heinemann, 1984, 358 p. Statistical appendix, bibl.: 335-50.

Written by a South African scholar, now a lecturer at the University of Witwatersrand, the essay in Namibia. The last colony is an
attempt to discuss the present political economy of Namibia in
terms of the expansion of capital in South Africa itself. After a
brief description of the development of the diamond industry and
the expansion of capitalist farming in the final years of German
rule, the author focuses on the changes which took place following
the South African takeover. He points out how the South African
state acted swiftly to transfer the control of the diamond industry
to Anglo American Corporation and to facilitate the growth of settlement. This form of development resulted in Namibia's growing
dependency on the South African economy, but due to depression and
drought the Namibian economy was characterised by stagnation and

and chronic underdevelopment in the interwar period. The main part
of the article concentrates on the economic expansion in the three
decades following the Second World War, in which South African
capital intensified its exploitation of mineral resources, fisheries
and karakul ranching to secure international purchasing power. The
author also argues that political control is organised through an
alliance of international monopoly capital (mining), local settler
farmers and appointed chiefs and headmen and their attendant bureau-
cracies and paramilitary units. The main ideas of this essay are
summarised in the article in Review of African Political Economy,
which also contains a brief and rather simplified discussion of SWAPO
and the liberation struggle. Anglo American and the rise of modern
South Africa is a factually detailed study of Anglo American
Corporation, based on the author's PhD thesis. There are few explicit
references to Namibia in the published version, but the analysis
of the Anglo American Corporation and the international diamond
industry throws light on the international context in which the
Namibian mining industry operates.

KILJUNEN, KIMMO, see no. 359.

369. KILJUNEN, MARJA-LIISA. "The white man's burden: Africans under
apartheid". In Namibia. The last colony, edited by Reginald
H. Green, Marja-Liisa Kiljunen and Kimmo Kiljunen, p. 87-111.
London: Longman, 1981.

A brief sketch of Namibian social history under South African
colonial rule, focusing on the land theft, the reserves, migrant
labour, public health, wages and education. The article is based
on data up to 1977.

370. KREMP, ARNOLD. Die wirtschaftsgeographische Entwicklung des ehemaligen Schutzgebiets Deutsch Südwestafrika. Königsberg, 1933, 145 p.
Bibl.: 137-45. (Dissertation, Albertus-Universität zu Königsberg).

Compared to most other German theses on the Namibian economy in the
interwar period, this study contains more information and less raw
propaganda. It is basically a straightforward and factual presentation of the main features of the economy with a wide range of statistics on agriculture, mining, fisheries, trade, banking, communications,
exports and imports.

371 KROGH, D.C. The national accounting framework of South West Africa.
University of Pretoria, 1958, 323 p. 46 tables, 3 charts, bibl.:
appendix, 4 p. (PhD thesis).

372. ------- "The national income and expenditure of South-West Africa
(1920-1956)". The South African Journal of Economics, 28, no. 2,
(March), 1960: 3-22.

A basic reference work for the study of the economic history of
Namibia, providing a factual framework for an analysis of the
economic structure and development of the territory in the period
1920-1956. The investigation was also undertaken to construct
a national accounting system which could readily be consolidated

with that of South Africa after the suspension of the collection of
separate trade returns for Namibia after 1957. The thesis contains a
detailed discussion of all sources and statistical series available
on production and trade, and draws heavily upon the Annual Statements
of Trade and Shipping and the Annual Reports to the League of Nations.
Among the subjects covered are GDP by type of industrial activity,
Gross National Income (both current and constant), disposal of GDP
(private consumption, government consumption and capital formation),
real and per capita National Income, Central Government General
Current Account, commodity imports and exports, Unit Value Index
of imports/exports and terms of trade. A major weakness of the
research is the lack of proper information on the activities of the
major private corporations and on peasant subsistence farming. The
article in the SAJE provides a brief summary of the unpublished
thesis. It presents a wide range of primary statistics organised
under standard national account categories, with notes and discussion
of sources. The author, a prominent South African economist and
businessman, was in 1983 appointed chief executive at Legal & General
Volkskas after having served as Governor of the Reserve Bank of
Rhodesia in the 1970s.

373. KROGH, D.C. "The economic relations between the Union of South Africa
and South West Africa, with special reference to the implications
of complete integration". Finance & Trade Review, no. 5 (June)
1959: 294-304.

The author spells out the grounds for regarding South Africa and
Namibia as comprising a single domestic territory for many administrative, political and economic purposes. Although several important
differences between the two countries are recognized, especially in
terms of the level of industrial development and dependence on
foreign capital, the aim of the article is to propose a more complete
integration. It is argued that this will guarantee Namibia a more
stable level of capital investment and supply of public services,
especially if a complete integration also allows for a transfer of
funds from the richer to poorer regions.

374. LEISTNER, G.M.E. "Public finance in South West Africa, 1945/46 to
1969/70". The South African Journal of Economics, 40, no. 1, 1972:
1-32.

The author, a leading South African economist, presents an empirically
detailed and authoritative outline of public finance in the 25 years
after World War II. It includes several tables calculating taxes,
revenue and expenditure, and touches upon foreign debts, investment
and other important aspects of fiscal and economic history in a
period characterised by economic expansion dominated by South
African and international capital. The article also describes the
new fiscal and administrative organisation introduced in 1969 to
tighten still further Namibia's incorporation into South Africa.
See also by the same author: "South West Africa's economic bonds with
South Africa", Bulletin of the Africa Institute of South Africa,
April 1971: 111-22, which argues that Namibia's "prosperity, progress
and stability" can continue only for as long as the close ties
with South Africa are maintained. This article is reprinted in

<u>The case for South West Africa</u>, edited by A. Lejeune, p. 213-23
(see no. 743).

375. LEMPP, FERDINAND. <u>Windhoek</u>. Windhoek: Afrika Verlag der Kreis,
1964, 215 p. Photos.

This is a tourist guide to "the happy town" of Windhoek, with many
photos and texts in Afrikaans, German and English. The picture
texts are often a source of information on particular aspects of
local economic history.

376. MASSMANN, URSULA. <u>Swakopmund - eine kleine Chronik</u>. Swakopmund zum
90. Geburtstag. Swakopmund: Gesellschaft für Wissenschaftliche
Entwicklung und Museum, 1982, 59 p. (English edition: <u>Swakopmund.
A chronicle of the town's people, places and progress</u>. 1984).

Published in conjunction with the 90th anniversary of Swakopmund, this
is a brief, conventional local history of events. Its value for the
study of economic history lies in scattered information on trade,
transport, railways and harbour activities.

377. MICHAELIS, ILSE. <u>Die wirtschaftlichen Kräfte Südwestafrikas</u>. Kiel:
Institut für Weltwirtschaft, 78 p. 55 tables, bibl.: 76-77.1944.

A sectoral survey of the Namibian economy in the early 1940s, with
statistical data from the interwar period. Few original insights
are offered, but there is a certain amount of factual information
on a period which is poorly covered in the general literature.

378. MOIR, SIDNEY M. and H. TEMPLE CRITTENDEN. <u>Namib narrow gauge</u>. Ling-
field: The Oakwood Press, 1967, 153 p. 43 illus. (Reprint,
Johannesburg: Kempton Park, 1982).

This history of narrow gauge railways in Namibia from c 1900 to
1960 places emphasis on the construction and operation of the Otavi
Railway and "the pioneering period" up to World War I. The authors
are mainly concerned with technical details, but there is also a
certain amount of information on the connections between the
running of the railways and the general economic history of the
territory during the interwar depression and in "the era of expansion
and prosperity" (1945-1960). The lack of a bibliography as well as
a discussion of the sources reduces the value of the book as a
reference work.

379. NAUEN, OTTO. "Zur Wirtschaftslage Südwestafrikas". <u>Koloniale
Rundschau</u>, 28, no. 7, 1937: 3-7.

380. ------- <u>Die Karakulzucht in Südwestafrika</u>. Leipzig: Reichs-Zentrale
für Peltzier - und Rauchwarenforschung, 1939, 18 p.

The brief article in <u>Koloniale Rundschau</u> provides a general survey
of the Namibian economy over the previous decade, dealing mostly with
settler stock-farming. The author outlines production and the
marketing of exports in some detail, with a number of statistics.
Some emphasis is also placed on the suborientation of Namibia to the

interests of home producers in South Africa. The particular interest
of the author was in karakul, and in the following year he published
a fuller study of karakul ranching in Namibia for a research institution in Leipzig, describing its history, methods of stock management, exports and marketing structure.

81. RÄDEL, FRITZ EMIL. Die Wirtschaft und die Arbeiterfrage Südwestafrikas.
(Von der Frühzeit bis zum Ausbruch des zweiten Weltkrieges). University of Stellenbosch, 1947, 533 p. 127 tables, 27 diagrams, bibl.:
523-27. (D. Comm. thesis).

This is one of the classic academic works on Namibian economic history,
still valuable on the interwar period. It is mainly descriptive,
drawing on a wide range of official reports, archival documents,
and interviews with farmers, and is empirically strong on agricultural
production, both commercial and subsistence, the migrant labour system
and working conditions on the farms. The main focus is on the period
between the two World Wars, but there is also a lengthy chapter on
the origins of wage labour and the economic structure of Namibia under
German rule. Written within the colonial framework, the thesis is
rather vague in analysis and deficient in firm conclusions, but the
wealth of factual data from an under-researched period make it a
fruitful primary source. The author has since become one of South
Africa's leading economists.

382. RÖHR, GUSTAV F. Die Feldspurbahnen Südwestafrikas. 1000 km. auf
600 mm Spur. Krefeld: Verlag und Büro für spezielle Verkehrslitera-
tur - Röhr, 1980, 408 p. C 300 photos + maps, tables, charts,
drawings. (Verkehr in Afrika: Nr. 39).

This is the second edition of a splendidly illustrated history of the
railways up to 1961, covering such aspects as the construction of
railways, ports, the economic impact, the role of workers, and the
technical specifications of locomotives. The text is enriched by
numerous excerpts from books, papers, journals and timetables,
and there are a large number of photos and detailed contemporary
maps of Swakopmund, Oranjemund, Lüderitzbucht and Walvis Bay. There
is also a statistical appendix, prepared by W.E. Wendt, based on
the National Archives in Windhoek.

383. ROGALY, J. "The condition of the people". In South West Africa:
A travesty in trust, edited by Ronald Segal and Ruth First, p.
166-77. London: Deutsch, 1967.

Based on the reading of several important documents, most notably
the Odendaal Report, the author's concern is to go beyond the
official average figures to find out how the wealth of Namibia
is really distributed. The conclusion - not surprisingly - is that
the impressive infrastructure is mainly related to the needs of
the mines, the fishing industry and the white farms; that there are
immense gaps between blacks and whites in such areas as education,
health services and land distribution; and that the existing structure
seems most likely to be perpetuated through the development plans
and the report of the Odendaal Commission. The author was a South
African economics journalist.

384. SOUTH AFRICA (UNION)., DEPARTMENT OF CUSTOMS AND EXCISE. Annual statement of the trade and shipping of the Union of South Africa and of the Territory of South West Africa. Pretoria: Government Printer, 1906-1955.

Published under this title from 1930 onwards, this annual report is a major source on Namibian economic history under South African rule. The report provides detailed statistics on exports and imports (volume and value) and the direction of trade, including trade between Namibia and South Africa. Unfortunately the South African authorities ceased publication of separate statistics for Namibia in 1954, although a few overseas export commodities specific to Namibia can be traced in the succeeding Foreign Trade Statistics, which embraces the whole of the Southern African Customs Union.

385. SOUTH AFRICA (UNION). Report of the commission on the economic and financial relations between the Union of South Africa and the mandated territory of South West Africa. Pretoria: Government Printer, 1935, 273 p. (U.G. No. 16-1935).

This is one of the most important official documents published in the interwar period, providing a survey of the economy after a long period of recession, drought and political dissatisfaction. The commission was appointed in 1932 to enquire into the financial relationships between South Africa and the "mandated territory", with special emphasis on railway rates, customs duties and the administration of railways and harbours. The report begins with a brief economic history and review of the economy in the early 1930s, then moves to a more detailed discussion of exports, imports, custom duties as well as railway traffic and rates. This is followed by a chapter on the financial position, which concludes that the existing financial relations are greatly in favour of Namibia. The report contains a substantial set of statistical annexures, including a list of periods of drought since 1771. A large part of the text consists of a lengthy and well documented minority report by Dr. H. Hirsekorn, p. 88-178, a leading spokesman for the German community, who argues strongly that the relations are not in favour of Namibia and that the economic prospects are much brighter than conceded by the Commission. This led to the reconvening of the Commission in 1933 to add a commentary on the minority report (p. 214-251), to which Hirskorn issued a further rejoinder (p. 251-273).

386. SOUTH AFRICAN RAILWAYS AND HARBOURS/SOUTH AFRICA, DEPARTMENT OF AGRICULTURE. South West Africa. Particulars concerning land settlement. Pretoria, 1923, 16 p. 7 photos.

387. SOUTH WEST AFRICA (ADM.). South West Africa. Its possibilities. Windhoek, 1925, 35 p. 22 photos, 12 maps, 3 tables. (Wembley Exhibition, 1925).

388. -------/SOUTH AFRICAN RAILWAYS AND HARBOURS. South West Africa. Its attractions and possibilities. Windhoek/Johannesburg, 1937, 40 p. 61 photos, 1 map.

These phamphlets were principal publicity instruments in South Africa's drive to "sell" its new colony abroad between the world

wars. The first was aimed mainly at white South African stock-farmers.
It gives a description by region of the farming environment, water
resources, and the potential for different kinds of stock; and details
the procedures for land allocation to settlers and the generous
grants and loans on offer. The second was designed to attract a wider
spread of settlers and foreign investors, primarily from Britain. Its
main sections cover geography, climate, communications, farming and
land settlement, minerals and mining, and game. There is considerable
factual information, supplemented by detailed original maps, providing
what in effect constitutes the first official economic survey of the
territory since South Africa's takeover a decade earlier. The third
pamphlet has fewer economic data and is pitched more at tourists and
potential urban settlers, with individual descriptions of most of
the towns and villages. Even more than its prececessor, it contains
a large number of panoramic photographs which include some of the few
published views of the principal towns of the period.

389. SOUTH WEST AFRICA (ADM.). Report of the Native Reserves Commission.
Windhoek: The Secretary for South West Africa, 1921, 25 p.

This is the outcome of a commission appointed by the SWA Administrator to report on the administration, size and conditions of native
reserves and locations in Namibia. The report addressed a central
issue in the formulation of "native policy" in the early 1920s, namely
the question of how to force blacks into employment as farm labourers
and domestic servants. The commission advocated the extension of
the policy of segregation to Namibia, the removal of black settlements from "white" areas, the creation of reserves for all blacks
and the closure of temporary reserves. It also recommended an end
to the leasing of land by whites to blacks (so-called "kaffir
farming") and the removal of "surplus" blacks from urban areas.
The report was followed by the establishment of a Native Affairs
Branch of the Administration, the appointment of a Chief Native
Commissioner and the promulgation of a new Masters and Servants
Law, Vagrancy Law and Pass Laws. It also prefigured the influx control
law of 1924, the Native (Urban Areas) Proclamation.

390. SUTCLIFFE, ROBERT B. "The economic relationship with South Africa".
In South West Africa: A travesty in trust, edited by Ronald Segal
and Ruth First, p. 151-65. London: Deutsch, 1967.

This contribution to the international conference on Namibia in
1966 is concerned with the question whether future prospects of
economic growth would be hampered in the event of an economic break
with South Africa. Based on an examination of trade and balance of
payment figures for the period up to the mid 1950s, when the release of all
relevant statistics was interrupted, it is argued there was a trade surplus and that Namibia was not dependent to any substantial degree
upon finance from any major external source for her remarkable postwar capital formation. Although a South African transfer of funds
to finance the railway deficit is noted, it is contended that this
must be considerably offset by Namibia's membership in the customs
union which has increased the price of major imports and robbed
Namibia of customs revenues and the opportunity to protect her own
industry.

TEMPLE CRITTENDEN, H., see no. 378.

391. TERRY, CAROLYN. The desert bankers: the story of the Standard Bank
in South West Africa. Cape Town: W.J. Flesch and Partners, 1978,
184 p. 72 illus. (In Afrikaans: Bankiers van die Dorsland. Die
verhaal van die Standard Bank in Suidwes-Afrika).

The publishing of this unambitious but numerously illustrated book
coincided with the launching of Standard Bank SWA Ltd. (a part of
the Standard Chartered Group) in 1978. The Bank began its operations
in Windhoek in 1915, and has been a financial pillar of the colonial
economy. The author was the Bank's archivist, and has put together
glimpses from the history of the Bank as well as from the general
economic history of Namibia. Excerpts from old inspection reports
give an insight into the economic conditions in the 1940s. Harry
Gundry, an accountant and branch manager in Namibia for more than
thirty years, contributes to the book with anecdotal reminiscenses.

392. UNITED KINGDOM, DEPARTMENT OF OVERSEAS TRADE/WILSON GOODE, J.L.
Report on the conditions and prospects of trade in the protectorate
of South-West Africa. London: HMSO, 1920, 50 p. (Cmd. 842).

This report by the British Trade Commissioner at Cape Town was prepared to advise the British government of opportunities for the
extension of trade, as well as reporting on financial and economic
conditions in general. The report outlines the main features of
communications, public finance, agriculture, mining and foreign
trade, and provides some statistical background, especially on
exports and imports for the year 1918.

393. WILKEN, J.J.J. and G.J. FOX. The history of the port and settlement
of Walvis Bay. Johannesburg: Perskor Publishers, 1978, 197 p.
62 photos, 4 maps.

This well designed book has the form of an antiquarian town history
and was published in conjunction with the 100th anniversary of the
British Cape annexation. One of the authors is the Town Clerk and
a pillar of the South African community, a fact which makes the book
a semi-official centenary volume. There are some demographic and
economic statistics, as well as chapters on local government and
the development of the fishing industry. The text also occasionally
reveals original information, such as the forced closure of the cold
storage plant in the late 1950s to make South Africa the sole market
and the only exporter of Namibia beef.

WILSON GOODE, J.L., see no. 392.

SEE ALSO:

22, 24, 29, 32, 36, 45, 46, 49, 51, 55, 66, 68, 74, 75, 81, 82,
83, 84, 95, 96, 102-4, chapter 5 a(220-76), chapter 6 c(394-456),
chapter 7 a(497-550), chapter 7 b(551-74), chapter 7 c(575-614),
640, 655, 667, 675.

C. Under military occupation (1966-1984)

AFRICA INSTITUTE, see no. 415.

394. AFRICA TODAY. Namibia and the West: multinational corporations and international law. Denver, 1983, 123 p. (Africa Today, special double issue, 30, nos. 1-2, 1983).

This special issue focuses on the economic, political and legal implications of the transnational corporations operating in Namibia. Most of the contributions are papers originally delivered to the International Seminar on the Role of Transnational Corporations in Namibia, held in Washington in December 1982. A complete list of conference documents and the final declarations are also repro- duced. The articles deal with the strategic importance of Namibia's natural resources, Decree No. 1 and the support of the transnational corporations and the Western powers for South Africa's continued illegal control. For separate annotations, see McDougall (no. 744), Morrell (no. 421), Cooper (no. 353), Marchand (no. 788), Walters (no. 812) and Taskforce ...(no. 605). Apart from the conference papers, a separate article, written by P. Stephenson, J. Sedney and J.P. Prentice, contributes to the discussion on Decree No. 1 ("En- forcing Decree No. 1 in the Courts of the United States", p. 69-82).

395. BUSINESS SOUTH AFRICA. "A toast to SWA/Namibia". Business South Africa, 13, no. 2, (February) 1978: 36-75.

Conducted by the staff of a South African business magazine in early 1978, this survey of the economic conditions in Namibia provides a very optimistic assessment of the future economic prospects. The discussion of the main economic sectors concludes that "whoever will take over this country will inherit a brilliant kick-off from South African development, investment and administration".

396. CASON, JAMES. Recent North American corporate activity in Namibia. Paper presented to The International Seminar on the Role of a Trans- national Corporations in Namibia, Washington, 1982, 12 p.

Based on official figures supplied by the US Department of Commerce, this conference paper shows that American direct investment in Namibia increased considerably in the ten years since International Court of Justice ruled South Africa's control over Namibia illegal. There is also detailed and up-to-date information on companies engaged in prospecting activities. The author works with the New York- based Southern Africa Committee.

397. CATHOLIC INSTITUTE FOR INTERNATIONAL RELATIONS. South African occu- pation and the Namibian economy. London: CIIR, 1984, 11 p.

Prepared for an international hearing on South African aggression

against neighbouring states (Oslo, 22-24 March 1984), this is a
brief, up-to-date survey of the Namibian economy in early 1984.
Based on information given in CIIR's series A Future for Namibia, it
demonstrates how South African occupation has created an extra-
ordinarily distorted and inequitable economy. After outlining the
basic "structures of injustice", the paper describes the current
economic crisis (drought, recession, etc.) and points to the economic
benefit of Namibia to South Africa. It concludes firmly that these
benefits overshadow the South African claim that "the Republic's
total assistance to South West Africa must surely be one of the most
generous foreign aid programmes anywhere in the world". For more
statistical information, see the CIIR briefing paper The Current State
of the Namibian Economy (London: CIIR, April 1984, 3 p.).

8. COLLETT, SUE. "The human factor in the economic development of
Namibia". Optima, 28, no. 4, 1980: 190-219.

This is an attempt to draw together basic data on the Namibian economy,
mainly derived from official sources, but supplemented by facts and
impressions gathered in the course of field trips to Namibia in
1977/78. The author, who is a South African economist, was able to
collect material from government circles as well as the private
sector at a time when access to data was even more restricted than
it is today. Her general assessment of the economy and the prospects
for future development is close to the conservative reformist position
of Wolfgang H. Thomas (no. 75). This article in Optima, an Anglo-
American Corporation magazine, is based on a more comprehensive
and unpublished manuscript: The Economy of South West Africa. Current
Conditions and some Future Prospects (Johannesburg, 1978, 45 p.),
which offers some independent calculations of the balance of payments
and growth of real GDP which differ from the official data. See also
by the same author: Input-Output Table for Namibia (1979).

9. COLLETT, SUE. "Small and medium-sized enterprises in Southwest
Africa/Namibia". The South Africa Journal of Economics, 48, no. 3,
1980: 276-87.

The purpose of this brief study is to argue that the ideas of "small
is beautiful" and intermediate technology are particularly pertinent
to Namibia. Drawing on her research on Namibia, the author suggests
that there is considerable scope for small-scale industrial enterprises
as manufactured goods form an important part of total imports. These
enterprises should be based on simple technology to be compatible
with shortages of capital and skilled labour.

DAVIS, JENNIFER, see no. 400.

0. COURTNEY, WINIFRED and JENNIFER DAVIS. Namibia: U.S. corporate
involvement. New York: The Africa Fund, 1972, 34 p. (Published
in cooperation with The Programme to Combat Racism, World Council
of Churches). Although part of the information is outdated and surveys of US corporate involvement have been published (see nos. 353,
407, 396), this general introduction to the role played by the US corporations in Namibia is still valuable as both an overview and an emperic-
al source. There is a detailed examination of the operations of the
Tsumeb Corporation in the period on the "oil rush" in the beginning of
the 1970s.

401. Eerste Nasionale Ontwikkelingskorporasie (ENOK). 'n Streekstudie van Namaland en aangrensende gebiede ten einde ekonomiese ontwikkelings- projekte waarvan die Eerste Nasionale Ontwikkelingskorporasie van SWA Bpk deel kan hê, te identifiseer. Windhoek, 1979, 26 p. 9 tables.

402. ------- 'n Streekstudie van die Rehoboth Gebiet... Windhoek, 1981, 82 p. 20 tables, 1 map.

403. ------- 'n Streekstudie van Damaraland... Windhoek, 1981, 155 p. 23 tables, 11 maps.

These reports complement an earlier set of studies produced at Stellenbosch University for the South African government (see nos. 450-52). The primary focus of each is similarly one of the bantu- stans, in this case in central/southern Namibia. There are nonethe- less marked differences between the two sets in both purpose and method. The ENOK studies are more properly regional, extending beyond the bantustan boundaries and taking some account of macro-econ- omic factors. They are also less concerned with institutional structures and planning than with present economic activity and the identification of local opportunities for ENOK to stimulate economic expansion, particularly in small-scale commerce and industry. The approach, while strictly defined by orthodox market economics and the profit criterion, is therefore more pragmatic and in addition to surveying natural resources and infrastructure, closer attention is given to economic description. The studies are important sources of demographic and economic data, much of it from unpublished sources. Like their Stellenbosch counterparts, the ENOK researchers have drawn heavily on two unpublished series of regional surveys carried out in the mid-1970s, the first of natural resources by the consultancy firm Loxton, Hunting and Associates, the second of the socio-economic structure of peasant households by the University of South Africa's Bureau for Market Research. Internal data from official sources at all levels of administration are also extensively used.

404. ENOK/FIRST NATIONAL DEVELOPMENT CORPORATION. Information for investors. Windhoek, 1984, 24 p.

The First National Development Corporation, generally known by the acronym ENOK from its Afrikaans title, was established by the South African regime in 1978 to take over the assets and functions of all the bantustan "development corporations" in Namibia. Apart from introducing ENOK and its activities, the main purpose of this glossy brochure is to attract foreign capital to Namibia, which is described as being "on the threshold of unprecedented growth". It is at pains to explain how conducive the legal and tax arrangements are for profit-making, how favourable is the business environment, and how many opportunities exist for foreign investment. For further infor- mation on ENOK, see ENOK in perspective/ENOK in perspektief (Wind- hoek, 1983, 24 p.).

405. FINANCIAL MAIL. Namibia. A survey. Johannesburg, 1983, 40 p. (A supplement to Financial Mail, July 22, 1983).

A report on the economic and political situation in Namibia in 1983, prepared by the staff of the leading South African business weekly.

The articles generally support the view that the economy is highly
vulnerable to external disruption, that the mining sector is a
high-risk and capital-intensive sector and that there is a crisis in
both capitalist and African agriculture. The 1983/84 budget is
critically analysed, and the inefficient and corrupt system of ethnic
authorities - as well as the strong capital outflow to the Republic -
are identified as among the major constraints on growth. The survey
is disappointingly thin on economic and social data, especially
statistical, compared to its predecessors (Financial Mail, 2 March 1973
and 20 August 1965), which assembled a great deal of factual information at times when very little was forthcoming from official sources.

5. GREEN, REGINALD H. Namibia. A political economic survey. University
of Sussex, 1979, 123 p. 10 maps, 32 tables, bibl.: 121-23. (Institute
of Development Studies, Discussion Paper, no. 144).

When it was published in 1979, this pioneering survey went a long
way towards filling the knowledge gap on Namibia's colonial/transitional
economy, while at the same time providing an alternative interpretation
- from a point of view close to SWAPO - to the analysis offered by
Wolfgang H. Thomas (see no. 75). It contains a brief historical
overview, a sectoral survey of the economy, background information
on geography and national resources, an informed comment on the
ideology of the liberation movement and the first assessments of
Namibia's potential role in SADCC. The second half of the study
(p. 60-120) is devoted to statistical series and tables, and brings
together a wide range of quantitative and qualitative information
to construct what remains today by far the most comprehensive and
authoritative baseline data on population, personpower, GDP/GNP,
balance of payments, and government revenue and expenditure. The
tables are supplemented by footnotes discussing the origins and
reliability of the statistical sources and the author's own calculations.
The section dealing with the economy of colonialism has been expanded
in later publications, as is the case also for the discussion of the
transitional stage (no. 470).

7. HOVEY, GAIL. Namibia's stolen wealth. North American investment and
South African occupation. New York: The Africa Fund, 1982, 52 p.
(Foreword by Sean MacBride).

The first part of this booklet provides a brief introduction to the
Namibian economy, apartheid society and the struggle for liberation.
It is followed by a description of the North American corporations
involved in the extraction of Namibia's wealth. The author, who is
research director of The Africa Fund, examines the role played by
these corporations in South Africa's war, and argues in the con-
cluding section that the Reagan Administration policy bears major
responsibility for the continued sufferings of the Namibian people.
See also Breaking the Economic Links with Namibia's Exploiters:
Divestment Action in the United States, a paper presented to the
International Seminar on The Role of Transnational Corporations in
Namibia, Washington, 1982, 10 p.

8. ILANGA, MÉDARD NYONSCHI. Le capital international et ses effets en
Namibia. Quebec: Editions Naaman, 1978, 243 p. Bibl.: 203-35.

(Collection "Thèses" Reproduction).

This political science thesis, submitted to the University of Quebec, offers a mainly descriptive account of the operations of the multi-national corporations in the Namibian economy. The focal point of the critical study is on the first part of the 1970s, based on annual reports and calculations of profits of the major corporations. There is also some information on the Namibian economy and the role of foreign investment in general. The book contains a comprehensive list of firms according to sectors, as well as several tables. The bibliography is especially valuable because of the inclusion of articles from the current affairs magazines such as Afrique-Asie. Jeune Afrique, Le Monde, and L'Economiste du Tiers Monde.

409. JESKE, JOACHIM. Verkehrsgeographische Strukturwandlungen im südlichen Afrika, 1975-1980. Hamburg: Institut für Afrika-Kunde, 1981, 256 p. 26 tables, 4 diagrams, 11 maps, bibl.: 245-56.

Taking the political changes in Southern Africa during the second half of the 1970s as its point of departure, this empirical study outlines their impact on intra-regional cooperation in the economic and transportation sector. South African control of railways and deep-sea harbours is described in detail, including a separate section on Walvis Bay (p. 78-87) and a review of the plans for a Trans-Kalahari railway (p. 107-28). There are several tables and maps, as well as a comprehensive bibliography.

410. KLEIST, KARSTEN E.B. VON. Some aspects of growth and income distribution in Namibia. Oxford, 1981, 163 p. 19 tables, 22 figures, bibl.: 159-63. (MA thesis).

411. ------- Aspects of poverty and education in Namibia. Paper presented to the Carnegie Inquiry into Poverty and Development in Southern Africa, Cape Town, April 1984, 31 p. 12 tables. (Conference Paper, 104).

Written by a Namibian economist, this MA thesis provides an interesting, albeit preliminary discussion of income distribution in Namibia. The first part of the study, which is set in a framework of neo-classical economics, is devoted to abstract considerations on how to conceptual-ise and measure inquality. The chapters dealing specifically with Namibia are based on income tax returns data (for white and "brown" income earners), census income data (1950 and 1970), household surveys of Ovamboland, Kavangoland and Namaland (conducted by the Bureau for Market Research at the University of South Africa in 1974-76) and different price indices. One of the conclusions is that average household incomes in the "homelands" are 6.3% of the average white incomes. It is also emphasized that there are signifi-cant inequalities within the "homelands", with some government officials, top income farmers and traders distinctly separated from the majority. The data on black urban wages also indicate wide income differentials between unskilled workers and the professional occupations (nurses, teachers and civil servants), a gap which has increased considerably as a part of the strategy of creating a "black middle class" in the 1980s. The author has also utilised the Windhoek Household Subsistence Level (HSL) data from the Institute of

Planning Research (University of Port Elizabeth), showing that 87% of all income earners in 1976 had average total earnings less than the HSL figure. The paper presented to the Carnegie Conference in 1984 summarises and updates some of the main findings of the thesis, and argues more explicitly the case for "a market economy that combines growth with a government commitment to poverty eradiction.". (The authour is undertaking further research for a PhD thesis.)

412. KLEIST, KARSTEN E.B. VON. Tourismus in Namibia. Förderung des Tourismus als Beitrag zur Gesamtwirtschaftlichen und Gesamtgesellschaftlichen Entwicklung von SWA/Namibia. Windhoek/Freiburg, 1981, 142 p. 34 tables, 32 figures, bibl.: 138-41.

This is one of the very few published discussions of tourism in Namibia, based on available statistics as well as a questionnaire answered by tourists in 1978. The author, who is an economist and consultant based in Windhoek, starts by examining the current state of tourism in Namibia today (the number of tourists, infrastructure, regional distribution, attractions, the effects of seasonality, etc.). The section dealing with tourism as a contribution to the overall economic development covers aspects such as foreign exchange, GDP, regional development, employment and inflation. The study also touches upon ecology as well as the negative socio-cultural effects of tourism, and concludes with detailed proposals for the promotion of tourism through private enterprise as well as state institutions.

413. KRITZINGER, LARRY O. Taxation in South West Africa/Namibia. Windhoek, 1982, 94 p.

Based on the Income Tax Act No. 24 of 1981, this handbook supplies general information on taxation in Namibia. A discussion of the distinctive features of the tax system is followed by a detailed outline of the administration of taxes, income tax rates, withholding taxes and business incomes.

414. LANG, ERIC. Address to the Interessengemeinschaft Deutschsprachiger Südwester (IG). Windhoek, 11 May 1982, 14 p; and 23 May 1983, 23 p. (Unpublished typescripts).

The aim of these two addresses by a prominent Namibian businessman was to expose publicly the exploitation and mismanagement of the crisis-ridden Namibian economy. The critique is based on neo-liberal capitalist principles and a profound scepticism of government spending in general and the abuses of the South African administration in particular. The speeches have been extensively quoted in the Namibian press, and have sparked off a heated debate involving government officials as well as representatives of the major mining corporations (especially CDM). Drawing on a close examination of government revenues and expenditures, as well as of the operations of the mining companies, Lang asserts that South Africa is largely to blame for the economic and political crisis in Namibia. He argues that the system of government - especially the second-tier ethnic administration - is expensive, inefficient and corrupt; that the agricultural sector has been governed in terms of the political interests of South Africa and the National Party; and that the management of commercial farming still lies firmly in the hands of South African interests. His sharpest criticism is directed against the lack of national control over the mining industry, which stands accused of large-scale transfer pricing, tax evasion and payment of excessive dividends instead of reinvestment in the country. The 1983 address, which includes a statistical annex covering the period 1953-1983, is also concerned with the rapid increase in the external public debt.

415. LEISTNER, ERICH et al. Namibia/SWA Prospectus. Pretoria: Africa Institute of South Africa, 1980, 66 p. 13 tables, 5 maps, photos.

Prepared by three staff members of the Africa Institute in Pretoria, this is one of the most valuable of the recent crop of pro-South African and official publications. Apart from documenting the endless negotiations over the future of Namibia, the main part of the report consists of a semi-authoritative survey of the Namibian economy. The team benefitted from access to hitherto unpublished statistics, some of which were later updated (see G.M.E. Leistner/Theo Malan: "SWA/Namibia - economic survey, Africa Insight, 11, no. 2, 1981: 79-95). The Department of Finance in Windhoek began to publish an official national accounts series soon afterwards (nos. 437, 442).

416. LEISTNER, G.M.E. "SWA/Namibia's economic problems viewed in Africa context". Africa Institute of South Africa Bulletin, 21, nos. 11-12, 1981: 81-96.

A brief comment on the Namibian economy by the director of the Africa Institute of South Africa, supplemented by a statistical appendix drawing on unpublished official sources. The author's main argument is that the economic structures created during the colonial period are often extremely persistent after independence and that they cannot be transformed fundamentally within a short spell of time without administrative and economic chaos. He also argues that rapid efforts to even out differentials in respect of income, land ownership and other wealth can only be undertaken at the cost of total economic collapse. This plea is therefore - not surprisingly - for "pragmatism and gradualism".

417. MCGREGOR, ROBIN. McGregor's who owns whom. Grabouw: Purdey Publishing Co., 1983, 487 p. (Third edition).

This is an indispensable reference tool for research on South African companies, including their operations in Namibia. The book provides a wealth of information on ownership structure, directors, investment, subsidiary and associate companies. The stated intention is to publish a new edition every year.

418. MARRIOTT, MARTYN, ROGER MURRAY and PAUL SPRAY. Periodic report on the activities of transnational corporations in Namibia. January 1982- June 1983. New York: UN Centre on Transnational Corporations, 1983, 35 p. (Paper submitted to Namibia High Level Workshop on Transnational Corporations, Brazzaville, 5-10 September 1983).

Forming a part of the continuing research and training under the UN Nationhood Programme, for which the UN Centre on Transnational Corporations is the executing agency, this periodic report is an

up-to-date study on the activities of the TNCs in Namibia. In spite
of the paucity of certain relevant data, the authors have succeeded
in gathering valuable information from corporate reports, business
news media and other external sources. The report opens with a
succinct overview of the Namibian economy up to mid-1983, stressing
the impact of the drought, the ravages of the war, the depressed
mineral prices and the rapid deterioration of Namibia's finances.
The major part of the report consists of a detailed examination of
the mining corporations during the period under review, documenting,
inter alia, the increasing role played by South African private and
parastatal companies. There are special sections devoted to the three
major companies - CDM, Rossing and Tsumeb - followed by a review of
the agricultural, fishing and financial sectors.

9. MENSAH, J.H. Review of the economic conditions in Namibia and South
   Africa. Part I - Namibia. Geneva: UNCTAD, 1981, 49 p. 21 tables.
   (TD/B/869, 26 August 1981).

   Prepared by a consultant for the UNCTAD Secretariat, this is a survey
   of the main features of the Namibian economy in the late 1970s. It
   is designed to focus attention on a number of problem areas which need
   further study. Supported by a wide range of tables, the review covers
   the different sectors of the economy, employment and wages, education,
   income distribution and external dependency. Although the author's
   perspective is close to that of the liberation movement, the empirical
   data is drawn largely from W.H. Thomas (see no. 75).

0. MOORSOM, RICHARD. Walvis Bay. Namibia's port. London: International
   Defence and Aid Fund for Southern Africa, 1984, 93 p. 6 diagrams,
   5 maps, 4 tables, 13 photos. (In cooperation with the United Nations
   Council for Namibia).

   A factually detailed and comprehensively referenced presentation of
   Namibia's only deepwater port, this is the best introduction to Walvis
   Bay and the legal and economic implications of the South African occupation. The opening chapter reviews the international legal context
   of the Walvis Bay enclave and the islands, challenging South Africa's
   claim in international law. The second gives an economic history
   of Walvis Bay as port and centre of the fishing industry. The third
   describes in detail the exploitation of black labour and Walvis Bay's
   significance as a centre of worker resistance. It is followed by an
   assessment of developments since the 1977 annexation and of the
   potential economic and military consequences of continued South
   African occupation, in both a local and a national context. The large
   number of references make the book an indispensable guide to the
   literature on Walvis Bay.

21. MORRELL, JIM. "The International Monetary Fund and Namibia". Africa
    Today, 30, nos. 1-2, 1983: 17-22.

    This short paper, written for a conference on transnational corporations
    in Namibia (Washington, 1982), surveys the IMF assistance to South
    Africa. The author argues that the loans greatly encourage transnational
    investors in both South African and Namibian economies, and that the
    1982 loan (US $1,1 billion) roughly equals the cost of the war in

Namibia and Angola over the past two years. The author is on the
research staff of the Center for International Study, Washington.

422. MURRAY, ROGER, et al. The role of foreign firms in Namibia. Studies
on external investment and black workers' conditions in Namibia.
Uppsala: Africa Publications Trust, 1974, 220 p.

Published as a volume in a series of reports from "The Study Project
on External Investment in South Africa and Namibia", this book presents a pioneering critique of the illegal South African occupation.
The first of its two principal essays offers an extended description
of the main sectors of the Namibian economy in the early 1970s. This
section, amounting to almost half the book (p. 21-127), was written
by Roger Murray, and is strongest on the role of mining corporations,
although in places methodologically weak in economic analysis. Included is a comprehensive list of foreign companies operating in
Namibia, with calculations of their profits and taxes. There is also
a survey of South African expenditure in Namibia. The second essay,
by Jo Morris (no. 668), provides a descriptive survey of the situation
of black workers. There is also an article on the legal aspects
of South African occupation and foreign investment, written by
Professor John Dugard at the University of the Witwatersrand. His
interpretation is challenged from a radical point of view in a brief
comment by Neville Rubin, a South African lawyer in exile.

MURRAY, ROGER, see no. 418.

423. NAMIBIA SUPPORT COMMITTE. "A country by country listing of foreign
companies operating in Namibia". In Trade Union action on Namibian
uranium, p. 71-86. London: SWAPO/NSC, 1982.

A detailed compilation of data, prepared by Namibia Support Committee,
on companies operating in Namibia. In addition to companies with
direct or indirect investments, those involved in trade, shipping
and finance are also listed. The information is updated to February,
1982.

424. NGAVIRUE, ZEDEKIA (comp.). Careers in SWA/Namibia. Windhoek: Private
Sector Foundation, 1982, 38 p. (Education and Training Series No. 1).

425. ------- A report on the 1981 Manpower Survey. Windhoek: Private
Sector Foundation, 1982, 62 p. (Manpower Survey Series No. 1).

426. TRUEBODY, CHARLES T. Labour relations in SWA/Namibia. A first assessment. Windhoek: Private Sector Foundation, 1982, 16 p. (Labour
Relations Series No. 1).

The Private Sector Foundation (PSF) was set up in 1981 to promote
"free market values" and support the small business sector. Together
with W.H. Thomas: Employment generation... (no. 445) these three
pamphlets were the first to appear in the series "Private Sector
Publications". Careers is a guide to training and job opportunities
in the private sector, partly based on a pamphlet prepared by Career
Research & Information Centre in Cape Town. A report... describes
the 1981 manpower survey conducted by PSF to determine the principal

employers and the prevailing skill shortages. Labour relations reports
on the second part of the survey, summarising information on working
conditions given by 263 firms. The survey did not include agricultural
and domestic workers.

7. RIJNEVELD, A.W. Economic exploitation: the case of Namibia. Rotterdam,
1977, 39 p.

This pioneering report on the economic exploitation of Namibia, prepared
by a Dutch economist at the request of SWAPO, addresses economic issues
of no small political relevance. Admitting that official data are
either unreliable, misleading or lacking, the author nevertheless
succeeds in highlighting the main mechanisms of exploitation in the
various sectors of the economy. There are some careful calculations
of gross profits at Consolidated Diamond Mines, Tsumeb and SWACO over
a period of 25 years (1950-1975), leading to the conclusions that
yearly profits over this period averaged at least US $200 per capita
and that the total outflow of capital was an estimated 25-40% of GDP.
To this have to be added the effects of internal exploitation expressed
in the highly unequal distribution of income, wealth and land. The
report also contains other economic data, such as estimates of total
exports of cattle, karakul pelts and fishery products (oil, canned
fish, fishmeal) in the 1955-1975 period.

8. ROGERS, BARBARA. Foreign investment in Namibia. New York: UN Council
for Namibia, 1975, 134 p.

Commissioned by the UN Council for Namibia, this comprehensive consultancy report was one of three to be completed by the same author
which remain among the best of their kind but, regrettably, unpublished
(see nos. 567, 599). The first part examines the role of foreign
investment and provides a survey of investment by country. It is
followed by a discussion of investment in Namibia as an international
issue. The critique of such investment is sharp, authoritative,
and buttressed by solid empirical research.

9. ROGERS, BARBARA. White wealth and black poverty. American investments
in Southern Africa. Westport, Connecticut/London: Greenwood Press,
1976, 331 p. (Center on International Race Relations, University of
Denver, Studies in Human rights, no. 2.).

The author of this survey of US corporate interests in Southern Africa
is a freelance writer and researcher, who in the mid-1970s produced the
first major studies for the UN Commissioner for Namibia. The main
focus is on South Africa and the role played by the multinational
corporations in preserving the structure of white power, but there
are also separate chapters on Namibia as well as Zimbabwe, Mozambique
and Angola. Namibia is discussed in chapter 5 (p. 170-216), and the
author documents how many US corporations are doing business in
Namibia as part of their South African operations. She also argues
strongly for corporate withdrawal.

0. SCHNEIDER-BARTHOLD, WOLFGANG. Namibia's economic potential and
existing economic ties with the Republic of South Africa. Berlin:
German Development Institute, 1977, 93 p. Bibl.: 90-3. (German

original: <u>Wirtschaftspotensial und wirtschaftliche Verflechtung</u>
<u>Namibias mit der Republik Südafrika</u>. Berlin, 1977, 90 p.).

Written by a senior economist at the German Development Institute,
this widely quoted report was one of the first serious attempts
to question the South African assertion that Namibia would have to
maintain close links with the "mother country" because of its economic
dependence. Based on a broad reading of official and non-official
sources, as well as a visit to Namibia, the study sets out to describe and examine the economic structure, the development bottle-
necks and the present heavy dependence on South Africa. The author
argues that even within the framework of a "free market economy", assum-
ing that no structural changes take place after independence, Namibia's
resources are extensive and varied enough to serve as a basis for a
self-supporting economic development. The conclusion is, however,
that this potential can only be exploited for the good of the Namibian
people after an independent government has abolished apartheid and
eliminated (or modified) the close economic links to South Africa.
There are also a large number of tables and a bibliography.

431. SEIDMAN, ANN and NEVA SEIDMAN MAKGETLA. <u>South Africa and U.S. multi-</u>
<u>national corporations</u>. Dar es Salaam, Tanzania Publishing House/West-
port, Connecticut: Lawrence Hill & Co., 1977, 252 p.

432. ------- <u>Outposts of monopoly capitalism. Southern Africa in the changing</u>
<u>global economy</u>. Westport, Connecticut: Lawrence Hill & Co./London:
Zed Press, 1980, 370 p.

Written by two leading US socialist economists, the first of these two
studies on the political economy of foreign investment in Southern
African contains a separate chapter on Namibia: "Namibia: an outright colony" (p. 162-73). Although there are few explicit references
to Namibia in the book published in 1980, this well-documented
survey provides a framework for the analysis of transnational corporations, underdevelopment and the prospects for regional integration
of utmost relevance to Namibia.

433. SIMON, DAVID. <u>The end of apartheid? Some dimensions of urban poverty</u>
<u>in Windhoek</u>. Paper presented to the Carnegie Inquiry into Poverty
and Development in Southern Africa Conference, Cape Town, April 1984,
31 p. 6 tables, bibl. 28-31. (Conference paper 22).

Mainly based on the author's D.Phil. thesis - <u>Aspects of urban changes,</u>
<u>Windhoek</u> (no. 102) - this conference paper is devoted to the question
of urban poverty and working class organisation. Despite the upward
mobility of a small coloured and black bourgeoisie since 1977, the
author shows that a racial class hierarchy still persists and that
most black workers earn poverty wages in an essentially unchanged
economic system. He also argues that "many Katutura and Khomasdal
residents have become poorer in real terms in recent years - as evi-
denced also by housing conditions, disease patterns, rising alcoholism,
unemployment and the growth of 'informal' activities". The paper also
discusses the factors which make the formation of strong trade unions
difficult, such as rising unemployment and active employer and official
resistance.

434. SOUTH WEST AFRICA (ADM.). <u>Ontwikkelingspotensiaal van Suidwes-Afrika:</u>
<u>eerste verslag van die tweede komitee van die Staatkundige Beraad.</u>
Windhoek: SWA Administration, Planning Dept., 1977, 132 p. 31 tables,
15 maps, 4 figures.

Drawn up by a subcommittee of the Constitutional Conference, this report
on the development potential of Namibia was intended to be the first
prospective development plan prepared by an "interim government" installed by South Africa. It includes chapters covering physical
setting, population, infrastructure, general economy, mining, agriculture, fisheries, forestry, tourism, and nature conservation.
Because of changes in the political context the report was never
released, but it is available for reference and consultation.

435. SOUTH WEST AFRICA (ADM.). <u>The economy of SWA/Namibia: problems,</u>
<u>future prospects and required policy measures.</u> Windhoek, Department
of Finance, 1978, 64 p. (In Afrikaans, <u>Die ekonomie van SWA/Namibië:</u>
<u>probleme, toekomsmoontlikhede en vereiste beleidsmaatreëls.</u> Windhoek:
Departement van Finansies, 1978, 65 p.).

This study of the Namibian economy originated from the Economic
Advisory Committee set up by the Turnhalle Conference to determine
the economic potential of the territory and to advise the "interim
government" on economic policy. The Committee did not submit its
report until 1978, when the Conference had already been dissolved,
and publication was delayed a further two years. The report gives
a brief survey of the different sectors of the economy, discusses
future forms of cooperation with South Africa and presents a large
number of specific recommendations. The orientation of the document
reflects the preponderance on the Committee of prominent South African
businessmen and representatives of multinational corporations. It
argues strongly against a national minimum wage and "a too rapid
equalisation of income differences", and it generally supports a
close association with the sophisticated South African economy. In
this regard the assertion that Namibia has been "exploited" is completely rejected. It also claims that favourable terms for mining
operations are necessary to compensate for the risks involved.

36. SOUTH WEST AFRICA (ADM.). <u>Verslag van die Kommissie van ondersoek na</u>
<u>die finansiële verhoudings tussen sentrale, verteenwoordigende en</u>
<u>plaaslike owerhede.</u> Windhoek, 1980. Vol. 1: 83 p. Vol. 2: 136 p.

This report on the financial aspects of the politico-administrative
system prevailing in 1980 takes the existing division of functions
between central government, second-tier ("representative") and local
authorities as given. The report outlines the fiscal set-up under the
old dispensation and presents detailed proposals for the financing
of the new system as well as for allocation of funds. The second
volume contains a wide range of tables which highlight the financial
and fiscal structure.

37. SOUTH WEST AFRICA (ADM.). <u>On the economic front.</u> Windhoek: Dept.
of Finance/SWA-Namibia Information Service. No. 1, April 1980,
9 p.; no. 2, June 1980, 26 p.; no. 3, January 1981, 26 p.; no. 4,
July 1981, 33 p.; no. 5, November 1981, 17 p.

These booklets were published as an occasional series during 1980-81 with the aim of directing public attention to the economic policies of the South African administration in Windhoek. No. 1 provides a very brief survey of GDP by economic sector for 1976-78. No. 2 reproduces the text of Dirk Mudge's first Budget Speech to the "National Assembly". No. 3 presents an analysis of GDP by the Department of Finance supplied with a brief discussion of the trends in each major sector for the period 1970-78. No. 4 contains Mudge's Budget Speech; while no. 5 comprises four brief pieces on the governmental system, the economic structure, economic policy, and the 1981/82 budget. The GDP statistics in no. 3 were the first time series to be issued officially following 20 years of secrecy and suppression. The 1983 Budget Speech, delivered by the South African Administrator General, has been published as a booklet: SWA/Namibia. Budget 1983-1984 / SWA/Namibia. Haushalt 1983-1984. Windhoek, 1983, 32 p.

438. SOUTH WEST AFRICA (ADM.). Private placing of R 40 m local registered stock, loans nos. 11, 12 and 13. Windhoek, 8 March 1982, 9 p.

439. ------- Private placing of R 40 m local registered stock, loans nos. 18, 19 and 20. Windhoek, 19 January 1983.

The South African central administration in Namibia, caught by a serious budget crisis, first entered the loan market on a substantial scale during 1981. The resulting prospectuses provide not only full details of the amount and terms of the loans themselves but also a fairly up-to-date assessment of the state of the economy, although clearly presented in as optimistic a light as possible. They contain a range of official data, including some not to be found in any other published source.

440. SOUTH WEST AFRICA (ADM.). Socio-Economic Conference= Sosio-Ekonomiese Beraad. Windhoek, 1983, 252 p.

441. ------- Development Conference 84= Ontwikkelingsberaad. Windhoek, 1984. Vol. 1: 207 p. Vol. 2: 166 p.

The first Socio-economic Conference was held in Windhoek in May 1982, and was followed exactly two years later by a Development Conference. The purpose of these conferences, convened by the South African authorities in Windhoek, was to give high-ranking officials and prominent business leaders an opportunity to discuss the Namibian economy and to exchange views on future economic policy. The proceedings, compiled by the Directorate for Development Coordination, reproduce the major background documents and addresses. Apart from sectoral reviews (agriculture, fisheries, mining, infrastructure, housing etc), papers and comments were submitted by the Private Sector Foundation, the Chamber of Commerce and Industries, the South West African Agricultural Union and other private interest groups and business organisations. Most of the text is in Afrikaans, but parts are in English.

SPRAY, PAUL, see no. 418.

442. THE SWA/NAMIBIA INFORMATION SERVICE. Statistical/economic review 1983.

Windhoek, 1983, 28 p.   16 figures, 32 tables.

Compiled by the Department of Finance, this most recent official
review of the Namibian economy reflects the increasing willingness
of the regime to release statistical data.   Apart from providing a
survey of the year 1981 (GDP, investment trends, balance of payments,
public finance and sectoral reviews), the major part of the document
consists of a statistical appendix covering the period 1970-81.   Walvis
Bay is excluded from the statistical series, and information on
population and wages are highly disputable.   The main problem, however,
is that there is no explanation of the many changes from the first
edition (1982) to the second edition.

3. SPARKS, DONALD L.   Walvis Bay, Plumpudding and Penguin Islands:
   their history and economic importance to Namibia.   Paper presented
   to the 22. annual meeting of the African Studies Association,
   Los Angeles, 1979, 22 p.

   Prepared by a researcher at the Office of Economic Research and Analysis,
   US Dept. of State, this brief paper examines the economic implications of the South African occupation of Walvis Bay.   It discusses
   the importance of Walvis Bay as a port and economic centre, and suggests
   that South Africa wants to use Walvis Bay and the islands as bargaining
   levers to extract fishing and mineral rights.   It also speculates
   that South Africa might - under an extreme scenario - dismantle
   the port and industrial facilities or keep the port and railway link
   closed in order to cut off an independent Namibia from the outside
   world.

4. THIMM, HEINZ-ULRICH.   Integrated rural development (IRD):   Kommentar
   zum Ontwikkelingsplan vir Owambo/Namibia.   Saarbrücken/Fort Lansdale:
   Breitenbach, 1980, 91 p.   Maps, 24 figures.   (Schriften des Zentrums
   für Regionale Entwicklungsforschung der Justus- Liebig-Universität
   Giessen, 14).

   The "development plan" discussed here is one of three on northern
   Namibian bantustans which were prepared at Stellenbosch University
   in the second half of the 1970s for the South African government
   (see nos. 450-52).   The commentary is part of a series on regional
   development plans published by the Zentrum für regionale Entwicklungsforschung, which all follow a uniform procedure.   The first half
   presents a straightforward summary of the Ontwikkelingsplan in terms
   of its own framework and concepts, and includes many of the tables
   and maps.   The second half analyses the plan in terms of a standard
   set of criteria derived from the concept of integrated rural development, to which the centre is committed.   It detects some positive
   features, but raises a large number of criticisms, some of them
   major.   The author is a leading West German expert on agriculture
   and rural development and paid a lengthy visit to southern Africa
   in 1979-80.

5. THOMAS, WOLFGANG H.   Employment generation in the context of a basic
   needs orientated development strategy for Namibia.   Windhoek: Private
   Sector Foundation, 1982, 23 p.   (Socio-Economic Development Series
   No. 1).

Based on a public lecture in 1981, this is the first in a series of
socio-economic studies published by the Private Sector Foundation (see nos
424-26). The author (see no. 75) sets out to update some of his
earlier calculations of population, labour force and employment estimates, concluding that un- and underemployment had increased considerably since 1978 due to the drought, the near-breakdown of the
fishing industry, and a slow-down in the mining sector. The final section
lists several policy recommendations for the government, such as
discouraging the rapid exodus of people from the peasant sector,
improvement in rural services and introduction of new crops, expansion
of the basic infrastructure in rural and black urban areas and greater
emphasis on the local production and processing of consumer goods.

446. THOMAS, WOLFGANG H. "The 1983/84 budget and Namibia's alleged financial
crisis". The Namibian Review, no. 29, (July-August) 1983: 1-10.

This is a brief and provocative comment on the current economic and
financial crisis in Namibia, designed to modify the widespread notion
that financial collapse, fiscal bankruptcy and a huge foreign debt
burden is imminent. The author accepts that the general perspective
is less optimistic due to the war, world-wide recession, the drought,
high rates of inflation, and the exodus of skilled manpower, but argues
that the underlying goal of some official documents might be to demonstrate that internationally recognised independence is financially
impossible for Namibia. Since the country is little more than another
(semi-independent) "homeland" of South Africa, he suggests that the
final responsibility for the fiscal consequences of the expensive
political structure - including ethnic authorities and the dominant
position of the conservative white administration - should fall upon
South Africa.

TRANSPORT RESEARCH CENTRE, see no. 453.

TRUEBODY, CHARLES T., see no. 426.

447. UNITED NATIONS COUNCIL FOR NAMIBIA. Activities of foreign economic
interests operating in Namibia. Paper presented to the International
Conference in Support of the Struggle of the Namibian People for
Independence, Paris, 1983, 33 p. 3 tables. (A/Conf. 120/4. A/AC.131/92
16 March 1983).

448. ------- List of transnational corporations and other foreign economic
interests operating in Namibia. Paper presented to the International
Conference in Support of the Struggle of the Namibian People for
Independence, Paris, 1983, 18 p. (A/Conf. 120/8, 4 April 1983).

Prepared by the UN Council for Namibia, these two reports present
up-to-date information on the transnational corporations operating
in Namibia. They illustrate the extent of Namibia's considerable
natural resources, their strategic and economic value to South Africa
and other foreign economic interests, and the role played by the
corporations in perpetuating the illegal occupation of the territory.
There are also sections dealing with working conditions, the exploitation of Namibia's human resources and the international campaign

against corporations collaborating with South Africa in defiance of
UN resolutions. The list of foreign corporations identifies close to
250 companies. See also Report of the Mission of the Council to
Contact Corporations, 30 July to 9 July 1982 (New York: UN Council
for Namibia, 1983. A/AC. 109/699). For a brief update, see Activities
of transnational corporations and measures being taken by governments
to prohibit investments in South Africa and Namibia. (New York: UN
Economic and Social Council, 1984, 12 p. E/C. 10/1984). The question
of governmental measures to prohibit investments is covered in
Responsibilities of home countries with the respect to the transnational
corporations operating in South Africa and Namibia in violation of
the relevant resolutions and decisions of the United Nations (E/C.
10/1984/19).

9. UNITED NATIONS COUNCIL FOR NAMIBIA. Social conditions in Namibia.
Paper presented to the International Conference in Support of the
Struggle of the Namibian People for Independence, Paris, 1983, 16 p.
(A/Conf. 120/5, A/AC.131/93, 16 March 1983).

In fulfilment of its responsibility to keep social conditions in
Namibia under constant review, the UN Council for Namibia prepared a
report for the Paris Conference in 1983. It documents the extent
to which racial discrimination and discriminatory laws continue to
govern education, housing, employment and all other aspects of the
daily life of Namibians. The review devotes special sections to
education, health facilities, living conditions, the status of
women, exploitation of labour and the refugee problem. There is
also a brief overview of oppressive legislation, maltreatment of
political prisoners, terrorisation of the general population, and
other violations of human rights.

0. UNIVERSITEIT VAN STELLENBOSCH, INSTITUUT VIR BEPLANNINGNAVORSING.
Evaluasie van die hulpbronne van Kaokoland en ontwikkelingsvoorstelle.
Stellenbosch, 1976, 20 p. 19 tables, 13 maps, 1 diagram.

1. ------- Ontwikkelingsplan vir Owambo. Stellenbosch, 1978, 79 p.
67 tables, 13 maps, 7 diagrams.

2. ------- 'n Raamwerk vir ontwikkeling van Kavango. Stellenbosch,
1980. 141 tables, 22 maps, 40 figures. Vol. 1: Report, 189 p.
Vol. 2: Atlas, 40 p.

These studies, which complement a later set produced by ENOK (see nos.
401-03), represent a major South African government effort to develop
an economic strategy for its bantustan administrations in northern
Namibia. Although precise circumstances differ, the major commissioning
agency was the frequently renamed Department of Bantu Administration
and Development, which to judge by the size of the research effort,
which also produced a number of unpublished preliminary and technical
reports as well as a large number of detailed maps, funded the programme on a large scale. Researched and prepared between 1973 and
1978, the reports are firmly located within South Africa's bantustan
policy, which defines their terms of reference and which they seek
to elaborate in the fields of economic and administrative planning.
Although they approximate to regional development plans, there is
virtually no consideration of the national economic or political

context except in terms of the administrative structures of a "separate
development". Despite progressive elaboration from a 20-page overview
to a 230-page two-volume report, little attention is given to "developmen
as a social, economic and political process. Discussion of the local
peasant economy and society is likewise sketchy from both empirical
and analytical points of view. The main preoccupation is to identify
natural resources suitable for commercial exploitation and to outline
institutional and infrastructural mechanisms for promoting agricultural
and industrial expansion within a free-market commercial framework. The
reports remain nevertheless one of the very few sources of recent data
on the northern bantustans, much of it derived from unpublished government reports and studies. Their main empirical strength lies in their
detailed examination of the local physical geography, ecology and infrastructure.

453. UNIVERSITY OF STELLENBOSCH, TRANSPORT RESEARCH CENTRE. Report on an
investigation into the potential development at Walvis Bay. Stellenbosch
1977, 148 p. 9 figures.

Submitted to the Town Council of Walvis Bay, this consultancy report
provides scattered data on harbour facilities, fisheries, canning
factories, secondary industry, trade, water supply, railway traffic,
employment and power supply. The chief purpose of its commissioning
was to discuss aspects of the proposal to declare the area a free port
or free trade zone, an idea which is periodically popular amongst
local whites wanting to retain South African protection after independence but nervous of the economic consequences of confrontation
over the status of Walvis Bay following the South African annexation.

454. VESPER, MICHAEL. Überleben in Namibia. "Homelands" und kapitalistisches
Weltsystem. Bonn: Informationsstelle Südliches Afrika, 1983, 273 p.
13 tables, 3 diagrams, bibl.: 235-38. (ISSA Wissenschaftliche Reihe
17).

The purpose of this scholarly work, originally submitted as a PhD
thesis in development sociology, is to focus attention on the Namibian
reserves or "homelands". The author argues that a serious under-
estimation and underevaluation of the subsistence sector characterise
most recent works on the Namibian economy and social formations,
including contributions from radical scholars, and that more consideration has to be given to the working and living conditions of small
peasants, artisans, women, children and old people in the "homelands".
The study is partly based on field work in 1977-79, but it is disappointingly thin on original data, which is restricted to central
and southern Namibia. The main value of the book lies in the summary
of the scanty secondary literature and in the theoretical discussion
of the highly controversial concept of "subsistence production", the
role of non-wage labour, and the subordination of the economic
activities of the people in the bantustans to capital accumulation
in the overall Namibian economy. The discussion tends, however, to
be rather abstract, and there is a stark contrast between the
theoretical ambitions and the lack of empirical data to support the
author's position.

55. WINDHOEK (MUNICIPALITY). <u>Die kleinhandel in Windhoek</u>. Windhoek: City
Engineers Department, Town Planning Section, 1978. Vol. I: Data
insameling en beskrywing van die rumtelike struktur. 121 p. 37 tables,
3 maps, 45 figures. Vol. II: Analise van rumtelike struktuur. 96 p.
18 tables, 10 maps, 18 figures.

A study of retail trade in Windhoek, packed with data on employment,
salaries and wages, sales and turnover. An attempt is made to analyse
the material with a view to defining the roles played by the separate
ethnic groups.

56. WOOD, BRIAN. "The militarisation of Namibia's economy". <u>Review of
African Political Economy</u>,no. 29, 1984: 138-44.

Originally prepared for a UN conference on the military situation in and
relating to Namibia in 1982, this is a succinct survey of the far-
reaching militarisation of the Namibian economy. It makes the point
that the foreign corporations operating illegally in the territory,
sustain South Africa's military effort through payments to state
revenues, contracts for military infrastructure, and the arming and
training of their staff. The author argues that the white settler
farmers are seen as a second line of defence and receive heavy government subsidies in order to stay on in their fortified farmhouses .
He concludes by recommending that those companies which materially
support South Africa's military occupation should be made liable to
specific claims for damages by a future government of Namibia. The
author was formerly executive secretary of the Namibia Support Committee
in London.

SEE ALSO:

2, 3, 9, 10, 11, 12, 17, 18, 29, 30, 36, 41, 42, 44, 45, 49, 51, 56,
60, 72, 74, 75, 78, 79, 87, 88, 92, 95, 96, 100, 102-4, 111, 296,
353, 359, 361-2, 366-8, 269, 376, chapter 6 d(457-96), chapter 7
a(497-550), chapter 7 b(551-74), chapter 7 c(575-614), 649-50,
680, 800, 896, 943, 970, 1021, 1037.

D. Planning for an independent Namibia

457. THE AFRICAN-AMERICAN SCHOLARS COUNCIL, INC. Zimbabwe. Namibia. Anticipation of economic and humanitarian needs. Transition problems in developing nations in Southern Africa. Washington, 1977, 338 p. + appendices. 35 tables, 26 maps, bibl.: Appendix I, 19 p.

This is the first of several US reports concerned with "transitional problems" in Namibia and the need for US assistance. Commissioned by the US Agency for International Development, it was produced in a hurry by a large number of consultants from the academic establishment and is based on a wide range of unpublished papers. One of the purposes was to create a data-base to be used by economic planners and political analysts, but there are few attempts to supplement or to examine critically the out-dated South African data on which the study is based. In terms of both data and analysis, the report is comprehensively superseded by another US AID study: Development Needs and Opportunities... (nos. 490-1). There are several factual appendices, such as an annotated bibliography and a list of institutions with research and training capabilities related to Southern Africa. For a critical examination of the report and its basic assumptions, see James Turner and Sean Gervasi: "The American Economic Future in Southern Africa", Journal of Southern African Affairs, 3, no. 1, 1978: 85-98.

458. ASOMBANG, WILFRED W. "Export marketing strategies for economic development in Namibia". SADEX, 2, no. 6, (November-December) 1980: 1-24.

459. ------- Trade policy options for independent Namibia. Lusaka: UNIN, 1982, 76 p. 21 tables. (Working Paper).

The aim of this working paper, written by an economist at the UN Institute for Namibia, is to focus on the existing trade patterns and practices and possible trade policy options after independence. The first part of the study examines internal trade, arguing that the local processing of minerals, cattle and fish will expand value added, employment, and domestic trade in manufactures. The second part is devoted to an analysis of the present composition and trends of Namibia's foreign trade and balance of payments, and leads to a detailed examination of product-by-product trade policy options. A final section outlines some of the policy options for services (transport, financial and technical services) which are today a major drain on foreign exchange earnings. Regional aspects are also considered, and the author argues strongly for an independent Namibia joining SADCC instead of the Rand Monetary Zone and South African Customs Union. The article in SADEX gives a summary of the main ideas and the statistical data.

460. ASOMBANG, WILFRED W. Transnational corporations (TNCs) and the Republic of South Africa (RSA) as partners in the exploitation of the people and the economy of Namibia. Paper presented to the International Seminar on the Role of Transnational Corporations in Namibia, Washington, 1982, 42 p.

This well-researched paper provides a survey of the role of TNCs in the political economy of Namibia, demonstrating that the government of a future independent Namibia will inherit an economy that has been run as an enclave of TNCs based in South Africa, Western Europe and the US. The author gives a concise summary of the numerous studies which have appeared on the TNCs in Namibia, especially in mining, and argues that there has been a tendency to propose more and more research projects rather than utilising the completed studies for the purpose of training Namibians and of formulating action to confront the home countries of the TNCs. He also makes the point that the TNCs have been stepping up production so as to strip Namibia of proven mineral deposits before handing over the country to Namibians. The final section of the paper is devoted to a discussion of the possibilities of rapprochement between the TNCs and the government of an independent Namibia.

ASOMBANG, W., see no. 461.

461. AULAKH, H.S. and W. ASOMBANG. Economic development strategy options for independent Namibia. Lusaka: UNIN, 1985. (Namibia Studies Series, edited by N.K. Duggal). In preparation.

462. BOMANI, M.D. and C. USHEWOKUNZE. Constitutional options for Namibia. A historical perspective. Lusaka: UNIN, 1979, 66 p. (Namibia Studies Series No. 2, edited by N.K. Duggal).

This is the second study in a series published by the UN Institute of Namibia, designed to stimulate discussion on the constitutional options for an independent Namibia. It opens with a wide-ranging historical survey of the evolution of the constitutional structure imposed upon the territory by South Africa after 1920. The Turnhalle Constitutional Conference is then critically examined, and it is argued that its interim draft constitution was structured on the assumption of the continued existence of the bantustan ethnic home- lands and racial segregation. The authors have deliberately refrained from making detailed proposals, leaving policy formulation to Namibians at a constitutional conference, but offer a sober discussion of the major policy options with regard to the functions of the executive, the legislature, the election process, the judiciary, citizenship, human rights, state succession, and the role of political parties. It does, however, come to the categorial conclusion that a unitary rather than a federal system of government is a necessity in order to transform the fragmented and ethnically based system.

463. DANIEL, PHILIP. Mining wages and national wage policy: international experience and the prospects for Namibia. University of Sussex, Institute of Development Studies, 1984, 21 p. (IDS Discussion Paper, 191).

Originally prepared for a seminar on mining industry at the United
Nations Institute for Namibia in 1983, the aim of this discussion
paper is to explore ways in which a wage system for the mining
sector can be reconciled with the wider national development prospects. One of the basic assumptions is that direct linkages between
mining and other industries in Namibia are negligible, and that
the short-term potential after independence for creating additional
employment or industrial linkages will not be great. The main purpose
of the mining sector is, therefore, to raise revenue and foreign
exchange for development programmes. Although there will be strong
pressure for increases in wages and salaries, the paper argues that
there are possibly stronger arguments on grounds of equity and
development strategy for resisting them. It points out that mine-
workers' wages have in the 1970s moved rapidly ahead of wages in other
sectors, and that it is implausible to expect mining wages to serve
as a standard in low-paying sectors of employment, such as ranching
and domestic services.

464. DEUTSCHES INSTITUT FÜR ENTWICKLUNGSPOLITIK. Multisektorstudie.
Namibia - Kurzbericht. Berlin: DIE, 1979, 155 p. (English edition:
Multi-sectoral study in Namibia. Summary. Berlin: German Develop-
ment Institute, 1979, 137 p. 8 tables, 9 maps.)

In 1978 the Federal Ministry for Economic Cooperation requested
the German Development Institute "to work out a multisectoral study
on Namibia which could serve as a foundation for a future bilateral
cooperation programme of the Federal Republic of Germany". The work
was to be based on the assumptions that a negotiated settlement and
free elections would take place, that all forms of racial discrimination would be abolished, that a large part of the white population
would remain in the country, and that the government would follow
the course of a mixed economy with priorities given to economic
growth, income redistribution and reduction of economic dependence
upon South Africa. The authors of the study visited Namibia and
South Africa in July-November 1978, and their reports were submitted
in early 1979. The sectoral studies on agriculture, industry, health,
education, material infrastructure and external economic relations
have been published separately (see nos. 502-04, 475, 712-14, 698,
492, 494-96), while the studies on fisheries, mining, manpower and
administrative structures remain unpublished. This condensed report
contains a brief section giving background data on the economic and
social structure, followed by a summary of the individual sectoral
studies with emphasis on programmes and projects for bilateral
cooperation with West German ministries, foundations and private
industry.

DEUTSCHES INSTITUT FÜR ENTWICKLUNGSPOLITIK, see GERMAN DEVELOPMENT
INSTITUTE, no. 467.

DUGGAL, N.K., see nos. 461, 462, 468, 476, 534, 536, 578, 692, 708.

465. ECONOMIC COMMISSION FOR AFRICA. Transport survey for Namibia:
report of a multidisciplinary team of experts. Addis Ababa, n.d.,
151 + 7 p. (annexes). Tables, diagrams. (UN Nationhood Programme

for Namibia, Project NAM/79/005).

As a preliminary survey this study has its limitations: railways are omitted altogether "because an expert in railways could not be recruited"; no field visit was possible; and only the very scanty published official documentation was available. It is nonetheless one of the more sub- stantial of the consultancy reports prepared under the Nationhood Programme. A considerable body of data was gathered from a wide range of sources, notably on physical infrastructure, facilities and ser- vices, traffic types and volumes, and to a certain extent administra- tive structures and procedures. Although in a few respects the data is outdated by the German Development Institute study and the National Atlas (see nos. 492, 111), some of the tabulations of technical and organisational information will remain valuable for planning purposes. A notable feature of the study is its concern with strategy and planning, both in the transitional period and longer-term, with an emphasis on practical requirements and pre-independence preparation. Following a general overview, the study is organised into separate chapters on roads, road transport, ports, shipping, maritime adminis- tration, and civil aviation. One of its more controversial conclusions is that there is no alternative to using Walvis Bay and that therefore a peaceful transfer should be sought "at all costs".

466. FABER, MIKE, REGINALD H. GREEN and CHARLES HARVEY. TNC-state relations and negotiations: fiscal and financial issues (with special emphasis on Namibia). University of Sussex, Institute of Development Studies, 1984. 92 p. (IDS Commissioned Studies Series).

Prepared by three prominent economists from the Institute of Development Studies (Sussex, UK) for the Namibia High Level Workshop on Trans- national Corporations (Brazzaville, 5-10 September 1983), the purpose of this discussion paper is to present some general fiscal and finan- cial issues which are relevant to determining state policy towards the TNCs. The last part discusses the specific situation in Namibia, arguing that the fact that none of the TNCs have entered the country after negotiations with a Namibian government constitutes grounds for initiating far-reaching renegotiations. Special emphasis is laid on taxation and participation options, using examples from mining, banking, manufacturing, foreign trade and the energy sector.

467. GERMAN DEVELOPMENT INSTITUTE. Perspectives of independent development in Southern Africa. The cases of Zimbabwe and Namibia. Berlin: GDI, 1980, 183 p. 12 tables, 2 diagrams, 2 maps.

The purpose of this book is to make available in English some of the information contained in the extensive GDI studies on Zimbabwe and Namibia in 1977-78. The information has been placed in a more general and theoretical framework, and an introductory essay by W. Schneider- Barthold discusses the concept of dependence in southern Africa. There are four chapters concerned with Namibia, drawing on the sectoral studies on agriculture, industry, health and external economic relations. For separate annotations, see Brandt (no. 504), Lachenmann (no. 713) and Zehender (no. 495). The overall strategy is set mainly within a "free-market" framework, modified by proposals to reform the most exploitative economic and social relationships. The chapters on industry, health and agriculture contain original information, but its origins and status are often difficult to establish.

468. GREEN, REGINALD H. Manpower estimates and development implications
for Namibia. Lusaka: UNIN, 1978, 72 p. 12 tables, 7 figures.
(Namibia Studies Series No. 1, edited by N.K. Duggal.).

A pioneering study which provided the first independent and coherent
analysis of employment patterns, the labour force., population estimates, education, training and manpower requirements for an independent
Namibia. The opening chapter outlines the basic features of the
colonial political economy and the problems confronting Namibia.
The ensuing discussion is based on the assumption that the development
strategy for an independent Namibia will follow the principles and
broad themes enunciated by the liberation movement. The author
estimates the high and middle level manpower requirements of key
sectors, and discusses important aspects such as employment for women,
the implications of ending contract labour and the role of the public
sector. There is also a separate chapter on expatriate personnel
requirements (cost, recruiting and control), and the final chapter
identifies areas for further study. The original draft, which was
not published, contained a wide range of data and estimates which
have served as a basis for a large number of studies by the author
himself (see nos. 29, 470) as well as by others.

469. GREEN, REGINALD H. "Economic co-ordination, liberation and development: Botswana - Namibia perspectives". In Papers on the economy
of Botswana, edited by Charles Harvey, p. 178-95. London: Heinemann,
1981.

This is one of the very few attempts to analyse the prospects for
Namibian independence. The author opens with a brief outline of the
aims and organisation of SADCC, and then discusses the scope for
economic integration between Namibia and Botswana. Among the projects
he considers are the Trans-Kalahari railway, Okavango River water
allocation and management, mining (exchange of geological surveys
and joint formulation of bargaining positions vis-à-vis foreign
firms), and research and training. Among his many capacities, the
author serves as a consultant to SADCC, the Government of Botswana,
SWAPO and the UN Institute for Namibia.

470. GREEN, REGINALD H. From Südwestafrika to Namibia. The political
economy of transition. Uppsala: Scandinavian Institute of African
Studies, 1981, 51 p. 7 tables, 3 maps. (Research Report No. 48).

This is one of the most stimulating and up-to-date discussions of
the period of transition in Namibia. It opens with a brief survey
of the basic features of the present economic structure, followed
by an anlysis of SWAPO's "political economy of liberation". The
author makes the point that the constraints on change, are
numerous and severe, and that they could become unmanageable
in the context of delayed transition and destabilisation by South
Africa. The discussion focuses on the need to loosen the economic
ties with South Africa (personnel, transport, trade), concluding
that a very substantial reduction in dependence can be achieved
within five years of independence. The author also considers
the prospect for regional cooperation within the SADCC framework,

and concludes by providing a checklist of priorities for Year One.
The research report is also published in a slightly revised form as
"One Namibia, one nation: the political economy of transition",
in Changing realities in Southern Africa, edited by Michael Clough,
p. 92-122. (Berkeley: University of California, 1982). See also
two briefer articles dealing with the same subject: "The political
economy of liberation", in Namibia. The last colony, edited by
Reginald H. Green, Marja-Liisa Kiljunen and Kimmo Kiljunen, p. 198-217,
(London: Longman, 1981) and "Transition to what? Some issues of
freedom and necessity in Namibia", Development and Change, 11, no. 3,
1980: 419-41. The author also presented a paper, The political
economy of transition, to a symposium on research priorities at the
Institute of Commonwealth Studies, London, 21-23 July 1984.

GREEN, REGINALD H., see no. 466.

HARVEY, CHARLES, see no. 466.

KGARABE, ALOYSIUS, see no. 473.

471. KUKURI, B.R. Options for a monetary system for an independent Namibia.
Bangor, Gwynedd, University of North Wales, 1981, 117 p. (MA thesis).

The object of this thesis by a Namibian economist is to undertake a
preliminary investigation into issues of monetary policy. The opening
chapters provide a brief survey of the Namibian economy, mainly based
on the works of R.H. Green. They are followed by a presentation of
the arrangements of the Rand Monetary Area (RMA) and a discussion of
the experience of Botswana, Lesotho and Swaziland in the post-independence
period. Against this background, the author argues strongly for an
independent monetary system in Namibia, coupled with a central bank,
as an immediate step after independence. Such a radical break with
the forced integration into the South African orbit is regarded as
essential in order to control the exchange rate and interest rate
policies, bank lending and the money supply. Any study in this field
is, of course, hampered by the unavailability of adequate data, but
it nevertheless succeeds in raising important questions. The author
is registered at the University of Sussex for doctoral research on
financial and monetary systems in Namibia.

472. NSEKELA, AMON J. (ed.). Southern Africa. Toward economic liberation.
London: Rex Collings, 1981, 274 p. 29 tables.

473. KGARABE, ALOYSIUS (ed.). SADCC - 2. Maputo. London: SADCC Liaison
Committee, 1981, 287 p.

474. SADCC. SADCC Maseru. The proceedings of the Southern African Development Coordination Conference held in Maseru, Kingdom of Lesotho,
on 27/28 January 1983. Gaborone: SADCC, 1983, 392 p. 12 tables,
14 figures. (Printed by Mambo Press, Gweru, Zimbabwe).

These three volumes bring together a large number of SADCC papers,
sectoral reviews, conference documents, statements and speeches,
emerging from four of the organisation's major conferences (from

Arusha in 1979 to Maseru in 1983). The books also contain informative tables and statistical series concerning trade patterns, transport, agriculture, energy, employment and migrant labour. Although SWAPO representatives have been present as observers at SADCC conferences, and there are several refereneces to Namibia in the important Lusaka Declaration of 1980, the prospects for an independent Namibia and the role of Namibia in the SADCC context are only marginally discussed. For future research on Namibia in the regional context, the volumes are, however, indispensable reference works. In addition to the three books, a large number of sectoral and technical papers are available from the SADCC secretariat in Gaborone, Botswana.

475. SCHNEIDER-BARTHOLD, WOLFGANG. Namibia. Sektorstudie Industrie. Berlin: Deutsches Institut für Entwicklungspolitik, 1979, 77 p.

Prepared as part of the German multi-sector report on Namibia, this study on the manufacturing industry was for several years the only published survey of any substance on an under-researched sector, in respect of which the lack of reliable data is particularly evident. The study proceeds from a presentation of the present structure to an outline of the future industrial strategy, based on the assumptions of a "mixed economy". Priority is given to employment and income creation, as well as elimination of geographical-ethnical imbalances. Several possible large- and small-scale industrial projects are identified, together with a more selective list of projects which might be executed with bilateral cooperation immediately after independence. The annexes contain an annotated list of most of the main industrial enterprises, invaluable for being based on field investigation. There is also a presentation of ENOK (the First National Development Corporation), the aims and constitution of the National Union of Namibian Workers and a selective description of a number of informal sector crafts, mainly in the bantustans. The author, a senior economist at the German Development Institute, has published several studies on Namibia (see no. 430). For a more recent and extensive consultancy study on industry, see no. 489.

476. SICHILONGO, MENGO D.F. Toward a new legal system for independent Namibia. Lusaka: UNIN, 1981, 74 p. (Namibia Studies Series No. 5, edited by N.K. Duggal).

This is the fifth in a series of studies concerned with policy options for an independent Namibia, focusing on the need for a fundamental change in the judicial structure. The first three chapters survey the present legal system, providing valuable information on the imposition of apartheid legal and administrative structures. The historical sections reveal the extent to which gradual incorporation into South Africa has taken place, leading to a legal system epitomizing racial inequality at all levels. The major part is devoted to an informed discussion of the options for a new legal system, based on the political goals of the liberation movement as well as the experiences of neighbouring countries.

477. SIMON, DAVID. Cities and settlement planning: problems for indepen-
     dent Namibia. Paper presented to the Conference on Research Priorities
     in Namibia, ICS, University of London, 23-25 July 1984, 26 p.   2
     tables, bibl.:   19-23.

     Taking the absence of a specifically urban element in the otherwise
     comprehensive UN research and planning programme for an independent
     Namibia as its point of departure, the author of this conference
     paper argues that urban areas are of great importance in economic
     and social planning and have to be discussed against a background
     of broader development strategy. It outlines the current state of
     urbanisation in Namibia, mainly based on data derived from the
     National Atlas of South West Africa (no. 111), and proposes a research
     agenda including such critical issues as urban squatting, alternative
     housing strategies, redistribution of social services and amenities,
     town planning systems, and the nature and process of post-colonial
     class and alliance formations.

478. SOUTHERN AFRICAN DEVELOPMENT COORDINATION CONFERENCE. Namibia.
     Arusha: SADCC Secretariat, 1979, 41 p.

     Prepared as a background study for the preparatory SADCC conference
     in Arusha, Tanzania in 1979, this paper offers a lucid introduction
     to the political economy of Namibia. The final section is concerned
     with regional cooperation and Namibia in the SADCC context, providing
     a brief sketch of potential early possibilities for increased links
     with Angola, Botswana, Zimbabwe and Zambia in the fields of water
     and power, transport and communication, personpower development and
     trade and production.

     SOUTHERN AFRICAN DEVELOPMENT COORDINATION CONFERENCE, see SADCC,
     no. 474.

479. SPARKS, DONALD L. "Namibia's future: prospects for the economy and
     foreign involvement". In Economist Intelligence Unit: Multinational
     Business, No. 1, p. 11-21. London: EIU, 1983.

     Written by a researcher at the Centre for Metropolitan Affairs &
     Public Policy, Charleston, USA, this brief study opens with a straight-
     forward review of the inherited structure of the Namibian economy.
     The aim of the report is then to outline the options and constraints
     that will confront an independent Namibia, and to discuss the economic
     policies likely to be followed by possible future governments. It
     argues that whatever government does emerge, it will need the re-
     sources of foreign investment and management. The author expects
     significant foreign involvement to take place in mining, agriculture
     and tourism, and he points especially to potential opportunities for
     the multinationals in Namibia's public sector and for infrastructural
     development in cooperation with aid agencies.

480. THOMAS, WOLFGANG H. "The economy in transition to independence".
     In Namibia: political and economic prospects, edited by Robert I.
     Rotberg, p. 41-91. Lexington/London: D.C. Heath & Co., 1983.

481. ------- Independence and beyond: two scenarios of probable future
     developments in SWA/Namibia. University of Stellenbosch, Unit for
     Futures Research, 1981, 76 p. (UFR Occasional Paper 81/4).

Thomas's aim in the first of these two studies is to update and revise
his previous writings, using recent official data, supplemented with
his own estimates, calculations and political assumptions. The effects
of the prolonged war and the political instability, the devastating
drought, the relatively slack uranium, diamond and base metal prices
as well as the indiscriminate exploitation by fishing companies,
lead the author to a less optimistic assessment than in his 1978 book
(no. 75). Emphasis is also placed on the increasing rate of under-
and unemployment, estimated to be 25-30% in 1982, together with a
decline in living standards for the great majority. It is also argued
that the short-term prospects for commercial agriculture are poor,
and that the internal government has been unable - for political
reasons - to bring about a "modernizing mobilisation" in the rural
areas. The article, which is well furnished with statistics, ends
with some abstract speculations about the economic policies an independent government is likely to "choose". The report commissioned
by the University of Stellenbosch is essentially an exercise in
political "futurology". It is argued that an "internal solution"
(without SWAPO) is less likely because of the impossibility for any
government linked to the status quo of meeting the demands of the black
population. In the discussion of "probable" scenarios for short-,
medium- and long-run political and economic development, the author
nevertheless claims that DTA and SWAPO "may differ widely in their
style of reform politics but far less in their goals".

482. THOMAS, WOLFGANG H. "Economic prospects". In Perspectives on Namibia:
past and present, edited by Christopher Saunders, p. 138-55, Cape
Town: African Studies Center, 1983.

Based on a lecture at the University of Cape Town in early 1983, this
is one of the most recent publications by a prolific and controversial
economist. The starting point is, interestingly, that much of the
writings on the prospects for the transition and the post-independence
period - his own major work (no. 75) included - have turned out to
be futile exercises. The alternative, he argues, is that for so long
as South Africa remains unwilling to allow international elections
leading to a SWAPO-oriented government, the Namibian economy should
be analysed as another "homeland". He claims that the recent trends
have demonstrated that Namibia is not the resource-rich and promising
economy which was suggested in the mid-1970s, that political changes
have brought about a comprehensive indigenisation of Namibian administrative and socio-economic structure, helping the local black elite
to widen and strengthen its position, and that drought, war and low
mineral prices have retarded economic and social development.
He also argues that in line with South Africa's dominant role, Namibia
has been heavily indoctrinated with "free market" ideology and that
income inequalities and social-political polarisation have increased.

483. TOSTENSEN, ARNE. Dependence and collective self-reliance in Southern
Africa. The case of Southern African Development Coordination Conference. Uppsala: Scandinavian Institute of African Studies, 1982.
170 p. 10 tables, 2 figures, bibl.: 163-70.

484. ------- Independent Namibia in the Southern African region. Paper presented to the Conference on Research Priorities in Namibia, ICS,

University of London, 23-25 July 1984, 28 p.

A valuable overall description of the relations of dependency between South Africa and its neighbours (trade, investment, transport, energy and labour migration), which also contains a wide range of data of relevance for the study of Namibia in the regional context. The author discusses the evolution, problems and prospects of SADCC, and touches upon such Namibia-related issues as the role of Walvis Bay and the Trans-Kalahari rail link. The conference paper notes that surprisingly little serious work has gone into placing the political economy of Namibia in a regional context, and goes on to sketch some possible scenarios of Namibia's position in the Southern African region after independence. The main focus is on the potential contributions of SADCC towards easing some of the problems of transition, particularly by providing alternative external linkages to those of dependence on South Africa. Against this background, the author surveys the existing projects within the fields of transport and communications (especially the Trans-Kalahari Railway), agriculture and food security, industrial cooperation, mining, and personpower development.

485. TUCKER, ADALBERT A. Administration system and establishment needs for an independent Namibia. Lusaka: UNIN. 1982, 329 p. (Working paper, New York: TCD/New York: Office of the Commissioner for Namibia/Lusaka: UNIN).

Conducted under the United Nations' Nationhood Programme for Namibia, this is a pioneering study on the administrative system for an independent Namibia. The paper is based on the assumption that the government of Namibia will be a SWAPO government which immediately begins to implement its programme of socio-economic transformation. The first part presents a historical overview of the administrative system under German and South African colonial rule. It is followed by a detailed and critical examination of existing institutional arrangements. The second part provides an outline of the objectives and strategy of restructuring the state machinery, with particular attention to personnel requirements for key elements of the preliminary state machinery. The study concludes by proposing a training strategy for independent Namibia, drawing on experiences from Zambia and Zimbabwe.

UNIDO, see UNITED NATIONS INDUSTRIAL DEVELOPMENT ORGANISATION, no. 489.

486. UNITED NATIONS CENTER ON TRANSNATIONAL CORPORATIONS. Role of transnational corporations in Namibia. New York, 1982. 305 p. + annexes. 19 tables. (Draft).

Prepared as part of the project on "training and research in transnational corporations" being carried out by the UN Center on Transnational Corporations under the Nationhood Programme for Namibia, this major study is an indispensable reference work on the foreign domination of the Namibian economy as well as a stimulating contribution to the discussion on policy options on foreign direct investment. The first part gives a brief overview of the role of natural resources

in the Namibian economy, the effects of South African control and
the legislative framework governing transnational corporations operating in Namibia. The second part consists of a detailed description
of foreign companies in the major economic sectors, with special
emphasis on mining. This section contains a wealth of information,
unfortunately not all of it accurate or correctly interpretated, on
the major producers, their company structure, subsidiaries, investments, taxation, profits and financial performance, with statistical
data going back to the early 1970s. Although more sketchy, the chapters concerned with agriculture, fisheries, banking and insurance
also offer insight into the operations of the transnationals, the
structure of production and the integration of these critical sectors
of the Namibian economy into that of South Africa. Part III
discusses alternative forms of foreign participation, drawing on
the experience of other African countries in the post-independence
period. Regrettably, the study remains unpublished (mid-1984).

487. UNITED NATIONS INSTITUTE FOR NAMIBIA. Planning for Namibian independence: manpower development strategies. New York: UN, 1983, 11 p.
3 tables. (A/Conf. 120/6, 21 March 1983).

Submitted by UNIN to the International Conference in Support of the
Struggle of the Namibian People for Independence (Paris, 25-29 April
1983), this report deals with the effects of apartheid on Namibia's
manpower resources, the most urgent of these being the acute shortage
of trained manpower. The paper stresses the need for large-scale
training programmes to produce professional, skilled and semi-skilled
personnel, and provides some estimates for the most pressing manpower
requirements of an independent Namibia. It also presents an outline
of the training programme presently being undertaken by UNIN, SWAPO
and the UN Nationhood Programme.

488. UNITED NATIONS INSTITUTE FOR NAMIBIA. Namibia: perspectives for
national reconstruction and development. A comprehensive study.
In preparation. To appear in 1985.

489. UNITED NATIONS INDUSTRIAL DEVELOPMENT ORGANISATION (UNIDO), REGIONAL
AND COUNTRY STUDIES BRANCH. Industrial development programme for
independent Namibia. Vienna: UNIDO, 1984, 278 + 32 p. 62 tables.
(Preliminary report).

This report, prepared by a consultancy working group, represents the
first major input by UNIDO to the UN Nationhood Programme for Namibia
and more particularly to the comprehensive study of post-independence
development strategy now under way at the UN Institute for Namibia
(see no. 488). As yet it is only at the stage of a preliminary
draft, and bears the hallmarks of hasty preparation and lack of
analytical integration. It is nonetheless one of the most extensively
researched of the crop of UN consultancy reports and contains a wealth
of statistical data on the most undeveloped sector of the Namibian
economy. After an introductory analysis of current structures and
policies in manufacturing, three chapters discuss the prospects for
resource-based industrialisation arising out of the major primary
sectors: agriculture, marine fishing and mining. A pioneering central

chapter assesses domestic demand for manufactured goods and sources
of local and imported supplies. Five subsidiary chapters then examine
infrastructural resources and specific policy areas: industrial skills
and training; women; science and technology; energy and water; and
transport. Two concluding chapters examine the international context
and present a summary of the argument and the main conclusions. Of
considerable value, especially empirical, are the background appendices
on agricultural and fish resources and transport. Although its quantitative assumptions may be criticised, two strengths of the study
are the detailed statistical projections in a 10-year scenario for
post-independence planning and the development of a method and framework of analysis which can accomodate revised data.

90. UNITED STATES AGENCY FOR INTERNATIONAL DEVELOPMENT. A report to the
Congress on development needs and opportunities for cooperation in
Southern Africa. Washington, 1979, 162 p. 5 tables.

91. ------- A report to the Congress on development needs and opportunities
for cooperation in Southern Africa. Annex A. Namibia. Washington,
1979, 129 p. Bibl.: 122-24.

In March 1979 the US Agency for International Development presented
a voluminous report (39 volumes) to the Congress. The report consists of study papers on economic sectors, problem areas and nine
individual countries in Southern Africa, prepared by consultants
and contractors from a wide range of firms and academic institutions.
The summary report is an overall document focusing on regional development prospects and priorities for US assistance. It contains some
useful data, but suffers from inadequate consultation with the governments or liberation movements of several of the countries (Angola,
Mozambique, Zimbabwe, Namibia) as well as from lack of explicit
discussion of political constraints to development, economic independence and a strategy for meeting "basic needs". This is particularly evident in the report on Namibia, which is very much a US perspective of what the needs of the Namibian people are and what opportunities an independent Namibia opens for the US. The study is based
on the assumption that Namibia is likely to receive foreign assistance
if the new government is acceptable to the UN "as well as the US
and other Western powers", and that "a gradual and orderly disentangle-
ment of the links between the two countries (Namibia and South Africa)
could be accomplished without affecting Namibia's development". The
strength of the report lies in the identification of some of the
main economic constraints, as well as in the discussion of the potential-
ly vital role an independent Namibia could play in a regional strategy.
When it comes to specific recommendations for economic policies and
priorities of assistance, the report can be regarded as a prescription
for a capitalist-oriented course with more emphasis on export
potential than on internal needs. There is a special review section
on the reports in Rural Africana, nos. 4-5, 1979: p. 131-59.

USHEWOKUNZE, C., see no. 462.

92. WALLER, PETER. Namibia. Sektorstudie Materielle Infrastruktur.
Berlin: Deutsches Institut für Entwicklungspolitik, 1979, 72 p.
7 tables, 7 maps.

This sectoral study on material infrastructure, prepared as a part of
the German multi-sector study, provides a certain amount of background
data on water supply, electricity supply, the roads and railway network, some of it derived from unpublished official sources. The
author notes that infrastructural costs are high compared to most
other developing countries, reflecting the requirements of the export-
oriented mining and animal husbandry sector, the adaptation of equipment to South African standards and the needs of the South African
army. He also points to the extreme imbalances between the European
and African areas, and argues that the facilities of the "white area"
have been installed at the expense of the more densely populated
"homelands". The survey concludes with a discussion of the immediate
manpower and financial problems facing an independent Namibia in
the light of the fact that most of the institutions connected with
material infrastructure are parts of the South African Administration and
of South African state corporations. There is also a brief section
dealing with the strengthening of ties with neighbouring African
countries.

493. WILCOX, STEPHEN C. A framework for US assistance in Southern Africa.
Country resource paper. Namibia. Washington/New Jersey: US Agency
for International Development, The Office of Eastern and Southern
Africa Affairs, 1977, 125 p. 35 tables, bibl.: 123-25.

This is one of the first of many country reports prepared by international agencies and consulting firms at a time when it was widely
believed that Namibia would become independent in the near future.
The report is a rather unimaginative, descriptive account of the
various economic sectors. In contrast to most other reports of the
kind, there are few attempts to discuss the prospects for the future
or to speculate about abstract policy options. The major part of
the statistical data is drawn from official figures (the Odendaal
Report, SWA Survey 1967 and 1974), but there are also some calculations based on independent sources (UN, FAO, US Bureau of Mines).
Most of the statistics cover the period up to 1973.

494. ZEHENDER, WOLFGANG. Namibia. Sektorstudie Aussenwirtschaft. Berlin:
Deutsches Institut für Entwicklungspolitik, 1979. 24 p.

495. ------- "Namibia's dependency in external economic affairs: options
for re-orientation". In Perspectives of independent development in
Southern Africa. The cases of Zimbabwe and Namibia, p. 163-83.
Berlin: German Development Institute, 1980.

496. ------- "Aussenwirtschaftspolitische Perspektiven für ein unabhängiges
Namibia". Afrika Spectrum, 15, no. 2, 1980: 135-45.

These three publications, which are almost identical, were originally
prepared as part of the German Development Institute's multi-sector
study on Namibia. Although the research team was able to visit
Namibia and South Africa to collect material in 1978, this study
reflects the lack of reliable data on Namibia's external economic
relations in the late 1970s. The description of external dependency
is very close to the more substantial work of W.H. Thomas (no. 75),
and the list of "options" to be considered by an independent government adds little to the existing literature, apart from the idea of
a "free trade zone" between Namibia and South Africa. Some of the

economic assumptions have proved over optimistic in the light of recent
developments.

    SEE ALSO:

    9, 10, 17, 18, 19, 40, 48, 67, 75, 85, 102, 430, 502-4, 511, 513,
    514, 531, 532, 534, 535, 536, 547, 557, 562, 564, 565, 572, 578,
    580, 595, 614, 692, 694, 695, 698, 700, 707, 708, 712-4, 896.

7. THE PRIMARY SECTORS

A. Agriculture

497. ANSCHEL, KURT and RUSSEL H. BRANNON. The agricultural sector of Namibia: a brief assessment. University of Kentucky, College of Agriculture, 1978, 69 p.

Prepared in cooperation with the South East Consortium for International Development, this is a substantial paper. It concentrates mainly on capitalist stock-farming and peasant agriculture appears only incidentally. Brief mention is also made of the fishing industry. The analysis, framed in terms of orthodox market economics, proceeds from a general geographical and political introduction to a survey of the present situation in agriculture. The data presented, although competently arranged, are limited by reliance on the small and often out-of-date range of published English-language literature. The report concludes with a brief assessment of constraints and priorities in post-independence agricultural development, concentrating on technical, institutional and environmental factors rather than political issues such as land tenure and income distribution. It advocates greater stock-farming output and the commercialisation of crop production in the northern bantustans.

498. BÄHR, JÜRGEN. Kulturgeographische Wandlungen in der Farmzone Südwestafrikas. Bonn, 1968, 212 p. 42 maps, 31 diagrams, 20 photos, 35 tables, bibl.: 125-137. (Bonner Geographische Abhandlungen, 40).

This is the most thorough general study of the economics of settler farming to have been completed in the postwar period. It is partly based on field research, which involved extensive contacts with white farmers and government officials. It is also informed by a comprehensive reading of theses, books and articles, German as well as South African and Namibian. It is primarily a descriptive work of economic geography, which, because of the author's concern with structural change, is also an economic history of commercial farming since the beginning of the colonial period. Spatial patterns and infrastructural expansion are prominently treated, in particular

land settlement, fixed investment and urban servicing centres. Of
great value is the wide range of economic and social data presented
in tables and graphs, some of which cover long time-runs. There
is also a large number of useful maps, town outlines, and plans of
farm settlement and land-use. The author has summarised his analysis
in several published articles, notably "Strukturwandel der Farmwirtschaft in Südwestafrika", Zeitschrift für Ausländische Landwirtschaft, 9, 1970: p. 147-59, and "Probleme der Wirtschafts- und Sozialstruktur in der Farmzone Südwestafrikas", Zeitschrift für Wirtschafts-
geographie, 13, no. 5, 1969: p. 129-39.

499. BÄHR, JÜRGEN. "Veränderungen in der Farmwirtschaft Südwestafrikas/
Namibias zwischen 1965 und 1980". Erdkunde, 34, no. 4 (December)
1981: 274-89. 4 diagrams, 4 maps, 6 tables.

During 1979-80 the author undertook a second field research visit
to assess the form and pace of structural change in the ranch sector
since his original research in 1965-6 (see no. 498). The result is a
brief but incisive and informative economic assessment, one of the
few in recent years to be based on first-hand research (compare
no. 502). His principal conclusions are that the concentration of
farm ownership has deepened, largely at the expense of middle-sized
units; that the camp system of pasture rotation has developed rapidly
to near its full potential, and that the quality of slaughter stock
has been increased rather than absolute numbers. However, although
associating "terrorism" with falling land prices, absentee farming
and the reduction of the farm labour force and noting the serious
marketing difficulties for cattle, his assessment of the structural
problems in the ranch sector is less severe than an alternative
recent analysis (see no. 532), and pays relatively little attention
to the impact of labour resistance and the liberation struggle. An
earlier research report ("Die neuere Entwicklung der südwestafrikanischen Farmwirtschaft unter dem Einfluss veränderter politischer
Bedingungen", Afrika-Informationen, no. 3, 1980: 15-25) gives preliminary results and a description of the research methods and resources used. A rather longer and more general structural analysis
is presented in a second "preliminary" article, drawing heavily on
the author's previous work ("Entwicklungsstufen der Farmwirtschaft
in Südwestafrika", Journal of the SWA Scientific Society, 34-5,
1979/80-1980/1: 113-37).

500. BATTELLE, GENEVA RESEARCH CENTRE. Study to determine possible
improvements to the effectiveness of the marketing of SWAKARA.
Geneva, 1981, 183 p.

In 1981 the International Karakul Secretariat in Windhoek commissioned
the Battelle Research Centre to undertake a close examination of all
aspects of the marketing of SWAKARA pelts, with a view to recommending the best course of action to overcome the decline of the
industry. The report contains a considerable amount of valuable information on the production, marketing, and consumption and promotion of
SWAKARA, and brings together a wide range of up-to-date statistics
on production and auction prices. The points are made that SWAKARA
suffers from a "grandmother" image in the critical West European
markets and the lack of penetration into the US market. Among the
recommendations are the cutting of production costs, rationalisation

of auctions, the setting up of a European central promotion office and concentrating on new markets, especially Japan and the US.

01. BOETTICHER, GERHARD. Die landwirtschaftlichen Produktions- und Siedlungsverhältnisse in Südwestafrika vor und nach dem Weltkrieg. Breslau, 1930, 132 p. Tables, 5 diagrams, bibl.: 9-14. (Dissertation).

The author, a settler farmer between 1913 and 1919, gives a generalised descriptive account of commercial farming up to the mid-1920s, based largely on a wide reading of German colonial literature. Successive chapters cover the natural environment, farming types and methods, markets, labour, the history of land settlement, and sources of capital. Statistics are scattered through the text, but there are also a few separate tables and graphs.

02. BRANDT, HARTMUT. Namibia: Sektorstudie Landwirtschaft. Berlin: Deutsches Institut für Entwicklungspolitik, 1979, 55 p. 5 tables, 1 diagram, 6 maps.

03. ------- "Perspektiven der Agrarentwicklung eines unabhängigen Namibia". Afrika Spectrum, 14, no. 2, 1979: 203-17.

04. ------- "Development perspectives for agriculture in an independent Namibia". In Perspectives of independent development in Southern Africa. The cases of Zimbabwe and Namibia, p. 75-99. Berlin: German Development Institute, 1980.

This study formed part of the German Development Institute's research project on Namibia (see no. 464). It is packed with data, of which perhaps the most useful are the economic statistics derived from the balance-sheets of settler ranches visited by the author during his research trip in 1978. Because the published sources used in this study are usually not attributed, and several which can be identified are questionable, some of the data, as well as the judgments based on them, are of varying utility. But the analysis itself is expert. The first section surveys briefly the historical evolution of the main forms of land use, the colonial land theft, and bantustan policy. The second examines production, income and food supply on the ranches and in the Owambo and Kavango bantustans. The third considers several aspects of development policy after independence: export dependence, ranch employment, increased production, land reform, training and research. The author advocates the retention of high-output, export-oriented ranching, substituting animals for vehicles to expand employment; medium-sized commercial stock- and crop-farms in the north; capital-intensive irrigation; practical training for black farmers; and problem-oriented research. The study is summarized in two other publications, though in both cases without most of the maps and tables.

BRANNON, RUSSEL H., see no. 497.

05. CARSTENS, N.E. An economic analysis of farming in the northern beef cattle areas of South West Africa, 1970. Pretoria: South Africa, Department of Agricultural Economics and Marketing, Division of Agricultural Production Economics, 1971. 79 p. (Economic Series no. 76).

An important survey, both empirically and analytically. It is one
of only a handful of detailed investigations of capitalist stock-
farming and the only one to be based on a statistically valid and
competently executed sample survey. Its results yield a wealth of
raw data on the micro-economics of cattle-ranching, covering capital,
income, costs, productivity, scale and branches of production as
well as profitability. The data are expertly arranged and carefully
analysed. The author states his chief purpose as being "to pinpoint
the less profitable and nonprofitable practices and to identify the
factors affecting the financial results of beef farming" in the survey
area. He is at pains to stress that "the tables in this report, with
the discussions that follow them, were meant only to serve as guidelines to the beef farmer to help him improve his financial results"
(p. 77). Nevertheless, two of his key conclusions are that "farmers
in the poorest group would not even realise a net farm income of
R 10 per R 100 of capital invested in stock and equipment only, even
if they were to get their land for nothing" and that the quality of
management is decisive in determining efficiency and profitability
(p. 76-77).

CHAMBERS, ROBERT, see no. 516.

506. CROSS, SHOLTO and DAVID GIBBON. A short evaluation of the agricultural
resources of Namibia. Rome: FAO, Action for Development/Freedom
from Hunger Campaign, 1975, 24 p. 3 tables, 7 maps.

This consultancy report was the first in a series of contributions
by the FAO to the Namibia Nationhood Programme (see nos. 510-14).
Although brief, it is densely written, based on a close reading of
the scanty sources then available, and expert in its analysis, being
especially strong on physical geography and agronomy. The social and
economic sections are more cursory, with a few factual errors and
a tendency to adopt apartheid tribal categories as the frame of
reference; and issues of land theft and labour exploitation are barely
mentioned. This is nonetheless a sound technical and economic
critique of farm policy and practice under South African rule, with
a welcome emphasis on peasant agriculture and local self-management
in future development.

507. CURSON, H.H. "Notes on eastern Caprivi strip". South African
Journal of Science, 43, (July) 1947: 124-59. Photos.

Primarily a botanical survey undertaken in 1945 by an official of the
South African Native Affairs Department, this article nevertheless
summarised rare information on local settlement and the peasant
economy. It also discusses the history of environmental change and
touches on the ecological relationships between land-use, vegetation
and seasonal flooding.

508. DENK, HANS. Lage und Entwicklung der deutschen Farmerschaft
Südwestafrikas, 1936-9. Stuttgart/Hamburg: Schriftendienst Übersee,
1942, 104 p.

An anthology consisting largely of addresses and articles by Hans
Denk, a pro-Nazi German farmer in Namibia during the years leading

up to the Second World War. In 1936 he founded the Landwirtschaftskammer with the intention of uniting German and Afrikaner farmers.
By 1939 it claimed 2460 members, 40% of them Afrikaner. Much of
the material reproduced reflects the concerns and activities of the
Landwirtschaftskammer, especially in the economic field, with a certain amount of factual information on farm production and exports.

09. ERKRATH, WILHELM. Die Voraussetzungen und Bedeutung der Farmwirtschaft in Südwest-Afrika. München: Technische Hochschule, 1936,
151 p. Bibl.: 149-51. (Dissertation).

An extensively researched and detailed survey of all branches of
settler farming, describing its evolution since the German colonisation
with a good deal of statistical background. The two main sections
cover official farm policy and agricultural production, the latter
with considerable emphasis on methods.

10. FAO. Namibia: a preliminary note towards a country development
brief. Rome: FAO, 1976, 51 p. 29 tables, 10 maps. (Draft report).

11. ------- Namibia: prospects for future development. Rome: FAO,
1977, 61 p. 20 tables, 5 maps. (Draft report).

Described as an "internal working document", the 1976 FAO report
constitutes a largely descriptive survey which devotes as much
attention to the economy in general as to agriculture and fisheries.
The bulk of the data is taken - usually without acknowledgement -
directly from South African official publications, in particular
the South West Africa Survey 1967, of which in places the text and
presentation become little more than a paraphrase. More seriously,
South African descriptive information and policy presentations,
which occupy the great bulk of the text, are rarely subjected to
critical analysis, even where blatantly inaccurate or politically
prejudiced. It is thus scarcely surprising that the "tentative
conclusions" should call for white settlers and South African technical and financial support to play a central role in agricultural
development, and for political disengagement and development policy
to be subordinated to the "stabilisation" of the white population.
The 1977 FAO report is a considerable improvement on its initial
effort, criticism of which by the UN Council for Namibia may have
been a spur to its being commissioned. While in places weak in
technical and economic analysis, it is sharpened by a radical
political economy which stresses the role of ownership and labour
exploitation in economic growth and of land theft and labour migration
in the expansion of commercial at the expense of peasant agriculture.
It concludes with an extended and wide-ranging discussion of agricultural development strategy, which, while shaky on economics and
vague on details, is valuable for stressing the need for structural
reform and for popular political participation. Like almost all
consultancy reports for the Nationhood Programme, this text, which
has the appearance of a rough first draft, remains unfortunately
unpublished and thus largely inaccessible to those to whom it would
be of greatest use - Namibians and supporters of Namibian independence.

12. FAO. Effects of apartheid on the African rural population of Namibia
and Zimbabwe/Rhodesia: Namibia. Annex to Special issue on Apartheid.

0

Ideas and Action, no. 127 (July-August) 1978: 2-7.

A readable short description of the history and present situation of
agriculture. Sections describe pre-colonial modes of land-use, the
land theft, the rise of settler stock-ranching, the creation of labour
reserves and the migrant labour system, the conditions of black
farmworkers as well as foreign domination of commercial farming.
The article is too short to contain much empirical data, but has a
clear historical analysis of the process of exploitation under
colonial rule.

513. FAO. Agriculture, fisheries and food security in Namibia. Background
paper presented to the planning workshop on the UN Nationhood Programme
for Namibia, Maputo, 1980, 38 p. Maps.

The first half of this paper provides a factual survey of Namibia's
demography, general economy and both peasant and ranch farming.
Much of the data is taken from old South African sources of 1960s and
early 1970s, and even recent sources are sometimes suspect. (The
quoted FAO crop estimates for 1971-76, for example, are wildly
inaccurate.) There is nonetheless some useful information, especially
on livestock production, marketing and diseases. A middle section on
agricultural policy issues consists mainly of a summary of some key
problems after independence and a survey of support services for
white farmers. The final section gives an informative short survey
of the fishing industry, especially its offshore trawler branch.
It also develops a perceptive analysis of the problems and priorities
in establishing proper control after independence, although its
recommendation that Namibia should join ICSEAF, of which South Africa
is a dominant member, may prove controversial. A conclusion summarises
land reform options, and ongoing projects in agriculture, fisheries
and food security under the Nationhood Programme are described in
an annex.

514. FAO. Food supplies and nutrition in Namibia. An assessment of food
needs, distribution requirements and policy options for food security
planning. Rome: FAO, 1982, 100 p. 10 maps and figures, 15 tables,
bibl.: 98-100. (AG:UNO/NAM/922. Field document. Prepared by
Overseas Development Group, University of East Anglia).

This report is a synthesis of a major research project and one of
FAO's principal contributions to the Nationhood Programme. As such,
it is likely to be a strategic guide for Namibian planners and
especially seconded foreign experts on contingency arrangements for
food supplies and agriculture after independence. It provides a
sophisticated, wide-ranging and clearly written analysis both of
likely needs and policy options. The first chapter offers a penetrating analysis of the background and political economy of food
scarcity and defines planning zones which for the first time break
from the bantustan framework. The second chapter describes food
production and deficiencies in each region, as well as the scope
for expansion. The third chapter estimates food import requirements
and considers the logistics of transport, distribution and storage.
The fourth chapter assesses policy options on food imports and
exports and on pricing and distribution. It also considers related
aspects of agricultural development, in particular land reform,

services to farmers, physical infrastructure and short-term
emergency actions. The final chapter briefly translates recommendations into project categories. Together with the two UNIN studies
(no. 536, 534) and the CIIR sectoral study (see no. 532), this is
by far the most closely argued and thoroughly researched analysis
in the agricultural development genre to date. Key differences
between the CIIR and the FAO studies include the latter's advocacy
of continued high livestock exports and its assumption that many
white farmers would probably stay on unless subjected to "radical
land reform". It might also be added that the CIIR study puts more
emphasis on political mobilisation.

15. GELLERT, J.F. "Klimabedingheit und wirtschaftsgeographische Struktur
der Farmwirtschaft in SWA". Erdkunde. 2, no. 4/6, 1948: 282-302.

An early attempt, complementing that of the Minimum Area of Farms
Commission two years earlier (no. 545), to assess the economics of
settler stock-ranching in terms of the ecological potential of the
land. Although the argument is based on somewhat abstract criteria,
its method is thorough. The author concludes that as of 1948 some
70% of southern ranches were below the minimum theoretical size
limit for long-term ecological viability, and that in general there
were 20% too many farms. See also by the same author Die Nieder-
schlagsschwankungen im Hochland von SWA. Berlin: Akademie Verlag,
1955, 70 p. + 18 maps. (Abhandlungen des Metereologischen und
Hydrologischen Dienstes der Deutschen Demokratischen Republik, 4,
no. 32).

GIBBON, DAVID, see no. 506.

16. GREEN, REGINALD H. and ROBERT CHAMBERS. "Agrarian change". In
Namibia. The last colony, edited by Reginald H. Green, Marja-Liisa
Kiljunen and Kimmo Kiljunen, p. 227-58. London: Longman, 1981.

This is a concentrated and thought-provoking analysis of the priorities,
obstacles and resources for agrarian reform, both short- and long-term.
For Green, this is a fuller expression of a section of his analysis
of the political economy of transition to independence, of which a
number of versions have been published (see no. 470); while Chamber's
research on Botswana is apposite to Namibian conditions. The
authors assume a difficult transition, with a SWAPO government but
a substantial flight of personnel and capital. A thumb-nail sketch
of the salient features of present-day agriculture leads to consideration of social and economic change in rural Namibia after independence in the light of policy criteria ("equity, employment, productivity,
marketed output and administrative feasibility"). The post-independence experiences of a number of African and Southeast Asian countries
are then compared, followed by a discussion, in greater detail, of
different ways of transforming the stock-ranching sector. After
a brief consideration of policy towards the peasant sector, the
authors point out in conclusion that "if it is to belong truly to the
Namibian people, the Namibian ranching sector must be radically
transformed". In contrast, to most other writers on Namibian development, they stress the validity of peasant and worker experience
and urge the value of grass-roots consultation and popular mobilisation.

Although so complex that its message at times is blurred, the
analysis is tightly integrated and frequently original and challenging.

517. GUNDERT, HELMUT. Die betriebswirtschaftlichen Verhältnisse auf
Karakulfarmen in den südlichen Distrikten von Südwestafrika. Hohenheim:
Landwirtschaftliche Hochschule, 1962, 128 p. 39 tables, bibl.:
113-14. (Dissertation).

A rare example of agricultural field research, this is a detailed
economic case study of 12 book-keeping karakul ranches. The investigation consists largely of a careful comparative analysis of the
farms' accounts for 1959, together with a description and assessment
of farm investment and production methods. A statistical appendix
gives key production and economic data for each farm through the
1950s. For five years preceding his research the author was himself
the manager of a large Namibian karakul farm, an experience which is
reflected in this study.

518. HANSSEN, C.P.A. "The agricultural economy of South-West Africa".
Agrekon, 5, no. 4, 1966: 30-38.

A short economic survey of commercial agriculture, useful mainly because of the scarcity of published data at this time. The author
was an official in the Agricultural Division of the South West Africa
Administration and obtained his data from a variety of unpublished
official sources. Although brief, the article gives factual
information on land allocation, livestock ownership, production and
marketing, particularly in its tables and statistics. The central/
southern reserves feature briefly in terms of livestock sales, the
northern reserves hardly at all. This article formed the basis of
the section on agriculture in the offical SWA Survey 1967 (no. 305).

519. HARRISON, J.E. (FARM CONSULTANTS) and UNIVERSITY OF STELLENBOSCH,
INSTITUTE OF AGRICULTURAL ECONOMICS. Proposals for the restoration
of profitability of farming in SWA/Namibia. 1983, 146 p. (2 vols).
54 tables. (SWA/Namibia, Administration for Whites, Draft report).

A major study of the economics of commercial farming, the first of its
kind since the 1940s. It was commissioned by the second-tier "white"
authority at a time of severe drought and deep structural crisis
in the ranch sector, and the terms of reference reflect official
concern at the adequacy of existing methods of data-gathering and
the long-term commerical viability of settler stock-ranching.
The report represents a radical attempt to rescue capitalist
stock-farming. It confirms the depth of the crisis, estimating
that 35-40% of existing farm businesses were too small to offer
an acceptable standard of living, that concentration of holdings
was well advanced, and that more than a quarter were run by week-end
farmers. It severely criticises the extent and application of state
subsidies, and recommends that they be ended for undersized farms,
that farms should be concentrated into larger, economically viable
units, and that the state itself should buy up undersized farms
for letting to larger farmers at high rents to promote efficient
management. Despite the shock tactics implicit in its attack on
some of the fundamental tenets of 60 years of South African farm

policy, the report is a narrowly focused business analysis and is
weakened by, for example, failing to take account of the relevance
of cheap black labour to white farm probitability. The second half
of the report consists of tables of economic data, much of it
drawn from unpublished census returns and a sample survey of agricultural credit records. It constitutes by far the most comprehensive
statistical analysis of the economics of commercial ranching in recent
years.

520. HASE, HANS JÜRGEN VON. "Die Auswirkungen der Dürrejahre in Südwestafrika und ihre Überwindung". Deutsche Tropenlandwirt, 65, 1964:
38-54.

21. ------- "Die Entwicklung der Karakulzucht in Südwest-Afrika". Deutsche
Tropenlandwirt, 66, 1965: 42-57.

The first of these two articles by a leading rancher is a plea for
improved ranch management and greater investment following a severe
and prolonged drought. The article contains long-run graphs of
rainfall and exports of cattle and karakul pelts. It also outlines
the range of official subsidies to white farmers, especially for
investment in fencing and water supply. The second article is an
account of the history and methods of karakul farming, breeding and
marketing, with a few production statistics.

522. HERRIGEL, OTTO. Namibian agriculture. The challenge ahead. Paper
presented to the Ditchley Park Conference on Namibia, 1981, 4 p.

This brief conference paper ascribes widespread and serious pasture
degradation to poor management by the majority of white ranchers
and to "communal usage of the land coupled with lack of scientific
knowledge of modern farming" in the central/southern bantustans.
According to the author, top priority in commercial ranching would
go to "scientific and productive management of farms"; in peasant
stock-farming to enclosure of the land in profitable economic units
and large-scale transfers of population to new urban employment. He
also advocates whole-basin development along the Okavango river.
The author has written a doctoral thesis on Namibian economic development (no. 363).

523. HURLICH, SUSAN. Reserves, migrant labour and the karakul industry
in Namibia: a historical perspective. University of Toronto, 1983,
478 + 25 p. Bibl.: appendix p. 1-25. (PhD thesis in preparation).

524. ------- Namibia, the karakul industry and the Hudson's Bay Company.
Paper presented to The International Seminar on The Role of Transnational Corporations in Namibia, Washington, 1982, 37 p.

This history of development of karakul sheep ranching pays particular
attention to the conditions of farm labourers and the role of the
Canadian-owned Hudson's Bay Company. It opens with a lengthy chapter
on the colonial conquest and the destruction of the pre-colonial
social formations, followed by an analysis of the migrant labour
system, the reserves and their impact on the role of women and a
discussion of the Odendaal blueprint for the creation of "homelands".
The production and marketing of karakul pelts is outlined in detail,

based on library and corporate research in North America and archival work and field investigation in Namibia. With extensive interviews, several tables and a full bibliography it serves as a valuable guide for further research on the political economy of Namibia. The author has summarised the main findings of her thesis in a conference paper, which retains some of the most important tables.

INTERNATIONAL KARAKUL SECRETARIAT, see no. 500.

525. KARAKUL BREEDERS ASSOCIATION OF SOUTH WEST AFRICA. Karakul Breeders Association of South West Africa 1919-1969. Windhoek: 1969, 160 p. Photos.

This publication marked the 50 years anniversary of the Karakul Breeders Association, the principal interest group of the karakul ranchers in Namibia. Amongst glossy advertisements and self-congratulatory articles, there are a few tables and some historical details.

526. KIRSTEN, G.J.C. "The production and marketing of karakul pelts". Agrekon, 5, no. 3, 1966: 22-29.

A brief summary of the history of karakul production and marketing by an official of the South African Meat Control Board. Its chief value lies in its description of the complex institutional structure and channels of marketing at the time.

527. KROGH, D.C. The karakul industry in S.W.A., with special reference to the marketing of karakul pelts. Windhoek: S.W.A. Karakul Advisory Board/SWA Scientific Society, 1954, 104 p. Tables, bibl.: 103-04.

528. ------- "Economic aspects of the karakul industry in South West Africa", The South African Journal of Economics, 23, no. 2, (June) 1955: 99-113.

Originating from an MA thesis, this book is one of the first attempts to provide an overview of karakul breeding and marketing. The author, a well-known South African economist, gives a historical account of karakul breeding from 1907 to the late 1940s, and reviews the importance of this industry in the economy as a whole. In a separate section, special emphasis is put on the export and marketing of pelts. There are several statistical series, particularly on trade and farm employment. The article in the SAJE provides a brief summary was well as an updating of some figures.

529. LANGLET, JOACHIM. "Die Karakulzucht in Südwestafrika". In Kühn-Archiv, 47, p. 197-315. Berlin, 1938. (12. Sonderband für Tierzucht).

A survey of karakul farming in the midst of its first phase of rapid expansion. Although much concerned with breeding, the author gives a detailed descriptive account, based on personal observation and unpublished official statistics, of production, stock ownership, marketing, and farming methods. Other forms of commercial farming, especially cattle, are also covered, although less fully.

30. MATHIESSEN, L. Socio-economic aspects of land use planning in the
non-white farming areas in SWA/Namibia. Paper presented to a meeting
of the Southern African Regional Commission for the Conservation and
Utilisation of the Soil (SARCCUS), Pretoria, 1980, 37 p.

The author, designated "Chief Planning Officer for the Northern SWA
Region of the Department of Agriculture and Nature Conservation",
presents a survey of agriculture and land tenure in each of the
Namibian bantustans, together with recommendations for "land use
planning". His data and recommendations are drawn largely from the
Stellenbosch University development plans (see nos. 450-52) and
the Odendaal Report (see no. 266). The survey is wholly uncritical
of apartheid and labour migration, and adopts a patronising and
hostile attitude towards the history, social organisation and farming
methods of the black peasantry. However, the author departs from
the former official endorsement of communal tenure and tribal control,
reflecting a recent shift in policy amongst South African planners and
pro-government politicians in Namibia, especially the DTA. "Communal
tenure" and "traditional" techniques are seen as the principal barrier
to development, whose most promising agent is identified as the "middle
class farmer" with individual control and profitable farming units.

31. MBAMBA, A. MAUNO. Possibilities for the future development of livestock ranching in an independent Namibia. Sussex: Institute of
Development Studies, 1977, 106 p. 25 tables, 6 maps. (MA thesis).

Written by a Namibian scholar, this is a general survey of commercial
ranching in the settler-owned farm zone. From a geographical introduction the study proceeds through a historical background outlining
the rise of settler agriculture to a more detailed description of
present-day cattle and karakul ranching, focusing mainly on the types
of farming, ownership of livestock and land, the economics of production, and state support. After a summary of ranch production and
exports, it is concluded by a general discussion of some possible
forms of development in the commercial ranching sector. This study,
amongst the first of a growing number over the past decade, is
hampered by the limited range, quality and accessibility of its sources.
Much of the data is from official sources of the 1950s and 1960s
and is on the whole presented rather than critically analysed.
Stock-raising in the bantustans is virtually ignored. The discussion
of development potential after independence is, however, illuminating
in raising a number of key social and political issues, including
competing claims to land, the forms of ownership and management, and
the scale and organisation of production.

32. MOORSOM, RICHARD. Agriculture: transforming a wasted land. London:
Catholic Institute for International Relations, 1982, 114 p. 5 maps,
17 tables, bibl.: 107-14. (A Future for Namibia, 2).

This is the first sectoral study in CIIR's series of booklets on the
economic problems of the transition to independence in Namibia, condensed
from a much longer and more empirically detailed original draft. It
is one of the most solidly researched of the recent development
studies, drawing on a wide range of secondary sources in Afrikaans
and German as well as English. It also benefits from the author's
previous historical work, especially on rural class formation and

labour migration (see nos. 56, 664, 667). Background is provided
by short chapters on the "agriculture of theft": a residual peasantry
and capitalist settler farmers locked together by the migrant labour
system. A central chapter analyses the exploitation and crisis-
ridden nature of present-day agriculture. The final chapter assesses
both the short- and long-term possibilities for agricultural development, setting SWAPO's commitment to social ownership and equality
in the likely context of post-independence Namibia. It states the
case for radical and early transformation, arguing inter alia that
collapse in the ranch sector can only be avoided through social
ownership, of which producer cooperatives may be the most desirable
form, that the technical scope for a large expansion of the area of
peasant cultivation in the north is considerable and that popular
participation is vital to success as well as social justice. In each
chapter the disadvantaged position of women, sidelined in much of
the literature, is integrated into the analysis. There is also a
full bibliography and a wide range of tables.

533. MSHONGA, S. Agricultural policies and programmes of the German and
South African administrations in Namibia (1884 to 1966). Lusaka:
UNIN, 1977, 27 p. (Draft).

Written by a former lecturer at the UN Institute for Namibia, this
is a well-informed survey of the agricultural policies and programmes
followed by the German and South African administrations. It
covers such aspects as land distribution, price policies, infrastructure, credit institutions and extension services. The author
argues that the policies of the colonial powers were the main causes
of the destruction of the African agricultural economy and the
propping up of white settlement, and that these policies would hold
any future Namibian government committed to egalitarian goals in an
economic and political straight-jacket.

534. MSHONGA, S. Towards agrarian reform: policy options for Namibia.
Lusaka: UNIN, 1979, 72 p. 3 tables, 9 figures, 7 maps. (Namibia
Studies Series No. 3, N.K. Duggal, editor).

This is one of the more sophisticated analyses of a rapidly-growing
genre and, because produced at Namibia's main external research
centre, likely to be the most influential with Namibian economic
planners. The discussion is equally balanced between the structure
and trends in present-day agriculture and policy-options for long-term
development. The first part of the study is devoted to natural environment and ecology, as well as the present economic and institutional
structures (land distribution, ownership, income, numbers and skills
of workers, marketing, transport, training and research facilities).
The author's agronomic expertise is evident, and the documentary
evidence has been reinforced by the direct experience of rural
Namibians. In the second half, a thoughtful structural analysis
of economic exploitation, constraints and development priorities leads
to an extended appraisal of alternative forms of land tenure and
production organisation - freehold, communal, tenancy from the state,
cooperative, collective, state farms - with a broad survey of
comparative African experience. Both the political goals of the
liberation movement and the political and economic realities of

post-independence Namibia are closely integrated into the discussion.
A final brief chapter assesses a number of policy issues common to
all variants of agrarian reform.

35. NIXON, CHARLES D. Land use and development in Namibia. The Hague:
Institute of Social Studies, 1980, 143 p. 6 maps, 13 tables,
bibl.: 139-43. (M.A. thesis).

The author sets out to "examine the production potential of the land
under the existing patterns of land use and reveal the exploitative
nature of the present social relations of production". He considers
that the development of Namibia and its people can only be obtained
in terms of a revolutionary change in which "the direct producers ...
overthrow the owners of land and capital ...." After an introductory
overview of Namibian politics and economics, the bulk of the dissertation is devoted to the evolution and present context of land use,
with chapters on geography and natural resources, colonisation and
land distribution, support services for white farmers and conditions
for black farmworkers and peasants. In the final section a largely
theoretical discussion of "development" in the context of class
struggle is concluded with a brief assessment of some of the practical
problems in transition and of the different forms of social ownership.
The analysis is at times rather simplistic and abstract, and the
empirical base is often out-of-date. But the study benefits from
the author's expertise in agronomy and the information gathered from
official sources during his brief research visit to Namibia in
1978. The latter is drawn together in his still useful summary
report to UNIN: Land use and development in Namibia, Lusaka, UNIN,
Division of Agriculture and Land Resources, 1978, 8 p.

36. OLOYA, J.J., et al. Agricultural economy of Namibia: strategies
for structural change. Lusaka: UN Institute for Namibia, 1984,
77 p. 23 tables, 4 maps, 8 figures. (Namibian Studies Series
No. 6. Edited by N.K. Duggal, based on the work of J.J Oloya, I.
Miclaus, F.A. Ishengoma and K. Aho).

This study, the second on Namibian agriculture to have been undertaken
by the staff of UNIN, differs from its predecessor (no. 534) chiefly
in its more specifically economic focus and greater depth of empirical
detail, drawn from an extensive range of academic, official and
current affairs sources. It also includes a chapter on fishing
(p. 27-36), the first attempt by UNIN to date to assess this important
sector. After a general introduction and statement of objectives,
separate chapters discuss the natural environment and water resources,
the different branches of livestock farming, arable farming, marine
and inland fishing, agricultural support services, nutrition and
food supply, and strategy options in each of the topic areas. Each
of the chapters discusses the present economic situation, resources
and constraints and future potential, the latter receiving more
extended assessment in the concluding section. The range of factual
information deployed, both descriptive and statistical, is one of
the study's more important features, but is not without drawbacks:
for the most part it covers only a narrow band of recent years,
which makes judgments on trends uncertain, and on occasion South
African data are used uncritically. The assessment of strategy
options for agricultural development covers a great deal of ground,

tending to discuss each policy area separately rather than
attempting a systematic integration of strategy. Although cautious
in evaluating the available alternatives, the general thrust is
towards centralised state control, technological and managerial
efficiency, and greater integration and self-sufficiency through
extended crop production, local processing and local manufacture
of intermediate inputs. Selective subsidies and the transfer of
surplus from the mining sector are also endorsed.

537. PAUL, JOHANNES. "Wirtschaft und Besiedelung im südlichen Amboland".
In Wissenschaftliche Veröffentlichungen, N.F. 2, p. 71-106. Leipzig:
Museum für Länderkunde, 1933. 18 photos, 6 maps, bibl.: 102.

A detailed and competent study of peasant agriculture and land
settlement in Ovamboland, based on field visits in 1929 and 1930.
The author argues, in opposing the establishment of European
plantations, that the preservation of peasant agriculture within
a reserve benefits the colonial economy more through cheap migrant
labour and sustaining the unemployed. In one sense this study can
thus be seen as a "forerunner" of more recent marxist analyses of
the role of the reserves in the apartheid economy.

538. SCHÄFER, HEINRICH and KARL WALTER SPITZNER. Die Karakulzucht in
Südwestafrika und das Haus Thorer. Cape Town: Thorer-Unternehmen,
1962, 92 p.

This history of karakul breeding and marketing in Namibia focuses
on the important role played by the Thorer company from the
beginning around the turn of the century up to 1962. The book,
published by the company itself, contains information and observations which shed light not only on the karakul business but
also on the economic history of Namibia in general. It shows how
the changing conditions of karakul breeding and international marketing have been related to depression, drought, war and the
political considerations of South Africa and its administration
in Windhoek. The book has, however, nothing to offer to readers
who are looking for information on wages, working and living
conditions for farm labourers. The wider history of the "Thorer
Haus" is to be found in Thorer/Hollender: 350 Jahre Thorer (Frankfurt, 1962, 223 p.), which also contains a separate chapter on
Namibia and South Africa ("Südwestafrika- Südafrika und das Haus
Thorer", p. 185-215). See also a brief text - in German, English
and Afrikaans - which deals with the operations of the Thorer
company in Namibia up to the mid-1930s, Otto Nauen: Karakulzucht
in Südwest-Afrika und die Firma Theodor Thorer (Windhoek: Meinert,
1935, 80 p.).

539. SCHMOKEL, WOLFE. The myth of the white farmer: commercial agriculture in Namibia, 1900-1983. Paper presented to the African
Studies Association Conference, Boston, 1983, 23 p.

Based on research in the National Archives (Windhoek), this is a
lucid overview of the history of commercial farming in the 20th
century by a historian at the University of Vermont. White commercial
agriculture is seen as primarily a parasitical phenomenon ("a curious

political-cultural activity"), which has failed to establish its viability in the capitalist economy despite the considerable economic and political support given by the government to the settler community as far back as from the beginning of the century. The final section of the paper focuses attention on the present agricultural crisis and the expensive measures taken by South Africa to prop up an uneconomic structure, making the farmers as a group "pensioners of the state, which placed and maintained them on the land for political reasons". The author concludes that this inheritance of a bankrupt agriculture presents severe dilemmas for a future independent Namibia, but that state farms, cooperatives and the encouragement of black land tenure in the traditional white farming areas may constitute possible strategies. The author has previously published a book on the German colonial movement in the interwar period: Dream of Empire: German Colonialism, 1919-1945 (New Haven/London: Yale U.P., 1964, 204 p.).

40. SCHNEIDER, HERBERT. Analyse der Tiergesundheitssituation in Südwestafrika/Namibia. Giessen: Institut für tropische Veterinärmedizin der Justus Liebig-Universität, 1977, 318 p. 65 illus. (maps and photos), 65 tables. (Dissertation).

Based on painstaking research and practical experience as a veterinary in Namibia, this empirically dense thesis provides a basic reference work on the incidence, control, eradiction and prevention of animal diseases in Namibia. The thesis is also of great value for the study of the history of a country where cattle and small-stock farming are economically vital. For this purpose, the sections on the Rinderpest (cattle plague) in the 1890s and foot-and-mouth-disease in the early 1960s are especially interesting. The author also shows how the well organised veterinary department has developed over the years. Numerous tables, photos, maps and references, as well as a comprehensive bibliography, add to the value of the study.

41. SOINI, SYLVI. "Agriculture in northern Namibia: Owambo and Kavango, 1965-70". Journal of the Scientific Agricultural Society of Finland, 53, 1981: 168-209. 13 figures, 2 maps, 9 tables.

At the initiative of the Evangelical Lutheran Owambokavango Church in 1964, the author was engaged by the Finnish Missionary Society to undertake an agricultural survey of the two northern bantustans in which the church was active. This study is a revised version of the slightly longer typescript report, submitted in 1971. Concentrating largely on Ovamboland, it provides a more detailed, if generalised, analysis of soils and vegetation and the scope for technical improvement in peasant farming than the hundreds of pages of the "development" plans undertaken for the South African government in the 1970s by Stellenbosch University (see nos. 450-52). Although limited in scope, it is valuable for the author's experience amongst local peasant farmers (1965-70), and for her close attention to the practical conditions and problems of peasant farming. These qualities are not seriously impaired by the lack of a social and economic framework and by the author's uncritical endorsement of official agricultural policy.

542. SOUTH AFRICA, DEPARTMENT OF BANTU ADMINISTRATION AND DEVELOPMENT.
Verslag van die interdepartementale komitee insake waterbenutting
en algemene landbouontwikkeling in die Oostelike Caprivistrook.
Pretoria, c 50 p., 1969. (Draft report).

Studies of any kind concerning the eastern Caprivi Strip have been
rare in the period of South African rule, and therein lies the
chief value of this unpublished report. Drawing on a field visit
by Pretoria-based officials of the Department of Bantu Administration
and Development, it provides a factual survey of the ecology,
economics and infrastructure of peasant agriculture in this remote
region, together with brief assessments of existing and possible
future "development" schemes. The report can be seen as preparing
the ground for the creation shortly afterwards of the East Caprivi
"homeland".

543. SOUTH WEST AFRICA (ADM.). Report of the farm industry commission.
Windhoek: Government Printer/Meinert, 1927, 39 p.

This is the much overlooked report of a commission appointed by the
Administrator for SWA to enquire into the position of the white-
owned farming industry. Its brief was to review the state of
commercial stock-farming agriculture and to present concrete proposals for the improvement of production and marketing. The first
part of the report contains a factual description of production
patterns and costs, transport and marketing. The recommendations
of the commission generally reflect the local farmers' disapproval
of what they claimed to be the official policy restricting financial
support and subsidies to the newly established settlers from
South Africa. The commission was also "impressed" with the apparent
ability of South African Railways and Harbours to resist all proposals for improvement of services. Apart from transport and
marketing, the commission's major concern was "the native supply
problem", advocating a "Native Labour Association" for white
farmers, greater restrictions on "native stock" and an even stricter
pass law than had already been imposed only a few years before.

544. SOUTH WEST AFRICA (ADM.). Land settlement commission. Windhoek,
1935, 22 p.

Appointed to enquire into the economic position of the ranchers, the
Land Settlement Commission reflects in its report the official
concern at the stability of this lynchpin of the colonial economy.
The Commission established that most settlers were living under
precarious financial circumstances due to a steep decline in prices,
prohibitive transport costs, want of markets, variable rainfall,
stock diseases, and the reckless taking up of loans. The report
did not, however, recommend further financial support, but argued
for other measures such as dam construction, improved infrastructure,
research into diseases and provision of markets.

545. SOUTH WEST AFRICA (ADM.). Report of the minimum area of farms
commission. Windhoek, 1946, 59 p.

The first and more limited in scope of the two important agricultural
policy reports to be commissioned in the 1940s (see no. 546), this

investigation was briefed to advise on general policy regarding
minimum farm size. It came down in favour of enforcement by legislation, largely on grounds of ensuring economic viability and pre-
venting pasture degradation. It also made a provisional demarcation
by district and sub-district, a detailed list of which forms an
appendix to the report. The commission was careful to consult the
white farmers extensively by public meeting and questionnaire, and
obtained an overwhelming mandate for legislation. The district
surveys give useful descriptive information on the local ecology
and conditions of farming in the settler zone.

546. SOUTH WEST AFRICA (ADM.). Report of the long-term agricultural
policy commission. Windhoek, 1949, 290 p. 28 tables, 7 diagrams,
4 maps, 20 photos.

This commission strongly influenced South African agricultural policy
in Namibia in the postwar decades, and in certain respects prefigures
recent discussion of post-independence development policy. It remains the only official investigation into agriculture in the 70
years of South African rule to have been given a comprehensive
brief; its nearest sequel is the recent and more specific Harrison
report on farm profitability (no. 519). The report is broad in
scope. A long introductory chapter describes the natural environment, the first systematic account of its kind, and farm economy
and society on white-owned ranches and, briefly, in the reserves.
Two short chapters on agricultural organisations and support services
and on soil and water conservation are followed by discussion of
methods of improvement, primarily in settler karakul and cattle
ranching, and an extended analysis of the marketing of livestock
products. A concluding section provides a useful summary of the
argument and main recommendations. The report bears the stamp of
thorough local knowledge, intensive investigation, and a pragmatic
problem-oriented approach. It contains much empirical detail, and
the statistical appendix provides valuable coverage of the first
25 years of South African rule. Although the reserves were not
entirely neglected, the commission's main concern was with settler
stock-farming, and nearly all its 50 public hearings were in white
farming localities, with the SWA Agricultural Union closely involved
in coordinating the evidence. The report is written in clear and
forthright style and is at times trenchantly critical of existing
farming practices and official policy, diagnosing a gathering
crisis in soil and pasture degradation. Its recommendations legiti-
mated the three foundations of official policy towards settler
ranching right up to present reconsideration: comprehensive
planning of water and pasture use; state-subsidised enclosure of
the open range into camps; and state-organized marketing, particularly
of exports. Interestingly, while endorsing the primary subsistence
role of the reserves, the commission recommended cash incentives,
facilities for marketing surplus production, and equal access to
services for peasant agriculture, in the north as well as the south -
aspects which were not so actively taken up by the government.

SPITZNER, KARL WALTER, see no. 538.

547. TJINGAETE, FANUEL. Grundelemente einer wirksamen Agrarreform unter besonderer Berücksichtigung Namibias. Berlin: Freie Universität, 1983, 96 p. (M.Sc.Econ. thesis).

This thesis, written by a Namibian economist, outlines some of the main elements in a policy for agrarian reform and agricultural improvement. The study is not based on primary research, but restricts itself to a general discussion - with examples from other third world countries - of questions like agricultural price policy, credit policy, agricultural research, education and training as well as taxation and subsidies. These are important aspects which are often overlooked in the literature on agrarian reforms, and the author claims that these shortcomings (or omissions) also characterise the UNIN study on agrarian reform in Namibia (see no. 534). Based on what is regarded as a failure of reform programmes in Tanzania and Egypt, the author especially underlines the need for higher producer prices and a credit system and a research policy in the service of small peasants. The case is also made for flexibility in allowing the coexistence of different organisational forms of agricultural production (communal, group, cooperative and private farming). The author is based in West Germany, preparing a PhD thesis and serving as the local representative of the South West Africa National Union (SWANU).

UNIVERSITY OF STELLENBOSCH, see no. 519.

548. URQUHART, ALVIN W. Patterns of settlement and subsistence in southwestern Angola. Washington, DC: US National Academy of Sciences/ National Research Council, 1963, 149 p. 85 illus., 9 maps. (Foreign Field Research Program, Report no. 18).

Although not directly concerned with Namibia, the area covered by this study includes the Angolan half of pre-colonial Ovamboland. As a detailed and expert field study of the agronomy, the forms of land use and the economy of peasant farming, it provides much valuable information, supported by numerous photos, plans and diagrams, on local conditions similar to those on the Namibian side of the border. Its value is the greater for the lack, even today, of any similarly detailed study of peasant farming in the northern Namibian bantustans, the nearest equivalent being the agronomic survey by Soini (see no 541).

549. VILJOEN, JOHANNES J. Die geskiedenis van die karakulboerdery in Suidwes-Afrika, 1907-50. Johannesburg: Randse Afrikaanse Universiteit, 1981, 198 p. 10 diagrams, 4 maps, 16 tables. (MA thesis).

A descriptive economic history of the founding and rise to prosperity of karakul ranching in southern and central Namibia, based largely on archival research. After a technical introduction, the study is divided into four periods: the introduction of karakul sheep in the latter years of the German regime, pioneer farming during the First World War and the 1920s, explosive expansion during the 1930s, and consolidation during the 1940s.

950. WERNER, WOLFGANG. "Production and land policies in the Herero reserves", 1925-1950. In Seminar on Namibian history, December 1982, p. 57-77. Windhoek: Namibian Review Publications, 1983.

Written by a Namibian scholar who is preparing a PhD thesis on the socio-economic history of the Herero, with a special emphasis on the period 1915-1950, this essay is concerned with the fundamental issue of production and reproduction in the Herero reserves. On the basis of extensive archival material, which is admittedly weak on the conditions of the poorer sections of the population, the author brings together original and valuable information on the number and unequal distribution of stocks and income from stock sales and dairy production. He also shows that the process of peasantisation and increasing social stratification was particularly strengthened by the development of dairy production. There is also a discussion of some of the political manifestions of the process of differentiation, such as the struggle between individual and communal forms of access to land and the agitation against white domination of the reserve economy. The hypothesis is advanced that despite the decline in the natural resources of the reserves, a number of peasants have managed to accumulate considerable wealth.

SEE ALSO:

29, 41, 49, 75, 84, 90, 91, 94, 95, 97, 107, 109, 111, 112, 322, 323, 340, 342, 349, 350, 357, 380, 381, 401-3, 444, 450-2, 454, 489, chapter 8 a(615-643), 649-50, 745, 887, 888, 949, 958, 961, 965, 966, 1036.

B. Fisheries

551. AHLGREN, C.S. The Namibian fishing industry: Africa's cannery row. Airgram, US Embassy, Pretoria to US Department of State, Washington, 9 June 1981, 8 p. 6 tables.

An economic survey of the fishing industry and, to a lesser extent, the Walvis Bay enclave. It is clearly informed by interviews with local business leaders and government officials. Such embassy reports, because unclassified and thus fairly easily obtainable, may continue to provide useful sources of current economic data and information on policy issues.

552. BÄHR, JÜRGEN. "Zum gegenwärtigen Stand der Fischereiwirtschaft in Südwestafrika". Mitteilungen der Österreichischen Geographischen Gesellschaft, 14, no. 1-2, 1972: 86-103.

A well-researched and informative survey of the inshore fishing industry, concentrating on the late 1960s. It contains much useful factual information, especially on rock lobster catches and production, processing methods, prices for raw fish and processed exports, employment and the new quotas awarded in the late 1960s.

553. BOOTH, ALAN R. "American whalers in South African waters". The South African Journal of Economics, 32, no. 4, 1964: 278-82.

A short historical analysis of economic interaction between the American long-distance whaling fleet and southern African coastal communities in the late 18th and early 19th centuries. Walvis and Lüderitz (Angra Pequena) Bays were major operational bases and barter trading with the Khoisan inhabitants was the earliest form of economic contact between Namibia and the Western capitalist economies. See also p. 32-40 in the author's book: The United States experience in South Africa 1784-1870 (Cape Town/Rotterdam: Balkema, 1976).

CLARK, W.G., see no. 573.

554. COOPER, ALLAN D. The politics of indirect investments: US corporate interests in Namibia. Draft paper, University of Wisconsin, 1976, 86 p. 7 diagrams.

Despite its general title, this is in fact a study of US corporate involvement in the Namibian fishing industry. Much of the text has been incorporated into the author's more recent book (no. 353), but a few significant points have not, and the paper remains an important case-study in its own right. It argues that US corporations were instrumental in equipping the Namibian processing factories during the collapse of the Californian sardine fishery after the Second World War and in marketing their products, particularly canned pilchards. Similarly, cargo facilities and promotion by the two main US shipping lines servicing Southern Africa gave access to a new and lucrative market for frozen lobster tails after 1945. The author deploys a wealth of factual evidence, based on extensive research, mainly in South African and US newspapers, journals and official sources.

555. CRAM, DAVID L. "Hidden elements in the developments and implementation of marine resource conservation policy: the case of the SWA/Namibian fisheries". In Resource management and environmental uncertainty, edited by M.H. Glantz and J.D. Thompson, p. 137-56. New York: Wiley Interscience, 1981.

This is an important and authoritative analysis of the collapse of the Namibian pilchard stock in the mid-1970s. The author was the South African government's chief marine scientist in Namibia during the 1970s and, as Deputy Director of the Sea Fisheries Division with responsibility for Namibia, in charge of official research and administration during the critical years of collapse. Although cautious in ascribing specific blame, he presents a damning indictment of official complacency and company greed, arguing that scientific influence in decisions over conservation policy was often rendered marginal by political and business interests, that scientific monitoring of the fish population was woefully inadequate and that widespread evasion of the already inadequate restrictions was not effectively stopped. He also assesses the economic motives of the companies for overfishing and presents an excellent concise overview of conservation policy over the 30-year history of the inshore industry, complementing an earlier and more detailed account (Cram, D.L., "Research and management of Southeast Atlantic fisheries", California Cooperative Oceanic Fishery Investigations (CalCoFi), Report 19, 1977, p. 33-56). The author's argument carries conviction, despite lack of documentation from first-hand sources and the fact that it is in part a defence of the professional reputation of the fishery scientists, whom critics have repeatedly accused of complacency.

556. CULLEY, MICHAEL B. The pilchard: biology and exploitation. Oxford: Pergamon Press, 1971, 256 p. 92 illus., tables.

The chapter on South Africa and Namibia (p. 181-207) gives an early account of the rise of the processing industry at Walvis Bay. Although primarily of scientific interest, it was written at the climax of the reckless expansion of the 1960s, when the factory ships were plundering the pilchard stock near to destruction, and contains interesting detail and policy statements from that period. The much more exhaustive case-study of the spectacular collapse of the Californian sardine canning industry in the 1940s offers a most instructive parallel to the disastrous history of its Namibian counterpart.

557. FAO. Fishery country information base: Namibia. Rome: FAO, 1979, 79 p. 1 map, 28 tables. (Unpublished draft).

This is an unpublished draft which follows the format of the series of FAO background reports on national fisheries. It draws heavily on Barbara Rogers' consultancy report for the UN Council for Namibia (see no. 564), the controversy over which may be the principal reason why it has not been circulated as an FAO document. In its present unedited form the study lacks a contents page and is poorly laid out, making it difficult to use. Although its research base is limited, it does gather together much useful information, particularly from the South African fishing trade journal and yearbook and from ICSEAF. After a general introduction on Namibia as a whole, the study covers living marine resources, catches, the state of the different fish stocks, conservation measures, fishing methods, inland water and fish resources, factory and trawler processing and marketing, the institutional structure (government, companies), research, and development recommendations. The latter place considerable emphasis on the training of Namibians, especially for government supervision, the gathering of policy-related data and the preparation of contingency measures to enable the post-independence Namibian government to impose effective controls. The study does not, however, analyse the implications of foreign exploitation of Namibia's fish resources or assess the strategic options for a national fisheries policy. These and other deficiencies are likely to be rectified in a major analysis of post-independence policy options for the Namibian fishing industry now in preparation by an FAO consultancy team and due for completion during 1984.

558. FOSTER, SUSAN D. and DENNIS M. WEIDNER. The lobster fisheries in the Republic of South Africa and Namibia, 1975-6. Washington: US National Marine Fisheries Service, 1978, 21 p. 20 figure, 4 tables, 8 app. (Foreign Fisheries Leaflet, 77, no. 5).

A concise and informative survey of the biology, economics and management of the South African and Namibian rock lobster industry, particularly useful on the ownership structure of the companies involved and on exports to the US, then by far the biggest market. Although Namibia tends to be merged with South Africa in the statistics, specific data are scattered through the text.

GULLAND, J.A., see no. 573.

559. HARRISON, HUMPHREY. Report on the South African fishing companies (?). Johannesburg, 1981, c 70 p. Tables.

This is a financial survey of the eight leading South African companies with fishing interests, most of them heavily involved in Namibia as well as South Africa. It was prepared by a Johannesburg firm of share analysts for sale to stock market investors and remains unpublished. The general introduction gives a brief but well-informed and trenchantly critical review of South African conservation policy and overfishing by the companies. The rest of the report applies a standardised framework of assessment to each company in turn.

Each section consists of a brief commentary, with useful details
of the company's ownership, investments and economic activities
as well as statistics from its accounts for the period 1975-79.
(The statistics can be a little difficult to interpret without a
knowledge of the terminology of accountancy.) A comparative
summary of the stock market data is also given together with a
chart of the ownership structure of the companies.

560. LEES, ROBIN. Fishing for fortunes: the story of the fishing industry in Southern Africa and the men who made it. Cape Town:
Purnell, 1969, 283 p. 9 photos, 1 map, bibl.: xiii-xv.

An important history of the fishing industry in South Africa and
Namibia. Although sources are rarely given for factual evidence,
the book appears to be based on extensive research, which is
competently deployed and, where verifiable, accurate. From
internal references the author appears to be the daughter of a top
executive of one of the major Namibian fishing companies, and
her knowledge indicates substantial assistance from leading
figures in the industry. With its wealth of detail, and at times
perceptive analysis, this book is therefore invaluable as an
inside view of the rise of the pelagic fish and lobster processing
industry in Namibia. It provides rare insight into a closed
managerial world, although it is not entirely uncritical of
company attitudes and government policy. Its major drawback is
that as a popular narrative history, factual information is
scattered in fragments throughout the text, making it difficult
to use for reference and analysis.

561. LIESEGANG, C. "Die Guanogewinnung auf den Inseln und an der Küste
Südwestafrikas". Erdkunde, 4, no. 1-2, 1950: 35-43.

A brief economic history of guano recovery along the Namibian coast
from its origins in the 1820s up to the late 1930s, researched from
a wide range of published sources.

562. MOORSOM, RICHARD. Fishing: exploiting the sea. London: Catholic
Institute for International Relations, 1984, 123 p. 7 diagrams,
14 tables, 2 maps, bibl.: 114-20. (A Future for Namibia, 5).

The second of Moorsom's contributions to the excellent CIIR series
on Namibia, this short book follows a similar format to its
companions, with a strong emphasis on rigorous but simplified
analysis and on the development strategy. The opening chapters
describe Namibia's wealth of marine resources and the history of
foreign fishing, both by South African companies and by long-distance
trawler fleets, which has all but destroyed them. The three middle
chapters analyse the political economy of overfishing, the economic
stake of the foreign interests involved, and the exploitation of
Namibian workers and fishermen in the ruthless scramble for profits.
The final and longest chapter analyses the prospects and alternative
strategies for development after independence, arguing, controversially,
that should South Africa hang on to Walvis Bay, a medium-term option
of rebuilding a moderate-size industry at Lüderitz would be viable.
Although empirical data is limited and highly selective, the tables

and diagrams provide a comprehensive set of up-to-date statistics
for a notoriously poorly served sector of the Namibian economy.
There is also a full bibliography. Two shorter articles by the
same author give slightly greater information on the specific
subjects they address, foreign exploitation, and the recent exodus
to Chile (The Namibian fishing industry, paper presented to the
International Seminar on the role of TNCs in Namibia, Washington,
1982, and "The plunder of Namibia's seas", African Business, July
1983).

563. NEWMAN, GARTH G. The living marine resources of the Southeast
Atlantic. Rome: FAO, 1977, 59 p. 23 tables, bibl.: 56-9.
(Fisheries Technical Paper 178).

Although primarily a synthesis of scientific knowledge on the state
of the fish stocks, this authoritative survey by one of South
Africa's most able marine scientists - since departed for Australia -
is valuable for its overview of the recent history of commercial
fishing and for its comprehensive catch statistics.

564. ROGERS, BARBARA. Question of the Namibia Fishery industries. New
York: UN Council for Namibia, 1975, 94 p. 3 diagrams, 14 tables +
statistical appendix. (Unpublished conference paper, 75/156).

This is one of the most comprehensive and best-researched studies
of the Namibian fishery to date, and it is unfortunate that it
remains unpublished. It was submitted as a consultancy report,
and draws extensively on material unused or not easily available to
other researchers, especially Lees' history (see no. 560), ICSEAF
documents and the trade journal and annual (see no. 976). Separate
sections cover the marine environment, pelagic fishing, trawling,
other marine products (mainly crayfish, seals, guano), marketing,
the processing companies, the international trawler fleet, and
ICSEAF, with an appendix giving FAO statistics for the Southeast
Atlantic for 1965-72. The author's analysis is penetrating and
strongly critical of foreign (including USSR) exploitation and
overfishing of Namibia's living marine resources. She argues that
ICSEAF, whose establishment and mode of operation is outlined in
detail, is no less illegal than the South African occupation regime
and urges, with a series of specific recommendations, that the UN
and FAO should act to protect Namibian marine resources.

565. ROTHSCHILD, BRIAN J. The fish resources of Namibia: present status
and options for future policies. Rome: FAO, 1982, 78 p. 1 map,
8 figures, 16 tables. (Unpublished report).

This is one of a number of consultancy reports prepared under the
most recent phase of the UN Nationhood Programme for Namibia. Like
most of the others it is as yet unpublished. The author is the
first non-South African fish population expert to assess the
Namibian fishery, and his report is a sophisticated technical
analysis, both of the present state of the fish stocks and of the
options for Namibian conservation policy after independence. His
recommendations are complex, interdependent and - because they
understandably tend to sidestep the controversial questions of

political choice - often conditional. The first section of the
report provides valuable data on catches and the state of the fish
stocks, largely drawn from ICSEAF sources. The author's comments
are authoritative, although in places all to brief and at times
too technical for non-experts to follow easily. The authors of
sources used are cited, but unfortunately no bibliography is attached.

RUSHBURNE, J.L., see no. 567.

SA Fishing Industry Handbook and Buyer's Guide, see no. 976.

566. SHAUGHNESSY, P.D. "The status of seals in South Africa and Namibia".
FAO Fisheries Series, 4, no. 5, 1982: 383-410. 10 tables.

As well as providing information on population and biology, this survey
is one of the few sources to give a detailed history and description
of the economic exploitation of the seal colonies.

567. SMIT, P.G. and J.L. RUSHBURNE. A survey of the fishing industry in
South Africa and South West Africa. Statsinform (Pty) Ltd., 1971,
158 p. 21 diagrams, 36 tables + summaries of company accounts.
(Statisform, Nedbank Group, Survey no. 4).

A detailed survey, mainly statistical, on conservation policy, catches,
production and the companies involved. Separate chapters cover
the inshore pelagic industry, deep-sea trawling, rock lobster and
whaling. In most of the tables and diagrams which relate largely
to the mid- and late 1960s, Namibia is distinguished from South
Africa, a practice which because it was not usually followed in
official publications of the time makes them particularly useful,
although the sources are not always given. Although much of the
text is taken up with a presentation of the statistics, there is
additional information on what was a murky episode in the history
of Namibian conservation policy. The final section summarises in
turn the accounts of 11 leading fish processing companies, with
brief notes on fish production, investment and dividends.

568. SOUTH AFRICA (REPUBLIC). Commission of inquiry into the fishing
industry of South Africa and South West Africa. Pretoria: Government Printer, 1972, 173 p. Maps, diagrams, tables. (RP47-72).

569. SOUTH WEST AFRICA (ADM.). Commission of inquiry into the fishing
industry. Windhoek, 1966, 70 p.

These two reports are the only official investigations into the
Namibian fishing industry to have been published. They were initiated
(in 1965 and 1967 respectively) partly in response to the gathering
crisis of over-exploitation of the pilchard in both the South
African and the Namibian inshore fisheries, with the companies
pressing for ever higher quotas and with open warfare between the
SWA Administration and the South African Department of Industries
over the licensing of fishmeal factory ships to operate off the
Namibian coast. The first commission, reporting at the end of 1966,
concentrated on the short-term problems of resource management.

Despite clearly registering scientists' warnings of inadequate
data and the risks of overexploitation, its response to the entry
of the factory ships was - perversely - to endorse additional
shore quotas. It also hastened the collapse of the rock lobster
by adopting the controversial argument of one of its members
(reproduced in an appendix) for the abolition of the restriction
on the minimum size allowed to be caught. Its successor, a more
substantial investigation with broad terms of reference, reported
late in 1971 after four years of deliberation and a series of
unpublished interim reports, at least three of which - on the South
African takeover of fisheries administration from the SWA Administration (1968), on stock assessment (1970), and on the pelagic
fish factories (1970) - included the Namibian industry. The final
report is a comprehensive and well organised survey of the South
African and Namibian fishing industries and remains a valuable
source of factual information. It includes histories of the rise
of the different branches of the shore-based industry, as well as
foreign offshore trawling; and sections on the living marine resources,
the forms of exploitation, the methods of resource management, and
the structures of administration and research. Text relating to
Namibia is scattered throughout the report, but is organised into
sub-sections and therefore easy to locate, although regrettably
most Namibian and South African statistics are merged. Its recommendations, cautiously framed, were directed mostly to the long
term rather than immediate issues. Few of the more important
of them were adopted.

570. SPARKS, DONALD L. Namibia's coastal and marine resource development
potential. Paper presented to a conference on Namibia, University
of Vermont, 1982, 36 p. 4 tables.

One of several recent papers (see nos. 479, 443) on economic and
political issues related to Namibian independence by a former
adviser in the US State Department during the Carter Administration
of the late 1970s. It provides a brief overview of mineral and
marine resources in the coastal Namib desert and the 200 mile
offshore zone which Namibia will be entitled to control after
independence, as well as a description of the present forms and
rates of economic exploitation. It is critical of South African
policy, but occasionally inaccurate and somewhat speculative in
argument. An appendix provides a useful summary history of South
Africa's legal claims to Walvis Bay and the offshore islands and
of the former's significance as a port (See also no. 1563).

571. STOOPS, W.H. "The South African fishing industry". The South
African Journal of Economics, 21, no. 2, 1953: 241-50.

While it contains few explicit references to Namibia, this article
provides a well-informed general account of the explosive rise
of the pelagic fish processing industry in South Africa and
Namibia during the 1940s and early 1950s, of which there are few
competent overviews. It discusses the economic factors behind the
expansion, the fishing fleet and the role of the state.

572. THOMESEN, INGE.   The fisheries of Namibia: a preliminary report.
University of Tromsø (Norway), Institute of Fisheries, 1978, 71 p.
11 figures, 6 tables.

This is a well-researched technical report, mainly but not only
concerned with present conditions. Its value is enhanced by the
author's expertise in fisheries research and by his field visit
in 1978, which, although restricted to two weeks by the South
African authorities, is one of the very few made by independent
researchers of the Namibian fishing industry. As well as personal
observation, the author uses several research reports by South
African scientists which are not easily available abroad. After
describing the living marine resources along the Namibian coast,
he outlines the history of conservation policy, catches and production in the land-based industry with its South African dominated
ownership structure. Separate chapters on Lüderitz and Walvis
Bay describe factory production and fishing methods, focusing in
particular on working conditions, the technology and the organisation
of local trawler fishing. An illuminating assessment of government
fisheries, research and administration is followed by a discussion
of policing the offshore fishing zone and the context of Walvis
Bay following South Africa's illegal annexation in 1977. In conclusion, the author advocates eventual nationalisation of
company-owned factories and boats; a separate and adequately funded
fisheries administration supervising a 200-mile offshore zone;
national nutritional planning; improvement in working conditions
and training programmes; labour-intensive investment and processing
for human consumption.

573. TROADEC, J.P., W.G. CLARK and J.A. GULLAND. "A review of some
pelagic fish stocks in other areas". In Rapports et Procès-verbal.
Conseil International pour L'exploration de la Mer, 177, 1980:
252-77. 8 tables, 3 figures.

A major part of this article, written by experts in FAO's Fisheries
Department, is devoted to Namibia, presenting probably the most
thorough and authoritative analysis to date of the history and
disastrous decline of Namibia's rich pilchard stock under commercial
exploitation. Although directed primarily to the scientific aspects
of fishery regulation, the catch and fishing effort data and
summary of management measures will be of particular economic
interest.

574. US DEPARTMENT OF THE INTERIOR, BUREAU OF COMMERCIAL FISHERIES.
The marine fishing industries of South Africa and South West Africa.
Washington DC, 1969, 28 p. (Foreign Fisheries Leaflet, no. 22).

A detailed and comprehensive survey of all branches of the fishing
industry, in the Namibian case incorporating most of the information
contained in a short review of the previous year (SWA's fishing
industries, 1966 and 1967, Foreign Fisheries Leaflet no. 21,
1968, 3p). Compiled by the Regional Fisheries Attaché, US Embassy,
Ivory Coast, it is a thoroughly researched and authoritative report,
giving some historical background but concentrating on recent
economic developments, marketing, and the organisation of the

industry. Written at the peak of the Namibian fishing boom, it pays particular attention to the factory ships controversy.

SEE ALSO:

25, 32, 49, 75, 95, 111, 353, 420, 489, 510, 513, 536, 729, 745, 976.

C. Mining

575. ANONYMOUS. "Tsumeb: three-year wonder". Fortune, 41, no. 2, 1950: 84-5.

A celebration of the success of the US-owned Newmont Mining Corporation in turning the derelict Tsumeb mine into a large-scale and hugely profitable operation. The article gives a valuable insight into management strategy, both towards investment and towards labour control, with economic information on the mine both under previous owners and since the US takeover in 1946.

576. ANONYMOUS. "A comprehensive survey of the mining position in South West Africa". SWA Annual 1951: 101-135.

An account of the postwar mining boom, packed with concise information on production and export of each of the minerals. There is also a section outlining the mining laws of the territory.

577. ANTI-APARTHEID-BEWEGUNG GRUPPE BREMEN. Uranabbau in Namibia. Gestohlenes Uran für die strahlende Zukunft der Bundesrepublik. Bremen: AG gegen die militärisch-nukleare Zusammenarbeit der BRD mit Südafrika in der Anti-Apartheid-Bewegung Gruppe Bremen, 1982, 114 p. Bibl.: 108-11.

A collection of articles and documents concerned with Namibia, uranium, South Africa's nuclear strategy and the role of West Germany in nuclear collaboration, bringing together a wide range of material from sources such as the UN hearings on Namibian uranium, the Information Centre on Southern Africa (ISSA), the SWAPO/Namibian Support Committee Seminar on Trade Unions and Namibian Uranium.

578. AULAKH, H.S., et al. The mining industry of Namibia. Legal framework and development strategy options (tentative title). Lusaka: UNIN. (Namibia Studies Series, edited by N.K. Duggal). In preparation.

579. BÜRG, GEORG. Die nutzbaren Minerallagerstätten von Deutsch-Südwestafrika. Berlin: Walter de Gruyter & Co., 1942, 305 p., 66 illus., maps, tables, bibl.: 293-305. (Mitteilungen der Forschungsstelle für Kolonialen Bergbau an der Bergakademie Freiburg, Nr. 2.)

An extensive and thorough survey of geology and mineral production in Namibia. Although the main focus is on geology and natural resources, there is also valuable information, especially in

respect of diamonds, on production, export, sales income and company
structure. There are separate chapters on copper, vanadium, tin,
diamonds, gold and iron ore, as well as smaller sections on minor
minerals. A comprehensive bibliography and a large number of
tables, maps and charts make the book a source of considerable
value.

580. CATHOLIC INSTITUTE FOR INTERNATIONAL RELATIONS. Mines and independence. London: CIIR, 1983, 155 p. 25 tables, 5 figs., 3 maps,
bibl.: 147-51. (A Future for Namibia, 3).

Published as the third volume in the CIIR series A Future for
Namibia, this study of the mining sector makes a valuable contribution to the discussion on the economic and political prospects for
an independent Namibia. The first part of the book provides a
factual, up-to-date and lucid analysis of the past and present
operations of the mining companies and their impact on the political
economy of Namibia. This part offers important insights into
mineral production, company ownerships, profits, and working
conditions, as well as the mining sector's links with the international markets and to the South African regime. It also reveals
how the mining boom in the 1970s turned into a slump in the 1980s,
leading to increasing unemployment and falling state revenues. The
second half is concerned with mineral policy issues after independence, and provides a detailed and realistic examination of the
options facing a Namibian government committed to social justice
and national control of a vital sector of the economy. Among the
issues considered are a national mining service, the building
up of strong trade unions, training of Namibians, the abolition
of the contract labour system, a revision of contracts and agreements with foreign companies and the use of mineral revenues for
general development purposes, thus benefitting the people as a whole.
The study will undoubtedly serve as a handy reference work with its
numerous tables in the text and appendix and with an extensive bibliography.

581. CDM (PTY) LTD. Consolidated Diamond Mines. Windhoek, 1981, 25 p.
15 photos, 6 figs., 2 tables.

Published by the company itself, this is a brief, informative
booklet on the operations of CDM in Namibia. Among the subjects
touched upon are the history of diamond mining, the geology of the
deposits, the mining process, the metallurgy as well as a PR-section
on employment practices. There are also detailed production figures
(1970-1979) and several figures which provide useful technical
information for non-experts.

THE CHAMBER OF MINES OF SWA/NAMIBIA. Annual Report, see no. 944.

582. THE CONSOLIDATED DIAMOND MINES OF SOUTH-WEST AFRICA LTD. Annual
reports and accounts. Windhoek: CDM, 1920-1974.

The annual report of the major mining company in Namibia, a subsidiary
of De Beers Consolidated Mining Ltd., is an important source on
diamond production, exports, labour and profitability. In 1974

De Beers bought out CDM's minority shareholders and stopped publication of the report. Since then only fragments of information have been revealed in its own annual report.

583. DEVERELL, JOHN and THE LATIN AMERICAN WORKING GROUP. Falconbridge. Portrait of a Canadian mining multinational. Toronto: James Larimer & Co., 1975, 184 p.

Published by a group of researchers in Toronto who investigate multinational corporations and Canadian foreign policy, this book takes a critical look at Falconbridge Nickel Mines Ltd. The company defied both the UN and the International Court of Justice when it opened a copper mine in Namibia in 1971 (Oamites Mining Co. (Pty) Ltd.), in partnership with the South African government. Ch. 8, "Profits from apartheid: Falconbridge in Africa" (p. 149-69) demonstrates how Falconbridge took full advantage of the repressive labour system in Namibia, with a rate of return (after tax) of 57% in 1973. Falconbridge sold its controlling interest in Oamites to Meteorex of South Africa in 1982, but its parent company, Superior Oil, is still involved in oil exploration.

584. EPSTEIN, EDWARD JAY. The diamond invention. An exposé of the international diamond monopoly. London: Hutchinson, 1982, 250 p.

This is a popular and somewhat superficial account of the international diamond industry, written by an American journalist. The book is based on extensive reading and investigations, including visits to several mines in Southern Africa, but contains a number of inaccuracies and is not as reliable and informative as the similar account by T. Green (no. 586). The major part of the book deals with the role of De Beers Central Selling Organisation, and chapter 4 - "Holding back the ocean" - is devoted to the operations in Namibia. The author describes how the cartel organises production and marketing on a global scale, and how it has repeatedly interfered in the internal political affairs of African states. He predicts a collapse of the monopoly and the disintegration of the industry, with profound effects on a country like Namibia which depends heavily on income from the export of diamonds. There is also a bibliographic guide to the vast literature on diamonds, mining and marketing (p. 239-56).

585. FERREIRA, EDUARDO DE SOUSA. "International capital in Namibia. Tsumeb and the CDM". Ufahamu, 3, no. 2, 1972: 49-64. (In German: "Internationales Kapital in Namibia", Blätter für deutsche und internationale Politik, no. 12, 1972; also distributed as a reprint by Informationsstelle Südliches Afrika, Bonn, 1972, 12 p.).

Based on information available in the late 1960s, this article identifies 44 foreign firms doing business in Namibia. The general discussion of the role of multinational companies is followed by an analysis of the two largest companies, Consolidated Diamond Mines and the Tsumeb Corporation. Among the issues covered are company structure, production, profits and dividends, taxes and the labour force.

586. GREEN, TIMOTHY. The world of diamonds. London: Weidenfeld and
Nicolson, 1981, 261 p.

Written with admirable clarity and authority, this is the most informative of several popular accounts on the mining and marketing
of diamonds. It is based on extensive travelling, including
a visit to Namibia, and succeeds in highlighting the main features
of what is described as a "ruthless, secretive and often illicit
business". The author, an experienced journalist, points to the
dominant role played by De Beers/Central Selling Organisation,
and devotes a separate chapter to "Namibia: the diamond desert"
(p. 63-74).

587. GREGORY, THEODOR. Ernest Oppenheimer and the economic development
of Southern Africa. Cape Town: Oxford University Press, 1962,
609 p. Bibl.: 599-609.

The author of this factually detailed book was originally commissioned
by Anglo American Corporation of South Africa to write a history
of that institution, but it was decided after the death of Ernest
Oppenheimer to link the company history directly to his name. As
a conventional company history, the book is strong on details but
devoid of any serious criticism of the company and its leaders.
The focus is on the mining and marketing of diamonds, and there are,
therefore, several references to the development of mining in
Namibia. The author shows, for example, that the acquisition of
monopoly control over the Namibian diamond fields through an Anglo
subsidiary, Consolidated Diamond Mines (CDM), played an important
role in the formation of the new syndicate in 1925. There is also
some information of the strategy of De Beers during the depression
in the 1930s, during which CDM was closed down altogether for several
years. For another study of the Oppenheimer empire, with fewer
details, see Edward Jessup: Ernest Oppenheimer: a study in power.
(London: Rex Collings, 1979, 357 p.). From a quite different perspective, Duncan Innes has recently published a well documented and
critical analysis of Anglo American Corporation (see no. 368).

588. JEPSON, TREVOR B. Rio-Tinto Zinc in Namibia. London: Christian
Concern for Southern Africa, 1977, 18 p.

This brief report formed an early, liberal-minded contribution to
the exposure of British involvement in the illegal production and
export of uranium from the Rössing mine. It urges the British
government to withdraw its commercial protection from investments
in Namibia and the churches to monitor closely RTZ policies on
wages, health protection and trade union representation.

589. KRAMER, REED and TAMI HULTMAN. Tsumeb. A profile of United States
contribution to underdevelopment in Namibia. New York: Corporate
Information Center of the National Council of Churches, 1973, 36 p.

This was the first case study to expose the exploitative role of
the Tsumeb Corporation, until recently controlled by two US-based
mining corporations, as Namibia's largest producer of base minerals,
and it remains one of the best researched. The authors analyse

the implications of Tsumeb's operations for Namibia and for the
United States, drawing attention to issues like migrant labour and
labour policies, profitability, wages and working conditions and
Tsumeb's contribution to South African control over the territory.
The tables, showing production figures (1949-1971), taxation and
return on investment (1963-1970), are valuable for compiling time
series of pre-1970 company data.

590. LANNING, GREG with MARTI MUELLER. Africa undermined. Mining
companies and the underdevelopment of Africa. Harmondsworth:
Penguin, 1979, 592 p. 38 tables, 24 figures.

This lucid and comprehensive survey of the international mining
corporations and their operations in Africa is written for a general
audience, having grown out of a close study of the Anglo American
Corporation. The authors are freelance writers who have carried
out extensive research and paid several visits to Africa. The book
shows how the mining corporations dominate the economies of the
Southern African region, undermining and distorting the social and
political structure, as they plunder the region's non-renewable
resources. A separate chapter (p. 468-81) is devoted specifically
to Namibia, but the general sections on mining, the marketing of
Africa's minerals, the world diamond monopoly and the Oppenheimer
complex contribute also to an understanding of the Namibian economy
and the prospects for the future.

591. LENZEN, GODEHARD. The history of diamond production and the diamond
trade. London: Barrie and Jenkins, 1970, 230 p. Bibl.: 212-219.
(German original: Produktions- und Handelsgeschichte des Diamanten.
Zeitlich geordnete Beiträge unter besonderer Berücksichtigung der
Preisbildung und der Konzentrationsbestrebungen der Urproduktion.
Berlin: Duncker & Humblot, 1966.)

Originally published in German, this is a solid description of
the fascinating history of diamond production and the diamond trade.
Nearly one-third of the book is concerned with the production and
trade of the diamond deposits of Africa from 1870 onwards. The
author pays due attention to the role played by Namibian diamonds
in the changes of the production and marketing structure which took
place in the period 1919 to 1933, eventually leading to the high
degree of concentration characterising the trade today.

592. LEVINSON, OLGA. Diamonds in the desert. The story of August Stauch
and his times. Cape Town: Tafelberg, 1983, 173 p. 156 photos,
bibl.: 167-68.

This well written anecdotal account of the early days of diamond
production in Namibia focuses on the settler pioneer August Stauch,
who has also become a legend among the settler community today. The
author gives a vivid description of the major diamond discoveries and
the rush for claims in 1908, followed by the struggle for control
and monopoly which eventually led to the takeover by De Beers. It
also deals with the political career of August Stauch as a member
of the old "Landesrat" and of the Legislative Assembly established
in 1926, and describes the fall of his business empire in Germany

and Namibia in the interwar period. The biography glorifies a
time which, in the overall history of diamond mining in Namibia,
is relatively unimportant, and tends to reinforce dearly held
colonial myths ("the men who made South West"). It is lavishly
illustrated with photos, drawings and facsimile prints of documents.

593. LUND, WENDA. Die Rössing-Uranmine in Namibia und ihre regionale
und internationale politische Bedeutung. Köln: Pahl-Rugenstein
Verlag, 1984, 208 p. 18 tables, 4 figures, bibl.: 200-08.
(Diplomarbeit, Univ. Bremen).

This is a comprehensive study of the Rössing uranium mine, covering
the origins of the project, its contemporary importance for the
world uranium market and the South African nuclear strategy, the
role of international finance and mining capital, and health and
working conditions at the mine. There is also a certain amount
of technical information. Special attention is paid to British
and West German connections and the support given by these two
countries to the continuing illegal occupation of Namibia. It
also points out that the requirements of the uranium mine were
one of the main reasons for building the controversial Ruacana
hydro-electrical power scheme, and that the heavy water consumption
at the mine could lead to a future ecological disaster.

594. MOMPER, JAMES A. "The Etosha basin reexamined". Oil & Gas Journal.
April 5, 1982: 262-87.

This is one of the few published reports on the petroleum potential of
the Etosha basin, focusing almost exclusively on the southern half
of the basin in Namibia. Although the article is strictly technical,
it also contains a brief survey of the exploration activities
and an informative bibliography listing unpublished and open reports
prepared by Etosha Petroleum Co. (Pty.) Ltd. The conclusion is
that the geological evidence for oil and gas is suggestive, but
that the basin's true potential can only be determined by drilling
more wells.

MUELLER, MARTI, see no. 590.

595. MURRAY, ROGER. The mineral industry of Namibia: perspective for
independence. A factual survey of existing mineral developments
in Namibia with descriptive analysis of their economic, fiscal and
legal implications. London: The Commonwealth Secretariat, 1978,
127 p. 10 tables, bibl.: 125-27.

Prepared as a consultancy report for the Commonwealth Fund for
Technical Co-operation at the request of SWAPO, this was one of
the first studies to appear on the Namibian mining sector and its
fiscal and legal dimensions. The first part is devoted to a descriptive, albeit uneven survey of mineral resources, production,
exports, processing capacity, employment, foreign investment and
prospecting rights. It is followed by case studies of two of the
major corporations, Consolidated Diamond Mines (CDM) and Tsumeb.
Special attention is then devoted to the legal aspects of mining
in a territory under South African control, and a chronology

as well as details of mining legislation are provided in appendices. There is also a general profile of the economy, which helps to place the mining sector in a proper perspective. A revised and partly updated edition is scheduled for publication in 1984, but compared to the more concentrated study by the Catholic Institute for International Relations (no. 580) it is neither as comprehensive in scope nor as authoritative in analysis.

NAMIBIA SUPPORT COMMITTEE, see no. 604.

596. RAMSEY, ROBERT H. Men and mines of Newmont. A fifty-year history. New York: Octagon Books/Farrar, Straus and Giroux, 1973, 339 p.

Although conventional and uncritical, as a company history this book nevertheless illuminates the important role played by the Tsumeb Corporation in providing Newmont with huge profits to be invested in mining and oil exploration in other parts of the world. Ch. 7: "Tsumeb- The Unique Orebody" (p. 126-145) deals exclusively with mining operations in Namibia, which Newmont, together with American Metal Climax, bought for a very low price after the German-owned mine had been confiscated by South Africa during the Second World War. According to the company's own calculations, few orebodies anywhere in the world have been as high grade in as many metals and have proved as profitable as has the Tsumeb mine.

597. ROBERTS, ALUN. The Rossing file: the inside story of Britain's secret contract for Namibian uranium. London: The Campaign against the Namibian Uranium Contracts (CANUC), 1980, 68 p. 6 photos.

This booklet is a classical example of politically directed radical research. Its publication was part of a carefully planned escalation of the campaign to end British imports of Namibian uranium, which included a hard-hitting television documentary ("Follow the yellowcake road", World in Action, Granada) and trade union action against the hitherto secret transport route, in both of which the author was centrally involved. Well-written and thoroughly researched, the pamphlet explains with admirable clarity how a major mining multinational, Rio Tinto Zinc, set up a lucrative mining operation by manoeuvring the British government into becoming its major customer and defender. It also exposes the duplicity of successive governments in protecting RTZ's illegal contract. It contains a good deal of useful information on the economics of the Rossing mine itself and the conditions for its black employees, and also reproduces key statements by SWAPO and by the Rossing workers. For a brief, and somewhat updated version, see a conference paper by the same author: The International Trade in Namibia's Uranium. An overview of the Expropriation of Namibia's uranium resources . (Washington: International Seminar on The Role of Transnational Corporations in Namibia, 1982, 8 p.).

598. RÖSSING URANIUM LTD: An introduction to Rössing, the largest uranium mine in the world. Windhoek: Rössing Uranium Ltd., 1980, 13 p.

Published by Rössing Uranium Ltd. to defend the company against its
many critics, this is a glossy introduction to uranium mining in
Namibia. It provides a certain amount of technical information
on the geology of the uranium deposits and the mining operations,
and paints a rosy picture of environmental control, training schemes,
community facilities and the achievements of the Rössing Foundation.

599. ROGERS, BARBARA. Namibia's uranium. Implications for the South
African occupation regime. New York: UN Council for Namibia, 1975,
81 p. (Unpublished working paper).

This is the first comprehensive study of the Rössing uranium mine
and its political implications, which is still a valuable source
for understanding the dynamics of mining expansion and the process of
Namibia's further economic and military integration with South
Africa and the West. The conclusion is that the Rössing mine
provides a major economic and strategic incentive for the South
African occupation regime to refuse to withdraw, and that the
huge project could never have been undertaken without foreign
companies and the backing of their governments.

600. SAVOSNICK, KURT. "Economics of the Namibian diamond industry".
Nairobi/Geneva: UNCTAD, 1978, 76 p. (Chapter 7 of an unpublished
report on the external sector of Namibia's economy).

Prepared as a self-contained study which was stated to be part of a -
still unpublished - report on the external sector of Namibia's
economy, this is a detailed examination of the economics of the
diamond industry. The estimates are based on the Annual Reports
of De Beers Consolidated Mines and additional information given
by De Beers directly to the consultant, but it is noted that certain
key information - such as the value of the Namibian diamonds sold
to Central Selling Organisation, the commission margin charged by
CSO and the cost and profit position of the marketing subsidiaries -
is still missing. Despite these limitations, the author has
attempted to undertake an analysis of costs, prices, profits and
taxes. All assumptions and data used are made explicit, so that
any errors of fact, judgement and reasoning can be evaluated and
corrected. The study reveals that in 1976-78 the production costs
and related expenditure appeared to be less than one-quarter of
the gross sales revenues from Namibian diamonds, concluding that
an independent Namibia will have a strong interest in ensuring
that profits arising from production and trading in Namibian
diamonds are taxed by and for Namibia.

601. SINGHAM, A.W. "Namibia and nuclear proliferation". Third World
Quarterly, 3, no. 2, April 1981: 277-286.

The author's concern in this brief article is the fundamental
role uranium is playing in the political destiny of Namibia.
He bases his treatment of the subject on the UN special hearings
on "The plunder of Namibian uranium" in 1980 (see nos. 606-7).
The exploitation of mineral resources in Namibia is placed in a
historical context, followed by a discussion of foreign investments,
the transportation of uranium and South Africa's nuclear capability.

602. SÖHNGE, G. Tsumeb. A historical sketch. Windhoek: SWA Scientific Society, 1967, 92 p. 32 photos. (Sec. ed., 1976).

The author, a geologist by profession, explains in the preface that this is not a history but a sketch compiled on a spare time basis. Given this obvious limitation, the book nevertheless contains a certain amount of historical data on copper mining. The chronicle is mainly based on files of the Otavi Minen- und Eisenbahn-Gesellschaft for the period 1906-1940. The author has also added two brief chapters on mining and explorations prior to 1906, as well as a section on the development of mining after the Second World War. The latter part gives some interesting technical descriptions. As a whole, however, the book is very much a narrow "company history", and readers looking for information on working and living conditions should not expect to be rewarded. It is illustrative of the approach that the author believes the main reason for the migrant labour system to be "the attractive conditions of work, good food and hospital facilities".

603. SOUTH AFRICA (UNION). The mineral resources of the Union of South Africa. With a summary of the mineral resources of South West Africa. Pretoria: Government Printer, 1936, xiv., 454 p. Maps, graphs, tables.

Compiled in the Office of the Geological Survey, Pretoria, this massive survey is mainly concerned with geology, but also contains information on the history of mining, economic factors, and companies. Namibia is referred to in the general chapters and in the statistical section, and there is also a very brief summary: "Economic Minerals of South West Africa", p. 415-22.

604. SWAPO/NAMIBIA SUPPORT COMMITTEE. Trade union action on Namibia uranium. London: SWAPO/NSC, 1982, 92 p.

This booklet originates from a workshop for West European trade unions on Namibia, the illegal uranium trade and the steps to be taken to stop the trade and to forge solidarity with Namibian workers. It contains several background documents on the Rössing mine, SWAPO's position on the contracts for Namibian uranium and the activities of the National Union of Namibian Workers (NUNW), as well as papers on the countries involved (West Germany, France, The Netherlands, Belgium and Great Britain). There are also a comprehensive annotated list of foreign companies operating in Namibia (see no. 423), a transcript of the seminar's press conference and the text of the final declaration.

605. THE TASKFORCE ON THE CHURCHES AND CORPORATE RESPONSIBILITY. "Canada and Namibian uranium". Africa Today, 30, no. 1&2, 1983: 33-50.

According to this detailed enquiry, several Canadian companies are involved in the exploration, extraction, transport, processing and sale of Namibian uranium. It argues that these activities raise serious questions about Canada's ability to seek a just independence for Namibia as a member of the "Contact Group". The findings of the paper are partly based on the 1980 UN Hearings on

Namibian uranium, (no. 606) and partly on investigations into the role played by Eldorado Nuclear Ltd. in importing, processing and exporting Namibian uranium. The Taskforce is an ecumenical coalition of the major Christian churches in Canada.

606. UNITED NATIONS COUNCIL FOR NAMIBIA. Report of the United Nations Council for Namibia, vol. III. New York: General Assembly, 1980, 67 p. (Official Records: Thirty-fifth Session, Supplement no. 24, A/35/24).

607. UNITED NATIONS. Plunder of Namibian uranium. Major findings of the hearings on Namibian uranium held by the United Nations Council for Namibia in July 1980. New York: UN, 1982, 35 p. 2 maps (Plans of the Rössing mine).

In 1980 a week of hearings was called by the UN Council for Namibia in order to focus attention on the plunder of Namibian uranium. The hearings drew experts, eye-witnesses and representatives of non-governmental organisations to give testimony before an international panel. The evidence presented at the hearings revealed the extensive scope of uranium mining, the role therein played by transnational corporations and certain Western governments, the dangers to the Namibian workers and the Namibian environment and the development of a South African nuclear capacity. The point was also made by many participants that uranium mining was illegal, following the revocation of the Mandate (1966), the International Court of Justice advisory opinion (1971) and the UN Decree No. 1 (1974). The main findings of the hearing are concisely summarised in Plunder...., which also lists the transnational corporations involved in the extraction, processing and sale of Namibian uranium, together with their South African connections. The text of this booklet is also reprinted in Objective: Justice, 14, no. 2, 1982: 20-55. The Report... constitutes part five of the report of the UN Council for Namibia covering the period from 1 November 1979 to 31 July 1980. The document contains "report of the Council on the Hearings on Namibian Uranium", which provides considerable information on the exploitation of uranium and its economic and strategic value. The comprehensive background documents and the verbatim records of the hearings should be consulted for a closer study of this highly topical subject.

608. UNITED STATES DEPARTMENT OF THE INTERIOR, BUREAU OF MINES. Namibia. Washington: Bureau of Mines, 1983, 57 p. 7 figures, 6 tables, bibl.: 47-55.

Prepared by the US Bureau of Mines with the purpose of providing the latest available data and information on mining and mineral resources in Namibia, this is a well-informed and useful reference work. The study covers regional geology, the history of exploitation, mining policies and legislation, production (including detailed tables on production and reserves 1970-1981) as well as water resources, energy supply, labour and transport. It argues that uranium has the greatest potential for long-term growth, and that elsewhere a pattern of diminishing ore reserves in the metals and to a lesser extent diamonds suggests a declining resource base. Shortages of water supplies, lack of artisans and skilled labour

and "the unresolved international dispute" are identified as
constraints to future growth in Namibia's mining industry.
There is a chapter outlining the main features of mining legislation, and a lengthy, mainly technical bibliography listing
close to 200 items. As a technical and economic survey, relying
heavily on information provided by the mining companies themselves,
the study has considerable value. As a guide to the political
economy of Namibia, it is, however, quite misleading. The UN
Decree No. 1 of 1974 is not mentioned at all, while two decades
of worker organisation, liberation struggle and harsh colonial
repression are dismissed in the assertion that "differences among
worker languages and interests have inhibited the formation of
a uniform political party or union". The study is notably weak
on labour and social conditions, wages and labour legislation.
For up-to-date information along the same lines, see Bureau of
Mines Minerals Yearbook, vol. III: Area Reports: International,
which contains a chapter on the mineral industry of Namibia.

609. WAGNER, PERCY ALBERT. The diamond fields of Southern Africa. Cape
Town: Struik, 1971, 374 p. (First ed. Johannesburg: Transvaal
Leader, 1914).

610. ------- The geology and mineral industry of South West Africa.
Pretoria: Union of South Africa, Government Printer, 1916, 234 p.
41 illus., 5 figures, 1 map. (Union of South Africa, Geological
Survey, Memoir 7).

These are two classic studies by the most influential South African
geologist at the time. The general study of Southern Africa provides
an introduction to the geology of the detrital deposits of Namibia,
supplemented by basic information on transport, water supply,
labour, working costs, taxation, and company structure. When
"German South West Africa" was annexed, the author was commissioned
by the Government of South Africa to compile a record of the geology
and mineral resources of the territory, and the Geological Survey's
Memoir brings together a wide array of scattered information.

611. WILLIAMS, ERIC LLOYD. "Diamond harvests of the Namib surf". Optima,
no. 2, 1978: 84-105.

This is a popular and somewhat glossy account of the history of
diamond mining in Namibia, focusing on the more recent operations
of the Consolidated Diamond Mines (CDM). It contains little hard
information. Originally published in the Anglo American Corporation
magazine, the article is also distributed as a reprint by CDM.

612. WILSON, WENDELL E. Tsumeb! The world's greatest mineral locality.
Bowie, Maryland: The Mineralogical Record, Inc., 1977, 128 p.
Bibl.: 101-10. (The Mineralogical Record 8, no. 3 (May-June) 1977).

Published as a special issue of the Mineralogical Record, this
lavishly illustrated book is the single most comprehensive work
concerned with Tsumeb. The articles and research papers concentrate
mainly on geology, describing the array of species varieties, but
there are also chapters providing background information on the
geography, history and politics of the Tsumeb locality and mining

business. There is, however, nothing on labour and working conditions.
The extensive bibliography lists nearly 150 books and articles.

613. WOOD, BRIAN. International capital and the crisis in Namibia's
mining industry. Paper presented to the International Seminar on
the Role of Transnational Corporations in Namibia, Washington,
1982, 16 p.

This perceptive paper opens with an attempt to periodise the plunder
of Namibia's mineral wealth, in order to provide the necessary
historical background for an understanding of the current crisis in
the Namibian mining industry. After surveying the role of mining
under German and South Africa colonialism, the author discusses
the recent efforts by some companies to promote a black comprador
stratum to counteract the militancy of the workforce and the increasing support for SWAPO. He also warns that the companies will
use all their financial, technological, managerial and marketing
power to demobilise any attempt to bring "their" resources under
social control at independence. The appendices contain detailed
statistics in which, among other things, reveal that the dramatic
slump   mineral prices, compounded by the increasing cost of the
war, threatens state revenue as well as the profits of the multinational corporations. The author was executive secretary of the
British-based Namibia Support Committee from 1978 to 1983.

614. ZORN, STEPHEN. The mineral sector in Namibia and strategic options
for an independent government. New York: UN Office of Technical
Cooperation, 1978, 129 p. Tables.

This thoroughly researched consultancy report, prepared by a world
expert on mining and mineral processing, provides important information on the current structure of the Namibian mining industry and
the policy options for a future government. The study opens with
a survey of the role of mining in the Namibian economy and a review
of the major current operations, including a discussion of the world-
wide industry structures of the minerals produced in Namibia. The
next section deals mainly with the legislative and fiscal arrangements, and outlines the basic strategy options. The discussion of
Namibia's future is set against a review of relevant examples from
the mining sector in other developing countries, with special
emphasis on manpower needs , the governmental structures required
for regulating the mining industry, and the scope and need for
pre-independence actions. The report is based on data from the
mid-1970s, but the frame of analysis and the discussion of policy
alternatives are in no way outdated. There are several tables, but
no bibliography.

SEE ALSO:

7, 20, 25, 28, 29, 32, 47, 49, 75, 95, 105, 111, 318, 319, 333, 400,
418, 422, 460, 463, 486, 489, 652, 763, 773, 812, 944.

8. WORKERS AND PEASANTS UNDER COLONIAL RULE

A. Anthropology and peasant society

ADAM, LEONHARD, see no. 638.

615. ALNAES, KIRSTEN. "Oral tradition and identity: the Herero in Botswana". In The Societies of Southern Africa in the 19th and 20th centuries, vol. 11/Institute of Commonwealth Studies, Collected Seminar Papers No. 27, p. 15-23. London: ICS, University of London, 1981.

Written by a Norwegian scholar based in London, this short paper is a pioneering essay in what might best be called political anthropology, representing "a preliminary attempt to analyse the perception of history - as it appears in oral tradition - as an expression of ethnic identity". It is based on fieldwork amongst the Herero community in Western Botswana, most of whose members have lived in exile since the German genocide of 1904-05, and concentrates on experiences of the flight to Botswana in 1904, relations with the local Tswana authorities, and attempts to return to Namibia.

616. ANONYMOUS. "Class formation and class consciousness in Namibia: some history of the Nama people and the Rehoboth Basters". NAMSO News, no. 3, (August) 1977, 10 p.

Published in a mimeographed newsletter of the Namibian Students' Association (NAMSO), this essay is one of the first attempts - admittedly very brief and preliminary - to come to grips with the process of class formation in the southern part of Namibia. It is suggested that the working class and the peasantry form the dominant class elements among the Nama, and that the conditions for popular support for the Turnhalle conference are conspicuously lacking in their present class structure. It is argued that this is not the case in the Rehoboth Gebiet, where a complex and heterogeneous class structure is identified: a few wealthy capitalist farmers, a large body of small-scale capitalist farmers, traditional petty-bourgeoisie (shopkeepers) and a large group of skilled and semi-skilled artisans and craftsmen.

617. BRUWER, J.P. VAN S. The Kwanyama of South West Africa. University
of Stellenbosch, 1961 (?), 152 p. 18 tables, 4 maps, 28 figures.

An unpublished anthropological study by an Afrikaner academic who
was to become a leading influence in the Odendaal Commission. The
author undertook extensive fieldwork during 1958-60. Having
official backing, he was one of the few researchers to have had
complete freedom of movement and access to unpublished records, in
this case the district files at Oshikango. His purpose was "to give
a general picture of life and activities in Ukwanyama today".
Later chapters largely pursue traditional anthropological concerns.
The first half of the study, however, discusses history, the colonial
administration, social structure and settlement, the peasant
economy and labour migration, with valuable unpublished economic
and demographic data. Both parts contain perceptive observation of
economic, social and ideological change in a society undergoing
fundamental structural transformation under the impact of the
contract labour system. A microfiche copy of the typescript is at
the Overseas Development Group, University of East Anglia.

618. BUDACK, K.F.R. "The Kavango: the country, its people and history".
Namib und Meer, no. 7, 1976: 29-43. (In German: "Der Kavango:
Geschichte, Land und Leute", Afrikanischer Heimatkalender, 46, 1976:
125-39.)

Written by an ethnologist working with the South African administration,
the main purpose of this brief introduction to the Kavango is to
demonstrate the government's achievements among an "industrious,
peaceful, friendly and hospitable rural people". The article gives
a historical outline, concentrating on travellers, missionaries
and colonial administrators, and provides some rudimentary information
on the economic, social and political organisation of the Kavango
people.

619. CARSTENS, PETER. "Opting out of colonial rule: the brown Voortrekkers
of South Africa and their constitutions", African Studies, 42, no. 2,
1983: 135-52.

The aim of this article, which forms part of a two-part study, is
to discuss the historical origins and the constitutional development
of the largely autonomous political communities which were set up
by the "Basters" in South Africa and Namibia in the second part of
the 19th century. The main focus is on the written law books and
constitutions that the various communities, such as the one at
Rehoboth, drew up in response to their specific local needs. The
author suggests that the creation of political institutions
("captaincy", "Volksraad", etc.) coincided with the tensions and
anxieties that stemmed from growing emphasis on private property,
local economic surpluses and the growing inequalities which arose
out of this development. The Rehoboth Constitution of 1872 is
analysed in some detail, and the point is made that no substantial
changes took place until the 1920s following the economic decline
which resulted from the loss of political autonomy and the growth

of settler capitalism in Namibia. The second part of the study
is scheduled for publication in African Studies, 43, no. 1, 1984.
The author, a professor of anthropology at the University of
Toronto, has studied the "Baster" communities for more than 20 years.
His PhD thesis (University of Cape Town, 1961) was on the Steinkopf
community in the Cape, and he is also the editor of the English
translation of M. Bayer: Die Nation der Bastards (no. 178). See
also "The inheritance of private property among the Nama of Southern
Africa reconsidered", Africa, 53, no. 2, 1983: 58-70.

DE VORE, IRVEN, see no. 631.

620. DU PISANI, ETIENNE. Die Nama van Gibeon: ' etnografiese studie met
besondere verwysing na sosiaal-ekonomiese aspekte. University of
Stellenbosch, 1976, 189 p. Bibl.: 178-89. (MA thesis).

This is a rather conventional ethnographical study of the Nama
people of Gibeon, written by a scholar of Namibian origins. Apart
from covering the historical background (mainly based on Vedder,
Bruwer and Budack) and ethnographic   aspects like kinship, rites
and mythology, the thesis also pays due attention to socio-economic
conditions, a full chapter (p. 118-64) being devoted to the economy
and material life (cattle-breeding, food and health, income sources,
migrant labour, etc.). There are also an extensive bibliography and
several interesting maps. For a vivid description of the community
and its present confrontation with the apartheid authorities, see
Helga and Ludwig Helbig: Mythos Deutsch- Südwest (no. 33), especially
p. 83-94.

621. ESTERMANN, CARLOS. The ethnography of southwestern Angola. New York:
Africana Publishing Co. Vo. 1: The non-Bantu peoples, the Ambo
ethnic group, 1976, 228 p. Vol. 2: The Nyaneka-Nkhumbi ethnic
group, 1979, 249 p. Vol. 3: The Herero people, 1981, 182 p.
Illus., maps, photos. (Portuguese original: Etnografia do sudoeste
de Angola. Lisbon: Junta de Investigacoes do Ultramar, 1957, 1957,
1961).

This is the English translation of the major work of Father Estermann,
who spent nearly all his adult life as a Roman Catholic missionary
in southern Angola, much of it in a leading capacity. A prolific
amateur ethnographer, the author organised his work in a traditional
anthropological format, divided by major tribal group. The text is
largely a generalised synthesis of personal observation and field
notes and is of limited interest to the political and economic
historian. As background to the narrative accounts and more recent
historical analyses of the peasant societies of the region, it nonetheless carries authority as the expression of a lifetime's careful
observation, and does occasionally record specific original detail.
The English edition is translated and edited by Gordon D. Gibson.
See also a collection of articles by Esterman: Etnografia de Angola
(Sudoeste e Centro), Colectânea de Artigos Dispersos, Vol. 1 (Lisbon:
Instituto de Investigação Cientifica Tropical, 1983, 483 p.).

622. FISCHER, EUGENE. Die Rehobother Bastards und das Bastardierungsproblem
beim Menschen. Anthropologische und ethnographische Studien am
Rehobother Bastardvolk in Deutsch-Südwest-Afrika. Graz (Austria):
Akademische Druck- und Verlagsanstalt, 1971. 323 p. + genealogical

tables. 21 tables, 112 photos, illus., bibl.: 303-06. (Original: Jena: Fischer, 1913).

This is mainly an exercise in physical anthropology and anthropo-biology, written within a racist, colonial framework by a geneticist who conducted research into the Rehoboth Baster community in 1908. The book also, however, contains contemporary observations on social stratification and the uneven distribution of land, and the author documents the material wealth, the control of political institutions and the high rate of class and family endogamy within a distinct group of families regarding themselves as a "superior" class.

623. GIBSON, GORDON D. "Himba epochs". History in Africa, 4, 1977: 67-121. Bibl.: 92-5.

Through painstaking field and archival research the author has con-structed a chronology of year-names used by the Himba of the Kaokoveld and southern Angola. These names, especially when correlated with documentary evidence from other sources, give an 83-year sequence (1882/3-1965/6) which records not only political events but also climatic and natural phenomena affecting economic life, especially variations in rainfall.

624. GIBSON, GORDON D., THOMAS J. LARSON and CECILIA R. MCGURK. The Kavango peoples. Wiesbaden: Franz Steiner Verlag, 1981, 275 p. 27 photos, bibl.: 271-5.

This is a synthesis of anthropological studies of the people living along the Namibian section of the Okavango River, in which the authors have supplemented their own field research with other source material. After a general introduction, consecutive chapters discuss each of the five "tribes", using the same comparative frame-work of presentation. Although historical change is regularly noted in passing, the essays are largely written in a timeless present, sometimes even when early sources are cited. Coverage of the peasant economy is variable, but the scattered factual detail is useful given the almost total absence of modern field studies.

GIBSON, GORDON D., see no. 621.

625. GORDON, ROBERT J. "The !Kung San: a labor history". Cultural Survival Quarterly, 7, no. 4, 1983: 14-16.

626. ------- Bushmen as bandits. Primitive accumulation and Bushman policy in South West Africa. Paper presented to American Anthropological Association, 1983 annual meeting, Chicago, 17 p.

Based on extensive archival research and fieldwork in Namibia, the author, a well-known anthropologist, presents a reinterpretation of the history of the San people (or "Bushmen"). Contrary to what is often believed, the author shows clearly that the "Bushmen" do not enjoy the happy hunting and foraging life constantly evoked in books and films, secluded in splendid isolation deep in the Kalahari desert, but that on the contrary of all peoples who have lived in Southern Africa, they have perhaps been the most victimised and discriminated against. The historical survey demonstrates how large

numbers of "Bushmen" have been super-exploited as labourers since
the turn of the century. The promulgation of a separate "Bushmanland"
reserve by the South African authorities after World War II is seen
as primarily an attempt to secure the supply of "Bushman" labour –
the "invisible proletariat" of Namibia – while at the same time extending
administrative control over the last remaining "forage-hunters".
The author concludes that the "Bushmen" are at present entering a new
phase in the process of incorporation, characterised by their militarisation as part of the South African army. This topic is elaborated
in "What future for the Kung of Nyae Nyae"?, to be published as an
Occasional Paper by Cultural Survival (Cambridge, Mass.). The author
has also completed a book-length study to be published by Ravan Press
(Johannesburg), tentatively entitled Overlording the last frontier:
the "taming" of the Bushmen.

627. HAHN, CARL HUGO L., et al. The native tribes of South West Africa.
London: Frank Cass & Co./New York: Barnes & Noble, 1966, 211 p.
63 photos. (First impression: 1928).

Published by the South African colonial administration in the late
1920s, the purpose of this book was to present to the League of
Nations a short sketch of each of the principal "tribes" in Namibia.
Three of the chapters were written by Heinrich Vedder ("The Herero",
"The Namas", "The Berg Damara"), while the chapters on "The Owambos"
and "The Bushmen" were written by C.H.L. Hahn and L. Fourie, two
South African colonial officials. The articles are mainly concerned
with "anthropological zoo-ism", and are quite interesting as a
distillation of the prejudices of colonial officials and as a reflection
of the knowledge they thought they had on the historical/ethnological
background of the peoples in the territory. The interest of the
authors lie in magico-religious beliefs and "superstition", physical
characteristics, puberty and initiation rites, laws and customs,
the holy fire, and marriage and courtship, while there is less information on social conditions, material culture, production and trade.
The contributions by Vedder contain some sections on history, based
on premises such as that "the history of the Berg Damaras commences
with the history of missionary activities amongst them". There are
several photos and a brief bibliography at the end of each chapter.

628. KÖHLER, OSWIN. "Die Topnaar-Hottentotten am unteren Kuiseb". In
Ethnological and linguistic studies in honour of N.J. van Warmelo,
p. 99-122. Pretoria: South Africa, Department of Bantu Administration
and Development, 1969. (Ethnological Publications Series no. 52).

This is a sequel to the same author's district ethnologies of the
1950s (see no. 640) and his field research appears to date from that
period. In this chapter, however, the weight of emphasis is on
demographic, economic and social history, based on narrative historical
accounts and providing probably the most detailed record of this
distinct community so far published.

KÖHLER, OSWIN, see no. 640.

LARSON, THOMAS J., see no. 624.

629. LEACOCK, ELEANOR and RICHARD LEE (eds.). Politics and history in band societies. Cambridge University Press, 1982, 500 p.

Originating from an international conference in 1978, this book contains several contributions which are directly concerned with the San people of Botswana and Namibia. In "Risk, reciprocity and social influences on ! Kung San economics" (p. 61-84), Polly Wiessner interprets ! Kung exchange in terms of production relations specific to foraging society, while Richard Lee sets out to revise and upgrade the role of women in light of their important economic role:"Politics, sexual and non-sexual, in an egalitarian society" (p. 37-60). There is also a separate chapter devoted to the militarisation of the San in Namibia, written by Susan Hurlich and Richard Lee (see no. 295).

630. LEBZELTER, VIKTOR. Eingeborenenkulturen in Südwest- und Südafrika. Wissenschaftliche Ergebnisse einer Forschungsreise nach Süd- und Südwestafrika in den Jahren 1926-1928. Leipzig: Verlag Karl W. Hiersemann, 1934, 306 p. 111 drawings, 26 photos.

This is the major work of an Austrian anthropologist who was a prolific writer in the 1920s and 1930s. The book, which is extensively illustrated with sketches and photos, contains one of the few first-hand studies of the Ovamboland peasantry in the early period of South African colonial rule ("Die Stämme des Ambolandes", p. 188-253). Although the author is mainly concerned with anthropological and political aspects of the societies, there are also direct observations on material culture, internal and external trade, migrant labour, methods of cultivation, the cost of living, and the penetration of the monetary economy. Other ethnic groups are also covered, especially the Damara, but these sections are less impressive in terms of original information. This study forms the second volume of Rassen und Kulturen in Südafrika, the first volume being a rather conventional presentation of what was at the time known about the prehistory of the area (Die Vorgeschichte von Süd- und Südwest-Afrika, Leipzig, Hiersemann, 1930). The author also published several articles in academic journals, and it is likely that a lot of unpublished material is available in Vienna.

LEE, RICHARD, see no. 629.

631. LEE, RICHARD B. and IRVEN DE VORE (eds.). Kalahari hunter-gatherers. Studies of the !Kung San and their neighbors. Cambridge, Massachusetts/ London: Harvard University Press, 1976, 408 p. 10 maps, 22 figures, 44 tables, 31 photos. Bibl.: 377-94.

This is a comprehensive account of the extensive research of the Harvard Kalahari Research Group, founded in 1963, comprising studies by 17 authors (anthropologists, medical doctors, archaeologists, etc.). The book is divided into four sections: 1) ecology and social change, 2) population and health, 3) child development, and 4) the cognitive world, and provides a full bibliography. The aim of the studies is to document how the San people sustain the demands of communal existence in a "subsistence ecology". It is also shown how the fencing and patrolling of the Namibia-Botswana border by

the South Africans in the mid-1960s induced a number of families to
settle at Chum !Kwe (Tshumkwe), where the South African authorities
supplied rations and some employment in return for increased social
control. There is, however, little discussion of other changes
during the colonial period which have forced the "Bushmen" into
an existence very different from the stereotypes of a "hunter/gatherer"
society as a stage in the development of humankind. See also the
substantial monograph by Richard B. Lee, mainly concerned with the
!Kung San in northwestern Botswana: The !Kung San. Men, women and
work in a foraging society (Cambridge U.P., 1979, 526 p.), and, for a
different perspective, Robert Gordon (no. 625-6).

632. LIMA, MARIA HELENA FIGUEIREDO. Paisagens e figuras típicias Cuanhama
     Angola. Lisbon: 1965, 200 p.

633. -------Nação Ovambo. Lisbon: Editorial Aster, 1977, 257 p. Bibl.:
     254-57.

Written by a Mozambican anthropologist who worked closely with Carlos
Estermann (see no. 621), these two books are mainly concerned with
the Kwanyama people in Southeastern Angola and across the Namibian
border. Nação Ovambo provides a useful historical chronology, a brief
survey of pre-20th century history (especially the Portuguese occupation
of the interior), and a presentation of the informants, followed by
a conventional anthropological discussion of family structure,
religion, rituals, art, oral literature, and material culture.
The second book is an album of photographs with texts in Portuguese,
English and French, which shows "some representative landscapes and
human types of Kwanyama".

MCGURK, CECILIA R., see no. 624.

634. MALAN, J.S. Peoples of South West Africa/Namibia. Pretoria/Cape
     Town: HAUM Publishers, 1980, 113 p. 44 photos.

Prepared on the basis of research for a doctoral thesis and the
author's service in the South African colonial administration, this
textbook is intended as a first year reader for students in anthropology. It does not cover all ethnic groups in Namibia, but concentrates on the Himba, the Herero, the Ovambo and the Kavango "tribes".
The focus is mainly on standard themes such as kinship, religion,
language and rites set in an "ethnographic present", but there are
also brief descriptions of natural environment and economic life.
Very little attention is paid to social differentiation and the
migrant labour system, or to the effects of the war, the liberation
struggle, and the policy of apartheid, but the Turnhalle Conference
is characterised as "the formalising of external political relations
between the various national groups".

635. MARSHALL, LORNA. The !Kung of Nyae Nyae. Cambridge, Massachusetts/
     London: Harvard University Press, 1976, xxiii, 433 p. Illus., maps.

Based on extensive fieldwork in the Nyae Nyae area since the early
1950s, this is a scholarly, detailed and readable account of the
life of a San community in Namibia. Several chapters are devoted to

material conditions, such as environment and settlement, plant
foods and gathering, animal foods and hunting. See also the less
scholarly and more widely read account by her daughter: Elizabeth
Marshall Thomas: The Harmless people, which was published as early
as 1959 and reprinted several times (London: Secker & Warburg,
1959, 266 p.).

636. OTTO, ANTJE. "Der Ost-Caprivi-Zipfel. Ein historisch-ethnographischer
Überblick". Afrikanischer Heimatkalender 1982: 87-100.

A brief review of the literature on the Caprivi Strip and its inhabitants, touching upon the historical and geographical background,
political organisation and material culture. The summary of earlier
writings is supplemented by the author's own observations during a
visit to the area to study and collect items (tools, handicraft products, etc.) for the State Museum in Windhoek. The author, an
anthropologist at the State Museum, is presently undertaking research
on the socio-economic position of Herero women.

637. PENDLETON, WADE. "Herero reactions: the pre-colonial period, the
German period and the South African period". In Profiles of self-
determination. African responses to European colonialism in Southern
Africa, 1652-present, edited by David Chanaiwa, p. 167-94. Northridge:
California State University Foundation, 1976.

This is a brief historical interpretation of the conflicts between the
Herero and other African groups over cattle and land in the 19th
century and of their resistance to the intrusion of German and
South African colonisers. The essays starts with a rather sketchy
description of pre-colonial Herero culture, and ends with the formation
of independent churches and the uprising in the Windhoek African
township in 1959. The essay discusses the various forms of resistance,
and documents how the Herero have paid a heavy price for their resistance, not the least in mass extermination and the destruction of their
economic system during the German colonial period and in the
"native reserves" policy of the South African occupying power. The
author is an anthropologist at San Diego State University (see no. 301).

638. SCHULTZ-EWERTH, E. and LEONHARD ADAM (eds.). Das Eingeborenenrecht.
Sitten und Gewohnheitsrechte der Eingeborenen der ehemaligen deutschen
Kolonien in Afrika und in der Südsee. Stuttgart: Verlag von
Strecker und Schröder. Vol. 1: Ost-afrika, 1929, 380 p. Vol. 2:
Togo, Kamerun, Südwestafrika, Die Südseekolonien, 1930, 728 p.

In the final years of the German colonial empire, an ambitious project
was undertaken to collect material on "native law", rules of inheritance
and property, criminal law, political structure and administration.
On the basis of a standardised questionnaire, German missionaries,
anthropologists and colonial officials were asked to answer more than
100 detailed questions. The original answers have not been published,
but can be found in some archives and libraries in the form of undated
brochures under the collective title: Beantwortung des Fragebogens...
The answers have been revised for the two-volume collected edition
covering all the former German colonies. From Namibia there exist
27 reports in all. The chapters on the customs, laws and political
organisation of the "peoples" of Namibia (vol. 2. p. 209-435) are

restricted to the Herero, the Nama, the Damara and the San
("Bushmen"), and have been edited by Heinrich Vedder and two German
lawyers: B. von Zastrow and M. Schmidt. For reasons not explained,
the original material concerned with the Ovambo (collected by the
missionaries M. Rautanen and A. Wulfhorst) is not included. Despite
its obvious limitations, the book contains a wealth of observations
not available anywhere else in this condensed form.

39. SHOSTAK, MARJORIE. Nisa. The life and words of a ! Kung woman.
Harmondsworth: Penguin, 1983, 402 p. (Original: Harvard University
Press, 1981/London: Allen Lane, 1982. In German: Nisa erzählt:
das Leben einer Nomadenfrau in Afrika. Reinbek bei Hamburg: Rowohlt,
1982, 341 p.).

This is the unique story of Nisa, a fifty years old woman living
on the northern fringe of the Kalahari desert. Marjorie Shostak is
a member of the Harvard anthropology team, specialising on collecting
in-depth life history materials from ! Kung women. Apart from
focusing on the sophisticated knowledge of the semi-arid savannah
environment, the major part of the book deals with women in society:
childhood, adolesence, sex, marriage, motherhood. Each chapter is
introduced by Shostak, who has also contributed a substantial introductory chapter as well as an epilogue. One could, however, have
expected some comments on the current political situation in the area
and a discussion of the factors threatening the seemingly idyllic
life of Nisa and other San people (See e.g. nos. 625, 626, 295).

40. SOUTH AFRICA, DEPARTMENT OF NATIVE AFFAIRS. Ethnological Publications
Series. Pretoria: Government Printer. Notes on the Kaokoveld, 1951,
64 p., 3 tables. (No. 26); A study of Okahandja District (SWA), 1957,
106 p., 30 tables. (No. 40); A study of Karibib District (SWA), 1958,
116 p., 46 tables. (No. 40); A study of Gobabis District (SWA), 1959,
108 p., 34 tables. (No. 42); A study of Omaruru District (SWA), 1959,
113 p., 30 tables. (No. 43); A study of Otjiwarongo District (SWA),
1959, 98 p., 32 tables. (no. 44); A study of Grootfontein District
(SWA), 1959, 85 p., 27 tables.

This series was published in the decade preceding the Odendaal Report
(see no. 266) and the launching of full-scale apartheid in Namibia
and at one level it was designed to supply the government with the
basic information it needed to reconstruct tribal identities amongst
the multi-ethnic communities of central-northern Namibia, its
area of coverage. However, these studies are also of major empirical
importance, being based on detailed geographical and demographic field
surveys and containing a wealth of historical and economic data, set
down descriptively. Each forms an integrated district study, divided
according to a standard format between zones (reserves, farms,
towns) and themes (historical, demographic, administrative, social,
economic, educational, and health). Although some of the initial work
was carried out by N.J. van Warmelo (no. 26) and C. Wagner (nos. 38,
40, 42, 43), the principal researcher and author was Oswin Köhler.
A study of Windhoek was also conducted, but it exists only in a
few typescript copies. This study is especially important for the data
on the Old Location of Windhoek in the 1950s.

641. SUNDERMEIER, THEO. Die Mbanderu. Studien zu ihrer Geschichte und Kultur. St. Augustin: Anthropos-Institut, Haus Völker und Kulturen, 1977, 267 p. 17 photos, bibl.: 179-83.

This book is a rare initiative in the field of oral history. The author, a Lutheran clergyman, conducted an extensive series of interviews between 1966 and 1973, and to a large extent the resulting account represents the collective view of the tribal leaders and elders of the rural Mbanderu community, who endorsed the enterprise in part as a means of defining a group identity distinct from that of the Herero. In the first section the oral narrative is presented, assessed and complemented by information from written sources. It concentrates on the late 19th century and the last great pre-colonial leader, Kahimemua. The second describes different aspects of Mbanderu society, politics and religion. The third, written by a Herero evangelist, presents a largely anthropological account of the Herero-speaking communities in the Kaokoveld. (Silas Kuvare: "Die Kaokoveld-Herero", p. 187-258).

VAN WARMELO, N.J., see no. 640.

642. VIVELO, FRANK ROBERT. The Herero of western Botswana: aspects of change in a group of Bantu-speaking cattle herders. St. Paul/New York: West Publishing Co., 1977, 232 p. 6 tables, 18 photos and sketches, bibl.: 221-29.

An anthropological study of the Herero community exiled in Botswana after the Battle of Waterberg in 1904. It is based on a reading of the extensive literature devoted to the Herero, especially by German missionaries, as well as on field research in the early 1970s. In contrast to the spuriously timeless anthropology of a generation earlier, its purpose is to explain the major transformations in Herero society which have occurred since the flight into exile. The three central chapters discuss in turn "locality and social structure, economy and the organisation of labour and polity, authority, order and control".

643. WAGNER, GÜNTHER. "Aspects of conservation and adaptation in the economic life of the Herero". Sociologus, N.F., 2, no. 1, 1952: 1-25. (Also published in African Studies, 13, nos. 3-4. 1954: 113-30, and in Selected abstracts in development administration: field reports and directed social change, edited by V.D. Hart, Syracuse University Press, 1962).

This article was written shortly before his death by an ethnologist on the staff of the South African Department of Native Affairs. Although cautious in approach, it marks a sharp departure from the patronising racism in much previous official and missionary writing on Namibian peasant societies. Using evidence from the files of reserve administrators and his own extensive anthropological fieldwork, Wagner argues that in the Herero reserves a thriving peasant economy was emerging, based on sales of cattle and cream and on the reinvestment of wages from urban employment. This study formed

part of a major official investigation of the Herero and Damara
reserves in the 1950s (see no. 640).

WAGNER, G., see no. 640.

SEE ALSO:

8, 38, 118, 119, 126, 129, 137-8, 138, 143, 146, 153, 156, 159, 178,
212, 266, 295, 307, 313, 401-3, 450-2, 454, chapter 7 a(497-530),
644-45, 653, 664, 678-9, 685, 696-7, 912-3.

B. Migrant labour, repression, worker resistance

644. BANGHART, PETER D. <u>Migrant labour in South West Africa and its effects on Ovambo tribal life</u>. University of Stellenbosch, 1969, 152 p. 2 maps, 36 tables, bibl.: 149-52. (MA thesis).

645. ------- "The effect of the migrant labourer on the Ovambo of South West Africa". <u>Fort Hare Papers</u>, 5, no. 4, 1972: 68-81.

For the credibility of its principal hypothesis, the timing of this thesis, and even more so the published article based on it, was unfortunate in that it was submitted just two years before the great national strike of Ovambo migrant workers against the contract labour system and the closely associated peasant uprising in Ovamboland itself early in 1972. The author addresses himself to those aspects of the anthropological literature on southern and central Africa which discuss the impact of recurrent labour migration on the labour-exporting peasant societies. He concludes that amongst the matrilineal Ovambo, in contrast to the patrilineal groups studied by Schapera and others, any "harmful effects" were "overruled by the more beneficial effects of migrant labour" and that there was "no evidence of a disintegration of tribal life and the village economy" partly because men contributed little labour to field cultivation. He also states that such changes as occurred "have had a stabilising effect at all levels of Ovambo cultural and social life". A sharply opposing assessment is to be found in Voipio's 1971 social survey (nos. 678-79) and Moorsom's historical analysis (see nos. 664, 667). Banghart's study is empirically valuable as one of the very few to be based on field research, and includes extensive statistical analysis of data from interviews with contract workers and a sample survey at the Tsumeb mine.

646. BOLTON, BRIAN. <u>The condition of the Namibian workers</u>. Paper presented to the UN Council for Namibia Seminar on the Activities of Foreign Economic Interests in the Exploitation of Namibia's Natural and Human Resources, Ljubljana, Yugoslavia, 16-20 April 1984, 14 p. (A/AC. 131/LSR/CRP. 7).

The main focus of this brief conference paper is on the conditions of black Namibian workers in the early 1980s, which are described as being considerably worse than in South Africa itself both in the mines and on the settler farms. The author, a research officer in Transport and General Workers Union, United Kingdom, also makes the point that the effectiveness of trade union organisation in Namibia is heavily circumscribed through selective and discriminatory representation, through suppression of all but collaborationist unions, and through rising unemployment. In spite of this fact, the author concludes that the National Union of Namibian Workers (NUNW), through its close association with SWAPO, has built up a substantial following, particularly in the mines.

647. CRONJE, GILLIAN and SUZANNE CRONJE. The workers of Namibia. London: International Defence and Aid Fund for Southern Africa, 1979, 136 p. 28 photos, 6 tables.

A solid and well-written report on the conditions of the black workers of Namibia, drawing extensively on the South African Labour Bulletin issue on Namibia (no. 674), the local press and a variety of other sources. It ties together the situation of the workers with the prominent position which they have played in the struggle for national independence. The book gives a general introduction to the apartheid economy, and provides a detailed account of the migrant worker system, living conditions, resistance against oppression and the fight for the right to organise. Separate chapters are devoted to the 1971/72 strike and the South African response to it. The authors emphasize SWAPO's roots in the labour force, and argue strongly that the history of the liberation movement cannot be sep- arated from the struggle of working people for improved wages and working conditions, and for their political rights. For an updating of the material concerned with workers and the transnational corpor- ations, see Wilfred Grenville-Grey: Labour conditions in the TNC, paper presented to The International Seminar on the Role of Trans- national Corporations in Namibia, Washington, 1982, 7 p. This paper also discusses the resources available for further research at the International Defence and Aid Fund for Southern Africa (London). IDAF is also preparing a Fact Paper on Namibian workers (1985), which will provide up-to-date information and serve as a supplement to The workers of Namibia.

648. DEKKER, L., et al. "Case studies in African labour action in South Africa and Namibia/South West Africa". In The development of an African working class, edited by R. Sandbrook and R. Cohen, p. 207- 38. London: Longman, 1975. (Also published in The Africa Review, 4, no. 2, 1974: 205-36).

The purpose of this contribution to a major reader on the African working class is to demonstrate that, even in the thoroughly repressive environment of South Africa and Namibia, workers have been able to organise informally to sustain extended strike campaigns. The authors argue that "labour power" is one of the few points of leverage against the apartheid regime, and that resentment against the contract system and the pass laws is a major potential source of collective action, providing grounds for politicised industrial- cum-political action among contract workers. The section on Namibia is related to the material gathered by John Kane-Berman immediately after the 1971-72 strike (see nos. 657-58).

649. GEBHARDT, F.E. BETTINA. "The socio-economic status of farm labourers in Namibia". South African Labour Bulletin, 4, nos. 1-2. (January- February) 1978: 145-73.

650. ------- Zur sozialökonomischen Lage der Farmarbeiter in Namibia.
Entwicklung in Vergangenheit und Zukunft. Universität Bremen, 1984,
380 p. 43 tables, 3 diagrams, 6 maps, 4 photos, bibl.: 352-63.

Written by a scholar who grew up in Namibia, the study published
in SALB is a solid piece of committed academic work. It is based
on several visits to Namibia in the 1970s, during one of which the
author conducted wide-ranging interviews with a cross-section of
330 farm workers. Among the subjects covered are the composition
and recruitment of farm workers, wages and working conditions,
the treatment of workers by farmers, the relations between employers
and workers and political activity. The material shows clearly
that for most workers farm labour means subordination, frustration
and alienation, and that their status and living conditions have a
devastating impact on their social life. The article is a summary
of a dissertation in German (Der soziale und ökonomische Status der
Farmarbeiter in Namibia/Südwestafrika, MA thesis, Frankfurt, 1975),
and appeared in its original form in F. Wilson, et al. (eds.):
Farm Labour in South Africa (Cape Town: David Philip, 1977) and in
Namibia Today, 4, nos. 5-6, 1980: 27-47 ("The socio-economic status
of the rural Namibian proletariat"). The work has recently been
expanded into a PhD thesis, based on a reworking of the original
data as well as on additional information. The thesis also gives
a historical introduction to farm labour and Namibian agriculture,
includes a brief review of the prospects for agrarian reform and
attempts to relate the Nambian experience to the general discussion
of dependency, development, exploitation and liberation. The value
of the study is enhanced by a large number of tables, diagrams and
references.

651. GORDON, ROBERT J. "A note on the history of labour action in Namibia".
South African Labour Bulletin, 1, no. 10, (April) 1975: 7-17.

Written to show that the 1971-72 contract workers' strike was by no
means the first manifestation of labour action in Namibia, this
brief article produces evidence that labour protests can be said to
have started immediately after the German conquest and have been a
constant feature of the labour scene ever since. The first part
quotes extensively from the diaries of the Mine Manager at the
Gross Otavi mines to describe a strike in 1893, while the second
part surveys labour actions (both "desertions" and "collective actions")
in the post 1945 period. This latter part is based on the files of
the Windhoek newspaper Die Suidwes-Afrikaner.

652. GORDON, ROBERT J. Mines, masters and migrants. Life in a Namibian
compound. Johannesburg: Ravan Press, 1977, 276 p. 17 photos, 3
diagrams, 26 tables, bibl.: 269-76.

The most substantial work to date of one of the leading labour
historians and anthropologists specialising on Namibia, this book
is the author's doctoral thesis revised for publication. It is all
the more valuable - indeed unique in recent literature on Namibia -
for being based on more than a year's participant observation while
employed during 1973-4 as a personnel officer during the construction
of a large new mine near Windhoek, the identity of which is not stated
but is almost certainly Otjihase. The opening chapters discuss the

contract labour system in its national context and, in illuminating
detail, the structure, methods and ideology of labour repression
on the mine. The rest of the book places black workers centre-stage,
and it is here that the author's explicitly committed standpoint is
best exemplified. A central chapter analyses their perceptions
of the totalitarian framework of authority to which they are subordinated and identifies the underground code of "brotherhood" as
the key mechanism of worker solidarity. The next two discuss
wages and working conditions and workers'earning, spending and
saving strategies. Finally, labour turnover and the cycle of
migration is analysed from the standpoint of workers' perceptions
and motivations. For much of the study the author's organising framework is that of the sociology of repressive, totalitarian institutions
and of the subjective perceptions and social relationships between
powerless and power-holders. Generalised statements are interspersed
with a wealth of observed instances; and there is also considerable
factual information on the mine, not least on wages and conditions
and on the operation of the contract labour system. The study is,
however, weak on economics and takes little account either of the
political economy which enables such mines to operate or of the wider
labour and political dimensions of worker consciousness, despite
being based on fieldwork only two years after the great contract
workers' strike of 1971-2. For a critical review of the book,
written by Renfrew Christie, see Social Dynamics, 3, no. 7, 1977:
69-71.

53. GORDON, ROBERT J. "Variations in migration rates: the Ovambo case".
Journal of Southern African Affairs, 3, no. 3, 1978: 261-94.

A significant contribution to the analysis of the dynamics of
labour migration in Namibia, this article presents a detailed historical account of the evolution of the contract labour system from
its origins up to the national strike of 1971-72. The first part
is concerned with the "demand" situation and the impact of the
overarching colonial superstructure, while the second part considers
the "supply" side by examining conditions in the sending area, with
special emphasis on ecology, social structure, land tenure systems,
population pressure and cash trading. The author's organising
principle is the concept of "regressive spiral migration". In
practice there is less concern with theorising or model-making
than with detailed historical presentation, which yields many useful insights despite an occasionally uncritical deployment of
evidence. The article's chief empirical value lies in its extensive
use of unpublished South African theses (e.g. Banghart, Olivier and
Rädel), supplemented by anthropological accounts and published South
African official literature and reports. An alternative discussion of
the same broad issues is to be found in an article published the
previous year by Moorsom (no. 664).

54. GORDON, ROBERT J. "The celebration of ethnicity: a "tribal fight"
in a Namibian mine compound". In Ethnicity in modern Africa,
edited by B.M. du Toit, p. 213-31. Boulder, Colorado: Westview
Press, 1979.

This article analyses a specific incident in 1974 towards the end

248

of the author's period of "participant observation" as personnel
officer on a new Namibian mine, on which his major study of
labour repression and worker consciousness is based (see no. 652).
The article in fact provides a handy condensation of much of the
central argument of that study. It develops a sophisticated critique
of the simplistic conventional interpretation of intergroup conflict
amongst mine-workers solely in terms on innate ethnic antagonism.
The author argues that in respect of this incident such an interpretation was the viewpoint of management and was adopted by workers
largely to conceal their more complex motivations and preserve
space for private activity in a repressive environment. In practice
the conflict served to reconsolidate the inherently unstable underground code of worker solidarity, "brotherhood", by reaffirming
its rules of behaviour and by identifying and penalising deviants.
The author concludes that the "tribal fight" was not an expression of
ethnicity but rather of antiethnicity.

655. GOTTSCHALK, KEITH. "South African labour policy in Namibia 1915-1975".
South African Labour Bulletin, 4, nos. 1-2, (January-February)
1978: 75-106.

A general survey of labour control and workers' resistance in Namibia
under South African rule, focusing on the migrant labour system and
the vast array of repressive laws and regulations. There is also a
brief discussion of the main labour actions from 1915 to the general
strike in 1971-72, as well as a summary of the available literature
on wages, health, housing and schooling.

656. INTERNATIONAL LABOUR OFFICE (prepared by NEVILLE RUBIN). Labour and
discrimination in Namibia. Geneva: ILO, 1977, 126 p.

A thoroughly documented and well organised survey of labour-repressive
and racially discriminatory legislation imposed on Namibians by the
South African administration, in which the author's legal expertise
is evident. Appendices reproduce the texts of two of the key legal
instruments of the contract labour system, the Employment Bureau
Regulations of 1972 and the Control and Treatment of Natives on
Mines Regulation of 1925, as well as the old and revised (1972)
terms of labour "contract" ("indenture" would be a more accurate
description). The booklet sets the legislation in the context of
a brief analysis of the economy, racial discrimination and deprivation in education, access to employment, wages and working and
living conditions, as well as repression of trade union and political
organisation. An updated report was presented to a ILO seminar in
Lusaka in 1981 and published in Nationhood Programme for Namibia.
Report on The Seminar concerning discriminatory legislation in
Namibia relating to labour matters (Geneva: ILO, 1983, 96 p.
ILO/78/NAM 007). This report also contains a classified list of laws
relating to the ILO study on discriminatory labour legislation in
Namibia.

657. KANE-BERMAN, JOHN. Contract labour in South West Africa.
Johannesburg: South African Institute of Race Relations, 1973, 37 +
xxxii p.

658. ------- The labour situation in South West Africa. Johannesburg; South African Institute of Race Relations, 1973, 6 p. (Lead-in paper, SAIRR, Forty-third annual council meeting).

An important primary as well as analytical source for the study of labour history in Namibia, written after a visit to the country in February 1972, in the midst of the general strike. The report provides an excellent reconstruction of the course of events, based on first-hand observations, press reports and discussions with workers, church leaders, businessmen and government officials. There is little on the evolution of the contract worker system, but wages and living conditions are well covered. The author argues strongly that the strike was not merely a labour dispute but a strike against the apartheid system as a whole. The second impression of the report examines the Employment Bureau Regulations of 30 March 1972, concluding that the essentials of the migrant system remained unchanged. The appendices contain several important documents, such as the minutes of the mass meeting in Ondangua in January 1972 and large extracts from the survey on migrant labour by Rauha Voipio (see no. 678). The 1973 paper focuses on the changes which took place in the year following the general strike. The author points out that the revised labour arrangements were tightened up when the employers wanted more rigorous controls, that influx controls were strictly enforced and that the emergency regulations of February 1972 made detentions widely used. It is also argued that using a "homeland" government to implement a hated system "is hardly a sound basis on which it can develop any degree of legitimacy or popular support". For a more general review, which summarises both papers, see "Focus on Labour" in South West Africa: problems and alternatives (University of Cape Town, 1975). The author, a well-known journalist and the present director of the South African Institute of Race Relations, was at the time research assistant at SAIRR.

659. KAULUMA, JAMES H. The migrant contract labour situation in Namibia and the response to it. Windhoek (?); n.d. (1977/78 ?), 67 p. Bibl.: 86-7.

Written by the present Bishop of the Anglican church this is a significant contribution to an understanding of the history and the mechanisms of the migrant labour system. The first part of the study is an autobiographical sketch, based on the author's own experience as a contract labourer in the 1950s. It contains a detailed description of the recruitment system, the working and living conditions on the farms, the behaviour of the "baas", the prison cells (after a desertion), life within the compound, and the role played by headmen and chiefs in assisting the South African authorities in their constant humiliation of the people of Ovamboland. The second part is concerned with the historical development of the contract system, tracing its roots back to the colonisation and the final destruction of the pre-colonial social formations. This historical account has its value in giving a lucid summary of the existing secondary literature as well as UN and ILO reports. The final part aims at demonstrating how the churches and the workers themselves have been responding to the system, and how family relations, the role of women in production and the whole social fabric in Ovamboland have been affected over

the years. The author concludes by arguing that "neither the employers
nor the administration have at any time shown the will or ability
to remove this kind of labor system which is so oppressive and
humiliating to the workers and their families" and that a solution
is not possible without complete independence from colonial rule.

660. KOOY, MARCELLE. "The contract labour system and the Ovambo crisis
of 1971 in South West Africa". African Studies Review, 16, no. 1,
(April) 1973: 83-105.

Mainly based on press reports, this is a straightforward descriptive
account of the contract system and the general strike in 1971-72.
As it was published at the time, it has served as a useful survey
of the events. It does not, however, contain any original material,
and has later been superseded by Moorsom and others (see no. 665)
both in terms of original information and a perspective which is
closer to the workers' own aspirations.

661. KURAISA, CHARLES. "The labour force". In South West Africa: A
travesty of trust, edited by Ronald Segal and Ruth First, p. 189-93.
London: Deutsch, 1967.

A very brief introduction to the origins of the labour reserves and
the contract labour system, outlining some of the proclamations,
rules and regulations aiming at controlling the black labour force.

662. LOFFLER, JOHN. Labour and politics in Namibia in the 1970s. York:
Centre for Southern African Studies, 1979, 68 p. Bibl.: 66-8.
(MA thesis).

Written with admirable clarity, this brief MA thesis surveys the
existing literature on the migrant labour system, workers'
resistance in a historical perspective, and the 1971-72 general
strike, benefitting from the studies by R.J. Gordon, R. Moorsom,
J. Kane-Berman and others. The author takes issue with those who
have portrayed the general strike as a spontaneous or populist
uprising, and argues convincingly that the process of proletarianisation and politicisation has a much longer history and that it
was the linkage between the workers and national political
developments which enabled the mass actions to occur. In this context, the role of SWAPO is also stressed. The final chapter deals
with "Reforms, repression and resistance 1972-1979", and gives an
account of the major aspects of the struggle and the changes in
labour relations. The author concludes by suggesting that more
importance be ascribed to the basic struggle between labour and
capital over recent years than is commonly attributed to it.

663. MELBER, HENNING. "National Union of Namibian workers: background
and formation". The Journal of Modern African Studies, 21, no. 1,
1983: 151-58.

This brief introduction to the recent history of the National Union
of Namibian Workers shows how the organisation of labour interests
is shaped by the specific characteristics of Namibia's deformed
socio-economic situation. The author argues that the need to modify
the apartheid system has allowed the creation of a more permanent

and qualified labour force, while at the same time the marginalisation of the overwhelming majority is increasing. N.U.N.W. is seen as the organisational expression of the majority of the black workers, at the same time as the fight for genuine national independence and the political goals of the union by far transcend the improvement of labour conditions under the existing system. For a shortened German version, see "Namibia", in Internationales Gewerkschaftshandbuch, edited by Siegfried Mielke, p. 1241-45 (Opladen: Leske und Budrich, 1983).

MERCER, DENNIS, see no. 669.

664. MOORSOM, RICHARD. "Underdevelopment, contract labour and worker consciousness in Namibia, 1915-72". Journal of Southern African Studies, 4, no. 1, (October) 1977: 52-87. 9 tables.

This article, the third in a trilogy (see nos. 123, 667), sets out to apply to Namibia some of the insights of recent historical materialist analysis of class formation and labour migration in Southern Africa, focusing on the contract labour system and worker resistance under South African rule. Taking the pre-colonial history and ecology of Ovamboland as his starting point, the author documents how food shortages, the growing pressure on internal subsistence resources and the structural exploitation of the migrant labour system have made wage-labour the only possible source of cash income for the vast majority. He also shows that in compelling contract workers' dependants and families to remain on the land, and by forbidding any semblance of negotiation, the system forced peasant agriculture to subsidise and service wage-rates low even by the extreme standards of South Africa. The latter part ends with a discussion of the main factors which led to the general strike of 1971-72, the course of the strike itself, and its aftermath. (See also no. 665).

665. MOORSOM, RICHARD. "Labour consciousness and the 1971-72 contract workers strike in Namibia". Development and Change, 10, no. 2, 1979: 205-31.

The second part of this article, analysing the course and implications of the 1971-72 strike in Namibia, is a revised extract from a previously published essay (no. 664), but the first part is an original and perceptive discussion of class position and labour consciousness in the context of the migrant labour system. Its point of departure is that contract labour not only binds the male migrant to a rigorous and inflexible work routine but also extends the labour-time spent by women in household and food production for themselves and their dependants. It is argued that the critical point at which the balance of objective class interest transfers from peasant to proletarian status occurs when the migrant's family becomes regularly dependent on his wages not merely for items of equipment but also for day-to-day living costs, in particular food. The turning point, the author argues, came for many peasant families with migrant workers in the 1950s and 1960s. Several examples are also given to support the contention that migrant workers have long since developed a perception of the need for collective

action and political struggle which goes beyond the concept of
"brotherhood" introduced by R.J. Gordon in his seminal study (no. 652).

666. MOORSOM, RICHARD. "The workers of Namibia". Action on Namibia, 1,
no. 4, 1979: 4-5, and 1, no. 5, 1979: 4-6.

A brief but analytical presentation of the position of black workers
under South African rule. The article includes recent employment
and wage data, a summary of labour legislation, and a history of
worker resistance and trade unionism, with excerpts from workers'
own accounts of their situation.

667. MOORSOM, RICHARD. "Underdevelopment and class-formation: the birth
of the contract labour system in Namibia, 1900-26". In University
of York, Centre for Southern African Studies, Collected Papers, 5,
1980, p. 17-44.

This is the second of a trilogy of papers on the origins and evolution
of the contract labour system (see nos. 123, 664). The published
version omits for reason of space two early sections of the paper
given at the CSAS seminar, which discuss the pre-colonial social
formation in Ovamboland and structural changes within it under the
impact of long-distance trade with industrial capitalism. The published version proceeds to analyse capital formation and labour
demand through the German and early South African colonial periods;
the growth of labour migration; cooperation and conflict between
the triangle of principal actors, Ovambo rulers,migrant peasant/workers,
and colonial authorities and employers; and the final struggle which
led to the imposition of the severely repressive contract labour
system. Particular attention is given to the workers' strategic
interests and tactics of struggle. As in its counterparts, the
author attempts to apply the method of class analysis to specific
questions in a concrete historical context, and the resulting
interpretation differs sharply from the more conventional accounts.

668. MORRIS, JO. "The black workers in Namibia". In The role of foreign
firms in Namibia, edited by Roger Murray, et al., p. 129-80. Uppsala:
Africa Publications Trust, 1974.

Commissioned by The Study Project on External Investment in South
Africa and Namibia (see no. 422), this article examines the composition
of the black workers in Namibia and wages and living conditions in
industrial and rural areas. The author concludes that the conditions
are even worse than in South Africa itself. There is also a brief
review of labour legislation and the migrant worker system, and a
discussion of the rising militancy of the workers and the confrontation
leading to a strike in 1971-72.

669. NDADI, VINNIA. Breaking contract. The story of Vinnia Ndadi.
Richmond, B.C.: Liberation Support Movement Press, 1974, 115 p.
(Life histories from the revolution, Namibia, SWAPO, 1). (German
translation: Kontraktarbeiter Klasse B. Mein Leben in Namibia.
Zurich: Unionsverlag, 1978, 179 p.).

This classic example of oral history, written with admirable stylistic authenticity and editorial clarity, gives a basic insight into the operation of the migrant labour system in Namibia. Based on extensive interviews with Vinnia Ndadi, recorded and edited by Dennis Mercer, the book tells the story of a contract labourer's life from his first recruitment by SWANLA at the age of 17 until he left Namibia to join SWAPO in exile in 1964. It is an account not only of suppression and exploitation at the work place (farms, factories, canneries), but also of how the workers fight back. It is also a valuable primary source, highlighting the active years of workers' resistance, strikes and political organising in the late 1950s, and eloquently complements academic writings on the same subject.

70. NEHOVA, HINANANJE SHAFODINO. "The price of liberation". In Namibia: SWAPO fights for freedom, edited by Liberation Support Movement, p. 69-87. Oakland, CA: LSM, 1978.

This excerpt from the life history of Hinananje S. Nehova provides a first-hand account of the origins of the 1971-72 general strike by one of its active organisers. Nehova was at the time working with one of the fish canneries at Walvis Bay, after having been expelled from a secondary school together with other leaders-to-be of the SWAPO Youth League. The story offers unique insight into the preparations for the strike in Walvis Bay, and how the workers' action spread to other parts of the country. Nehova was later arrested, tortured and handed over to the Portuguese secret police (PIDA) in Southern Angola, and was held in prison under horrific conditions until the Portuguese coup d'etat in 1974.

571. ROGERS, BARBARA. "Notes on labour conditions at the Rössing mine". South African Labour Bulletin, 4, nos. 1-2, (January-February) 1978: 140-44. (In German: Die Lage der Arbeiter im Uranbergbaubetrieb Rössing. Bonn: ISSA Archiv Aktuell, 1977, 8 p.

A brief note on the conditions for labourers at the Rössing uranium mine in Namibia, pointing to the enormous gap between the promises of Rio Tinto Zinc and the daily realities of low wages, long working hours, overcrowded workers' quarters, poor diets and discriminatory health care.

RUBIN, NEVILLE, see no. 656.

672. SCHILLING-JAEGGI, JOHANNA. Das Problem der Land - Stadt-Wanderung in Namibia vor und nach 1977. Universität Basel, 1982, 83 p. 6 maps, 18 tables, bibl.: 81-3.

This brief dissertation is an attempt to assess the trends and the principal factors determining labour migration before and after the lifting of some of the pass law restrictions in October 1977. The main sections discuss the causes of labour migration in terms of a simple "push-pull" paradigm, and outline the changes in the migration rate and their social and economic consequences. The last chapter concentrates mainly on assessing population, labour-force and migration statistics and indicators, which are drawn from a rather selective range of secondary sources, in particular Thomas (no. 75) and the

UN Institute for Namibia (no. 468), and from recent press cuttings. Alternative historical analyses, such as Gordon (no. 653) and Moorsom (no. 664) are largely ignored.

673. SIMONS, RAY E. The Namibian challenge. Paper presented to the International Conference on Namibia, Brussels, 1972, 45 p. + appendix.

Prepared for an international conference on Namibia in Brussels in 1972, this unpublished report is a contemporary account of the migratory labour system and the general strike in 1971-72. The author is a South African trade union activist who was involved in organising unions among fish canning workers in Namibia in the early 1950s and who later left South Africa after having been banned by the apartheid regime. The first part of the paper surveys the oppressive apparatus of labour laws, SWANLA contracts and working conditions akin to slavery. It is followed by a detailed account of the course of the events in 1971-72. The author argues strongly that the most remarkable feature of the strike was its political character, as revealed in the workers' demands for the termination of the contract labour system, a central pillar of colonial rule. Several important documents are included as appendices, such as the strikers' demands and examples of contracts and labour laws.

674. SOUTH AFRICAN LABOUR BULLETIN. Focus on Namibia. Durban: 1978, 194 p. (Double issue, January-February 1978, 4 nos. 1-2).

Edited by Richard Moorsom, the focus of this special issue of the South African Labour Bulletin is on the history and current concerns of black workers in Namibia. It offers a collection of excellent articles as well as a wide range of documents and a selection of interviews, recorded in 1977, which give workers a rare opportunity to speak for themselves. The first part contains edited extracts from the interviews, organised in thematic sections covering labour laws, wages and living conditions, industrial relations, workers' consciousness, collective action, and women workers. There is also a special section dealing with the black student revolt in 1976-77 and the Nama teachers' strike, providing insight into one of the bitterest and longest labour disputes in Namibia. The second part consists of scholarly articles on labour history and action, for which see separate annotations of Gebhardt (no. 649), Rogers (no. 671) and Gottschalk (no. 655). Amongst the documents reproduced are the strikers' manifesto of January 1972 and the first fully revised edition of the famous "strike diary".

675. SOUTH WEST AFRICA (ADM.). Report of the S.W.A. Native Labourer's Commission, 1945-1948. Windhoek, 1948, 68 p.

The point of departure for this important commission of inquiry is the "native labour problem" in the years following the Second World War, mainly as a result of the increased demand for farm workers and the anticipated expansion in mining and industry. The commission, which worked for almost three years, recognizes the need for an improvement in wages, housing conditions and diet for farmworkers in order to increase the labour supply to a highly unpopular field of employment. It also recommended that the agreement between SWANLA (the recruiting agency) and the Witwatersrand Native Labour Association

Ltd. (WENELA), under which 3,000 mine workers a year were recruited for the mines in South Africa, should be terminated. The report provides a wealth of factual information on the operations of SWANLA, working and living conditions, health and the attitudes of the employers (especially farmers), making the document an invaluable primary source. There are also several interesting appendices, such as standard contracts, recommendations for housing and an outline of the health examination regulations.

76. SWAPO OF NAMIBIA, DEPARTMENT OF LABOUR. The struggle for trade union rights in Namibia. London: SWAPO, 1984, 46 p. Illus. (Published on behalf of the National Union of Namibian Workers).

77. THOMPSON, ELISABETH. Organized labor activities among Namibian workers: 1910-1950. Paper presented to the International Conference in Solidarity with the Struggle of the People of Namibia, Paris, 1980, 10 p.

This brief essay is the result of preliminary research for a PhD thesis on the history of the Namibian working class. The author is one of the few to have researched this subject from archival sources both in Namibia and West Germany. She argues that Namibian workers have presented their employers and the colonial governments with an organised and active struggle to maintain and better their position, and that the repressive measures taken by both the German and the South African regime against the workers were in part a response to these actions. This contention is supported by examples mainly drawn from the copper and diamond mining industry in the period from 1907 to the Second World War.

78. VOIPIO, RAUHA. KONTRAK soos die Owambo dit sien. Braamfontein: Christian Institute of Southern Africa, 1971, 35 p.

79. ------- "Contract work through Ovambo eyes". In Namibia. The last colony, edited by Reginald H. Green, Marja-Liisa Kiljunen and Kimmo Kiljunen, p. 112-31. London: Longman, 1981.

Prepared by a Finnish missionary, this seminal report appeared as a booklet in the middle of the 1971-72 general strike. It is mainly concerned with the destructive role of the contract labour system on family life, living conditions and the social fabric and provides a graphic descriptive exposure of deep social distress. The report is based on questionnaires sent out to the workers and their wives as well as some Christian workers in Ovamboland, almost 100 of which were returned. The major part of the booklet was translated into English and published as an appendix in Kane-Berman: Contract labour in South-West Africa (see no. 657). The main findings are summarised in the contribution to Namibia. The Last Colony, which also describes developments since 1972, concluding that the new contract system does not differ essentially from the former one and that the present situation in many respects is even worse than at the beginning of the 1970s.

SEE ALSO:

22, 23, 29, 39, 52, 54, 55, 74, 118, 123, 146, 211, 317, 328,
346-8, 356, 357, 381, 389, 420, 424-6, 523, 532, 537, 562, 580,
597, 604, 635-6, 685, 1015.

9. WOMEN

80. ALLISON, CAROLINE. Women, work and family in contemporary Namibia. (Draft, 89 p. IDS, University of Sussex). In preparation.

81. ------- The effects of war and political repression: women in Namibia. (Draft, 149 p. IDS, University of Sussex). In preparation.

82. COLLINS, CAROLE. This is the time. Interview with two Namibian women. Chicago: Chicago Committee for African Liberation, 1977, 28 p.

83. ------- "SWAPO images of a future society: women in Namibia". Issue, 7, no. 4, 1977: 39-45.

84. MUSIALELA, ELLEN. "Women in Namibia: the only way to free ourselves", in Third world, second sex. Women's struggle and national liberation, edited by Miranda Davies, p. 83-7. London: Zed Press, 1983. (Originally published in Anti-Apartheid News, March 1981).

Based on interviews with two SWAPO militants in 1976, the booklet edited by Carole Collins is one of the very few publications mainly concerned with the role of Namibian women in society and in the liberation struggle. Netumbo Nandi and Mathilda Amoomo provide a vivid description of their experience under colonial rule, the oppressive conditions both in rural areas and in towns, and the activities of SWAPO Women's Council. The article in Issue discusses the same subjects very briefly, while the interview with Ellen Musialela, a leading SWAPO activist, is a more recent comment on the position of women in the struggle for an independent Namibia. There is also a brief section on Namibia (p. 82-90) in G. Wellmer (ed.): Frauen im Befreiungskampf (Bonn: ISSA, 1979).

85. HISHONGWA, NDEUTALA SELMA. Women of Namibia. The changing role of Namibian women from traditional precolonial times to the present. Stockholm: By och Bygd, 1983, 103 p. 35 photos, bibl.: 102-03. (Also distributed by International Defence and Aid Fund for Southern Africa, London).

Although sketchy and not very penetrating in its analysis, this is
a welcome contribution to the very sparse literature on women in
Namibia. Written in a popular style by a Namibian who has lived in
exile in Sweden since 1974, the book starts with a brief description
of life in pre-colonial Ovamboland. It then discusses the impact
of the colonial system in general and the effects of migrant labour
on family structure and living conditions in northern Namibia. The
author also deals with the role of women in SWAPO and the liberation
struggle, and ends with an elaboration of some of the problems
facing women in an independent Namibia.

686. INTERNATIONAL DEFENCE AND AID FUND FOR SOUTHERN AFRICA. To honour
women's day. Profiles of leading women in the South African and
Namibian liberation struggles. London: IDAF in cooperation with UN
Centre Against Apartheid, 1981, 56 p. 41 photos.

Describing the lives and experiences of women who have all made outstanding contributions to the struggle for a democratic and non-racial
Southern Africa, this collection of brief biographies was produced
as a tribute to the fighting women of South Africa and Namibia on the
occasion of the 25th anniversary of South Africa Women's Day and the
protests against the pass laws. Seven Namibians (Libertine Amathila,
Lucia Hamutenya, Ida Jimmy, Gertrude Kandanga, Ellen Musialela,
Rauna Nambinga, Nahambo Shamena) are among those selected as representatives of women who have been banned, detained, tortured, imprisoned and driven into exile for their participation in the
liberation struggle. See also: You have struck a rock. Women and
political repression in Southern Africa (London: International
Defence and Aid Fund for Southern Africa, 1980, 24 p.).

687. LAPCHICK, RICHARD E. and STEPHANIE URDANG. Oppression and resistance.
The struggle of women in Southern Africa. Westport, Connecticut/
London: Greenwood Press, 1982, 198 p. 10 illus., 10 tables, bibl.:
185-89. (Contributions in Women's Studies, no. 29).

Based on background papers and the discussions at the World Conference
of the United Nations Decade of Women (Copenhagen, 1980), this is
one of the few studies of women in Southern Africa. There is a brief
chapter dealing specifically with women in Namibia, which also offers
some rudimentary information on health and employment ("The role
of women in the struggle for independence in Namibia", p. 110-17).

688. MURRAY-HUDSON, ANNE. "SWAPO: solidarity with our sisters". Review
of African Political Economy, no. 27-28, 1983: 120-25.

Written by a member of the British-based SWAPO Women's Solidarity
Campaign, this is a brief review of the role of women in the struggle
for liberation. The article discusses the aims and objectives of
the SWAPO Women's Council, socio-economic conditions for women, the
effects of the war on civilians (forced removals, torture, rape),
and the victimisation of women for their SWAPO activities. There is
also a bibliographic note.

MUSIALELA, ELLEN, see no. 683.

89. NAMIBIA SUPPORT COMMITTEE/SWAPO WOMEN'S SOLIDARITY CAMPAIGN. Women in Namibia (Tentative title). In preparation.

0a. PFOUTS, ANITA. "Changing times: women in Namibia". Ufahamu, 11, no. 3, 1982: 49-60.

This is the text of an address during a panel discussion on women in Southern Africa, which was part of the African Activist Association Conference in 1981. The aim of the lecture was to give a brief outline of the division of labour between men and women in pre-colonial Namibia, to discuss the impact of German and South African colonialism on women and to highlight the role of women in the SWAPO's struggle for liberation. These important questions are merely touched upon in this brief text, but it has its value in directing attention to a much neglected field of research.

0b. SOUTH WEST AFRICA PEOPLE'S ORGANISATION. Namibia: women in the struggle. Luanda: SWAPO Dept. of Information & Publicity, 1984, 24 p. Illus.

A pamphlet describing the role women have come to play in the struggle for national and social liberation, covering such topics as the heroism of women in the Windhoek Uprising (1959), participation in the armed struggle and the activities of SWAPO Women's Council in working out programmes for learning, for productive labour and cultural creativity.

SWAPO WOMEN'S SOLIDARITY CAMPAIGN, see no. 689.

URDANG, STEPHANIE, see no. 687.

SEE ALSO:

74, 167, 468, 489, 532, 629, 639, 717.

10. EDUCATION AND CULTURE

591. ADVIESKOMITEE VIR GEESTESWETENSKAPLIKE NAVORSING IN SWA/NAMIBIË.
Ondersoek na die onderwys in SWA/Namibië. Windhoek. 1: Verslag
van die Komitee insake riglyne vir 'n stelsel van onderwysvoorsiening.
1982, 43 p. 2: Verslag oor demografie en onderwysstatistiek vir
SWA/Namibië. 1982, 111 p. 3: Verslag van die navorsingsprojekkomitee: Kurrikulering. 1982, 150 p. 4: Verslag van die
navorsingsprojekkomitee: Knelpunte in 'n veeltalige onderwyssituasie.
1982, 196 p. 5: Verslag van die navorsingsprojekkomitee: Onder-
wysstelselbeplanning. 1983, 223 p.

In 1980, the Advisory Committee for Human Sciences Research in
SWA/Namibia was asked by the Department of National Education to
review the present education system in Namibia and to consider the
need for changes in the structure and the curriculum. Three years
later the committee submitted a five-volume report, which unfortunately
is published only in Afrikaans. The report contains a critical
examination of the failure of the existing system, and provides a
wealth of facts and figure, (See especially vol. 2, which is concerned
with demography and education statistics and vol. 5 which includes
an assessment of the economy.) The report also makes detailed
proposals for the establishment of a revised educational structure.
Two important principles are, firstly, that education and vocational
training must be combined and, secondly, that educational policy
and support services must be centralised to avoid the present fragmentation and inefficiency of the ethnic administrations. The school
syllabus stresses functional literacy and the need for giving the
students "modern value-orientations" and "a healthy work-ethic". It
also urges that the role of the private sector in education be
reinforced, especially through training colleges funded by mining
corporations. Critics have pointed out that the plan lacks a serious
discussion of making education compulsory, that there is no commitment
to English and that the overall thrust of the recommendations is to
keep black Namibians in subordinate positions. For a summary in
English of the main proposals, as well as a criticial review, see
Justin Ellis: Education, Repression and Liberation: Namibia (no. 695).

692. CHAMBERLAIN, R., et al. Toward a language policy for Namibia. English as the official language: perspectives and strategies. Lusaka: UNIN, 1981, 123 p. 15 tables, 6 figures. (Namibia Studies Series no. 4, N.K. Duggal, editor).

Published in a series designed to provide basic data and to provoke discussion on policy options for an independent Namibia, this study examines the practical, educational, cultural and political aspects of introducing English as the official language. There is also a background chapter outlining the structure of education in Namibia, which is followed by a discussion of teacher training and the language content of education.

693. ELLIS, JUSTIN. Formal and nonformal education in Namibia. University of Manchester, 1980, 91 p. (Dipl. in Adult Education diss.).

694. ------- Basic adult education in Namibia after independence. University of Manchester, 1981, 221 p. Bibl.: 208-21. (M.Ed. thesis).

Based on the author's own experience as a teacher in Namibia (Bureau of Literacy and Literature, Christian Centre) until his expulsion in 1978, the first of these two studies outlines the history of the educational system in Namibia and the changes introduced in the 1970s. It also covers the various forms of nonformal education (by, for instance, churches, community development, correspondence clubs and SWAPO political education). As the author himself acknowledges, one of the merits of the study is to make some of the main ideas of Henning Melber (see no. 702) available in English. Basic Adult Education is more specifically concerned with educational reform after independence. Several models for planning participatory adult education programmes are discussed, and proposals are made for the training of adult educators. For a further development of the themes covered by these two dissertations, see no. 695.

695. ELLIS, JUSTIN. Education, repression and Liberation: Namibia. London: Catholic Institute for International Relations/World University Service, 1983, 94 p. 11 tables, 4 figures, 11 illus., bibl.: 88-94. (A Future for Namibia, 4).

Published as the fourth volume in the CIIR series on Namibia, this is an informative and perceptive study of the past, present and future education system. The first chapter focuses on the ways in which missionary education was used to impose a European culture, and how the introduction of the Bantu Education system contributed to ethnic fragmentation and the subjugation of the black majority. The author also notes that recent political changes have made the eleven ethnic governments responsible for primary and secondary education, with the effect of perpetuating segregation and inequality. The examination of the present state of education, both formal and informal, amply demonstrates the decline in its quality. It also shows how the secondary schools have been places of conflict between young Namibians and the South African authorities, resulting in mass expulsion of pupils, the sacking of teachers and the victimisation of supposed "agitators". A separate chapter is devoted to "education through exile", especially in the refugee communities in Angola and Zambia, where SWAPO is providing education for 10-15,000 pupils as well as mass adult education programmes, vocational training and teacher training. The book finally considers the prospects for a new education system after independence, based on the policy guidelines emerging from SWAPO. The value of the study is enhanced by its challenging critique of the 1000-page report of Namibian education submitted in 1983 and published only in Afrikaans (see no. 691). There is also an excellent bibliography.

696. KNAPPERT, JAN. Namibia. Land and peoples, myths and fables. Leiden: E.J. Brill, 1981, vii + 201 p. (NISABA. Religious texts translation series, vol. 11).

697. SCHMIDT, SIGRID. Märchen aus Namibia. Düsseldorf/Köln: Eugen Diederich Verlag, 1981, 284 p.

Being the first of its kind in English, the merit of the book edited by Knappert lies in the collection of oral literature, legends, myths, fables and proverbs it presents. The compiler is a Dutch linguist who has previously published several books on Swahili language and culture. The traditional stories are, however, set in a static context which fails to take into account processes of social change and the profound impact of colonisation and occupation. The introductory survey of Namibian history is mainly an unsophisticated summary of the "myth and fables" of European explorers, missionaries and traders, and the background information on the country is often inaccurate and biased. In this sense, the book underlines the urgent need for oral literature and history to be based on the experiences and values of the indigenous population. For an acute comment by a Namibian social scientist, see the critical review by Peter H. Katjavivi in International Journal of African Historical Studies, 16, no. 1, 1983: 95-8. The book edited by Schmidt, a West German folklorist with a long research experience in Namibia, presents more than 130 Nama and Damara folktales, with a scholarly and imaginative analysis of each. It does, however, tend to suffer from the same limitations as the Knappert volume.

698. LACHENMANN, GUDRUN. Namibia. Sektorstudie Bildungswesen. Berlin: Deutsches Institut fürEntwicklungspolitik, 1979, 85 p. 13 tables, 4 figures, bibl.: 83-5.

This is one of the best documented of the several sectoral studies prepared by the German Development Institute, outlining the main features of the present educational system based on regional and ethnic inequality and discrimination. The author argues that the quantitative expansion of recent years has not been matched by any qualitative improvement in a rudimentary service for blacks. She presents a strategy for an independent Namibia in some detail, based on a functional concept of education related to the living conditions of the people and the needs of development. She also stresses that women have to be regarded as a special target group. For these goals to succeed, she urges that not only is action required in the education system as such, but that profound social and economic changes must also take place.

699. LEU, CHRISTOPHER A. "Colonial education and African resistance in
Namibia". In Independence without freedom. The political economy
of colonial education in Southern Africa, edited by A.T. Mugomba
and M. Nyaggah, p. 152-71. Santa Barbara, California/Oxford:
ABC- Clio, 1980. (Published in a slightly revised form as
"Opposition to apartheid in Namibia; the role of education, religion
and the contract labour system". Ufahamu, 9, no. 1, 1979: 111-37).

This contribution to a reader on education in Southern Africa argues
that the imposition of the apartheid educational system on Namibia
has assisted the South Africans in their policy of fragmenting the
opposition into different "homelands" and "nationalities", and
that it had the effect of keeping the African population educationally
inferior to the whites. This interpretation is backed by a historical
survey of the educational system from the time of its missionary
origins, which links colonial education to the emergence of political
awareness. The author also argues that the role of the churches in
recent times has legitimised opposition, and that the contract labour
system can be regarded as a form of "political education" enhancing
African perceptions of inequality and exploitation.

700. MBAMBA, A. MAUNO. Primary education for an independent Namibia.
Planning in a situation of uncertainty and instability. Stockholm:
Almqvist & Wiksell International, 1982, 244 p. 68 tables, 19 figures,
bibl.: 233-44. (PhD thesis).

The objective of this dissertation, written by a Namibian scholar
and SWAPO member, is to examine the implementation of South Africa's
apartheid education and the implications of this policy for planning
primary education in an independent Namibia. The first part surveys
the historical development of the educational system, and provides
a more detailed description of the 1962-1978 period, supported by
a wide range of - mainly official - statistical information. It is
followed by a chapter on the organisation and administration of
SWAPO's educational activities, which also contains a brief outline
of the liberation movement's strategies for socio-economic and
educational development. These background chapters lead to an
examination of future educational needs and requirements, focusing
on strategies for quantitative and qualitative planning. In order
to gather essential information for the planning of primary education,
a large number of projections on primary enrolment, school classes
and teacher requirements are carried out for the 1984-1990 period.
The author concludes by discussing briefly some of the major constraints on the planning and implementation of a new educational
policy in an independent Namibia, such as lack of financial resources
(especially in the case of compulsory and universal primary education)
and political resistance from conservative forces and groups with
vested interests in the status quo.

701. MCGILL, MARCIA KENNEDY. "Education policy and results". In
South West Africa: A travesty of trust, edited by Ronald Segal and
Ruth First, p. 194-212. London: Deutsch, 1967.

A brief historical analysis of official education policy and conditions,
with statistics on attendance and finance. The author concentrates
mainly on the imposition of "Bantu Education" and its consequences
for Africans.

702. MELBER, HENNING. Schule und Kolonialismus: Das formale Erzieh-
ungswesen Namibias. Hamburg: Institut für Afrika-Kunde, 1979,
319 p. 108 tables, 7 figures, bibl: 288-99.

This study is the result of a major research effort to describe and
analyse Namibia's institutionalised system of colonial education,
placing it in its wider socio-economic context. The first chapter
surveys the history of formal education from its introduction by
the missionaries in the pre-colonial period through German rule
and the continuation of colonial administration by South Africa. It
is followed by an analysis of the specific ideology of Christian
National Education (for the whites) and "Bantu Education" (for
blacks). The final section deals with the present educational
structure, and includes a review of criticism and opposition by
Namibian students and teachers. The author concludes that a complete transformation of the educational sector is required, but
warns that an educational system can never be more progressive than
the society in which it is established and operating. Containing
more than 100 tables, 400 references and a full bibliography,
this study will remain for many years the standard work on colonial
education in Namibia, and it is only to be regretted that it is not
available in English.

703. MELBER, HENNING (ed.). It is no more a cry. Namibian poetry in
exile. Basel: Basler Afrika Bibliographien, 1982, 60 p.

A collection of poetry written by students at the United Nations
Institute for Namibia (Lusaka), reflecting the hopes and commitment
of the younger generation to the struggle for independence and
national reconstruction in Namibia. The editor has contributed an
introductory essay - "Colonialism, culture and resistance: the case
of Namibia" (p. 11-23) - outlining the historical process and the
ideological character of colonial rule in Namibia. He shows
how non-European cultures were objects of violent conquest, and
that the prevailing ideology denied any meaningful sense to the
existence of indigeneous cultures. In the present era, he argues
the aim of the National Party has been to integrate cultural
aspects on a tribal basis as a tool of perpetuating colonial
structures under the cover of "separate development".

704. MELBER, HENNING. "Eine Waffe im Befreiungskampf... Erziehungsstrategie
und Bildungsmassnahmen der SWAPO für ein unabhängiges Namibia". In
Pädagogik: Dritte Welt. Jahrbuch 1983, edited by Walter Sülberg,
p. 87-113. Frankfurt: Verlag für Interkulturelle Kommunikation,
1984.

A well documented essay dealing with educational progress under the
auspices of SWAPO, the movement's educational objectives and results,
as well as the programme developed so far for the transformation of
formal education in an independent Namibia. It is argued that - much
as the efforts in this field are appreciated - the transformation of
the Namibian and the success of the new educational strategy depend
far more on the solution of other socio-political issues than on
changes within the sphere of education itself. There is also a
valuable list of publications concerned with education in Namibia.

705. O'CALLAGHAN, MARION. <u>Namibia: the effects of apartheid on culture and education.</u> Paris: UNESCO, 1977, 169 p. 77 tables.

This volume in the UNESCO series on Southern Africa does not attempt to present the "Namibia question" in general, but provides an analysis of the effects of South African rule within the fields of education and culture. As a background to the detailed description of the educational system as an instrument for perpetuating white supremacy, the first and in fact longest part of the book outlines Namibian history since the conquest and the present economic structure. The book covers the central features of South African rule, and is packed with tables and lengthy quotations from official reports. The author concludes that racial discrimination, denial of human rights, tribalism and cultural domination "are the inevitable result of the social structure of Namibia, its history of conquest, of the pattern of its economy and of the method of capital accumulation".

SCHMIDT, SIGRID, see no. 697.

706. SOUTH WEST AFRICA (ADM.). <u>Report of the commission of inquiry into Non-European education in South West Africa.</u> Windhoek, 1958. Part I: <u>Native education,</u> 164 p. 19 tables. Part II: <u>Coloured education,</u> 99 p. 9 tables.

While a report on the improvement of "European education" was published in 1956, these reports two years later provided the blueprint for the imposition of apartheid education in Namibia. The investigation was a substantial effort, following an outline of the origins of "native education" with an extensive survey of the system in operation at the time. The reports contain a wealth of data which goes well beyond the strictly educational to include , for instance, demographic and economic statistics from unpublished official sources. Not surprisingly they recommended an end to the almost total government indifference towards "native education" and the takeover or replacement of the mission schools by an expanding state system segregated in terms of the ethnic rules of apartheid - this despite some acknowledgement of church criticism of the inferiority and racial discrimination of the prevailing laissez-faire policy. Although education for Whites had already been made obligatory under the Education Proclamation of 1921 and 1926, the Commission recommended that "the Department of Education should not take the initiative to introduce compulsory education in native schools". See also <u>Memorandum of education policy adopted with reference to Reports of Commission of enquiry regarding European and Non-European education.</u> (Windhoek: Education Department, SWA Administration, 1959, 36 p.). These reports eventually led to the <u>Education Ordinance no. 27/1962.</u>

707. TJITENDERO, MOSE P. <u>Examination of an alternative: a look at the primary and secondary education in Namibia.</u> University of Massachusetts, 1976, 116 p. (D.Ed. thesis).

The aim of this thesis, written by a Namibian scholar and leading SWAPO educationalist, is to prepare the groundwork for formulating

educational policy and planning curriculum development for
independence. It opens with a discussion of the historical roots
of "Bantu education", which is seen as an instrument of oppression
designed to perpetuate white domination. The analysis of the
current system focuses on the character of the curriculum objectives
at both primary and secondary levels, underlining the enormous tasks
of educational reorganisation which will be required to adjust the
educational system to the needs and goals of an independent and just
society. The thesis also contains two case studies (of Tanzania
and Ghana) as a means of identifying issues and ideas relevant
to the Namibian situation. One of these issues is the introduction
of English as the medium of instruction, a policy which was subsequently adopted by SWAPO (see no. 692). For a more recent paper,
see Policy options for basic education (Lusaka: SWAPO Seminar on
Education, 20-25 September 1982, 17 p.). The author is also preparing a major study on education policy options in an independent
Namibia, to be published in the Namibia Studies Series (UN Institute
for Namibia) in 1985.

SEE ALSO:

71, 411, 487, 790.

11. HEALTH

708. ANDERSSON, NEIL. <u>Health sector policy options for independent Namibia</u>. Lusaka: UNIN, 1984, 154 p. 31 tables, 1 map, 3 figures. (Namibia Studies Series, No. 7, edited by N.K. Duggal).

Commissioned by the UN Institute for Namibia, this is a pioneering study on the existing state of health and health services and policy options for independent Namibia. The first part concentrates on the major health problems and the historical origins of inequalities both in health status and health care, documenting the "production of ill-health" through economic exploitation, occupational disease, malnutrition and the policy of apartheid. A large number of tables, drawn mainly from official sources (especially Municipality of Windhoek reports, SWA Administration White Papers and Anglo American Corporation medical reports), document the disease and death patterns as well as diseases and accidents in the diamond mines. The author's careful analysis of the present health care infrastructure shows the extent to which the services mostly benefit a small minority, are biased towards the towns and have a distinct curative orientation. This system contrasts sharply with the proposals for a "peoples' health program", based on the health experience of the liberation movement, the primary health approach and the experiences of other Third World countries striving for radical transformation. The primary health care approach embodies three basic ideas: firstly, that the promotion of health depends fundamentally on improving socio-economic conditions; secondly, that in this process the mass of people should be both activists and the main beneficiaries; and thirdly, that the entire health care system should be restructured to support health activities at the primary level. The final chapters comprise a detailed outline of the institutional framework for the health sector, health personnel development, the primary health care implications for resource allocations and budgets, health legislation and the need for a pharmaceutical policy. The appendices contain information on existing hospitals and clinics, health sector personnel requirements, budget estimates for the first year of independence and an essential drugs list.

709. HINSBEECK, F.C.S. "Public health and medical services in South West Africa". South African Journal of Science, 34, 1937: 317-27.

Although brief, this survey is valuable for being one of the very few published between the wars. It comments on public health and sanitation in the latter years of the German period, and describes the public health legislation and medical services of the mid-1930s. It also provides a summary of the principal diseases which, although lacking in statistics, gives a revealing insight into the prevalence of serious endemic diseases such as malaria, TB, typhoid, typhus, venereal disease and even bubonic plague amongst the black population.

710. INTERNATIONAL DEFENCE AND AID FUND FOR SOUTHERN AFRICA. Health in Namibia. (Tentative title). London: IDAF Fact Paper. In preparation.

711. KRIEGER-HINCK, CARLA. Über die medizinische Versorgung der ehemaligen Kolonie Deutsch-Südwest-Afrika. München: Ludwig-Maximilians-Universität, 1973, 81 p. (Dissertation).

The title of this thesis is quite misleading, as the study is primarily concerned with the organisation of hospitals and health services for the German colonial troops ("Die Schutztruppen"). The health condition of the great majority of the population is discussed only to the extent that their diseases and problems have implications for their ability to serve the Europeans as labour power.

712. LACHENMANN, GUDRUN. Namibia. Sektorstudie Gesundheitswesen. Berlin: Deutsches Institut für Entwicklingspolitik, 1979, xi, 143 p. 29 tables, 8 figures, bibl.: 141-43.

713. ------- "Perspectives for decolonising health in Namibia". In Perspectives of independent development in Southern Africa. The cases of Zimbabwe and Namibia, edited by German Development Institute, p. 128-62. Berlin: GDI, 1980.

714. ------- "Die "getrennte Entwicklung" der Gesundheit in Namibia". Afrika Spectrum, 15, no. 2, 1980: 147-62.

The point of departure for this carefully researched analysis of the health problems in Namibia is that underdevelopment has to be conceived as a process of continued deterioration - in either absolute or relative terms - of the living conditions of the majority of the population. The author points out that although environmental conditions are conducive for certain tropical diseases, it is bad living conditions and poverty-induced malnutrition which lower people's resistance both to tropical and other infectious diseases. The high risk of occupational disease and injury is also discussed, and the few available data on life expectancy, mortality and incidence of diseases are skilfully put together to give a coherent picture. The study concludes by arguing for the principle of primary health care and a basic-needs-oriented development strategy instead of the present urban-biased and racially based system. The report, which was prepared as one of several sectoral studies prepared by the German Development Institute, is summarised in two subsequent articles in English as well as German.

15. LACHENMANN, GUDRUN. Entkolonisierung der Gesundheit. Theorie und Praxis der Gesundheitsversorgung in Namibia und Benin. Diessenhofen: Verlag Rüegger, 1982, 341 p. 15 tables, bibl.: 309-41. (Konkrete Fremde, 4).

16. ------- Primary health care and basic-needs orientation in developing countries. Berlin: German Development Institute, 1982, 138 p.

This major thesis offers a theoretical discussion of health and basic needs in developing countries. The data on health conditions and health care in Namibia are largely drawn from the German develop-ment Institute sectoral study (see no. 712), and are supplemented with a similar examination of Benin. Primary health care is a briefer discussion of the same subject in English.

17. LOBSTEIN, TIM and THE NAMIBIA SUPPORT COMMITTEE HEALTH COLLECTIVE (eds.). Namibia. Reclaiming the people's health. London: Namibia Support Committee, 1984, 151 p. Illus., tables.

Most of this book is derived from papers given at the International Seminar on Health in Namibia, organised in London on September 1983 by the Namibia Support Committee in cooperation with the SWAPO Department of Health and Social Welfare. The book contains additional material written by participants at the seminar and other contributions through the NSC Health Collective, and the foreword on "The effects of colonialism in health" is written by the SWAPO Secretary for Health, Dr. Iyambo Indango. As well as general introductions to the "politics of health", health education and health planning, there are several informative chapters which address themselves to present social inequalities and the corrupt health administration in Namibia. Among the aspects covered more specifically are women and health, urban and industrial health, medical and pharmaceutical supplies and the reorganisation of health care in an independent Namibia. Detailed lists of organisations and publications for information and further reading are given.

MCLELLAN, DONNA L., see no. 718.

18. MAY, JAQUES M. and DONNA L. MCLELLAN. The ecology of malnutrition in seven countries of Southern Africa and in Portuguese Guinea. New York: Hafner Publishing Company, 1971, 432 p. (Studies in medical geo-graphy, vol. 10).

The authors of this broad survey have brought together valuable infor-mation on food resources and their nutritional adequacy. The chapter on Namibia (p. 61-103) is, however, rather weak due to lack of statistics and original research. On the basis of the available material, the chapter concludes that the people living in the reserves do not command adequate food resources, and that the only alternative is to retain meat, fish and dairy products for the local population instead of exporting food products for profit.

THE NAMIBIA SUPPORT COMMITTEE HEALTH COLLECTIVE, see no. 717.

719. SIMON, DAVID. "The crisis in Namibian health services". The
Namibian Review, 28, (April-June) 1983: 15-23.

This article forms part of the author's D.Phil. (no. 102), and shows
clearly that the health services are in a state of crisis. It is
argued that little change other than ethnic fragmentation has
taken place since 1977, and that the state-run services remain
totally segregated. The population's state of health is regarded
as an issue directly linked to wide socio-economic divisions:
low housing standards, low income and education levels, rising
unemployment and racial discrimination. The supporting tables
demonstrate medical staff shortages and an alarming rate of
alcoholism among blacks in Windhoek. The article does not, however,
consider other important contributions to the crisis, such as the
takeover of some church hospitals by the state, closure of clinics
in the North, and the increased influence of South African military
personnel in the health services.

720. SOUTH WEST AFRICA (ADM.). Report of the health commission for South
West Africa, 1945-46. Windhoek, 1946, 66 p.

The report of this commission, one of a number appointed immediately
after the Second World War, is concerned with nutrition and medical
services on a national basis. Unfortunately, although it covered
all sections of the population, the commission confined its investigations to the "Police Zone", and there are consequently no references to the northern reserves where some 60% of the population live.
The report points to the widespread malnutrition and the grave
health problems of the African population, and recommends increased
production of fruit and vegetables, a national minimum wage to be
laid down by law, improved housing (especially for farm workers),
increased hospital services and concerted efforts to reduce the
high incidence of venereal diseases. For the European population,
a new Central Hospital with all modern equipment is given the
highest priority. A useful feature of the report is its compilation
of the available data on medical and dental services and their costs.

721. SOUTH WEST AFRICA (ADM.). Die Verslag van die Kommissie van Ondersoek
na Gesondheidsdienste in Suidwes-Afrika aan die Administrateur-
General vir die Gebied Suidwes-Afrika. Windhoek, 1982, 441 p.

A lengthy inquiry into the health services in Namibia, with particular
emphasis on their administration, prepared by a five-man committee
of South African lawyers, medical doctors and economists, under the
chairmanship of C. Broeksma. The report was submitted in August 1982,
but was not released until one year later, after mounting public
pressure. The politically most controversial recommendation was
that the health services should be taken away from the ethnic second-
tier authorities, and transferred to the Department of National Health
and Welfare to avoid further fragmentation and lowering of standards.
This idea encountered fierce resistance from the Administration for
Whites and certain members of the SWA Medical Society. The Commission,
however, puts forward the proposal that the ethnic authorities should
retain the right to reserve hospital wards, if they so wished, for
the exclusive use of a particular "population group". The report
also deals with a wide range of other administrative matters, and

its many recommendations are brought together in an appendix:
Aanbevelings van die Kommissie van Ondersoek na Gesondheidsdienste
in Suidwes-Afrika (24 August 1982, 30 p.).

22. STRODTMANN, LOUISE H.B. Die Entwicklung des Gesundheitszustandes
und der Hygiene in Südwestafrika seit dem Weltkriege. Hamburg:
Hans Füsslein, 1937, 55 p. (Dissertation, Institut für Schiffs- und
Tropenhygiene in Hamburg).

The chief merit of this disappointingly thin thesis on health conditions in Namibia, focusing on the period 1925-32, is to bring
together some detailed statistics concerned with the major diseases
occurring in Ovamboland and among mine workers. The high risk of
contracting tuberculosis and pneumonia in mining towns is noted,
and there is a brief discussion of the high rate of venereal diseases (both among Africans and Whites). The dissertation is obviously
not based on fieldwork and the statistical material is mainly
drawn from the Administrators' annual reports.

SEE ALSO:

102, 536, 540, 671, 675.

12. NAMIBIA AS AN INTERNATIONAL ISSUE

A. UN and international law

723. ASMAL, KADER. Namibia: the international law dimension. Paper presented to the International Conference in Solidarity with the Struggle of the People of Namibia, Paris, 1980, 32 p.

This paper, written by a senior lecturer in law and chairperson of the Irish Anti-Apartheid Movement, touches upon several important aspects of the Namibian question: the revocation of the mandate, Decree No. 1 on natural resources, the status of the UN Council for Namibia, SWAPO as the authentic representative of the Namibian people, South African aggression, war crimes, mercenaries and Walvis Bay.

724. ASMAL, KADER. Walvis Bay: Self-determination and international law. New York: UN Council for Namibia, 1982, 41 p. (UN General Assembly A/AC.131/SLI/L.2. 27 January 1982).

Originally presented at a UN seminar on legal issues concerning the question of Namibia in 1981, this paper focuses on the international law dimension of the dispute over Walvis Bay. The main arguments for regarding Walvis Bay as an integral part of Namibia are out-lined, with special emphasis on the right to self-determination in international law. The author concludes by arguing that a continued South African refusal to leave Walvis Bay becomes an additional reason for the imposition of mandatory economic sanctions under Ch. VII of the UN Charter.

725. AUSTIN, R.H.F. Namibia and Zimbabwe: decolonisation and the rule of international law. London: Stevens & Sons, 1982, 29 p. (Reprinted from Current Legal Problems 1982, p. 203-32).

This essay, written by a Zimbabwean expert on international law, takes as its point of departure the fact that Namibia remains one of the outstanding cases of a dependent territory still awaiting

self-determination despite the development of elaborate legal norms
and UN procedures towards that end. The author sets as his task
to examine and explain some of the reasons for this contradictory
situation. He emphazises that the Western powers have restricted
their response to the continued illegal occupation to purely verbal
condemnation, and argues that South Africa has not only delayed the
implementation of Security Council Res. 435/78 by means of massive
military repression, but also demanded and obtained important changes
in the UN plan. The essay analyses the Western constitutional
proposals and their "non-paper" presented in 1981, and concludes that
these documents meet South Africa's desire for a perpetually
dependent Namibia and try to ensure that Namibia would be unable
to support the war of national liberation which already is being
waged in South Africa itself.

726. BOOYSEN, H. and G.E.J. STEPHAN. "Decree No. 1 of the United Nations
Council for South West Africa". South African Yearbook of International
Law = Suid-Afrikaanse Jaarboek vir Volkreg, 1, 1975: 63-86.

This analysis of the Decree No. 1 was undertaken to support the South
African official position. It argues that the decree is not valid
from the point of view of international law, and that it was issued
"in the true tradition of all non-representative or dictatorial
governments".

727. CARROLL, FAYE. South West Africa & the United Nations. Westport,
Connecticut: Greenwood Press, 1975, 123 p. (Original: Lexington:
University of Kentucky Press, 1967).

Based on a PhD thesis submitted in 1963, this is a concise survey
of the Namibia dispute. As well as outlining the history of the
mandate, the author focuses on criticism of South Africa in the
League of Nations and in the UN, concluding that the failure to find
a solution was due not to legal issues but to the policy of apartheid.

728. COCKRAM, GAIL-MARYSE. South West African mandate. Cape Town: Juta,
1976, 531 p. Bibl.: 517-25.

The purpose of this examination of Namibia's international status is
to argue the South African case against the United Nations. The
book covers all the major issues from the conquest of Namibia by
South Africa and the origins of the mandate to the present international
confrontation. A separate chapter is devoted to Ovamboland in
the early 1970s. The inclusion of cartoons from South African newspapers underscores the propagandist slant of the book.

729. DREYER, RONALD F. Walvis Bay and its importance to Namibia: past,
present, future. Paper presented to a conference on Namibia,
University of Vermont, 1982, 20 p.

This paper concentrates mainly on the history and the future context
of the Walvis Bay enclave as a subject of international political
and legal dispute. It also contains economic information on the
town's role as the main port and the centre for the fishing industry.
See also no. 1549.

730. DUGARD, JOHN (ed.). The South West Africa/Namibia dispute. Documents
and scholarly writings on the controversy between South Africa and
the United Nations. Berkeley/London: University of California Press,
1973, 585 p. Bibl.: 543-63. (Perspectives on Southern Africa -9).

This comprehensive collection of documents and scholarly writings
on the politico-legal aspects of the Namibia dispute is by far the
most substantial in an overcrowded literature. There are three
background chapters covering the period up to 1945, but the main
focus falls on the UN and the International Court of Justice.
There is also a brief chapter on political developments (1960-66),
as well as an excellent bibliography. The editor is Professor of
law and director of the Centre for Applied Legal Studies at the
University of the Witwatersrand, and has written extensively on South
Africa and Namibia from the standpoint of a liberal critique of
apartheid and the South African occupation.

731. EVBOROKHAI, A.O. (comp.). Texts of United Nations resolutions on
Namibia (1946-1978). Lusaka: UNIN, 1980. Part I, 341 p. Part II,
70 p.

These two volumes bring together the large number of resolutions on
Namibia over a period of more than twenty years. Part I consists of
150 General Assembly resolutions, while resolutions passed by the
Security Council and the Economic and Social Council are reproduced
in Part 2. The entries are arranged in chronological sequence.

DAVIS, MICHAEL I., see no. 740.

732. HUARAKA, TUNGURU. "Walvis Bay and international law", India Journal
of International Law, 18, no. 2, 1978: 160-74.

Written as a response to the South African transfer of the administration of Walvis Bay to the Cape Province in 1977, this article is
largely confined to the legal issues relating to the alleged acquisition
of sovereignty by Great Britian over Walvis Bay in the late 1870s.
The main argument, which appears somewhat legalistic as well as
historically questionable, is that the annexation was per se invalid
by the then norms of international law, and that consequently
neither the British proclamation in 1878 nor the Cape Colony Act of
1884 had any legal significance. The author also discusses the OAU
principle of respecting colonial borders, taking the view that this
principle is concerned with decolonisation and not with maintaining
colonial rule and that as a non-member, South Africa is not entitled
to benefit from the legal norms of the charter of the OAU.

733. HUARAKA, TUNGURU. Namibia by resolutions: a legal analysis of
international organisations' attempts at decolonisation. Geneva:
University of Geneva, 1982, 430 p. Bibl.: 409-30. (PhD thesis).

Written by a Namibian in exile, this is the most comprehensive and
up-to-date of several scholarly accounts of the Namibian question in
international law. The focal point of the study is the United Nations
legal approach to decolonisation, and the final chapter is devoted
to a discussion of the failure to implement the UN's decisions

through the UN Council for Namibia and Decree No. 1. The extensive
bibliography reflects the large legal literature on Namibia, the
mandate system, the UN and the International Court of Justice.

HUMAN RIGHTS JOURNAL, see no. 747.

734. INTERNATIONAL COURT OF JUSTICE. International status of South West
Africa, advisory opinion of July 11th, 1950, Leyden: Sijthoff,
1950. 373 p. (Pleadings, oral arguments, documents. no. 46).

735. ------- South West Africa cases (Ethiopia v. South Africa, Liberia v.
South Africa): judgment of 21 December 1962 . The Hague, 1962,
662 p. (Reports of judgments, advisory opinions and orders).

736. ------- South West Africa cases. (Ethiopia versus South Africa,
Liberia versus South Africa), 1966. The Hague, 1967-70. 1008 p.
Vols. 1-12. (Pleadings, oral arguments and documents).

737. ------- South West Africa cases. (Ethiopia versus South Africa,
Liberia versus South Africa), second phase. Judgment of 18 July 1966.
The Hague, 1966, 505 p. (Reports of judgments, advisory opinions
and orders).

738. ------- Legal consequences for states of the continued presence of
South Africa in Namibia (South West Africa) notwithstanding Security
Council resolution 276(1970): advisory opinion of 21 June 1971. The
Hague, 1971, 345 p. (Reports of judgments, advisory opinions and
orders. Also published in International law reports 49, 1976:
1-355).

These documents constitute the main body of the International Court
of Justice's publications concerned with Namibia, containing the
complete texts of the judgments and advisory opinions, as well as
separate and dissenting opinions, written and oral statements, etc.
For a bibliography of the extensive literature on the ICJ and its
dealings with Namibia, see Elna Schoeman: The Namibia issue 1920-
1980 (no. 906).

739. LANDIS, ELIZABETH. Human rights in Namibia. Paper presented to the
International Conference on Namibia and Human rights, Dakar, 1976,
73 p. (A French translation is published in Revue des droits de
l'homme/Human rights journal, 9, nos. 2-3, 1976: 283-339).

This paper is a detailed documentation of the denial of human rights
in Namibia, contrasting articles of the Universal Declaration of
Human Rights with articles in Namibian law. Excerpts from the
paper are published as "Denial of human rights in Namibia",
Objective: Justice, 8, no. 1, 1976: 32-47.

740. LANDIS, ELIZABETH and MICHAEL I. DAVIS. "Namibia: impending inde-
pendence?". In Southern Africa. The continuing crisis, edited by
Gwendolen M. Carter and Patrick O'Meara, p. 141-74. London:
MacMillan, 1979. (First ed.: Bloomington/London: Indiana University
Press, 1977).

This is one of the best introductions to Namibia as an international
issue, providing a readable overview of Namibian history, the role

of the UN and the International Court of Justice, the liberation
struggle, the diplomatic manoeuvres, the South African strategy
in the 1970s and the Turnhalle Conference. The presentation is,
however, rather weak on economic and social affairs.

741. LANDIS, ELIZABETH. If it quacks like a duck... Walvis Bay, Namibia
and estoppel. Paper presented to the UN Seminar on Legal Issues
Concerning Namibia, The Hague, 1981, 27 p.

Written by a leading expert on Namibia in the context of international
law, the purpose of this fully referenced conference paper is to
demonstrate that the principle of estoppel applies to Walvis Bay.
This principle arises where a party fails to assert a right of
which it is aware and where the party knows that this failure
may be interpreted as an abandonment of the right. The principle
may then be invoked to prevent the party from belatedly enforcing
the right to the detriment of those induced to rely on its abandonment. The author sets out the most important grounds on which an
argument of estoppel can be based, demonstrating that neither the
Cape Colony nor South Africa itself ever treated the enclave as
an integral part of their metropolitan territory. She also shows
that much of the evidence is to be found in the legislation applied
to the Territory by South Africa and in decisions in South African
and Namibian courts. The author concludes that the development of
the Territory has been shaped by the legal, political and administrative joining of Walvis Bay to Namibia, and that the enclave
remains an integral part of Namibia as a matter of conventional law,
as well as of history, economics, cultural, political necessity and
the modern principles of international law regarding self-determination.

742. LANDIS, ELIZABETH S. Namibian liberation: self-determination, law
and politics. New York: Episcopal Churchmen for South Africa,
1982, 19 p. (Also presented as a paper to the African Studies
Association annual meeting 1982: International law and Namibian
liberation).

This is a clear, succinct and up-to-date analysis of the Namibian
issue, containing both a brief historical survey and a discussion
of recent Western policy. The main conclusion is that "the Western
Five" have interfered with the Namibian right of self-determination
by vetoing proposals for sanctions against South Africa, by
weakening Resolution 425/78, by failing to insist on the return of
Walvis Bay to Namibia, and by the demand of Cuban withdrawal from
Angola.

743. LEJEUNE, ANTHONY (comp.). The case for South West Arica. London:
Tom Stacey, 1971, 245 p. (In French: L'Affaire du Sud-Ouest
Africain. London: Tom Stacey, 1971, 268 p.).

This compilation of articles and documents is published with the
explicit purpose of expressing the South African government's
point of view. The major part of the book is occupied by the complete text of the two dissenting judgments given in the International
Court of Justice's 1971 advisory opinion. It also contains an
article by G.M.E. Leistner on the economic bonds between South
Africa and Namibia (see no. 374).

744. MCDOUGALL, GAY J. "The Council for Namibia's Decree No. 1: enforcement possibilities". Africa Today, 30, nos. 1-2, 1983: 7-16.

A brief discussion of the purpose of and the legal battle for
Decree No. 1, which concludes that the exploitation of Namibian
natural resources is illegal on the strength of Security Council
Resolutions and the opinion of the International Court of Justice
alone, and that this illegality is further compounded by Decree No. 1.
The author concedes that there are political as well as constitutional
impediments to successful litigation to enforce the decree, but
maintains that these impediments should not be considered insur-
mountable. The author is Director of the Southern African Project
under the US-based Lawyers' Committee for Civil Rights under Law.

745. MOORSOM, RICHARD. Decree No. 1 and the protection of Namibia's
agricultural and fishery resources: problems and prospects for
action. Paper presented to the UN Council for Namibia Regional
Symposium on International Efforts to Implement Decree No. 1 for
the Protection of the Natural Resources of Namibia, Geneva, 27-31
August 1984, 16 p.

The purpose of this conference paper is to review the implementation
of Decree no. 1 and to discuss the scope for increasing its effectiveness. While recognizing that the wording of the Decree suggests that
its main concern is the extraction of minerals, the author stresses
that it also forbids the extraction, processing, export and distribution of animal and vegetable resources of agriculture, forestry and
fishing. The point is also made that Namibia has one of the last
of the world's great fisheries not to be regulated by an exclusive
fishing zone, making the Decree a weak instrument for protecting
the major fish resources. The paper gives an informative overview
of present structures of exploitation - drawing on the author's
studies on Namibian agriculture and fisheries (nos. 532, 562) - and
shows that the destruction of resources gives a desperate urgency
to the objectives of the Decree. The final section demonstrates
that there is a great variety of concrete steps to be taken by
governments, non-governmental organisations and by the Council
itself, but that there is a need for a clear articulation of
strategies and tactics as an essential preparation for actions.

746. PRINSLOO, DANIEL STEPHAN. Walvis Bay and the Penguin Islands:
background and status. Pretoria: Foreign Affairs Association,
1977, 28 p. 2 maps., bibl.: 27-8. (FAA Study Report, no. 8).

The objective of this study report, written by a South African
political scientist, is to argue that South Africa's claim to
sovereignty over Walvis Bay is indisputable. Apart from presenting
a legal case for this position, the main argument is that a South
African military presence would be in the best interest of Namibia
as well as for the West "as long as political and economic instability threatens South Africa". See also a similarly motivated
study by J.A. Faris: "The administration of Walvis Bay", South
African Yearbook of International Law, (Pretoria), 5, 1979:
63-91.

747. REVUE DES DROITS DE L´HOMME/HUMAN RIGHTS JOURNAL. Conférence
international de Dakar sur la Namibie et les droits de l´homme:
d´hier à demain. Paris, 1976. Vol. 9, nos. 2-3, 1976: p. 210-
569.

This special issue of Human Rights Journal is exclusively devoted
to the proceedings of the important Dakar Conference on Namibia
and Human Rights (January 1976). The issue contains several
addresses, speeches and declarations, in addition to substantial
working papers concerned with international law and human rights
in Namibia in general (Elizabeth S. Landis), UN activities, the
use of flogging (Felix Ermacora), the UN Decree No. 1 (Francois
Rigaux), the churches in Namibia (Lukas de Vries) and a SWAPO discussion document on the constitution of an independent Namibia.

748. RICHARDSON, HENRY J. "Constitutive questions in the negotiations
for Namibian independence". The American Journal of International
Law, 78, January 1984: 76-120.

Written by a professor of law at Temple University, this is one of the
most up-to-date, well researched and comprehensive surveys of the
negotiations for Namibian independence from the perspective of
international law. The main focus of the inquiry is on the negotiations conducted between the "Contact Group" (the US, Canada,
France, the United Kingdom and West Germany) and South Africa,
with SWAPO and the Frontline States as the other principal participants. Following recent studies by Elizabeth Landis (no. 742)
and R.H.F. Austin (no. 725), the author argues that the "Contact
Group" is violating international law by significantly revising the
original UN peace plan and by co-operating with South Africa in
undermining the Namibian people's right to self-determination. The
insistence on the departure of Cuban troops from Angola in return
for South African acceptance to quit Namibia is regarded as an
imposition of conditions totally extraneous under law to the realisa-
tion of the right to self-determination. The existence of proposals
for "constitutional guarantees" safeguarding the interests of South
African settlers and foreign companies, as well as proposals for
restricting an independent Namibia's right to make its own foreign
policy decisions vis-a-vis the apartheid regime, are similarly seen
as substantial modifications of Security Council Res. 435/78.

749. RIGAUX, FRANCOIS. The Decree on the natural resources of Namibia
adopted on 27 September 1974 by the United Nations Council for
Namibia. Paper presented to the International Conference on
Namibia and Human Rights, Dakar, 1976, 19 p. (French original:
"Le decret sur les resources naturelles de la Namibie adopté le
27 Septembre 1974 par le Counseil des Nations-Unies pour la
Namibie", Revue des droits de l´Homme/Human Rights Journal, 9,
nos. 2-3, 1976: 467-83).

This valuable paper, written by a professor at the Law Faculty of
the Catholic University of Louvain, argues that the Decree No. 1
applies two fundamental principles of existing international law:
the rights of the Namibian people both to self-determination and
independence and to permanent sovereignty over their wealth and
natural resources. These principles thus provide the grounds for

the courts of the industrialised countries to declare null and void any contract the object of which is the illicit export of natural resources from Namibia. The author does, however, concede that the acceptance of seizure of goods and ships would be more problematic.

750. SAXENA, S.C. Namibia: challenge to the United Nations. New Dehli: Sundeep Prakashan, 1978, 316 p. Bibl.: 303-12.

Derived from a PhD thesis, this is yet another study of the Namibian conflict cast in an international law framework. Although it does not add very much to the existing literature, the analysis facilitates an understanding of the weaknesses of the UN when the economic interests of some major powers are involved. This observation leads the author to conclude that a delay in finding a solution would be detrimental to the interests of Namibia, as material wealth is being drained out of the country at an alarming rate while at the same time the roots of apartheid penetrate deeper and deeper.

751. SCHERMERS, H.G. "The Namibia Decree in national courts". The International and Comparative Law Quarterly, 26, Part I, 1977: 81-96.

Written by a professor of law at the University of Amsterdam, this is an authoritative discussion of the implications of the Decree No. 1 of the protection of natural resources. It argues that the legal basis for the promulgate laws and decrees by the UN Council for Namibia is to be found in Article 81 of the UN Charter, but notes that pressure on companies operating in Namibia will diminish if no actual seizure of illegal mineral resources follows. It suggests, therefore, that the next step must be such a seizure in an important port of an industrialised nation, and that the binding force of the Decree could be pleaded – on grounds of established public international law – before a national court.

752. SHOCKET, GEORG R. "Enforcement in the United States courts of the United Nations Council for Namibia's Decree on natural resources". Yale Studies in World Public Order, 2, no. 2, 1976: 285-342.

This well documented essay explores the possibilities of enforcing the Decree No. 1 on Namibian natural resources through litigation in US courts. Although US policy supports the conclusion that licenses and concessions granted by South Africa after the revocation of the mandate are not valid, the author recognizes that there are several problems involved in the implementation of the decree. The article concludes that the significance of successful action to enforce the decree would lie in demonstrating the viability of national courts as means for supporting the authoritative decisions of the UN.

753. SINGH, L.P. The United Nations and Namibia. Nairobi: East African Publishing House, 1980, 151 p. Bibl.: 149-51.

This is one of several introductions to the international dispute over Namibia and covers the whole of the period from the German colonisation to the liberation of Angola in the mid-1970s. The author outlines the basic issues in a simple language, and pays more attention to the historical background and the strategic and economic interests involved than is usually the case with brief surveys of this kind. The treatment of internal forces in Namibia and the liberation struggle is, however, cursory and less impressive. The book contains several UN documents as appendices.

754. SLONIM, SOLOMON. South West Africa and the United Nations: an international mandate in dispute. Baltimore/London: The Johns Hopkins University Press, 1973, 409 p. Bibl.: 385-98.

Based on a PhD thesis, this is one of the most authoritative and readable of the large range of books examining the international law aspects of the dispute over Namibia. It offers a concise outline of the international conflict from the creation of the League of Nations' Mandate system through the lengthy proceedings of the International Court of Justice to the revocation of the mandate and the direct confrontation between the UN and South Africa. There are also an extensive bibliography and excerpts from several important historical documents.

755. SOUTH AFRICA (REPUBLIC). South West Africa. South Africa's reply to the Secretary-General of the United Nations (Security Council resolution 269 of 1969). Pretoria/Cape Town: Government Printer, 1969, 115 p.

Published by the South African Department of Foreign Affairs, this document argues against the UN position that the occupation of Namibia denies its people the right to self-determination and that their struggle against the illegal presence of the South African authorities is legitimate. The annexure (p. 51-115) consists of a survey of social and economic conditions, mainly based on the 1967 Survey (no. 305).

STEPHAN, G.E.J., see no. 726.

756. UNITED NATIONS. A trust betrayed: Namibia. New York: UN Office of Public Information, 1976, 44 p. (Also available in French, German and Spanish).

This UN publication gives a brief introduction to the history of Namibia, the role played by the UN, the main features of the exploitative economic system and the struggle for Namibian independence. It supersedes a previous publication: A Principle in Torment. The United Nations and Namibia (New York, UN, 1971).

757. UNITED NATIONS. Objective: Justice. Special Issue on Namibia. New York, 1982, 55 p. (Objective: Justice, 14, no. 2, 1982).

Apart from reprinting the booklet Plunder of Namibian Uranium (no. 607), this special issue of Objective: Justice contains the Arusha Declaration on Namibia (adopted by the UN Council for Namibia at Arusha 14 May 1982) as well as excerpts from some of the statements delivered at the UN Council's meeting on 26 August 1982 to observe Namibia Day. See also Objective: Justice, 15, no. 1,

1983, which reproduces several important documents, such as the 1983 Paris Declaration and Programme of Action on Namibia.

758. UNITED NATIONS. Namibia: a unique UN responsibility. New York: UN, 1983, 38 p.

The purpose of this booklet is to document the various UN actions in support of the struggle for Namibian independence for the period 1966-83. The major part consists of a year by year survey of meetings, resolutions and activities. This edition updates the original 1980 edition by the same title.

759. UNITED NATIONS. Report of the International Conference in Support of the Struggle of the Namibian People for Independence. New York, 1983, 171 p. (A/Conf. 120/13).

This report from the Paris Conference in 1983, which was attended by as many as 138 governments, reflects the extent of international opposition to the continued illegal occupation of Namibia, the militarisation of the territory and South Africa's aggression against Frontline States. It reproduces statements made at the opening and closing plenary meetings, the report of the Committee of the Whole, the Paris Declaration and the Programme of Action on Namibia.

760. UNITED NATIONS. Relevant resolutions and decisions on Namibia, adopted by the United Nations, the Organization of African Unity and the Movement of Non-aligned Countries and excerpts from the Advisory Opinion of the International Court of Justice of 21 June 1971. New York: UN, 1983, 117 p. (A/Conf. 120/CRP.1, 6 April 1983).

Prepared for the International Conference in Support of the Struggle of the Namibian People for Independence, held in Paris in April 1983, this is the best and most up-to-date collection of resolutions and international statements on Namibia. It contains all the major Security Council resolutions in the period 1968-1978, the most important General Assembly resolutions from the revocation of the mandate in 1966 to the 1982 General Assembly, the 1980-82 resolutions adopted by the Council of Ministers of OAU as well as excerpts from declarations and communiques adopted by the Movement of Non-aligned Countries during 1981-83. The final part of the documentation reproduces the main sections of the 1971 Advisory Opinion of the International Court of Justice.

761. UNITED NATIONS COUNCIL FOR NAMIBIA. Report of the delegation of the Council to the seminar on legal issues concerning the question of Namibia held at the Hague from 22 to 24 June 1981. New York, 1981, 12 p. (A/AC. 131/L. 218, 9 October 1981).

In 1981 the UN Council for Namibia held a seminar on legal issues to examine various ways and means of implementing Decree No. 1 for the protection of the Natural Resources of Namibia and preserving the territorial integrity of Namibia. A considerable body of legal experts and jurists participated and made presentations on the legal principles underlying the Decree and the indispensability of Walvis Bay to Namibian territorial integrity. This report by

the Council's delegation provides a concise summary of the issues
discussed, the papers presented and the statement issued by the
seminar. For annotations of the major conference papers, see nos.
447, 448, 449, 487, 760, 762, 802, 803. The verbatim records of the
seminar are available as UN General Assembly documents A/AC. 131/SLI/
PV 1-6.

62. UNITED NATIONS COUNCIL FOR NAMIBIA. Implementation of Decree No. 1
for the Protection of the Natural Resources of Namibia. Paper presented to the International Conference in Support of the Struggle
of the Namibian People for Independence, Paris, 1983, 13 p. (A/Conf.
120/11, 8 April 1983).

This is one of the most up-to-date accounts of the international
efforts to implement Decree No. 1. It begins with a historical
background to the establishment of the UN Council and the enactment
of the Decree, and proceeds to discuss its legal character. The
report also deals with the enforcement efforts of the UN Council,
such as research, international hearings, and seminars and consultations with Western governments which so far have not implemented
the Decree. The document makes it clear that no country has so far
implemented the Decree, and that the Council itself faces great difficulties in its efforts to have it established as an accepted part
of international law.

63. VERHEUL, J.P. Namibian uranium. New York: UN General Assembly,
1982, 17 p. (A/AC. 131/SLI/L.1, 27 January 1982).

Originally presented at the UN Seminar on Legal Issues concerning
Namibia (The Hague, 1981), this paper by a professor of international
law at the University of Leiden, the Netherlands, argues that
a further dealing in exploitation of Namibian uranium is
contrary to international law. This judgment is based on Security
Council resolutions and the advisory opinion of the International
Court of Justice, and is further supported by the UN Council
Decree No. 1. As commercial transactions in uranium from Namibia
take part in Almelo, where there is an enrichment plant for deliveries to West Germany and the United Kingdom, the paper suggests that
an action for damages (or for a prohibitory injunction) instituted
by the Council for Namibia in a Dutch court against the Kingdom
of the Netherlands might succeed.

SEE ALSO:

3, 8, 11, 12, 21, 43, 46, 47, 71, 76, 77, 228, 394, 420, 595, 597,
606-7, chapter 12 b(764-813), 878, 892, 906, 1011, 1018.

B.   International relations

764. ABRAHAMS, KENNETH. "Namibian independence negotiations: approaching a neo-colonial settlement". The Namibian Review, no. 25, (July-August) 1982: 1-14.

In this article, the editor of The Namibian Review argues that during 1981-82 the international negotiations were being directed towards a broad neo-colonialist settlement whereby South Africa, supported by the US, would dominate the whole sub-continent. He also suggests that the South African strategy is to delay the negotiations in order to squeeze concessions from the liberation movement and the Frontline States, while at the same time attempting to foster a black middle-class with a strong stake in a neo-colonial solution. The same theme is developed further in three subsequent articles, see "The brigadiers take over: a review of the year", no. 26, (September-December) 1982: 1-11, "Present imperfect, future indefinite: Namibia in early 1983", no. 27, (January-March) 1983: 1-15 and "From Nkomati to Lusaka: The implications for Namibian independence", no. 31, (January-September) 1984: 1-21.

765. AFRICA TODAY. Namibia: crisis for the international community. Denver, 1979, 96 p. (Africa Today, 26, no. 2, 1979).

This special issue of Africa Today on Namibia contains articles on the collapse of the Western Contact Group's settlement plan (Georg W. Shepherd, jr.), a survey of forces and factions in Namibian politics (William Johnston), Namibia and its neighbours (Robert L. Dillingham, jr.) and SWAPO's war of liberation in international law (Christos Theodoropoulos). There are also several book reviews. See also the updated - and sharpened - analysis by Georg W. Shepherd, jr.: "Breaking the Namibia Impasse", Africa Today, 29, no. 7, 1982.

766. ANGOLA (PEOPLE'S REPUBLIC). White paper on acts of aggression by the racist South African regime against the People's Republic of Angola, 1975-1982. 1983, 174 p. 2 maps, 54 photos. Published by the Ministry of External Relations of the People's Republic of Angola, printed in United Kingdom and distributed by Angola Information (London).

Chronologically organised and vividly illustrated, this is a graphic account of acts of aggression, casualities and material damage inflicted upon Angola by South African forces operating from Namibia. The white paper also contains official Angolan statements, the related UN Security Council resolutions, and the evidence and testimony of visits by international missions of inquiry. The

documentation reveals clearly how closely the Namibian struggle
for independence and the Angolan struggle for survival are inter-
linked, and how extensively the territory of Namibia is used by the
occupying power as a base for attacks against neighbouring countries.

67. BARRATT, JOHN. "Namibia in the international arena". Journal of
Contemporary African Studies, 1, no. 2, 1982: 269-80.

68. ------- "The outlook for Namibian independence: some domestic constraints". International Affairs Bulletin, 7, no. 1, 1983: 14-24.

The main argument in these two comments on the Namibia issue is that
the concern of the South African government can be ascribed less
to economic considerations than to questions of security and
political influence. The author considers that Namibia under a future
SWAPO government is perceived as a national security threat (involving
USSR and Cuba), and that politically a SWAPO victory in elections
is likely to cause a right wing domestic reaction among white South
Africans and a raising of expectations and aspirations among blacks.
He concludes, therefore, that these South African concerns will have
to be taken into account in order to reach a negotiated settlement.
The author is Director of the Johannesburg-based South Africa
Institute of International Affairs.

69. BLEY, HELMUT. "Namibia, die Bundesrepublik und der Westen: 15
Jahre Krisenverschärfung". In Hilfe+Handel=Frieden ? Die Bundes-
republik in der dritten Welt, edited by Reiner Steinweg, p. 109-38.
Frankfurt: Suhrkamp, 1982.

Written by the author of a major study of the German colonisation
of Namibia (see no. 179), this essay provides a survey of Namibia
as an international issue since the early 1970s. The main focus
is on the diplomatic manoeuvres of the Western powers in general
and of West German foreign policy in particular. The author points
to the deepening of West German economic and technological collaboration with South Africa over the years, and argues that the government is partly responsible for the lack of Western pressure on
South Africa to accept a negotiated settlement along the lines of
the UN proposals. See also by the same author: "Die Bundesrepublik,
der Westen und die internationale Lage um Namibia", in Afrika und
Bonn. Versäumnisse und Zwänge deutscher Afrika-Politik, p. 145-68..
(Reinbek-Hamburg: Rowohlt, 1978).

70. BROHMAN, JOHN A. and DAVID B. KNIGHT. "Some geopolitical aspects
of the conflict in Namibia/South West Africa". In Political studies
from spatial perspectives. Anglo-American essays on political geography, edited by Alan D. Burnett and Peter J. Taylor, p. 489-513.
Chichester: John Wiley & Sons, 1981.

This essay attempts to analyse the Namibia conflict "in conjunction
with the global superpower rivalry and the racial struggle in southern
Africa", and is basically presented within a hard-line cold war
perspective. Apart from a few pages in the final section outlining
the basic geography of Namibia, it is mainly concerned with Soviet
"expansionism" and the prospects for a solution which will make a
"dialogue" and a mutual understanding between Black Africa and South

Africa possible in the future. To make it easier for the reader to
grasp the political message, the military forces of SWAPO are
referred to as "terrorist squads".

771. CALLAGHY, THOMAS M. (ed.). South Africa in Southern Africa. The
intensifying vortex of violence. New York: Praeger, 1983, 423 p.
Bibl.: 405-12.

Originating from a conference in Pennsylvania in 1980, this is an
updated collection of 14 well-researched essays on the Southern
African region. The main focus is on the apartheid regime in
South Africa and its economic, military and political impact on the
neighbouring states. There is one article dealing specifically
with Namibia (John Seiler: "South Africa in Namibia", p. 165-189,
see no. 793), but the contributions on SADCC, Southern Africa in
the World System, and South Africa's relations with Mozambique and
Angola also throw light on questions highly relevant to the future of
Namibia.

772. CANADIANS CONCERNED ABOUT SOUTHERN AFRICA. Canadian complicity in
Namibia. Paper presented to the International Conference in
Solidarity with the Struggle of the People of Namibia, Paris, 1980,
15 p.

The main objective of this outline of Canada's economic involvement
in Namibia is to draw attention to the fact that Canada condemns the
South African illegal occupation of Namibia while simultaneously
allowing an increase in trade and investment. The paper shows that
the investments of Canadian multinational corporations in Namibia
are by no means insignificant, and that they profit from the discriminatory wage practices. It also provides a historical overview
of the Canadian official position at the United Nations on the
Namibian question, and concludes that Canada's participation in the
Western Contact Group and its diplomatic manoeuvres means that its
objective support for the South African regime can no longer be
camouflaged by moralising rhetoric.

773. ČERVENKA, ZDENEK and BARBARA ROGERS. The nuclear axis. Secret
collaboration between West Germany and South Africa. London:
Julian Friedmann, 1978, 464 p.

The purpose of this well researched book is to expose the secret
West German collaboration with South Africa in the field of nuclear
and military technology. There is also a detailed chapter (p. 108-
156) on "The Rössing connection", documenting the uranium rush in
Namibia, the West German involvement in the Rössing mine, and the
South African uranium marketing strategy.

774. CLOUGH, MICHAEL (ed.). Changing realities in Southern Africa.
Implications for American policy. Berkeley: University of California,
Institute of International Studies, 1982, 318 p.

This uneven collection of essays on the international aspects of the
conflict in Southern Africa brings together seven contributions
by authors with quite different political perspectives. In addition

to articles on Zimbabwe, SADCC and South Africa's regional policy,
there are two essays dealing specifically with Namibia. "From
South West Africa to Namibia" (p. 61-91) is written by the editor,
an assistant professor at the Naval Graduate School. The main concern of the author is to urge the US Administration to promote
an international settlement by putting pressure on South Africa,
arguing that a prolongation of the conflict "will shift the balance
of power within SWAPO in favor of the factions most hostile to the
United States and less willing to compromise". In "One Namibia, one
nation: the political economy of transition" (p. 92-122), R.H. Green
focuses on the colonial economy and the transitional period from
a position close to SWAPO. (For a separate annotation of this
article, see no. 470).

775. DALE, RICHARD. "Walvis Bay: a naval gateway, an economic turnstile,
or a diplomatic bargaining chip for the future of Namibia?". RUSI,
Journal of the Royal United Services Institute for Defence Studies,
172, no. 1, (March) 1982: 31-36.

This brief article discusses the military and strategic importance
of Walvis Bay, emphasizing the extent to which Walvis Bay has been
integrated into the command structure of the South African Navy.
The author argues that South African naval planners are concerned
with the use of Walvis Bay as a staging post for a blockade or
even an invasion in the future, and that military considerations,
in addition to economic and diplomatic interests, play an important
role in official South African policy-making in the area.

DE BEER, DAVID, see no. 794.

776. DUIGNAN, PETER and L.H. GANN. South West Africa - Namibia. New York:
American African Affairs Association, 1978, 37 p.

Apart from providing some basic background data on Namibia, this
booklet by two right wing US scholars is primarily concerned with
Namibia and SWAPO in the context of the Cold War. Its main asser-
tions are that a SWAPO victory would weaken the strategic position
of Western powers in the South Atlantic and that Namibia might become
a Soviet "client". In their assessment of SWAPO, which closely
follows the South African propaganda line, the authors maintain that
white communists were instrumental in launching the movement, that
the leaders of SWAPO are "poorly educated and unsophisticated" and
that SWAPO faces opposition from non-Ovambo population groups. They
conclude that a Namibia led by DTA would be the best solution
for Western interests, but that its chances - "unfortunately" - are
not good.

777. DU PISANI, ANDRÉ. "Namibia: the search for alternatives". South
Africa International, July 1981: 292-302.

778. ------- "Prospects for an international settlement". In Perspectives
on Namibia: past and present, edited by Christopher Saunders,
p. 128-37. Cape Town: Centre for African Studies, University of
Cape Town, 1983.

779. ------- "Namibia: the quest for legitimacy". <u>Politeia</u>, 2, no. 1,
     1983: 43-51.

780. ------- "The Namibian enigma: variations on a theme". <u>Indicator
     South Africa</u>, 1, no. 1, 1983: 22-26.

     Written by a prominent political scientist with a Namibian background
     (see nos. 282-83), this set of articles assesses diplomatic and politi-
     cal developments in the two years following the abortive Geneva
     conference in January 1981. According to the author, the conference
     was "another opportunity for South Africa to demonstrate the
     inability of the West to bring pressure to bear on it to relinquish
     its control over the international territory of Namibia". He
     also suggests that the electoral vulnerability, the internal frag-
     mentation and the crisis of legitimacy of the DTA have been important
     factors in explaining why South Africa acquiescence in the UN peace
     plan has not been forthcoming. His conclusion is that the prospects
     for a settlement have been improved by the downturn of the South
     African economy, the escalating costs in defence spending, and
     the need of the Frontline States for a settlement because of their
     tremendous suffering from South African destabilisation and
     military operations. On the other hand, he notes that
     Pretoria seems to want to avoid an outright SWAPO victory and that
     there is a fear that Namibian independence will lead to a radicalisa-
     tion of Black politics inside South Africa, coupled to stronger
     reactionary thinking amongst whites. See also: "SWA/Namibia update:
     1981 to April 1984", <u>Africa Insight</u>, 14, no. 3, 1984: 176-90.

     GANN, L.H., see no. 776.

781. GRUNDY, KENNETH W. <u>The rise of the South African security establish-
     ment. An essay on the changing locus of state power</u>. Braamfontein:
     The South African Institute of International Affairs, 1983, 39 p.
     (Bradlow Paper No. 1).

782. ------- <u>Soldiers without politics. Blacks in South African armed
     forces</u>. Berkeley: University of California Press, 1983, 297 p.

     Written by a US political scientist and authority on the role of
     the military in African affairs, this is a challenging and well-
     researched essay on the South African armed forces, "the security
     establishment" and the militarisation of domestic as well as foreign
     policy. Its main thesis is that the South African Defence Force
     and supporting institutions are active participants in decision-
     making at all levels, and that high-ranking SADF officials have
     come to occupy political and advisory positions close to the
     Prime Minister and the real centre of state power (the State
     Security Council). He also points to the heavy involvement of
     industry and the transnational corporations in the security estab-
     lishment. A special section of the essay is devoted to foreign
     policy, destabilisation and the regional dimension. The author
     argues that the Namibia war enhances the domination of the SADF in
     foreign policy and allows it a virtual veto over any settlement
     proposals, in reflection of which top SADF officers participate
     directly in the negotiating process. He also considers that the
     military men favour the view that the Republic can best be defended
     from forward positions, and that SADF wants to delay a settlement

that might lead to a SWAPO government. Recent developments, however, have clearly shown that there are forces within the military establishment who question the wisdom of a forward defence strategy and who would rather opt for a pull-out from Angola and for an "Orange river defence line". Soldiers without politics is a major study of the "africanisation" of sections of the SADF. It includes a separate chapter discussing the establishment of "tribal armies" and black commando units in Namibia ("The use of indigenous forces in Namibia", p. 249-72). The author concludes that this process prolongs the struggle and makes postwar settlement less stable and more bitter.

783. HOLNESS, MARGA. Apartheid's war against Angola. New York: Centre against Apartheid/Oslo: World Campaign against Military and Nuclear Collaboration with South Africa, 1983. 24 p.

The author's purpose is to document the extent to which the People's Republic of Angola has become the victim of South African aggression since 1975-76. Total damage is estimated to more than 10 billion US $, and has severely disrupted national reconstruction and development programmes. It is pointed out that Angola is in a strategic geographical position, has considerable mineral wealth and plays an important part in supporting the struggle for decolonisation and liberation in Namibia, a territory with which Angola shares an extensive border. The booklet has been translated into several languages, including German, Danish and Norwegian.

784. JENKINS, SIMON. "Destabilisation in Southern Africa". The Economist, 16 July 1983: 15-28.

A journalistic and well-informed review of the rise of South Africa as a "regional superpower", focusing on the military and economic destabilisation of the frontline states. A section of the survey is specifically concerned with the attacks against Angola and the occupation of Namibia. The author holds a pessimistic view of the future for South Africa's neighbours because of the strength of the apartheid regime, and consequently sees few possibilities for the independent states in the region to counter the political, economic and military power of the apartheid regime.

KNIGHT, DAVID B., see no. 770.

785. LEONARD, RICHARD. South Africa at war. White power and the crisis in Southern Africa. Westport, Connecticut: Lawrence Hill, 1983, 280 p.

This is an up-to-date, sharp and well written analysis of the militarisation of the South African society and the South African aggression against its neighbouring states. The book provides a detailed and careful examination of the transition from a police to a military state in South Africa, and pays close attention to regional destabilisation and "total strategy". There is also a wealth of material documenting the military and political collaboration with the major Western powers. The war in Namibia is dealt with in a separate chapter (p. 59-97), which places the continuing

occupation and military escalation within the context of South
Africa's regional strategy of control. The author is a journalist
associated with the American Committee on Africa and serves as a
consultant to the National Council of Churches.

786. LÖWIS OF MENAR, HENNING VON. Namibia im Ost-West-Konflikt, Köln:
Verlag Wissenschaft und Politik, Berend von Nottbeck, 1983, 176 p.
Bibl.: 175-76.

As suggested by its title, the purpose of this book is to examine
developments in Namibia in terms of the East-West conflict rather
than the illegal South African occupation, the apartheid system and
the right to self-determination. As such, it is a representative
example of a flourishing literature which depicts SWAPO as a
communist (especially East German) puppet. The author applauds
Prime Minister P.W. Botha for stating that South Africa would never
allow "the red flag to be hoisted in Windhoek", while the West
German government is accused of being "soft on communism" and
too eager to please SWAPO. The author is research fellow at the
Forschungsinstitut für Politische Wissenschaft und Europäische
Fragen der Universität zu Köln. For a similar - or even cruder -
approach, see, inter alia, Hans Germani: Rettet Südwest (Berlin/
München: Herbig Verlagsbuchhandlung, 1982, 188 p.), Fritz Sitte:
Schicksalsfrage Namibia (Graz/Wien/Köln: Verlag Styria, 1983,
235 p.) and Rüdiger H. Tronje: SWAPO. Die Geissel Südwest- Afrikas
(Berg am See: Vowinckel Verlag, 1983, 158 p.). For a critique
of the book by Löwis of Menar, see an article by Henning Melber
in Informationsdienst Südliches Afrika, no. 12, (December) 1983.
The books by Germani and Sitte are reviewed in the same magazine in
no. 7-8, (July-August) 1983.

787. LUTHERAN WORLD FEDERATION/WORLD COUNCIL OF CHURCHES. Documentation
on U.N. pre-implementation meeting on Namibia, Geneva, January 7-14,
1981. Geneva: LWF/WCC, 1981, 234 p.

A comprehensive compilation of c 60 documents which together explain
why the Geneva conference in 1981 failed. The documentation is
divided into five parts: official statements by UN representatives,
the South African Government and SWAPO; documents by official
observers; descriptions of church activity relevant to the conference
documents evaluating the result of the conference; and background
material.

788. MARCHAND, JACQUES. The French-Namibian connection. Paper presented
to the International Seminar on the Role of Transnational Corporation:
in Namibia, Washington, 1982, 14 p. (A section of the paper is
published as "Namibia and the Government of France", Africa Today,
30, nos. 1-2, 1983: 45-50).

The aim of this conference paper is to discuss French-Namibian
connections since the coming to power of a socialist government
in 1981, with special emphasis on the question of uranium imports
and processing as well as on the role of French corporations
operating in Namibia. Stating that it is as difficult as ever
to get information about contracts concerning Namibian uranium,

the author concludes that Namibian uranium is still arriving in
France, probably under a South African label. The absence of any
move towards applying sanctions is also noticed, and the plea is
made for a strengthening of the solidarity campaign run by
trade unions and the French Anti-Apartheid Movement. The author
is a past president of the Mouvement Anti-Apartheid of France.

789. MEINARDUS, RONALD. Die Afrikapolitik der Republik Südafrika. Von
der outwardlooking policy bis zur Gegenwart. Bonn: Informationsstelle Südliches Afrika, 1981, 491 p. Bibl.: 452-81. (ISSA –
Wissenschaftliche Reihe 15).

In what was originally a political science thesis, the author sets
out to describe and analyse South African economic control and
military destabilisation in the region as a whole. There are also
thoroughly-researched chapters on each country, paying attention
to political/diplomatic manoeuvres as well as economic strategy,
military aggression and the struggle for independence. Two chapters are devoted to Namibia, and there is also a comprehensive
bibliography.

790. MELBER, HENNING (ed.). Focus Federal Republic of Germany-Namibia.
Paper presented to the International Conference in Solidarity with
the Struggle of the People of Namibia, Paris, 1980, 29 p.

The aim of this conference paper, prepared by the Anti-Apartheid
Movement in the Federal Republic of Germany and West Berlin, is
to show that the FRG makes a considerable contribution to the
perpetuation of the colonial system in Namibia. The document
comprises four essays, covering relations in the economic and
military field (Wolff Geisler), the role of the pro-DTA German-
speaking pressure groups in Namibia and the FRG (Gottfried
Wellmer), cultural ties with special reference to the German
private schools in Namibia (Henning Melber), and church relations
(Peter Ripken).

ROGERS, BARBARA, see no. 773.

791. SANO, HANS-OTTO, et al. Namibia and the Nordic countries. Uppsala:
Scandinavian Institute of African Studies, 1981, 44 p.

This booklet by four research fellows at the Scandinavian Institute
of African Studies is the by-product of an international seminar
on "Namibia and the Nordic countries", outlining the positions
of the Nordic governments. The emphasis is on the debates in the
UN and on assistance towards the liberation of Namibia, including
assistance from solidarity groups and other non-governmental
organisations. There is also information on bilateral trade,
which is regarded as a support to the South African occupying
power. See also Eric Erichsen, et al.: Scandinavia and Namibia:
Policies and Actions (Washington: International Seminar on The
Role of Transnational Corporations in Namibia, 1982, 13 p.).

792. SEILER, JOHN and GERHARD TÖTEMEYER. "South West Africa/Namibia: a study in polarization and confrontation". In Southern Africa since the Portuguese coup, edited by John Seiler, p. 79-96. Boulder, Colorado: Westview Press, 1980.

793. SEILER, JOHN. "South Africa in Namibia: persistence, misperception and ultimate failure". The Journal of Modern African Studies, 20, no. 4, 1982: 689-712. (Also published in South Africa in Southern Africa, edited by T.M. Callaghy, p. 165-89. New York: Praeger, 1983).

The aim of the first of these two articles is to provide an overview of the Namibian political arena in the period following the Portuguese coup in 1974. The authors point out that the events in Portugal and the independence of Angola marked an important upturn in black Namibians' long-frustrated hopes for political independence, while at the same time making it easier for SWAPO to bring military pressure to bear on South Africa. They also, however, note the South African military build-up before and during the South African intervention in Angola, and that the South African Defence Force and Police have increasingly taken over the administration of northern Namibia. There is also a brief survey of the Turnhalle conference and the international negotiations, which leads the authors to conclude that the most likely course to be followed by South Africa is a kind of "internal solution". In the second article, John Seiler argues that the prospects for peaceful change have been ebbing during the Reagan administration. He finds the main reasons for this state of affairs in the "incorrect perceptions" of the US, the failure of the South African government to provide an alternative to SWAPO, and the "miscalculations" of the depth of African commitment to genuine independence. See also John Seiler: "Policy options in Namibia", Africa Report, 29, no. 2, 1984: 61-63. The author was in 1984 visiting professor, U.S. Army's John F. Kennedy Warfare Center, Fort Bragg, N.C.

794. SHIPPING RESEARCH BUREAU. Oil and tanker interests that facilitate the exploitation of Namibia's natural resources. Amsterdam: Shipping Research Bureau, 1984, 16 p. (Paper presented to UN Council for Namibia Seminar on the Activities of Foreign Economic Interests in the Exploitation of Namibia's Natural and Human Resources, Ljubljana, Yugoslavia, 16-20 April 1984).

Founded in 1980 by two Netherlands-based anti-apartheid groups, the principal purpose of the Shipping Research Bureau is to conduct in-depth research on the means whereby South Africa is circumventing the oil embargo. This seminar paper argues that oil keeps South Africa's illegal occupation of Namibia operative, and that without a constant flow of petroleum products and petrochemicals, the exploitation and export of Namibia's natural resources would soon come to a halt. It shows that about 9000-12,500 barrels per day of petroleum are shipped to Walvis Bay by the major oil companies operating in South Africa (Shell & BP, Caltex, Mobil, Total and SASOL), in addition to petrochemicals and high value petroleum products shipped to Namibia almost exclusively from Europe (70%) and the Far East (20%). The study also lists the shipping and tanker companies responsible for the oil transport to South Africa and

Namibia as well as the oil companies known to have sold most of the
crude oil to South Africa for refining. The paper ends with a set
of recommendations for actions to be taken by governments, trade
unions, non-governmental organisations and the UN Council for
Namibia to implement sanctions, to monitor Southern African ports
and to publish lists of tankers and of companies involved in oil
deliveries to South Africa and Namibia.

795. SOLANDER, JOHAN (ed.). Namibia - negotiations and "elections".
Stockholm: SIDA, 1979, 47 p. (In Swedish: Förhandlingar och
"val" i Namibia. Stockholm: SIDA, 1979).

This is a succinct survey of the international negotiations and
the South African efforts to hold an "election" in Namibia in
1978. The main text, written by Justin Ellis (see no. 285), is
supplemented by a compilation of the most relevant UN and other
documents.

796. SOUTH AFRICA (REP.). South West Africa. Basic documents. 30 January
1976 to 2 May 1979. Cape Town: Department of Foreign Affairs,
279 p.

This substantial collection of documents and political statements,
compiled by the Department of Foreign Affairs, covers an important
period of recent diplomatic history. Among the 69 documents are
several exchanges of letters between the South African government
and the United Nations, which clearly demonstrate the South African
unwillingness to accept the UN peace plan. Included are also a
large number of UN resolutions and statements from SWAPO, Namibia
National Front and the "Constituent Assembly of South West Africa".

797. STOKKE, OLAV and CARL WIDSTRAND (eds.). Southern Africa. The UN-OAU
Conference, Oslo 9-14 April 1974. Uppsala: Scandinavian Institute
of African Studies, 1973. Vol. I: Programme of action and conference proceedings, 275 p. Vol. II: Papers and documents, 346 p.

This collection of conference proceedings and papers from the Oslo
Conference in 1973 reflects the growing international concern in
the early 1970s with the apartheid system and South Africa's
illegal occupation of Namibia. There are several references to
Namibia in both volumes, and a special section in vol. 2 (p. 97-136)
contains papers by SWAPO, Elizabeth Landis and Barbara Rogers
on the liberation struggle, the legal aspects of the conflict and
economic exploitation.

798. SWAPO. WESTERN EUROPE OFFICE (ed.). U.S. State Department documents
on Southern Africa leaked to American press. May-June 1981. London,
1981, 28 p.

The documents contained in this booklet, which were leaked to the
press and reproduced by SWAPO, reflect the extent to which the US
administration is willing to cooperate with the South African regime
in subverting the UN plan for elections and independence in Namibia.
They also show that Southern Africa is regarded as a key arena of
the cold war. The collection of documents consists of a "memorandum

of conversations" based on the talks between Assistant Secretary
of State for Africa, Chester Crocker and top South African officials
in Pretoria in April 1981 as well as background papers prepared for
the visit of the South African Foreign Minister to Washington in
May the same year.

TÖTEMEYER, GERHARD, see no. 792.

799. TRANSAFRICA. Namibia. The crisis in United States policy toward
Southern Africa. Washington: TransAfrica, 1983, 49 p.

Reproduced by TransAfrica and 23 other non-governmental organisations
in the United States, this booklet describes itself as "a story of
a failed effort of five Western nations to compel South Africa to
live up to norms of international law and conduct". It provides a
critical survey of the negotiations in the 1976–1982 period, arguing
that the Reagan administration has encouraged the hostile position
of South Africa, and proposes, specifically, that the US should remove
the issue of the Cuban presence in Angola from the negotiations for
Namibian independence. The appendices contain several UN and
SWAPO documents. The booklet is also distributed as a UN Security
Council document (S/15781/23 May/1983).

800. UNITED NATIONS COUNCIL FOR NAMIBIA. "The continuing economic exploitation and militarization of Namibia". Objective: Justice, 14, no. 1,
(April) 1982: 20–39.

The Standing Committee II of the UN Council for Namibia has been
mandated to recommend policies to counter the support given to
foreign economic interests operating in Namibia to the illegal South
African administration, and to consider the nature and scale of
South Africa's military installations and operations in Namibia.
Excerpts from two recent reports of the committee are reprinted in
this article, serving as a brief introduction to the wealth of
evidence gathered by the Council on these two important subjects.

801. UNITED NATIONS COUNCIL FOR NAMIBIA. Report of the delegation of
the Council to the seminar on the military situation in and relating
to Namibia, held at Vienna from 8 to 11 June 1982. New York: United
Nations, 1982, 30 p. (A/AC.131/L.268, 9 November 1982).

For the purpose of obtaining information on South Africa's increasing
militarisation of Namibia, on military and strategic collaboration
with South Africa, on the involvement of mercenaries, and on the
attempts to destabilise other African states, the UN Council for
Namibia held a seminar in June 1982. The report of its delegation
offers a concise summary of the papers presented and the information
given by the expert participants. The final section reproduced the
conclusions and recommendations adopted for submission to the
Council. See also the extensive verbatim records of the seminar,
which together amount to approx. 300 pages. (A/AC.131/SMS/PV. 1-7,
21 July – 27 July 1982).

802. UNITED NATIONS COUNCIL FOR NAMIBIA. The military situation in and
relating to Namibia. New York: UN, Department of Public Information,
1983, 25 p.

In recent years, South Africa's increasing use of military force to
suppress popular resistance in Namibia and to destabilise neighbouring
countries has been a cause of grave concern to the international
community. The present report, now available as a booklet,
focuses on the events in 1982-83, and is partly based on the testimonies and documents presented to a UN Council seminar at Vienna
in June 1982. The booklet highlights the South African military
build-up in Namibia, the introduction of compulsory military service
and "tribal armies", the recruitment of mercenaries, and the use
of Namibia as a launching pad for acts of subversion and aggression
against neighbouring states. An annex lists Security Forces bases
and units permanently stationed in Namibia.

803. UNITED NATIONS COUNCIL FOR NAMIBIA. Political developments related
to Namibia. Paper presented to the International Conference in
Support of the Struggle of the Namibian People for Independence,
Paris, 1983, 26 p. (A/Conf. 120/7. A/AC. 131/94, 31 March 1983).

The purpose of this UN report is to provide a review of the major
political developments since the UN General Assembly terminated
South Africa's mandate and assumed direct responsibility for the
Territory in 1966. The report begins with a survey of the events which
led to the Security Council Res. 435/78, and then discusses the
efforts to implement the UN peace plan. The next section deals with
the current situation in Namibia, with emphasis on the continued
illegal occupation, the acts of aggression against Angola, the
intensification of the struggle of the Namibian people and the
activities of the international community. The final part is concerned with the Western attempts to modify and obstruct the UN
plan, especially by bringing in extraneous questions such as the
presence of Cuban forces in Angola.

804. UNITED STATES, HOUSE OF REPRESENTATIVES. Critical developments in
Namibia. Hearings before the Subcommittee on Africa of the Committee
of Foreign Affairs, 93 Congress, second session, 21 February +
4 April 1974. Washington: US Government Printing Office, 1974, 300 p.

805. ------- Namibia: the United Nations and U.S. policy. Hearings before
the Subcommittee on International Organisations of the Committee
on International Relations, 94 Congress, second session, 24 and 27
August 1976. Washington: U.S. Government Printing Office, 1976,
223 p.

806. ------- Resources in Namibia: implications for U.S. policy. Hearings
before the Subcommittee on International Resources, Food and Energy
of the Committee on International Relations. Washington: US
Government Printing Office, 1976, 165 p.

807. ------- Namibian update. Hearing before the Subcommittee on Africa
of the Committee on Foreign Affairs, 96 Congress, second session,
9 September 1980. Washington: U.S. Government Printing Office,
1981, 39 p.

808. ------- Regional destabilization in Southern Africa. Hearing before the Subcommittee on Africa of the Committee on Foreign Affairs. Washington: U.S. Government Printing Office, 1982, 175 p.

809. ------- United States policy toward Southern Africa. Focus on Namibia, Angola, and South Africa. Hearing and markup before the Subcommittee on Africa of the Committee on Foreign Affairs. Washington: U.S. Government Printing Office, 1983, 61 p.

These six comprehensive reports of important US hearings on Namibia and Southern Africa contain a wealth of material on US policies, developments inside Namibia, the role of foreign companies, international law and the liberation struggle. Included are numerous testimonies and statements prepared by government officials as well as by individual experts and representatives of the liberation movement and US organisations working for peace and independence in Namibia. There is also valuable statistical material, covering, inter alia, US trade and investments in the region.

UNITED STATES, STATE DEPARTMENT, see no. 798.

810. UYS, STANLEY. "Namibia: the socialist dilemma". African Affairs, 81, no. 325, (October) 1982: 569-76.

This brief article is the text of a talk given to a joint meeting of the Royal African Society and the Royal Commonwealth Society in April 1982, based on the two assumptions that there will be a settlement in Namibia and that SWAPO would win the resulting elections. The author spells out the constraints that would operate on a SWAPO government in a country which has been administered as a fifth province and a tightly controlled economic colony, and argues that these circumstances will impel SWAPO towards compromise and pragmatic decisions. The author is London Editor of the South African Morning Newspaper Group. See also no. 67.

811. VESPER, MICHAEL. Über die Beziehungen zwischen der Bundesrepublik Deutschland und Namibia. Bonn: Informationsstelle Südliches Afrika, 1980, 12 p. (ISSA Archiv Aktuell, No. 19).

Summarising the economic and political relations between the Federal Republic of Germany and Namibia, this brief pamphlet focuses mainly on the support given to the Democratic Turnhalle Alliance (DTA) in the late 1970s by German business groups and political organisations.

812. WALTERS, RONALD W. "The United States and the Southern African-Namibian uranium options". Africa Today, 30, no. 1&2, 1983: 51-59.

In an article in 1978 ("Uranium Politics and U.S. Foreign Policy in Southern Africa", Journal of Southern African Affairs, 4, no. 3, 1979: 281-300), the author argued that there was a growing interdependence between US and Namibia, based on the urgent problems of energy and the availability of uranium reserves at favourable prices in Namibia. In this more recent article he suggests that the "option" has now become a chosen strategy. He argues that US demand for foreign-source uranium is increasingly being supplied by "South African" sources which undoubtedly include Namibian uranium, and

concludes that all dealings with South Africa - including enrichment
of raw uranium for re-export to South Africa for domestic end-use -
should therefore be prohibited. The author is professor of
political science, Howard University, Washington.

WIDSTRAND, CARL, see no. 797.

813. WOOD, BRIAN and ANNE HUDSON. "Namibia: behind the diplomatic
charade". <u>Journal of African Marxists</u>, no. 4, (September) 1983:
79-83.

Written by two authors associated with the Namibia Support Committee
(London), this article gives a critical assessment of the role of
the Western Contact Group and discusses the peculiarities of
Namibia's colonial heritage and struggle for independence. It
argues that the members of the Contact Group have worked out their
plans in accordance with the interests of the South African regime
as well as their own economic stake, but that a neo-colonial solution
is most unlikely given the strength of SWAPO and the weaknesses of
the tiny black petty bourgeoisie. See also Brian Wood: "Impasse in
Namibia", <u>Marxism Today</u>, July 1983: 25-8.

WORLD COUNCIL OF CHURCHES, see no. 787.

SEE ALSO:

3, 4, 11, 12, 14, 15, 17, 20, 21, 34, 36, 37, 41, 42, 43, 54, 56,
58, 61, 64, 66, 68, 71, 72, 74, 80, 110, 303, 304, 353, 421, 429,
443, 577, 593, 599, 601, 604, 605, 613, chapter 12 a(723-63), 835,
837.

13. THE STRUGGLE FOR NATIONAL LIBERATION

A. African nationalism, SWAPO and the liberation movement

814. ANSPRENGER, FRANZ. Die SWAPO. Profil einer afrikanischen Befreiungs-bewegung. Bonn: Katholischer Arbeitskreis Entwicklung und Frieden, 1983, 160 + 11 + vi p. Bibl.: i-vi. (KAEF Arbeitspapier Dokumentation 31).

Commissioned by the West German Catholic Commission for Justice and Peace, this is one of the very few serious attempts to discuss the history and political development of SWAPO from outside. The author, a political scientist who has written extensively on the process of decolonisation and liberation in Africa, has made use of a wide range of SWAPO documents as well as secondary literature. The first part gives a brief background to the situation in Namibia in 1983, partly based on a visit to the territory, and leaves little doubt that the majority are likely to vote for SWAPO if the opportun-ity is ever offered. It is followed by an outline of SWAPO's his-tory, with considerable emphasis on the Tanga Conference in 1969 and the 1975-76 conflict inside the movement. This part of the study reflects a lack of familiarity with the mobilisation and struggle undertaken by SWAPO under severe repression inside Namibia, and there are few attempts to understand Namibian society in terms of class forces. The discussion of the political profile of SWAPO also takes place in a social vacuum, and is mainly pre-sented as a conventional content analysis of the official documents. The final part concentrates on international negotiations, arguing that SWAPO has demonstrated a high degree of flexibility, while South Africa - in collusion with the Reagan administration in the United States - has prevented the implementation of Res. 435/78. A revised version of the working paper is expected to be published in 1984.

815. BARNARD, W.S. "Die geografie van 'n revolusionêre oorlog: SWAPO in Suidwes-Afrika", South African Geographer, 10, no. 2, 1982: 157-74.

This study, undertaken by a University of Stellenbosch academic and author of a major general geography of Namibia (see no. 83), is one of the relatively few attempts at scholarly analysis of the liberation struggle from a pro-South African perspective amongst the flood of simplistic propaganda. Employing McColl's three-stage typology of armed revolutionary change and a rather eclectic comparative framework, the author assesses the development of the war from both a geographical and a logistical perspective, and concludes that SWAPO stands little chance of a purely military victory. Familiar stereotypes of PLAN "terrorists" and SWAPO's "dictatorial" political practice and "tribalist" base amply express the author's hostility to the liberation movement, but he does at least concede that SWAPO has majority political support.

816. BRAGANÇA, AQUINO DE and IMMANUEL WALLERSTEIN (eds.). The African liberation reader. Documents of the national liberation movements. London: Zed Press, 1982. Vol. 1: The anatomy of colonialism, 202 p. Vol. 2: The national liberation movements, 196 p. Vol. 3: The strategy of liberation, 219 p.

Originally published in Portuguese, this three-volume work brings together many of the key documents of the liberation movements in Southern Africa and Guinea-Bissau. It provides a valuable introduction to the history of the armed struggle for national liberation in the words of the protagonists themselves. The reader contains material up to 1974. The three volumes are thematically organised and each section has an introduction by the editors. The selection reflects the editors' intimate knowledge of the former Portuguese colonies, and SWAPO is surprisingly under-documented. The work does, however, make it easier to understand the Namibian struggle as part of the broad movement to liberate Southern Africa from minority rule, racism and exploitation.

817. CULLINAN, SUE. "SWAPO and the anti-colonial struggle". Work in Progress, no. 23, 1982: 27-43.

This is a straightforward account of the history of SWAPO since the late 1950s, opening with a discussion of the origins of the movement among the contract workers. It shows how disillusionment with the international community led to preparations for armed struggle, and how SWAPO was able to broaden its base in the 1970s in spite of severe suppression by the apartheid regime. The author concludes by suggesting that awareness of the grassroots support for SWAPO is one of the main reasons for South Africa's unwillingness to accept the UN plan for independence. See also nos. 14-15.

818. DALE, RICHARD. African insurgency and German and South African counterinsurgency in Namibia in 1904-1907 and 1922: legacies for African nationalism and protracted guerrilla warfare. Southern Illinois University, Department of political science, 1982, 37 p.

Delivered to a conference on Namibia at the University of Vermont in April 1982, this discussion paper makes a plea for a comparative study of insurgency and counterinsurgency. The author's main preoccupation is to show the discontinuities between the "rebellions"

in the first part of the century and the present guerrilla warfare.
He argues that in contrast to the former campaigns, waged in an era
that glorified imperial rule, the "insurgents" today enjoy a degree
of legitimacy and that SWAPO, as the de facto government-in-exile,
is in a position to negotiate for funds, military hardware, diplomatic
protection and technical assistance. It is also noted that in
the present situation the churches are more openly antagonistic to
the civil and military authorities than their mission forebears. In
an earlier article, the author has surveyed the political history
of the South African Defence Force in Namibia from 1914 to 1979, see:
"The armed forces as an instrument of South African policy in
Namibia", Journal of Modern African Studies, 18, no. 1, 1980: 57-71.

819. EMMETT, ANTHONY BRIAN. The rise of nationalism in Namibia, 1915-1966.
University of the Witwatersrand, PhD thesis, In preparation.

GEINGOB, GOTTFRIED H., see no. 821.

820. GIBSON, RICHARD. African liberation movements. Contemporary
struggles against white minority rule. London: Oxford University
Press, 1982, 350 p. (Published for the Institute of Race Relations).

The purported aim of this book is to give an overview of the liberation
struggle in Southern Africa in the 1960s. It includes a separate
chapter on Namibia (p. 107-141). After a brief introduction to
the country and the history of resistance against colonial rule,
a section which contains a number of inaccuracies, the author discusses the origins and activities of SWANU and SWAPO up to 1970.
The main focus is on personalities, ethnic rivalries, conflicts
between groups in exile and the Sino-Soviet split, while there is
vitually no attempt to relate the background of the movements and
the development of the struggle to socio-economic conditions
and the social forces at play in Namibia. There is not, for instance,
a single reference to the migrant labour system or to working class
support for SWAPO. Although some of the detail is of apparent
interest, the author presents few means of verification. In general,
the narrow and distorted political perspective and the factual
errors rule this chapter out as a serious historical interpretation
or reliable source.

821. HAMUTENYA, HIDIPO L. and GOTTFRIED H. GEINGOB. "African nationalism
in Namibia". In Southern Africa in perspective. Essays on regional
politics, edited by Christian P. Potholm and Richard Dale, p. 85-94.
New York: The Free Press/London: Collier-MacMillan, 1972.

This early account of the origins of Namibian nationalism and the
rise of the liberation movement SWAPO, is an important document
of the Namibian liberation struggle. Written by two scholars and
prominent members of SWAPO's leadership, it provided from within
the liberation movement an authoritative strategic analysis and
overview, whose influence is reflected in later SWAPO publications
in the 1970s. Although brief, the analysis is precise and coherent,
and is supplemented by comments on pre-colonial history designed
to refute the colonialist mythology of endemic ethnic conflict.

822. HARNEIT, AXEL. SWAPO of Namibia - Entwicklung, Programmatik und Politik seit 1959. Hamburg: Institut für Afrika-Kunde, 1985. In preparation.

823. KILJUNEN, KIMMO. "National resistance and the liberation struggle". In Namibia. The last colony, edited by Reginald H. Green, Marja-Liisa Kiljunen and Kimmo Kiljunen, p. 145-71. London: Longman, 1981.

A brief presentation of the history of the struggle against colonial rule from the early resistance in the late 19th century to the armed struggle for national independence in the 1960s and 1970s. It has its value as a descriptive rather than analytical account. The discussion of SWAPO's ideology is further developed by the author in another article in the same book: "The ideology of national liberation", p. 183-95.

824. LIBERATION SUPPORT MOVEMENT (ed.). Namibia: SWAPO fights for freedom. Oakland, California: LSM Information Center, 1978, 124 p.

This is a valuable collection of a variety of documents and interviews on SWAPO and the liberation struggle, put together with the goal of conveying some of the perspectives and experiences of people who have dedicated their lives to the fight for an independent Namibia. The book opens with extended interviews with the President of SWAPO, the Political Commissar of the People's Liberation Army of Namibia (PLAN), and two women militants, followed by a first-hand account of the beginning of the strike in 1971 by Hinanjane Shafodino Nehova (no. 670). The final section reproduces several important SWAPO documents. Much of the material appeared originally in LSM News, nos. 11-12. (October) 1976.

825. MERCER, DENIS. Andreas Shipanga. Richmond, B.C.: Liberation Support Movement Information Center, 1973, 27 p. (Interviews in depth: Namibia, 1).

At the time of this interview Andreas Shipanga, a founder member of SWAPO who was later expelled and returned to Namibia to start one of the small "internal parties" (see nos. 850-51), was still SWAPO Secretary for Information. The interview covers a wide range of topics, and is a valuable source on the origins of SWAPO in the late 1950s, the decision to prepare for armed struggle, the role played by SWAPO in the general strike of 1971-72, and the position of women in the liberation struggle.

826. NUJOMA, SAM. "The state of the liberation struggle". In Namibia. The last colony, edited by Reginald H. Green, Marja-Liisa Kiljunen and Kimmo Kiljunen, p. 172-82. London: Longman, 1981.

This is an authoritative statement on the liberation struggle in Namibia, conducted in the form of an interview in 1979. In it, the president of SWAPO reviews the recent history of the political and military struggle, outlines the social basis and the ideology of SWAPO and discusses the most urgent problems to be solved in an independent Namibia. For another extensive interview with Sam Nujoma, see no. 824.

SHIPANGA, ANDREAS, see no. 825.

827. SOUTH WEST AFRICA PEOPLE'S ORGANISATION. Discussion paper on the constitution of independent Namibia. Lusaka ?: 1975, 12 p.

This is an informal discussion paper, the aim of which was to stimu-late informed discussion on the constitutional future of Namibia. It was circulated to coincide with the opening of South Africa's "Turnhalle Constitutional Conference". The proposals include a Bill of Rights, eradiction of all forms of racialism and ethnic fragmentation and an electoral system based on majority voting in numerically equal constituencies. The document has been widely reproduced, but has not the status of an official SWAPO position paper.

828. SOUTH WEST AFRICA PEOPLE'S ORGANISATION (SWAPO). Constitution of the South West Africa People's Organisation. Lusaka: SWAPO Dept. for Publicity and Information, 1976, 35 p.

829. ------- Political program of the South West Africa People's Organisa-tion. Lusaka: SWAPO Dept. for Publicity and Information, 1976, 14 p.

These two major SWAPO documents were both adopted by the augmented Central Committee at its politically vital meeting in Lusaka from 27 July to 1 August 1976. The Constitution outlines the aims and objectives of SWAPO, the conditions for membership, the organisational structure and the duties and functions of the National Officers. The Program opens with a brief survey of SWAPO's history, and then moves on to a presentation of the major policy principles on foreign relations, the armed struggle, economic reconstruction, education and culture, and health and social services.

830. SOUTH WEST AFRICA PEOPLE'S ORGANISATION (SWAPO). Information on SWAPO. An Historical Profile. Lusaka: SWAPO Dept. of Information and Publicity, 1978, 31 p.

831. ------- Information on the people's resistance 1976-1977. Lusaka: SWAPO Dept. of Information and Publicity, 1978, 28 p.

832. ------- Information on Namibian political prisoners. Lusaka: SWAPO Dept. of Information and Publicity, 1978, 42 p.

833. ------- Laws governing the Namibian people's revolution. Lusaka: SWAPO Dept. of Information and Publicity, 1978, 55 p.

834. ------- Conference reports 1976-1977. Lusaka: SWAPO Dept. of Publicity and Information, 1978, 45 p.

These five booklets, some of them illustrated, were all published in the same year as a part of a concerted publicity compaign by SWAPO. The first three provide a brief, clear history of the liberation struggle, a detailed account of the politically critical years 1976-77 and a hard-hitting description of political repression in Namibia, including a list of known political prisoners and letters from Robben Island. Laws Governing... consists of four "revolutionary decrees" adopted by the Central Committee on 24 September 1977. Conference reports... provides information on three important SWAPO

conferences in 1976-77, which reorganised the party machinery and
revised the Constitution and the Political Programme. (National
Congress, Walvis Bay, 29-31 May 1976; the enlarged meeting of the
Central Committee, Lusaka, 28 July - 2 August 1976; Central Committee,
Lubango, 21-24 September 1977).

835. SOUTH WEST AFRICA PEOPLE'S ORGANISATION (SWAPO). "Namibia's independence held ransom: SWAPO memorandum submitted to the 7th Conference
of the Heads of State/Government of Non-Aligned Countries, New Dehli,
7th-11th March 1983". SWAPO Information Bulletin, (March) 1983:
6-20.

This is a representative statement by SWAPO, reviewing the continued
South African illegal occupation of Namibia, the state of the
liberation struggle and the role of the international community. The
report concludes that the year 1983 will go down in the history of
the Namibian independence struggle as yet another year of sacrifice,
and urges the non-aligned movement to remain firm in its rejection
of the US/South African attempt to impose a "linkage" between the
Namibian question and the withdrawal of Cuban troops from Angola.

836. SWAPO YOUTH LEAGUE. The manifesto of the SWAPO youth to the Namibian
people. 1971, 28 p. (German edition: Manifest der SWAPO-Jugend
an das namibische Volk. Hamburg: Redaktion Harambee, 1971, 28 p.).

Although principally a political tract and a call to arms, this
pamphlet, powerfully written despite its rough-hewn, ungrammatical
English, develops an original critique of South African colonial
rule from the perspective of radical political economy, one of the
earliest to originate from the ranks of the liberation movement.
Composed shortly after SWAPO's crucial party congress (at Tanga,
Tanzania) at the turn of the decade, at which the Youth League itself
was formed, it predates the World Court ruling of June 1971, the
1971-2 contract worker's strike, and SWAPO's 1976 Political Programme, and prefigures the inspiring and courageous leadership of
the Youth League during the early 1970s in the struggle inside Namibia.

837. UDUGO, EMMANUEL IKE. South West Africa People's Organization of
Namibia as a non-state actor in the Namibian issue. Southern Illinois
University at Carbondale, 1980, 184 p. Bibl.: 163-74 p.
(PhD thesis).

This thesis is an attempt to study SWAPO as a "non-state actor",
offering a brief assessment of the role of SWAPO in the political,
diplomatic and military struggle for independence. It opens with
a survey of the South African strategy for maintaining control,
followed by a rather sketchy description of SWAPO's formation,
structure and actions. Although the thesis is at times inaccurate
and superficial, it is a welcome contribution to the very sparse
literature on the liberation movement.

WALLERSTEIN, IMMANUEL, see no. 816.

838. YA-OTTO, JOHN. Battlefront Namibia. An autobiography. New York:
Lawrence Hill & Co./London: Heinemann, 1981, 151 p. (With Ole
Gjerstad and Michael Mercer).

John Ya-Otto is the present SWAPO Secretary for Labour, and this book
is a personal account of his life and struggle against South African
occupation and oppression of the Namibian people. The autobiography
is based on a mass of taped conversations in 1975-76, and demonstrates
clearly why so many Namibians have been drawn into the liberation
struggle. The book contains several chapters of historical interest,
such as the first-hand account of the Windhoek massacre in 1959 which
led many Namibians into nationalist politics. Ya-Otto's life
story also exposes the brutality of the South African regime in
suppressing SWAPO and its supporters. Trained as a teacher, Ya-Otto
was arrested and tortured on several occasions, and was eventually
persuaded to leave Namibia to continue his work for SWAPO in exile.
For a Dutch translation, see: Frontlijn Namibie (Leuven: 1982,
179 p.).

SEE ALSO:

3, 4, 10, 11, 17, 22, 29, 30, 33, 36, 37, 38, 40, 41, 42, 43, 45,
49, 50, 51, 52, 53, 54, 57, 63, 73, 74, 245, 293, 312, 356, 367, 604,
647, 663, 669, 670, 676, 682-4, 685, 686, 687, 688, 689, 695, 699,
704, 765, 797, 853, 854, 857, 858, 860, 862, 867, 918, 981, 1014, 1024.

B.   Other political organisations

839. ABRAHAMS, KENNETH. "The Reverend Peter Kalangula and the failure of reformism". The Namibian Review, no. 24, (May) 1982: 1-19.

840. ------- "The 'Waserauta' phenomenon. Additional notes on the Namibian elite". The Namibian Review, no. 25, (July-August) 1982: 21-31.

Written by the editor of The Namibian Review, who is also a prominent member of the small National. Independence Party, these two articles contribute to the debate on the origins and functioning of the Namibian elite. The first article focuses mainly on the role played by Rev. Peter Kalangula, a former DTA leader who in 1982 established his own ethnic party in Ovamboland (see no. 841). The second article is a stimulating discussion of the emergence of the "Waserauta" (a corruption of the word "sell-out"), the size of this group, its elite income and its political significance in contemporary Namibia.

BEAVON, K.S.O., see no. 849.

841. CHRISTIAN DEMOCRATIC ACTION. Constitution of the Christian Demo-cratic Action for Social Justice. 1982, 18 p.

In 1982 Peter Kalangula, leader of the bantustan authority in Ovamboland, left the Democratic Turnhalle Alliance (DTA) and established his own party. The main part of this document consists of the constitution of CDA, but there is also a brief section outlining the general aims and the principles of the party. Among the goals of the party are an independent Namibia which will main-tain close ties with all its neighbours, "consensus by means of consultation and exchange of ideas with all interested groups", free enterprise and "a prosperous and satisfied population".

842. DTA. Demokratiese Turnhalle Alliansie/Democratic Turnhalle Alliance. Windhoek, 1978 (?), 35 p.

This is probably the most representative policy document published by DTA. It opens with the constitution and a list of members of the Alliance, followed by a reproduction of the Constitutional Principles for "the Republic of South West Africa/Namibia", as accepted by the Turnhalle Conference (see no. 308). A brief list of very general economic principles, adopted by the founding meeting of DTA, is also included. The principles are based on "the maximum economic participation by private initiative" and "the encouragement of foreign investment through incentives and security measures". The document is also available in German (DTA Grundsatz) and in Afrikaans (Konstitusie van die DTA).

843. DU PLESSIS, A.H. Nine questions about South West = Neun Fragen über Südwest = Nege vrae oor Suidwes. Windhoek: The National Party of South West Africa, 1979/80 (?), 30 p.

Written by the then chairman and senior leader of the SWA National Party, this document is a representative expression of the party's views on the key political issues, which have often been opposed to South Africa's "reformist" colonialism of recent years. The booklet outlines the kind of "independence" acceptable to the National Party, rejects Security Council Resolution 435/1978 as a basis for negotiations and reaffirms the principles of the Turnhalle draft constitution of 1977.

844. INTERESSENGEMEINSCHAFT DEUTSCHSPRACHIGER SÜDWESTER (IG). Inter-essengemeinschaft Deutschprachiger Südwester (IG). Windhoek, 1982, 24 p.

The purpose of this booklet is to present the objectives and activities of the Interessengemeinschaft Deutschsprachiger Südwester, which was formed in 1977 as a political, social and cultural forum for the German-speaking community. The guidelines make it clear that the IG regards a "free market economy" and the protection of the rights of the German-speaking community to be among the main pillars of an independent Namibia. The booklet also contains three brief articles on the Namibian economy and the constitutional development of Namibia (1884-1981). The document was published before the recent efforts by IG to seek an understanding with the liberation movement and to distance itself further from the South African occupying regime.

845. LEVINE, VICTOR (ed.). Encyclopedia of African Political Parties. Westport, Connecticut/London: Greenwood Press. (Contains a section on Namibia, prepared by John J. Grotpeter). In preparation.

846. NAMIBIA NATIONAL FRONT. Policy manifestos and alternatives. Windhoek: NNF, 1978, 16 p.

This interesting political document emanated from the short-lived attempt to form a "moderate and centrist" coalition in Namibia. The main purpose of the Namibian National Front (N.N.F.), which was set up as an umbrella organisation of independent parties and groups such as the National Independence Party, Federal Party, SWANU, and the Damara Council, was to contest the independence elections which were expected to take place in 1978. The pamphlet opens with a series of attacks on SWAPO on the left as well as on the DTA, the National Party and the Herstigte Nasionale Party on the right, followed by N.N.F.'s own policy declaration. The manifesto is mainly concerned with constitutional and economic principles, and states that "private economic initiative may be exercised freely,

subject to measures against unhealthy monopolistic conditions", and
that "the right of everyone to private property, and to transfer
the same during life or at death shall be guaranteed". Although
it declares a commitment to the fair distribution of wealth as a
major goal, the manifesto is strongly geared to business interests.
The document is also published in German (Das Manifest und die
Alternative) as well as in Afrikaans (Beleids- manifesto en Alternatie-
ve).

847. NAMIBIAN CHRISTIAN DEMOCRATIC PARTY. N.C.D.P. Program and aim.
Windhoek/Tsumeb, (n.d.). 13 p.

A brief presentation of the political views of the N.C.D.P. This
small political grouping, led by Hans Röhr, regards itself as belonging
to the "centre" in the Namibian political spectrum. According to
the guidelines, N.C.D.P. favours an independent and sovereign
Namibia, a democratic party system based on "Christian principles",
a free market economy and the forming of a broad middle class. The
pamphlet was written in the early 1980s, and the party has since
moved to the left in white Namibian terms. In 1983/84 N.C.D.P.
exposed the terror and violence inflicted upon the civilian population,
especially in Kavangoland, walked out of the "Multi-Party Conference",
and endorsed the UN peace plan (Res. 435/78).

848. O'LINN, BRYAN. Die Zukunft Südwestafrikas in realistischer Sicht.
Windhoek: Meinert, 1975 (?), 200 p.

Written by a leading Windhoek lawyer, this is primarily a liberal
plea for an independent Namibia and a political compromise to
avoid what is described as a catastrophic and violent confrontation
between whites and blacks. The book outlines the history of the
international dispute over Namibia, as well as the social and
economic structure. It concludes by presenting the political and
constitutional ideas of the Federal Party, which was founded in 1975
with O'Linn as its chairperson, after the demise of the old United
Party. The book is an updated and revised version of a publication
which first appeared in Afrikaans: Die toekoms van Suidwes-Afrika
gebou op die werklikheid (Windhoek: Verenigde Pers, 1974, 127 p.).

PIRIE, G.H., see no. 849.

849. ROGERSON, C.M., K.S.O. BEAVON and G.H. PIRIE. "The geography of
the Afrikaner Broederbond in Namibia". Social Dynamics, 5, no. 2,
1979: 13-17.

This is a brief but original contribution to the discussion of the
forms and extent of "white power" in Namibia. Documenting the
growth and composition of the Afrikaner Broederbond, the authors
argue that this class of "super-Afrikaners" is strongly represented
at all levels in the contemporary power structure in Namibia.
Broeder cells are located in nearly all the major concentrations
of white population, but are relatively strongest in the rural areas
and in the military zones in the north. The conclusion is that
the greatest opposition towards structural changes in the political
economy of Namibia will occur in the rural farming areas. Without

an unlikely volte-face in white attitudes or a likely exodus of
the farming community, the prospects for rural change and land
reforms are consequently rated as exceedingly low.

850. SWAPO-DEMOCRATS. Constitution of SWAPO-Democrats. Windhoek, (n.d.),
21 p.

851. ------- Basic documents. Windhoek, 1978, 22 p.

These two documents present the organisational structure and the
broad aims of "SWAPO-Democrats", a small political group which was
formed in 1978 by Andreas Shipanga, a SWAPO leader until his expulsion
in 1976. The documents are also available in German.

852. THE SOUTH WEST AFRICA NATIONAL UNION. Basic documents of the South
West Africa National Union. Stockholm: Pogo Print, 1976, 27 p.

This pamphlet consists of two important SWANU documents: the Constitution of SWANU and the Programme for the Liberation and Reconstruction of South West Africa (Namibia). The programme has few
details regarding economic policies, and reflects the revolutionary
rhetoric of the organisation at the time of its adoption (December
1974). SWANU later adopted a new political programme, but
this document has not yet (1983) been made public. The decision to
join the "Multi-Party Conference" caused a major split in the organisation, and a party congress in September 1984 elected a new leadership, withdrew from the MPC and decided to establish links of
cooperation with SWAPO.

SEE ALSO:

22, 34, 37, 46, 49, 73, 245, 304, 312, 765, 790, 918, 939, 947, 956.

C. The churches

853. (THE ANGLICAN CHURCH). Namibia. A report to the Archbishop of
Canterbury by the Anglican delegation after their visit of October
1983. London, 1984, 38 p.

In October 1983 an international delegation from the Anglican church
spent two weeks in Namibia with the purpose of reporting both to
the Archbishop of Canterbury and to the Archbishop of Cape Town.
The delegation spent six days in the northern war zone, visited
mission stations, met clergymen, teachers and community leaders,
and visited South African Defence Force (SADF) bases. The delegation also held discussions with the general managers of the three
major mining companies and met the South African Administrator-
General and his staff. The report contains a brief history of
Namibia, extracts from conversations, the conclusions of the dele-
gations, and its recommendations, as well as a documentary appendix.
Among the conclusions are that there is a desire among the majority
for the opportunity to be free of South African oppression, that
the occupation by the South African Defence Force is causing hard-
ship, distress, fear and loss of life, that there is an almost total
rejection of the present 11 ethnic governments, and that it appears
that SWAPO has overwhelming support not least from the main-line
churches and their leaders.

854. BRITISH COUNCIL OF CHURCHES. Namibia - a nation wronged. London:
BCC, Division of International Affairs, 1981, 34 p.

This report of a visit to Namibia by a delegation from the British
Council of Churches documents by direct testimony the enormous
suffering inflicted upon the civilian population by South African
repression, the strong support of Namibians for SWAPO and the
liberation struggle, and the widespread suspicion of the Western
"Contact Group". An appendix records twenty cases of brutality
and terror by the South African military forces. The visit took
place in November 1981 at the invitation of the Namibian Council
of Churches. The conclusions and recommendations arising out of
the Report, as approved by the board of the BCC's Division of
International Affairs, are reproduced in PCR Information, no. 14,
1982: 59-63 (no. 1019). See also the pamphlet Namibia (London:
British Council of Churches, 1978, 23 p.).

855. COUNCIL OF CHURCHES IN NAMIBIA. Statements by churches in Namibia. Windhoek, (1981?), 16 p.

Published by the Council of Churches, this pamphlet reproduces ten of the most important documents issued by the Namibian churches in the period from 1971 to 1980. They include the historic open letter to the South African prime minister (1971) and a letter to the UN Secretary-General (1980). The documents bear testimony to the prominent role played by the churches in the drive for a negotiated settlement.

856. DE VRIES, JOHANNES LUKAS. Mission and colonialism in Namibia. Braamfontein: Ravan Press, 1978, 216 p. (In German: Namibia: Mission und Politik (1880-1918). Neukirchen- Vluyn: Neukirchener Verlag, 1980, 324 p.).

Originally submitted as a dissertation (theology) at the University of Brussels, this book is mainly concerned with German colonialism and the role of the Rhenish Missionary Society during the colonial period in Namibia. Although the church is defended against some of it critics, the author demonstrates how the mission supported the supression of the people's fight against exploitation. The author concludes that the church must avoid repeating the past error of failing to speak up against an unjust society. De Vries was one of the foremost church leaders in Namibia before he resigned to join the South African administration in 1980. In 1983-84 he was one of the leading spokesmen of the "Multi-Party Conference".

857. ELLIS, JUSTIN. "The church in mobilization for national liberation". In Namibia. The last colony, edited by Reginald H. Green, Marja-Liisa Kiljunen and Kimmo Kiljunen, p. 132-44. London: Longman, 1981.

Written by a church worker and educationalist who was deported from Namibia in 1978, this is a general account of the prominent role played by the churches in the struggle for national independence. The author points out that this position is a relatively recent occurrence, and the main focus of the essay is on the historical change from complicity with colonialism to organised opposition against South African colonial rule and occupation. He also shows that repressive action against the churches has tended to be counter-productive.

858. FROSTIN, PER, PETER KATJAVIVI and KAIRE MBUENDE (eds.). Church and liberation in Namibia. In preparation.

A collection of essays by the three editors, two Namibian scholars and SWAPO members and a Swedish theologian, supplemented with a contribution by Zedekia Mujoro and Emma Mujoro, two Namibian pastors. The book covers the role of the church in the struggle for liberation, church and class in Namibia, Christianity versus capitalism, and Namibian "Black Theology".

859. HELLBERG, CARL-J. A voice of the voiceless. The involvement of the Lutheran World Federation in Southern Africa 1947-1977. Lund: Skeab/VERBUM, 1979, 236 p. Bibl.: 232-36.

This study gives an informative introduction to the involvement of
the Lutheran World Federation in Southern Africa, the main emphasis
being laid on inter-church relationships and cooperation between the
LWF and its member churches in the region. A substantial chapter
is devoted to Namibia ("Lutheran churches in Namibia, 'The voice
of the voiceless', 1971-1977", p. 175-214), documenting the growing
involvement of the churches in the struggle against South African
occupation. The chapter opens with a discussion of the political
and theological implications of the open letter to the South African
prime minister in 1971 and the subsequent conversation between J.B.
Vorster and the church leaders. The author notes that the 1971-72
general strike led to increased political awareness and activity
among churchmen, but he also argues that the period covered by the
study was characterised by internal tension between those politically
engaged on the side of SWAPO and forces more cautious in their
political involvement. The author, a Swedish theologian in the
service of the LWF since 1966, has written extensively on Namibia
and South Africa.

KATJAVIVI, PETER, see no. 858.

860. MAY, HANS- CHRISTOPH. Der Kampf der Befreiungsbewegung SWAPO von
Namibia und die Stellung der Kirchen. Universität Würzburg, 1981,
342 p. Bibl.: 329-41. (Diplomarbeit).

This thoroughly researched theology dissertation focuses on SWAPO
and the role of the churches in Namibia, drawing on a wide range
of primary documents from the liberation movement as well as from
the different churches. The major part of the thesis is concerned
with the history and ideology of SWAPO, providing a broad outline
of its political and military activities. The second part is a much
briefer account of the involvement of the churches in the struggle
for independence. Although the author indicates the various forms
of cooperation which exist between the churches and individual
SWAPO members, he regards the significant disagreements within and
between the churches as well as their ambiguous position on armed
struggle as factors which weaken the prospects for a united front
in the liberation struggle.

MBUENDE, KAIRE, see no. 858.

861. THE OBLATES OF MARY IMMACULATE. The green and dry wood. Documentation. The Roman Catholic Church and the Namibian socio-political
situation 1971-1981. Newcastle (SA): Zulu Publications, 1983,
269 p.

This is an extensive documentation of the Catholic church's involvement in the struggle for Namibia over the last decade, bringing
together a wide range of letters, statements, articles, reports
and newspaper clippings on issues of concern to the church. The
collection goes beyond leadership positions to reflect the occasionally sharply differing standpoints within the church itself. Of
special interest is the part of the book dealing with violation
of human rights, including the deportation of Father Heinz Hunke

for his active involvement in the exposure of widespread torture.
A separate chapter documents the cooperation with other churches in
Namibia. The report of the Southern African Catholic Bishops'
Conference on Namibia (no. 862), as well as the following exchange
of letters with the South African prime minister, are also reproduced.

862. THE SOUTHERN AFRICAN CATHOLIC BISHOPS' CONFERENCE. Report on Namibia.
Pretoria, 1982, 40 p. (In German: Bericht Namibia. Die katholischen
Bischöfe aus dem südlichen Afrika: Bericht über Namibia. Frankfurt:
Evangelischer Pressedienst, 1982, 37 p. In Afrikaans: Verslag oor
Namibië. Uit gereik deur Die Suid-Afrikaanse Katolieke Biskoppe-
konferensie. Windhoek, 43 p.).

Based on a visit to Namibia in September 1981, followed by an extensive discussion within the Southern African Catholic Bishops'
Conference, this valuable report is mainly concerned with the attitudes of Namibians towards the South African occupation. Its assessment is that most Namibians consider the DTA regime to be a device
to ensure South African control of Namibia and the imposition of a
structure and policy dictated by South Africa. It provides a graphic
account of the widespread intimidation of the civilian population,
including use of torture, in the operational areas in the north.
There is also a section focusing on the role of SWAPO, concluding
that "support for SWAPO is massive and that it would be easily vic-
torious in any free and fair election held under United Nations
supervision". The report, which subsequently was banned, also contains two South African government statements on the main findings
of the commission.

863. SUNDERMEIER, THEO. Wir aber suchten Gemeinschaft. Kirchwerdung und
Kirchentrennung in Südwestafrika. Erlangen: Luther-Verlag/ Witten:
Verlag der Ev. - Luth. Mission, 1973, 359 p. Bibl.: 337-51.
(Erlanger Taschenbücher).

This is a detailed and scholarly account of the establishment of
independent African churches in the 1940s and 1950s in the central
and southern part of Namibia, an important precursor to the formation of the national liberation movement in the 1960s. The study
is also concerned with the response of the missionary churches to
this cultural, political and theological challenge. For another
treatment of the same subject, see Katesa Schlosser: Eingeborenenkirchen in Süd- und Südwest-Afrika. Ihre Geschichte und Sozialstruktur (Kiel: Mühlau, 1958), especially ch. III: "Eine Abfall-
bewegung von der Rheinischen Missionsgesellschaft im Namaland"
(p. 71-124).

864. WINTER, COLIN. Namibia. The story of a bishop in exile. Guildford
and London: Lutterworth Press/Grand Rapids, Michigan: Eerdmans
Publishing Comp., 1977, 234 p.

Colin Winter was the Anglican bishop in Namibia up to his expulsion
by the South African authorities in 1972, and thereafter championed
the cause of national liberation as bishop in exile until his death in
1982. In this personal story he chronicles the contributions which the
churches, with his own courageously in the forefront, have come

to make towards national independence in Namibia. Of special interest are the chapters dealing with living conditions for Africans in Windhoek, the migrant labour system, the strike in 1971-72, his visit to Ovamboland and the trial of 12 Namibians accused of having "incited" workers to stay away from work. The bishop also brings a sober indictment against the churches who have been unwilling to confront the colonial regime.

865. WORLD COUNCIL OF CHURCHES. The churches' involvement in Southern Africa. Geneva: 1982, 76 p. (Special issue of PCR Information, Reports and Background Papers, no. 14, 1982).

Published as a part of the Program to Combat Racism, this special issue of PCR Information contains several articles on recent developments in Southern Africa and the role of the churches. Among the documents reproduced are statements by the Namibian Council of Churches to the US delegation on its visit to Namibia (12 June 1981) and to the Prime Minister of South Africa during his visit to Windhoek (26 February 1982), a statement by the synod of the Evangelical Lutheran Ovambokavango Church in 1982, and a statement approved by the Board of the British Council of Churches' Division of International Affairs arising out of the BCC Report on Namibia (see no. 854).

SEE ALSO:

9, 11, 17, 29, 32, 37, 39, 41, 43, 45, 73, 192, 233, 296, 312, 787, 804, 940, 942, 1019.

14. BIBLIOGRAPHIES

A. Bibliographies on Namibia

866. AFRICAN BIBLIOGRAPHIC CENTER. <u>SADEX. The Southern Africa development information/documentation exchange</u>. Washington: ABC, 1979-1983.

This excellent information and documentation guide, published bi-monthly for four years, provides a wide range of information on publications, projects and international cooperation efforts related to the SADCC, Frontline States and Namibia. The bibliography was published by African Bibliographic Center, under a contract from the Africa Bureau of the US Agency for International Development (AID). Each issue comprises a feature section, consisting of articles and special bibliographic essays; an information section that includes details of forthcoming publications, conferences and research in progress; a book review section; a bibliographic section arranged by country and an author index. For a bibliographic essay on Namibia in the regional context, see no. 890.

867. ANSARI, S. <u>Liberation struggle in Southern Africa. A bibliography of source material</u>. Gurgaon/Haryana: Indian Documentation Service, 1972, 118 p.

This is a useful bibliography for students of the liberation movements in the period 1961-1971, listing a large number of books, articles, and documents originating from UN and from the liberation movements themselves. The bibliography is confined to material published in English. The main focus of the Namibia section (p. 8-38) is on UN reports, resolutions and petitions which are listed in chronological order.

868. BIELSCHOWSKY, LUDWIG. <u>List of books in German on South Africa and South West Africa published up to 1914 in the South African Public Library, Cape Town</u>. Cape Town: School of Librarianship, University of Cape Town, 1949, 84 p.

As indicated by the title, this is a library holding list of books
in German on South Africa and Namibia up to World War I. Books
translated into German are not included, nor are periodical
articles unless they are treated as a separate volume. The bibliography also excludes schoolbooks and fiction. The section on Namibia
takes up the final part (p. 58-76), and lists a number of rare items,
some of which are briefly annotated. For a follow-up, see Plaat
(no. 899).

869. BOTH, ELLEN LISA MARIANNE. Books and pamphlets published in German
relating to South Africa and South West Africa, 1950-1964. Cape Town:
University of Cape Town Libraries, 1969, 132 p.

Containing close to 500 briefly annotated entries, this bibliography
lists books and pamphlets in German as found in the South African
Public Library. The works are entered alphabetically by author and
indexed alphabetically by subject. The bibliography is restricted
to material published between 1950 and 1963, but there are also some
entries prior to this date to supplement the bibliographies of
Bielschowsky (no. 868) and Plaat (no. 899).

870. BOTHA, LAURETTE ISABELLA. The Namib desert. Cape Town: University
of Cape Town Libraries, 1970, 26 p.

Including 139 entries with brief annotations, this bibliography
lists books and periodical material relating to the Namib desert.
The focus is on description and travel, botany, diamond mining and
rock paintings. The arrangement is by subject and then alphabetically
by author. There is also an author index. No material published
later than 1967 is included.

871. BRIDGMAN, JON and DAVID E. CLARKE. German Africa. A select annotated
bibliography. Stanford, California: The Hoover Institution on War,
Revolution, and Peace, 1965, 119 p. (Hoover Institution Bibliographical
Series: XIX).

Based on the extensive Hoover Institution German Africa collection,
this bibliography contains more than 900 entries, some of them with
brief annotations. Five hundred items are concerned with German
colonialism in general, followed by regional lists on each colony.
The section on "German Southwest Africa" includes 102 publications
(p. 82-95). There are also an introductory note on German official
and semi-official publications, a list of serials and a list of
microfilmed British confidential documents dealing with German Africa.

872. BROSE, MAXIMILIAN. Die deutsche Kolonialliteratur von 1884-1895.
Berlin: Die Deutsche Kolonialgesellschaft/Elsner, 1897, 158 p.

873. ------- Die deutsche Kolonialliteratur im Jahre 1897. Berlin:
Meinecke, 1898, 28 p.

874. ------- Die deutsche Kolonialliteratur im Jahre ++++. Berlin: Die
deutsche Kolonialgesellschaft/Süsserott. vol. 3 (1898), 38 p.;
vol. 4 (1899), 58 p.; vol. 5 (1900), 63 p.; vol. 6 (1901), 66 p.;
vol. 7 (1902), 63 p.; vol. 8 (1903), 74 p.; vol. 9 (1904), 78 p.;
vol. 10 (1905), 86 p.; vol. 11 (1906), 86 p.; vol. 12 (1907), 104 p.;

vol. 13 (1908), 92 p.; vol. 14 (1909), 107 p.; vol. 15 (1910), 118 p.;
vol. 16 (1911), 118 p.; vol. 17 (1912), 116 p.; vol. 18 (1913),
140 p.; vol. 19 (1914), 89 p.

Started by Maximilian Brose, the librarian at the German Colonial
Society, this was by far the most extensive bibliography covering
German colonialism. The work was continued by Hubert Henoch from
1907 onwards, but was brought to a halt during the World War I.
Organised by subject, the bibliography still serves as an indispensable
reference tool for students of German colonialism and Namibia.

875. CARLSON, ANDREW R. German foreign policy, 1890-1914, and colonial
policy to 1914: a handbook and annotated bibliography. Metuchen,
New Jersey: The Scarecrow Press, 1970, 333 p.

This is a handy reference work and guide to German foreign policy
in general and colonial policy in particular, covering the period from
the dismissal of Bismarck to the outbreak of World War I. The
major part of the book consists of an extensive, partly annotated
bibliography. Apart from references to a large number of books,
periodicals and documents relevant for the study of Namibia, there
are also 73 entries specifically concerned with the territory.

876. DE JAGER, THEO (comp.) and BRIGITTE KLAAS (ed.). South West Africa/
Suidwes-Afrika. Pretoria: State Library, 1964, 216 p. (Bibliographies No. 7).

This is one of the largest general bibliographies on Namibia, containing close to 2000 entries. The aim is to provide a checklist
of books, entered alphabetically by author. Periodic articles
are not included except when available as reprints or pamphlets.
The subject index suffers from inaccuracies as quite a number of
the entries have not been checked against the original works. The
coverage of official publications is very thin, and there are no
annotations.

877. DUIGNAN, PETER and L.H. GANN. A bibliographical guide to colonialism
in Sub-Saharan Africa. Cambridge University Press, 1973, 552 p.
(Colonialism in Africa 1870-1960, vol. 5).

This extensive bibliography on colonialism contains also a special
section on German colonial rule (p. 386-411). The number of entries
dealing specifically with Namibia is rather limited, but the
section as a whole provides a careful selection of literature. The
annotations reflect the conservative inclinations of the authors
(see no. 776).

878. EVBOROKHAI, A.O. (comp.). A descriptive list of United Nations
reference documents on Namibia (1946-1978). Lusaka: UNIN. 1980,
167 p.

Based on the large accumulation of UN material accessioned by the
UN Institute for Namibia, this list of publications covers the
various organs concerned with Namibia, notably the Security Council,
the General Assembly, the Council for Namibia, the Commissioner
for Namibia, the Special Committee of 24 on Decolonization, the

UN Fund for Namibia, the Special Committee on Apartheid, the Centre
against Apartheid, the Commission on Human Rights, the Economic
Commission for Africa, etc. There are also records of the Trusteeship Council and the International Court of Justice. Although the
list is not exhaustive, it serves as a guide to a wide range of
important documentary material. General Assembly and Security Council
resolutions are excluded, as they are available in another compilation
(see no. 731).

879. GESELLSCHAFT FÜR WISSENSCHAFTLICHE ENTWICKLUNG. Ferdinand Stich
     Africana. Swakopmund, 1977, 134 p. (Bibliotheka, Heft 2, 1977).

This list describes the collection of more than 2000 items donated
to the library of the Gesellschaft für Wissenschaftliche Entwicklung
in Swakopmund by Ferdinand Stich, a bookseller and bibliophile resi-
dent in Swakopmund. The main value of the list lies in the inclusion
of several local and rare publications, especially from the German
period, which are not to be found on other bibliographies.

880. HALSTEAD, JOHN P. and SERAFINO PORCARI. Modern European imperialism:
     a bibliography of books and articles 1815-1972. Boston: G.K.
     Hall, 1972. Vol. 1: General and British empire, 508 p. Vol. 2:
     French and other empires & regions, 501 p.

The second volume of this general bibliography on colonialism covers
the German empire (p. 290-312) and "South West Africa" (p. 312-15).
It adds little to other bibliographies of the kind, but it does
contain some interesting items and is readily available in many
libraries.

881. HILLEBRECHT, WERNER. "Bibliographical aids for studies on Namibia.
     A supplement to Martin Vogt's list". Basler Afrika Bibliographien
     Nachrichten/Newsletter, no. 3, 1982: 39-54.

Designed to supplement the list of bibliographical aids prepared by
Martin Vogt (no. 919), this annotated bibliography contains 83 entries.
Most of the items included are general bibliographies which are also
of interest for researchers in Namibian affairs. It also indicates
in which West German libraries the bibliographies can be consulted.

882. HILLEBRECHT, WERNER W. Hochschulschriften zu Namibia unter Einbezie-
     hung von Arbeiten zur deutschen Kolonialpolitik, Kolonialrecht und
     Kolonialwirtschaft sowie zum Völkerbundsmandatsrecht. Kassel:
     Namibian Bibliographical Data, 1984, 57 p. (A revised edition is schedu-
     led for publication in 1985 by Basler Afrika Bibliographien, Basel.)

This list of 800 dissertations and theses concerned with Namibia and
German colonial policy is the most comprehensive to date. It
includes theses from Belgium, the Federal Republic of Germany, the
German Democratic Republic, Finland, France, Great Britain, Canada,
Kenya, the Netherlands, Austria, Switzerland, USSR, US, South
Africa and the Vatican. The author is compiling a comprehensive
bibliography of all Namibiana in West German libraries. He
can be contacted at his private address, see p. 405.

83. INSTITUT FÜR WELTWIRTSCHAFT, KIEL. Regionenkatalog, Band 41. Boston:
G.K. Hall, 1967, 773 p.

This volume in the series of catalogues of the library of the Institut
für Weltwirtschaft, Kiel (Library of the Institute for World Economics)
lists all its holdings on Namibia up to the mid-1960s (p. 327-51).
The catalogue reproduces close to 600 index cards on Namibia, some
of which appear more than once. There have, however, been many
new acquisitions since 1965. The library is especially strong on
German material from the turn of the century and on official South
African documents and statistics. The catalogue is one in a series
of 52 volumes dealing with countries and regions, in addition to
which there is a wide range of catalogues concerned with persons,
companies, titles, subjects and periodicals.

84. THE INSTITUTE FOR CONTEMPORARY HISTORY, UNIVERSITY OF THE ORANGE FREE
STATE. Bibliographies on South African political history. Boston:
G.K. Hall & Co., 1979-1982. (Edited by O. Geyser, P.W. Coetzer and
J.H. Le Roux. Vol. 1: Register of private document collections on
the political history of South Africa since 1902, 1979, 150 p.
Vol. 2: General sources on South African political history since
1902. 1970, 763 p. Vol. 3: Index to periodical articles on South
African political and social history since 1902, 1982, 616 p.

These three volumes contain a guide to archives and an extensive
bibliography on South African and Namibian history, with special
emphasis on political history in the 20th century. The register of
document collections (vol. 1) gives the contents of private
collections of several administrators and colonial politicians
involved in Namibian affairs, and there are separate chapters on
Namibia in vol. 2 (256 items, p. 663-83) and in vol. 3 (658 items,
p. 545-64). The sections on Namibia provide an unannotated list of
books, theses, articles and documents, some of which are not
easily available outside South Africa. The bibliographies are linked
to the Institute for Contemporary History, University of the Orange
Free State. INHC has one of South Africa's best collections of
primary source material on contemporary political history, including
the archives of the Namibian branch of the National Party. It has
also an extensive press clipping system, and more than 20,000
articles and reports are selected each month from 33 South African
newspapers and professional journals.

85. INTERNATIONAL AFRICA INSTITUTE. Cumulative bibliography of African
studies. Boston: G.K. Hall, 1973, 5 vols.

86. PEARSON, J.D. (ed.). International African Bibliography 1973-1978.
Books, articles and papers in African studies. London: Mansell,
1982, 392 p.

These two cumulative bibliographies are based on the work started by
the International Africa Institute (London) in 1929. From this year
up to 1970 a quarterly bibliography of current books and articles
was published in the journal Africa, and thereafter in a special
bulletin, International African Bibliography. Cumulative Bibliography..., published in 5 volumes, covers the period up to 1972, and
contains a classified catalogue as well as an author catalogue. The

classification is regional, and regions are then divided by country
and subject. The subject headings ethnography and linguistics are
further subdivided into ethnic groups and languages respectively.
The bibliography reflects the main interests of the International
Africa Institute, and is especially strong on ethnography and linguistics. The section on Namibia (p. 501-512, vol. 3) lists more
than 350 entries. In 1971 the compilation of the International African
Bibliography was taken over by the School of Oriental and African
Studies (University of London), and the cumulative bibliography
by the same title covers vols. 3-8 (1973-78) of the quarterly
bulletin. Additionally, some 3000 titles not previously indexed
in the bibliography have been inserted. The arrangement is roughly
the same as that of its predecessor. The 1973-78 bibliography
lists 155 items concerned with Namibia.

887. KAHN, EVELYN RUTH. Karakul sheep in South West Africa and South
Africa: a bibliography. Cape Town: School of Librarianship,
University of Cape Town, 1959, 27 p.

Although it was published 25 years ago, this partly annotated
bibliography of books and journals is still of specialist use for
students of economic history.

888. KINSEY, B.H. and K.A. MUIR. Agriculture, food and rural development
in Namibia: a select annotated bibliography. Norwich: University
of East Anglia, Overseas Development Group/FAO, 1981, 95 p.
(Working Paper No. 1).

889. CROSS, SHOLTO et al. A select development bibliography of Namibia.
Norwich: University of East Anglia, Overseas Development Group/FAO,
1981, 27 p. (Working Paper No. 2).

The objective of these two bibliographies, which were prepared in
conjunction with a FAO/UN Nationhood Programme study on Namibian
agriculture and food security (see no. 514), is to make available
information on literature of interest to those engaged in agricultural planning in Namibia and those concerned with broader devel-
opmental issues. Agriculture, food and rural development is an
annotated computer-produced list organised by subject and using
key words, author and short title indexes. It contains 175 entries,
of which the German and Afrikaans titles are also translated into
English. The promised revised and expanded edition has unfortunately
not yet appeared. A select development bibliography... is an unannotated list of more than 300 publications, not all of them directly relevant to Namibia.

890. KORNEGAY, FRANCIS A. Jr. and JOYCE R. MORTIMER: "Namibia's transition
and regional cooperation in Southern Africa". SADEX, 3, no. 1,
(January-February) 1981: 1-24.

This is a lengthy and useful bibliographical essay which surveys
the recent literature concerned with the Namibian economy, Western
economic involvement, South Africa's strategic interest and Namibia
in the regional context of Southern Africa. The article also
provides insight into current sources relevant for documenting
Namibia.

891. LIBRARY OF CONGRESS (US). <u>Africa south of the Sahara. Index to</u>
<u>periodical literature, 1900-1970.</u> Boston: G.K. Hall, 1971. 4 vols.

This index to periodical literature reproduces catalogue cards of
the Africana Section, General Reference and Bibliography Division,
Library of Congress. It is organised by country and thereunder by
subject. The section on "South West Africa" (vol. 4, p. 149-74)
contains close to 600 references to articles in journals, some of
them rare. Two supplementary volumes have also been published so
far: 1973 (p. 328-30) and 1982 (p. 293-303).

892. LOENING, LOUISE S.E. <u>A bibliography of the status of South-West-Africa</u>
<u>up to June 30th 1951.</u> Cape Town: University of Cape Town Libraries,
1951, 27 p. (Reprint 1969).

This is a list of books, articles and documents on the legal and
international aspects of Namibia in the immediate postwar period
(1945-51). It includes debates in the South African Parliament
and newspaper reports in the <u>Cape Times</u> and <u>Windhoek Advertiser.</u>

893. LOGAN, RICHARD F. <u>Bibliography of South West Africa. Geography</u>
<u>and related fields.</u> Windhoek: SWA Scientific Society, 1969,
152 p. (Scientific Research in South West Africa, 8th Series).

The aim of this extensive bibliography, which contains more than
2000 entries, is to serve as a guide to sources on the geography
of Namibia. It covers books and articles published up to the mid-
1960s. The bibliography is not restricted to geography in a narrow
sense, but includes a selection of works within the fields of
anthropology, history, economy, politics and culture. The entries
are organised alphabetically by author, but there is also a subject
index. More than half of the items are annotated. The comments
reflect the strongly pro-South African bias of the author, a US
professor of geography, and are often too brief to be particularly
useful. There is also a large number of misprints, especially
in German titles.

894. MELVILLE J. HERSKOVITS LIBRARY OF AFRICAN STUDIES, NORTHWESTERN
UNIVERSITY. <u>The Africana conference paper index.</u> Boston: G.K. Hall,
1982, Vol. 1: 737 p. Vol. 2: 738-1460 p.

The Melville J. Herskovits Library of African Studies at the Northwestern University holds a unique collection of conference papers,
and has recently made this important research literature accessible
through a two-volume index listing 562 conferences and over 12,000
individual papers. The first volume contains a register of the
conferences, with the indexed papers listed alphabetically by
author, while the second volume provides an extensive keyword index.
Although the list of conference papers reflects the paucity of
scholarly work on Namibia during the 1960s and the early 1970s, it is
nevertheless possible to find references to some valuable material.
All papers are held by the Northwestern University Library and are
available for either loan or by photocopy through the interlibrary
loan department.

895. MOKOBANE, SIMON RAPULE. A select bibliography on South West Africa/
Namibia. Johannesburg: South African Institute of Race Relations,
1980, 25 p.

This reading list of 287 items concerned with Namibia contains materials
up to the end of 1979. There are no annotations, and the list is
alphabetically organised without subject division or index.

896. MOORSOM, RICHARD. Namibia library collection: a working list of
titles. Bergen: Development Research and Action Programme, Christian
Michelsen Institute, 1985, 79 p.

This bibliography lists 450 items collected together as a resource for
the UNIDO study of industrial development strategy for independent
Namibia. (no. 489), the preliminary draft of which was prepared at
DERAP. The list is neither comprehensive nor representative, but
is nonetheless strong on recent economic literature and on UNIN and
UN development studies prepared under the Nationhood Programme, many
of which remain unpublished. The list contains articles, theses
and unpublised drafts as well as books and government publications.
It is filed on a computer diskette and is to be issued in early 1985
in the DERAP Working Papers series. The majority of the items are
either in stock or to be acquired by the DERAP library. The list is
arranged by rough subject division and also by author, and indicates
where items are held in the DERAP and Scandinavian Institute of
African Studies libraries.

897. MULLER, C.F.J., et al. South African history and historians - a
bibliography. Pretoria: University of South Africa, 1979, 411 p.

This is the standard guide to South African historical literature,
compiled by four prominent historians and listing more than 4500
items. There are also several references to Namibia, mainly in
section 18 (South Africa in Southern Africa). A detailed subject
index makes the bibliography easy to consult, but there are no annotations.

898. MUNGER AFRICANA LIBRARY. South African political ephemera. California
Institute of Technology, 1975, 124 p. (Munger Africana Library
Notes, no. 29, March 1975).

This is an alphabetically organised list of 1400 pamphlets, broad-
sides, serials and manuscripts in the Munger Africana Library.
There are about 60 items on Namibia from the turn of the century
to the present, some of them rare enough not to have been listed
in other bibliographies.

899. PLAAT, A.F. German Africana in the South African Library, Cape Town,
published after 1914. Cape Town: School of Librarianship,
University of Cape Town, 1951, 61 p.

Restricted to books and pamphlets in German found in the South African
Public Library, this compilation covers both South Africa and Namibia.
It is intended as a continuation of Bielschowsky (see no. 868), but
differs; slightly by including fiction and books translated into
German. Of 322 entries, occasionally annotated, 100 are concerned

with Namibia (p. 38-56). Works are entered under broad subject headings in alphabetical order of authors' names.

900. POLLAK, OLIVER B. and KAREN POLLAK. Theses and dissertations on Southern Africa: an international bibliography. Boston: G.K. Hall, 1976, 236 p.

An extensive list of 2400 dissertations on Southern Africa. It covers the period 1884-1974, and includes theses from 30 countries in 9 languages. The bibliography is organised by subject and country, and there is also an author index. For theses on Namibia, see especially nos. 198-229, 668-704, 980-990, 1586-1646. 1886-1893 and 2188-2300.

901. POLLER, ROBERT MANFRED. Swakopmund and Walvis Bay. Cape Town: School of Librarianship, University of Cape Town, 1964, 25 p.

This is an incomplete but useful compilation of material relating to the towns of Swakopmund and Walvis Bay, compiled with the needs of local historians in mind. It includes 148 items, some of them with brief scope notes. The list is arranged by subject, and under each, chronologically, according to the period covered by the item.

902. ROBERTSON, ELIZABETH (comp.). Subject list and index of the laws of South West Africa from 1915, in force in 1969. Johannesburg: University of Witwatersrand, 1973, 68 p. (Department of Bibliography, Librarianship and Typography, Diploma).

This is a basic finding-list of laws in force in Namibia at the end of 1969. The laws listed are arranged alphabetically under broad subject headings, under each of which they are grouped into two sections: Acts of the Parliament of South Africa,which apply to the territory,and Laws of South West Africa. Unfortunately regular financial legislation is among the items excluded from the list.

903. ROGERS, BARBARA. "Namibia". In American-Southern African relations. Bibliographical essays, edited by Mohamad A. El-Khawas and Francis A. Kornegay, p.: 47-114. Westport, Connecticut/London: Greenwood Press, 1975.

This is one of the most substantial contributions to Namibian bibliography, published in a collection of essays concerned with US-Southern African relations. The essay opens with a discussion of the recent trends in the writings on Namibia, and continues with a brief discussion of some of the most important works and a list of more than 700 publications. The bibliography includes books, articles, theses, papers, statements, and UN documents arranged by subject. The list reflects the large volume of publications dealing with legal aspects, but works on Namibian history, economy, the liberation struggle and the South African occupation are also well covered, and include a number of rare or unpublished items, several not referenced in other bibliographies.

904. ROUKENS DE LANGE, E.J. South West Africa 1946-1960. Cape Town: School of Librarianship, University of Cape Town, 1961, 51 p.

Designed as a continuation of Welch (no. 921), this bibliography
provides a general and very briefly annotated introduction to publications on Namibia in the postwar period up to 1960. It is restricted
to works examined in the collections of the South African Public
Library and the University of Cape Town Library, with the exception
of a few theses. A qualitative selection has been made, especially
with regard to periodical articles, while articles in newspapers
have been excluded. Among the 322 titles, there are several entries
on geography and the different sectors of the economy.

905. SCHLETTWEIN, CARL. "Bibliographie Südwestafrika ("Namibia") 1971".
Mitteilungen der Basler Afrika Bibliographien, Heft 2/3, 1972:
17-74.

This is one of the first attempts to provide a rudimentary "national
bibliography" of Namibia. It concentrates on the year 1971, and
serves as a forerunner to the work of Eckhard Strohmeyer (see nos.
914-916). The bibliography includes 256 titles, of which the great
majority have been published in Namibian, a subject index and an
author index. It is available as an offprint.

906. SCHOEMAN, ELNA. The Namibian issue 1920-1980. A select and annotated
bibliography. Boston: G.K. Hall, 1982, 247 p.

This substantial bibliographical work focuses mainly on international
relations, diplomacy and legal proceedings, but also includes minor
sections on economics, politics, resources, labour, administration
and the role of the churches. It contains close to 1500 entries,
covering books, documents as well as articles from a wide range of
periodicals. Most of the entries are annotated, but the annotations
are brief and not very informative. South African and Western standpoints are covered extensively, while coverage of African opinion
is thin and SWAPO material and anti-apartheid publications are
scarcely touched. For many students, the sections on UN documents
and International Court of Justice material will, however, provide
a useful working resource. The author, who is a librarian at the
University of Witwatersrand, restricted her research to library
resources available in Johannesburg and Pretoria. The bibliography
includes a chronology (1883-1980), a subject guide and an author
index. This work is an expansion and updating of a previous
publication: South West Africa/Namibia: An International Issue,
1920-1977. A Select Bibliography (Johannesburg: South African
Institute of International Affairs, 1978). See also two bibliographies
which concentrate on UN and South Africa's foreign relations:
Gail L. Rogaly: South Africa's Foreign Relations, 1961-1979. A
select and partially annotated bibliography (Johannesburg: SAIIA
1980, 462 p.) and Elna Schoeman: South Africa and the United Nations
(Johannesburg: SAIIA, 1981, 244 p.).

907. SPOHR, OTTO HARTUNG. German Africana. German publications on South-
and South West Africa. Pretoria: State Library, 1968, 332 p.
(The State Library Bibliographies no. 14).

This is a comprehensive unannotated list of all publications in German
on South Africa and Namibia in South African libraries in the mid-
1960s, indicating in which libraries the items can be found. There
are 3423 entries, the great majority of them on Namibia. The items
are arranged in one alphabetical sequence by author, but there is
a separate and detailed subject index on Namibia (p. 292-308).

908. STANDING CONFERENCE ON LIBRARY MATERIALS ON AFRICA (SCOLMA).
Periodicals from Africa: a bibliography and union list of periodicals
published in Africa. Boston, 1977, xiii, 619 p. (Compiled by
Carole Travis and Miriam Alman, edited by Carole Travis).

This list comprises periodicals published in African countries, organised by country in alphabetical order with a periodical title index.
The section on Namibia contains more than 130 publications (papers,
magazines, bulletins, etc.), covering both current publications
and publications which have ceased to exist. The location is given
for periodicals held by UK libraries.

909. STENGEL, HEINZ WALTER. Bibliographie Wasserwirtschaft in Südwestafrika. Basel: Basler Afrika Bibliographien, 1974, 65 p. (Mitteilungen der Basler Afrika Bibliographien, Heft 10, 1974, in cooperation
with Afrika-Verlag der Kreis bei Lempp Verlag, Schwäbisch Gmünd).

Compiled by the leading water affairs engineer in Namibia, this list
is devoted to publications dealing exclusively or partly with water,
water affairs, rainfall, irrigation, and dam building. It is also
invaluable for referencing unpublished official material (reports,
essays, etc.), especially by Stengel himself. The bibliography
covers the period from the first European travellers up to 1973,
and contains more than 500 entries, an author index, a subject index
and a geographical index.

910. STRANDMANN, HARTMUT POGGE VON and ALISON SMITH. "The German empire
in Africa and British perspectives: A historiographical essay".
In Britian and Germany in Africa, edited by P. Gifford and Wm. R.
Louis, p.: 709-95. New Haven/London: Yale University Press, 1967.

911. STRANDMANN, HARTMUT POGGE VON. "The German role in Africa and
German imperialism". African Affairs, 69, no. 277, (October) 1970:
381-89.

This is a most valuable and informative historiographical essay by
two prominent historians, covering the period up to the mid-1960s.
The survey examines the great range of literature dealing both with
the bid for colonies, the Anglo-German rivalry and the history of
the African colonies under British and German rule. Apart from a
discussion of the major books, the essay contains a section on
sources (archival material, official publications, papers and
magazines) and an extensive bibliography. The purpose of the review
article, published in African Affairs three years later, is to
draw attention to the fast-growing body of works which appeared in

the period 1966-69. It points out that much of the more recent
literature underlines the African context of German colonial rule
and stresses African reactions and initiatives.

912. STROHMEYER, ECKHARD and WALTER MORITZ. Umfassende Bibliographie der
Völker Namibiens und Südwestangolas, Band I. Kampala, Uganda/Spenge,
West Germany: 1975, 349 p.

913. STROHMEYER, ECKHARD. Umfassende Bibliographie der Völker Namibiens
und Südwestangolas, Band 2. Karben: 1982, 400 p.

Based on access to material in several libraries and archives in
Namibia, these two volumes comprise one of the largest listings of
material on Namibia to date, with close to 5000 titles. There is a
particularly broad coverage of ethnology and linguistics while
politics, economics and sociology are treated more cursorily. The
bibliography is arranged by different "population groups", divided
into sub-sections covering history, ethnology, physical anthropology,
linguistics, religion and culture. The sub-sections on economics and
material culture are rather weak, and unfortunately the author has
made the decision to exclude titles concerned with wars of resistance,
uprisings and the liberation struggle. The comprehensive index
covers both author and titles, and makes the bibliography particularly
valuable as a reference work. Some of the titles are briefly
annotated, and the libraries and archives in which rare material
can be consulted, are indicated. The bibliography can be ordered
through the author, see the address on p. 405.

914. STROHMEYER, ECKHARD. Namibische National Bibliographie/Namibian
National Bibliography 1971-1975. Basel: Basler Afrika Bibliographien,
1978, 242 p. (Mitteilungen der Basler Afrika Bibliographien, vol.
20, 1978),

915. ------- Namibische National Bibliographie/Namibian National Bibliography 1976-1977. Basel: Basler Afrika Bibliographien, 1979, 168 p.
(Mitteilungen der Basler Afrika Bibliographien, vol. 21, 1979).

915. ------- Namibische National Bibliographie/Namibian National Bibliography 1978-1979. Basel: Basler Afrika Bibliographien, 1981, 215 p.
(Mitteilungen der Basler Afrika Bibliographien, vol. 24, 1981).

In the absence of an authoritative national bibliography run by a
national archive or a national library, this series of meticously
compiled bibliographies is a welcome substitute. The three cumulative
volumes which have appeared so far, tapping a wide range of sources
from inside and outside Namibia, list of more than 4500 entries. The
scope of NNB is all written materials of Namibian concern, no matter
where or in which language they have been published. The NNB consists of two parts: a classified list of title-entries according to
subject and an author/title index. The principle of "autopsy" has
been used systematically, so that only titles which have been
catalogued by personal inspection are listed, and in most cases
the location of the items has been indicated. The publishing of
the NNB has hitherto been possible through joint efforts of the
compiler and the Basler Afrika Bibliographien. The next volume, which
is scheduled for publication in 1985, will be published by the compiler
in cooperation with Brandberg Verlag.

917. TÖTEMEYER, GERHARD. South Africa - South West Africa/Süd-Afrika-
Südwestafrika. A bibliography, 1945-1963. Freiburg: Arnold
Bergstraesser- Institut für Kulturwissenschaftlicher Forschung,
1964, 285 p.

This extensive, unannotated bibliography of books and articles on
South Africa and Namibia concentrates on history, anthropology,
politics, social sciences, education, religion and philosophy.
There is also a useful list of periodicals, yearbooks and bibliographies. The bibliography reflects the scarcity of published literature on Namibia in the period 1945-1963.

918. UNISA DOCUMENTATION CENTRE FOR AFRICAN STUDIES. List of material on
South West Africa/Namibia. Pretoria: University of South Africa,
1981, 18 p. (Acc. 245).

This is a list of more than 400 smaller items held in the Namibia
collection at the University of South Africa. The material is
mainly related to political developments inside Namibia in the
1970s, and a large number of rare documents originating from SWAPO,
DTA, The Turnhalle Conference, Namibia National Front and other
movements and groupings are listed.

919. VOGT, MARTIN. "Bibliographical aids for studies on South West Africa".
Mitteilungen der Basler Afrika Bibliographien, vol. 13, 1975:
21-32.

The bibliographical aids for studies on Namibia listed here are all
available for consultation at the reference library of the Basler
Afrika Bibliographien. It includes 68 briefly annotated titles.
See also the supplementary list prepared by Werner Hillebrecht
(no. 881).

920. VOIGTS, BARBARA. South West Africa imprints. Cape Town: School of
Librarianship, University of Cape Town, 1964, 50 p.

This valuable bibliography covers books, pamphlets and periodicals
published or printed in Namibia from 1892 up to 1961. The entries
are arranged in chronological order with an author index, and the
location of all items has been indicated. The bibliography includes
345 titles, and is particularly useful for tracing official and semi-
official reports printed in Windhoek.

921. WELCH, FLORETTA JEAN. South-West Africa. Cape Town: School of
Librarianship, University of Cape Town, 1967, 41 p. (First print:
1946).

This incomplete and unannotated general bibliography concentrates
mainly on the period 1919-1946. It contains 343 titles, which almost
all have been personally examined in the collections of the South
African Public Library and the University of Cape Town Library.
The material is divided by subject, and the entries appear in each
section in chronological order. This is also the system to be
found in the subject catalogue of the Library of the Royal Empire
Society (now: the Royal Commonwealth Society) in London, on which

the compiler relies heavily. See also de Lange (no. 904), which is
a follow-up covering the period 1946-1960.

B. Current bibliographies

922. The African Book Publishing Record. Oxford: Hans Zell Publishers
     (an imprint of K.G. Saur). Quarterly. 1975 –

     Edited by Hans M. Zell, ABPR provides extensive bibliographic cover-
     age of new and forthcoming publications (books, pamphlets, reports,
     magazines) in English and French, as well as significant titles in
     the African languages. It also features short reviews. The criter-
     ion for inclusion of a title is that is has been published in
     Africa. The bibliography is arranged by subjects, and there are
     subject and author indexes. All entries are cumulated and listed
     in the two-yearly African Books in Print.

923. Africana Journal. A Bibliographic Library Journal and Review Quarterly.
     New York: Africana Publishing Company (a division of Holmes & Meier
     Publishers). 1969 –

     A quarterly current bibliography, containing bibliographic articles
     and essays, brief books reviews and a special review section relating
     to one general topic.

924. Ausgewählte neuere Literatur. A selected bibliography of recent liter-
     ature. Hamburg: Institut für Afrika-Kunde/Dokumentations- Leitstelle
     Afrika. Quarterly. 1973 –

     Published four times a year, this annotated bibliography contains a
     selection of new entries to the catalogue of the Dokumentations-
     Leitstelle Afrika (Africa Documentation Center). The main emphasis
     is laid on the economic and social sciences, with special reference
     to development planning and policy. The titles are arranged
     according to region and country, and within each country according
     to subject. There is also a list of periodicals indexed.

925. A Current Bibliography on African Affairs. Farmingdale, N.Y.:
     Baywood Publishing Comp. Quarterly. 1968 –

     Compiled by the independent African Bibliographical Center (Washington),
     this quarterly journal provides a comprehensive guide to current books
     and articles from journals specialising in African studies. The
     entries are arranged by general subjects and countries, with an author
     index. It also includes book reviews and bibliographic essays.
     Analytical entries are made for distinctive parts of collective works,
     and brief annotations are made where necessary for further explana-
     tion of titles.

926. Current Contents Africa. New Series. Frankfurt: Stadt- und Universitätsbibliothek Frankfurt. (In Kommission bei K.G. Saur, München). Quarterly. 1976 –

The City and University Library, Frankfurt, has been responsible since 1964 for collecting literature on Africa South of the Sahara under an agreement with the German Research Council (Deutsche Forschungsgemeinschaft). Current Contents Africa is published as part of the information services of the library, providing full details, in the form of facsimile reproductions of the title or content pages, of the current contents of almost 200 major periodicals.

927. Documentatieblad. The Abstracts Journal of the African Studies Centre Leiden. Leiden: Afrika- Studiecentrum. Quarterly. 1968 –

Compiled by the library and documentation staff of the ASC, this quarterly publication provides up-to-date coverage of articles in recent periodicals and books on Africa in the field of the social sciences and the humanities. Each issue contains approximately 500 informative abstracts, a geographical index and a subject index. The abstracts are based on 100 periodicals received by the ACS and articles published in books, and are abstracted in the languages of the article (English, French, Dutch, Afrikaans). All articles listed are available in the library of the ASC.

928. Index to South African Periodicals. Johannesburg: City of Johannesburg Public Library. 1940 –

An annual index to periodical literature published in South Africa. Scholarly periodicals are indexed systematically, while more general and popular journals are indexed selectively. There is a separate section on Namibia, covering on average 15–40 entries, but several important Namibian periodicals are not indexed.

929. International African Bibliography. Current books, articles and papers in African studies. London: Mansell. 1971 –

Compiled at the Library of the School of Oriental and African Studies, University of London, in association with the International Africa Institute, this quarterly bibliography covers the whole of Africa except Egypt, and is devoted primarily to the arts and humanities. Publications included are monographs, pamphlets, conference papers and symposia, periodical articles and new periodical titles. It is arranged geographically, and entries are listed alphabetically under each country heading. An annual name index appears in the fourth issue of each volume. The bibliography was founded by IAI in 1929, and appeared as a supplement to its journal Africa until it was launched as a separate publication in 1971. For a cumulation of entries up to 1981, see no. 886.

930. Joint Acquisition List of Africana (JALA). Evanston, Illinois: Northwestern University Library. 1962 –

This comprehensive acquisition list is compiled by the Melville J. Herskovits Library of African Studies on a bi-monthly basis. Annual cumulations, beginning with 1978, are published by G.K. Hall Company of Boston. The 1980 edition contains approximately 15,000

computer-produced entries. It lists books, journals and microfilm
acquisitions from 20 leading African studies libraries, notably
Yale, Northwestern, Boston, Stanford and California Universities,
the Hoover Institution on War, Revolution and Peace, and the Library
of Congress. It also indicates from which library the bibliographic
data have been contributed. The list is arranged in two sections:
author and geographic area.

931. Namibia Abstracts. Guide to selected literature on Namibia and other
Southern African countries. Lusaka: The Information and Documentation Division, United Nations Institute for Namibia. Quarterly.
1981 –

Compiled by C.O. Kisiedu and D.C. Kulleen, the purpose of this annotated bibliography is to bring literature on Namibia and Southern
Africa to the notice of scholars engaged in research on Namibia.
Material for abstracting consists largely of articles taken from
journals, but increasing attention is being paid to reports,
pamphlets, monographs and other documents that are contributed to
the Library of UNIN. The entries are arranged by subject.

932. South African National Bibliography=Suid-Afrikaanse Nasionale Biblio-
grafie (SANB). Pretoria: State Library. Quarterly/annual. 1959 –

SANB is compiled and printed by the State Library, and appears in
three softcover quarterly issues and the final annual hardcover
edition, in which all four quarters are cumulated. It includes all
material received in terms of the legal deposit stipulation of the
Copyright Act, such as monographs, pamphlets, government publications,
microforms, maps, technical reports and unpublished conference papers.
To a certain extent this also includes material originating from
Namibia. The bibliography consists of a classified sequence of main
entries, according to the Dewey schedules. There is also a useful
alphabetical index which provides access to these full entries via
title, as well as names of personal and corporate authors, joint
authors, translators, editors, compilers and illustrators.

15. PERIODICAL PUBLICATIONS

A. The German colonial period

933. Amtsblatt für das Schutzgebiet Deutsch- Südwest-Afrika. Windhoek: Kaiserliches Gouvernement, 1910-1915. (Printed and distributed by Swakopmunder Buchhandlung).

Published fortnightly during the last six years of German colonial rule in Namibia, this is an informative source on tariffs,taxes, customs and excise, weather reports, rainfall and production and trade statistics. A monthly supplement was devoted to agriculture (Landwirtschaftliches Beilage des Amtsblatts...).

934. Beiträge zur Kolonialpolitik und Kolonialwirtschaft. Berlin: Süsserott, 1899-1914. (Deutsche Kolonialgesellschaft).

Published under the title Zeitschrift für Kolonialpolitik, Kolonial-recht und Kolonialwirtschaft from 1904, and as Koloniale Monats-blätter and Zeitschrift für Kolonialrecht from 1913, this was the monthly periodical of imperial Germany's most influential colonial interest group. Each issue contained a large number of articles, many of them concerned with Namibia. With an annual index and an extensive bibliographic supplement (see nos. 872-74), the journal is an important reference work. The Deutsche Kolonialgesellschaft also published a more propagandist weekly magazine, Deutsche Kolonial-zeitung, as well as an agricultural journal, Der Tropenpflanzer, Zeitschrift für tropische Landwirtschaft. See also the reports of the Kolonialwirtschaftliches Komitee, the economic committee of the Society, which provides important information on economic con-ditions in Namibia.

935. Deutsch-Südwestafrikanische Zeitung. Swakopmund, 1901-14.

This was the leading mouthpiece of the German settlers in Namibia, taking over from Windhoeker Anzeiger (1898-1900). In 1912, it merged with the Swakopmunder Zeitung. The other important newspaper was Windhuker Nachrichten, Windhoek, 1904-10, which had a reputation for settlers' criticism of the colonial administration. Later it was renamed Der Südwestbote (1911-1915).

936. Die Deutsche Kolonial-Gesetzgebung. Sammlung der auf die deutschen
Schutzgebiete bezüglichen Gesetze, Verordnungen, Erlasse und inter-
nationalen Vereinbarungen. Berlin: Mittler, 1893-1910.

An important source for colonial legislation and international treaties,
with annotations and a detailed subject index .

937. Deutsches Kolonialblatt. Amtsblatt für die Schutzgebiete des
Deutschen Reiches. Berlin: Mittler, 1890-1921.

This government gazette, published by the Ministry of Foreign Affairs
(the Auswärtiges Amt) and after 1907 by the Colonial Office (Reichskolonialamt) , was the official periodical on the German colonies.
The Reichskolonialamt prepared annual reports to the Reichstag
(Weissbücher), which were published as supplements to the Kolonialblatt (Jahresbericht über die Entwickelung der deutschen Schutzgebiete
in Afrika und der Südsee) and from 1909 independently (Die deutschen
Schutzgebiete in Afrika und der Südsee. Amtliche Jahresberichte) until
1914. These reports are especially valuable for their economic information and detailed statistics. The Reichskolonialamt also published
the scholarly journal Mitteilungen aus den deutschen Schutzgebieten
(1888-1929) as well as a number of monographs and Medizinal-Berichte
über die deutschen Schutzgebiete (1903/4 - 1911/12).

938. Koloniale Rundschau. Monatschrift für die Interessen unserer Schutzgebiete und ihrer Bewohner . Berlin, 1910-1943.

This monthly magazine was initially published by the Gesellschaft für
Eingeborenenschutz, with changing subtitles, publishers and affiliated
societies after 1915. Intermittently edited by Diedrich Westermann,
a well-known Africanist, it partly reflected a somewhat critical
and humanitarian opinion, and contained several scholarly accounts.

B.   Namibian

939. A.D.K. "Information". Windhoek. 1974 -

Published by the right-wing Afrikaans-Duitse Kultuurunie (SWA)/Afrikaans-
Deutsche Kulturgemeinschaft (SWA), this is an irregular (4-6 issues a
year ?) news bulletin in English, German and French editions. Editor
is Erno Gauerke, who is also chairman of A.D.K. and the author of a
series of pamphlets (A.D.K. Booklet - Facts and figures/A.D.K. Schrift-
enreihe, Daten und Fakten).

940. Afrikanischer Heimatkalender. Windhoek. 1930 -

This annual, published by the Evangelical German Lutheran Church in
Namibia, has been issued continuously since 1930. As well as
articles concentrating on the role of the church itself, the yearbook
contains contributions on a broad range of subjects (history, anthropology, arts, philosophy, etc.).

941. Allgemeine Zeitung. Windhoek. 1919 -

The only daily newspaper in German in Africa. Its origins goes back
to the end of World War I, when John Meinert bought the existing
newspapers. Under new owners since the late 1970s, the editorial
policy of the Allgemeine Zeitung is close to the Democratic Turnhalle
Alliance (DTA). It has been issued daily since 1938.

942. CCN-Information. A newsletter of the Council of Churches in Namibia.
Windhoek. 1979 -

Edited by D.J.K. Tjongarero, the Council of Churches monthly news
bulletin contains information on the activities of the CCN as well
as comments on current affairs in Namibia. It reflects the important
role played by the CCN in the struggle against South African occupation. The major churches in Namibia also have separate newsletters
and journals.

943. The Chamber of Commerce and Industries of South West Africa/Namibia.
Council's Annual Report. Windhoek.

Presented by the president of the Chamber, this annual report surveys
the activities of the Chamber and its standing committees and discusses matters of special concern to its members, such as the general
economic situation, economic policies, manpower development, monetary
policy, and liaison with the public sector. In this sense, it is
a valuable source, reflecting the interests of local urban commerce

and industry. The 1983 report was the Chamber's 61st.

944. The Chamber of Mines of SWA/Namibia. Annual Report. Windhoek. 1979 -

The annual report of the Chamber of Mines is a valuable source of
information on the mining sector and the policies of the major companies. The first part contains the president's report, outlining
the impact of the recession on the profitability of the mines and the
decline in the sector's contribution to tax income and employment.
There are also separate sections on the major minerals, such as
diamonds, uranium, copper, lead, zinc, tin and silver. The annexures
give information on metal prices, employment, wages, and accidents.

945. Cimbebasia: SWA-Navorsing=SWA Research=SWA-Forschung. Windhoek.
1962 -

Published by the State Museum in Windhoek, Cimbebasia has since 1967 been
divided into two series of scholarly reports: A (Natural history)
and B(Cultural History). Irregular.

946. Dinteria. Windhoek. 1968 -

Named after the prominent botanist M.K. Dinter, the subject of this
journal is botany in Namibia. Articles are published in English,
German and Afrikaans. Dinteria is edited by Willy Giess, and published irregularly by the SWA Scientific Society. 17 issues have
been published up to 1984.

947. IG-Kurier. Windhoek, 1981 -

The newsletter of the Interessengemeinschaft Deutschsprachiger Südwester (see no. 844), IG-Kurier is a forum for discussion on the
role of the German-speaking community and for information on the
activities of the IG.

948. Journal. - The South West Africa Scientific Society. Windhoek. 1925/26

This is the most substantial scholarly journal to be published in
Namibia and usually contains 6-8 articles in German and English.
The scope of the Journal is very wide, and covers arts and humanities
as well as natural sciences. Each issue has a complete list of
contents of all previous volumes, as well as books published by
the Society. Since 1959 the SWA Scientific Society has also produced
a monthly Newsletter/Mitteilungen/Nuusbrief, which reports on the
activities of the Society and its working groups. There are also
two supplements: Botanische Mitteilungen and Mitteilungen der
Ornithologischen Arbeitsgruppe (renamed Lanioturdus in 1984).

950. KONTAK. Windhoek. 1978 -

Issued bi-monthly, this is the official publication of the South
African parastatal First National Development Corporation (ENOK).
It is mainly concerned with the activities of ENOK, but also contains bits and pieces of information on the Namibian economy in
general.

951. <u>Logos</u>. Windhoek. 1981 –

Published twice a year by the Academy for Tertiary Education, this is a general journal on Namibian politics and culture. The idea is obviously to turn it into a prestigieous academic journal, but so far the quality of the contributions (in English, German and Afrikaans) has been very mixed and the publication has a very limited circulation.

952. <u>Madoqua</u>. <u>Journal of nature conservation and desert research</u>. Windhoek. <u>1969</u> –

Up to 1975 Madoqua was published in two series, but scientific papers of the Namib Desert Research Station and articles more generally concerned with nature conservation are now published in one journal. The publisher is the Department of Agriculture and Nature Conservation.

953. <u>Namib Times</u>. Walvis Bay. 1958 –

Published twice a week (Tuesday and Friday), this conservative local newspaper in Afrikaans and English contains valuable information on fisheries, shipping and other economic activities in the Walvis Bay area.

954. <u>Namib und Meer</u>. Swakopmund. 1970 –

The annual publication of the Swakopmund Museum and the Society for Scientific Development, Swakopmund. The journal is tri-lingual (German, English, Afrikaans) and gives summaries of its articles in alternate languages. The aim of <u>Namib und Meer</u> is to make available new information from all disciplines related to research on the Namib desert and the ocean on which it borders. Apart from natural sciences, there are several articles concerned with history and ethnology. The Museum also distributes a quarterly newsletter (<u>Nachrichten</u>) which lists new additions to the library as well as information on the activities of the Museum and the Society.

955. <u>The Namibian Review</u>. <u>A Journal of Contemporary South West African Affairs</u>. Windhoek. 1976 –

Edited by Kenneth Abrahams and Ottilié Abrahams since the journal was started (in exile in Sweden), more than thirty issues of the Review have appeared up to 1984. Although mimeographed and with limited circulation, the journal presents well-informed, stimulating and controversial articles and topical comments. The editors are associated with the Namibia Independence Party, which has vehemently refused to take part in South African efforts towards an "internal solution" to bypass UN and SWAPO. The journal has also attracted liberal and progressive scholars from outside Namibia, and is the publisher of <u>Namibian Review Publications</u> (see nos. 1, 177).

956. <u>The Namibian Struggle</u>. Windhoek, 1981 –

The official mouthpiece of the Democratic Turnhalle Alliance (DTA), edited and published by its Information Department. It appears irregularly in English and German editions.

957. Namibiana. Communications of the ethno-historical study group. Windhoek. 1979 -

Published twice a year by the ethno-historical study group of the SWA Scientific Society, each issue presents 4-6 articles in English, German or Afrikaans. Most of the contributions are within the framework of conventional anthropology, supplemented with reminiscences from the colonial period.

958. Oranjemund Newsletter and Weekly Bulletin. Oranjemund.

Published on a weekly basis by the Public Relations Department of Consolidated Diamond Mines (CDM). It is primarily an in-house newsletter, and reflects the image CDM has sought to build.

959. Die Republikein. Windhoek. 1977 -

This daily newspaper was started in late 1977 as a mouthpiece of the Democratic Turnhalle Alliance, at a time when the Republican Party, led by Dirk Mudge, split away from the National Party.

960. Rössing Magazine. Windhoek. 1979 -

A glossy magazine, published three times a year, which contains well illustrated and some times well researched feature articles on Rössing and uranium mining as well as on other topics.

961. Rössing Uranium News/Nuus. Windhoek. 1981(?) -

A weekly newspaper succeeding Rössingazette=Uranuus (1975 -), published by Rössing Uranium Ltd. for its employees. Reflecting the position of the company, it contains some interesting information on safety, labour turnover, production and costs.

962. The Student Voice. A paper from, by and for Namibian students. Windhoek. 1983 -

This mimeographed newsletter, distributed by a group of students in Namibia, is mainly concerned with the role played by students at the Academy for Tertiary Education and other institutions of higher education in Namibia. The publication has no clear political line, but the contributions generally reflect a critical attitude to the South African occupation. In 1984 students in Namibia formed a national organisation, Namibia National Students Organisation (NANSO), which adopted The Student Voice as the official newsorgan.

963. Die Suidwester. Windhoek. 1945 -

The official organ of the National Party in Namibia, published twice a week - and later three times a week - since August 1945.

964. S.W.A. Annual. Jaarboek. Jahrbuch. Windhoek. 1945 -

This yearbook was edited for 35 years by Sam Davis, since 1981 by Jean Fischer and Peter Meinert. It has over the years carried a

wide range of articles on history, economic growth, geography,
wildlife and history, with a number making original contributions
to economic history. They are brief, popular in style, often well
illustrated and sometimes thoroughly researched in the antiquarian
tradition. The annual is a particularly valuable source on the
business community and   economic development in the late 1940s
and the 1950s, where it regularly covered mining, fisheries, and
karakul breeding and published foreign trade statistics.

965. Swakara Nuus. Windhoek. 1973 -

Published by Hudson's Bay & Annings, this bi-monthly newsletter -
mainly in Afrikaans - provides useful information on the karakul
industry, production and sales statistics, prices, pelt types
and auctions.

966. SWALU. Suidwes-Afrikaanse Landbou-Unie/South West Africa Agricultural
Union. Jaarverslag/Annual Report. Windhoek.

Apart from a general review by way of introduction, this annual
report of the Agricultural Union is largely a descriptive summary
of the administrative and representational activities of the Union,
its branches and the Control Boards (see no. 1036), in which it
plays an influential part. There are few economic statistics,
but informative coverage of policy discussions and initiatives
with the South African administration on a range of issues, notably
drought relief, debt, credits, levies, etc.

967. Yearbook of the Karakul Breeders Association of Southern Africa.
Windhoek. 1958 -

Published under slightly different titles since 1958, the articles
in this mainly technical yearbook are directed to a highly specialised
branch of stock-farming in which breeding is critical. There are,
however, occasional articles concerned with economic developments
and reviews of the Society's activities.

968. Windhoek Advertiser. Windhoek. 1919 -

The only daily English newspaper in Namibia. Since the takeover
by a West German publishing house in 1978, it has generally been
supportive of the Democratic Turnhalle Alliance. Under the
editorship of David Pieters since 1983 it has, however, become more
open for independent journalism.

969. Windhoek Observer. Windhoek. 1978 -

Edited by Hannes Smith, ousted in 1978 from the editorship of
Windhoek Advertiser and Namibia's most controversial journalist,
this independent weekly newspaper has vehemently opposed the South
African administration and military occupation of Namibia. The
newspaper mixes serious political reporting and analysis (especially
in the form of a weekly column written by Gwen Lister) with sen-
sationalism and an obsession with "sex and crime". During 1984 the
newspaper subjected to increasingly severe legal harassment by the
South African regime, and several issues were banned in mid-year.

The ban was subsequently lifted only under stringent political conditions. Soon, afterwards, Gwen Lister was effectively sacked and several other progressive journalists resigned in sympathy.

970. <u>Wirtschaftsbericht Südwestafrika.</u>   Windhoek.   1977 –

A mimeographed monthly newsletter in German, compiled by Dr. H.J. Rust and distributed by the firm Keller & Neuhaus Trust. Based on press reports and business intelligence, it provides succinct and frequently unreported information on current economics and politics.

C.   South African

971. <u>Africa insight</u>. Pretoria: The Africa Institute of South Africa.
1970 -

Published three times a year by The Africa Institute of South Africa,
which over the years has devoted considerable attention to Namibia
(see no. 415). The magazine has carried several articles on Namibian
economics and development strategy by G.M.E. Leistner, Theo Malan
and other economists.

972. <u>Braby's Commercial Directory of South, East and Central Africa</u>.
Durban.

This is one of the two major trade directories for Southern Africa,
the other being the <u>Cape Times Directory of Southern Africa</u> (Cape
Town). Both devote a country section to Namibia, within which entries
are arranged alphabetically, by town and by trade classification.
Braby now publishes a separate directory for Namibia, the most
recent being <u>SWA 1984. Braby's Business Directory</u>. The directories
provide an index of individual businesses, with varying potted
information on the nature, products and services of the enterprise.
They cover the great majority of manufacturing and commercial undertakings, but their classified sections are eclipsed by the <u>Yellow
Pages</u> of the <u>SWA/Namibia Telephone Directory</u>.

973. <u>Financial Mail</u>. Johannesburg. 1959 -

This is South Africa's premier weekly business magazine giving
Namibia limited but regular coverage. Commentary on current political
and economic affairs is complemented by standardised assessments
of company annual reports, for Namibia mainly those operating in
the mining and fish processing sectors. <u>Financial Mail</u> has also
published several special supplements on Namibia (see no. 405).

974. <u>International Affairs Bulletin</u>. Johannesburg. 1977 -

Published three times a year by the South African Institute of
International Affairs. There are many articles concerned with South
Africa in the regional context, including Namibia, written mainly
from a broadly pro-government perspective.

975. <u>Journal of Contemporary African Studies</u>. Pretoria. 1981 -

An interdisciplinary bi-annual journal, published by the Africa
Institute of South Africa, containing scholarly articles as well as
book reviews. Vol. 2., no. 1, 1982 presented two essays on Namibia

by André du Pisani (no. 282) and John Barratt (no. 767). The
contributions are written from a broad range of political perspectives, but the majority are within the liberal, "enlightened"
framework.

976. SA Fishing Industry Handbook and Buyer's Guide. Cape Town: Thomson
Publications SA.

This yearbook, which is published every two years, is a mine of
information for all students of South African and Namibian
fisheries. The 1982/83 edition (244 p.) contains an extensive review
of the performance of the fish industry during the 1981 and 1982
seasons, with tables giving fishing quotas and licences, as
well as local and world statistics of catches, landings and values.
There are also a register of more than 900 fishing vessels (including
160 Namibian), details of more than 80 public and private fishing
companies and information on registrations, licences, processing
factories, and organisations serving the industry. The associated
monthly trade journal, South West African Shipping News and Fishing
Industry Review (1946 -), is an important and frequently unique
source of economic and technical data on the industry, including
catch statistics.

977. South African Review. Johannesburg: Ravan Press/SARS (South African
Research Services), 1983 -

This excellent and comprehensive annual review is edited by a
Johannesburg-based research and information agency which also
publishes Work in Progress (no. 980). It appeared for the first
time in 1983, sub-titled Same Foundations, New Facades? A special
section devoted to "South Africa and Southern Africa" contained
several articles on SADCC, destabilisation and Namibia (see no. 15).
The review is intended by its publishers to contribute to the
development of a critical perspective on contemporary economic,
social and political developments in Southern Africa.

978. Southern Africa Record. Braamfontein. 1975 -

Published quarterly by the South African Institute of International
Affairs, this Record contains the original texts of important
statements by political leaders (mainly South Africa), government
representatives and international relations in the Southern African
region.

979. A Survey of Race Relations in South Africa. Johannesburg. 1951/52 -

This is a standard reference work on current affairs in South Africa,
published annually by the liberal South African Institute of Race
Relations. All volumes contain a chapter on Namibia (c 20 pages),
focusing on the international negotiations, racist legislation,
political repression, the war and internal developments.

980. Work in Progress. Yeoville (SA). 197?

Published by the Southern African Research Services (SARS), WIP
provides an up-to-date analysis, from a progressive and not

infrequently neo-marxist point of view.   It covers current developments in South Africa, with particular emphasis on the labour scene
and the resistance to the apartheid system.   It has also published
several articles on Namibia, for example by Sue Cullinan (no. 14).
The South African Review (no. 977) is produced by the same editorial
collective.

D. Outside South Africa/Namibia

981. Action on Namibia. London. 1979 -

The bulletin of the Namibia Support Committee, containing news briefs, articles and information on campaign activities in support of the liberation struggle. The analysis is sharply anti-imperialist and some of the information, especially from liberation movement sources, is unreported anywhere else. The bulletin was published bi-monthly through 1979 and has since appeared irregularly in the form of a serie of thematic issues. The current news coverage has since been translated to Namibia News Briefings (See no. 1013). In addition The Campaign against the Namibian Uranium Contract, one of NSC's campaigning arms, has so far published three issues of CANUC News.

982. Africa. The international business, economic and political magazine. London. 1971 -

This is one of four general monthly magazines concerned with current developments in Africa. There is a broad coverage of Southern African affairs.

983. Africa Bureau Fact Sheet. London. 1970 -

Published periodically by the Africa Bureau as an insert to its bi-monthly newsbriefing X RAY (see no. 1029), each Fact Sheet analyses and presents background information on a topical Southern Africa issue. Namibia is regularly covered; of particularly value has been a review of the economy which has appeared more or less annually since 1978. Alternating irregularly with the Fact Sheet has been a Document Paper,which has featured a number of important Namibian documents not easily accessible through other sources. Neither series has appeared since the incorporation of X RAY into the Lincoln Letter in January 1984.

984. Africa Confidential. London. 1968 -

Published fortnightly, AC is supplied on the condition that the information is treated as confidential. Each issue - usually 8 pages - provides up-to-date comments, mostly political, on a few selected subjects. The idea is to reveal "inside information", but the comments on Namibia often contain factual errors.

985. Africa Contemporary Record. Annual survey and documents. London: Europa Publications/New York: Holmes & Meier. 1968 -

Edited by Colin Legum, ACR is the single most important reference work on current developments in Africa. There are substantial country surveys and articles concerned with specific topics as well as a wide range of documents. The section on Namibia (c 20 pages) is especially valuable for its analysis of current economic affairs, in recent years written by Reginald H. Green.

986. Africa Economic Digest. Weekly business news, analysis and forecast. London: MEED Ltd. 1980 -

An up-to-date weekly magazine specialising on business news. Apart from brief country-by-country sections, there are also longer background articles and surveys. There are from time to time comments on Namibian economic affairs, and the Southern African region (apart from South Africa itself) is well covered.

987. Africa Guide. Essex: Saffron Walden. 1977 -

A reference work in the format of an annual handbook covering current events. The section on Namibia in the 1984 edition (p. 227-230) is written by Colm Foy, and gives a brief survey of political and economic development.

988. Africa News. A weekly digest of African affairs. Durham (US).

Now in its 22nd volume, Africa News is published weekly, except the last two weeks of June and December. It provides up-to-date comments on current events, with a particularly broad coverage of the Southern African region. The viewpoints of the liberation movements are reflected through extensive interviews.

989. Africa Now. London: Pan-African Publishers. 1981 -

This is the youngest of the general monthly magazines covering current African events, and like its main competitors it covers the Southern African region regularly.

990. Africa Report. New Brunswick, N.J.: Transaction Periodicals Consortium. 1955 -

A bi-monthly publication of the African-American Institute, which describes itself as "non-partisan". It contains a section of news briefs as well as longer articles and book reviews. There are often articles and comments relating to Namibia and Southern Africa, and special attention is focused on US policies and interests in the region.

991. Africa Research Bulletin. Exeter. 1964 -

This press digest , a unique aid to the study of contemporary Africa, is published in two series: political, social and cultural, and economic, financial and technical. ARB is published monthly, and consists of information gathered from the African, European and American press and radio, as well as from international news agencies and African governments. All sources are acknowledged, each issue is comprehensively indexed and cross-references are made to previous issues of the bulletin.

992. Africa South of the Sahara. London: Europa Publications. 1971 -

A standard annual reference work on Africa, containing general articles as well as country surveys, which are updated each year. The Namibia

section in the 1983-84 edition (p. 603-18) was originally written
by Ruth First and revised by Guy Arnold.

993. Africa Today. Denver. 1953 –

A quarterly journal on African affairs, mainly written by scholars
with a more general readership in mind. There have recently been two
special issues on Namibia: Namibia and the West: Multinational
Corporations and International Law (vol. 30, nos. 1 & 2, 1983) (see
no. 394) and Namibia, South Africa and the West (vol. 29, no. 1,
1982) (see also no. 765). Africa Today offers an excellent book
review section and a list of publications received.

994. African Business. London: IC Publications. 1978 –

A monthly magazine focusing on African economic development, containing
longer feature stories, country briefings, sectoral surveys (e.g.
mining, banking, energy) as well as business news. AB provides
regular information on Namibia, especially on mining, fisheries
and transnational corporations. Among the contributors is Roger
Murray (see nos. 422, 595).

995. Afrique-Asie. Paris: Societé d'editions Afrique, Asie, Amerique
Latine). 1972 –

996. AfricAsia. Paris: Societé d'editions Afrique, Asie, Amerique, Latine).
1984 –

This is a progressive, independent and widely read French periodical.
It covers Africa, Middle, East, Asia and Latin America with a network of local correspondents. The French edition has been published
fortnightly since 1972, while the English edition was started as
a monthly in 1984. It is partly based on Afrique-Asie, but gives
greater attention to countries and questions of concern to English-
speaking readers. There is a broad coverage of the Southern African
region, including Namibia.

997. Aktueller Informationsdienst Afrika. Hamburg. 1981 –

Published fortnightly by Institut für Afrika-Kunde/Documentations-
Leitstelle Afrika in Hamburg, this is a current affairs information
service based on clippings from African newspapers. The selection
pays special attention to   social and economic development.
The section on Namibia consists mainly of excerpts from Allgemeine
Zeitung, The Star(SA) and Financial Mail(SA).

998. Anti-Apartheid News. London. 1959 –

The monthly newspaper of the British Anti-Apartheid Movement presents articles and comments on current developments in the region,
British collaboration with apartheid, and campaigning activities.

999. Bulletin. London: Angola Information, 1982 –

Although mainly concerned with Angola, this news bulletin occasionally
provides information on the South African war against the Namibian

people. Based on the official Angolan news agency, it includes
statements and communiques related to the Namibian struggle for
independence as well as to the international negotiations.

1000. The Combatant. The Organ of the People's Liberation Army of Namibia
(PLAN). Luanda. 1979 –

Published monthly, this is the official organ of PLAN, the military
wing of SWAPO of Namibia. Its aim is to "serve as the main vehicle
of PLAN in disseminating to the Namibian oppressed masses and the
outside world information on political and military activities by
PLAN against the forces of the illegal occupationist racist regime
of South Africa in Namibia".

1001. Dateline: Namibia. New York. 1982 –

A publication of the Division for Mission in North America of the
Lutheran Church in America. The main focus is on the role
played by the churches in Namibia and the activities of the Lutheran
Church in America in supporting the struggle for Namibian independence.

1002. Facts and Reports. Amsterdam. 1971 –

A wide-ranging selection of press cuttings on Southern Africa
published twice a month. Its sources are mainly British, South
African, Namibian and Zimbabwean newspapers, international magazines
and radio reports. The coverage is primarily of political events,
but feature articles and economics are far from ignored, and a basic
index by country and subject is a distinctly useful feature. It is
published by the Holland Comittee on Southern Africa (Angola Comité).

1003. Focus on Political Repression in Southern Africa. News bulletin of
the International Defence and Aid Fund. London. 1976 –

This informative press digest of the International Defence & Aid
Fund, the continuation of the twice yearly Information Service Manual
(1967-1974), is published six times a year. Its purpose is to pub-
licise political repression in South Africa and Namibia and the
military build-up of the apartheid regime, in support of the
campaign for the release of all political prisoners. On Namibia
it has the widest press coverage of the available current affairs
sources, is expertly compiled, and like all IDAF publications exhibits
a high and consistent standard of factual accuracy. Coverage of
economic affairs is unfortunately outside its scope, but the social
and economic effects of repression and exploitation are regularly
featured. A comprehensive index, which covers 10 numbers at a time,
serves as a powerful finding aid. Subscribers to FOCUS also receive
the IDAF Briefing Papers, some of which are devoted to Namibia (see
nos. 42, 292).

1004. ICSA Bulletin. London. 1979 –

Published irregularly by the International Committee against Apartheid,
Racism and Colonialism in Southern Africa. ICSA's objects are to
promote support for and solidarity with the national liberation

struggles being waged by the ANC of South Africa and SWAPO of Namibia.

1005. <u>Information and Comment</u>. SWAPO of Namibia. London. 1979 –

This is a wide-ranging bi-monthly selection of press cuttings arranged by subject, mainly from the British and Namibian press, as well as SWAPO statements and commentaries. It is distributed by the SWAPO Western European office. A similar publication by the same name is also irregularly distributed by the SWAPO Scandinavia office (Stockholm).

1006. <u>Informationsdienst südliches Afrika</u>. Bonn. 1975 –

The monthly magazine of the Anti-Apartheid Movement in the Federal Republic of Germany and Informationsstelle Südliches Afrika. It contains well-researched articles in a popular style, book reviews and information on campaigning activities. Namibia is covered extensively, and no. 7/8 1983 was a special issue on Namibia (see no. 41).

1007. <u>Internationales Afrikaforum</u>. München: Weltforum Verlag. 1965 –

Quarterly magazine published in cooperation with the IFO-Institut für Wirtschaftsforschung, Entwicklungsländer/Afrikastudienstelle and the Europäisches Institut für politische, wirtschaftliche und soziale Fragen. Each issue contains a brief chronicle of current events in most African countries, supplemented by a few longer and more analytical essays on specific themes or countries.

1008. <u>Jeune Afrique</u>. Paris. 1980 –

An influential weekly magazine in French, published by La Societé Africaine de Presse. Its main focus is on North Africa and the French-speaking part of the continent, but Namibia and the rest of Southern Africa are also regularly covered.

1009. <u>Journal of Southern African Studies</u>. Oxford: Oxford University Press. <u>1974</u> –

Published twice a year, this is the leading scholarly journal concerned with Southern African studies. The contributions are of high academic quality. The lack of studies on Namibia is reflected in the Journal, and up to 1984 there has only been one article relating to Namibia: Richard Moorsom (no. 664).

1010. <u>Nachrichten/Newsletter</u>. Basel. 1977(?) –

The quarterly bulletin of the Basler Afrika Bibliographien containing book reviews and information on its activities, such as library acquisitions, publications, conferences, etc.

1011. <u>Namibia Bulletin</u>. New York. 1973 –

Published by the United Nations, the main purpose of this irregular bulletin is to present information on recent developments inside Namibia as well as on the activities of the United Nations.

1012. Namibia in Focus. London. 1981 -

Distributed free of charge to schools, trade unions, mass media and politicians by the South African propaganda agency Namibia Informa- tion Service, which is run by the public relations company Lloyd-Hughes Associates Ltd. NIS was set up in 1980 to promote the views of the South African government and the Democratic Turnhalle Alliance. NIS has also produced several glossy booklets and "fact sheets".

1013. Namibia News Briefing. London. 1983 -

A two-page news briefing produced monthly by the Namibia Support Committee, mainly in the form of a press digest. It provides packed and up-to-date information on current events, with sub-sections on repression, militarisation, internal developments, the economy, the churches and the liberation struggle.

1014. Namibia Youth. Luanda. 1980 -

The official bulletin of the SWAPO Youth League, published bi-monthly.

1015. The Namibian Worker. Luanda. 1983 -

The first and apparently only issue of this official organ of the National Union of Namibian Workers (NUNW) appeared in October 1983.

1016. New African. London. 1966 -

Under the name African Development, this was the first monthly magazine on Africa to appear in English. It is published by IC Publications and, complementing its counterpart, Africa Business, specialises in political affairs and up-to-date comments on current events, with a broad coverage of Southern Africa.

1017. New African Yearbook. London. 1977 -

Published by IC Publications (see also nos. 994, 1016), this is a handy reference work on political history, current events and socio-economic conditions. There are separate chapters on each African country as well as more analytical articles on selected topics. The chapters on Namibia have since 1981 been written by Richard Moorsom. From 1983/84 the yearbook has been divided into two volumes: West & Central Africa and East & Southern Africa.

1018. Objective: Justice. New York. 1969 -

Published by the UN Department of Public Information, this is a quarterly review of UN activities against apartheid, racial discrim- ination and colonialism. As well as reports, it summarises and re- produces important UN documents, studies, statements and resolutions on Southern Africa, and occasionally devotes a whole issue to Namibia (see no. 757).

1019. PCR Information. Reports and background papers. Geneva. 1979 -

A journal published by the Programme to Combat Racism of the World

Council of Churches. Its primary purpose is "to provide churches, support groups and individuals with a background documentation and analysis on the major issues in combating racism". Apart from general articles, WCC documents and book reviews, it also contains statements from the Namibian churches (see e.g. no. 14, 1982 and no. 17, 1983). No. 2, 1979 and no. 11, 1981 were special issues on recent developments in Namibia.

1020. Pressedienst. Bonn. 1980 –

Distributed by the "Namibia Information Office", this monthly news service in German presents the views of the South African government, the Democratic Turnhalle Alliance and the Multi-Party Conference. Longer background articles with the same purpose are also published as separate documents (Dokumentation).

1021. Quarterly Economic Review of Namibia, Botswana, Lesotho, Swaziland. London: The Economist Intelligence Unit. 1960 –

This descriptive survey is one of the most authoritative sources on Namibian economic affairs, published quarterly with an annual supplement. The section on Namibia (c 15 p.) provides a wealth of up-to-date information, supplemented by statistics where available.

1022. Resister. Journal of the Committee on South African War Resistance. London. 1979 –

This bi-monthly magazine is written and produced by COSAWR (UK), which was set up in 1978 by exiled South African war resisters. Using inside information as well as a wide range of public sources and documents, Resister documents South Africa's military build-up, the attacks against neighbouring countries and the occupation of Namibia. Nos. 27, 1983-30, 1984 presented a four-part article on Namibia under siege (nos. 278-81). COSAWR has also published State of war. Apartheid South Africa's decade of militarisation (1984).

1023. South Africa/Namibia Update. New York. 1977 –

A monthly news briefing monitoring economic and political developments in South Africa and Namibia. It is published by the Africa Policy Information Center of the African-American Institute, and partly overlaps with the Update section of Africa Report (no. 990).

1024. SWAPO Information Bulletin. Luanda. 1982 –

Succeeding Namibia Today (1977-1983), this monthly journal is published by the SWAPO Dept. of Information and Publicity. It contains official SWAPO statements, interviews and comments, mainly on topical issues and events. Before the launching of the official party journal SWAPO's Western European Office (London) published Namibia News (1968-1976).

1025. SWAPO of Namibia. Informations-Bulletin. Bonn. 1983 –

A monthly bulletin in German, distributed by the SWAPO mission to the Federal Republic of Germany. It contains brief articles and comments on current events, with special emphasis on issues relevant to a West German audience.

1026. <u>TCLSAC Reports</u>. Toronto. 197? –

A journal produced six times a year by the Toronto Committee for the Liberation of Southern Africa, providing information on current events in the region from the liberation movements' perspective as well as on campaigning activities in Canada.

1027. <u>United Nations Council for Namibia</u>. <u>Report of the Council</u>. New York. 1968 –

The annual report of the UN Council for Namibia is an indispensable reference document, reflecting the role of the Council as the legal administrative authority for Namibia until independence and as a major policy-making organ of the UN. The report reviews at length the statements and activities of the Council, the General Assembly, the Security Council and other UN bodies, and considers recent economic, political, social and military development in Namibia. There is also full information on the UN Fund for Namibia, the Nationhood Programme and the UN Institute for Namibia.

1028. UNITED NATIONS ECONOMIC AND SOCIAL COUNCIL. <u>Violations of human rights in Southern Africa</u>. New York. (Progress report of the <u>Ad Hoc</u> Working Group of Experts).

Reports in this series have been prepared annually since 1967 and form one of the most comprehensive historical records of political, social and economic violations of human rights in white-ruled Southern Africa, combining the testimony of victims and representatives of the liberation movements with a wide-ranging survey of documentary evidence. Also of considerable value are the voluminous verbatim records. The section on Namibia (p. 74-95) in the most recent report (1984) starts with a brief survey of the efforts to secure a negotiated settlement, the South African moves towards the imposition of an internal settlement, the militarisation of Namibia and attacks against Angola. This is followed by a carefully documented examination of the treatment of political prisoners and captured freedom fighters, including evidence of torture. Attention is then focused on the situation of Black workers and the conditions of the civilian population in the bantustans. The final part gives information on persons suspected of being guilty of serious violations of human rights.

1029. XRAY on Current Affairs in Southern Africa. Huntington (UK). 1970 –

A bi-monthly news briefing which follows a standard four-page format. It has a liberal perspective, is well informed, and concentrates on key issues and illustrative case studies; its tight editing making it highly readable. Namibian coverage is, however, in fragment. Issued for 15 years by The Africa Publication Trust associated with The Africa Bureau, <u>X Ray</u> was in January 1984 incorporated into the UK-US bimonthly <u>Lincoln Letter</u>, following a similar format and perspective and edited by Donald Woods.

E. Government publications

1030. The Land and Agricultural Bank of South West Africa. Report of the Board of Management. Windhoek. 1932 -

An annual statement of the assets and liabilities of this powerful official credit agency and of its lending activities. The report includes statistics and brief comments, and is the only source of these important data on an economic and political lynchpin of the colonial order, although its accounts appear in the Official Gazette.

1031. On/Op Record. Windhoek.

Published by the SWA/Namibian Information Service every three weeks, and distributed free of charge. It reflects the official position of the South African administration and the Multi-Party Conference, and reproduces articles and comments from Die Republikein, Allgemeine Zeitung, Windhoek Advertiser , etc.

1032. Official Gazette of South West Africa/Offisiële koerant van Suidwes-Afrika. Windhoek. 1921 -

The gazette is the legal instrument of South Africa's colonial administration in Windhoek, and contains laws, regulations, proclamations and directives issued by the SWA Administrator and, from 1977, the Administrator-General. In the period 1915-1921 it was published under the title Official Gazette of the protectorate of SWA in military occupation of the Union Forces. Some of the bantusan authorities also publish their own gazettes, such as the Ovambo Official Gazette. It should also be noted that up to 1977 it does not contain certain legislation applied directly to Namibia by the South African Parliament (Acts) and State President (Proclamations) and that after 1977 Walvis Bay is excluded altogether. For both these exclusions it is necessary to check the South African Government Gazette.

1033. South Africa 19--. Official Yearbook of the Republic of South Africa. Johannesburg (Chris van Rensburg Publications). 1974 -

Compiled and edited by the Department of Foreign Affairs, this massive yearbook - about 1000 pages - covers geography, history, economy as well as the official view of current events. There is no separate chapter on Namibia, but there are many references to the country in the various chapters.

1034. South Africa (Rep.). Departments of state, annual reports. Cooperation and Development (formerly Bantu Administration and Development);

Coloured and Nama Relations and Rehoboth Affairs; Agricultural
Technical Services; Agricultural Economics and Marketing; Sea
Fisheries Branch. Pretoria/Cape Town.

The annual reports of several central government departments were
significant if variable sources of information on Namibia between
the transfer of many administrative functions to Pretoria in 1969
and their return to the Administrator-General in Windhoek in 1978.
Of the series indicated, the report of the Cooperation and Development department contains virtually nothing on Namibia, leaving a
huge area of policy and administration unreported from the time of
its takeover of "Native Affairs" in the mid-1950s. Coloured Relations
is brief, but contains primary descriptive and statistical data on
the Rehoboth and Nama reserves. Agricultural Economics and Marketing
reveals occasional scraps of economic information, mainly on stock
imports from Namibia. Agricultural Technical Services devotes brief
attention to state veterinary administration and disease control in
Namibia. Sea Fisheries is the fullest of the quintet, providing
statistics as an appendix to the main report. Since the Administrator-
General's takeover, annual reporting of any kind by government departments has virtually ceased except in the cases of Water
Affairs (see no. 1038) and Finance (see no. 437).

1035. South West Africa (Adm.). White paper on the activities of the
different branches for the year ----. Windhoek. 1962 -

This official publication is the nearest approach to a conventional
series of annual colonial reports, and as such is an approximate,
if belated, continuation of the interwar SWA Administrator's Reports
to the League of Nations (see no. 258). Its coverage reflects the
dual status of the administration whose activities it reports, being
responsible both for the affairs of the white colonists, and thus
excluding altogether such pillars of the machinery of repression
as "Bantu Administration" and labour, and for a range of national
functions, especially finance and economics. The transfer to South
African government departments of most of the latter functions, on
which the reports at times give considerable description and statistical information, deprived the series of its most valuable political
and economic content from 1969 onwards, and this is only partly made
up in sections of annexes of the South African departmental reports.
Confusion has only deepened with the reconstruction since 1977 of
the national colonial administration, which appears to publish no
information on its activities at all.

1036. South West African (Agricultural) Control Boards. Dairy Industry/
Grain/Karakul/Meat. Windhoek.

The agricultural control boards reflect the extension to Namibia
of the South African interventionist strategy in the marketing of
farm products. For lack of any annual reports from the appropriate
sections of the colonial administration, they are invaluable
sources of primary data on climate, production, trade, prices and
marketing conditions, although frequently the coverage is rudimentary
and varies from year to year. The Dairy Industry Board was dissolved in 1969 after the dramatic decline in dairy output, and the
Grain Board followed in 1973. The Karakul Board was merged with its

South African counterpart in 1969, but marked its reconstitution in
1979 with a substantial annual report reviewing the historical
evolution of the sub-sector with time-series of production data.
The report of the Meat Trade Control Board, which allocates and
control quotas for slaughter stock exported to South Africa, gives
details on prices, numbers of cattle slaughtered, and exports of
hides and livestock . The reports of these boards are not widely
circulated and are unfortunately difficult to obtain outside Namibia.

1037. South West Africa (Adm.). Estimates of revenue and expenditure for
the financial year ending 31 March 19--. Windhoek.

This is the most recent title of the budget presented by the SWA
Administration (Central Revenue Fund). It was previously published
as Estimates of the Expenditure to be defrayed from the Revenue Account
and Estimates of the Expenditure from the Territorial Development
and Reserve Fund and Estimates of Revenue to be defrayed from the SWA
Account, and should be consulted with the annual budget speeches.
Each bantustan (or "Representative Authority" after 1980) has its own
budget. Especially after the 1969 transfer and the proliferation
of bantustans, precise tracking of categories of expenditure becomes
impossible becuase of the maze of "block grant" transfers.

1038. South West Africa (Adm.). Report of the Secretary for Water Affairs.
Windhoek.

Published annually, this extensive report gives a range of information
on water supply, rainfall, irrigation, and dam contents, as well as
on the Department of Water Affair's construction programme, planning
and administration. The report covering the period 1 April 1982 to
31 March 1983 is more than 100 pages long.

F.   Company reports

Information published by or obtained from business enterprises,
especially company annual reports, is an important source of statistical and policy data. For lists of currently operating companies,
see UN Council for Namibia: List of transnational corporations and
other foreign economic interests operating in Namibia (no. 448);
UN Centre on Transnational Corporations: Role of transnational
corporations in Namibia (no. 486); Namibia Support Committee; "A
country by country listing of foreign companies operating in Namibia"
(no. 423); Richard Moorsom: Exploiting the sea (no. 562); and
Catholic Institute for International Relations: Mines and independence (no. 580). McGregor's who owns whom is also an important source
(no. 417).

16. THESES

1039. AARNI, TEDDY. The Kalunga concept in Ovambo religion from 1870 onwards. PhD, University of Stockholm, 1982, 166 p.

1040. ADAMS, M. The British attitude to German colonisation, 1880-85. MA, London, 1935.

1041. ADEBAYO, O.J. (Project). Namibia: A study of the interests, attitudes and approaches of the internal and external parties to the conflict, 1960-1980. MA, Univ. Keele. In preparation.

1042. AHMAD, SYED SHAHZAD. The South West Africa dispute and the International Court of Justice. PhD, Knoxville, Univ. Tennessee, 1971, 285 p.

1043. ALLISON, CAROLINE. (Project). The subordination of Namibian women. Historical evolution, recent trends and possible future directions. PhD, Univ. Sussex. In preparation.

1044. AUSTERHOFF, AUGUST. Die Banken in den deutschen Kolonien. Diss., Univ. Greifswald, 1918 (Publ.: Borna, Leipzig: Noske, 1918, 41 p.).

1045. AYDELOTTE, WILLIAM O. Bismarck and British colonial policy: the problem of South-West-Africa 1883-1885. PhD, Univ. Michigan, 1935. (Publ.: Philadelphia: Univ. of Pennsylvania Press/London: Humphrey Mulford, 1937, 179 p. Reprint: New York: Russel & Russel, 1970, 207 p.).

1046. BAARD, FREDERICK R.L. Die ontwikkeling van die visbedryf in die Republiek van Suid-Afrika en Suidwes-Afrika. M.Com., Univ. South Africa, Pretoria, 1968.

1047. BAARD, FREDERICK R.L. 'n Kritiese beskouing van die ontwikkeling van die bestuur en organisasie van die visnywerheid in die Republiek van Suid-Afrika en Suidwes-Afrika. D.B.A., Univ. Stellenbosch, 1971.

1048. BACH, ROSEMARIE. Die Deutschen in Namibia seit dem Ende der deutschen Kolonialherrschaft. Diplomarbeit. Univ. Bremen, 1980, 80 p.

1049. BACKEBERG, HEINRICH E.W. Duitse kolonisasieplanne in suidelike Afrika, 1844-1885. MA, Univ. Pretoria, 1944.

1050. BACKEBERG, HEINRICH E.W. Die betrekkinge tussen die Suid-Afrikaanse Republiek en Duitsland tot na die Jameson-inval, 1852-1896. D.Phil., Univ. Pretoria, 1949. (Publ.: Argiefjaarboek wir Suid-Afrikaanse geskiedenis, 12, deel 1, 1949).

360

1051. BADE, KLAUS J. Friedrich Fabri und der Imperialismus der Bismarckzeit: Revolution, Depression, Expansion. Diss., Erlangen
Univ., 1972. (Publ.: Zürich/Freiburg: Atlantis, 1975, 579 p.).

498. BÄHR, JÜRGEN. Kulturgeographische Wandlungen in der Farmzone
Südwestafrikas. Diss., Marburg Univ., 1967. (Publ.: Bonn:
Dümmler in Komm., 1968, 137 p.).

1052. BAERMANN, HULDA E. German annexation of Southwest Africa. MA, Iowa
Univ., 1935.

1053. BAHTA, B.M. The international status of South-West Africa. MA,
Univ. Illinois, 1959.

1054. BAKER, N.A. The Nazi dream of empire. A study of the effects of
African colonies on German policy, 1919-1941. MA, East Texas State
College, 1963/64.

1055. BALLARD, BROOK B. South-West-Africa 1945-1950: Union province or
United Nations trusteeship territory. MA, Univ. Chicago, 1955, 117 p.

644. BANGHART, PETER D. Migrant labour in South West Africa and its effects
on Ovambo tribal life. MA, Univ. Stellenbosch, 1969, 152 p.

1056. BARNARD, NICO. Die staatkundige ontwikkeling in Suidwes-Afrika vanaf
die wêreldhofuitspraak in 1966 tot die aankondiging van die Turnhalle-
beraad. MA, Univ. Oranje-Vrystaat, Bloemfontein, 1980.

1057. BARNARD, WILHELM S. Staatkundig-geografiese aspekte van Suidwes-Afrika.
MA, Univ. Stellenbosch, 1959.

83. BARNARD, WILHELM S. Die streekpatrone van Suidwes-Afrika. PhD,
Univ. Stellenbosch, 1964, 393 p.

1058. BARRY, LOUIS M. Wangedrag en die administratiese tugproses ten
opsigte van onderwys in staats- en staatsondersteunde skole in die
Unie en Suidwes-Afrika: 'n krities-vergelykende studie. M.Ed.,
Univ. Stellenbosch, 1954.

1059. BAUMANN, JULIUS. Mission und Ökumene in Südwestafrika. Dargestellt
am Leben und Werk von Hermann Heinrich Vedder. Diss., Marburg Univ.,
1964, 57 + 7 p. (Publ.: Mission und Ökumene in Südwestafrika,
dargestellt am Lebenswerk von Dr. Hermann Heinrich Vedder. Leiden/
Köln: E.J. Brill, 1965, 168 p.).

1060. BEEGER, H. Besiedlung und wirtschaftliche Erschliessung der Küstenge-
biete in Südwestafrika. Staatsexamens-Hausarbeit, Univ. Mainz,
1969, 130 p.

1061. BEHRENDT, PETER. Was hat der Gesundheitsdienst in den deutschen
Kolonien Afrikas geleistet? Diss., Hamburg Univ., 1940, 53 p.

118. BERGER, LOTHAR. Der Einfluss der Grenzziehung auf die Ovambo.
Diplomarbeit, Univ. Mainz, 1980, 148 p.

1062. BERRY, LUTHERINE L. 'n Kritiese beskouing van die internasionale
geregshof as regs-politieke orgaan and die versoenbaarheid van sy
judisiële en politieke funksies met verwysing na die revokasie van
die Suidwes-Afrika mandaat deur die Algemene Vergadering van die
Verenigde Volke-Organisasie. LL.M., Univ. Suid-Afrika, Pretoria, 1977.

221. BERTELSMANN, WERNER. Die Minderheitenrechte der deutschsprachigen
Bevölkerung in Südwestafrika. Diss., Göttingen Univ., 1970, xxxiv,

361

169 p. (Publ.: <u>Die deutsche Sprachgruppe Südwestafrikas in Politik und Recht seit 1915.</u> (Windhoek: SWA Wissenschaftliche Gesellschaft, 1979, xxxiv, 172 p.).

351. BEWERSDORF, RICHARD. <u>Die Industrialisierung der Südafrikanischen Union und Deutsch Südwestafrikas.</u> Diss., Univ. Bonn, 1940. (Publ.: Berlin: Mier & Glasemann, 1939, 99 p.).

1063. BISSON, JEAN. <u>Le statut international du Sud-Ouest Africain.</u> Thèse doct., Paris, 1954, 175 p.

1064. BIXLER, RAYMOND W. <u>Anglo-German imperialism in South Africa, 1880-1900.</u> PhD, Ohio State Univ., 1929. (Publ.: Baltimore: Warwick & York, 1932, 181 p.).

1065. BLAAUW, CHRISTOFFEL E. <u>Propagandametodes van swart en bruin partye in Suidwes-Afrika.</u> MA, Univ. Potschefstroom, 1978.

179. BLEY, HELMUT. <u>Der Kampf um die koloniale Sozialordnung in Deutsch-Südwestafrika 1894-1914: Obrigkeit, Gesellschaft und Stamm.</u> Diss., Univ. Hamburg, 1968, 390 p. (Publ.: Kolonialherrschaft und Sozialstruktur in Deutsch-Südwestafrika, Hamburg: Leibniz, 1968, 390 p. and South-West Africa under German rule, London: Heinemann/Evanston: Northwestern Univ. Press, 1971, 303 p.).

1066. BLUMHAGEN, HANS ERNST. <u>Die Doppelstaatigkeit der Deutschen im Mandatsgebiet Südwestafrika und ihre völkerrechtlichen Auswirkungen.</u> Diss., Univ. Halle, 1939, 95 p. (Publ.: Reimer, 1938, 90 p.).

182. BOCHERT, CHRISTIAN H.K. <u>The Witboois and the Germans in Southwest-Africa. A study of their interaction between 1863 and 1905.</u> MA, Univ. Natal, Durban, 1980, 207 p.

501. BOETTICHER, GERHARD. <u>Die landwirtschaftlichen Produktions- und Siedlungsverhältnisse in Südwestafrika vor und nach dem Weltkrieg.</u> Diss., Friedrich-Wilhelms-Univ. zu Breslau, 1930. (Publ.: Breslau: Hochschulverlag, 1930, 132 p.).

119. BORKOWSKY, CHRISTOPH. <u>Zu einigen Aspekten des Ovambolebens.</u> Diplomarbeit, Freie Univ., Berlin, 1975, 122 p.

1067. BORNEFELD, OTTO. <u>Das Bergrecht in den deutschen Schutzgebieten unter besonderer Berücksichtigung der Erlangung des Bergwerkseigentums</u> Diss., Heidelberg Univ., 1910. (Publ.: M(önchen)-Gladbach: Hütter, 1910, 72 p.).

1068. BOSCH, JOHANNES L. <u>Die Shambiu van die Okavango: 'n volkekundige studie.</u> PhD, Univ. Stellenbosch, 1964, 373 p.

1069. BOSHOFF, FREDERIK. <u>Die rol van lone in die volkshuishouding: en 'n ondersoek na die loonstruktuur van hoogekwalifiseerde mannekrag in die Republiek van Suid-Afrika en Suidwes-Afrika.</u> M.Com., Univ. Pretoria, 1973.

224. BRADFORD, ROBERT LAROY. <u>The origin and concession of the League of Nations' class "C" mandate for South West Africa and fulfilment of the sacred trust, 1919-1939.</u> PhD, Yale Univ., 1965, 493 p.

84. BRANDMAYR, JOSEF. <u>Eine Landeskunde von Südwestafrika mit besonderer Berücksichtigung der ethnisch und historisch-politisch bedingten Raumprobleme.</u> Diss., Univ. Salzburg, 1977, 553 p.

352. BRENNER, HARRO. Südwest-Afrika und sein Aussenhandel. Diss., Univ. Berlin, 1933, 87 p.

1070. BROMMER, OTTO. Das Budget der deutschen Schutzgebiete. Diss., Univ. Leipzig, 1920, 180 p.

1071. BUDACK, KUNO F.R.H. ´n Volkekundige studie van die Tses-reservaat, (Distrik Keetmanshoop, Suidwes-Afrika), met besondere verwysing na die geskiedenis en interetniese verhoudinge van die bewoners. MA, Univ. Pretoria, 1965.

1072. BUDACK, KUNO F.R.H. Die traditionelle politische Struktur der Khoe-Khoen in Südwestafrika (Stamm und Stammesregierung, auf historischer Grundlage). D.Phil, Univ. Pretoria, 1973, 341 p.

1073. BURGER, ANDRIES PETRUS. Die koste van watervoorsiening te Windhoek: ´n gevallestudie. M.Com., Univ. Potchefstroom, 1972.

1074. BURGER, NICOLAAS ALBERTUS. Die dorslandtrek: ´n histories-geografiese studie, 1870-1954. D.Phil, Univ. Bloemfontein, 1979.

727. CAROLL, FAYE. South West-Africa in the United Nations. PhD, Univ. Kentucky, Louisville, 1963. (Publ.: Lexington, Univ. of Kentucky Press, 1967, 123 p. Reprinted: Westport/Connecticut: Greenwood Press, 1975, 123 p.).

1075. CENTURIER-HARRIS, OLIVER M. Estimate of size and interaction of the South African anchovy and pilchard populations. M.Sc., Univ. Cape Town, 1977.

1076. CERFF, SEVÉRUS M. Die pligte en bevoeghede van blanke onderwysers in staats- en staatsondersteunde skole in die Unie en Suidwes-Afrika: ´n vergelykende studie. M.Ed., Univ. Stellenbosch, 1954.

86. CHRISTIE, RENFREW L. The political economy of the Kunene River hydro-electric schemes. MA, Univ. Cape Town, 1975, 242 p.

1077. CILLIERS, ANDRIES C. The South West African mandate in United Nations context. LL.D., Univ. South Africa, Pretoria, 1976, 314.

124. CLARENCE-SMITH, WILLIAM GERVASE. Mossamedes and its hinterland, 1875-1915. PhD, SOAS, Univ. London, 1975, 448 p. (Publ. in revised form: Slaves, peasants and capitalists in southern Angola 1840-1926, Cambridge U.P., 1979, 132 p.).

1078. CLASS, PAUL. Die Rechtsverhältnisse der freien farbigen Arbeiter in den deutschen Schutzgebieten Afrikas und der Südsee. Diss., Univ. Heidelberg, 1913, 101 p.

186. CLAUSS, RAINER. Reaktionen auf Kolonialismus und Imperialismus: Untersuchung der Völker Namibias. Diss., Freie Univ., Berlin, 1977, 104 p.

1079. COETZEE, E.R. Die geskinedenis van landelike vestiging van blankes in Suidwes-Afrika, 1915-1931. MA, Randse Afrikaanse Univ., 1982.

1080. CRONJE, PIETER KAREL. Die aanvangsonderwysstelsel vir blankes in Suidwes-Afrika: ´n pedagogiese evaluering. D.Ed., Univ. Suid-Afrika, Pretoria, 1977.

288. CROWELL, WILLIAM U. The evolution of South African control over South West Africa (Namibia). PhD, St. Johns Univ., NewYork, 1975, 434 p.

1081. CULLINAN, SUE. (Project). Political developments in Namibia since 1960: a study of the South West African People's Organisation (SWAPO). MA, University of Cape Town. In preparation.

1082. CURRY, F.G. The land policy of the South African government in South West Africa, 1915-1939. MA, SOAS, Univ. London, 1967.

354. CZAYA, EBERHARD. Der deutsche Imperialismus in Süd- und Südwestafrika. Ein Beispiel für Kontinuität und Elastizität der deutscher kolonialen Bestrebungen. Diss., Berlin (DDR), Humboldt-Univ., 1967, 476 p.

1083. DALE, RICHARD. The United Nations, the Union of South Africa, and the international status of South West Africa, April 25, 1945 - November 1, 1947: a case study in political motivation and behaviour. MA, Ohio State Univ., 1957.

1084. DALE, RICHARD. The evolution of the South West African dispute before the United Nations, 1945-1950. PhD, Princeton Univ., 1963, 357 p.

121. DAVIES, JOAN H. Palgrave and Damaraland. MA, Grahamstown, Rhodes Univ., 1939. (Publ.: Archives Yearbook for South African History, 1942, part II, p. 93-203).

1085. DEDERING, TILMAN, "Mein Arm ist nicht gelähmt, solange des Herrgott ihn als Zuchtrute gebrauchen will". -Zur Geschichte der religiös-politischen Bewegung von Hendrik Witbooi in Südwestafrika/Namibia. MA, Freie Univ., Berlin, 1984.

1086. DEEKEN, MATTHIAS. Das Geldwesen in den deutschen Kolonien. Diss., Univ. Münster, 1913. (Publ.: Münster: Westfälische Kreisdruckerei, 1913, 73 p.).

1087. DE KLERK, CORNELIUS H. Karakoelboerdery in "Rehoboth-gebiet". M.Agric., Univ. Pretoria, 1967.

1088. DE KLERK, CORNELIUS H. Menskundige en omgewings-invloede op praktykaanvaarding en reproduksie doeltreffendheid in die höepotensiaal bees-boerdery gebiede van Suidwes-Afrika. D.Inst. Agrar., Univ. Pretoria, 1980.

1089. DE KOCK, ANDRIES J. Die kleinhoewestelsel in Suidwes-Afrika gedurende die Duitse bewind, 1884-1915. MA, Univ. Stellenbosch, 1965.

1090. DE KOCK, GERHARDUS L. Die evolusiegang van die padroetenetwerke in Suidwes-Afrika. MA, Univ. Stellenbosch, 1973.

1091. DE KOCK, JOHAN. Die strukturering van 'n geintegreerde Blanke residensiële en woonhuismodel vir Windhoek: 'n faktorekologiese universum-studie van die 1975 sensusopname. MA, Univ. Oranje-Vrystaat, Bloemfontein, 1979, 163 p.

1092. DE KOCK, WILLEM W.J. Ekstraterritoriale vraagstukke van die Kaapse regering (1871-1885) met besondere verwysing na die Transgariep en Betsjoeanaland. PhD, Univ. Stellenbosch, 1947. (Publ.: Argief-jaarboek vir Suid-Afrikaense geskiedenis, 11, deel I, 1948).

1093. DEMASIUS, BERND W.W. Die kleinhandelstruktuur van Windhoek: 'n geografiese studie. MA, Randse Afrikaanse Univ., Johannesburg, 1979.

319. DEMUTH, JEAN. Der Diamantenmarkt mit besonderer Berücksichtigung der deutsch-südwestafrikanischen Ausbeute. Diss., Heidelberg, 1913. (Publ.: Karlsruhe: Braun, 1912, 132 p.).

1094. DENISOV, I.M. Kolonial' naya voina germanskogo imperializma v Yugo-Zapadnoi Afrike v 1903-1907 g bez meta. Diss., Univ. Moscow, 1944. (Colonial wars of German imperialism in South West Africa, 1903-1907).

1095. DENTLINGER, URSULA. Social and spatial mobility along the Kuiseb River in the Namib Desert, Namibia, MA, Univ. Cape Town, 1983.

356. DEUTSCHLAND, RUTH. Die Lage der afrikanischen Bevölkerung Süd- westafrikas und ihr Kampf um nationale Befreiung (1945-1959). Diss., Humboldt Univ., Berlin (DDR), 1967, 284 p.

1096. DE VRIES, IZAK DANIËL. Suidwes-Afrika/Namibië: ontleding van 'n potensieël revolusionêre situasie, 1978-1979. MA, Johannesburg, Randse Afrikaanse Univ., 1980.

896. DE VRIES, JOHANNES L. Sending en kolonialisme in Suidwes-Afrika: die invloed van die Duitse kolonialisme op die sendingswerk van die Rynse Sendinggenootskap in die vroeëre Duits- Suidwes-Afrika (1880- 1914/1918). D.Theol., Brussel Univ., 1971, 372 p. (Publ.: Namibia: Mission und Politik (1880-1918). Neukirchen-Vluyn: Neukirchener Verlag, 1980, 324 p./ Mission and colonialism in Namibia, Johannesburg: Ravan Press, 1978, 216 p.).

1097. DIEHL, HANS-HARTMUT. Carl Hugo Hahn in Suidwes-Afrika, 1842-1872. MA, Randse Afrikaanse Univ., Johannesburg, 1973, 212 p.

1098. DITTON, ERNST. Etatsrecht und Etatswesen in den deutschen Schutz- gebieten. Diss., Univ. Heidelberg, 1940, 47 p.

357. DOWD, HERBERT W. The non-white land and labour policies of the South African administration of South West Africa, 1918-1948. PhD, Fletcher School of Law and Diplomacy, Tufts Univ., 1954, 397 p.

188. DRECHSLER, HORST. Der Kampf der Nama und Herero gegen den deutschen Imperialismus (1884-1915). Habil.schrift, Univ. Halle (DDR), 1963, 568 p. (Publ.; Berlin: Akademie-Verlag, 1966, 372 p./"Let us die fighting". The struggle of the Herero and Nama against German imperialism (1884-1915), London, Zed Press, 1980, 278 p.)

1099. DRESCHER, C. Genossenschaftliche Kolonisationsarbeit in Deutsch Südwest-Afrika durch Deutschland, in Lybien durch Italien und in Mandschukuo durch Japan. Frankfurt Univ., 1940, 79 p.

1100. DUNGAN, MARY V. South-West-Africa. A study of the international problems resulting from the European colonization and subsequent conquest and mandatory administration of the Union of South Africa. MA, Stanford Junior Univ., 1927, 336 p.

620. DU PISANI, ETIENNE. Die Nama van Gibeon. 'n Etnografiese studie met besondere verwysing na sosiaal-ekonomiese aspekte. MA, Univ. Stellen- bosch, 1976, 189 p.

1101. EFIMENCO, NICHOLAS M. Imperialism and the League experiment with the mandate system. PhD, Univ. Minnesota, 1949, 243 p.

191. EIROLA, MARTTI. Ambolaisten vastarinta Saksan siirtomaavaltaa vastaan, 1885-1908. (The Ovambo peoples' resistance to German colonialism, 1885-1908). MA (pro gradu), Univ. Oulu, 1982, 150 p.

693. ELLIS, JUSTIN. Formal and nonformal education in Namibia. Diss., Diploma in Adult Ed., Univ. Manchester, 1980, 88 p.

694. ELLIS, JUSTIN. Basic adult education in Namibia after independence. M.Ed., Univ. Manchester, 1981.

1102. ELMENHORST, WILHELM L.G. Das Haus in Südwestafrika. Diss., Univ. Hamburg, 1926, 64 p.

1103. ELONHEIMO, MARJATTA. Luonnonmaantieteelisten tekijöiden vaikutus amboheimojen asitukseen ja elinkeinoihin. MA (pro gradu), Univ. Helsinki, 1967. (The influence of nature and geography on settlements and economic activities among the Ovambos).

819. EMMET, ANTHONY B. The rise of African nationalism in Namibia (1915-1966). Univ. Witwatersrand, PhD, in preparation.

192. ENGEL, LOTHAR. Die Stellung der Rheinischen Missionsgesellschaft zu den politischen und gesellschaftlichen Verhältnissen Südwestafrikas und ihr Beitrag zur dortigen kirchlichen Entwicklung bis zum Nama-Herero-Aufstand 1904-1907. Diss., Hamburg Univ., 1972, 504 p.

1104. ENGELS, HARALD. Ansätze des sozialen Wandels in Bildungswesen der Rheinischen Missionsgesellschaft in Südwest-Afrika (Namibia). Bochum Univ., 1976, ii, 170 p.

1105. ERAKER, STEINAR. Kirchliche Mission und politischer Kolonialismus in Namibia. Wissenschaftliche Hausarbeit, Phillipps- Univ. Marburg, 1984, 40 + v p.

509. ERKRATH, WILHELM. Der Voraussetzungen und Bedeutung der Farmwirtschaft in Südwestafrika im besonderen als koloniale Rohstoff- und Nahrungs- mittelquelle, unter Berücksichtigung der Entwicklungsmöglichkeiten. Diss., Techn. Hochschule, München, 1935, 151 p.

193. ESTERHUYSE, JAN H. Suidwes-Afrika 1880-1894. PhD, Univ. Cape Town, 1964. (Publ.: South West Africa, 1880-1894: The establishment of German authority in South West Africa. Cape Town: Struik, 1968, 225 p.).

1106. EVANS, LUTHER HARRIS. The mandates system and the administration of territories under C mandate. PhD, Univ. Stanford, 1927, 373 p.

1107. FEGBEUTEL, JÜRGEN PHILIPP. Die staatkundige betekenis van die Turnhalle-beraad in die proses van onafhanklikheidswording van Suidwes-Afrika/Namibië. MA, Univ. Pretoria, 1980.

1108. FLACHBERGER, INGEBORG. Das Glaubensleben der Namaqua von 1777 bis 1837 mit einer Einführung in die Stammesgeschichte. PhD, Wien, 1971, 255 p.

1109. FORBES, VERNON S. The expanding horizon: a geographical commentary upon routes, records, observations and opinions of travellers at the Cape 1750-1800. PhD, Rhodes Univ., Grahamstown, 1957. (Publ.: Pioneer travellers of South Africa ...., Cape Town/Amsterdam: Balkema, 1965, 177 p.).

1110. FORKEL, HELMUT. Das Küstengebiet Südwestafrikas und seine wirtschafts- geographische Bedeutung. Diss., Univ. Rostock, 1926. (Publ.; Rostock: Beckmann 1926, 111 p.).

1111. FULLER, BEN. (Project). Rural economic changes in Namibia brought about by the introduction of colonial market forces. PhD, Univ. Boston. In preparation.

322. GAD, JOHANNES. Die Betriebsverhältnisse der Farmen des mittleren Hererolandes, Deutsch Südwest-Afrika. Diss., Univ., Jena, 1915. (Publ.: Hamburg: Friedrichsen, 1915, 147 p.).

1112. GAGLIONE, ANTHONY GABRIEL. Anti-colonialism and the South West Africa case: a study in majoritarianism at the United Nations. PhD, Rutgers Univ., New Brunswick, 1971, 303 p.

1113. GAUL, JOHANNES BERNHARD ADOLF. Finanzrecht der deutschen Schutzgebiete unter besonderer Berücksichtigung der Steuergesetzgebung. Leipzig Univ., Diss., 1909. (Publ.: Leipzig: Milde, 1909, 172 p.).

1114. GEBHARDT, F.B.E. (Bettina). Der soziale und ökonomische Status der Farmarbeiter in Namibia/Südwest-Afrika. MA, Univ. Frankfurt, 1975, 110 p.

650. GEBHARDT, F.E. Bettina. Zur sozialökonomischen Lage der Farmarbeiter in Namibia. Entwicklung in Vergangenheit und Zunkunft. Diss., Univ. Bremen, 1984, 378 p. (?).

1115. GERHARDT, HANS. Das moderne Bergwerkskonzessionswesen in den deutschen Schutzgebieten: Staatsrechtliche Fragen vom Marmoraprozess in Südwest. Diss., Univ. Würzburg, 1914. (Publ: Borna-Leipzig: Noske, 1914, 128 p.).

1116. GERTENBACH, L.P.P. The marine fishery industries and commerce of the Union of South Africa and South West Africa: A statistical, economic and political study of their rise and development, during the last hundred years, seen in their national and international context. PhD, Univ. Cape Town, 19??.

1117. GILDENHUYS, JOHAN. Die siekteprofiel van die Ovambo en ʼn oorsig van die belangrikste voorkomingsmatraeëls. M.D., Univ. Pretoria, 1975.

1118. GLASS, PAUL R. Die Buschmänner in Deutsch.-Südwestafrika. Diss., Königsberg , 1939. (publ.: Königsberg : Gräfe und Unzer, 1939, 95 p.).

1119. GOABAB, SIMON NAMA. Imperialism and colonialism: a case study of Namibia. BA(Hons.), Preston Polytechnic, 1983.

1120. GOABAB, SIMON NAMA. (Project). The political economy of imperialism. Case study: Namibia. Centre for Southern African Studies, Univ. of York. In preparation.

1121. GOLANT, W.J. Vosstanija v afrikanskych kolonijach Germanii v 1904-1908. (The uprising of the German African colonies 1904-1908). Diss., Univ. Leningrad, 1952.

1122. GOLDSMITH, W. The German Social Democrats and the "Hottentot" election of 1907. MA, Univ. California, 1958, 83 p.

1123. GORDON, ROBERT J. Some sociological aspects of verbal communication in Okombahe, S.W.A.: a community study. MA, Univ. Stellenbosch, 1972.

652. GORDON, ROBERT J. Mines, migrants and masters: An ethnography of labour turnover at a Namibia mine. PhD, Univ. Illinois, 1977, 341 p. (Publ.: Mines, masters and migrants: life in a Namibian compound. Johannesburg: Ravan Press, 1977, 276 p.).

1124. GOTTSCHALK, KEITH (Project). South African imperialism, with special reference to the formation of colonial policy in Namibia, 1915-1925. PhD, Univ. Cape Town. In preparation.

1125. GRAHAM, ANN. The response of African societies in Namibia to white administration, 1915-1939. MA, SOAS, Univ. London, 1971.

1126. GRESSMANN, ARNE. 'n Ondersoek na die groeipotensiaal van die inheemse Owambo beestipe en die produksiepotensiaal van Oshonaweiveld. M.Sc., Univ. Stellenbosch, 1979.

1127. GROBBELAR, BAREND J. 'n Ondersoek na die verandering van die lewe van die !Kung op tegnologiese en ekonomiese gebiede. MA, Univ. Pretoria, 1967.

1128. GRÜNDER, HORST. Christliche Mission und deutscher Imperialismus: eine politische Geschichte ihrer Beziehungen während der deutschen Kolonialzeit (1884-1914) unter besonderer Berücksichtigung Afrikas und Chinas. Habilitationsschrift, Univ. Münster, 1980/81, 444 p. (Publ.: Paderborn Schöningh,1982, 444 p.).

1129. GRYGER, F.M. Southwest Africa in the United Nations. MA, Carleton Univ., 1969.

517. GUNDERT, HELMUT. Die betriebswirtschaftlichen Verhältnisse auf Karakulfarmen in den südlichen Distrikten von Südwestafrika. Diss., Hohenheim Univ.,1962, 128 p.

1130. HADKINS, V.R. Comparative study of the economic development of the mandated territories in Africa. M.Sc., Univ. Sheffield, 1940.

1131. HAGOLANI, ELHANAN. Das Kulturmodell der bantu-sprechen den Rinder-nomaden Südwestafrikas. PhD, Univ. Köln, 1967, 74 p. (Publ.: New York, 1968).

1132. HAIKOLA, MAJA. Ambokavangokyrkans politiska roll i Namibia. (The political role of the Ovambokavango Church in Namibia). Helsinki, Social- och kommunalhögskolan, 1976.

1133. HALENKE, HERBERT. Akklimatisation und Tierzucht in Afrika mit besonderer Berücksichtigung der Rinderzucht in Deutsch-Südwestafrika. Diss., Berlin Univ., 1941, 100 p. (Publ.: Viehwirtschaft in Deutsch-Südwestafrika. Probleme der Akklimatisation und Tierzucht. Berlin: de Gruyter, 1942, p. 61-148 in Mitteilungen der Gruppe Deutscher Kolonialwirtschaftlicher Unternehmungen 5).

1134. HALL, RICHARD M. The United Nations and South West Africa. MA, Kent State Univ., 1969, 104 p.

1035. HANSSEN, CHRISTIAN C.P.A. Agro-ekonomiese vergelyking tussen drie beesweistreke in Suidwes-Afrika. M.Sc.Agric., Univ. Pretoria, 1967.

822. HARNEIT, AXEL. Geschichte der SWAPO of Namibia - zur historischen und programmatischen Entwicklung 1959-1982. MA, Univ. Hannover, 1983. (Publ.: SWAPO of Namibia - Entwicklung, Programmatik und Politik seit 1959. Hamburg: Institut für Afrika-Kunde, 1984).

1136. HAUTH, DIETER. Die Reedereiunternehmungen im Dienst der deutschen Kolonialpolitik. Diss., Technische Univ., München, 1943, 212 p.

1137. HAYWOOD, CARL NORMAN. American whalers and Africa. PhD, Boston Univ., 1967, 253 p.

1138. HEESE, CARL PIETER. Die verband tussen onderwys en sendingswerk in Suidwes-Afrika 1806-1870. M.Ed., Univ. Stellenbosch, 1978. (Publ.: Sendingonderwys in Suidwes-Afrika 1806-1870: 'n kritiese beskouing van bepaalde aspekte. Cape Town, Goodwood: Nasionale Boekdrukkery, 1980, 208 p.)

1139. HEESE, HANS F. Genealogie as hulpwetenskap van geskiedenis met verwysing na die Boeretydperk in Angola 1881-1928. MA, Univ. Cape Town, 1974.

1140. HEESE, HANS F. Die Afrikaners in Angola 1880-1928. PhD, Univ. Cape Town, 1976.

1141. HEESE, JOHANNES A. Onderwys in Namakwaland, 1750-1940. D.Ed., Univ. Stellenbosch, 1942.

1142. HEINZ, HANS-JOACHIM. The social organization of the !Ko Bushmen. MA, Pretoria, Univ. South Africa, 1966.

1143. HELMER, ELIZABETH. The mandates system in the B and C territories. PhD, Univ. London, 1928. (Publ.: van Maanen-Helmer, E.: The Mandates system in relation to Africa and the Pacific Islands, London: King, 1929, 331 p.).

363. HERRIGEL, OTTO. Studien zur Bevölkerungs- und Wirtschaftsentwicklung Südafrikas. Diss., Univ. Basel, 1971, 123 p.

364. HEYER, ADOLF BERNHARD. Die wirtschaftliche und finanzielle Lage Südwest-Afrikas. Diss., Univ. Marburg, 1937, 112 p.

239. HILDEBRAND, KLAUS. Von Reich zum Weltreich: Hitler, NSDAP und koloniale Frage, 1919-1945. Diss., Univ. Mannheim, 1967. (Publ.: München: Fink, 1969, 955 p.).

1144. HODGE, AMELIA L. Angra Pequena. PhD., Univ. München, 1936, 80 p. (Publ.: München: Heller, 1936, 91 p.).

1145. HOFF, JOHANNA A. Melk by die Nama in volkekundige perspektief, met besondere verwysing na die /Hai-/Khauan van Berseba. MA, Univ. Pretoria, 1981.

365. HOPPE, THEODOR. Wirtschaftsstruktur und Wirtschaftsentwicklung von Deutsch-Südwestafrika. Diss., Handels-Hochschule, Leipzig, 1936, 109 p.

1146. HOUGHTON, F.L. Missions and government in Ovamboland 1870-1940: A survey of the forces for change in a Southwest Africa reserve. MA, Michigan State Univ., East Lansing, 1965, 73 p.

1147. HRISS, ALFRED. Die Entwicklung der Finanzen der deutschen Kolonien in Afrika bis zum Kriege. Diss., Univ. Heidelberg, 1924, 251 p.

1148. HUANG, THOMAS T.F. The South-West-Africa question. Harvard Univ., Cambridge, Mass., PhD, 1951, 337 p.

733. HUARAKA, TUNGURU. Namibia by resolutions: a legal analysis of international organisations' attempts at decolonisation. PhD, Univ. Geneva, 1982, 430 p.

37. HUBRICH, HEINRICH-GEORG/MELBER, HENNING. Entstehungsgeschichte und aktuelle Probleme der Turnhallen-Konferenz (Namibia) unter Berück-

sichtigung ihrer Auswirkungen auf die Bundesrepublik Deutschland.
MA, Freie Univ., Berlin, 1977, 296 p. (Publ.: revised and updated:
Namibia-Geschichte und Gegenwart. Zur Frage der Dekolonisation einer
Siedlerkolonie. Bonn: ISSA, 1977, 274 p.).

523. HURLICH, SUSAN. (Project). Reserves, migrant labour and the karakul
industry in Namibia: A historical perspective. PhD, Univ. Toronto.
In preparation.

1149. IGBOELI, THEOPHILUS N. The internal politics of the United Nations:
a case study of Namibia's independence, 1967-1972. PhD, Howard Univ.,
1973, 194 p.

408. ILANGA NYONSCHI, MÉDARD. Le capital international et ses effects en
Namibia. Thèse de Maitrise, Univ. Quebéc, 1978. (Publ.: Sherbrooke/
Quebéc: Editions Naaman, 1978, 244 p.).

1150. IMISHUE, R.W. The South West Africa mandate as a problem in inter-
national politics. PhD, Univ. London, 1964/65. (Publ.: South
West Africa. An International Problem. London: Pall Mall/IRR.
A Race Relations Publication, 1965, 80 p.).

1151. IMMEL, FARILT. Schule und Mission im vorkolonialem Südwest-Afrika:
Untersuchungen zur Rolle der Rheinischen Missionsgesellschaft vor der
deutschen Besitzergreifung. Exam. VEM (Vereinigte Evangelische Mission),
Wuppertal, 1974, 80 p.

368. INNES, DUNCAN. Monopoly capital and imperialism in Southern Africa:
the role of the Anglo American group. PhD, Univ. Sussex, 1980.
(Publ.: Anglo American and the rise of modern South Africa. Johannesburg: Ravan Press/London: Heinemann, 1984, 358 p.).

325. JÄCKEL, HERBERT. Die Landgesellschaften in den deutschen Schutzgebieten. Diss., Univ. Halle-Wittenberg, 1909, 88 p.

1152. JAHANBANI, MANSOUR E. The question of Southwest Africa. MA, Columbia
Univ., 1956, 139 p.

1153. JOHNSON, FRANCES E. Operation of the mandate system in Southwest
Africa for 1927. MA, Univ. Atlanta, 1983.

1154. JOHNSON, O. The United Nations and South-West-Africa. LL.M.,
Univ. Belfast, 1962.

1155. JONES, WILLIAM BUREN JR. The international status of South West
Africa. MA, West Virginia Univ., 1962, 103 p.

1156. JOOSTE, G.P. Die administrasie van die mandaat vir Suidwes-Afrika.
M.Admin., Univ. Pretoria, 1943.

1157. JOUBERT, PIETER S. Partypolitieke groepering in Suidwes-Afrika sedert
1915. MA, Univ. Oranje-Vrystaat, Bloemfontein, 1959, 291 p.

1158. JUBBER, ARNOLD ERIC. The economic feasibility of a cement plant in
South West Africa. M.B.L., Univ. South Africa, Pretoria, 1971.

1159. KAAKUNGA, ELIA MBAHAHIZA. Colonial capitalist development: the case
of Namibia (1884-1977). MA (pro gradu), University of Helsinki,
1982, 86 p.

1160. KAAKUNGA, ELIA MBAHAHIZA. (Project). Foreign capital and economic growth. PhD, University of Helsinki. In preparation.

1161. KAAKUNGA, MARY OMAGANO. Education and manpower development in Namibia. MA, University of Helsinki, 1984, 87 p.

45. KATJAVIVI, PETER H. Some aspects of Namibian political sociology. MA, Univ. Warwick, 1980, 164 p.

1162. KATJAVIVI, PETER H. (Project). The rise of nationalism in Namibia and its international dimensions. D.Phil, St. Antony's College, Oxford. In preparation.

1163. KATZAO, J. Formal education in Namibia with special attention to German and South African influence up to 1980, and the implications for future development. M.Ed., University College, Cardiff, 1981.

1164. KATZAO, JOHN JACOB. A critical appraisal of post primary education (including technical) in Namibia and its contribution to the growth of the national economy. PhD, University College of Cardiff, Wales, 1983.

1165. KAVINA, S.B.D. The South-West Africa dispute: a political study. M.Sc., Univ. Edinburgh, 1967.

1166. KAZAPUA, ZACHEUS J.N. Towards an integrated approach to education in Namibia. M.Ed., Univ. Manchester, 1982.

198. KIENETZ, ALVIN. Nineteenth century South West Africa as a German settlement colony. PhD, Univ. Minnesota, 1976, 959 p.

1167. KIENZLE, WILLIAM R. Jr. German policy towards the Union of South Africa, 1933-1939. PhD, Pennsylvania State Univ., 1974.

240. KILJUNEN, MARJA-LIISA. South African colonialism in Namibia: from segregation to "ethnic democracy". MA, Univ. Sussex, 1977, 61 p.

1168. KIRSTEN, GIDEON J.C. 'n Kritiese studie van die produksie en be-marking van karakoelpelse in die Republiek van Suid-Afrika en Suidwes-Afrika. M.Sc., Univ. Pretoria, 1962, 132 p.

1169. KLAUSS, KLAUS. Die Deutsche Kolonialgesellschaft und die deutsche Kolonialpolitik von den Anfängen bis 1895. Humboldt Univ., Berlin (DDR), 1966, 292 p.

1170. KLEINZ, NORBERT. Die drei germanischen Sprachen Südwestafrikas — politische und soziologische Gesichtspunkte ihrer Lage und Entwicklung. Diss., Univ. Bonn, 1981, 434 p.

410. KLEIST, KARSTEN E.B. VON. Some aspects of growth and income distribution in Namibia. MA, Univ. Oxford, 1981, 163 p.

1171. KLEIST, KARSTEN E.B. VON. (Project). Aspekten von Einkommenverteilung und Armut in Namibia. Univ. Freiburg./ The economic effectiveness of the Namibian educational system, Univ. Oxford.

1172. KOFFSKY, P.L. The transfer of power over the German colonies, 1914-1922. MA, Univ. Wisconsin, Madison, 1965.

1173. KOTZE, CAROL E. The establishment of a government in Ovamboland, 1915 - 1925. MA, Univ. South Africa, Pretoria, 1984.

1174. KOTZÉ, DIRK ALBERTUS. Duits- inboorlingsverhoudinge in Suidwes-Afrika, 1880-1914. 'n historiese studie. PhD, Univ. Pretoria, 1970.

175. KOTZE, JOHANNES C. Die Kuanjama van Ovamboland, Suidwes-Afrika, ´n studie van waarde-opvattinge, MA, Univ. Stellenbosch, 1968.

176. KOUVALAINEN, MARJA LIISA. Ambomaan siirtotyöläsyyden synty. (The origins of the migrant labour system in the Ovamboland). MA, (pro gradu), Univ. Helsinki, 1980.

370. KREMP, ARNOLD. Die wirtschaftgeographische Entwicklung des ehemaligen Schutzgebietes Deutsch-Südwestafrika. Diss., Königsberg Univ., 1933, 145 p.

711. KRIEGER-HINCK, CARLA. Uber die medizinische Versorgung der ehemaligen Kolonie Deutsch Südwest-Afrika. Diss., Ludwig-Maximilian Univ., München, 1973, 82 p.

177. KRITZINGER, JOHAN JACOB. Sending en kerk in Suidwes- Afrika: ´n Ondersoek na die kerk onder die Nie-Blankes van Suidwes-Afrika. D.D., Univ. Pretoria, 1973.

527. KROGH, DESMOND CHARLES. The karakul industry in South West Africa with special reference to the marketing of the karakul pelts. MA, Univ. Cape Town, 1953. (Publ.: Windhoek: John Meinert, 1954, 101 p.).

371. KROGH, DESMOND CHARLES. The national accounting framework of South West Africa. (A study in applied economics and statistics). PhD, Univ. Pretoria, 1958, 323 p. + tables.

178. KRÜGER, WOLFGANG F. Die theoretische Auseinandersetzung um den gesellschaftspolitischen Auftrag der lutherischen Kirchen in Südwest-Afrika/Namibia, 1970-1974. Diss., Hamburg Univ., 1982, 272 p.

241. KÜHNE, HORST. Die nazistische Kolonialpropaganda - eine Hauptmethode der ideologischen Vorbereitung des zweiten Weltkrieges. Diss., Institut für Gesellschaftswissenshaften beim Zentralkomitee der SED, Berlin (DDR), 1960, 200 p. (Publ.: Faschistische Kolonial-ideologie und zweiter Weltkrieg. Berlin: Dietz Verlag, 1962, 227 p.).

471. KUKURI, B.R. Options for a monetary system for an independent Namibia. MA, Bangor, Gwynedd, North Wales, 1981, 117 p.

179. KUKURI, B.R. (Project). Toward options for a financial system for an independent Namibia. D.Phil., Univ. Sussex. In preparation.

715. LACHENMANN, GUDRUN. Entkolonisierung der Gesundheit. Theorie und Praxis der Gesundheitsversorgung in Namibia und Benin. Diss., Univ. Konstanz, 1982. (Publ.: Diessenhofen: Rügger, 1982, 341 p.).

180. LAKOWSKI, RICHARD. Die Kriegsziele des faschistischen Deutschland im transsaharischen Afrika. Humboldt Univ., Berlin (DDR), 1970, 236 p.

181. LANE, ROBERT B. The United Nations Committee on South West Africa, 1953-1961. MA, The American Univ., 1964, 104 p.

182. LANGE, HILDE. Das europäische Handwerk in Deutschsüdwest- und Deutschostafrika vor dem Weltkriege. Diss., München Univ., 1942, 185 p.

183. LANGSDORFF, ALFRED. Rechtshistorische und rechtliche Grundlagen des deutschen Anspruchs auf Deutsch-Südwestafrika. Diss., Univ. Heidelberg, 1940. (Publ.: Philippsburg: Kruse, 1940, 72 + 10 p.).

1184. LARSON, THOMAS J. The ecological adaptation of the Mbukushu, a Bantu tribe in Ngamiland. PhD, Univ. Michigan, Ann Arbor, 1962.

1185. LATEGAN, MARTHA M. Sending- en staatsonderwys vir die inheemse bevolking van die Kavango: 'n histories-pedagogiese besinning. M.Ed., Univ. South Africa, Pretoria, 1980.

131. LAU, BRIGITTE. A critique of the historical sources and the historiography relating to the 'Damara' of pre-colonial Namibia. BA, Univ. Cape Town, 1979, 105 p.

133. LAU, BRIGITTE. The emergence of Kommando politics in Namaland, southern Namibia, 1800-1870. MA, Univ. Cape Town, 1982, 388 p.

1186. LAVERS, L.A. Walfish Bay and Angra Pequena. MA, Columbia Univ., New York, 1923.

1187. LAWRENCE, HENRY V. A survey of the water resources of the Windhoek region, South West Africa. M.E., Univ. Witwatersrand, 1971, 131 p.

1188. LEE, RICHARD B. Subsistence ecology of Kung Bushmen. PhD, Univ. California, 1966, 219 p.

1189. LEHMANN, ADOLF. Wirtschaftsgeographische Kritik der Statistik in den Jahresberichten über die Entwicklung der deutschen Schutzgebiete. Diss., Univ. Jena, 1911. (Publ.: Kirchain: Schmersow, 1911, 55 p.).

1190. LEMKE, MICHAEL. Die Funktion der katholischen Missionskongregationen in den ehemaligen deutschen Kolonien Afrikas (1884-1918) im System des deutschen Kolonialismus. Diss., Potsdam, Pädagogische Hochschule, 1971, 443 p.

1191. LEMMER, CECIL J.C. Onderwys in Suidwes-Afrika. PhD, Univ. South Africa, Pretoria, 1935.

1192. LEUSNER, HERMANN. Die Entwicklung des Schulwesens in den deutschen afrikanischen Kolonien, jetzigen Mandatsgebieten, vom Ende des Weltkrieges bis zur Gegenwart. Diss., Univ. Köln, 1938. (Publ.: Köln: Orthen, 1938, 283 p.).

327. LEUTWEIN, PAUL. Die Leistungen der Regierung in der südwest-afrikanischen Land- und Minenfrage. Diss., Friederich-Wilhelms-Univ., Berlin, 1911. (Publ: Berlin: Süsserott, 1911, 130 p.).

242. LEWIS, GAVIN L.M. The Bondelswarts rebellion of 1922. MA, Rhodes Univ., Grahamstown, 1978.

1193. LIEBENBERG, HENDRIK BADENHORST. Aspekte van die vleisnywerheid in Suidwes-Afrika en die Republiek van Suid-Afrika, MA, Univ. Stellenbosch, 1967.

1194. LIEBENBERG, PETRUS W. Die inlywing van Suidwes-Afrika by die Unie van Suid-Afrika: 'n Ontleding van die geskil met die Verenigde Nasies tydens die 1946 sitting. MA, Univ. Pretoria, 1971.

1195. LÖTTY, SEPPO. The Ovambo Sermon. A study of the preaching of the Evangelical Lutheran Ovambo-Kavango Church in South West Africa. Diss. Theol., Univ. Helsinki, 1971. (Publ.: Tampere : Tampereen Keskuspaino, 1971, 173 p.).

662. LOFFLER, JOHN. Labour and politics in Namibia in the 1970s. MA, Univ. York, 1979, 68 p.

196. LOOTS, J.H. The health conditions of the native population in Ovamboland, and its bearing on the development of South-West-Africa. Med.D., Univ. Edinburgh, 1930.

197. LOS, LAURENCE JOHN. The mandate for Southwest Africa, 1920-1939. M.Phil., Univ. Toronto, 1969.

140. LOTH, HEINRICH. Die destruktive Rolle der Rheinischen Missions-gesellschaft beim Prozess der Staatsbildung in Südwestafrika. Diss., Univ. Leipzig, 1961, 213 p. (Publ.: Die Christliche Mission in Südwestafrika, Berlin (DDR): Akademie-Verlag, 1963, 180 p.).

198. LOTZ, MARTHINUS E. Die aanstelling en diensvoorwaardes van blanke onderwysers onder die provinsiale afministrasies en Suidwes-Afrika: 'n vergelykende studie. M.Ed., Univ. Stellenbosch, 1952.

199. LOUW, WALTER. Die sosio-politieke stelsel van die Ngandjera van Ovamboland. MA, Univ. Port Elizabeth, 1967.

200. LÜHRSSEN, FRIEDRICH. Die Schulen der deutschen Schutzgebiete. Diss., Univ. Leipzig, 1914. (Publ.: Borna-Leipzig: Noske, 1914, ix, 113 p.).

201. LUERSSEN, HANS. Beitrag zur Kenntnis der Viehzuchtverhältnisse, insbesondere der Rindviehzucht in Gross Namaland, Südwestafrika. Diss., Tierärztliche Hochschule, Berlin, 1925. (Publ.: Berlin: Melzer, 1929, 34 p.).

593. LUND, WENDA. Die Rössing-Uranmine in Namibia und ihre regionale und internationale politische Bedeutung. Diplomarbeit, Univ. Bremen, 1983. (Publ.: Köln: Pahl-Rugenstein Verlag, 1984, 208 p.).

202. LUTTIG, HENDRIK G. The religious system and the social organization of the Herero. A study in Bantu culture. D. Litt. et Phil., Univ. Leiden, 1933. (Publ.: Kemink, 1933, 123 p.).

1203. MCCARROL, VERNELL. The operation and administration of the mandate system in South West Africa for 1931. MA, Howard Univ., Washington, 1944, 111 p.

1204. MACFARLANE, ALISTAIR. (Project). Management strategies in the Namibian mining industry. PhD. Univ. Oxford. In preparation.

1205. MCLETCHIE, JAMES K. Germany's acquisition of South West Africa: a study in British imperial policy 1880-1885. MA, McGill Univ., Montreal, 1929.

1206. MAGER, GÜNTER. Die deutsche Sozialdemokratie und die Aufstände der Herero und Nama in Südwestafrika, 1904-1907. Diss., Univ. Halle, 1966, 231 p.

1207. MALAN, JOHANNES S. Dubbele afkomsberekenings by die Himba, 'n Hererosprekende volk in Suidwes-Afrika. PhD, Randse Afrikaanse Univ., Johannesburg, 1972, 259 p.

1208. MALLORY, CHARLES S. Some aspects of the mission policy and practice of the Church of the Province of South Africa in Ovamboland. MA, Rhodes Univ., Grahamstown, 1972.

167. MAMOZAI, MARTA. Frauen und Kolonialismus: Thesen, Hypothesen, erste Arbeitsergebnisse. Diplomarbeit, Freie Univ., Berlin, 1981. (Publ.: in rev. edition: Herrenmenschen. Frauen im deutschen

Kolonialismus. Reinbek bei Hamburg: Rowohlt, 1983, 312 p.).

860. MAY, HANS-CHRISTOPH. Der Kampf der Befreiungsbewegung SWAPO von Namibia und die Stellung der Kirchen. Theol. Diplomarbeit, Würzburg Univ., 1981, 342 p.

1209. MARSHALL, JOHN. Ecology of the !Kung Bushmen of the Kalahari. Senior hons. thesis, Harvard Univ., Cambridge, Mass., 1957.

1210. MAYER, OTTO. Die Entwicklung der Handelsbeziehungen Deutschlands zu seinen Kolonien. Diss., Univ. Tübingen, 1913. (Publ.: München: Finsterlin, 1913, 195 p.).

1211. MBAMBA, A. MAUNO. Namibia, traditional and modern economic sectors development strategies. MA, (Fil.kand.), Univ. Gothenburg (Göteborg), 1975.

531. MBAMBA, A. MAUNO. Possibilities for the future development of live-stock ranching in an independent Namibia. MA, Univ. Sussex, 1977, 96 p.

700. MBAMBA, A. MAUNO. Primary education for an independent Namibia. Planning in a situation of uncertainty and instability. PhD, Univ. Stockholm, 1982. (Publ.: Stockholm: Almqvist & Wiksell International, 1982, 244 p.).

1212. MBUENDE, ELISABETH. (Project). Teacher education for independent Namibia. PhD, University of Lund, in preparation.

51. MBUENDE, KAIRE. (Project). Namibia - The broken shield: anatomy of imperialism and revolution. PhD, Univ. Lund (Sweden) In preparation.

1213. MEHNERT, WOLFGANG. Schulpolitik im Dienste der Kolonialherrschaft des deutschen Imperialismus in Afrika (1884-1914). Habil.schrift, Univ. Leipzig, 1965, 325 p.

789. MEINARDUS, RONALD. Die Afrikapolitik der Republik Südafrika: von der outward-looking policy bis zur Gegenwart. Diplomarbeit, Univ. Hamburg, 1981. (Publ.: Bonn: Informationsstelle Südliches Afrika, 1981, 491 p.).

702. MELBER, HENNING. Schule und Kolonialismus: das formale Erzieh-ungswesen Namibias. Diss., Univ. Bremen, 1980. (Publ.: Hamburg: Institut für Afrika-Kunde, 1979, 319 p.).

1214. MENGES, HANS E. Die Rechtsstellung von Süd-West-Afrika nach dem 2. Weltkrieg. Diss., Univ. Bonn, 1955, 104 p.

1215. MEYER, ERWIN. Das Finanzwesen der deutschen Schutzgebiete. Diss., Univ. Erlangen, 1912. (Publ.: Erlangen: Junge, 1912, viii, 155 p.).

1216. MEYER, FELIX. Skorbuterkrankungen unter den kriegsgefangenen Eingeborenen in Südwestafrika in den Jahren 1905/07. Diss. Med., Univ. Berlin, 1920.

1217. MEYNTJES, ELLA M. Suid-Afrika en die Vrede van Versailles. MA, Univ. Potchefstroom, 1974.

1218. MILLER, RICHARD I. The United Nations Trusteeship System and educational advancement. PhD, Columbia Univ., New York, 1958, 287 p.

100. MITCHELL, PAUL. The politics of water with particular reference to the Cunene River Scheme. MA, Univ. York, 1976, 101 p.

1219. MÖLLER, BARBARA. Die Tage buchaufzeichnungen des Hottentottenkapitäns Hendrik Witbooi aus der deutschen Kolonisation in Südwestafrika, 1884-1894. Zulassungsarbeit, Univ. Freiburg, 1977, 88 p.

55. MOORSOM, RICHARD. Colonisation and proletarianisation: An exploratory investigation of the formation of the working class in Namibia under German and South African rule. MA, Univ. Sussex, 1973, 257 p.

1220. MOSTERT, LOUIS. A comparative study of beef brands and dual purpose breeds with regard to their beef production potentialities under ranching conditions in South West Africa. D.Sc.Agr., Univ. Orange Free State, Bloemfontein, 1972.

1221. MUJURO, ZEDEKIA KAPIRIKIRUE. Christ at the centre of culture. The Namibian experience. MA, Wartburg Theological Seminary, Dubuque, Iowa, 1984, 81 p.

1222. NEL, JACOBUS ANDREAS. Kritiese studie van die ontwikkeling teling en versorging van die Neudam-Karakulstoet. M.Sc., Univ. Stellenbosch, 1950. (Publ.: The Neudam Karakul stud. Windhoek: Meinert, 1955/ Eine kritische Betrachtung über die Entwicklung, Zucht und Haltung der Neudamer Karakul-Stammschaftzucht. Windhoek, 1954).

1223. NENGENGE, JOYCE (Project). Industrial relations in Namibia. PhD, University of Lund. In preparation.

1224. NEUBERT, ALFRED. Die Schutzherrschaft in Deutsch-Südwestafrika, 1884-1903. Eine Untersuchung zum Wandel kolonialer Herrschaftsformen im Zeitalter des heraufkommenden Imperialismus. Diss., Würzburg Univ., 1954, 216 p.

1225. NEULAND, ERNST WILHELM. ˊn Kritiese bedryfskoste-analise van privaat lugdienste in die Republiek van Suid-Afrika en Suidwes-Afrika. D.B.A., Univ. Potschefstroom, 1977.

1226. NEWMAN, ALLEN RAY. South Africa and the post-war question of the incorporation of South West Africa. MA, Univ. North Carolina, 1968.

245. NGAVIRUE, ZEDEKIA. Political parties and interest groups in South West Africa - a study of a plural society. PhD, St. Antony's College, Oxford, 1972, 424 p.

1227. NIEMAND, CORNELIS MEYER. Onderwys aan die Swart volke van Suidwes-Afrika tot 1970. M.Ed., Univ. Potschefstroom, 1980, 289 p.

1228. NIEWOUDT, MATTHYS M. Die kerkregtelike ontwikkeling van die Nederduitse Gereformeerde Kerk in Suidwes-Afrika: ˊn kerkhistories - kerkregtlige studie, 1: Pionierstyd, 1875-1902. M.Theol.,Univ. Stellenbosch, 1967.

1229. NIEWOUDT, MATTHYS M. Die Nederduitse Gereformeerde Kerk in Suidwes-Afrika: woordbediening in pioniersomstandighede op weg na ˊn self-standige sinode; ˊn kerkhistoriese studie. Univ. Stellenbosch, D.D., 1978, 565 p.

146. NITSCHE, GEORG J.K. Ovamboland. Versuch einer landeskundlichen Darstellung nach dem gegenwärtigen Stand unserer geographischen Kenntnis. Diss., Univ. Kiel, 1913. (Publ.: Kiel: Donath, 1913, 154 p.).

535. NIXON, CHARLES D. Land use and development in Namibia. M.Dev., ISS, The Hague, 1980, 143 p.

1320. NOBLE, JOHN. Education in Namibia. M.Ed., Univ. Nairobi, 1977, 128 p.

1231. NORTHCOTT, W.C. Life and work of Robert Moffat, with particular reference to the expansion of mission and white settlement north of the Orange River, 1817-1870. PhD, SOAS, Univ. London, 1960.

1232. NUSSBAUM, MANFRED . Vom "Kolonialenthusiasmus" zur Kolonialpolitik der Monopole: Zur deutschen Kolonialpolitik in den Jahren 1880-1885. Diss., Humboldt-Univ., Berlin (DDR), 1960, 229 p. (Publ.: Vom "Kolonialenthusiasmus" zur Kolonialpolitik der Monopole: Zur deutschen Kolonialpolitik unter Bismarck, Caprivi, Hohenlohe. Berlin, Akademie-Verlag, 1962, 167 p.).

1233. OBOZUWA, A. UKIOMOGBE. The Namibian question. Legal and political aspects. PhD., Northwestern University, Chicago, 1970. (Publ. revised and updated: Benin City, Ethiope Publishing Corp., 1973, 256 p.).

1234. O'CONNEL, JOHANNES P. Die interindustrietransaksies van landbou en bosbou in Suid-en Suidwes-Afrika. D. Litt. et Phil., Univ. South Africa, Pretoria, 1974.

332. OELHAFEN VON SCHÖLLENBACH, HANS. Die Besiedlung Deutsch-Südwest-Afrikas bis zum Weltkriege. Diss., Univ. Würzburg, 1922, 116 p. (Publ.: Berlin: Reimer, 1926, 136 p.).

1235. OLIVEIRA, INÁCIA OLIMPIA TEIXEIRA C. DE. A evoluçãodo historica dos Cuanhamas. Univ. Lisboa, Diss., 1962.

247. OLIVIER, MATTHEUS J. Inboorlingbeleid en administrasie in die mandaatsgebied van Suidwes-Afrika. D.Phil., Univ. Stellenbosch, 1961.

1236. OPPERMANN, DANIËL P.J. Die stryd van die Duitser om die behoud van sy eie op die gebied van die skoolwese in Suidwes-Afrika. M.Ed., Univ. Potchefstroom, 1968.

1237. OTTO, ANTJE. ʼn volkekundige studie van die sosio-ekonomiese posisie van Hererovrouwe in Katutura, Windhoek, Suidwes-Afrika/Namibië. MA, Univ. Stellenbosch, 1981, 264 p.

1238. PEACHEY, R.A. The United Nations and South West Africa. MA, Columbia Univ., 1951.

1239. PEARSON, PATRICK. (Project). MA thesis - the Renoboth community. Univ. Witwatersrand Johannesburg. In preparation.

301. PENDLETON, WADE CARLTON. A study of ethnicity and conjugal unions among Africans in Windhoek, South West Africa. PhD, Univ. California, 1970, 145 p. (Publ.: Katutura, a place where we do not stay: the social structure and social relationships of people in an African township in South West Africa. The San Diego University Press, 1974, 197 p.).

1240. PETERS, WALTER. Baukunst in Südwestafrika 1884-1914: die Rezeption deutscher Architektur in der Zeit von 1884 bis 1914 im ehemaligen Deutsch-Südwestafrika (Namibia). Diss., Univ. Hannover, 1980. (Publ.: Windhoek; S.W.A. Wissenschaftliche Gesellschaft, 1981, 338 p.).

1241. PFOUTS, ANITA. (Project). Linguistics and Namibian history. PhD, Univ. California. In preparation.

301. PICKERING, ARTHUR. Law, state and social control in contemporary Namibia. LL.M., Univ. Warwick, 1983, 150 p.

170. PIERARD, RICHARD V. The German Colonial Society 1882-1914. PhD, State Univ. Iowa, 1964, 407 p.

1242. PÖLLITZER, PHILIPP. Die eigene Kerze anzünden. Untersuchung zu Entstehung, Lehre, Leitung und Leben in der Oruuano. (The Protestant Unity Church of South West Africa). D.Theol., Univ. South Africa, Pretoria, 1979, 256 p.

204. POOL, GERHARDUS. Die Herero-opstand 1904-1907. MA, Univ. Stellenbosch, 1976, 466 p. (Publ.: Cape Town: H.A.U.M., 1979, 311 p.).

334. POOL, GERHARDUS. Die Staatsbahn in Duits-Suidwes-Afrika, 1897-1915. PhD, Univ. Stellenbosch, 1980, 334 p. (Pub.: Pionierspoorweë in Duits-Suidwes-Afrika, 1897-1915. Durban: Butterworth, 1982, 301 p.).

1243. PRETORIUS, JACOBUS W.F. Die staatkundige ontwikkeling van Suidwes-Afrika met besondere aandag aan die invloed van die bevolkingssgroepe in die verband. MA, Univ. Oranje-Vrystat, Bloemfontein, 1960.

1244. PRETORIUS, JOHANNES L. The Fwe of the eastern Caprivi Zipfel: a study of their historical and geographical background, tribal structure and legal system, with special reference to the Fwe family law and succession. MA, Univ. Stellenbosch, 1974, 156 p.

335. QUIRING, ERICH. Die Eisenbahnen Deutsch Südwestafrikas und ihre Bedeutung für die wirtschaftliche Entwicklung der Kolonie. Diss., Erlangen, 1911. (Publ.: Borna-Leipzig: Noske, 1911, 63 p.).

381. RÄDEL, FRITZ EMIL. Die Wirtschaft und die Arbeiterfrage Südwestafrikas von der Frühzeit bis zum Ausbruch des 2.Weltkrieges. D. Comm., Univ. Stellenbosch, 1947, 522 p.

1245. RAITHEL, HELLMUTH. Der "Schulstreit" in Südwest, 1919-1921. Ein Beitrag zur Geschichte von Südwestafrika nach dem Ende der deutschen Schutzherrschaft. Diss., Univ. München, 1977, 233 p. (Publ.: München: Salzer, 1977, 233 p.).

1246. RATH, ALFRED H. A study of South West Africa, 1915-52. MA, S. California, 1955.

1247. REINECKE, REINHARD. Das Finanzrecht der deutschen Schutzgebiete. Univ. Strassburg, Diss., 1912. (Publ.: Hildesheim: Borgmeyer, 1912, 121 p.).

1248. RHEINEN, OTTO. Die Selbstverwaltung der Gemeinden in Deutsch-Südwestafrika. Diss., Univ. Jena, 1913. (Publ.: Berlin: Gutenberg, 1913, 89 p.).

1249. RICHTER, LISELOTTE. Die Finanzierung der Kolonialgesellschaften. Diss., Technische Hochschule, Dresden, 1940.

1250. RIEGNER, GEORG. Das Sachenrecht der Herero vor dem Eindringen fremder Rechtsbegriffe. Univ. Heidelberg, Diss., 1911. (Publ.: Borna-Leipzig: Noske, 1911, ix, 80 p.).

1251. ROBERTS. H.L. The Southwest African mandate. Columbia Univ., New York, MA, 1933.

1252. RODENBERG, HARRY. Die Kulturen der Hirten, Jäger und Sammler Südwestafrikas in ihrer Abhängigkeit von der Landschaft. Diss., Univ. Hamburg, 1931. (Publ.: Bad Segeberg: Wäser, 1931, 181 p.).

1253. ROSEN, HARRIET B. The South West Africa case and the future effectiveness of the International Court of Justice. MA, Trinity College, Oxford, 1968, 124 p.

1254. ROSSOUW, JOHANNES G. Die dinamika van boereverenigings in Suidwes-Afrika. M. Agric., Univ. Pretoria, 1973.

1255. ROSSOUW, N.J. Onderwysaangeleenthede van die Witbooistam. B.Ed., Univ. Stellenbosch, 1939.

1256. ROUNDS, HAROLD B. German Southwest Africa under mandate, 1919-1939. PhD, Univ. Wisconsin, 1944.

1257. RUTHERFORD, MICHAEL CHARLES. Aspects of ecosystem function in a woodland savanna in South West Africa. PhD, Univ. Stellenbosch, 1975.

1258. SAGAY, ITSEJUWA. South-West Africa - its international status and other legal problems. PhD, Cambridge, 1970. (Publ.: The legal aspects of the Namibia dispute, Ile-Ife: University of Ife Press, 1975, 402 p.).

1259. SCHIEFEL, WERNER. Bernhard Dernburg 1865-1937: Kolonialpolitiker und Bankier im wilhelminischen Deutschland. Diss., Univ. Münster, 1972. (Publ.: Zürich: Atlantis, 1974, 277 p.).

672. SCHILLING-JAEGGI, JOHANNA. Das Problem der Land-Stadt-Wanderung in Namibia vor und nach 1977. Lizentiats-Arbeit, Univ. Basel, 1982, 83 p.

1260. SCHLEYER, MICHAELA SUZAN. Kolonialkrieg und öffentliche Meinung: der Herero-Aufstand 1904-1907 im Spiegel von kirchlicher und säkularer Presse. MA, Univ. München, 1981, 177 p.

1261. SCHLIMM, KARL. Das Grundstücksrecht in den deutschen Kolonien. Univ.Tübingen. Diss, 1905. (Publ.: Leipzig-Reudnitz: Hoffmann, 1905, vii + 126 p.).

1262. SCHLOSSER, KATESA. Neue Sozialverbände der Eingeborenen in Süd- und Südwestafrika. Ihre Entstehung und Struktur. Habil.schrift, Univ. Kiel, 1953. (Publ.: Eingeborenenkirchen in Süd- und Südwestafrika. Ihre Geschichte und Sozialstruktur. Ergebnisse einer völkerkundlichen Studiereise 1953, Kiel: Mühlau, 1958, 355 p.).

1263. SCHMAHL, OSKAR. Das koloniale Diamantenrecht. Univ. Münster, 1919, 145 p.

341. SCHMIDT, CARL. Geographie der Europäersiedlungen in der ehemaligen Kolonie Südwestafrika. Diss., Univ. Marburg, 1922, 223 p. (Publ.: Geographie der Europäer-Siedlungen im deutschen Südwest-Afrika. Jena: Fischer, 1922, 132 p.).

1264. SCHMITT, GERHARD. Die Wasserwirtschaft in Südwest-Afrika. Wiss. Hausarbeit, Univ. Mainz, 1975. (Publ.: Worms, 1975, 122 p.).

171. SCHMITT-EGNER, PETER. Kolonialideologie im Wilhelminischen Reich. Diss., Univ. Frankfurt, 1974. (Publ.: Kolonialismus und Faschismus. Eine Studie zur historischen und begrifflichen Genesis faschistischer Bewusstseinsformen am deutschen Beispiel. Giessen/ Lollar: Achenbach, 1975, 224 p.).

1265. SCHNEIDER, A.H.R. Die Süd-West-Afrika-Frage vor den Organen der Vereinten Nationen: Ein Beitrag zur rechtlich-politischen Analyse dieses Konflikts. Diss., Univ. Würzburg, 1975, 115 p.

540. SCHNEIDER, HERBERT. Analyse der Tiergesundheitssituation in SWA/Namibia. Vergangenheit und Gegenwart. Dr.Vet., Justus-Liebig-Univ., Giessen, 1977, 318 p. (Publ. in series "Aus dem Institut für Tropische Veterinärmedizin", Giessen).

1266. SCHOEMAN, STEFANUS JOHANNES. Suidwes-Afrika onder militêre bestuur 1915-1920. MA, Univ. South Africa, Pretoria, 1976.

1267. SCHOLTZ, PETRUS J. Die ontwikkeling van inboorling-onderwys binne die suidelike sektor van Suidwes-Afrika 1915-1962. M.Ed., Univ. Pretoria, 1973.

1268. SCHRANK, GILBERT I. German South West Africa: social and economic aspects of its history, 1884-1915. PhD, Univ. of New York, 1974, 283 p.

1269. SCHROEDTER, FRIEDRICH. Über die Syphilis bei den Eingeborenen Südwestafrikas. Diss., Leipzig Med. Fak., 1908. (Publ.: Leipzig: Georgi, 1908, 47 p.).

342. SCHUBERT, EMMERICH. Landwirtschaft und ihre Nebenbetriebe in Südwestafrika. Diss., Univ. Heidelberg, 1913. (Publ.: Heidelberg: Winters Universitätsbuchhandlung, 1913, 112 p.).

1270. SCHÜLEIN, FRIEDRICH H. Rekruteringstudie oor die Suidwes-Afrikaanse sardyn, Sardinops ocellata, 1954-1958. M.Sc., Univ. Stellenbosch, 1971.

1271. SCHULTE, DIETER. Die "Ära Dernburg" (1906 bis 1910): zum Charakter der Herrschaft des Finanzkapitals in den deutschen Kolonien. Diss., Humboldt-Univ., Berlin (DDR), 1976, 377 p.

1272. SCHULTE, THEODOR. Das Bergrecht der deutschen Schutzgebiete. Univ. Leipzig, Diss., 1910. (Publ.: Cöln: Pahl, 1910, 83 p.).

1273. SCHUTTE, CHRISTOFFEL H.J. Kleurlingsonderwys in Suidwes-Afrika. M.Ed., Univ. South Africa, Pretoria, 1942.

1274. SCUPIN , ERNST-OTTOMAR. Die völkerrechtliche Stellung der deutschen Schutzgebiete. Univ. München, Diss., 1963. (Publ.: München: Schön).

1275. SEARLE, D.E. The foreign policy of the Gladstone administration of 1880-1885, with special reference to German policy in South-West Africa. MA, Univ. Wales, 1933.

1276. SEILER, JOHN J. The formulation of U.S. policy toward Southern Africa, 1957-1976: the failure of good intentions. PhD, Univ. Connecticut, 1976.

1277. SILAGI, MICHAEL. Von Deutsch-Südwest zu Namibia: Wesen und Wandlungen des völkerrechtlichen Mandats. Univ. München, Diss., 1977. (Publ.: Ebelsbach: Gremer, 1977, x, 165 p.).

102. SIMON, DAVID. Aspects of urban change in Windhoek, Namibia, during the transition to independence. D.Phil., Linacre College, Oxford, 1983, 546 p.

754. SLONIM, SOLOMON I. South West Africa and the United Nations: a struggle over international accountability. PhD, Columbia Univ., New York, 1967, 380 p. (Publ.: South West Africa and the United Nations: An international mandate in dispute. Baltimore/London: The John Hopkins University Press, 1973, 409 p.).

1278. SMALBERGER, JOHN M. Aspects of the history of copper mining in Namaqualand, 1846-1931. MA, Univ. Cape Town, 1969. (Publ.: Cape Town/Johannesburg: Struik, 1975, 152 p.).

1279. SMALL, ALDEN COLT. The United Nations and Southwest Africa: a study in parliamentary diplomacy. PhD, Fletcher School, Harvard Univ., 1969/70.

1280. SMIT, JACOBUS H. Suid-Afrika en die Verenigde Nasies 1946-1952: die internasionale stryd teen die Suid-Afrikaanse rassebeleid begin. MA, Univ. Bloemfontein, 1979.

1281. SMIT, PHILIPPUS. Die betekenis van Walvisbaai as hawe vir Suidwes-Afrika. MA, Univ. Stellenbosch, 1962.

1282. SMITH, I.C. The international role of Jan Christiaan Smuts, with special reference to the mandates system and South West Africa. B.Phil., Univ. St. Andrews, Fife, 1970.

1283. SOELLING, ERICH M. Die Gebiete ohne Selbstregierung, in Sonderheit Südwestafrika, unter der Obhut der Vereinten Nationen. Diss., Univ. Kiel, 1960, xi + 245 p.

1284. SOLLARS, JAMES W. African involvement in the colonial development of German South West Africa. PhD, Univ. Washington, Seattle, 1972, 196 p.

1285. SPENCER, LEON PHARR JR. The American role in the South West Africa question. MA, Indiana Univ., 1967.

1286. SPIECKER, WALTER. Die Rheinische Missionsgesellschaft in ihren volks- und kolonialwirtschaftlichen Funktionen. Diss., Berlin, 1921. (Publ.: Gütersloh: Bertelsmann, 1922, 81 p.).

1287. STALS, ERNST L.P. Die geskiedenis van die beesteelt in Suidwes-Afrika tydens die Duitse tydperk 1884-1915. MA, Univ. Stellenbosch, 1961. (Publ.: Die Argiefjaarboek vir Suid-Afrikaanse Geskiedenis, vol. 25, 1962.).

211. STALS, ERNST L.P. Die aanraking tussen Blankes en Owambos in Suidwes-Afrika, 1850-1915. D.Phil., Univ. Stellenbosch, 1967. (Publ.: Die Argiefjaarbock vir Suid-Afrikaanse Geskiedenis, vol. 31, Deel 2, 1968, p. 219-349).

1288. STEENKAMP, J.A.J. Die christelike sending langs die benede-Oranje. M.Theol., Univ. Stellenbosch, 1953.

1289. STEYN, DANIEL MARTHINUS. An investigation of the relationship between acculturation, achievement and affiliation in Ovambo. PhD, Grahamstown, Phodes Univ., 1977.

1290. STEYN, HENDRIK, P. Pastoralisme by die Himba van Suidwes-Afrika:

'n kultureel-ekologiese studie. PhD, Univ. Stellenbosch, 1977.

1291. STRÄHUBER, HERMANN. Die Entwicklung des landwirtschaftlichen Kreditwesens in Deutsch-Südwestafrika. Ein Beitrag zur Wirtschaftsgeschichte dieser Kolonie. Diss., Friedrich-Alexander Univ., Erlangen, 1915. (Publ.: Nürnberg: Heydolph, 1915, 109 p.).

1292. STRAUSS, FREDERIK JOHANNES. Die politieke en judisiële organisasie van die Herero. MA, Univ. Pretoria, 1974, 188 p.

722. STRODTMANN, LUISE H.B. Die Entwicklung des Gesundheitszustandes und der Hygiene in Südwestafrika seit dem Weltkriege. Diss., Univ. Hamburg, 1938, 55 p. (Publ.: Hamburg: Füsslein, 1937, 55 p.).

1293. STROM, TERENCE M. Newmont Mining Corporation: Southern African operations. MA, (PhD?), Columbia Business School, 1972.

1294. STRYDOM, J.P.L. 'n Regionale studie van die distrik Outjo Suidwes-Afrika. MA, Bloemfontein, Univ. Oranje-Vrystaat, Bloemfontein, 1964.

1295. STUMPF, HARRY P. South West Africa: the question of its incorporation into the Union of South Africa. MA, Washington Univ., 1958, 135 p.

1296. SUCKERMANN, NEAL MERLE. The sacred trust of South West Africa. MA, Washington Univ., Seattle, 1968, 55 p.

1297. SUCKOW, CHRISTIAN. Die Bantu- und Khoisanbevölkerung Südafrikas unter den Bedingungen der europäischen Kolonialexpansion von der Mitte des 17. Jh. bis zur Mitte des 19. Jh. im Spiegel der Berichte deutscher Reisender. Diss., Humboldt Univ., Berlin (DDR), 1973, 493 p.

213. SUDHOLT, GERT. Die deutsche Eingeborenenpolitik in Südwestafrika. Diss., Ludwig-Maximillians-Univ., München, 1975. (Publ.: Hildesheim/ New York: Olms, 1975, 241 p.).

1298. SUNDERMEIER, THEO. Mission, Bekenntnis und Kirche: Missionstheologische Probleme des 19. Jahrhunderts bei C.H. Hahn. Diss., Theol., Univ. Heidelberg, 1961. (Publ.: Wuppertal: Verlag der Rheinischen Missions-Gesellschaft, 1962, 215 p.).

1299. TAYLOR, PAULINE RITA. The Union government's treatment of the South West African mandate 1915-1944. MA, Univ. Cape Town, 1944, 118 p.

1300. TERHAG, HERBERT. Walvis Bay und Swakopmund: ein wirtschaftsgeographischer Vergleich zweier südwestafrikanischer Küstenstädte. Diplomarbeit, Univ. Köln, 1972, 132 p.

1301. THIEL, GUDRUN E.K. Deutsche Literatur in Südwestafrika 1890-1920. MA, Johannesburg, Univ. Witwatersrand, 1981, 313 p.

1302. THOMPSON, ELIZABETH. (Project). Organized labour activities among Namibian workers, 1910-1950. PhD, Western Case Univ. (?). In preparation.

1303. THOMSEN, HANS. Die Verteilung des landwirtschaftlichen Grundbesitzes in Südafrika. Diss., Univ. Kiel, 1928. (Publ.: Jena, Fischer, 1927, 165 p.).

1304. TIMMINS, JAMES F. The United Nations and South West Africa: implications of illegitimacy. MA, San Diego State Univ., 1967, 174 p.

547. TJINGAETE, FANUEL. Grundelemente einer wirksamen Agrarreform unter besonderer Berücksichtigung Namibias. M.Sc.Econ., Freie Univ., Berlin, 1983, 96 p.

707. TJITENDERO, MOSE P. Examination of an alternative: A look at the primary and secondary education in Namibia. D.Ed., Univ. Massachusetts, 1976, 123 p.

1305. TLALÊ, SEGAJANE S.S. Völkerrechtliche Probleme des Kampfes des Volkes von Namibia (Südwestafrika) um politische Unabhängigkeit. Diss., Univ. Leipzig, 1973, iv. 305, 95 p.

313. TÖTEMEYER, GERHARD K.H. Die rol van die Wambo-élites in die politieke ontwikkeling van Owambo. D.Phil., Univ. Stellenbosch, 1974. (Publ.: Namibia old and new. Traditional and modern leaders in Ovamboland. London: Hurst, 1978, 258 p.).

1306. TOWNSEND, MARY E. Origins of modern German colonialism, 1871-1885. PhD, New York, Columbia Univ., 1921.

1307. TRÜMPELMANN, GEORG P.J. Die Boer in Suidwes-Afrika. PhD, Univ. Pretoria, 1946. (Publ.: Argiefjaarboek vir Suid-Afrikaanse Geskiedenis vol. 11, 1948, deel 2, p. 1-166).

1308. TUUPAINEN, M. Marriage in a matrilinial African tribe. A social anthropological study of marriage in the Ondonga tribe in Ovamboland. PhD, Univ. Helsinki, 1970. (Publ.: Helsinki: Academic Bookstore, 1970, 171 p.).

837. UDOGU, EMMANUEL I. South West Africa People's Organization of Namibia as a non-state actor in the Namibian issue. PhD, Carbondale Univ., Southern Illinois, 1980, 196 p.

1309. UEBERHORST, PAUL. Die Arbeiterfrage in den deutschen Kolonien. Diss., Münster, 1926, 320 p.

1310. UNGLEICH, THOMAS R. The defence of German Southwestafrica during World War I. MA, Univ. Miami, 1974, 258 p.

1311. VAN DER COLF, ADRIANUS P. Die problematik van die politiesgeografiese akkomodasie van die bevolking van Suidwes-Afrika/ Namibië. MA, Univ. Oranje-Vrystaat, Bloemfontein, 1980.

1312. VAN DER MERWE, JOHANNES J.K. Die geskiedenis van die Rynse sendinggenootskap in Suidwes-Afrika tot 1880. M.Theol., Univ. Stellenbosch, 1951, 92 p.

1313. VAN DER MERWE, PAUL S. Die ontwikkeling van selfbestuur in Suidwes-Afrika 1919-1960. MA, Univ. South Africa, Pretoria, 1964, 204 p.

1314. VAN DER WAAL, BENJAMIN C.V. 'n Visekologiese studie van die Liambezimeer in die Oos-Caprivi met verwysing na die visontginning deur die Bantoebevolking. PhD, Johannesburg, Randse Afrikaanse Univ., Johannesburg, 1977.

1315. VAN DER WESTHUIZEN, JANNIE B. Die teleologiese uitlegmetode soos aangewend in die 1971-opinie van die Internasionale Geregshoof oor Suid-Wes-Afrika. LL.M., Univ. South Africa, Pretoria, 1979.

1316. VAN NIEUWENHUISEN, MAURITS E. Tuberculosis in Ovamboland. PhD, Univ. Stellenbosch, 1968.

1317. VAN RENNINGS, HEDWIG. Die Entwicklungskonzeptionen der nationalen politischen Kräfte in Namibia und ihre Rahmenbedingungen. MA, Univ. Hamburg, 1984, 167 p.

1318. VAN RENSBURG, HELGARD M.J. Die internasionale status van Suid-wes-Afrika: 'n kritiese beskouing van die Internasionale Hof van Justisie se raadgewende mening van 11 Julie 1950. Univ. Leiden, 1953. (Publ.: Leiden: Luctor et emergo, 1953, 154 p.).

1319. VAN ROOYEN, PETRUS H. Die inheemse reg van die Kavango. MA, Univ. Stellenbosch, 1977.

1320. VAN SCHALKWYK, MARTIN J. Die werk van die Wesleyaanse Metodiste Sendinggenootskap in Klein - en Groot Namakwaland, vanaf 1816 tot 1850. MA, Univ. South Africa, Pretoria, 1964.

1321. VAN TONDER, LOUIS L. Leadership, power and status: stratification, with reference to Bushmen, Hottentot and Owambo Society. MA, Univ. Stellenbosch, 1963, 138 p.

1322. VAN TONDER, LOUIS L. The Hambukushu of Okavangoland. An anthropological study of a South Western Bantu people in Africa. D.Phil., Univ. Port Elizabeth, 1966, 455 p.

1323. VAN WYK, JACOBUS T. Aspekte van die Onderwysontwikkeling in Suidwes-Afrika, 1915-1960. D.Ed., Univ. Potchefstroom, 1965.

1324. VAN WYK, THEODOR. Die Ontwikkeling van selfbestuur in Duits Suidwes-Afrika voor 1915. MA, Rhodes Univ., Grahamstown, 1944.

1325. VASIN, V. Kolonialnaja politika Germanii v Jugo-Zapadnoj Afrika (Vosstanie Herero i Hottentotov v 1904-1907). Diss., Univ. Moscow, 1950.

454. VESPER, MICHAEL. Die Homelands in Namibia. Zur Funktion von Überlebensproduktion. Diss., Univ. Bielefeld, 1982, 367 p. (Publ.: Überleben in Namibia: "Homelands" und kapitalistisches Weltsystem. Bonn: ISSA, 1983, 273 p.).

549. VILJOEN, J.J. Die geskiedenis van die karakoelboerdery in SWA 1907-1950. MA, Randse Afrikaanse Univ., Johannesburg, 1981.

642. VIVELO, FRANK ROBERT. The Herero of Western Botswana: aspects of change in a group of Bantu-speaking cattle herders. PhD, Rutgers Univ., 1975, 248 p. (Publ.: New Brunswick, St. Paul: West Publishers, 1977, 232 p.).

345b. VOELTZ, RICHARD A. The origins and early years of the SWA Company Ltd. A study of a British concession company in German South West Africa. PhD, Univ. California, Los Angeles, 1980, 260 p.

1326. WACKERBECK, LOTHAR. Die deutschen Kolonialgesellschaften: ihre Entstehung, Entwicklung und Sonderstellung im Gesellschaftsrecht. Diss., Münster Univ., 1977, 233 p.

1327. WAGNER, RUTH H. South West Africa: A jurisdictional dispute. MA, Denver Univ., 1957.

215. WALLENKAMPF, ARNOLD V. The Herero rebellion in South West Africa, 1904-06. A study in German colonialism. PhD, Univ. California, Los Angeles, 1969, 409 p.

1328. WARMBOLD, JOACHIM. Deutsche Kolonial-Literatur. Aspekte ihrer Geschichte, Eigenart und Wirkung, dargestellt am Beispiel Afrikas. Diss., Univ. Basel, 1982, 292 p. + Anhang. (Publ.: "Ein Stücken neudeutsche Erd...": Deutsche Kolonialiteratur; Aspekte ihrer Geschichte, Eigenart und Wirkung; dargestellt am Beispeil Afrikas. Frankfurt: Haag + Herchen, 1982, 292 p.).

1329. WATTS, ANSLEY DOUGLAS. The early hunters and explorers in South West Africa, 1760-1886. MA, Pretoria, Univ. South Africa,126 p.

1330. WEDER, WALTER H. Die regsposisie van die Rehoboth Basters. LL.D., Univ. Stellenbosch, 1946.

346. WEGE, FRITZ. Zur Entstehung und Entwicklung der Arbeiterklasse in Südwestafrika während der deutschen Kolonialherrschaft. Diss., Univ. Halle, 1966, 359 p.

1331. WEHRSTEDT, KARL. Die handelspolitische Bedeutung der deutschen Kolonien. Diss., Univ. Hamburg, 1926. (Publ.: Hildesheim: Borgmeyer, 1926, 240 p.).

159. WERNER, WOLFGANG. An exploratory investigation into the mode of production of the Herero in pre-colonial Namibia to ca. 1870. B.Soc. Sc. (Honours), Univ. Cape Town, 1980, 112 p.

1332. WERNER, WOLFGANG. (Project). A socio-economic history of the Hereros of Namibia with special reference to the period 1915-ca. 1950. PhD, Univ. Cape Town. In preparation.

1334. WERTHER, RUDOLF. Die Kalahari. Diss., Leipzig Univ., 1935. (Publ.: Wissenschaftliche Veröffentlichungen des Museums für Länderkunde zu Leipzig, N.F. 3, Leipzig, 1935, p. 33-90).

1335. WESSELS, JACOBUS J. Die toepassing van koste- en kosprysbeheer in die visbedryf van Walvisbaai. D.Comm., Potchefstroom Univ., 1964.

1336. WESSELS, LOUIS HERMAN. Die mandaat vir Suidwes-Afrika. Diss., Univ. Leiden, 1937. (Publ.: s'Gravenhage: Nijhoff, 1937, 152 p.).

1337. WIEDORN, KURT. Die Staatsangehörigkeit im C-Mandat Südwestafrika. Diss., Univ. Greifswald, 1934, 83 p. (Publ.: Greifswald: Adler, 1934, 83 p.).

1338. WILCOX, K.L. South West Africa as a German colony. MA, Berkeley, Univ. California, 1930 , 98 p.

1339. WILLEMSEN, PAUL. Das Credit- und Bankwesen in den deutschen Kolonien Afrikas. Diss., Ruprecht-Karls-Univ., Heidelberg, 1915. (Publ.: Haselünne: Lammersdorf, 1915, 83 p.).

1340. WINKELMANN, GÜNTER. Territoriale Autonomie und Selbstverwaltung der Weissen in Südwestafrika? Dargestellt an den Verhältnissen vor und nach dem Weltkriege. Diss., Univ. Leipzig, 1936, 231 p.

1341. WINQUIST, ALAN H. Impact of Scandinavians on the cultural, social and economic development of pre-1948 South Africa. PhD, New York Univ., 1976, 620 p. (Publ.: Scandinavians and South Africa: their impact on the cultural, social and economic development of pre-1902 South Africa. Cape Town: Balkema, 1978, 268 p.).

1342. WITSCHER, WALTER. Die Entwicklung der Wirtschaft in Deutsch Südwestafrika mit besonderer Berücksichtigung der Handelsbeziehungen zu Deutschland. Diss., Univ. Frankfurt, 1925, 82 p.

176. WORCH, HERBERT. Die Entwicklung der deutschen Kolonien in Afrika. Ihre Bedeutung als Erzeuger und Verbraucher. Diss., Friederich-Wilhelms-Univ., Berlin, 1939. (Publ.: Berlin: Saladruck, 1939, 143 p.).

1343. WRIGHT, MILTON S.J. Die Wirtschaftsentwicklung und die Eingeborenen-politik in den ehemaligen afrikanischen Schutzgebieten Deutschlands von 1884 bis 1918. Diss., Heidelberg Univ., 1932. (Publ.: Wertheim: Bechstein, 1932, 64 p.).

1344. WÜHLISCH, FREIA VON. Die Windhuker "Allgemeine Zeitung" und die deutsche Frage von 1933 bis 1933. Diss., Heidelberg Univ., 1945, 128 p.

1345. YESUS, HAGOS GABRE. South-West Africa and the United Nations. MA, Univ. Illinois, 1962.

17. CONFERENCE PAPERS

A. INTERNATIONAL CONFERENCE ON SOUTH WEST AFRICA

Oxford, 23-26 March 1966. Sponsored by the British Anti-Apartheid Movement and the Africa Bureau.

180. BLEY, HELMUT. German South West Africa.
225. BRADFORD, ROBERT L. Blacks to the wall.
1346. THE CONFERENCE STEERING COMMITTEE. The case for international action.
1347. THE CONFERENCE STEERING COMMITTEE. The conference findings.
1348. GEINGOB, GOTTFRIED H. Experiences as a student and teacher.
358. GERVASI, SEAN. The South West African economy.
1349. GOTT, RICHARD. The defence position.
1350. KOZONGUIZI, J. and A. O'DOWD. The legal apparatus of apartheid.
661. KURAISA, CHARLES. The labour force.
1351. MACBIGGON, IAIN. The legal case.
1352. MACGIBBON, IAIN. Postcript: the International Court decides?
701. MCGILL, MARCIA K. Education policy and results.
1353. MONDLANE, EDUARDO C. From Mandates to Trust.
331. NGAVIRUE, ZEDEKIA. The land theft.
383. ROGALY, JOHN. The conditions of the people.
254. SIMONS, H.J. Techniques of domination: South Africa's colonialism.
390. SUTCLIFFE, ROBERT B. The economic relationship with South Africa.
276. VILAKAZI, ABSALOM. The Odendaal Report: social and economic aspects.

All the papers are published in Ronald Segal and Ruth First (eds.): South West Africa. A travesty of trust (see no. 71).

B. NAMIBIA'S FIGHT FOR FREEDOM

Brussels, May 1972. Convened by SWAPO of Namibia.

1354. APPOLUS-AMATHILA, LIBERTINE. The health system in Namibia.

227. BUNTING, BRIAN. Namibia between the two World Wars.

585. FERREIRA, EDUARDO DE SOUSA. International capital in Namibia: Consolidated Diamond Mines and the Tsumeb Corporation

286. FIRST, RUTH. The Bantustans: implementation of the Odendaal Report.

1355. GAROEB, MOSES M. African resistance: the early days.

1356. KATJAVIVI, PETER H. Namibia: strike and political protests.

1357. KATJAVIVI, PETER H. The new era.

1358. MURRAY, ROGER. The expropriation of Namibia's mineral resources.

1359. PIERSON-MATHY, PAULETTE. Namibia: a case for international action.

1360. SHIPANGA, ANDREAS Z. Struggles of the Namibian people.

673. SIMONS, RAY E. The Namibian challenge.

1361. VIGNE, RANDOLPH. Namibia's place in the world – some strategic questions.

C. INTERNATIONAL CONFERENCE ON NAMIBIA AND HUMAN RIGHTS

Dakar, 5-8 January 1976. Organised by the International Institute of Human Rights in collaboration with the International Commission of Jurists and the International Association of Democratic Lawyers, convened on the invitation of the Government of the Republic of Senegal, under the sponsorship of the United Nations Council for Namibia.

1362. ERMACORA, FELIX. Flogging in Namibia. +

1363. EZE, OSITA, C. Labour regime and the Namibian worker: some reflections on human rights.

1364. DE VRIES, LUKAS. La responsibilite˜ chretienne en Namibie. +

1365. INTERNATIONAL INSTITUTE OF HUMAN RIGHTS. Self-determination: techniques of implementation and the United Nations. Selected aspects. (By a member of the staff of the Institute...).

1366. INTERNATIONAL INSTITUTE OF HUMAN RIGHTS. Independent Namibia: survey of methods utilized to ensure the protection of minorities. (By a member of the staff of the Institute...).

1367. KISS, A.C. La Namibie et les conventions internationales des droits de l˜homme. +

739. LANDIS, ELIZABETH S. Human rights in Namibia. +

1368. M˘BACKE, M. La situation juridique des habitants de Namibie sous le régime illegal actuel. +

1369. PREMONT, DANIEL. Les Parlements, la Namibie et les droits de l˘homme. +

 749. RIGAUX, FRANCOIS. The Decree of the Natural Resources of Namibia adopted on 27 September 1974 by the United Nations Council for Namibia. +

1370. SENGHOR, LEOPOLD S. The importance for Africa and the world of the struggle for human rights in Namibia.

1371. SORNORAJAH, M. Self-determination: its continuing validity.

1372. SOUTH WEST AFRICA PEOPLE'S ORGANISATION (SWAPO). A) Namibia and the international rule of law. + B) Discussion paper on the constitution of independent Namibia. C) Constitution of SWAPO. D) Case histories from Namibia - exposing the South African illegal regime's brutalities against the Namibian people.

1373. TAMARO, DIALLO. La situation sociale en Namibie. +

1374. UNITED NATIONS, THE DIVISION OF HUMAN RIGHTS. Selected aspects of the activities of the United Nations concerning Namibia and human rights. +

See also a separate publication, Dakar International Conference on Namibia and Human Rights, 5-8 January 1976. A report. Strasbourg, 1976, which contains the Declaration and the Programme of Action passed by the conference.

Items marked with + are published (in French) in Revue des droits de l˘homme/Human rights journal, vol. 9, Nos. 2&3, 1976, p. 210-569, which is a special issue concerned with the Dakar Conference. (See no. 747).

D. INTERNATIONAL CONFERENCE IN SOLIDARITY WITH THE STRUGGLE OF THE PEOPLE OF NAMIBIA

Paris, 11-13 September 1980. Organised by the United Nations.

 723. ASMAL, KADAR. Namibia: the international law dimension.

 772. CANADIANS CONCERNED ABOUT SOUTHERN AFRICA. Canadian complicity in Namibia.

1375. COMMITTEE OF SOUTH AFRICAN WAR RESISTANCE. Some aspects of the South African military occupation of Namibia. (Prepared by the Preparatory Committee with the assistance of COSAWR).

1376. DANISH SOLIDARITY ORGANISATIONS. A brief survey of activities and publications specifically dealing with the situation in Namibia.

1377. INTERNATIONAL DEFENCE AND AID FUND FOR SOUTHERN AFRICA. Constitutional developments in Namibia- South Africa's internal settlement.

1378. INTERNATIONAL DEFENCE AND AID FUND FOR SOUTHERN AFRICA. Political prisoners and detainees in Namibia.

 780. MELBER, HENNING (ed.). Focus Federal Republic of Germany - Namibia. On relations and cooperation in the political, military, cultural and ecclesiastical fields.

1379. MURRAY, ROGER. Foreign control, investments and interests in the Namibian economy.

1380. NAMIBIA SUPPORT COMMITTEE (ed.). "The people have said so; ...and not us".

1381. NATIONAL UNION OF NAMIBIAN WORKERS. N.U.N.W.

1382. NOVATI, GIAMPAOLO CALCHI. Material aid; its political importance from a Western perspective.

1383. NUJOMA, SAM. Address by the President of SWAPO at the opening plenary session.

1384. PILLAY, VELLA. Focus on Five; the role of Britain in the Namibian question.

1385. SEIDMAN, ANN and NEVA SEIDMAN MAKGETLA. United States' transnational corporations in Namibia.

1386. SHOLTEN, JAN NICO. Plea for an oil boycott against South Africa.

1387. SWAPO. Namibia - Towards genuine independence

1388. SWAPO WOMEN'S COUNCIL. Namibia's women and their role in SWAPO's struggle.

 677. THOMPSON, ELISABETH. Organised labour activities among Namibian workers, 1910-1915.

1389. VESPER, MICHAEL. South African control of the Namibian economy.

See also the Declaration of the International Conference in Solidarity with the Struggle of the Namibian People, Report of the Action Committee, and Report of the Political Commission.

E. SEMINAR ON NAMIBIA AND THE NORDIC COUNTRIES.

Helsinki, 9-11 March 1981. Organised by the Scandinavian Institute of African Studies.

 470. GREEN, REGINALD H. One Namibia, one nation. The political economy of transition.

1377. INTERNATIONAL DEFENCE AND AID FUND FOR SOUTHERN AFRICA. Constitutional developments in Namibia- South Africa's "internal settlement".

1390. MODISE, BILLY. Education in Namibia- problems and prospects.

1379. MURRAY, ROGER. Transnational corporations in Namibia.

791. SANO, HANS-OTTO et al. The relations of the Nordic countries with Namibia.

1387. SWAPO OF NAMIBIA. Namibia. Towards genuine independence. SWAPO political paper.

1391. THORNBERRY, CEDRIC. Present situation as regards the implementation of Security Council resolution 435 (1978).

F. SEMINAR ON LEGAL ISSUES CONCERNING THE QUESTION OF NAMIBIA.

The Hague, 22-24 June 1981. Organised by the UN Council for Namibia.

724. ASMAL, KADER. Walvis Bay. Self-determination and international law. 41 p.

741. LANDIS, ELIZABETH S. If it quacks like a duck... Walvis Bay, Namibia and estoppel. 27 p.

1392. UNITED NATIONS COUNCIL FOR NAMIBIA. Relationship between Decree No. 1 of the UN Council for Namibia and certain Security Council resolutions. 23 p. (By a consultant).

1393. ROBERTS, ALUN. Consideration on the question of contacts, seizure and compensation in respect of Namibian natural resources. 3 p.

763. VERHEUL, J.P. Namibia uranium. 16 p.

1394. Statement issued by the Seminar on Legal Issues Concerning the Question of Namibia.

See also UNITED NATIONS COUNCIL FOR NAMIBIA: Report of the delegation of the Council to the seminar on legal issues concerning the question of Namibia (no. 761).

G. TRADE UNION SEMINAR ON NAMIBIAN URANIUM TO STOP THE ILLEGAL TRADE IN WESTERN EUROPE

London, 29-30 June 1981. Organised by SWAPO in co-operation with Namibia Support Committee.

Statements, background papers, messages, summaries of the proceedings, a transcript of the press conference and the declaration of the seminar are published in Trade union action on Namibian uranium (see no. 604).

H. NAMIBIA. AFRICA'S LAST COLONY: PROSPECTS FOR FREEDOM AND DEVELOPMENT.

Burlington, University of Vermont, 5-6 April 1982. Sponsored by International Nutrition Project, Center for Area and International Studies and University of Vermont Cross-cultural Committee.

1395. BEILSTEIN, JANET C. SWAPO's political economy and the prospects for development in Namibia after independence. 29 p.

818. DALE, RICHARD. African insurgency and German and South African counterinsurgency in Namibia in 1904-1907 and 1922: legacies for African nationalism and protracted guerrilla warfare.

729. DREYER, RONALD F. Walvis Bay and its importance to Namibia: past, present, future. 20 p.

1396. GROTPETER, JOHN J. African politics in settler states. A comparative study with implications for Namibia. 30 p.

1397. KAMARA, JEMADARI. Namibia: perspectives on transition in Southern Africa. 20 p.

570. SPARKS, DONALD L. Namibia's coastal and marine resource development potential. 36 p.

I. SEMINAR ON THE MILITARY SITUATION ON AND RELATING TO NAMIBIA.

Vienna, 8-11 June 1982. Organised by the UN Council for Namibia.

1398. AJALA, ADEKUNLE. (Nigerian Institute of International Affairs). Implications of the military occupation of Namibia for international peace and security.

1399. CAWTHRA, GAVIN (Committee on South African War Resistance). Some aspects of South Africa's military occupation of Namibia.

1400. CONRAD, THOMAS (NARMIC/American Friends Service Committee). Strategic technology - U.S. trade with Pretoria and the war in Namibia.

1401. CHECOLE, KASSAHUN (International Oil Working Group). The oil embargo, South Africa's militarization and illegal occupation of Namibia.

1402. DAVIS, JENNIFER (American Committee on Africa). South Africa in search of allies. Latin American connections.

1403. DEALE, FRANK (Center for Constitutional Rights, New York). The role of US Courts in enforcing UN resolutions.

1404. GEISLER, WOLFF. (Anti-Apartheid Bewegung, the Federal Republic of Germany & Berlin). The military capacity of the racist regime due to ongoing transfer from the Federal Republic of Germany.

1405. GONZALES, CARMEN (Centre for Studies on Africa and the Middle East, Havana). Namibia and the imperialist military complex.

1406. GREENSTREET, MIRANDA (University of Ghana). The implications of Southern African involvement in Namibia for international peace and security.

1407. GROFF, REGIS (State Senator of Colorado, USA). The implications of the military occupation of Namibia for international peace and security.

1408. GUPTA, VIJAY (Nehru University, New Dehli). The militarization of Southern Africa and international peace and security.

1409. INTERNATIONAL DEFENCE AND AID FUND FOR SOUTHERN AFRICA. The capture and treatment of guerrilla combatants and other prisoners-of-war by South African forces operating in Namibia.

1410. JOHNSTON, WILLIAM (Episcopal Churchmen for Southern Africa). The South African war against the people of Namibia.

1411. LEONARD, RICHARD (USA). The arms embargo and South African self-sufficency in military production.

1412. MARWAH, ONKAR (Programme for Strategic and International Security Studies, Geneva). Namibia: a strategic assessment.

1413. MINTY, ABDUL SAMAD (World Campaign against Military and Nuclear Collaboration with South Africa). The hemispheric implications of South Africa's military and nuclear build-up.

1414. MOLEAH, ALFRED T. (Temple University, USA). The historical/political context of South Africa's onslaught against SWAPO and the aggression against the front line states.

1415. OGAWA, T. (Japan Anti-Apartheid Committee). The military situation in and relating to Namibia (Japanese connections).

1416. PRITVOROV, ANDREI (Institute of African Studies, USSR). Namibia: the occupation regime's crisis.

1417. UNITED NATIONS COUNCIL FOR NAMIBIA. Namibian uranium.

1418. UNITED NATIONS COUNCIL FOR NAMIBIA. The military situation regarding Namibia.

1419. UNITED NATIONS COUNCIL FOR NAMIBIA. The military situation in and relating to Namibia. Report of Standing Committee II.

456. WOOD, BRIAN (Namibia Suppport Committee, London). The militarization of Namibia's economy.

See also the seven volume Verbatim Records of the meetings, United Nations General Assembly, A/AC.131/SMS/PV. 1-7. July 1982, as well as United Nations Council for Namibia: Report of the delegation of the Council to the seminar on the military situation in and relating to Namibia, held at Vienna from 8 to 11 June 1982. (See no. 801).

J. SEMINAR ON NAMIBIAN HISTORY

Windhoek, 10-12 December 1982. Sponsored by The Namibia Review.

1420. ABRAHAMS, KENNETH. Namibia and its past: does it matter?

177. ALEXANDER, NEVILLE. The Namibian war of anti-colonial resistance, 1904-1907.

237. GOTTSCHALK, KEITH. South African colonial policy in Namibia.

134. LAU, BRIGITTE. The Kommando and the 1860's traders' and missionaries' war of liberation.

246. NGAVIRUE, ZEDEKIA. Economic competition between the Germans and the South Africans in Namibia.

550. WERNER, WOLFGANG. Production and land policies in the Herero reserves, 1925-50.

All the papers are published in Kenneth Abrahams (ed.): Seminar on Namibian history (no. 1).

K. INTERNATIONAL SEMINAR ON THE ROLE OF TRANSNATIONAL CORPORATIONS IN NAMIBIA.

Washington DC, 29 November - 2 December 1982. Organised by the American Committee on Africa, with the support of the UN Council for Namibia.

1421. AMNESTY INTERNATIONAL. Documents from Amnesty International: Human Rights violation in Namibia- An Amnesty International briefing, September 1982; Namibia: A country under the control of South Africa where detention without trial, torture of political detainees, extrajudicial executions occur; Urgent Action: Namibia: about 25 arrests (November 26, 1982).

460. ASOMBANG, WILFRED W. Transnational corporations (TNCs) and the Republic of South Africa (RSA) as partners in the exploitation of the people and the economy of Namibia.

1422. BJORNDAHL, STERLING (Inter-Lutheran Committee for Nuclear Responsibility, Canada). Saskatchewan and Namibia; the uranium connection.

1423. BOLTON, BRIAN (Transport and General Workers' Union, U.K.) Multinational companies operating in Namibia: an overview.

396. CASON, JAMES (Southern Africa Committee, U.S.A.) Recent North American corporate activity in Namibia.

1424. CHILD, CRIS (British Anti-Apartheid Movement). Campaigning in Britain against economic collaboration with the illegal South African occupation of Namibia.

1425. COLLINS, CAROLE (Campaign to Oppose Bank Loans to South Africa, U.S.A.). Campaign to oppose bank loans to South Africa (COBLSA): Report on activities and some proposals.

1426. COOPER, ALLAN D. An overview of American corporate investments in Namibia.

1427. DE BEER, DAVID. The role of transnational corporations in Namibia.

1428. ERICHSEN, ERIC (Danish Association for International Cooperation) et al. Scandinavia and Namibia: Policies and actions.

1429. GROFF, ELIZABETH (American Friends Service Committee). Report on the research and organizing work of the American Friends Service Committee Southern Africa Program.

1430. HOVEY, GAIL (American Committee on Africa). Breaking the economic links with Namibia's exploiters: divestment action in the United States.

 524. HURLICH, SUSAN (Oxfam-Canada). Namibia, the karakul industry and the Hudson's Bay Company.

1431. INTERNATIONAL DEFENCE AND AID FUND FOR SOUTHERN AFRICA. Labor conditions in the TNCs. (Presented by Wilfrid Grenville-Grey).

1432. KITAZAWA, YOKO (Pacific Resource Center). Report on Japan.

1433. KYLE, PAT (Southern Indiana United Methodist Churches in and Others in Support of Southern Africans). Southern Indiana United Methodists support Southern Africans.

1434. MACBRIDE, SEAN. Opening address to the International Seminar on the Role of Transnational Corporations in Namibia.

 744. MCDOUGALL, GAY J. (Southern Africa Project, Lawyers' Committee for Civil Rights Under Law, U.S.A). Decree No. 1 for the Protection of the Natural Resources of Namibia.

 788. MARCHAND, JACQUES (Mouvement Anti-Apartheid, France). The French-Namibian connection: I) France and Namibian uranium, II) The French government and Namibia, III) Solidarity with SWAPO in France.

 203. MELBER, HENNING. Shadows of the past: the consequences of colonisation and German colonial rule in Namibia.

1435. MOORSOM, RICHARD. The Namibian fishing industry.

 421. MORRELL, JIM (Center for International Policy). The International Monetary Fund and Namibia.

1436. NAMIBIA ASSOCIATION, NORWAY. A short introduction to "Namibia-foreningen".

1437. ROBERTS, ALUN R. The international trade in Namibia's uranium (An overview of the expropriation of Namibia's uranium resources).

1438. SHOTT, TERRY (End Loans to South Africa, ELTSA, U.K.). Banks and Namibia.

1439. SOUTHERN AFRICA TASK FORCE OF HOUSTON. "Educate to liberate".

 605. THE TASKFORCE ON CHURCHES AND CORPORATE RESPONSIBILITY, CANADA. Canada and Namibian uranium.

1440. THE TORONTO COMMITTEE FOR THE LIBERATION OF SOUTHERN AFRICA (TCLSAC). Education and mobilization around Namibia.

1441. VAN HEUKELOM, JAN (Aktiekomite Zuidelijk Afrika, Belgium). Paper presented to the "International Seminar on the Role of the TNCs in Namibia".

812. WALTERS, RONALD W. The U.S. and South African/Namibian uranium options.

1442. WELLMER, GOTTFRIED (Anti-Apartheid Bewegung, Federal Republic of Germany). Background paper on relations between the Federal Republic of Germany and Namibia as occupied by the armed forces of South Africa.

613. WOOD, BRIAN (Namibia Support Committee, U.K.). International capital and the crisis in Namibia's mining industry.

1443. ZALENT, KIM (Lutheran Coalition on Southern Africa, U.S.A.). A report from the Lutheran Coalition on Southern Africa.

L. INTERNATIONAL CONFERENCE IN SUPPORT OF THE STRUGGLE OF THE NAMIBIAN PEOPLE FOR INDEPENDENCE.

Paris, 25-29 April 1983. Organised by the United Nations.

1444. MINTY, ABDUL S. Namibia: a review of developments since the 1980 international conference. 13 p.

760. UNITED NATIONS. Relevant resolutions and decisions on Namibia adopted by the United Nations, the Organization of African Unity and the Movement of Non-Aligned Countries, and excerpts from the advisory opinion of the International Court of Justice of 21 June 1971. 117 p. (A/CONF. 120/CRP. 1. 6 April 1983).

449. UNITED NATIONS COUNCIL FOR NAMIBIA. Social conditions in Namibia. 16 p. (A/CONF. 120/5. A/AC. 131/93, 16 March 1983).

803. UNITED NATIONS COUNCIL FOR NAMIBIA. Political developments related to Namibia. 26 p. (A/CONF. 120/7. A/AC. 131/94, 31 March 1983).

1445. UNITED NATIONS COUNCIL FOR NAMIBIA. Assistance to the Frontline States. 9 p. (A/CONF. 120/10, 7 April 1983).

447. UNITED NATIONS COUNCIL FOR NAMIBIA. List of transnational corporations and other foreign economic interests operating in Namibia. 17 p. (A/CONF. 120/8, 4 April 1983).

448. UNITED NATIONS COUNCIL FOR NAMIBIA. Activities of foreign economic interests operating in Namibia. 33 p. (A/CONF. 120/4. A/AC. 131/92, 16 March 1983).

762. UNITED NATIONS COUNCIL FOR NAMIBIA. Implementation of Decree No. 1 for the Protection of the Natural Resources of Namibia. 13 p. (A/CONF. 120/11, 8 April 1983).

802. UNITED NATIONS COUNCIL FOR NAMIBIA. The military situation in and relating to Namibia. 27 p. (A/CONF. 120/3. 28 March 1983).

487. UNITED NATIONS INSTITUTE FOR NAMIBIA. Planning for Namibian independence: manpower development strategies. 11 p. (A/CONF. 120/6, 21 March 1983).

See also Report of the International Conference in Support of the Struggle of the Namibian People for Independence (no. 759).

M. INTERNATIONAL SEMINAR ON HEALTH IN NAMIBIA

London, 14-16 October 1983. Organised by the Namibia Support Committee in co-operation with SWAPO, Department of Health and Social Welfare.

1446. BARKER, CAROL. Pharmaceuticals policy for an independent Namibia. 6 p.

1447. INDONGO, IYAMBO (SWAPO Secretary for Health and Social Welfare). The effects of colonialism on health. 4 p.

1448. LOEWENSON, RENE. Questioning development and aid in a post-independent situation. 2 p.

1449. NAMIBIA SUPPORT COMMITTEE. Apartheid and the parasites of Namibia (Background paper). 13 p.

1450. SANDERS, DAVID. The politics of health. 26 p.

1451. SCHIKWAMBI, AIRAH. The health of women. 2 p.

1452. ZINKIN, PAM. Child care and material health. 3 p.

1453. ZOYSA, ISABELLA DE. The importance of water and sanitation. 5 p.

1454. WALKER, GODFREY. Reorganization of health systems in post-independent Namibia. 8 p.

1455. WERNER, DAVID. Health workers and their relationship to the social and political dimensions of a country. 12 p.

1456. WERNER, DAVID. Health education and the training of health workers where the goal is health and social justice for all. 25 p.

The papers are available in a collected set from the Namibia Support Committee. See also Tim Lobstein and Namibia Support Committee (eds.): Namibia. Reclaiming the people's health. (no. 717).

N. SEMINAR ON THE ACTIVITIES OF FOREIGN ECONOMIC INTERESTS IN THE EXPLOITATION OF NAMBIA'S NATURAL AND HUMAN RESOURCES.

Ljubljana, 16-20 April 1984. Organised by the UN Council for Namibia.

1457. BABING, ALFRED. Suppression of the Namibian people. Control through deprivation. (A/AC.131/LSR/CRP.6).

647. BOLTON, BRIAN. The condition of the Namibian workers. (A/AC.131/LSR/CRP.7).

794. DE BEER, DAVID. Oil and tanker interests that facilitate the exploitation of Namibia's natural resources. (A/AC. 131/LSR/CRP.5).

1458. DABESCU, IULIAN. Namibia: exploitation of mineral resources. (A/AC.131/LSR/CRP.3).

1459. GALE, JIM. The nature of co-operation between foreign economic interests and the illegal South African regime. (A/AC.131/LSR/CRP.11).

1460. GONZALES, CARMEN. Nature of Namibia's colonial economy. (A/AC.131/LSR/CRP.2).

1461. GUROV, GEORGE. Namibia's natural resources – foreign economic activities, strategic interests and political consequences. (A/AC.131/LSR/CRP.9).

1402. JAEGER, ALFRED L. Exploitation of agricultural resources and exploitation of fisheries of Namibia. (A/AC.131/LSR/CRP.4).

1463. KITAZAWA, YOKO. On the illegal Japanese uranium deals. (A/AC.131/LSR/CRP.12).

1464. KLIMAS, WACLAW. South Africa's occupation of Namibia. The exploitative policies of South Africa and other foreign economic interests. (A/AC.131/LSR/CRP.1).

1465. MORRELL, JIM. The IMF and Namibia. (A/AC.131/LSR/CRP.10).

1466. SLIPTSCHENKO, S. The strategic interests in Namibia's resources and its political consequences. (A/AC.131.LSR/CRP.8).

O. REGIONAL SYMPOSIUM ON INTERNATIONAL EFFORTS TO IMPLEMENT DECREE NO. 1 FOR THE PROTECTION OF THE NATURAL RESOURCES OF NAMIBIA.

Geneva, 27-31 August 1984. Organised by the UN Council for Namibia.

1467. BROKENSHIRE, TARIN. Namibian uranium and British nuclear weapons: the Trident D5 programme. (A/AC.131/GSY/CRP.17). 14 p.

1468. CONFEDERATION GENERALE DU TRAVAIL(CGT). Note on the importing of Namibian uranium. (A/AC.131/GSY/CRP.10).

1469. DAS, SUJATA and INTA MINTA. The activities of transnational corporations in Namibia. (A/AC.131/GSY/CRP.18). 29 p.

794. DE BEER, DAVID. Oil and tanker interests that facilitate the exploitation of Namibia's natural resources. (A/AC.131.GSY/CRP.5).15 p.

1470. FAUNDEZ, JULIO. Namibia: is there still a role for international law? (AC/AC.131/GSY/CRP.2). 8 p.

1471. GERRITSMA, A.M. Implementation of Decree No. 1 in the Netherlands. (A/AC.131/GSY/CRP.1). 8 p.

1472. HINZ, MANFRED O. et al. Preliminary report on Decree no. 1. (A/AC.131/GSY/CRP.16). 26 p.

1473. HUISMAN, RUURD. Opposition in the Netherlands to the violation of Decree No. 1. (A/AC.131/GSY/CRP.9). 43 p.

1474. ISAK/AGIS. Sweden, Namibia and Decree no. 1. (A/AC.131/GSY/CRP.19) 5 p.

1462. JAEGER, ALFRED L. Exploitation of agricultural resources and exploitation of fisheries of Namibia. (A/Ac.131/GSY/CRP.4). 15 p.

1463. KITAZAWA, YOKO. On the illegal Japanese uranium deals. (A/AC.131/GSY/CRP.12). 13 p.

1475. LYALL, ANDREW. Violations of Decree No. 1 for the protection of the natural resources of Namibia. (A/AC.131/GSY/CRP.3). 10 p.

745. MOORSOM, RICHARD. Decree No. 1 and the protection of Namibia's agricultural and fishery resources: problems and prospects for action. (A/AC.131/GSY/CRP.15). 16 p.

1476. OFSTAD, ARVE. Proposals for the implementation of Decree No. 1 for the protection of the natural resources of Namibia and some problems. (A/AC.131/GSY/CRP.11). 9 p.

1477. ROBERTS, ALUN. Efforts to assist the implementation of Decree No. 1 in the United Kingdom. (A/AC.131/GSY/CRP.14). 30 p.

1478. SCHRIJVER, NICO J. The status of Namibia and of its natural resources in international law. (A/AC.131/GSY/CRP.13). 79 p.

1466. SLIPTCHENKO, S. The strategic interests in Namibia's resources and its political consequences. (A/AC.131/GSY/CRP.8). 13 p.

1479. TRANSPORT AND GENERAL WORKERS UNION. International efforts to implement Decree No. 1. Action by trade unions. (A/AC.131/GSY/CRP.6). 7 p.

1480. VERHOEVEN, JOE. The implementation of Decree No. 1 for the protection of the natural resources of Namibia. (A/AC.131/GSY/CRP.7). 12 p.

P. NAMIBIA 1884-1984. 100 YEARS OF FOREIGN OCCUPATION, 100 YEARS OF STRUGGLE.

London, 10-13 September 1984. Organised by The Namibian Support Committee in cooperation with SWAPO.

1481. AKWEENDA, SACKY. The wounds of martial law: Namibia in military occupation of the Union Forces, 1915-1920 and beyond. (55). 10 p.

1482. ALLISON, CAROLINE. Women in waged employment: some basic information and questions of relevance to a future independent Namibia. (69). 5 p.

1483. ANGULA, HELMUT. Namibia before the conquest. (72). 49 p.

1484. ANGULA, LOHMEIER SIMON. Theories fall apart: an exploration into the class position of the Namibian migrant worker. (53). 4 p.

1485. ANGULA, THEO M. Namibia, the United Nations and the West. (49). 10 p.

1486. ASMAL, KADER. The role and status of SWAPO in international law. (13). 26 p.

1487. ASMAL, KADER. Juridical aspects of the Berlin Conference (1884-1885): contribution to a colonial order. (15). 29 p.

1488. AWASEB, H.L. Namibia, the United Nations and the West. (54). 5 p.

317. BEINART, WILLIAM. Cape workers in German South-West Africa, 1904-1912: patterns of migrancy and the closing of options on the Southern African labour market. (12). 22 p.

1489 BENSON, MARY. Notes on research and personal experiences relating to Namibia, the United Nations and Britain's role. (7). 11 p.

1490. BOVIN, A. Presentation by a representative of Soviet Afro-Asian Solidarity Committee. (73).

1491. BRATH, ELOMBE (Patrica Lumumba Coalition). Efforts by the international community towards the settlement of the Namibian question particularly since the adoption of Security Council Resolution 435 (1978). (26). 11 p.

1492. BROKENSHIRE, TARIN and CANUC. British military use of Namibian uranium. (9). 14 p.

1493. CLARENCE-SMITH, W.G. The Angolan connection in Namibian history. (35). 4 p.

278-81. COMMITTEE ON SOUTH AFRICAN WAR RESISTANCE (COSAWR). The South African military occupation of Namibia. (11). 25 p.

1494. COOPER, ALLAN D. Namibia in the world economy. (1). 15 p.

1495. CULLINAN, SUE. South African public opinion and Namibia: the potential impact of independence. (51). 5 p.

1496. CULLINAN, SUE. South African attitudes towards Namibia: the case of the Windhoek Observer. (52). 16 p.

1497. EMMETT, TONY. Popular resistance in Namibia, 1920-1925. (40). 43 p.

1498. END LOANS TO SOUTH AFRICA (ELTSA). Partners in crime - banks in Namibia. (33). 9 p.

1470. FAUNDEZ, JULIO. Namibia. Is there still a role for international law? (20). 8 p.

1499. FORBES, DEREK. British press coverage of the 1981 South Africa invasion of Angola. (3). 16 p.

1500. GALE, JIM. The long road to freedom: Namibia in 1984. (17). 12 p.

1501. GEINGOB, H.G. (on behalf of the United Nations Institute for Namibia). Impediments to the settlement of the Namibia question. (29). 22 p.

1502. GEINGOB, H.G. The role of research in the struggle against colonialism: UNIN's role in the Namibian liberation struggle. (68). 9 p.

1503. GOTTSCHALK, KEITH. South African strategy in Namibia: from colonialism to counter-revolution. (67). 8 p.

1504. GREEN, REGINALD H. Namibia- notes on the political economy of transition: an applied planning and policy perspective. (5). 13 p.

1505. HAIKALI, ERASTUS. Churches and the liberation struggle in Namibia. (39). 5 p.

1506. HAMUTENYA, HIDIPO. One century of imperialist occupation and anti-colonial resistance: a historical flashback. (58). 21 p.

1507. HILLEBRECHT, WERNER. How to find out what has been written about Namibia. (23). 7 p.

1508. HISHIKUSHITJA, MICHAEL. Adaption of traditional stories for a European audience. (41). 17 p.

1509. HOLLAND COMMITTEE ON SOUTHERN AFRICA. International solidarity work in Holland. (60). 2 p.

1510. HOLNESS, MARGA. Angola Women's congress. (48) 5 p.

1511. HOLNESS, MARGA. Who are the Angolan bandits? (57). 11 p.

1512. HUNKE, HEINZ. The role of European missionaries in Namibia. (19). 11 p.

1513. HURLICH, SUSAN. One day in the life of a migrant worker. A docu-drama in three parts. (65). 11 p.

  45. KATJAVIVI, PETER H. The development of anti-colonial forces in Namibia. (44). 65 p.

1514. KATONA, EMIL. Power relations and politico-economic aspirations in Southern Africa. (28). 17 p.

1515. KOENIG, BARBARA and NAMIBIA SUPPORT COMMITTEE. South Africa's propaganda efforts in Britain: the Namibia Information Service. (4). 7 p.

1516. LANDIS, ELIZABETH. Namibia in the international context: the frustration of independence. (10). 22 p.

1517. LAWRENCE, JOHN C. Media bias on Namibia. (16). 6 p.

1518. LEE, RICHARD. The Gods must be crazy, but the state has a plan: government policies towards the San in Namibia and Botswana. (37). 7 p.

1519. LINDEROS, SUSANNE. Scandinavian studies on Namibia. (64). 4 p.

1520. MBAKO, SIMON ZHU. The Namib paradise- poems of Namibia. (38). 14 p.

1521. MELBER, HENNING. New tendencies of an old system: neo-colonial adjustments within Namibia's system of formal education. (6). 30 p.

1522. MKANDLA, STRIKE. Culture and tradition as a weapon of struggle: notes on a double-edged weapon. (63). 4 p.

1523. MUSHI, S.S. Namibia: South African strategy and independent Namibia. (14). 11 p.

1524. NAMIBIA SUPPORT COMMITTEE. New successes for Namibian resistance.... as SWAPO students and people unite. (34). 2 p.

1525. NDOPU, EDWARD IMASIKU. Writing on Namibia. (45). 5 p.

1526. NGHATANGA, MAGDALENA et al. Women's oppression and liberation. (42). 5 p.

1527. PATEMANN, HELGARD. Namibia: the double heritage of colonialism. (66). 4 p.

149. PFOUTS, ANITA. Economy and society in pre-colonial Namibia - a linguistic approach (c.500-1800 A.D.). (30). 27 p.

249. PIRIO, GREGORY ALONSO. The role of Garveyism in the making of the Southern African working classes and Namibian nationalism. (Extracts). (24). 19 p.

1528. REDDY, E.S. (UN Centre against Apartheid). Statement at the NGO conference for the independence of Namibia and the eradication of apartheid, Geneva, 2 July 1984. (22). 7 p.

1529. ROBERTS, ALUN. The development and role of transnational corporations in the colonial occupation of Namibia with reference to violations of international law. (71). 11 p.

1530. SHAMAPANDE, YOBERT K. Perspectives for post-independence development in Namibia. (61). 15 p.

1531. SHEFEENI, JULIA et al. The struggle for education - a play. (46). 19 p.

1532. SHEKWA, VICKY NGHI, MAGDALENA NGHATANGA and PAT BRYDEN. Witbooi- a dramatic interpretation of events on Namibia's past. (21). 19 p.

1533. SHITHIGONA, TSUUTHENI NERURU. Trends in the development of property relations in Namibia before 1884. (50). 9 p.

794. SHIPPING RESEARCH BUREAU. Oil and tanker interests that facilitate the exploitation of Namibia's natural resources. (27). 15 p.

1534. SINDAB, JEAN. United States nuclear and military collaboration with South Africa. (25). 13 p.

1535. SOROSES, A.M. Development of underdevelopment. (43). 4 p.

1536. SULTON, JAMES. Linkage, constructive engagement and the anatomy of American foreign policy toward Namibia. (31). 28 p.

1537. SWAPO. Namibia in the context of imperialism. (59). 19 p.

1538. SWAPO WOMEN'S SOLIDARITY CAMPAIGN. Education for subservience and liberation: another perspective. (2). 7 p.

1539. SWAPO WOMEN'S SOLIDARITY CAMPAIGN. Class, gender and race: theoretical perspectives and implications for building solidarity in Britain with Namibian women. (8). 26 p.

1540. SWAPO WOMEN'S SOLIDARITY CAMPAIGN. Women in production and reproduction. (36). 12 p.

688. SWAPO WOMEN'S SOLIDARITY CAMPAIGN. SWAPO: solidarity with our sisters. (48). 6 p.

1541. THIONG'O, NGUGI WA. Literature, education: the struggle for a patriotic national culture. (47). 31 p.

1542. TOIVO, ANDIMBA JA. Opening statement. (70). 5 p.

1543. UNTERHALTER, ELAINE. White supremacy, the colonial state and the subordination of women: some notes and questions. (32). 4 p.

1544. VIGNE, RANDOLPH. Imperialism at one remove: Britain and South Africa 1785-1915. (56). 9 p.

1545. WELLMER, GOTTFRIED. South Africa's policy in the framework of its regional policy. (62). 8 p.

1546. WERNER, WOLFGANG. Struggles in the Namibian countryside 1915 to 1950 - some preliminary notes. (18). 13 p.

18. ADDRESSES

UNITED KINGDOM

Anti - Apartheid Movement,13 Mandela Street, London NW1 0 DW.

British Library of Political and Economic Science, (London School of Economics and Political Science), 10 Portugal Street, London WC2A 2HD.

Catholic Institute for International Relations, 22 Coleman Fields, London N1 7AF.

Centre for Southern African Studies, University of York, (J.B.Morrell Library), Heslington, York YO 15DD.

City Business Library, Gillett House, 55 Basinghall Street, London EC2V 5BX.

Committee on South African War Resistance (COSAWR), B.M. Box 2190, London WC1N 3XX.

Green,Reginald H. IDS, University of Sussex, Falmer, Brighton BN1 9RE.

Institute of Development Studies, University of Sussex, Falmer, Brighton BNI 9 RE

International Defence and Aid Fund for Southern Africa, Canon Collins House, 64 Essex Road, London N1 8LR.

Institute of Commonwealth Studies, University of London, 27 Russel Square, London WC1B 5DS.

Institute of Development Studies, University of Sussex, Falmer, Brighton BN1 9RE.

Katjavivi, Peter H. St. Antony's College, Oxford OX2 6JF.

Moorsom, Richard, 49 A Vicarage Road, Oxford OX1 4RE.

Namibia Communications Centre, P O Box 286, London WC1X OEL.

Namibia Refugee Project, 22 Coleman Fields, London N1 7AF.

Namibia Support Committee, 53 Leverton Street, London, NX, or P O Box 16, London NW5 2LW

Rhodes House Library, University of Oxford, South Parks Road, Oxford OX1 3RG.

Public Records Office, Chancery Lane, London WC2.

The Royal Commonwealth Society, Northumberland Avenue, London WC2N 5BJ.

School of Development Studies/Overseas Development Group, University of East Anglia, Norwich NR4 7TJ.

School of Oriental and African Studies, University of London, Malet Street, London WC1E 7HP.

Simon, David. Institute for Transport Studies, University of Leeds, Leeds LS2 9JT.

Standing Conference on Library Materials on Africa, SCOLMA, c/o Institute of Commonwealth Studies, 27-28 Russel Square, London WC1B 5DS

SWAPO, 96 Gillespie Road, London N5.

FEDERAL REPUBLIC OF GERMANY

Bundesarchiv, Am Wöllershof 12, D-5400 Koblenz.

Deutsches Institut für Entwicklungspolitik (German Development Institute), Fraunhoferstrasse 33-36, D-1000 Berlin 10.

Deutsches Institut für Tropische und Subtropische Landwirtschaft, Steinstrasse 19, D-3430 Witzenhausen.

Hillebrecht, Werner. Namibian Bibliographic Data Project, Graudenzer strasse 3, D-2800 Bremen.

Informationstelle Südliches Afrika, Blücherstrasse 14, D-5300 Bonn.

Institut für Auslandsbeziehungen, Charlottenplatz 17, D-7000 Stuttgart.

Institut für Afrika-Kunde/Dokumentations-Leitstelle Afrika, Neuer Jungfernstieg 21, D-2000 Hamburg 36.

Institut für Weltwirtschaft an der Universität Kiel, Düsternbroocker Weg 120-122, Postfach 4309, D-2300 Kiel 1.

Institut für Wirtschaftsforschung/Hamburgisches Weltwirtschaftsarchiv HWWA, Neuer Jungfernstieg 21, D-2000 Hamburg 21.

Melber, Henning. Gesamthochschule Kassel. Fachbereich 5. Heinrich-Plett-Strasse 40, Postfach 10 13 80, D-3500 Kassel-Oberzwehren.

Niedersächsische Staats- und Universitätsbibliothek, Prinzenstrasse 1, Postfach 318, D-3400 Göttingen.

Projekt Politische Landeskunde Namibias, Universität Bremen, Fachbereich 5, GW II, Bibliothekstrasse, D-2800 Bremen 33.

Staatsarchiv Bremen, Präsident- Kennedy-Platz 2, D-2800 Bremen.

Stadt- und Universitätsbibliothek Frankfurt, Bockenheimer Landstrasse 134-138, D-6000 Frankfurt am Main.

Strohmeyer, Eckhard. c/o Brandberg Verlag, Assenheimer Strasse 10, D-6367 Karben 1. (Namibian National Bibliography - NNB).

Übersee-Museum Bremen, Bremer Afrika Archiv (BAA), Bahnhofplatz 13, D-2800 Bremen.

Universitätsbibliothek Bremen, Postfach 33 10 60, D-2800 Bremen 33.

Vereinigte Evangelische Mission, Rudolfstrasse 137-135, D-5600 Wuppertal 2.

GERMAN DEMOCRATIC REPUBLIC

Deutsches Zentralarchiv Potsdam, Historische Abteilung I, Berliner Strasse 98-101, DDR-15 Postdam.

THE NETHERLANDS

Holland Committee on Southern Africa, O.Z. Achteburgwal 173, 1012 DJ Amsterdam.

SWITZERLAND

Basler Afrika Bibliographien (Carl Schlettwein), P O Box 2037, CH-4001 Basel.

Antiquariat am Klosterberg, Klosterberg 21, CH-4001 Basel.

ITALY

IDOC (Heinz Hunke), 30 Via S. Maria dell'Anima, 00186 Rome.

THE NORDIC COUNTRIES

Christian Michelsens Institutt/The Development Research and Action Programme (DERAP), Fantoftveien 38, N-5036 Fantoft, NORWAY.

Eriksen, Tore Linné. Husebygrenda 11 A, Oslo 3, NORWAY.

Nordiska afrikainstitutet (Scandinavian Institute of African Studies), Sysslomansgatan 7, P O Box 2126, 750 02 Uppsala, SWEDEN.

Norsk Utenrikspolitisk Institutt/The Norwegian Institute of International Affairs, P O Box 8159, Oslo Dep, Oslo 1, NORWAY.

University of Joensuu, Institute of History, P O Box 111, SF-80101 Joensuu 10, FINLAND.

UNITED STATES OF AMERICA

African Studies Association, 255 Kinsey Hall, Los Angeles, California 90024.

American Committee on Africa, 198 Broadway, Suite 401, New York, N.Y. 10038.

Cooper, Allan D. Saint Augustine's College, Department of History and Government, Raleigh, North Carolina 27611.

Cooperative Africana Microform Project (CAMP/The Center For Research Libraries, 5721 Cottage Grove Avenue, Chicago, Illinois 60637.

Episcopal Churchmen for South Africa, (William Johnston), 853 Broadway, New York, N.Y. 1003.

Gordon, Robert J.   University of Vermont, Anthropology Department, Burlington, Vermont 05405.

Landis, Elizabeth S. 1095 Park Avenue, New York, N.Y. 10128.

TRANSAFRICA, 1325 18th Street, N.W. Suite 202, Washington D.C. 20036.

United Nations, The Office of the Commissioner for Namibia, UN, 1-DC 328, New York, N.Y. 10017.

Yale University Library, African Collection, New Haven, Connecticut 06520.

CANADA

CIDMAA (Centre d´information et de documentation sur le Mozambique et l´Afrique australe), 6738 St-Dominique, Montréal, Québec, Canada H2X2X9.

Toronto Committee for the Liberation of Southern Africa, 427 Bloor Street West, Toronto, Ontario.

Hurlich, Susan. 472 Brunswick Avenue, Toronto, Ontario M5R 2Z5.

REPUBLIC OF SOUTH AFRICA

Africa Institute of South Africa, P O Box 603, Pretoria 0001.

Alexander, Neville. SACHED Trust, 5 Church Street, Mowbray, Cape Town 7700.

Cullinan, Sue. 861 Third Avenue, Crown Mines, Johannesburg 2092.

du Pisani, André. University of South Africa, P O Box 392, 0001 Pretoria.

Gottschalk, Keith. 6 Suffolk Street, Claremont, Cape Town 7700/
Political Science Dept., University of Western Cape, Private Bag
X17, Bellville 7530.

Government Archives Depot, Queen Victoria Street, Private Bag 9025
Cape Town 8000.

Human Sciences Research Council, Private Bag X41, Pretoria 0001.

The Institute for Contemporary History, University of the Orange Free
State, P O Box 2320, Bloemfontein 9300.

Johannesburg Public Library, Market Square, Johannesburg 2001.

Potchefstroom University of Higher Education/Ferdinand Postma
Library, Potchefstroom 2520.

Rhodes University Library/Cory Library for Historical Research,
P O Box 184, Grahamstown 6140.

South Africa Institute of International Affairs, Jan Smuts House,
P O Box 3159, Braamfontein 2017.

South African Institute of Race Relations, 68 de Korte Street,
P O Box 97, Johannesburg 2000.

South African Library, Queen Victoria Street, Cape Town 8001.

The State Library, P O Box 397, Pretoria 0001.

Thomas, Wolfgang H. Economics Dept., University of Western Cape, Private
Bag X17, Bellville 7530.

Tötemeyer, Gerhard. Political Studies Dept., University of Cape Town,
Rondebosch 7700.

University of Cape Town, J.W. Jagger Library, Rondebosch 7700.

University of South Africa Library/Documentation Centre for African
Studies, P O Box 392, Pretoria 0001.

University of Stellenbosch Library, Private Bag 5036, Stellenbosch 7600.

University of the Witwatersrand Library, Private Bag 31550, Braamfontein 2017.

NAMIBIA

Academy for Tertiary Education, Private Bag 13301, Windhoek.

Administrative Library, Private Bag 13186, Windhoek 9100.

Council of Churches in Namibia, P O Box 41, Windhoek 9000.

Lau, Brigitte. c/o National Archives, Private Bag 13250, Windhoek 9000.

The Namibian Review (Kenneth Abrahams, Ottilie Abrahams),
P O Box 21075, Windhoek 9000.

National Archives/Department of National Education, Private Bag 13250,
Windhoek 9000.

Society for Scientific Development and Museum (Gesellschaft für Wissenschaftliche Entwicklung und Museum), P O Box 56, Swakopmund 9180.

SWA Scientific Society (SWA Wissenschaftliche Gesellschaft), P O Box 67, Windhoek 9000.

State Museum, P O Box 1203, Windhoek 9100.

Werner, Wolfgang. P O Box 6253, Ausspannplatz, Windhoek 9000/Department of Economic History, University of Cape Town, Private Bag, Rondebosch 7700, SOUTH AFRICA.

Windhoek Public Library, Private Bag 13183, Windhoek 9000.

ZAMBIA

United Nations Institute for Namibia, P O Box 33811, Lusaka.

ANGOLA

SWAPO Provisional Headquarters, P O Box 953, Luanda.

19. AUTHOR INDEX

Key to section location of item numbers:

Section	Item numbers	Section	Item numbers
1	1 - 81	10	691 - 707
2	82 - 112	11	708 - 722
3	113 - 159	12	723 - 813
4	160 - 219	13	814 - 865
5	220 - 316	14	866 - 932
6	317 - 496	15	933 - 1038
7	497 - 614	16	1039 - 1345
8	615 - 679	17	1346 - 1546
9	680 - 690		

20. ADDENDA

1547. ABRAHAMS, KENNETH (ed.) The people's seminar on education in Namibia. Windhoek: The Namibia Review, 1985, 30 p. (Namibia Review Publications no 4).

1548. ANSPRENGER, FRANZ. "Namibia - trübes Licht am Ende des Tunnels?" Internationales Afrikaforum, 20, no. 4, 1984: 379-86.

1549. DREYER, RONALD: "Dispute over Walvis Bay - origins and implications for Namibian independence". African Affairs, 83, no. 333, 1984: 497-510.

1550. DU PISANI, ANDRÉ. "SWA/Namibia update: 1981 to April 1984", Africa Insight, 14, no. 3, 984: 176-90.

1551. GARNIER, CHRISTINE VON. La Namibie vue de l'interieur. Paris: Berger-Levrault, 1984, 189 p. Bibl.: 183-9.

1552. GRANBERG, PER. An attempt to estimate some rudimentary economic data for Namibia 1980, with special emphasis on the production and consumption of manufactured products. Bergen: Chr. Michelsen Institute, 1984, 21 p. 19 tables. (DERAP Working Papers, A 324).

1553. GRANBERG, PER. A note on the production and consumption of manufactured products in Namibia. Bergen: Chr. Michelsen Institute, 1984, 72 p. 50 tables. (DERAP Working Papers A 316, Restricted).

1554. HANGALA, LEAKE S. Structure of Namibian mineral industry and a strategy option of institutional framework for mineral sector development for independent Namibia. New York: Department of Technical Co-operation for Development, U.N., 1984, 87 p. + appendix. 13 tables, 7 figures, bibl.: 84-6.

1555. INTERNATIONAL DEFENCE AND AID FUND. This is Namibia. A pictorial review. London: IDAF, 1984, 39 p. 53 photos.

1556. INTERNATIONAL DEFENCE AND AID FUND. Repression and resistance in Namibia. A review of developments in 1983-4. London: IDAF, 1984, 4 p. (IDAF Briefing Paper no. 14 - November 1984).

1557. INTERNATIONAL DEFENCE AND AID FUND. A nation in peril. Health in apartheid Namibia. London: IDAF with the cooperation of the Namibia Support Committee, 1985. (Fact paper).

1558. LIEDTKE, WOLFGANG and HEINZ SCHIPPLING. Quellen zu Geschichte und Gesellschaft der Bevölkerung des nordlichen Namibia (Ovambo).

1559. MOORSOM, RICHARD J.B., K.H. JOHANSEN and T. SANDE. Computerised data-base on the economy of Namibia: selected statistics. Bergen: Chr. Michelsen Institute, 1985. (DERAP Working Papers).

1560. ROCHA, GEISA MARIA. In search of Namibian independence: the limitations of the United Nations. Boulder: Westview Press, 1984, 129 p.

1561. SCHOEMAN, ELNA and STANLEY SCHOEMAN. Namibia. Oxford, England/Santa Barbara, California/Denver, Colorado: Clio Press, 1984, 186 p. (World Bibliographical Series. vol. 53).

1562. SIMON, DAVID. "Urban poverty, informal sector activity and inter-sectoral linkages: evidence from Windhoek, Namibia". Development and Change, 15. no. 4, 1984: 551-76.

1563. SPARKS, DONALD L. "Namibia's coastal and marine development potential". African Affairs, 83, no. 333, 1984: 477-96.

1564. TJITENDERO, MOSE P. Education policy for independent Namibia. Some fundamental considerations. Lusaka: UNIN, 1984, 56 p. 9 tables. (Namibia Studies Series. no. 8, ed. by N.K. Duggal).

1565. WEAVER, TONY. "Namibian review". In South African Review 2, p. 211-27. (Braamfontein: Ravan Press, 1984).